Chet Holifield

Member, U. S. House of Representatives
1942 – 1974

Chet Holifield

Master Legislator and Nuclear Statesman

Richard W. Dyke

Francis X. Gannon

With a Foreword by the Honorable Gerald R. Ford,
Former President of the United States

and

An Afterword by the Honorable Carl Albert,
Retired Speaker, U.S. House of Representatives

University Press of America, Inc.
Lanham • New York • London

Copyright © 1996 by
University Press of America,® Inc.
4720 Boston Way
Lanham, Maryland 20706

3 Henrietta Street
London, WC2E 8LU England

Library of Congress Cataloging-in-Publication Data

Dyke, Richard Wayne
Chet Holifield: master legislator and nuclear statesman / Richard W.
Dyke, Francis X. Gannon; with a foreword by Gerald R. Ford and an
afterword by Carl Albert.
p.   cm.
Includes index.
1. Holifield, Chet, 1903-. 2. Legislators--United States--Biography.
3. Statesmen--United States--Biography. 4. United States. Congress.
House--Biography. 5. Nuclear industry--Government policy--United
States. 6. Nuclear energy--Government policy--United States. I.
Gannon, Francis X. (Francis Xavier). II. Title.
E840.8H65D95   1995   328.73'092--dc20   95-44386 CIP

ISBN 0-7618-0171-5 (cloth: alk: ppr.)

⊖™The paper used in this publication meets the minimum
requirements of American National Standard for information
Sciences—Permanence of Paper for Printed Library Materials,
ANSI Z39.48—1984

This book is dedicated

in

Loving Memory

to

Vernice "Cam" Caneer Holifield

Whose inspiration, loyalty over six decades, common sense, and unfailing kindness to family, friend, and foe of Chet Holifield, helped transform a tenacious idealist into a peerless legislator of Twentieth Century America.

Cam, Chet's wife of 68 years, died on June 12, 1991 without having seen this book about her husband's life. Chet died at 91 years of age, on February 5, 1995, knowing that the book was soon to be published.

THE BUILDER

I watched them tearing a building down,
    A gang of men in a busy town,
With a ho-heave-ho and a lusty yell
    They swung a beam and a side wall fell.

I asked the foreman, "Are these men skilled
    As the men you'd hire if you had to build?"
He gave a laugh and said, "No indeed.
    Just common labor is all I need.
These men easily wreck in a day or two
    What builders have taken a year to do."

I asked myself as I went my way,
    "Which of these rules have I tried to play,
As a builder who works with care
    Measuring life by the rule and square
Shaping my deeds to a well laid plan,
    Patiently doing the best I can, or
Am I a wrecker who walks the town
    Content with the purpose of tearing down?"

Francis Sherman

Contents

Photos follow page 190

Abbreviations

ABM	antiballistic missile (system)
AEC	U.S. Atomic Energy Commission
ANL	Argonne National Laboratory
ANS	American Nuclear Society
APPA	American Public Power Association
ATR	Advanced Test Reactor
BNL	Brookhaven National Laboratory
BN-350	a Soviet Union breeder reactor
BRC	Breeder Reactor Corporation
BWR	boiling water reactor
CIA	U.S. Central Intelligence Agency
CRBR	Clinch River Breeder Reactor
DC	direct current (electricity)
DENR	U.S. Department of Energy and Natural Resources (proposed)
DOD	U.S. Department of Defense
DOE	U.S. Department of Energy
DOT	U.S. Department of Transportation
DNR	U.S. Department of Natural Resources (proposed)
DSG	Democratic Study Group
EBR	Experimental Boiling Water Reactor
EBR-I	Experimental Breeder Reactor No. 1
EBR-II	Experimental Breeder Reactor No. 2
EEI	Edison Electric Institute
EPIC	End Poverty in California program (proposed)
ERDA	U.S. Energy Research and Development Administration
FARET	a small fuels test reactor at ANL
FBI	Federal Bureau of Investigation
FDR	(U.S. President) Franklin Delano Roosevelt
FFTF	Fast Flux Test Facility
FHLB	Federal Home Loan Bank
FY	Fiscal Year
GAC	(AEC) General Advisory Committee
GAO	U.S. General Accounting Office
GE	General Electric
GOP	Grand Old Party (Republican Party)
GSA	U.S. General Services Administration
HUD	U.S. Department of Housing and Urban Development
ICBM	intercontinental ballistic missile
JCAE	(House-Senate) Joint Committee on Atomic Energy
KAPL	Knolls Atomic Power Laboratory
LASL	Los Alamos Scientific Laboratory
LMFBR	Liquid Metal Fast Breeder Reactor
LOFT	Loss of Fluid Test (Facility)
LSR	Large Ship Reactor
LWR	light water reactor
MVGC	Mississippi Valley Generating Company
NATO	North Atlantic Treaty Organization
NEC	U.S. Nuclear Energy Commission (proposed by Holifield)
NEPA	National Environmental Policy Act of 1969
NR	Naval Reactors (Organization)
NRC	U.S. Nuclear Regulatory Commission
N-reactor	New Production Reactor/Hanford Reactor/dual-purpose reactor

NRECA National Rural Electric Cooperative Association
NROTC Naval Reserve Officer Training Corps
NRTS Naval Reactor Testing Station
Mwe megawatt
OMB Office of Management and Budget
OPEC Organization of Petroleum Exporting Countries
OPS Offshore Power Systems
ORNL Oak Ridge National Laboratory
PAC political action committee
PAL Permissive Action Link
PBF Power Burst Facility
PDP Project Definition Phase
Phoenix a French breeder reactor
PHS U.S. Public Health Service
PMC Project Management Corporation
PNL Pacific Northwest Laboratory
PRDC Power Reactor Development Company
PSC (PMC's) Project Steering Committee
PUC public utility commission
Pu239 plutonium, a fertile isotope with an extremely long half-life
PWR pressurized water reactor
QA quality assurance
R&D research and development
RDT AEC Division of Reactor Development and Technology
RRD AEC Division of Reactor Research and Development
SAC Strategic Air Command
SANE National Committee for a Sane Nuclear Policy
SDI Strategic Defense Initiative
SEFOR Southeast Fast Oxide Reactor
SIR Submarine Intermediate Reactor
SNAP System for Nuclear Auxiliary Power (device)
SNUPPS Standardized Nuclear Utility Power System
STR Submarine Thermal Reactor
TMI Three Mile Island (nuclear plant complex)
TMI-II Three Mile Island Unit No. 2
TVA Tennessee Valley Authority

UEA Uranium Enrichment Associates
UPI United Press International
U-235 an isotope of uranium used in bombs and nuclear plants
U-238 a nonfissioning isotope of uranium ("natural" uranium)
V1/V-1 German World War II-vintage rocket
V2/V-2 German World War II-vintage rocket
WPPSS Washington Public Power Supply System
YMCA Young Men's Christian Association

Gerald R. Ford

Foreword

Writing a foreword for a book on a close personal friend and a long time colleague in the U.S. House of Representatives brings back wonderful memories of our treasured relationship. The friendship transcended political partisanship and included many enjoyable social activities with Cam and Betty. Chet and I embraced and sought to further the fundamentals of our government and society, although on occasion we might differ. In the following pages, let me share some personal views on my dear friend, Chet Holifield and his outstanding public career.

The Congress of the United States is the central political forum wherein public issues that concern our democracy are debated on a day-to-day basis. After only two centuries of existence, ours is already the world's oldest functioning democracy. Within the crucible of the Congress the competing and often conflicting hopes and aspirations of our citizens are put to the legislative test.

Those legislators who are closest to our local communities are the 435 members of the House of Representatives. They must represent the views of local citizens and go before their constituencies every two years for re-election. This places a high premium on their political and legislative skills. First and foremost, they must satisfy their own consciences that the legislation they support is beneficial both to their own districts and to the nation. Citizens expect their Representatives in Congress to reflect their governmental grievances, concerns, and interests.

Over a given decade hundreds of public-spirited men and women are elected to the House of Representative. Not all remain in Congress, either by their own choice or by that of the voters. But some manage to ride out the perils and responsibility and trust in the House. This requires a willingness to study and abide by the rules of the Congress, an unflinching determination to serve the people and a rare political and legislative sensitivity. Perhaps the most difficult virtue for a legislator to learn is how to disagree without being disagreeable. Those who master such legislative skills are the ones who leave an indelible imprint on the American Republic.

Chet Holifield stands high in the ranks of 20th century Representatives who have made major contributions to the Congress for 32 years, his record is one of sterling achievement, dedication to the common good and unyielding personal integrity.

To his legislative peers the name Holifield was synonymous with that of the peaceful atom. On nuclear energy his was the dominant voice in the House. Together with such associates as the late Craig Hosmer, Republican of California, and Mel Price, Democrat of Illinois, he set a standard of legislative excellence in the highly technical area of nuclear energy that will be hard to surpass. On many issues his legislative mastery of the nuclear field was so thorough that when he spoke, most members of the Congress not only listened carefully, but usually followed the course he recommended. Few legislators in my lifetime enjoyed the trust Chet did as a consequence of his study and knowledge of this new source of energy--the atom. Not only the Congress but the nation owes him a profound debt of gratitude.

As House Minority Leader, as Vice President and as President of the United States, I had my share of differences with Chairman Holifield on public and legislative policies.

For the most part, however, our views coincided on the great central problems of national defense, disarmament and nuclear energy. When we disagreed on the course we usually found a way, through the normal give-and-take of the legislative process, to reach our common goal.

Chet Holifield was and is, above all, a gentleman open to reasoned argument. He understood the positions of those who disagreed with him. While in the political arena, he was a partisan Democrat; when it came to national security his approach was non-partisan, objective and profoundly compassionate.

I have been privileged to work closely with and enjoy the friendship of Chet Holifield of California. Betty and I count Cam and Chet Holifield among the warmest friends we made in Washington. We all can be proud of this story of an American patriot whose vision and political courage enriched the cause of freedom and the lives of men and women everywhere.

Gerald R. Ford

Preface

This is the story of Chet Holifield, or Mr. Atomic Energy, as he was known by many colleagues in Washington. As a congressional leader of far-reaching influence in postwar America, this Californian helped the United States and, indeed, the world community, to recognize and adjust to both the perils and the opportunities of the atomic age. His powerful legislative leadership also contributed in important ways to efficiency and responsibility in government, long-term energy security, a strengthened national defense, and the domestic well-being of the American people and others abroad.

Holifield is an American success story. As his saga reveals, he began as a poor, but highly motivated farm boy from Arkansas who set out on his own to make his fortune in the "Golden West." Having never finished high school, he educated himself as he built his own small business in California. As a young haberdasher, he established a reputation of integrity and fairness which marked him for leadership. It seemed only natural that during the despairing times of the Great Depression the people in his community would ask Chet to represent them. Before long, his fellow citizens had propelled him from local political activities to long-term service as their representative in Congress. First elected in 1942, he was overwhelmingly reelected by his constituents for sixteen terms until he voluntarily retired in 1974--a record thirty-two years of service, unequalled by any other California congressman.

Chet Holifield was still a fledgling representative when the war in the Pacific ended in 1945 with the atomic bombings of Hiroshima and Nagasaki. An amazed and deeply troubled humanity found itself living suddenly in the nuclear age. In the U.S., the Congress responded to this new world by creating one of the most unusual and powerful committees in the history of the Republic: the Joint Committee on Atomic Energy, (JCAE), which endured from 1945 until it was formally abolished in 1977. Initially, JCAE membership included some of the most senior and prestigious members of both houses of Congress. Two of its founding members, though, Chet and his close friend Melvin Price of Illinois, were conspicuous in a different way. In 1945 they had been junior members of the House Armed Services Committee, ranking second and third in seniority from the bottom of this committee. From this relative obscurity, they were selected by Speaker Sam Rayburn to serve on the newest, most distinguished House-Senate committee of its time on Capitol Hill. From charter members, Holifield and Price eventually became the JCAE's dominant leaders from the late 1950s into the 1970s, together with senators Clinton Anderson of New Mexico and John O. Pastore of Rhode Island, and Republican House member Craig Hosmer of California.

Why did Speaker Rayburn, one of the strongest Speakers in U.S. history, select these two individuals for this unprecedented assignment? On the answer to this question hangs only the beginning of the story of Holifield's influence. Holifield eventually became a national figure as he pursued his JCAE career. But he also had a dominating influence on the larger story of the evolution of Congress in postwar America. Dedicating profuse time to immerse himself in the myriad rules, traditions, protocols, and legislative methods, Chet became one of a handful of master legislators in the House, and a reformer as well. His ability to use and adapt democratic processes and advances in technology, and then take hold of and move the issues, was exceptional. Word quickly spread: "If you want it done, see Chet." As a result, he acquired leadership roles in ever-widening spheres of influence.

Were Holifield to return to Congress today, his style and approach would probably not be as successful. Following the tradition-shattering reforms of the House Democratic Caucus during the 1970s, the House is no longer what it was for most of this century. Most efforts by congressmen today routinely give way to a sense of futility and wasted effort. The legislative authority which Holifield systematically acquired is all but impossible to obtain under present conditions. One can be sure, however, that if Holifield were younger and in Congress, he would be among those most determined to restore the capacity to govern in order to meet the nation's long-term public needs.

To examine anew the issues that dominated Holifield's legislative horizons from the mid-1940s to the mid-1970s is to plunge headlong into a cloud of uncertainty which masks a plethora of incredibly costly energy security problems. These problems have all but destroyed America's capability to carry out high-priority national energy commitments. They include such matters as the national debt and the budget deficit; dependence on imported oil; assuring high standards of excellence in clean generation of electricity, and protecting national defense and the environment; establishing and sustaining leadership in long-term energy security; avoiding the hazards of nuclear terrorism and warfare; assuring nuclear safety, international safeguards, and nuclear disarmament; and exploiting the full potential of atomic power and the peaceful atom. On all of these matters, Holifield's arguments--whether dating from the 1940s, 1950s, 1960s, or 1970s--are as pertinent and challenging as today's headlines. Many of Holifield's arguments which depended in an earlier time on insight and judgment, have been subsequently validated and reinforced by experience. Unfortunately, the nation seems to have forgotten about how the Holifield-JCAE type of dynamic leadership led to significant postwar progress. Hopefully, this study may suggest some ways in which such leadership could once again serve as a model in this more critical time of need.

One lesson of Holifield's life and career is that human beings can cope with and master even the most sophisticated technology when they are open to learning, willing to take the time and work hard, and able to interact fairly with sincere and intelligent opponents on issues, as he was. These factors are exactly what makes Holifield's story exceptional and worthy of note. Few, if any, thoughtful persons could resist Holifield's determination or sensitivity, passion, and eloquence to awaken the nation to the realities and potential of the peaceful atom. He became a powerful advocate for supporting its many uses, for example, for medical diagnostics and treatment; food storage; clean electricity for homes, industry, hospitals, and transportation; cleaning up the air and water as a substitute for fossil fuels; recycling natural resources and wastes; and reducing America's deficit and dependence on imported oil.

Having celebrated his ninety-first birthday a few months before he died in February 1995, Holifield sustained his hope that America's leadership would have the vision and commitment to again recreate productive legislative forums, like the JCAE, to invigorate and educate other centers of government and society. He saw the JCAE as a means to educate Americans on the value of clean electricity and other vital products of the atom. While essential and available to most modern societies, atomic applications are also needed by billions around the world in developing nations who also aspire to a better life. Holifield believed that too few Americans have an appreciation of how the peaceful atom has been satisfying some of the needs of the World Health Organization, the United Nations Food and Agriculture Organization, and the International Atomic Energy Agency. He insisted that much more must be done by America's leadership, the media, and our schools to educate the public about the vast potential benefits of using the atom.

Chet Holifield's work and continued aspirations and philosophy were summed up well in one of his personal notes written in his eighty-fifth year to his daughter Betty Holifield Feldmann in the fall of 1988:

> In the closing years of my life and the ending year of our Nation's second century, I earnestly pray that the people of the world will respect the possibility of a catastrophic nuclear war. I pray that the atom will be used only for service and blessing to the people of our Nation and the world.

This book was begun in 1983 by the late Dr. Francis X. Gannon at the request of Chet's close friend, the late Thomas E. Clark, as a limited project of essays on Holifield's nuclear energy views. The project rapidly developed into Chet's sole authorized biography, with no holding back from "telling it like it was." Tragically, Dr. Gannon's work was cut short by a fatal heart attack in late 1988. Contacted in March 1990 by Milton Shaw and Betty Holifield

Feldmann, I agreed to complete this book for a number of reasons, not the least of which is the friendship that my wife Paula and I developed with Chet and Cam Holifield. We came to know them well during numerous interviews and visits in the course of completing my doctoral dissertation and later book on Chet's role in atomic energy affairs.

Although Dr. Gannon and I worked at different times, this book is co-authored in every sense of the word. I have made extensive revisions and some deletions in the text, as well as added most of the endnotes, but Gannon's viewpoints still come through along with mine. The Holifield Book Associates, a group of Chet's close associates and friends organized to assist Gannon, deserve enormous credit for their continuing involvement during this manuscript's preparation. While we benefitted from a significant amount of technical input, review, and comment by the Associates, Dr. Gannon and I retained full rein in developing our conclusions and perspectives.

Books are not created in a vacuum by authors only. Many persons are owed sincere thanks for their help. The Acknowledgements attempt to list with thanks all of those who assisted on this twelve-year project. A few persons deserve special recognition here, however, for their extraordinary efforts and commitment. Milton and Natalie Shaw and Robert and Betty Feldmann of the Associates are two couples who have virtually lived day and night with this book before and since Gannon's death. Without their personal experience, insights, and unswerving persistence, this work would never have been published. Other nuclear power pioneers among the Associates with highly relevant experience and contacts with Chet and the JCAE--Ed Bauser, Wally Behnke, John Conway, Jack Crawford, Jim Ramey, and John Reich--provided extensive semantic, literary, and technical input that greatly enhanced the accuracy and clarity of many of the issues, ideas, and factual material. Finally, the authors' wives also must be accorded special thanks. Before he died, Dr. Gannon began a draft of the preface, in which he wrote: "One person, though, made a sustained, many-sided and indispensable contribution; my wife, Patricia Murphy Gannon, served as a sounding board, researcher, editor of drafts and did preliminary editing." Likewise, I extend my sincere thanks to my wife, Paula Radcliffe Dyke, for the losses she endured, the editorial criticisms she provided, and the positive ways she found to lighten my work during these last five and a half years.

In closing, the Holifield Book Associates and this author extend our sincere appreciation to President Gerald Ford and Speaker Carl Albert for their contributions to this book.

Los Angeles, California   Richard W. Dyke
September 1995

Acknowledgements

A multitude of friends, colleagues, individuals, and organizations, in addition to those mentioned in the Preface, are owed enormous thanks for their wide-ranging contributions that assisted in publication of this book. At the top of the list are the Holifield Associates, who granted in-depth and often multiple interviews and also helped identify the most credible and authoritarian sources from among the voluminous speeches, studies, hearing records, and other documents generated during the highly productive Holifield era. Together with Holifield personally, the Associates made significant contributions to the structure and content of this work. Most importantly, they reviewed many drafts and kept subsequent revisions alive with their generous time and financial support, wise counsel, and indispensable literary and technical contributions. Because most of the Holifield Associates were in Washington, D.C. and Dyke was in Los Angeles, Milton Shaw and Holly Gregory, certainly, as well as others, materially assisted the effort by collecting, compiling, and synthesizing a large variety of comments from the Associates on the various chapter drafts for transmittal to Dyke. In addition to those already mentioned here and in the Preface, the Holifield Book Associates included: Phillip Bayne, Robert Bergland, Shelby T. Brewer, Francis P. Cotter, Daniel Donoghue, Edward M. Davis, Harry Finger, Larry Hobart, Dwight Ink, Thomas Kuhn, Byron Lee, Kenneth Mansfield, Alex Radin, Jack Young, and Leo Wright.

Dr. Gannon's early efforts to obtain access to some classified JCAE files, then in a lengthy process of being declassified, were facilitated by Senators Robert Byrd (D-WV) and Robert Dole (R-KS), and George Murphy, Richard Kimmel, Robert Kepley and John Lane. Early counsel and help was generously given by William Carrigan, Sam Ashelman and Jerald R. Schultheis. Typing and word processing of Dr. Gannon's handwritten drafts was performed with aplomb by Betty Usmiller, Marge Korff Doe, Muriel Rice, Peg Spellacy, Sue Lerner and especially, Anna C. Gaskins. Barbara Murphy Edwards and William Ryan, in addition to many others mentioned herein, provided suggestions and editing in the earlier chapters. Selection of the photographs for this volume was headed by Betty Holifield Feldmann, with technical help from Dolly Seelmeyer and Keith Jewell, plus critical assistance from Carol Mason Feldmann, who generously lent her expertise in the photographic lay-outs and the book jacket. Warren Unna made an invaluable contribution through his unpublished typescript on Holifield, provided by Holifield to the authors. During the entire period, Miles Q. Romney generously provided historical information and the benefit of his long, continuing experience on the Government Operations Committee.

Many other persons were helpful and supportive in innumerable ways, either in the early period with Gannon or later in the process as Dyke brought the work to completion. Together they included Fleming Campbell, Dave Sweeney, Michael Brennan, John O'Shinski, J. C. Turner, Thomas Donahue, Robert Georgine, Carl Walske, Arline Roback, Harold Levine, John Simpson, Octave DuTemple and Mary Beth Gardner, Norman Jacobson, Congressmen Dante Fascell (D-FL), Frank Horton (R-NY) and the late Melvin Price (D-IL), Frank Alexander, Jo Ann (Holifield) and Robert Ward, Millie and Boyd Winfree, Elizabeth and Nathan Snyder, Carmen and Louis Warshaw, Susie and Robert Clifton, Bill Spodak, Joseph Rauh, Snyder and Selzer Attorneys, Lois (Holifield) and William Mulholland, Jack Newman, Adam Klein, John Harris, Charles Luce, and Joe Glazer.

The participation and help of many of the individuals mentioned above was enhanced measurably by help from friends and others in organizations with which they were affiliated. This book would not have been possible without the support of the following organizations: American Nuclear Energy Council, American Nuclear Society, American Public Power Association, Bechtel, Building & Construction Trades - AFL-CIO, California Labor Federation, Combustion Engineering Corporation, Commonwealth Edison, Diane & Guilford Glazer Fund, Doub & Muntzing, Eastern Conference of Teamsters, Edison Electric Institute, General Electric Corporation, International Union of Operating Engineers, United States Committee for Energy Awareness, Los Angeles Water Authority, National Rural Electric Cooperative Association, Northeast Utilities, Nuclear Management & Resources Council, Pacific Gas & Electric, San Diego Gas & Electric, Southern California Edison, Stone & Webster Engineering Corporation, Westinghouse Electric Corporation, and White, Verville, Fulton & Saner.

Dyke gratefully acknowledges many forms of assistance from the library staffs of the Edward L. Doheny, Jr. Memorial Library and satellite libraries at the University of Southern California; the University Research Library at the University of California, Los Angeles; the Robert Andrews Millikan Library at the California Institute of Technology; and the Honnold-Mudd Library of the Claremont Colleges. Special mention should be made of USC library staff Dace Taube (Holifield Papers) and Julia Johnson (Government Documents Section, Doheny Library), who went out of their way to assist Dyke in accessing important documentation.

1

The Meaning of Bikini

An Educator of Presidents

As he sat in the rear section of *Air Force One* flying between Washington, D.C. and California on March 29, 1971, California Congressman Chet Holifield was fully aware that his sometime political nemesis, President Richard M. Nixon, had not invited him along merely to pass the time of day. Indeed, as chairman of the Government Operations Committee in the U.S. House of Representatives, Holifield was an important key to achieving the President's ambitious initiatives in domestic policy. Nixon had proclaimed his desire to create "a new American Revolution" by reorganizing the federal bureaucracy from top to bottom to improve efficiency in government, and he needed Holifield's agreement to hold hearings on his proposals.[1]

For his part, Holifield also had an agenda for this meeting. In addition to his chairmanship of Government Operations, Holifield was one of very few congressmen to hold a second chairmanship. Since 1961 he had been chairman, or alternately vice chairman, of the House-Senate Joint Committee on Atomic Energy (JCAE). As such, he had a powerful role in atomic energy development and other matters affecting domestic energy security. Holifield viewed the meeting as an opportunity to win presidential support for a re-enforcement of the federal role in nuclear energy research and development (R&D) and more particularly, for the Liquid Metal Fast Breeder Reactor (LMFBR) or "breeder," as it was commonly known. Holifield fervently wanted a higher national priority for the breeder, with intensive R&D employing the highest levels of engineering management and technical excellence exemplified by Admiral Hyman G. Rickover for the Navy and by some utilities. He believed the breeder to be central to achievement of American energy independence over the long term.

Long before the Arab Oil Embargo which was to be inflicted (in October 1973) by the Organization of Petroleum Exporting Countries (OPEC), Holifield had been voicing concerns about America's worsening energy situation. He had issued many warnings about air pollution and other adverse consequences of burning fossil fuels and also had pointed out the alarming rate of depletion of irreplaceable hydrocarbon resources. Holifield had also expressed grave concern about the mounting threat to America's energy security and well-being from increasing dependence on imported oil, prophetically advising public, congressional, and industrial audiences of severe consequences from such dependence. Even prior to his meeting with Nixon, he had called for action on a broad front, emphasizing the nuclear option and the breeder with its potential for efficient, safe, and clean baseload electrical energy. He saw his role as educating Congress, the public, and now the president, on data amassed since the 1940s that viewed the breeder as a long-term, and environmentally safe solution to the nation's growing energy needs.[2]

Soon the door of the plane's forward compartment opened, and senior presidential aide John Erlichman invited Holifield to come forward to visit with Mr. Nixon. The Democratic congressman and the Republican president had a pleasant chat. Nixon was primarily concerned about his reorganization plans which had been drafted by a commission chaired by Roy Ash, a leading industrialist. But the conversation ultimately advanced to the subject of energy security and the breeder in particular. Holifield discovered that the president knew very little about the breeder. As Holifield remembered it, the president leaned over to him and said, "Chet, you and I are non-scientists. So explain to me the breeder's principles. Use layman's language. Scientists tell me about it, but I still can't make heads or tails of what they're saying."

Holifield thus found himself in the position of presidential educator, a role not unfamiliar to him. Since Harry S Truman's presidency, he had such a role at various junctures during his quarter century on the JCAE. He knew that simplicity and clarity were necessary. Presidents, with so much on their agendas, had to get to matters immediately and then move rapidly to the next problem. An image flashed suddenly across his mind: Nixon in front of the White House fireplace. Nixon preferred the reflective mood of this fireplace so much that sometimes he would sit there even during Washington's blistering summer, with the air conditioning turned up full blast. Holifield decided to use the fireplace and its ashes as an analogy for the breeder.

The Nuclear Phoenix: Even More Power from the Ashes

Holifield never referred to any president in less than formal terms, although as a fellow congressman he had been friendly with John F. Kennedy, Lyndon B. Johnson and Nixon while they served in the House. "If I told you, Mr. President," he began in response to Nixon's inquiry, "that the ashes left from burning logs in this fireplace contained more energy that the logs themselves, you'd say I was a liar and a fool. You'd be right on both counts! With the breeder, though, that's precisely what happens."[3] He then began a comparison of the ashes to the two large sources of nuclear waste products.

First, there was "the radioactive waste material in used fuel rods from our many civilian power reactors," that were stored in pools of water at utility plants and other approved sites. Holifield explained to Nixon that "these rods were originally filled with uranium in the form of pellets, pellets consisting mostly of U-238, with about three percent U-235." Holifield explained that the much rarer U-235 was the major fissionable material and vital for success with reactors. U-235 is "burned" in reactors in a controlled fission process to produce the heat source critical to developing electricity, just as oil or coal is burned to produce heat for conversion into electricity. Holifield told Nixon that the spent fuel rods--waste or "ashes" from the process--contained fission products and unused U-235, as well as plutonium (Pu239), a highly-fissionable element not found in nature that was natural uranium (U-238) before it was converted by neutrons released in the fissioning of U-235. He continued:

> Plutonium, Mr. President, is better known for its use in bombs. Plutonium 239 is far more powerful than the Uranium 235 used in the original atomic bomb. From the dawn of the Atomic Age, scientists have always believed that we could turn this tremendous force and source of energy in these materials into a great benefit for humankind and world development.[4]

Holifield explained that Pu239 was fissionable like U-235, "except that when it fissions in a high-temperature fast reactor, it produces far more energy than U-235 or Pu239 does in light water reactors."[5]

Holifield then explained to the president that the second source of nuclear waste was even greater in quantity than the first. Enormous amounts of nuclear waste products were being stored in barrels on the grounds of the government's enrichment plants at Oak Ridge, Tennessee, and Paducah, Kentucky. The waste products had been building since the plants began operating during the World War II Manhattan Project. "Unlike the ashes from the logs in your fireplace, Mr. President," Holifield told Nixon, "the waste . . . from the years of operating the enrichment plants can produce enormous new amounts of energy." This was true because a major portion of the nuclear waste was depleted (natural) uranium (U-238), the residue from separating the much rarer U-235 (much less than one percent of natural uranium) from natural uranium through a massive physical separation process for military applications. Since the mid-1950s, slightly enriched uranium (about three percent U-235) was needed as fuel for U.S. commercial reactors. "That's why we built the huge Manhattan Project, to carry out this enrichment process and why we are still operating enrichment plants," Holifield added.[6]

Aside from his discussions of U-238, U-235, and plutonium (Pu239), Holifield kept technicalities to a minimum as he explained how both sources of radioactive waste products could be used as a virtually inexhaustible supply of fuel for future reactors. Holifield told Nixon that, through the use of the breeder, "energy would be simultaneously and efficiently created to produce electricity for many, many generations. No longer useless, all the plutonium, U-238, and recycled U-235 would, therefore, become highly useable energy." Then came the Holifield punch line: "These ashes will be nothing more than waste until we process them and place them in breeders as fuel."

Holifield later felt that he had concluded in an almost pleading tone:

> Mr. President, we have more potential energy stored up and lying around in a few small acres of nuclear wastes than in all of the fossil fuel reserves known to humankind. That's true, if we demonstrate concretely that U.S. industry has the option of going to the breeder when needed. We're all set to move ahead. Of course, industry must use great care, and the highest engineering standards and rigorous quality control demanded of this new and more complex, but much more efficient technology.
>
> We desperately need a strong R&D program, along with a conservatively planned demonstration plant program, to get the practical experience with the breeder. In the 1950s we needed a successful demonstration of a civilian light water power reactor. This first electricity generating plant built at Shippingport, Pennsylvania was highly successful and created the high level of confidence everyone needed. Unless we build a few comparably successful breeder demonstration plants, the R&D community, the industry, and the public can't get the practical experience and confidence with this concept.[7]

Nixon seemed pleased by Holifield's informal assessment of the breeder. As they left *Air Force One*, however, both men agreed they would not discuss this matter with the waiting press; rather, the president would talk about his plans for reorganizing the government. Although he was personally skeptical of Nixon's reorganization plans, at the press briefing Holifield supported the president by indicating that he had agreed that his committee would hold hearings on Nixon's proposals. Holifield had not, however, gone away empty-handed; Nixon arranged for Holifield, AEC Chairman Glenn T. Seaborg, AEC Commissioner James T. Ramey, and AEC Division Director Milton Shaw to speak to the cabinet on this issue.

Holifield never presumed that his personal intervention with Nixon was primarily responsible for the president's decision to support the breeder or other energy projects. But from that point forward, Nixon's interest in the breeder and in the potentially serious nature of the nation's energy outlook did become intense. On June 4, 1971, in the first presidential energy policy message ever sent to Congress, the president emphasized that the breeder was "our best hope today for meeting the Nation's growing demand for economical clean energy." Nixon proposed that the development and demonstration of the breeder become the pivotal and highest-priority element in the U.S. effort to achieve long-term energy security. In 1973, after the OPEC-Arab oil embargo, President Nixon included the breeder as the central research and development plank in *Project Energy Independence*.[8]

Holifield was personally gratified by Nixon's actions on the breeder. For many years prior, he had been at the forefront of bipartisan efforts to give substance and stability to national energy policies and strategies. From his vantage point on the JCAE, he was among the few who recognized early that electricity had become a pervasive, indispensable element of modern society. There was a subtle, but definitely increasing dependence on electricity in most domestic, industrial, and defense activities that seemed to grow more widespread with each passing year. This was due, in part, to electricity's flexibility and its unique form, which permits its creation through various energy sources that affect its value, quantity, and quality. But more importantly, there were no reasonable substitutes for most of its uses, including many economic, labor-saving mechanisms in the home, work place, and industry. Holifield realized that electricity had become vital to the health, safety, and general welfare of the country, and to its defense. It had become as essential to everyday life in industrialized society as wholesome air, food, and water, and efficient transportation and recycling activities.

With such a clear appreciation for electricity himself, Holifield hoped to provide the leadership necessary to educate the public about the best methodologies for producing necessary "power" in future decades. He focused many JCAE hearings on fully developing and utilizing fission, which he believed to be the cleanest and most promising of America's baseload electric energy options. He also expended considerable effort in comparing fission energy with the other available options--coal, oil and gas--on the premise that all were needed and the subject of energy options "is far more important to the welfare of the Nation and the welfare of the people of the world than almost any domestic type problem that we can bring before us."[9]

Haberdasher on Capitol Hill

Holifield's personal meeting with Nixon was not the first time he had influenced decision-making by a president of the United States. He had advised Harry S Truman on the hydrogen bomb in the 1950s, John F. Kennedy on North Atlantic Treaty Organization (NATO) installations in 1960, and Lyndon B. Johnson on a multi-state power project and many other issues in the 1960s. This was high status and power, indeed, for a congressman who had never completed high school and who, as a small-town businessman, still maintained his haberdashery shop in California while serving in Congress. On one level, Holifield's story is an American success story, demonstrating how an ordinary American, possessing a limited formal education, albeit a high degree of intelligence, can nonetheless come to master even the most complex and intractable public issues, and "do something about them to help others make things come out right."[10]

It was not clear from the beginning of Holifield's life that he was destined to reach the apogee of national leadership and so influence events that U.S. presidents would accept his judgment on the shape and direction of public policy. Indeed, Holifield was thirty-nine years of age when he began his thirty-two year stint as a member of Congress. Up to that time, he was a self-made haberdasher who had come from his childhood home in Arkansas to the bright lights and opportunities of California. Born in Kentucky, raised in Arkansas, the youthful Holifield went west and settled in Montebello in 1920, then a booming oil town of 1800 people. He started his business with a loan cosigned by his father, and his first counter for his customers was a plank atop two wooden crates. From clothes cleaning and pressing, he expanded his business steadily until he was able to open a haberdashery called "Chet's House of Style." Although he became well-known in his community and began participating in civic activities, he had no real ambition to become a politician. It took the failure of his business during the Great Depression and a hunting accident that gave him time during recuperation to think about his and others' plights to make him a politically active citizen.

When he did enter politics, Holifield brought with him a philosophy that reflected his upbringing and experience as a small town businessman. His father was a lay preacher in the Christian Church and the young Holifield was exposed to a mixture of religious and "socialistic" ideas that colored his thinking and made him a "liberal" Democrat. He supported many of the social programs of the 1960s which had been viewed as radical, left-wing ideas during the 1930s. At the same time, his native intelligence, willingness to study issues fairly and persistently, ample common sense, and fair-minded spirit would make him acceptable to a wide spectrum of political groups. If he sometimes evidenced an unyielding determination on certain issues, Holifield also exhibited a warm personality and a simplicity of approach to life. As a person and politician (there was seldom a dichotomy in his public and private lives), he dealt with others on an "eyeball to eyeball" basis and supported with unflinching tenacity those who earned his trust by their integrity and deeds. For the most part, Holifield seemed to liberals and conservative "free enterprisers" alike a populist defender of the public interest, forever on guard against monopolies and other unfairness. Despite his liberalism, he had one viewpoint in common with small business conservatives: he looked at the marketplace through free enterprise lenses, possessing an innate wariness about "chain stores" and large industries of any kind.

Holifield could never quite forget his trade as a haberdasher during his thirty-two years in Congress. One of Holifield's staff members, Michael McGinn, who had been a naval officer during the Vietnam War, offered personal testimony to Holifield's continued commitment to tailoring in

Washington. During his first visit with his austere and prestigious chairman, McGinn was all business, nervously pointing to amendments, speeches, and ideas concerning a Cabinet-level office for Spanish-speaking Americans. This, too, was a subject close to Holifield's heart, but McGinn found himself interrupted several times. "That button is hanging off your coat. Let me fix it," he said. Handing over his jacket--all the while anxious that the chairman not miss a floor debate--McGinn stood agog as Holifield took out a pair of scissors, needle, and thread, snipped off the errant button, and then sewed it back on! Then both raced off to the floor of the House of Representatives![11]

The Road to Power: The Atomic Energy Act of 1946 and the JCAE

Holifield's road to power was long and not without the twists and turns of hardship and disappointment. He did, however, have some good luck along the way. Good fortune, mixed with long years of hard work and attention to duty, figured prominently in his ascent to two powerful chairmanships in the House. His first stroke of good luck was being selected as a junior member of the Military Affairs Committee not long before that committee would consider the nation's first atomic energy legislation. Holifield was astounded by the atomic discovery, and thereafter became a lifelong student of atomic energy. His future role in Congress was in fact grounded in a courageous stand he took in 1945. Joined by another young representative on the Military Affairs Committee, Melvin Price (D-Illinois), Holifield registered a striking legislative dissent against the otherwise unanimous judgment of the Democratic majority on the committee, insisting that control of the atom belonged in civilian rather than in military hands.[12]

Holifield's stand was a genuinely isolated and perilous stand for a junior member of Military Affairs, especially since notable scientists such as J. Robert Oppenheimer, Vannevar Bush, and James B. Conant were content to let the Pentagon maintain its untrammelled control of the atom. Yet Holifield believed that such military control could undermine American democracy. Ultimately, public opinion reinforced his position, and the Atomic Energy Act of 1946 firmly established control of the atom in civilian hands. Holifield thus caught the attention of the beleaguered Truman White House and Truman appointed him to serve as a member of the President's Civilian Evaluation Commission for the 1946 nuclear tests in the Bikini Islands. Speaker of the House Sam Rayburn (D-Texas) was also impressed, and appointed him to the new House-Senate JCAE created by the act.[13]

Much of Holifield's legacy as a congressman and legislative craftsman is tied to the JCAE. Among the few House-Senate joint committees created by Congress, only the JCAE possessed both the oversight and legislative functions. Endowed, in retrospect, with almost astonishing power and authority, the JCAE monitored and supervised the nation's vast atomic establishment for almost thirty years. By 1961 Holifield became chairman and for his remaining fourteen years in Congress was one of the committee's prime movers, along with Senator John O. Pastore (D-Rhode Island), with whom he shared the helm in alternate congresses. Holifield's tenacious determination to work closely with JCAE members and staff and to master everything he could about the atom and the ways of Congress lay at the heart of his capacity to dominate the JCAE and atomic energy affairs.

By the mid-1960s, the JCAE had compiled an enviable record on Capitol Hill. Its achievements were universally recognized, as was its comprehensive manner in approaching nuclear issues. According to contemporary journalist Oscar Johnson, "longtime committee members such as Holifield have over the years absorbed enough knowledge to amaze scientists and Atomic Energy Commission officials who deal with them." Johnson also noted that the JCAE sometimes brought in "panels of top scientists . . . for 'round-table' sessions on nuclear topics," and the results were "often printed and used as basic texts by graduate schools of physics around the country." By the time he retired, Holifield's JCAE influence was considerable enough that he was known by his friends and colleagues variously as "Mr. Atom" and "Mr. Atomic Energy."[14]

The Government Operations Committee

As with his leadership on the JCAE, Holifield was a major influence on the Government Operations Committee which he joined in 1946 when it was called the Committee on Expenditures in the Executive Departments. He served as chairman of some of its subcommittees before becoming *de facto* leader (acting chairman) in the late 1960s. In 1970, he became the chairman due to the death of Chairman William Dawson (D-Illinois).[15]

Government Operations' subpoena power and its unusually far-reaching mandate--to review government reorganization plans and to investigate any government problem touching on economy and efficiency--placed Holifield in a position to influence the very design of twentieth century American government. His contributions were enormous. In 1948-49 he was floor manager of the bill establishing the Department of Defense (DOD). In the 1960s he had the key House role in establishing two other Cabinet-level departments: Housing and Urban Development (HUD) and Transportation (DOT). With regard to these two bills, Holifield became the only representative in U.S. history to take the lead in creating two cabinet-level departments during a single Congress. Some of his other notable work on the committee included topics as diverse as creating the General Services Administration and the Commission on Government Procurement, fighting government excesses and abuses by big business, examining monopoly control by private industry over patent rights, investigating complaints against the Home Loan Bank Board, and criticizing proposals of the Second Hoover Commission.

Holifield's work on Government Operations encompassed far more than meets the eye, since his activities dealt with not only the organization of government, but its integrity. He never wavered from his determination to protect civil liberties and set the highest possible standards for integrity and commitment in government. His Government Operations work was also critical to his work on the JCAE. He influenced the nation's long-term energy security, development of all promising energy options, and nuclear safety by separating the AEC into the Energy Research and Development Administration (ERDA) and the Nuclear Regulatory Commission (NRC) in the mid-1970s. He thus laid the groundwork for the U.S. Department of Energy in 1977 created two years after his retirement. Unfortunately, he and others who relied on his leadership were not around by then to "help others make things come out right" for the new Cabinet-level department.

Achievement of Legislative Mastery

Given the breadth of his activities and his eagerness to learn all aspects of the legislative process, Holifield eventually became one of the two dozen or so congressmen in his generation recognized as master legislators by their peers. In achieving legislative mastery, Holifield knew there was no other way than to take the time--much time--to learn what he termed "the temper of the House" on the many issues presented in each Congress over the span of thirty-two years. His story is not replete with constant episodes that gave him prominence in the public eye. Most of his early legislative achievements were, in fact, made out of the limelight. This changed when he became Dean of the California congressional delegation, still the largest in Congress. He continues to hold the record for the highest number of special recognitions and commendation awards made to California representatives by the prestigious California Congressional Recognition Program.[16] As he aged and moved up in the ranks, he came to be appreciated as one of the House's master tacticians; thus, he was able to exercise a degree of legislative influence rarely equalled. His long tenure and diverse committee and other political experience, combined with strong personal traits, were important training grounds for his mastery of the art of legislating.[17]

Holifield's mastery of legislating extended far beyond committee work and attention to California affairs. In the late 1950s he was a founding member of the Democratic Study Group, a group of reform-minded Democratic House members intent upon reforming the House Rules Committee, whose chairman had made a science of killing legislation by failing to report it back to the House. Holifield increased his stature as a legislator by serving as a balancing force between the House leadership and the more radical members of the Democratic Study Group. Ultimately, the Study Group succeeded in getting House leaders to limit the power of the Rules Committee.

Holifield's keen legislative skills were put to the test many times during his tenure in office. He won some long, hard-fought battles when many before him had failed, such as during the early 1960s when he obtained an interstate agreement on a Pacific Electric Intertie to coordinate "firm" power supplies among several major public and private electrical suppliers along the West Coast. Holifield and many others consider this project among his major long-term accomplishments. But some of his legislative successes had negative side effects as well. During his efforts to protect individual privacy by reforming the General Accounting Office's reporting practices, he was falsely accused of attempting to destroy this government watchdog agency. Later, Holifield's rejection of the Republicans' request for specific minority party staff on House committees also won him much political enmity.

Holifield was a curious blend of partisan Democrat and nonpartisan legislator. He was a loyal Democrat, who attended most national conventions and helped write the party platforms; he could be fiercely partisan in political tugs of war with Republicans. As a legislator and committee chairman, however, he was nonpartisan and most would say fair-minded in his dealings. His willingness to deal equitably with others won both praise and criticism. Some Democrats were angry about Holifield's willingness to deal equitably with Nixon on the breeder, for example. Other observers were impressed with his nonpartisan attitude in this and similar instances. Dwight Ink, a former AEC official with experience also in the Bureau of the Budget and the General Services Administration, offered this assessment:

> Chet was a partisan Democrat when it came to elections; he would tell President Nixon, for instance, that the Democrats would catch the GOP at the next polling opportunity. But when it came to examining and voting on public issues, he would study and vote on a straight up-and-down basis, simply considering them on their merits. His sense of personal and public integrity was so fixed that each succeeding presidential administration, Republican or Democratic, found it easy to confide in and trust him.[18]

Holifield's Relationships With His Staffs

Holifield's fair-minded attitudes extended to both his personal staff and his committee staff. Both Ed Bauser, the last Executive Director of the JCAE, and Adam Klein, Holifield's last, long-serving administrative assistant, agree that he drew no lines between his personal staff and committee staff. Bauser had only praise for Holifield's committee leadership and relations with staff:

> Chet's leadership qualities, his energy and ability to get things done were quickly recognized in the Congress. In recognition, the leadership of the House assigned responsibilities to him normally reserved for members of greater seniority. His ability to take hold and move the issues, even in such completely new areas as atomic energy,

exceeded his colleagues' expectations. The word quickly spread: "If you want it done, see Chet." As a consequence Chet became involved in many major issues.

One of Chet's outstanding characteristics runs throughout his congressional service and warrants special recognition. This was his ability to get the help and cooperation of all of his associates, peers and subordinates alike, as well as others in government and industry who were involved in making things come out right. He knew the importance of this asset to the attainment of success and he knew how to develop it. His relations with his staff illustrates this.

He stressed and encouraged independence and initiative. The degree to which he carried this was always at first a shock to his new people. He made it clear that their work was critical to getting the job done. His alert mind and intellectual curiosity provided a challenge that brought out the best. He concentrated on getting people with the highest professional qualifications and a track record of success. Once proven, he gave them full rein. Of course, Chet always knew what was going on and wanted to be informed of the reasons behind the activities. All of his staff knew the moral and professional standards of excellence he expected to be followed. One item he stressed--to the point approaching a fetish--was his demand that no one should delay an instant in telling him if he was doing anything wrong. He made it clear that failure in this respect was unpardonable. Chet was always available to listen, counsel, and help. He was always generous in acknowledging the support and contributions of his people. There was no limit his staff wouldn't go to for him.[19]

As a staff person, Adam Klein concentrated mostly on matters other than those in the nuclear arena. He recalled his early years of committee service and his impressions of Holifield as a congressman:

By the 1960s Holifield had gained sufficient seniority to obtain a subcommittee chairmanship on the Government Operations Committee and become Chairman of the new Military Operations Subcommittee, formed in 1970, with jurisdiction over the Department of Defense. His previous experience on the Military Affairs and JCAE committees and his participation in organizing the Department of Defense were very helpful. As he saw it, the rapid growth of government, particularly the large military buildup of strategic forces and increased military R&D programs begun under the Kennedy administration, had outpaced the oversight ability of Congress and its capability to account to the taxpayer for the expenditure of funds. A small, competent professional staff was a necessity and Holifield was determined to get the best to work with him.

Without any question, Holifield found the bedrock for his coverage in these areas in Herbert Roback, an intelligent, hard-working, tough-minded and meticulous but unassuming man who was highly recommended by Senator "Scoop" Jackson and others who had worked with him. For legal counsel for his subcommittee staff he chose Douglas Dahlin, an experienced and highly qualified Harvard law graduate and as analysts, Paul Ridgely and Joseph Lumen. Ridgely had been a congressional page before returning to college and back to Chet's staff, and Lumen had served in the Korean war and become an attorney before ending up with Chet. Of course, there were others, but these seemed to be the most prominent from my contact with them.

Chet's transition in acting for and eventually replacing Chairman William Dawson on the Government Operations Committee gave him sufficient confidence in that strong, highly competent professional staff. They responded to Chet's leadership in an outstanding manner. It appears that Miles Q. Romney, counsel for the committee, is the last of that group and from what I hear, he continues to perform in an exemplary manner. Others that I can easily recall because of their unique capabilities and long-term commitments are Elmer Henderson, Staff Director and formerly Chief Counsel, and James Lanigan, Chief Counsel.[20]

As other staff members also stressed, Klein emphasized Holifield's nonpartisanship and close attention to work. "He never asked any staff member what his political preference was before he was hired," Klein noted. "Competence and ability were far more important." In summing up Holifield's attention to duty, Klein explained: "Chet attended every committee meeting that he could, read voraciously, listened and reasoned, and became a self-made expert in government procurement and administration, in addition to other areas he felt were his responsibility."[21]

Klein was also impressed by the amount of work that Holifield performed. "Most of the time," Klein explained, "it seemed like there were several major bills in the works at one time; committee meetings in the morning; House sessions in the afternoon; staff meetings in the office from 6:00 p.m. to 8:30 or 9:00 p.m.; and commission meetings on Saturdays and often Sundays--week after week." To enhance the prospects for his bills, Klein noted that Holifield often held working sessions at his Prospect House apartment on Saturdays and Sundays over brunch served by his understanding wife Cam.[22]

Holifield and the 1946 Bikini Tests

If there were any single guideposts or events in the early years of atomic energy that greatly influenced Holifield, they were the Bikini Island nuclear tests of 1946. These tests were the first atomic explosions witnessed by Holifield. His appointment by President Truman to the Civilian Evaluation Commission allowed him to witness first-hand the tremendous power of the atom. He was deeply impressed that July by the obliteration of the Bikini Atoll and the wholesale sinking of retired warships. First at Bikini and throughout his career, he understood the overriding necessity of containing the dangerous fission products present whenever nuclear energy is released. The Bikini blasts led him to conclude that humanity should never fight a nuclear war that no one could contain or win. The fundamental issue for Holifield was control: not only physical control of the dangerous by-products, but the methods of controlling the atom from both military and civilian standpoints that would contribute most toward the nurturing of democratic societies. For Holifield, effective control was critical to the continuance of American democracy and other Western governments.

Holifield believed in the ideal of world disarmament; one of his first pieces of atomic energy legislation asked that "negotiations with the United Nations be undertaken" with the objective that "a realistic hope of Peace be substituted for the present universal fear of mass annihilation through atomic war."[23] He also worked hard to improve the International Atomic Energy Agency and its safeguard efforts to prevent the spread of nuclear weapons. He was also fully behind the Nuclear Test Ban Treaty of 1963 and the Treaty on the Nonproliferation of Nuclear Weapons in 1968. As Dwight Ink, former Assistant General Manager of the AEC, remarked, "Holifield was frequently [at] center stage . . . through his chairmanship of the JCAE, and later the Subcommittee on Legislation and Military Operations of Government Operations, which he later chaired."[24] Despite his interests in peace and nonproliferation, however, Holifield's common sense also led him to push for practical deterrence measures, as in his 1949 support for development of the hydrogen bomb as a counterbalance to Soviet atomic bomb development.

Beyond control, the Bikini tests provided a lasting challenge to Holifield to develop nuclear energy for multiple purposes. He knew that military aspects could not be avoided, but he did not let these aspects nor their imperatives for safety overwhelm his judgment about potential peaceful applications. As he had stated in his dissent on the 1946 legislation, Holifield believed that the atom could be harnessed to produce electricity and provide other peacetime benefits, resulting in jobs, economic growth, and other societal benefits.[25] The tests only added to his vision and resolve to see the atom serve, rather than destroy, humanity. Holifield wanted to put the atom to work in such highly diversified fields as medicine, outer space, agriculture, telecommunications, health products, and processing and preserving food. Consistent with his Christian upbringing, he sought to use the atom quite literally to help feed the hungry, heal the sick, and provide jobs and other benefits to Americans and all humanity. The evidence of his success is reflected in many peacetime uses. He was proud of the peaceful atom's achievements during the last forty years:

> In the annals of mankind, we have never seen an industrial record like that of the peaceful atom. It has over 3,000 peacetime uses all developed in a brief span of 30 years. Its record of accomplishments in health, safety and other beneficial uses has no parallel, whatsoever, whether industrial or medical, in human history.[26]

Perhaps the most significant "fallout" for Holifield from the Bikini tests was that he was able to achieve a balance in promoting the military and peaceful applications of the atom. Very early on, he considered the military and civilian facets of the subject together in educating the public on both the effects of radiation and the vast costs and practical impossibilities associated with civil defense. Shortly after he returned from the Bikini tests, he wrote that "For all practical purposes, in the Atomic Age a defense is impossible."[27] He eventually developed and chaired some of the most comprehensive hearings on radiation hazards and civil defense in the nation's history. His activities should, in retrospect, make him almost a patron saint of advocates of a "nuclear freeze" or those committed to world disarmament. "I always believed there was no defense against atomic weapons," Holifield later commented, "but the hearings I chaired gave others a chance to comprehend this fact." Holifield's hearings during the 1950s offered extensive scientific evidence to sustain his judgment at Bikini: "There is no complete or effective defense against the destructive features of atomic warfare."[28] In addition to his civil defense and radiation hazards hearings, Holifield melded still other military and civil aspects. He strongly supported development of the hydrogen bomb and Admiral Hyman G. Rickover's efforts to create a nuclear-powered Navy, both actions designed to strengthen America's military might. A political realist, he was ever mindful that the U.S. must counterbalance the Soviet Union during the Cold War that raged during most of his tenure.

Holifield and the Military Atom

The military atom took precedence during the early years, and Holifield followed suit. In fact, there was little time to adjust to the new organizational arrangements under the 1946 act before a major crisis erupted. In October 1949, JCAE members and then the public learned that the Soviet Union had detonated an atomic bomb. The question of whether the U.S. should keep technologically ahead of the Russians by developing the "super" or hydrogen bomb became a divisive issue within the government, and pitted the JCAE against the AEC, the other major organization created by the 1946 act. Although he had argued for civilian control, Holifield now supported development of the hydrogen bomb wholeheartedly as a necessary expedient. His investigation of the feasibility of the hydrogen bomb and report to the JCAE and President Truman enhanced his own status within the JCAE. Truman's decision to develop the hydrogen bomb would further enhance the prestige of the JCAE and its primary role in overseeing and guiding the atom.

Holifield remained ever the epitome of the Cold War Warrior, always mindful of the need for vigilance in international affairs at a time when communism was on the upswing throughout the world. Although the world order has changed much during 1989-1995, Holifield then held few illusions about the threat to U.S. security and world peace posed by the Soviet Union from the end of World War II into the late 1980s. The expansive Soviet presence along the Mongolian border and the northern chain of islands above Japan and Soviet support for insurgencies in North Korea and Vietnam, Holifield believed, had revealed the Soviets' overriding objective to make Communist states in the countries of the Far East. In his view, not only were the Soviets determined to command the region's natural resources, but most importantly, their main historical thrust, consistent with centuries of Russian imperialism, was to control the industrial capacity and genius of Japan. Along with other U.S. leaders, Holifield was determined to thwart this objective, and events of the early 1990s have made such a result less likely.[29]

Vietnam proved to be part of the Far East puzzle that Holifield, like others, was unable to solve. The California congressman was a consistent supporter of every administration's policy in Indochina, including President Johnson's Gulf of Tonkin Resolution and Nixon's policies. For Holifield, support of Johnson's decision to expand the war was a difficult choice, but one he felt bound to make. As Vietnam dragged on interminably, support for the war became politically unpopular. After 1968, Holifield found his views divergent from those of new and younger Democrats, especially after the traditional Democratic coalition gave way under the Vietnam burden. Never one to hold views simply to be "politically correct," he continued to support Johnson's and later, even Nixon's, Vietnam policies. In fact, he received two personal letters of thanks from Nixon for supporting the Republican administration's efforts to extricate the U.S. from the Vietnam quagmire.[30]

By 1972, Holifield was troubled and even insulted by the McGovern forces' takeover of the national convention, and he refused to attend as a delegate. That the Vietnam military action was not ultimately successful in keeping South Vietnam from communist control was, Holifield later recognized, a major tragedy in American history. Nonetheless, from his perspective, the U.S. had been bound legally by its treaties with South Vietnam and its own national self-interest to oppose communist takeovers of other societies by force. In Holifield's opinion, the U.S. intervention in South Vietnam did succeed to some degree in its larger purposes of delaying, and perhaps restraining, Soviet pursuit of larger objectives in the Far East.

Admiral Rickover: Holifield's Bridge to the Peaceful Atom

Holifield's support for Admiral Hyman G. Rickover had vital implications for the Cold War and the military atom, but also for the peaceful atom. Holifield gained his legislative and technical spurs in atomic energy and national security not merely in the halls of Congress, but by reaching out constantly to support and protect Rickover. A captain at the time, Rickover was forced to fight the Navy brass to get them to accept nuclear-powered submarines and later, a nuclear surface fleet. Rickover faced determined opposition in attempting to exploit basic practical technological innovations for national security. Holifield was aware of this and joined a coterie of about a half dozen other advocates on the JCAE who assisted Rickover over three decades in building the "nuclear Navy." Holifield and his allies were also directly involved in obtaining Rickover's promotions to rear admiral and vice admiral to allow him to continue to serve the nation. As of June 1993, over 215 of Rickover's pressurized water nuclear plants had been applied to over 180 U.S. Navy combatant vessels, which boasted an impeccable safety record of over 4,000 accident-free reactor-years of power operations.[31]

Holifield's belief that a nuclear navy, especially the nuclear submarine, was indispensable to national security was the reason he firmly backed Rickover's proposals. By the early 1950s, the Californian had become convinced that a defense system centered on bombers and intercontinental rockets would eventually prove vulnerable. On the other hand, nuclear-powered submarines, proven capable of long-term submersion, stealth, and mobility, and mated with ballistic missiles or other unique features, would remain relatively invulnerable for decades. He was convinced that such submarines would become the principal foundation of U.S. strategic defense.

Holifield's most significant ties to the peaceful atom were solidified in July 1953, when Congress authorized Rickover to turn his vision, talents, and irrepressible energy to the challenge of building the world's first, full-scale civilian nuclear power plant. Holifield and AEC Commissioner Thomas E. Murray were convinced that this was the quickest and surest way of moving forward on this and other unclassified projects that the AEC and nuclear communities elsewhere were only dreaming about. The sweeping success of the Shippingport plant, which reached full power in December 1957, made it the centerpiece and most substantial and visible embodiment of President Eisenhower's widely heralded "Atoms for Peace" Program. This success and Holifield's continuing in-depth exposure to Rickover and his prudent and highly disciplined methods and leadership convinced Holifield that equivalent managerial and technical approaches would be absolutely essential for a civilian nuclear power industry and for the AEC's programs. Holifield continually stressed that without comparable management, the nation would not be able to achieve uniform success with nuclear power commitments nor be able to sustain, for long, public confidence in the atom as a relatively safe and benign instrument to serve humanity.

By normal standards, Holifield believed, public confidence should reflect the remarkable public health and safety record of U.S. nuclear reactors. In the last 35 years, over 400 U.S.-designed light water reactor (LWR) plants have operated throughout the world, with over 5,400 reactor-years of operation in widespread naval and commercial use. During this time, no member of the public nor any civilian plant operator is known to have died or sustained a serious injury from radiation attributable to reactor operation, even though many commercial plants have suffered serious malfunctions, dangerous fires, and spectacular "accidents," including the most serious and costly accident at Three Mile Island in 1979.[32] Holifield acknowledges that such a remarkable record may be difficult, if not impossible, to sustain, particularly since the demands are mounting for improved performance from aging LWRs. Experience suggests, however, that with high standards and qualified management, even if problems do occur, the results will not be catastrophic, but rather will include only isolated injuries and deaths that are almost inevitably encountered in an industrial society.

Dawn of the Nuclear Power Industry

In the early 1950s, Holifield at first objected to the development of nuclear power by private industry because he feared that industry was not qualified nor committed to discharge all responsibilities entailed in this new venture. Accordingly, he fought very hard, but unsuccessfully, against revisions to the 1946 act proposed by the Eisenhower administration. The Atomic Energy Act of 1954 passed over his strenuous objections, although it did reflect his legislative handiwork. Holifield also resisted JCAE efforts to produce a bill to provide government indemnification insurance for private industry in the event of a nuclear accident, still arguing that nuclear power was too new and untried to be trusted exclusively to private enterprise. When industry was unable to follow through on its 1954 mandate to accelerate atomic power development, Holifield cosponsored legislation with Senator Albert Gore (D-Tennessee) to build demonstration plants on federal reservations in order to "iron out any kinks" before unleashing nuclear power into the civilian marketplace. While the Gore-Holifield bill narrowly failed passage, it set off a chain reaction in Congress and the AEC which increased JCAE oversight and authorization powers over all nuclear power activities.

By 1957, Holifield had accepted the entry of private industry into nuclear power development, but he continued to insist on strengthening management and engineering standards. Having personally visited a large number of utilities and suppliers and garnered voluminous information from other sources, he found that only a few businesses seemed able to manage nuclear power in a disciplined, and safe manner. Holifield's views in this regard led many in industry to classify him as an anti-business zealot, but this did not cause him to change his opinions. In the 1960s he placed his legislative prestige on the line by backing the AEC's decision to impose stronger managerial and engineering discipline on AEC laboratories and contractors. He also urged that standardization policies be established to reduce nuclear plant costs, and enhance performance and public confidence.[33]

The Holifield-Ramey-Shaw Alliance

In his crusade to ensure safe and efficient nuclear power, Holifield relied heavily on his last two JCAE executive directors, John Conway and Edward Bauser. At the AEC, Holifield turned to Commissioner James T. Ramey and Milton Shaw, director of the Division of Reactor Development and

Technology (RDT). Ramey was a former JCAE executive director and personal friend of Holifield, and the AEC's longest-serving commissioner (1962-1973). Shaw also became a close friend, and was the longest-serving director of the AEC's reactor R&D programs, from 1964 to 1973.[34] While Holifield knew Conway, Bauser, and Ramey from their JCAE service, he had not known Shaw well until 1964, even though Shaw had been a principal Naval Reactors (NR) official since 1950. When Holifield first heard Shaw testify before the JCAE, Holifield quickly concluded that the AEC had found in this Rickover protege the managerial and engineering leadership it required to inject a sense of hard-nosed technical direction and realism into nuclear R&D programs. In the eyes of the JCAE, the AEC's approach was too laboratory-oriented, and not forceful and definitive enough to meet the nation's energy commitments. Shaw was blunt-speaking and not always politically sensitive, but he did enjoy the full confidence of Rickover and most other national engineering leaders, and that was sufficient for Holifield.

After getting to know Shaw, Holifield and Ramey formed a close alliance with him in order to upgrade management and technical capabilities in RDT programs. They strongly supported Shaw's determination to attract the nation's most experienced professionals and promising young engineers and scientists. They also supported RDT fully in its efforts to improve performance of laboratory and industrial units involved in nuclear R&D, operations, safety, and security. All three men agreed that R&D support from AEC laboratories on complex programs should be directly accountable to the RDT Director. With this support, Shaw carefully monitored and coordinated laboratory efforts, fully expecting them to fulfill their responsibilities in a safe, timely, cost-effective, and environmentally acceptable manner.

Holifield's Later Years: The Breeder and its Opposition

Holifield's meeting with Nixon was only the tip of the iceberg in the JCAE's and AEC's efforts to develop and demonstrate the breeder. The Holifield-Ramey-Shaw doctrine of management and engineering excellence and centralized coordination faced various barriers and met with considerable opposition from most AEC laboratories and contractors. Judging from the real accomplishments throughout Shaw's career, Shaw and his talented RDT associates and laboratory-contractor-utility teams probably would have produced a viable breeder demonstration plant in a reasonable period but for the unprecedented, disruptive changes in the political winds of Washington.

The political environment in Washington that was indispensable in the development of nuclear power disappeared during the last few years of Holifield's career. In Congress, Representative Richard Bolling (D-Missouri) proposed sweeping committee reforms, including elimination of the JCAE, an action that had the support of a new generation of liberal Democratic congressmen. Holifield bitterly opposed Bolling's JCAE proposal and was able to stave off such an effort as long as he remained in office. On the domestic front, the new Republican administration of Richard Nixon brought a new political orientation to the AEC. Under AEC Chairman Dixy Lee Ray, the AEC became hostile to the Holifield-Ramey-Shaw alliance, resulting in the forced retirements of Ramey and Shaw in 1973. With the retirement of stalwarts Holifield and Craig Hosmer (R-California) in late 1974, the JCAE also lost its battle for survival under Bolling's reorganization axe. The real loser in the fray was the breeder program, still the nation's best hope for demonstrating a virtually inexhaustible and clean domestic energy source.

In addition to adverse Capitol Hill politics and skirmishes with the Nixon AEC, Holifield also faced opposition on a new front. The environmental opposition to nuclear power was born in the 1960s, and had adherents in Congress and around the country by the time Holifield retired. He found himself increasingly classified as a member of the Atomic Establishment, along with most JCAE members and the AEC.[35] Part of his problems with environmentalists stemmed from his consumerism rows with Ralph Nader and Nader's allies in the House, but also from Holifield's refusal to give in to individual scientific views that were counter to consensus opinions of reputable scientific organizations. Ironically, Holifield had always considered himself to be a consumer advocate and an environmentalist, having introduced many consumer protection and environmental bills during the 1960s and 1970s. He had often conceded that nuclear power was in trouble due to a multiplicity of problems and felt that there was "enough blame to go around" for these problems, including the "weaknesses even of some major participants and companies in the nuclear arena." He also allowed that "There's also been a decline of forceful leadership in science, government, and industry, blind political partisanship, and the growth of environmental reactionaries." Yet Holifield was particularly upset with the media's sensational and mostly negative coverage of nuclear power and extreme environmental views that did not take into account the many positive aspects of nuclear power:

> Even now [Holifield wrote these words in 1992], fear and total ignorance of scientific and technological facts cause opponents of nuclear power to ignore its broad and profoundly different spans of application. They are unaware of its potential for humanity's future. They overlook an amazing and successful record in many peaceful uses of the atom. These routinely benefit the public. Electricity has been generated and war deterred despite many failures attendant on nuclear development. Few people seem to understand that from the beginning specific actions were taken to have scientists and engineers, doctors and technicians develop unprecedented and conservative practices and safety measures for controlling nuclear power or its other uses. And these are put to daily use for public well-being. But, there are few real options if these were not available.

Opponents have played on popular fears generated by the dropping of the atomic bomb on Japan.   There have also been uncalled-for failures and economic catastrophes such as those at TMI and at Chernobyl in Russia. Fear-mongers, zealot Luddites and an ultra-sensational news media constantly frighten many people into blind opposition to the atom. Never before has such a benefit to mankind been so abused by mindless people. Moreover, the 'anti's' have been helped by thoughtless officials in government and industry who attempt to bypass basic management and technological imperatives which are indispensable to its safe use. Scaremongers exaggerate legitimate concerns and problems affecting the weakest links in the government and nuclear industry but they totally ignore the successes of the majority of the participants in the nuclear field and the continuing improvements.[36]

Although he would have liked to continue the fight and overcome through education the many unfair aspersions cast on nuclear power, age and family concerns were catching up on Holifield. As he made a hard decision to retire from Congress after sixteen terms (thirty-two years) at seventy-one years of age, Holifield must have known that an era in atomic energy had come to an end. With his and Craig Hosmer's simultaneous retirements, the JCAE lost what the AEC had already lost: a generation of leaders fervently committed to the federal government's safe development of both the military and peaceful atom. With the demise of the JCAE and the AEC's simultaneous reorganization into separate R&D and regulatory agencies at the beginning of 1975, no individual congressman or single congressional committee would have a similar opportunity to impact atomic energy in the future, certainly not in the direct ways in which JCAE members like Holifield had.

To a large extent, Chet Holifield's story is a microcosm of the political history of the postwar period in the United States. As a leader of the JCAE, he helped to guide the route taken by atomic energy in both its military and peaceful applications for much of the second half of the twentieth century. As a leader of the Government Operations Committee, he participated in creating many of the government agencies which administered both defense and social services programs. As a dedicated and fervent Democrat, he was a mover and shaker in the liberal Democratic majority that controlled the Congress in all but a few sessions from 1932 to 1994. Finally, as a human being, family man, businessman, and politician, Holifield exemplified many, if not most, of the values and ideas that held sway during the last half century, from the sufferings he endured in the Great Depression that awoke his social consciousness and convinced him that government should intervene in the social and economic arenas, to his experiences in World War II that weighted his thinking on the contest between the U.S. and the Soviet Union for world hegemony, culminating in what he later believed to be the tragedy of Vietnam. In all of these ways and more, Holifield's story is worth telling for the contributions that it can make toward understanding United States history in the twentieth century.

2

Mr. Atom Goes Critical

Encounter with the Atom

When Chet Holifield reached Capitol Hill in January 1943, scientists were already at work on the atomic bomb. Because the research was conducted with utmost secrecy, Holifield was not even aware that such a bomb of mass destruction was in the works. Even less did he realize that events during his second term in Congress would transform him into one of the nation's premier legislators in the field of atomic energy. The atomic explosions at Hiroshima and Nagasaki would pique his interest in atomic energy, but Holifield's ascent to legislative power would begin with his opposition to the Truman administration's proposals for a postwar organizational framework for atomic energy. Holifield took the road less traveled in objecting to continued military control of atomic energy, but he was ultimately assisted in his efforts by a groundswell of other legislators, scientific organizations, and the public. The civilian-oriented Atomic Energy Act of 1946 bore the results of his and others' handiwork, and his appointment to the Joint Committee on Atomic Energy (JCAE) provided a base of operations for further contributions. Holifield and the JCAE became even more firmly entrenched as the nation's most important policy-making body for atomic energy largely due to their contributions to President Truman's hydrogen bomb decision of January 1950, which occurred hardly thirty months after the inception of the new committee.

Civilian vs. Military Control of the Atom

As a layman, Holifield was not privy to the technical research and philosophical ruminations of scientists studying atomic structure prior to World War II. Scientists were hopeful from the beginning that splitting the atom would have beneficial peacetime, as well as military, applications. Even after the war began, some scientists were concerned about developing a peacetime framework for exploiting nuclear materials for peaceful applications. They speculated often about medical, power, and other applications. Prior to the war, one widely-published news story pointed out that a penny contained enough energy to power a ship to England and back!

Once World War II was in full swing, the military atom got the most attention. Scientists such as Albert Einstein had foreseen that enormous amounts of energy in the atom's nucleus could be unlocked if a specific key were uncovered. This key was found before the war, in 1932, with the discovery of the neutron, a tiny uncharged particle in the nucleus. In 1938, two German scientists, Otto Hahn and Friedrich Straussman, hit upon the process called fission by determining that a nucleus of uranium split into fragments and released energy when it absorbed a neutron. In 1941, scientists demonstrated a chain reaction with the fission process, resulting in the release of a tremendous amount of energy. In fact, a fission process employing one ton of uranium 235 theoretically could generate an estimated equivalent fuel value of some three million tons of coal or up to 12 million barrels of oil!

To turn this tremendous energy into atomic bombs, the ultra-secret Manhattan Project was formed in 1942 and managed by the Army. It became the largest R&D program in world history. The small band of nuclear scientists knew their findings were sensitive and had imposed a security ban on themselves, refusing to divulge their work unless absolutely essential. With the Manhattan effort underway, these and other scientists nonetheless chafed under the tight security arrangements, contending that the head of the Manhattan Project, Colonel (later General) Leslie Groves, did not seem to fully appreciate the constraints placed on technological innovation. They felt that wartime concentration on weapons was leading to neglect of broader uses of the atom to protect national security. Some scientists were particularly fearful about military prohibitions being extended into the postwar era.[1]

The May-Johnson Bill

In July 1944, one year before the war ended, various proposals were advanced within the government for a postwar domestic body to control atomic energy. By July 1945, the War Department had unified the proposals into a bill calling for a part-time, nine-member commission, including members of the Army and the Navy. This bill was introduced by Andrew J. May (D-Kentucky), chairman of the House Military Affairs Committee, and Edwin C. Johnson (D-Colorado), ranking member of the Senate's Military Affairs Committee. The May-Johnson bill was not without opposition. Critics charged that the bill was merely an extension of wartime practices, and that it would restrict scientific research, peaceful applications, and freedom of opinion. To complicate matters further, the Senate seemed preoccupied with carving out a role for itself; this led to a resolution for a joint congressional committee to examine atomic energy. Freshman senator Brien McMahon (D-Connecticut), who had introduced the first bill proposing a new atomic control board composed of Cabinet officers and other federal officials, was subsequently named chairman of a special Senate committee of eleven members appointed in October by the Senate's pro tempore leader, Kenneth McKellar (D-Tennessee). While others seemed logical contenders to head this committee, Vice President Alben Barkley and McKellar settled on McMahon. At the White House, President Truman had not yet decided what to do about postwar atomic development. While May-Johnson was the administration's measure, Truman did not support its specific provisions.[2]

In the House, May scheduled what he foresaw as quick and short hearings. The hearings took exactly one day, October 9, 1945. After a message from Truman was read, Secretary of War Patterson outlined the major provisions in the bill: creation of a part-time, nine-member commission; "minimum interference" in private research by the commission; stringent security provisions; and an administrator for running the day-to-day affairs. Groves testified in favor of the bill, stating that the nation would not use atomic power for commercial purposes in the immediate future. Leading scientists also supported the bill. No one scheduled to testify had any major criticisms.[3]

Holifield, a low-ranking committee member, listened intently, but as a junior legislator he could ask only one question. In a way, he was unique on the committee. When he heard news reports of the Hiroshima bombing, he read all the material he could get on atomic energy. In fact, he and Senator William Fulbright (D-Arkansas) were the only two legislators who had read Henry DeWolf Smyth's report on the atomic bomb.[4] Other members were almost completely unprepared to deal with the subject. Only a few caught the basic import of the War Department's proposal: the part-time, military-assisted commission would have total control over atomic energy. Congress, aside from appropriations, would have no role. Several members wondered out loud about the idea of excluding Congress, the bill's ill-defined security provisions, and the presumption that the public would not benefit much in the short run from nuclear power. Overall, however, the bill was unhampered by substantial criticisms. Chairman May had set the tone for the committee's deliberations by brushing aside any in-depth reviews. To one representative who inquired whether uranium was mixed with other metals or found by itself in nature, the chairman replied: "I wonder if that is not going a little bit too much into detail?" Such reactions tended to stifle any meaningful opposition.[5]

News of the short hearings should have created a political thunderclap across the country, with scientists finding the security provisions excessive and alarming. But no such thing occurred, in large part due to timing. In October 1945, scientists were flocking away from the nation's atomic laboratories toward the peacetime academic market. With little informed opposition in Washington, the House was about to accept the May-Johnson bill almost without discussion and by an overwhelming majority.

Chet Holifield and a smattering of House legislators and scientists were the few holdouts to the House's inattention to May-Johnson. As has happened at other critical junctures in U.S. history, a small group would turn the tide. Holifield and his allies were aroused to action by the peremptory and brusque decision of May to hold only one day of hearings. Holifield, for one, protested heatedly to May. The Kentucky Democrat, whose entire concern about the atom, Holifield believed, revolved around what it would do to the coal industry, got pressured from other sectors as well, and reluctantly agreed to schedule another hearing for October 18, 1945.[6]

The new hearing was much different from the first. This time, three prominent scientists--Herbert Anderson, Leo Szilard, and Arthur Compton--testified against the proposal. Holifield's friend and political mentor, Representative Jerry Voorhis, also testified about the bill's shortcomings. Still another protest by scientist Harold Urey was placed in the record, because Holifield could not reach Urey in time to testify.[7] Holifield was also more vocal and assertive at the October 18 hearings. He extended his questioning along more detailed lines, realizing that Congress and the public had to be educated. He was particularly concerned with the military versus civilian control issue, the make-up of the commission, and the security provisions, but he devoted most of his time to the more esoteric subject of patents.

On the military versus civilian control issue, Holifield found an able military defender in the "father of the atomic bomb," Dr. J. Robert Oppenheimer. When he asked Oppenheimer if a military-dominated commission "would be conducive to full and free scientific research," and whether it would be wise to place atomic energy in the hands of the military completely, Oppenheimer replied that he could not think "of an administrator in whom I have more confidence than General [George C.] Marshall." Oppenheimer did allow that such an organization "might be unwise, but I think it is a matter not what uniform a man wears but what kind of a man he is." Holifield was not to be put off so easily, however. He asked Oppenheimer whether R&D "might be done along military lines rather than along civilian lines" in a military-dominated commission. Oppenheimer's response and Holifield's rejoinder capsulized this basic difference in opinion between the two men:[8]

Oppenheimer:	It might. It would certainly be so--
Holifield:	Naturally, would it not?
Oppenheimer:	No. I was going to say that if the administrators were chosen as representatives of the services to carry out work of consequence to the services, then it might be so.

Holifield countered that he favored military control of military applications, but that he would hesitate to turn over all R&D because the military might not look upon civilian research as favorably as some. Oppenheimer replied that this might be true, but that May-Johnson was an attempt to get atomic energy out of the War Department, not into it. Holifield asserted that he was not so certain on that score. May interrupted this colloquy, declaring "the War Department discovered the weapon. Why can they not keep the secret?"

The scientific testimony made it clear that there was not yet a consensus on a postwar framework for atomic energy. Holifield asked Arthur Compton whether the commission should be full-time or part-time, and more pointedly, whether the commission could "render a service commensurate with the importance of this affair and be composed only of part-time men." Compton thought it "doubtful public policy to put a majority of full-time men on this commission" because it should be composed of "men with broad interests." There was also a divergence of opinion on freedom of research. Compton thought that security restrictions would be better left to the new commission. Szilard felt the government "should have the power to carry out the needed development itself, but not the power to prevent other people from carrying out development work . . . government control can be carried too far."

If there were any overriding philosophical principles expressed at the hearings, they were provided by Voorhis. Closely mirroring Holifield's views, Voorhis believed that the guiding principles of the legislation should be "widespread dissemination" of atomic energy's benefits to the people, and avoidance of atomic warfare. To ensure benefits to all Americans, Voorhis argued that "the basic right of all patents" should rest with the government. On the possibility of atomic warfare, Voorhis predicted that atomic technology would be known by other nations "within a very few years." "The most short-sighted policy that could be followed," he observed, "would be . . . to set in motion an unlimited armament race which ultimately must lead to an atomic war. . . ." Voorhis was clearly in favor of a civilian commission. For him, the commission was "all-important" and he was emphatic that "I do not think that the board should be composed of part-time people." Rather, they should be well paid, and "it would be proper for the bill to prescribe that a certain number of [the commission positions] . . . be held by scientists."[9]

Holifield and the Patent Issue

Holifield also quizzed Compton and Leo Szilard at length on the intricate question of patents. This issue was at the top of Holifield's list and would be a continuing interest in his career, since patents are at the heart of the U.S. industrial system. At this hearing, Holifield's major concern appeared to be that single individuals and companies not be allowed to monopolize and profit from the government's multi-million-dollar atomic R&D efforts. He hoped to protect the interests of the government while also ensuring fairness and even-handedness in distributing technologies developed by the government. In another question directed to Compton, he asked: "What is your attitude toward scientists retaining for their own private welfare or private financial interests patents on a thing that is fraught with such terrible world-wide consequences?" He continued: "Do you feel that any scientist should be allowed to retain patent rights or royalty rights on a thing as big as this?" Compton responded that patent rights had to remain in national hands.

Not completely satisfied, Holifield then posed the question more concretely: "Let us say that scientist A invents a method of procedure for the better production of this. Do you think that the Government . . . should have to pay him a royalty for that knowledge?" Holifield was worried that the U.S. had financed all R&D upon which all "improvements" would depend, and it did not seem proper that scientists gain profit from such work. Compton grasped the implications more fully this time, and responded more comprehensively:

> . . . it depends upon how that knowledge has been obtained. I would say that a person who makes an invention is entitled to fair compensation for the work that he has done in making that invention. . . . if the man has already been compensated for his work in terms of salary or by some other method, then presumably the right to further compensation no longer exists, because he presumably was employed so that he would make this invention. But if he has made the invention privately, I see no objection from the point of view of justice to appropriate compensation being paid him by the Government if it takes over control of his invention.[10]

Holifield wanted to know the differences between patents for military and civilian uses. It was clear that the patent and royalty system would operate adequately for inventions in the civilian field, but Holifield wanted to know about military inventions. He questioned Compton on what would happen "if this man invented some method or procedure which would be adopted by the military," specifically, "do you expect the Government of the United States to pay him a royalty if it used that procedure in the construction of a superbomb, beyond that which we are now able to make?" Compton saw no reason "that the fact that it becomes of national interest lessens the Nation's obligation to pay the individual an appropriate amount for his services."

Holifield's foray into patents was ultimately interrupted by May, who grew exasperated by the detailed nature of the questioning and complained that "I doubt if that is pertinent to this issue . . . [since] we are not going to take patents away from anybody, unless they are military patents." Although patents are hardly the stuff of high national drama and the colloquy appeared to bog down in minutiae, Holifield had an instinctive grasp of some of the essential issues at stake on patents. He wanted to ensure that all firms entering this field had equal access under the law without having to pay royalties, as was the practice in Great Britain.[11]

The short hearings only heightened Holifield's interest in atomic energy. "It is impossible to recapture precisely why," Holifield later commented, "but my attention was riveted on this concentrated form of energy." He had been "fascinated by the explosion of the A-bomb, and I studied everything I could lay my hands on about it." Holifield was alarmed and dismayed by the Committee's abrupt decision to send the May-Johnson bill to the floor for a vote. The military-dominated commission boded ill, particularly for peacetime applications. As Holifield viewed the matter:

> Unlike many others, I looked upon [atomic energy] as an energy source as well as a weapon. The danger was that if the military were given exclusive control of it, there would be little advance toward peacetime applications. The only way to prevent this from happening was to put it under control of a full-time [civilian] commission.[12]

The Holifield-Price Dissent and the Fight for Civilian Control

Although he was only in his second term in Congress, Holifield determined that he had to do something to register his dissent against the May-Johnson measure. He decided to pencil his objections in long hand so they could be attached to the committee report as a dissenting report. Byron Miller, a skilled lawyer and close associate, then polished the statement to give it the proper legal tone. Holifield also enlisted the help of Mel Price (D-Illinois), a fellow committee member whose views fully paralleled Holifield's.[13]

The Holifield-Price dissent may have been overshadowed by the majority's views, but it was powerful in its arguments and represented growing sentiment against May-Johnson. The two men enunciated five basic principles. First, they believed that the commission "should be composed of full-time, well-paid members." They also posited that commission members "should be removable by the president whenever he deems it in the national interest." They also wanted the day-to-day administrator to be a civilian and further, appointed by the president. Finally, they believed that the government "should be the exclusive producer and owner of plutonium and other fissionable material."[14]

Holifield and Price provided convincing arguments in support of their recommendations. They noted scientists had testified that atomic energy was "the most significant discovery since the discovery of fire," and a part-time commission thus gave "not only inadequate attention [to the commission's [work]," but would also "permit the possible maintenance of private interests by members of the Commission which may either conflict with or be divergent from the Commission's responsibilities." They perceived the commission's quarterly meeting schedule as wholly inadequate. Holifield and Price were also critical of the method for appointing commissioners. They pointed out that "in most cases the President would have to be elected for two successive terms before he would be in a position to appoint a majority of the Commission." They also observed that the bill's provision for selection of the administrator by the commission itself was "inconceivable" in view of the importance of the field, especially "at a time when literally hundreds of government executives who hold positions of much less concern to the public must be appointed by the President with congressional approval."[15]

Holifield and Price emphasized the peacetime atom in arguing for a civilian administrator. In their view, "the constructive possibilities of the use of atomic energy in our civilian life far exceeds the importance of atomic energy for military purposes." "To consider the field of atomic energy as one of primarily military significance," they argued, "is to overlook totally the tremendous possibilities which it offers for improving the public welfare, increasing the standard of living, and generally easing the burdens of each of us." They noted that scientists had testified that "harnessing of atomic energy for civilian purposes can produce a degree of human comfort the like of which the world has never seen or even imagined."[16]

On the final point of exclusive government production and ownership of fissionable materials, the dissenting report reflected Holifield's ideas gleaned from the October 18 hearings. Holifield's inquiry into patents and also Voorhis' testimony convinced him that ownership and production of atomic materials should be a government monopoly, at least for the time being. He and Price believed that these materials should be at least in the same class as U.S. currency, since "it would seem reasonable to consider these materials of greater value than money." They recommended that the commission be "specifically prohibited from licensing any private concern to produce, refine, or process [atomic] materials except on a research basis."[17]

If the Holifield-Price dissent did anything, it provided a rallying point for opponents of the administration's first proposal on atomic energy. Holifield was unable to prevent the House from passing the May-Johnson bill, but his dissenting report served as an educational brochure for the Senate, where the May-Johnson bill would later be replaced by a totally new piece of legislation authored by McMahon's Special Committee on Atomic Energy. McMahon gave serious consideration to Holifield and Price's recommendations.

The fight for civilian control of atomic energy was long and hard. In the Senate, the political dust did not settle until June 1, 1946 when McMahon's bill was finally approved by the Senate. Negotiations with the House finally resulted in a bill both houses could send to President Truman. On August 1, 1946, fully ten months after the first House hearings on atomic energy legislation, the president signed the Atomic Energy Act of 1946 into law.[18]

Holifield believed that the effort to "demilitarize" the atom succeeded for many reasons. There was a realization that not merely control of atomic energy, but the nature of the U.S. democratic system itself, was at stake.

Scientists were forced to come down from their ivory towers, learning from hard experience that their ideas, no matter how exciting and reasonable, could only take hold in a free society through the rough and tumble business of politics. Scientists, like other interest groups, were forced to organize. The battle for civilian control led to the founding of important scientific organizations, including the Federation of American Scientists, the Federation of Atomic Scientists, and the National Committee on Atomic Information.[19]

Holifield was a friend and ally of the many scientists who made their way to Capitol Hill to work against military control. Prominent scientists, including Henry Dewolf Smyth, Leo Szilard, Edward Condon, and Harold Urey, worked with Holifield during the critical months prior to passage of the final legislation. In fact, Holifield and his House allies formed an ad hoc committee with scientists and civilian control proponents (including McMahon) in the Senate to keep abreast of amendments and to discuss legislative strategies for ensuring civilian control.[20]

Holifield also worked with scientists at perhaps the most critical juncture threatening civilian control. In the Senate, Arthur Vandenburg proposed the creation of a Military Liaison Committee (MLC) to advise and consult with the proposed commission on all subjects it deemed appropriate for national security. As proposed, the MLC could appeal to the President to override the commission on issues it deemed critical to national security. This amendment would have ensured indirect military control. Holifield and his legislative and scientific allies began a massive public education and lobbying effort to overturn the Vandenburg Amendment. The centerpiece of this effort was the "Emergency Conference for Civilian Control of Atomic Energy" held in the House Caucus Room on March 22, 1946, with a night session scheduled at the National Press Club. Holifield helped to organize the Emergency Conference and chaired the morning session at which McMahon and other prominent figures blasted the Vandenburg Amendment. Hundreds of scientists and thirty congressmen attended the session. Later at the National Press Club, an even larger crowd heard the arguments against military control. The conference was aided by local "emergency" meetings across the nation organized by local scientific groups. Facing reelection, Senator Vandenburg was impressed by the public outcry. He changed his amendment, retaining the MLC but clearly subordinating it to the commission.[21]

The Atomic Energy Act of 1946 and the JCAE

Holifield could take pride in the Atomic Energy Act of 1946. The new law embodied the principles he and Price set forth in their dissent. The act mandated full civilian control of the new Atomic Energy Commission (AEC). It provided for presidential appointment of full-time commissioners, subject to Senate confirmation, who would serve for specific, staggered terms. The new law also established exclusive government ownership and production of fissionable materials. To be sure, the military was not excluded entirely. The president was given unrestricted authority over available fissionable materials and over atomic weapons to be produced and transferred by the AEC to the military. The MLC was retained in an advisory capacity. A civilian panel, the General Advisory Committee (GAC), composed of scientists, was also included in the law as a vital counterweight to the MLC.[22]

The organizational structure that Holifield did not anticipate was the JCAE, created by the new law. During the hearings of the Senate Special Committee on Atomic Energy, senators recognized that the military affairs committees in the two houses were not equipped to handle the growing, unique workload of atomic energy. In a bold step, the Special Committee created the JCAE, to be comprised of nine members from each house. The JCAE was to be a permanent oversight body with unprecedented powers. Unique among joint committees, the JCAE could have bills referred to it by both chambers for hearings, reports, and even legislative recommendations. Its authority extended over the entire spectrum of "the development, use, and control of atomic energy." One of the well-springs of the JCAE's power was the requirement for the AEC to "keep the Joint Committee fully and currently informed with respect to the Commission's activities." Thus, no civilian or military program secrets could legally be kept from the JCAE.

Although all atomic energy activities were referred to the JCAE, the committee did not at first have clear control over the AEC. A weak spot in the JCAE's armor was its lack of power to authorize annual appropriations for the AEC, which meant that JCAE had to deal with separate appropriations committees in each house during the first decade of its existence. When Congress saw fit to give even this power directly to the JCAE, the committee became even more powerful. No joint committee or committee in either house had ever held such sweeping powers over a federal agency. The JCAE's prestige was reflected when it brought its bills to the floor of Congress; they were adopted almost without opposition.[23]

Holifield liked to cite the reasoning which helped to induce Congress to establish this super power within its walls. "We were very much impressed with the need for secrecy then because we had information that a parallel effort might be going on in the Soviet Union," Holifield noted. Toward the end of the World War II, the U.S. learned that the Soviet Army had overrun a scientific laboratory in Peenemunde, a town on the Baltic Sea, capturing 300 German scientists. The U.S. presumed the scientists "were put to work to make ballistic missiles with atomic warheads," which made the U.S. atomic R&D effort an overriding national priority requiring extraordinary measures.[24]

Chet Holifield became a charter member of the JCAE from its inception in August 1946 and would remain a member until his retirement at the end of 1974. His selection was quite exceptional, since he and Mel Price were almost at the bottom in House seniority and initially, JCAE membership included some of the most senior and prestigious members of both houses. Speaker of the House Rayburn appointed Holifield and Price, most probably due to their role in insisting on civilian control of the atom, after he conferred with congressional leaders and President Truman.[25]

Holifield at Bikini

Strangely enough, although he was chosen for the JCAE, Holifield was not present when the final vote on the 1946 act was taken. As the year-long debate was concluding, Holifield was thousands of miles away at sea witnessing the 1946 Bikini Atoll nuclear tests. He was part of the President's Atomic Bomb Evaluation Commission, which included two members each from the House and Senate and five civilians. In addition to himself and Walter G. Andrews (R-New York), the commission included senators Carl Hatch and Leverett Saltonstall; scientists Karl Compton and Edward U. Condon; industrialists W. S. Newell and Bradley Dewey; and Fred Searles, Jr. from the Department of State. Holifield became well acquainted with Condon in particular at Bikini. Months later, he would become Condon's staunch defender when, as head of the Bureau of Standards, Condon was assailed as a "security risk" by Congressman J. Parnell Thomas (real name: Joseph Feeny) of the House Committee on Un-American Activities.[26]

Holifield's trip to Bikini to witness the first tests on naval vessels was not accidental. Speaker Rayburn had listened with interest to the alternative arguments Holifield had posed on civilian control of the atom. Over at 1600 Pennsylvania Avenue, President Truman also was pleased that a party loyalist had been willing to buck his fellow Democrats on the House Military Affairs Committee and support the president by arguing for greater presidential prerogatives in the Atomic Energy Act. In the spring of 1946, Holifield's name was foremost as a logical choice when Truman decided to appoint military and civilian commissions to review the Bikini naval tests.

Although he was for civilian control, Holifield also supported a strong U.S. military presence in the postwar world. On March 11, 1946, when the House debated the imminent tests, Holifield countered the arguments of congressmen who expressed reservations. Congressman Johnson commented that sinking 100 ships "would no doubt be a great show," but that he would "not get enjoyment or satisfaction in seeing 100 ships or a fewer number sent to the bottom of the ocean . . . especially when I know that 18 of them are new ships." Holifield responded that the tests were necessary "so we can know the effect of atomic energy explosions upon naval vessels." The data, he believed, was vital to future military planning, and would be considered "when we arrive at the [future] type of ships and size of Navy," and also "the type of Army we are going to have" as dictated by the new atomic realities.[27]

For Holifield, the trip to Bikini Atoll was a memorable one, and he set down his reminiscences in a notebook that would later be published in a limited edition for his constituents. On July 1, 1946, the day of the first test code-named ABLE, Holifield arose at 6:00 a.m. to go for an early-morning swim. The California congressman was impressed by the idyllic scenes he encountered at the beach. The water was so clear that the coral bottom, perhaps 20 to 30 feet deep, seemed only a foot or two below the surface. Brightly-colored fish swirled all around as Holifield went on his swim.

A few minutes before 9:00 a. m., Holifield was on the bridge of the USS *Haven* with the other commission members, preparing to witness the ABLE blast. Even though he was 18 miles away from the bombing site, his eyes had to be protected by goggles with special dark lens that enabled him to look directly at the sun and see only a golden sphere. Minute by minute, the ship's loudspeaker drummed out the time as a plane headed toward the naval targets in the lagoon. Precisely at 8:59 a.m. came the call: "Bomb Away!" A searing flash enveloped the lagoon as the fourth atomic weapon in history was detonated. Even with the thick, air-tight goggles, it took Holifield a few seconds to refocus his eyes. With the danger to his eyes over, he ripped off his glasses to witness the awesome power of the atomic bomb. A billowing tower of fire and smoke--"a violent writhing upsurge" of orange, pink, and yellow against a "cloudless azure sky"--rose some thirty thousand feet above the sea. At twenty thousand feet, a mushroom cloud formed at the top, turbulent and boiling, spreading out "like the top of an umbrella." The sound of the detonation came two minutes later, "muffled and deep like thunder."[28]

Six hours after the blast, the *Haven* was permitted to enter the lagoon. Holifield was now 10 to 12 miles from the ships. He was issued powerful Navy binoculars to observe the damage: three ships had been sunk, two were listing heavily, and many more smoldered from fires. Superstructures, lines, and rigging of many of the surviving ships were askew. Two days after the test, the commissioners were permitted to inspect the damaged ships. They were accompanied by a scientist carrying a Geiger counter to steer the group away from high levels of radiation on board. This tour was an eye-opener for Holifield. "This feature of the Atomic bomb has not been adequately publicized," he reported on his return. He noted that "The A-bomb not only has the properties of blast and intense heat, but it also emits gamma and other radiation which are highly dangerous to human life." Holifield learned that "These radiations affect human tissue, the blood and the bone marrow," and "the result may be instant death or the victim may linger for days and weeks." Holifield shuddered to think that "the casualties would have been massive" if sailors had been on board. It was a lesson for future reference.

Holifield and other members visited the Philippines and Japan while the 40,000 military personnel at Bikini Lagoon prepared for the BAKER test, which would be an underwater nuclear explosion. At the Philippine island of

Corregidor, Holifield paused to consider the plight of General Jonathan Wainwright's army, which had made a valiant, but futile attempt in 1942 to hold back the Japanese advance. Holifield noted that "our great Democracy had asked the impossible from our military outpost," and that Wainwright had also been defeated by "our indifference and isolationism." In solemn tones, he lamented that "The blood of the heroes of Bataan and Corregidor will remain a stain on our national conscience, a constant reminder of our cruel indifference and refusal to bear our responsibility."[29]

Japan was next. General Douglas C. MacArthur, chief of the U.S. occupation forces in Japan, invited several commissioners, including Holifield, to visit him. Anxious for commissioners to observe the atomic destruction of Hiroshima and Nagasaki, the general arranged for a military plane to take commission members on a tour of the ravaged cities. Outfitted with a door that was partially open on one side but with bars riveted across the opening, the plane flew low on a slant so that the visitors felt like they were almost gliding across the top of the wreckage itself.

Later the commissioners went to MacArthur's house for lunch with the general and his family. MacArthur impressed Holifield with his plan for recovery in Japan, including broad land reform. When he returned home to his district, the Californian praised MacArthur's vision and courage in speeches to Rotarians, Lions, and members of the Kiwanis Club. Holifield contended that "The general's plan for forcing Japanese post-war recovery through land reform was a model we should have followed in other countries." Many of the conservative, small businessmen in Holifield's audiences were shocked when he told them that MacArthur had probably saved Japan from communism by breaking up the great Japanese estates and redistributing the land. "At that time," he explained, "similar action by our government at home would have brought outcries about the reforms being Communist-inspired." Holifield noted that "I usually kept the punch line until the end--that is, the General had confiscated the land using long-term Japanese bond payments that had low appraisal rates." Since Holifield was "merely praising action by a national hero," the audience response was favorable. When MacArthur was fired by Truman a few years later, Holifield's support of Truman's action did not damage him politically, probably since "the fact that I had previously defended the General's good qualities left me with a favorable image among the voters. Few were alarmed about my support for the President."[30]

Holifield's tour of Corregidor, where vegetation was swarming over the scars of war, and his tour of the atomic devastation in Japan left an indelible impression. These experiences reinforced his growing conviction that atomic war must never recur, and that the nation must constantly be on guard to defend freedom. Holifield thus promoted world peace and American defense as twin international goals. As part of these goals, he became a dedicated Cold War warrior, ever ready to defend America against communism.

Following his side trips, Holifield returned to Bikini to see the BAKER test of July 25, 1946. This time the pyrotechnics seemed less spectacular as the underwater explosion threw millions of tons of water into the air along with an enormous ball of fire and smoke. In other ways, the results were different. "Ninety percent of the ships in the target area," Holifield observed, "were deluged with sea water from the great column of water caused by the explosion." The water surrounding the ships contained radioactive fission fragments and the steel ships were "contaminated heavily." He noted that the water around the ships remained "hot" for some time, and "the oil scum from the sunken vessels apparently absorbed a heavy amount [of radioactivity]."[31]

Holifield and the Early JCAE

When Holifield returned from the tests in the South Pacific, he attended the first organizational session of the JCAE, held on August 2, 1946. At this first session, Senator Brien McMahon was elected as committee chairman. His chairmanship was short-lived, however; the Republicans gained majorities in both houses in the 1946 elections. When the Eightieth Congress convened, McMahon was replaced by Bourke B. Hickenlooper (R-Iowa), although McMahon would return again as chairman in the Eighty-First Congress.

The composition of the first JCAE reflected opposite polls in the Senate and the House. On the Senate side, almost all appointees had been members of the Special Committee on Atomic Energy. Almost to a man they were chairmen of standing committees or ranking minority members. Arrayed alongside this senatorial force were nine House members, none of whom were major national political or legislative figures. With much less clout, House members could not hope to dominate the JCAE. In fact, the Senate, particularly McMahon, dominated the JCAE in its early years, except for the Eightieth Congress. It would take a Holifield-inspired rebellion in the fifties for the House to gain parity in chairmanships on the JCAE. Later, under Holifield's leadership, the House would come to dominate the JCAE.[32]

From the outset, Holifield was an enthusiastic JCAE member. He could be counted on to support McMahon with work on the many issues facing the committee. From 1947 through most of 1949, much of the work revolved around confirmation of the first AEC commissioners, renewal of their tenure, and partisan wrangling over alleged security violations and communist infiltration within the AEC. The AEC's first chairman, David E. Lilienthal, was heavily criticized by the Republicans. In 1949, Hickenlooper charged him with "incredible mismanagement" and demanded an investigation. The AEC chairman was exonerated, with Democrats supporting him most vigorously.[33]

The one item that JCAE Democrats and Republicans could agree on and move forward on was protecting national defense. As Holifield described it:

We were busy improving atomic weapons, building the foundation for a nuclear Navy, and assuring national security. . . .

We also had to make our weapons smaller and less heavy so they could be carried in airplanes and on intercontinental missiles. The average atomic appropriations then were about four billion dollars a year. We built additional major laboratories besides Oak Ridge. The JCAE helped the AEC expand or build seven laboratories during the period 1946-1954, costing nine billion dollars. This expanded the nation's scientific research base and provided fundamental research tools for working on the atom.[34]

If any single event prompted expanded military research after 1949, it was the news that the Soviets had detonated their first atomic bomb. As Holifield viewed matters, military developments took on a "definite urgency" from 1946 to 1954, and "This was quite evident in 1949 when the USSR exploded its first atomic weapon as a result of the treachery of Klaus Fuchs."[35]

On September 23, 1949, news of this explosion ended the complacent and partisan forms of wrangling within the JCAE and between the AEC and the JCAE. A new intra-government struggle emerged, largely blocked from the public eye, over a new "super-weapon," whose power and force would dwarf the atomic bomb. On January 31, 1950, President Truman ended the struggle by ordering the AEC to develop the hydrogen bomb, a weapon which relied mainly on energy released in a fusion, rather than fission, process.

Unbeknownst to him, Holifield was destined to play a major role in Truman's hydrogen bomb decision. He first heard about the "superbomb" in a meeting in August 1949. McMahon had invited him to meet privately with scientist Edward Teller in McMahon's office. This luncheon impressed Holifield, since McMahon had steaks from the Senate dining room delivered to his office, a privilege not available in the House. The meeting occurred shortly after the JCAE learned that Fuchs, a refugee from Hitler's Germany and former Manhattan Project scientist, was a Communist agent. Teller, a war refugee from Hungary, had flown to Washington for meetings, first with McMahon and Holifield and then with other JCAE members in the JCAE's security-guarded back room. Holifield remembered that Teller argued that Fuchs' treachery meant "Now we've got to go after the hydrogen bomb."[36]

Neither McMahon nor Holifield knew what a hydrogen bomb was; McMahon asked Teller to "explain that to us." According to Holifield, "Teller then said that he was advocating using hydrogen in a fusion process instead of uranium in a fission process." As a theory, the concept of a hydrogen bomb or thermonuclear reaction was not new. The "H-bomb" had excited debate within scientific and military circles both during and after World War II. Several scientists, including Stanley Ulam, George Gamow, and Teller had worked on it, although Ulam was credited with the theoretical insights. Practical applications for fusion at first appeared impossible because, as Teller told McMahon and an utterly-amazed Holifield, it would be very difficult to duplicate on earth "the [heat] conditions found in the interior of the stars." The atomic bomb had to come first, in effect providing the heat source and serving as a trigger to surround the fusion of two forms of hydrogen, tritium and the naturally-occurring deuterium. The A-bomb was also first because the U.S. had decided that the atomic bomb had to be produced at all costs before Hitler's scientists could produce a similar bomb for Germany. Even during wartime, however, a few scientists were convinced that once the war ended, both Germany and Russia, if they had the atomic bomb, could also then produce the "H-bomb" within a short period, and the U.S. also must follow suit. But opponents argued against the H-bomb as "morally repugnant" or contended that the development of the "super" would make international problems even more intractable than ever. Despite such intense debate within senior military and scientific circles, the thermonuclear bomb was not brought to President Truman's attention until after the Russian explosion.[37]

By mid-October 1949, the lines between advocates and opponents of H-bomb development were clear. Both the JCAE and the Pentagon agreed that the super weapon must be developed. JCAE members expressed considerable anxiety about national survival if the USSR produced the super first. In questioning AEC officials, the legislators wondered whether sufficient supplies of tritium would be available for use in making the super weapon. They urged the AEC commissioners to give the matter priority attention.

There was general reluctance within the AEC, however, to proceed with development. Three of the five AEC commissioners opposed developing the H-bomb, as did the GAC headed by J. Robert Oppenheimer. Only two commissioners, Admiral Lewis L. Strauss and Thomas E. Murray, voiced unequivocal support. Lilienthal wanted to delay a decision until a U.S. strategic doctrine review showed relative worth of increasing conventional forces while reducing dependence on large-scale nuclear weapons.[38]

Holifield's JCAE Subcommittee on the Hydrogen Bomb

For McMahon, the Soviet explosion showed that the USSR could and would acquire the super before the U.S. if something were not done soon. Alarmed by what he perceived as inertia within the AEC and the GAC, he sought to galvanize Congress into action by using the JCAE as a springboard for action. McMahon decided to create a special ad hoc subcommittee chaired by Holifield. The subcommittee's job would be to review the AEC's possibilities for creating the H-bomb. Other JCAE members appointed to the subcommittee were Mel Price and Carl Hinshaw (R-California) and senators Henry Jackson (D-Washington) and William Knowland (R-California).

Holifield's appointment as subcommittee chairman was very unusual for a junior congressman. In some measure it demonstrated his increasing stature on the JCAE and also his close working relationship with McMahon and McMahon's trust in his judgment. McMahon's staff director Bill Borden believed that Holifield was selected because "Chet was a driving, almost kinetic individual with a gregarious nature and a gargantuan capacity for work." As Borden saw it, "Chet couldn't be bowled over by scientific expertise and meandering talk. He could even impress on his listeners the urgency of the JCAE mission, even when some were not really listening to him."[39]

Holifield viewed the subcommittee's mission as fact-finding. He planned to visit the laboratories directly involved in the H-bomb and discover firsthand what knowledge was available about its technology, feasibility, and the time frame required to complete the R&D. This would entail visits to the Los Alamos Weapons Laboratory in New Mexico and the AEC laboratory at Berkeley during the upcoming congressional recess. The trip was necessary because the JCAE had almost no information on the super weapon, despite the provisions of the 1946 act that the AEC was to "keep the committee fully and currently informed." McMahon and Borden believed the AEC was dragging its feet. According to Borden:

> We were operating under the assumption that the AEC was keeping us, as the statute required, "fully and currently informed." Much to our dismay we discovered that the Commission itself, through its own laboratories, was not fully informed on atomic weapons development, let alone the "super"!
>
> The Committee was already partially aware of the incredible failure of the military services or the AEC to stockpile nuclear weapons after the war ended. Our atomic weapons cupboard was empty and continued in this condition long after the war. The scientists dispersed from Los Alamos, work on the "super" was episodic and muddled along. Only limited improvements had been made in nuclear technology.[40]

The subcommittee trip was scheduled for October 27-29, 1949. The first stop was at Los Alamos Weapons Laboratory in New Mexico on October 27, followed the next day by a visit to Berkeley. Holifield initiated a third visit to the AEC's Idaho site on the following day. JCAE staff members Borden and Walter A. Hamilton accompanied the subcommittee, but neither they nor members of the subcommittee kept notes on the visits. (Holifield normally took notes except for matters dealing with atomic secrets, and in those cases, he only read classified materials in the presence of a security guard and returned such files to the guard for placement in a safe.) Upon return, Hamilton was asked to prepare a highly classified report on the subcommittee's findings and conclusions. In 1986 this report (with deleted sections) was declassified. The Hamilton report serves as the record of the Holifield subcommittee, and together with Borden's recollections, were part of the material used by McMahon to write his 5,000-word letter to Truman.[41]

The subcommittee, with Knowland absent, garnered a major portion of its data at Los Alamos. There was a morning meeting with Dr. Norris Bradbury, the laboratory's director, an afternoon session with Teller, and an evening session at Dr. Bradbury's home. In the morning session, Bradbury explained that theoretically there was no limit on the size and destructive power of hydrogen bombs, but their weight presented practical delivery problems for large sizes. Further, "no piloted air vehicle could expect to get away from the explosion." The super weapon would consist of "a conventional [atomic] bomb as an initiator, a mass of tritium and deuterium as a booster, and finally a mass of deuterium alone." The radioactivity from the atomic bomb initiator "would be completely dissipated by the blast," so the Soviets probably would not be able to detect any bomb tests by conventional means.[42] Bradbury was hopeful that the H-bomb could be developed "in an orderly, step-by-step process . . . by about 1958 or 1960." "On the basis of the supposition that the Russians are now developing a super weapon," Bradbury assured the subcommittee that the development period could be shortened considerably under a "speeded up program . . . which would yield a proven super weapon by mid-1952." He outlined the two development alternatives.

Teller's afternoon session considered "the realm of the political and military strategy of the problem." Teller noted that he had been "spark-plugging" efforts to start up the super weapon program at Los Alamos and "had taken it upon himself to sound out other scientists, both locally and nationally." His inquiries convinced him that such a program was not possible "unless firm moral and political assurance was given" by the president and Congress to the scientists that the program "would be used in a positive and perhaps even dramatic manner to achieve Russian compliance with Western aims." He seemed to have some sort of "open challenge to Russia" in mind.

In the evening discussion, the subcommittee felt that it had heard enough to send Hinshaw back as a personal messenger to McMahon to request an executive session of the JCAE within the next two weeks to hear Bradbury's proposal for a "crash" program on the super. They also agreed that Borden should telephone McMahon to prepare him for Hinshaw's visit and that Borden should also contact Knowland to try to get him to attend the meeting with Dr. Ernest O. Lawrence in Berkeley the next day. In a third action, the subcommittee planned work on a legislative amendment regarding export of enriched materials to Canada so that the U.S. "might get the benefit of possible tritium production from the Chalk River heavy water pile."[43]

The next day the Holifield subcommittee reassembled in Berkeley, this time with Knowland in attendance. "This was not an official subcommittee meeting," Hamilton wrote later in his report. "Its purpose was to permit Dr. Lawrence to express his views on the subject of the Super Weapon to the members present." Several other scientists attended this meeting, including Dr. Donald Cooksey, Dr. Edward MacMillan, Dr. Robert Thornton, and Dr.

Isodore Pearlman. Also in attendance from the AEC were Harry Fider, Area Manager, and Everett Hollis, Deputy General Counsel.

In his presentation, Lawrence supported Bradbury's belief "that a Super Weapon is entirely feasible." Moreover, Lawrence asserted that "the evidence on hand indicates that the Russians are already or will soon be well on their way to its production," and that the U.S. had "no time to lose" in getting development underway. Lawrence then outlined three methods to increase tritium production for an accelerated development program. These methods included construction of a specific heavy water pile design, modification of the Materials Test Reactor in Idaho, and construction of a cyclotron or particle accelerator. Lawrence "made it clear that he saw no security hazard to the construction of either the giant cyclotron or a heavy water pile installation at Berkeley and that he had even gone so far as to select a tentative site."

In the conversations following Lawrence's presentation, MacMillan stated that the urgency of the situation "warranted a philosophy of 'a production pile in every backyard.'" Lawrence agreed with him, as did others. In his report, Hamilton noted that "A cross between a note of hysteria and a tremendous enthusiasm seemed to underlie this part of the discussion."[44]

From Berkeley, Holifield, Borden, and Hamilton traveled to Idaho Falls to see "the degree of preparedness of the new Idaho office to take on construction of a tritium production facility." Hamilton later noted that the trip "bore no official connotation" and "was an entirely independent effort on the part of Mr. Holifield and his staff for the purpose of being somewhat informed in the event that such a possibility should arise." Holifield and his staff met with Mr. L. C. Johnston, the AEC Area Manager, and ascertained that "there were neither labor nor other construction problems which would hinder the rapid development of . . . such a production facility."[45]

Results of the Holifield Subcommittee Trip

In speaking of the subcommittee trip, Borden later noted that "This field trip was an eye-opener not only for Chet but the entire Joint Committee."[46] It was especially important for the wealth of new information it provided the JCAE. The trip also served to unite the subcommittee members and almost the entire JCAE in total support of a crash program on the H-bomb. Virtual JCAE unanimity helped to convince Truman of the necessity for this effort.

The subcommittee provided all JCAE members with several important, non-technical conclusions about the hydrogen bomb. First, the destructive force of this bomb would be far greater than anything seen before by humanity. Second, the Russians probably were already at work, or would soon be at work, on this new super weapon. Finally, the United State's own self-interest dictated that this country had no choice but to build the H-bomb.

Holifield himself put the issue in even darker terms: "if we didn't get that weapon first, we were wide open to blackmail or potential surrender."[47]

Holifield was upset with the hydrogen bomb's opponents, but particularly the AEC scientists who expressed opposition during his trip. "When we left Los Alamos to head for Berkeley, Holifield was almost in a rage at the nonchalant attitude of some of the scientists," Borden remembered. "He was perplexed by their unwillingness to roar ahead so as to get the hydrogen bomb before the Soviets did."[48] Holifield was especially stunned by scientists who realized that the Russians not only possessed the basic ideas for the super weapon, but also the production facilities to make it. He respected their expertise and saw nothing sinister nor subversive in their views, but he thought they were incredibly naive and lacking in common sense. Unlike many other legislators, when the House Committee on Un-American Activities sought to discredit scientists such as Edward U. Condon and J. Robert Oppenheimer in the late 1940s and early 1950s, Holifield was among the first to vigorously defend their honesty, integrity, and public record on the House floor.[49] An unflinching civil libertarian in a postwar era scarred by a virulent anti-Communist hysteria, Holifield fought pitched battles with anyone who attempted unjustly to impugn the record of scientists or political enemies.

There have been less-than-kind assessments of the subcommittee's real mission and importance. Some McMahon enthusiasts, for instance, still claim that McMahon did not really need its input, since he took a similar trip later before writing to Truman. Others claim that the subcommittee, with three Californians out of five members, was chiefly set up as a free trip home for West Coast House members who were complaining about presidential hopeful McMahon's singlehanded running of the JCAE. Such views do not take some realities into consideration. McMahon needed the JCAE's concurrence with his position, so what better method than a fact-finding trip by a subcommittee? Also, selection of members was last-minute due to the suddenness of the problem, and probably based on members' availability during the recess. McMahon did take a later trip to supplement the subcommittee's (Hamilton) report, but this is not unusual, since most complex subjects usually require clarifications. To suggest that McMahon appointed a boondoggling subcommittee or that subcommittee members were merely validating a course he already chose seems a disservice to both him and them.

After the congressional recess on January 27, 1950, Holifield reported the findings of the ad hoc subcommittee to the JCAE in the executive session the subcommittee members had requested. Holifield told his fellow JCAE members that "some scientists were dubious about going ahead because of the enormous heat needed to get the fusion process going." "But we came back from our tour," he added, "convinced this was feasible." Holifield continued:

We also believed the Russians were working on the H-bomb. We had little information about the Russians except that they had overrun Peenemunde in the Baltic, capturing all the German scientists working there. Some of those scientists were concentrating on making heavy water. We also found out that certain metals needed for fusion research were being exported from Czechoslovakia to Russia. I don't know if it was a gut decision or a lucky one, but we came to the conclusion that the Russians were indeed experimenting on the "super," the hydrogen-tritium bomb.[50]

After hearing this report, the JCAE voted 16 to 2 to recommend the H-bomb R&D effort to President Truman. The two members opposed were Sterling Cole (R-New York), who later would become JCAE chairman, and Charles Elston (R-Ohio). McMahon then set up a meeting at the White House with President Truman and invited Holifield to participate.

Shortly before Holifield's subcommittee reported its findings, the GAC dropped a bombshell into the nation's political atmosphere by launching a broad attack against the super. With Glenn Seaborg the only one of nine members absent, Oppenheimer's GAC unanimously concluded that all work should stop for three reasons. First, testing the super weapon would reveal its frightening power. Second, its destructive power was highly immoral because of its capability to destroy countless human beings, and third, no one could tell if the weapon had any nonmilitary applications.

AEC Chairman Lilienthal and two of the other four commissioners made up a majority at the AEC opposed to the super. Lilienthal in particular had been wary of the JCAE and the subcommittee trip to Los Alamos and Berkeley. Lilienthal complained in his diary that "the visiting firemen [the subcommittee members] saw a group of scientists who can only be described as drooling with the prospect and 'blood-thirsty.'" Lilienthal distributed the GAC report throughout the government, including the Department of State and the White House, in order to give it as wide a hearing as possible. By this time, he was desperate to counter the activities of the JCAE.[51]

McMahon and Holifield Meet with Truman

McMahon again wanted Holifield to be with him when the time came for the meeting with Truman. It was good politics to do so. Holifield and Truman had been close associates while both served in Congress. Holifield also knew personally the president's key military aide, Admiral Sydney Souers, who had worked with Charlie Baker, Holifield's cousin, at Missouri Life Insurance when it went bankrupt during the Great Depression. Souers was left with nothing, but Baker had some funds left because his father Elijah, who did not trust banks, had presciently buried his money in jars in the ground inside of a mule barn. No one, Elijah felt, would ever enter his barn to face the large and cantankerous mules![52]

At the meeting with the president, McMahon, Holifield, and a couple of other JCAE members were given 45 minutes or so to explain the JCAE's position on the H-bomb. Following some initial comments by McMahon, Holifield made a presentation to the president on the ad hoc subcommittee's findings. Truman listened intently and Holifield recalled that the president promised McMahon that he would get back to McMahon and the JCAE soon. As Holifield remembered it, Truman said, "This is important. I'll give you an answer very soon, November or later in December." McMahon had previously convinced his colleagues that they should leave Truman something to study and show to his advisors. When the group got up to leave, McMahon gave the president a now-famous, 5,000-word letter.[53]

The 5,000-word letter left with Truman had been drafted by JCAE Staff Director Borden and later revised by McMahon in a Los Angeles hotel room on November 21, 1949 during a trip to the West Coast that McMahon and Borden made as a follow-up to the Holifield subcommittee trip. At the January 27, 1950 JCAE executive session, McMahon acknowledged that he "went out West and made a tour of the installations and followed the path of the [Holifield] subcommittee which preceded me by a couple of weeks." "In Los Angeles," McMahon continued, " I [and Borden] wrote this eight-page letter to the President in which I tried to somewhat exhaustively discuss the problems and I read that to the Committee when I read the views of the GAC." McMahon believed Truman was favorably impressed, since "I subsequently talked with him about it and he expressed great interest in it and he said that he had read it twice, and had gotten copies of it in the hands of the Secretary of Defense and the Secretary of State, and also the Chairman of the Atomic Energy Commission." McMahon acknowledged that "I had no right to commit the Committee," but that "I knew that I spoke the views of the subcommittee because they had been delivered to me by Mr. Hinshaw."[54]

The GAC's opposition to hydrogen bomb development was in fact an underlying focal point in the McMahon letter. In nearly 5,000 words, McMahon sought to analyze and discredit all of the arguments opposing the hydrogen bomb. McMahon found "a fundamental inconsistency" in the opposition argument that "the super is unique . . . yet its military worth is dubious" because ordinary atomic weapons can provide adequate retaliation. To this argument, McMahon responded first with a rhetorical question: "If the super can accomplish no more than weapons already in our arsenal, then why single it out for objection?" "If, on the other hand," McMahon continued, "the super represents a wholly new order of destructive magnitude--as I think it does--then its military role would seem to be decisive."

To critics, including the GAC, who charged that the hydrogen bomb "would inevitably exterminate hosts of civilians and therefore constitute a pure weapon of genocide," McMahon responded that he could see "no moral dividing line . . . between a big explosion which causes heavy damage and many smaller explosions causing equal or still greater damage." The Connecticut senator pointed out that "its [the super's] use against cities could be preceded by a warning" and that "evacuees moving from city to country might hamper the enemy's war effort more seriously even than mass casualties." But getting to the heart of his argument, McMahon asked pointedly, "What happens if supers are aimed at New York, Chicago, Los Angeles, and Washington? Will we possess our own supers ... or will we lack such weapons and suffer defeat and perhaps utter annihilation as the result?" America's need to be armed properly against all possible future aggressors was a necessity that McMahon believed Truman could not ignore.[55]

The pressure from opposing sides in his official family ultimately brought decisive action from Truman. In December, he appointed a special National Security Council subcommittee to study the issue and report back to him. Truman's selection of Louis Johnson, Secretary of Defense, and Dean Acheson, Secretary of State, along with David Lilienthal from the AEC, foretold what the final result would probably be. Johnson was firmly behind the Pentagon's push for the H-bomb and personally disliked Lilienthal, while Acheson had not been persuaded by the AEC's opposing arguments. Thus, Lilienthal found himself in the minority on this important body.

Even though Truman took this action, the JCAE still continued to exert considerable pressure. Once Holifield himself had concluded that presidential action was essential, he pressed his point of view at the AEC and with Senator McMahon. At the January 27, 1950 JCAE executive session, with AEC commissioners present, Holifield was emphatic:

> I do think, however, that Dr. Smyth and some of the scientists who have been holding back on this have a certain justification both from a moral standpoint and from a psychological standpoint in obtaining the real cooperation of the scientific group on this point. Unless a high policy is developed in the State Department and in the Executive Branch, which will utilize this decision in the political field and in the international political field to our greatest advantage, to at least place us on the high moral plane by coming out again with a challenging declaration of some sort of the peoples of the world, that now that this great thing is possible, that we do intend to go into it unless some agreement can be reached which will be a real agreement.

> Then I think once having done that and putting ourselves on the correct moral plane in the eyes of the people of the world and in our own eyes and consciences, I think that we must go forward with full speed ahead on this program. This is my personal attitude.[56]

On January 18, 1950, McMahon again wrote to Truman because he "thought it would be well to advise you of the sentiment here." Although McMahon did not specifically mention Holifield, the Connecticut senator emphasized to Truman that some of the Democrats on the JCAE were restless because the President was not moving faster in arriving at a decision.

As proof, he quoted from a Borden memo. According to Borden, an unidentified JCAE member had expressed concern over the delay of an AEC test related to H-bomb development and believed McMahon should convey to Truman that things must move faster "or loyalty to the Administration would not prevent [the unidentified member] from sounding off on the Floor."

An adroit politician himself, Truman may have sensed that McMahon, who was not above using wily tactics in pressing his views, had perhaps prodded Holifield and other liberal Democrats to keep pressure on the president. In any event, Truman did not bite at the political bait. Rather, he responded rather stiffly to McMahon that he thought "the very best plan for you and me to pursue is silence on the subject and to carry out the business in the best interests of the United States." Truman did, however, soften his reply with a friendly handwritten note concerning McMahon's reelection campaign. The president did not want to discourage the JCAE, especially since he would soon be in full agreement with them.[57]

The Hydrogen Bomb Decision

A few days after McMahon wrote to Truman the second time, Holifield recalled that McMahon telephoned him and said, "Come on over, I've got news." Holifield hurried over to McMahon's office. McMahon was elated: "The President is going to go ahead." After calling McMahon to the White House to advise him of his decision, Truman gave the actual order to the AEC to build the hydrogen bomb a few days later, on January 31, 1950.[58]

A scientific uproar still continued as Oppenheimer, the GAC and other scientists remained opposed. The scientists on the GAC continued to insist that it was "immoral" to develop such a tremendous force for destructive purposes. Some scientists refused to participate in hydrogen bomb development. "But Truman had the courage," Holifield later observed, "to go against them." The California congressman saw the situation much differently than the opposing scientists:

> We made the right decision. We were able to develop a fusion bomb in which we achieved the tremendous heat required. Our idea was not that we wanted to get the bomb to destroy anything. It was that we had to get it before the Soviet Union did. If we did not, we would have been subject to blackmail by a nation which is not subject to Christian moral restraints. One demonstration of its awesome power on a modern city would have, in my opinion, brought about world subjection to Soviet domination.[59]

Eighteen months after President Truman's go-ahead, the H-bomb proved feasible. U.S. leaders had guessed correctly that the Russians were probably experimenting on a similar weapon. Stalin, many concluded, would have his own super weapon in two or three years. Even this estimate did not prove generous enough. The Russians managed to explode a hydrogen bomb just nine months after the United States tested its super weapon. "Incredibly," Holifield noted, "where ours was only a device, we determined that theirs was an active weapon. We had beaten them by nine months only!"[60]

Holifield saw the hydrogen bomb decision and his role in it as a high point in his career. He later wrote a short summation of the episode and entitled it "The Day I was Proudest to be an American." On August 25, 1959, the *New York Times* did a profile on Holifield using the title Holifield himself had coined. In the article, Holifield was quoted as saying: "Members of the Joint Committee discharged their responsibility to make the United States second to none in the field of military power." "They fulfilled their obligation as a committee," he continued, "to see that the right thing was done even beyond proposals which the military advanced. The Joint Committee was always too aggressive for the Pentagon."[61]

For Holifield, the U.S. nuclear umbrella over Europe, reinforced by the tritium-hydrogen bomb, gave the Western Europeans time to reestablish themselves. It also gave the Russians pause in seeking any further territorial aggrandizements. According to Holifield, atomic and hydrogen bombs may have sobered international relations in a way traditional diplomacy could not:

> Nuclear weapons have brought about a condition of peace in the world that has lasted since 1945. We were driven into this race by the traditional rivalry between nations. Such rivalry has invariably resulted in wars. But instead the United States has moved toward world peace. This is not to ignore brush fires like Korea and Vietnam. Perhaps we moved towards peace because of man's primitive and most basic instinct of all, that he must survive. Warning for thermonuclear war today is a matter of minutes rather than of months as before the atomic age. Maybe fear of the terrible instruments man has created has led us down the path we chose. Their massive destructive powers and the fear of retaliation has brought about a peace which diplomacy and ideological dedication to peace could not achieve.[62]

On the domestic front, the "race" for the hydrogen bomb and the further competition it engendered with Russia had important repercussions. Postwar domestic politics, gripped by an oversized national fear of imminent Soviet domination of the world, proved to be highly abrasive and injurious to many reputations. Within this context, honest opposition to developing the hydrogen bomb frequently began to be viewed as akin to treason. The acknowledged leader of the earlier atomic bomb, J. Robert Oppenheimer, found his record tarnished and his career ended as a result of anti-Communist hysteria. Similar attacks were made on other, lesser-known scientists.

Chet Holifield did not abide these attacks in silence. For the Montebello politician, such tactics were destroying a basic foundation of American democracy: the constitutional right of an individual to be secure in holding his opinions. This did not mean or imply that every utterance known to mankind had to be given full protection of freedom of speech, a point Holifield made later in his career regarding the involuntary receipt of pornographic material by homeowners in their mailboxes. Sometimes rights did clash and a prudent judgment had to be made in giving one right precedence over another. But political name-calling, slander, and false and malicious innuendos and public attacks, especially made under congressional immunity where the citizen had little chance to respond, was outrageous to Holifield. This behavior, especially as practiced by the House Committee on Un-American Activities, violated for Holifield the fundamental tenets of public civility that held the American community together. In consequence, he rose to challenge such behavior with force and vigor, even going so far as to introduce legislation to limit some practices of congressional investigating committees.[63]

In turn, of course, political opponents jumped all over the California congressman for his stands in the immediate postwar period. Since he was a small businessman himself, they could not, as some Republicans hoped to do, assail him as a foe of free enterprise. And since he was a member of the increasingly prestigious JCAE, none dared to attack his patriotism, especially in light of his role in the hydrogen bomb decision. What his opponents could and did do, however, was to classify him as an ultra-idealistic liberal, a "one worlder" like President Roosevelt and Wendell Wilkie, an American dreamer like Representatives Jerry Voorhis and Helen Gahagan Douglas, a statesman who, like W. Averell Harriman, should be colored "pink" since Holifield dared to think it was possible for a freedom-loving U.S. to coexist peacefully in the international arena with the Soviet Union. In the long run, however, Holifield's judgment that the U.S. had to both deter and yet live with the Soviets would prove to be correct. Holifield's enemies would never quite understand how the son of an Arkansas preacher, now a small-town haberdasher from Montebello, California, could be such a dedicated defender of civil liberties, a passionate advocate of social justice, especially for minorities, and yet a principal proponent of a strong military defense.

The JCAE and Holifield Rise to Prominence

The hydrogen bomb decision had one other important consequence. This was the rise of the JCAE, and Holifield along with it, to national prominence. After the H-bomb decision, both the JCAE and Chet were deemed as forces to be reckoned with. Holifield was personally viewed by many of his colleagues as one of the active and important JCAE members who was destined to become a dominating force on the JCAE. He had already become, in a way most representatives would not, a truly national figure. Chet ensured that his views would not be ignored by a combination of traits, including an intense drive to understand all aspects of atomic energy, long hours of hard work, and a keen eye for political opportunities and realities.

3

A Haberdasher Presses Into Politics

Idealist and Pragmatist

Chet Holifield confounded friend and foe alike in his early years in Congress. During the passage of the Atomic Energy Act of 1946, the partisan wrangling of the JCAE's early years, and the months leading up to the hydrogen bomb decision, he seemed to embody a strange combination of ultra-liberal idealism and tough-minded pragmatism. At the same time that he opposed military control of the atom and was forging a reputation as an unyielding defender of civil liberties, he also promoted development of the H-bomb as a military necessity. He was even willing in the spring of 1949, moreover, to forego an AEC fellowship program charged with employing communists, urging scientists to make a "strategic retreat" owing to "the hysterical nature of the atomic project in the public press."[1]

These were not the only apparent contradictions in his character. This small-town businessman had a socialistic bent and avidly supported the reforms of the Roosevelt and Truman years. He did not blindly support the interests of business, either, particularly big business. Throughout his career, Holifield opposed the predatory and self-serving activities of businesses who cloaked themselves in the mantle of defenders of free enterprise. While he supported the H-bomb, he was even more interested in peacetime applications of the atom; yet he did not buy the GAC's argument that development of the H-bomb had no potential peacetime applications.

If all of these apparent contradictions made it difficult to determine exactly where Holifield stood philosophically, there were reassuring elements in his character which made him attractive to important persons in government, including President Truman, Speaker of the House Sam Rayburn, and JCAE Chairman McMahon. These elements included his individualism and willingness to fight for what he sincerely believed in; his relentless determination to master the subjects and tasks in which he was involved; a political word that could be trusted absolutely; a fair-minded spirit in dealing with public figures, legislative peers, and his staff; and a deep loyalty to the ideals and interests of the Democratic party. Yet, above all, Holifield had a good native common sense; he knew where partisanship should end and where concern for the national interest should begin. His reasonableness and sensitivity to other political viewpoints, in particular, tended to give him increasing credibility among centrist legislators, Democrats and Republicans alike, and perhaps even grudging admiration from some of his enemies and detractors. His credibility would stand him in good stead even when he came under painful political cross-fire during some incidents in his career.

Holifield's blend of contradictions and character traits were not entirely accidental. His background and important events in his early life provide at least a partial explanation of how he came by his liberal Democratic ideas, and yet why he also remained eminently practical in his approach toward life and politics. His exposure to a combination of Christian and socialist ideas, coupled with practical training in business and a life-threatening accident, plus the economic misery he suffered during the Great Depression, all worked to develop his unique world view and political philosophy. These factors would make him a distinctive presence on the American political landscape for over three decades. His character traits, moreover, would remain constant, from childhood to Congress to his senior position as California's Legislative Dean.

Spanning Two Worlds

In a way, Chet Holifield's life spanned two very different worlds. The one in which he was born was very unlike the one in which he would live as an adult. His life and congressional career encompassed one of the greatest periods of change in American history--technologically, economically, politically, socially, and militarily. He was born in December 1903, just as the industrial revolution was rising to fever pitch and technological "marvels" began to proliferate, a trend accelerated by World Wars I and II. From an economic and political standpoint, he experienced the Great Depression and its deprivations as well as supported and celebrated Roosevelt's political and social reforms. Militarily, the two world wars would change the political geography of Europe and the U.S. would emerge in the postwar world as the major military leader and defender of the "free world," pitted against the Soviet Union and its allies in a seemingly endless struggle.

Few of these major changes were on the horizon in 1903. Technology was still in its infant stage. In recalling his birth year, Holifield once noted that "the year I was born, the Wright brothers flew their first flight at Kitty Hawk, North Carolina, in their primitive plane." It was a less populous world, with only 80 million people in the U.S., less than one-third of today's total. Most people still lived on farms rather than in large cities. Holifield observed that "it was an entirely different society, an agrarian society in the main." "Our principal fuels," Holifield noted, " were wood and coal and the oil and gas age was in its infancy," and further, "it was decades before radio and television."[2]

Even transportation and methods of lighting were different. Holifield remarked that "in 1903 only a few experimental automobiles existed," and that "In my youth, horse-drawn buggies and wagons were the vehicles of local transportation." "Our road system," Holifield remembered, "consisted of gravel, dirt, and dust in the summer and mud in the winter." The only long distance transportation was the railroad, in contrast to today's "great highway and freeway systems of concrete and asphalt." Electricity was not yet in widespread use. "For our lighting," Holifield explained, "we depended, at least in our rural areas, mostly on kerosene lamps and lanterns and candles, so activity ceased at dark."[3] Atomic energy had not even been dreamed of.

Revealing the social consciousness developed early in his life, Holifield noted that many Americans in 1903 did not have the economic opportunity and privileges that they would enjoy in later decades. "Eight decades ago," he commented, "there were no Federal programs such as old age pensions, medical care, vocational or educational training." The "great social programs of today," as Holifield called them, were not in existence "until Franklin Roosevelt and Harry Truman brought in the New Deal and the Fair Deal." When Holifield was born, "there was no protection for the organization of workers into unions for decent wages and working conditions," and "The 12-hour day, 6-day week, without job rights or vacations, was the common practice in commerce and industry." Miners in Holifield's native state of Kentucky "were jailed for striking" and "On the farm, owners and employees worked from dawn until dark, as did many members of my own family."[4]

Holifield's individualism can be explained partly by his descent from a long line of Southern planters that stretches back to the founding of the U.S. The first known member of the family, a Virginian, William Holifield, fought with General George Washington during the Revolutionary War. The Holifields "were part of the Scotch-Irish-English stock whose parents and grandparents had migrated from the Eastern seacoast colonies and states of Virginia and the Carolinas into the areas that became Kentucky, Tennessee, Arkansas, Oklahoma, and Texas."[5] The "fiercely independent" Holifields were "pioneers in a harsh and savage land" where "only the strong survived." In describing the frontier life of his Kentucky forebears, Holifield noted that "The long Kentucky rifle, the hunting knife and the axe were as much a part of their daily life as the log cabin, their riding and work horses, and the primitive plows, hoes and scythes they used to till the soil for food." These pioneers, Holifield believed, bequeathed to their children, grandchildren, and later descendants like himself, many sound character traits, including a strong sense of independence, courage, love of country, deep religious convictions, a willingness to work hard, and an adventurous spirit to explore new lands and subjects.[6]

Holifield's ancestors proved to be loyal to the South when the Civil War came. His grandfather, John R. Holifield, was a Confederate cavalry officer in General Nathan Bedford Forrest's regiment. He was wounded at the Battle of Shiloh by a "mini-ball" that pierced his wrist, permanently restricting the use of his left hand. After the South's surrender at Appomattox Court House in April 1865, John Holifield and other Southern soldiers were allowed to retain their sidearms and also their horses so they could return home for spring planting. John returned to his father's farm near Pryorsburg, Kentucky, only to find that the house and barns had been burned and the livestock stolen or killed, either by Yankee soldiers or the so-called "bushwhackers," civilian criminals who looted and killed indiscriminately on the fringes of both armies. Working behind the lines, the bushwhackers were feared most by families of Confederate soldiers who were fighting far from home to preserve the values in which they believed so fervently.[7]

The end of the War Between the States did not put an end to the privation and suffering of the people in the Southern and Border states. The years of Reconstruction were long, painful, and difficult. Progress was slow and tortuous for several decades, as uprooted Southerners tried to reestablish themselves in their former lives. The mental and physical wounds of this national tragedy lingered, particularly in the minds of the surviving Confederate soldiers and their families. Every Southern town had its own record of men lost or maimed in the Civil War. Young children, including the children and grandchildren of John Holifield, were reared with the stories of bravery, heroism and privation that had occurred during the war.

In the postwar period, John Holifield married Julia Ann Dodson and reared five sons. One of the five sons, Erscie, was Chet's father. John returned to raising tobacco on the family farm and slowly rebuilt the family's fortunes, with the help of his former slave, Tom, who had been his body servant during the four years of war. Industrious and hard-working just as Chet would be, John also found time to earn a medical degree, and he practiced medicine as a country doctor until his death in Pryorsburg in 1910.[8]

John's former slave, Tom, assumed the family name of Holifield and lived with his wife Mary on John's former plantation until his death. Chet, who strongly supported civil rights for all minorities, recalled:

> His name was Tom and his family had a special place in the life of Dr. John's family. They were considered and treated as human beings. They were loved and cared for by the doctor. Their first boy, Bob, who was the same age as Erscie, was educated by Dr. John and earned a degree in pharmacy. He was helped to start a small drug store in the town of Mayfield where both I and my father, Erscie, were born.[9]

Chet's father Erscie proved to be as industrious and hardworking as his father John. Chet remembered that one of Erscie's first accomplishments was building "his own 'gun barrel,' unpainted, two-room house on his father's farm." Chet referred to the house as the "successor" to the log cabin, "not exactly a log cabin, more country saw mill." Erscie learned the carpenter's trade more by happenstance than by design. Since the short Spanish-American War of 1898 was over by the time Erscie joined the Kentucky State Guard, he ended up building barracks rather than fighting in the war. Chet later wrote that Erscie "came out a jackleg country carpenter," with the skills he needed to build his first home.

In 1902, at age 19, Erscie decided to marry Bessie Lee Brady, a girl of 17 years with "beautiful blue eyes and the coal black hair of her Irish heritage." Bessie played the violin at country dances, and as Chet later explained, "this added to her charm when Erscie courted her."[10] Chet Holifield was born about one year after his mother and father were married. In his words:

> I was their first born, at 2 a.m. on December 3, 1903, on a night when sleet and snow were falling. Erscie made sure there were enough logs in the fireplace to keep the little house warm, put on thick clothes and boots, gave a few words of encouragement to his wife, and then reached for his old-fashioned lantern and walked the half-mile up the hill to the farm house of the country doctor, his father. "Papa, Bessie's time is near," he used to recount to me, as he shook my grandfather's shoulder to wake him up. Grandfather delivered me within an hour of reaching our cabin and told his son his first-born was a boy. I was named Chester Earl Holifield, but it was abbreviated to "Chet" by friends and relatives before I was even ten.[11]

A year after Chet was born, Erscie moved to improve his lot, just as his father and grandfather had done before him. He moved his family across the border to Paragould, Arkansas, where he worked for a relative who was in the cleaning and pressing business. Erscie learned the trade of a "bushelman," an alterations man who was not really a full-time tailor. That is what Chet would have been, had he stayed in the trade. Erscie also used his carpentry skills to help build a new church for the town. When Erscie felt he knew the business, he moved the family again, this time to Springdale, Arkansas. Chet's parents had four children in their ten years of marriage. Besides Chet, there was Madge, J.T. and Margaret. Madge died of typhoid fever at the young age of four, and she was soon followed in death by her mother. Bessie succumbed to "consumption"--tuberculosis--when she was 27 years old, and Chet was still a young boy of nine. With three small children to raise, Erscie soon remarried Hazel Osterland, a German-American woman. Three more children were added to the family by this union: Maxine, Lloyd, and Robert.

The period between his mother's death and his father's remarriage was a trying time for Chet. The family lived in a small one-room house, and Chet helped Erscie in the dry cleaning shop. One of Chet's daily jobs was to help clean coats with gasoline from a five-gallon can. Coats could not be cleaned with soap and water because their shoulders would be ruined; gas, on the other hand, would cut any type of grease. Young Chet also served as shop reliever for his father. At noon, the young boy raced from school to watch the shop while his father rested in a boarding house. Keeping a sharp eye on the street, Chet would dash back to class when he saw his father leaving the boarding house to return to work. He received no payment for his work, but a larger house was an indirect reward when his father remarried.

Young Chet was imbued with a basic social philosophy during his boyhood in Springdale. Erscie was a lay preacher in the Christian Church, and he encouraged his children to read and understand the Scriptures. Chet later recalled that he had read the Bible through more than once during his childhood. His father's cleaning shop was also a gathering place for the townsmen, and Chet's eager young mind soaked up many ideas from the lively discussions of religion and politics. His father Erscie, moreover, was an "avowed socialist." Thus, Chet became a socially conscious individual who believed in both the spiritual and social welfare of his fellow human beings. His religion reinforced his sense of responsibility, and the theories of socialism were not that far removed from his religious beliefs.[12]

In Springdale, Chet also became well attuned to the world of work. He not only trained as a haberdasher in his father's shop, but also displayed signs of entrepreneurship and adventurousness that would characterize his later life. As a young boy, Chet devised a business to earn his own spending money. Each winter he made "figure-four" rabbit traps to catch some of the area's numerous wood rabbits, which he could sell for ten cents each. Even on cold winter mornings, Chet was persistent in making his rounds to check the traps he had set.[13] Although he dropped out of high school, his adventurousness was probably increased by his avid reading of adventure stories. He slept in the loft of the family home and read books under the covers by lantern light. Holifield liked Wild West novels, and California held a particular fascination for him. "For me," as Holifield later remembered it, "California was the land of glamour, the finding of gold and oil, the setting of the Wild West novels."[14] Even as a young boy, he determined that someday he would go there.

Holifield's adventurousness was only a part of his general inquisitiveness, which manifested itself in his many homely "inventions." Sometimes he learned by example, as in building special rabbit traps. But he also "invented" on his own. One of his biggest confrontations with his father was because he wanted to plant strawberry plants "his" way. Later in life when he was a congressman, he made his own dark cloth shades for riding on airplanes from Washington to the West Coast, because his eyes were ultra-sensitive to light. In his eightieth year, he conceived of another "invention": a velcro strap to wrap around his head to prevent snoring. He did this not only because the snoring bothered his wife of six decades, but because he claimed proper breathing kept one healthy! He was always creative, whether it was in business or politics, or simply for his personal satisfaction.[15]

The Young Adventurer

Eventually, Holifield's adventurous spirit and his desire to improve his lot got the better of him. As he described it:

> When I was fourteen, there was an epidemic of Spanish flu. It was December, 1917, my birthday month, and the schools were closed because so many people were dying. I read in the paper that they were looking for pressers in Springfield, Missouri, so I took the railroad to Springfield, paying the fare of two cents a mile for the 60-mile trip, applied and got a job pressing pants for a firm which had a contract to make Marine uniforms. I was paid 20 cents per hour and worked six days of 10 hours each week.[16]

At twelve dollars a week, Holifield was elated at what he considered a small fortune. He saved even more money by learning to "ride the rods," essentially hitching rides on trains by riding on the three axles or rods beneath the box cars. "It was a skill that had to be learned," he remembered. "You hooked your foot under one [rod] and your knee over another and let your butt hang down between, with your arms hanging on the side." Due to the precarious position and the danger of falling onto the tracks, he noted "You didn't go to sleep." He felt lucky if he found a plank to rest between the rods so he could rest his back. Whatever the disadvantages, it did save money and "Anyway, you were protected from the rain."[17]

Holifield was scarcely back from his first adventure when he went on another. By the summer of 1918, most able-bodied men had been drafted for World War I, and a call went out from national defense officials for men over 45 years old and boys under 18 years to help harvest wheat in the nation's grain belt. Young Chet decided to answer the call. Laborers got unusually good wages: 50 cents per hour. The harvest season lasted about six weeks, followed by the threshing season, lasting another six to eight weeks. Chet traveled to Oklahoma and Kansas to work in the wheat and barley, and he also worked in Oklahoma's Winona Oil Fields.

After earning 50 cents an hour for ten hours each day of a six-day work week, young Chet returned home at the end of the summer with $300 in his bank account--more money than he ever thought existed in the entire world! The $5 a day was clear because each threshing machine operator fed his workers free of charge from a "cook shack," and the workers had bed rolls which they put on fresh straw that had been threshed during the day. With no expenses, including no travel expenses because he had learned to "ride the rods," Chet sent postal money orders home regularly. It was a lesson the fourteen year old boy, going on fifteen, would not forget: acquiring wealth required hard work. In later years, Holifield believed that his early lessons of hard work helped to forge the relentless working habits that marked his career. These experiences also deepened his sense of personal independence and his persistent concern for protecting the rights of every individual.[18]

On the lighter side, Chet's trips away from home provided the substance for a good-natured joke on one of his first subcommittee chairmen when Holifield later went to Congress. Twenty-five years after his trip, in a conversation with Representative Ross Rizzley of Oklahoma, Holifield told Rizzley that he had served time in the town jail of Enid, Oklahoma when he was fourteen years old. Rizzley, a former lawyer in Enid, was horrified until Holifield explained. As it happened, young Chet had stopped in Enid for the night, and rain clouds were forming. Many men and boys had left the train and crowded into the town park to sleep under newspapers. More resourceful than most, Holifield walked to the town's fire and police department and asked a fireman if there was a place to sleep for 50 cents. The fireman did not know of any, but suddenly came up with an idea. He noted that the jail cells were unoccupied and that the women's committee had recently cleaned the jail house, burned the old mattresses, and stuffed new ones with fresh straw. Holifield then paid the jail custodian 50 cents, and was allowed to sleep on a cell floor until dark. Then, he was permitted to sleep on one of the new mattresses. Torrents of rain came down, but Holifield spent a warm, dry, and peaceful night--in jail! When he finished his story, he asked Rizzley for forgiveness for his jail-bird status in Enid. Rizzley laughed and said Holifield would make a great congressman and a fine member of the Committee on Executive Expenditures, since its main objective was to improve government efficiency, including efficiency in local jails![19]

On to California

Holifield's increasing independence became hard to contain and he began to set his sights on a longer trip. "The following spring [of 1919]," he remarked, "I became restless and spoke to two friends about going to California." Holifield decided to leave when he did, however, due to his conflicts with his parents. He later acknowledged that "At home, relations with my father and stepmother were not good." The conflicts were normal ones that most adolescents have with their parents. He vividly remembered the final conflict with his father that sparked his decision to leave home:

> On April Fool's Day--I remember the day well--I was helping my father with our planting. We got into an argument about how I was planting strawberry plants with a special knife; my father, who was a Church of Christ lay preacher and very intelligent, but very authoritarian, said: "You're not planting them the way I told you to plant them."
>
> I argued and said, "Well, I don't see any reason why your way is any better than mine."

My father then said: "Well, Chester, the day you're too big to get things done the way I want them done is the day you are too big to put your feet under my table."[20]

Chet was determined not to put his feet under his father's table any longer. He remembered telling his father, "That suits me fine." He put his strawberry knife on the ground, put a few personal items in a red bandanna, and set off. This time, he did not do as well. He was able to earn only $1 a day, so he returned home for short stays. Soon, however, he set off for California with two high school friends. He was fifteen years old, not yet out of high school.[21]

Holifield's wanderings in the summer of 1919 took him and his two friends to Los Angeles and Pasadena, California. He first took a job as a presser in Los Angeles, but after a few weeks switched to a job as a presser in a Pasadena dry cleaning shop. His two friends, however, preferred the oil fields of Montebello, a small oil town of about 1800 people about ten miles southeast of Los Angeles. Chet visited his friends there on weekends. Together, the three spent the summer scouting out their new environment, intrigued by the different society, culture, and climate of Southern California. Holifield was gradually drawn to Montebello by his many friends there.[22]

At the end of the summer, Holifield's two friends returned to Arkansas. But Chet, intrigued by California life, decided to remain. In 1920 he settled in Montebello, which was growing fast because of the oil fields. Always the entrepreneur, Holifield realized that the growing city could use a laundry and dry cleaning shop. He opened a pressing business in a rented building, with packing crates as a counter. He bought an old Model-T truck and commuted 10 miles to Los Angeles to the wholesale dry cleaners, starting out at 5 a.m. each day and working until late to meet his customers' needs. There were many Spanish-speaking people working in the area, so he began to learn Spanish. Soon, he stocked clothing, and the business became a haberdashery.

To get the $200 loan he needed to open his business, Holifield had written home to request his father to cosign his loan. He used this and other opportunities to tell his father how promising things looked in his adopted home. Erscie was intrigued by what he read, and took Chet up on an offer to start a business together. With such a strong Southern family tradition, Chet's rebellion against his father's rules had never caused a serious rift; their relationship had healed with the passage of time. Soon Holifield was joined in California by his father, wife Hazel, and the rest of the family.[23]

With Erscie's financial contribution, Chet and his father were able to open an expanded cleaning and haberdashery shop in Montebello, and business continued to increase during their partnership. The joint business venture lasted about a year, when the two men got into a dispute over Chet's new "inventions." Chet wanted to advertise and also wanted a new window display to attract business into the store. Erscie thought that advertising and the window display were wasteful. Both of the owners were strong-willed and wanted their way, although this time, father and son were able to settle their dispute more amicably. Erscie was interested in moving to Oregon, so Chet agreed to buy Erscie's part of the business and Erscie agreed to sell.[24]

Holifield's first action as the sole proprietor of his shop was to grow a mustache. If he was going to be boss, he knew he needed to look the part:

> Having bought out my father's share of our shop, I decided I had better grow a mustache. In that way, people coming in and seeing a 20-year old youth would stop asking "Where's the boss?"[25]

Chet Marries Vernice ("Cam") Caneer

One day during the year Chet was in business with his father, two high school seniors came into the shop selling tickets to their class play. Chet teasingly told the women that he might buy a ticket if one of them would go out with him. When they left, Chet turned to his father and said: "You know that dark-haired girl on the right? That is the one I am going to marry." Chet was referring to Vernice ("Cam") Caneer, who had a lead role in her class play. The two were married on September 14, 1922. Since he was not even 19 years old, Chet had to get his father's written permission.[26]

Thereafter in reference to his and Cam's chance meeting, Holifield was fond of quipping that it always pays to treat customers well. From playing the lead role in her class play, Cam came to play the lead role in Chet's life. Chet and Cam became an inseparable team in Washington, where Cam joined Chet at many official congressional functions. She also served for years in his congressional office. At their Golden Wedding Anniversary party in 1972 in Washington, Chet and Cam enjoyed a receiving line of four daughters, four sons-in-law, 15 grandchildren, and one great granddaughter. Their marriage also became one for the Holifield record books: on September 14, 1990, they reached their sixty-eighth year of marriage.[27]

During the 1920s and the early 1930s, the couple had a family of five daughters: Lois Anita, Betty Lee, Patricia Jean, Willa Mae, and Jo Ann. The middle daughter, Patricia Jean, died in 1932 while still very young. Willa Mae, the only daughter who smoked, died in 1974 after a valiant fight with cancer. Young Chet had a souring experience smoking "Cheroots" with his friend, E. R. "Cotton" Lavender. He became so ill that he had to lay under a horse-drawn wagon (to escape the hot summer sun) for an entire day before going home. He never forgot the experience and never smoked again.

During the remainder of the 1920s, Chet and Cam worked very hard to increase their haberdashery business while raising a family. It was not an easy task. The Holifields lived quite frugally, saving all that they could for reinvestment into the haberdashery, "Chet's House of Style." While many of their friends went out on Saturday nights and bought new cars, the Holifield's single "extravagance" was accommodating one of Chet's customers from the St. Helens Oil Company, a youth who told Chet he was going to go to work for Metropolitan Life Insurance Company. Holifield promised to buy his first insurance policy, although he was in financial straits. Chet kept his promise. Later, following his 1931 hunting accident, Holifield received $100 a month for 30 months on the policy, a saving grace during the Great Depression.[28]

Holifield was convinced that advertising was the key to business growth. Another of his early "inventions" was to hold a raffle for a new Ford automobile. Anyone buying $5 worth of merchandise became eligible to receive five tickets for the drawing, which was held after six months. Holifield put the new Ford in the display window as an enticement, and held the drawing in front of all of his customers on Christmas Eve.   To the townspeople, this event was like the Fourth of July and was in fact the biggest promotional event ever to hit Montebello up to that time.

Holifield became well-known in Montebello from his business activities and was soon asked to join social and civic groups. He joined the local chamber of commerce, the Young Men's Christian Association (YMCA), and the Lions Club. Before long, he was even asked to become a stockholder in the new First State Bank of Montebello to replace a friend who had just died. Holifield had to borrow the money to come up with $900 to pay for the six required shares of $150 each to join the bank. He thus met his twin goals of helping out the widow of his friend who needed to liquidate her shares and of working more closely with the local business community.[29]

If the 1920s were tough, the 1930s proved to be even tougher for the Holifields. In a space of two years, from 1931 through 1932, a series of disasters struck, forever transforming their lives and for a while distressing them greatly. The first disaster occurred in March 1931, when Chet was accidentally shot in the leg during a hunting trip to Santa Catalina Island. He never knew who shot him, but was laid up for three full years until March 1934, during the height of the Great Depression. The failure of his business followed, also in 1931. If this were not enough, the family was then traumatized by the sudden and unexpected death of Patricia Jean in 1932. Cam was still tearful when recalling the event fifty years later. Patricia Jean was stricken suddenly and rather mysteriously while playing at home. While she was taken to the hospital quickly, it was not possible to save her. This shocking loss magnified their heartaches during this very difficult time, but their firm religious beliefs sustained them.[30]

Holifield's gunshot wound was a serious one that was not healing. While he was at home recovering, he got another jolt: Metropolitan Life notified him that his policy had expired. Since he could do very little at home in a physical sense, he got out the policy and studied it. He came to the conclusion that where the policy indicated that "12 $100 payments" was to be the entire benefits under the policy, there was fine print which gave the reader a feeling that the company was obligated for additional liability. When he tried to get additional information from the local Metropolitan Life office, he was rebuffed. So he went to an attorney, with largely the same result. Finally, when he wrote a letter to Metropolitan's headquarters, he was told there was no additional liability. By now, 18 months had passed, and most people would have given up, but Holifield was persistent. Cam drove him to San Francisco to see the top man in Metropolitan's West Coast headquarters. Chet walked in on crutches and later remembered that the top manager said, "You seem to be getting around all right. It must not be very bad." Holifield's next move caused the executive to turn pale:

> I just sat down and pulled my pants up my leg, yanked the pad off the wound and showed him a hole going right into the bone, and said: "Do you mean to tell me you are not going to give me food to feed my children?" He [the executive] turned white upon seeing the size of the wound. And I got $1,800 out of the deal, which was mighty welcome for my family in those depression days. Until then, I had been saving the $5 a time it cost to go to a doctor. I dressed the wound myself, heating a 20-penny nail over the gas stove, taking off the dead flesh, and then using a Kotex pad for a bandage with several changes a day.[31]

The economic woes of the Holifields matched Chet's physical condition. The economic trauma of the Great Depression reverberated on the streets of Montebello, and the Bank of Montebello closed its doors in 1931. With the failure of the bank, the Holifields were suddenly faced with debts exceeding their assets, since their business account had vanished with the bank. "Meanwhile," Holifield observed, "our store profits were down to zero." State Conservator Ed Scofield told Holifield that he owed $2,500 to the bank immediately. Holifield's only assets were $1500 in merchandise. "I told the bank they could foreclose," Holifield later remembered, "but then I would have to declare bankruptcy and they would get nothing." Holifield worked out an agreement whereby he could keep his business operating and repay the bank at $50 per month for 50 months. This payment schedule proved to be difficult, but Holifield noted that Scofield "trusted me and the merchandising wholesalers said, 'We know you, we'll back you.' And they restocked us." He was later proud to recount that "Ed Scofield said we were the first to pay off our full obligation to his bank in those depression days."[32]

The Holifield family struggled against the storms that besieged them in the early 1930s. With Chet unable to work, Cam and Chet's boyhood friend, Cotton Lavender, tended the store, even as business declined. The two older daughters did the housework and prepared dinner after they came home from school. A family friend of many years, Fannie Brown, served as a baby sitter for the two younger daughters. Even with the help, however, the Holifields were unable to keep their home, which had been mortgaged to save the business. They finally lost it and rented another from Cam's brother.

The Holifields were down, but not out. In 1934, they moved "Chet Holifield's Store for Men" to East Los Angeles. Holifield recounted that "We knew they needed a dry-cleaning, pressing and haberdashery store, but we didn't realize how badly." During the first month at the new location, the Holifields tripled their business volume. The change was thus a total success, except for customer parking. As the years passed, parking became more of a problem, prompting Holifield during the early 1950s to move the business a final time to Norwalk, a sleepy, one-street town where a shopping center was being built with ample parking. Holifield thought the move was a good gamble and it proved to be, with the store remaining there for more than a generation until he sold it in 1975, soon after his retirement from Congress. Lavender, whose only contract was a hand shake, managed the haberdashery during most of Holifield's service in Congress.[33]

Holifield Turns to Politics

From 1931 to 1934, Holifield was not sure his business would recover from the Great Depression. He did not lie idly in his bed during this time. He thought constantly about the effects of the Great Depression and began to read and speak out about the need for political reforms. He could no longer be just a businessman, blind to the effects that politics had on economics:

> I knew everybody was losing everything in the Depression. But as I lay in bed I began to do a lot of thinking: How come a person like me who has worked hard and scraped and saved is in the very same boat as somebody else who spent a lot of money on Saturday night good times and buying new cars? Other people who lost their jobs came to visit me and my bedside became a sort of corner drugstore. They told me they didn't have the money for their next bag of groceries. I listened and I read and I began to do a lot of reflecting on problems of every variety, national and international. Books of all kinds provided me with new ideas over those three years. I guess this period was the real crucible for my future political beliefs. I decided there must be something wrong with our economic system. And while I couldn't yet go back to work in the store, I did start going to political meetings and, eventually, making speeches.[34]

If and when he got into politics, there was no question that Holifield would be a liberal Democrat, even though he lived in largely Republican Montebello. He had been influenced by his family's Confederate heritage, his strong religious background coupled with his father's peculiar brand of nondoctrinaire socialism, and most importantly, his bitter experience during the Depression that convinced him of the need for political reforms. At age 21, he had voted for the Democratic presidential candidate in 1924, and he remained a dedicated Democrat thereafter. In 1932, he supported Franklin D. Roosevelt, as he would for all of Roosevelt's four terms.[35]

The year 1934 was especially significant for Holifield's development as a politician, just as it was for his business success. By this time, he had become well-known and respected in Montebello. As member of the local chamber of commerce and several nonpartisan clubs, he actively participated in civic affairs, became acquainted with many people, and found that he liked to interact with groups. His businessman status also was important. In 1934, his Democratic colleagues in Montebello were looking for a businessman to represent them as a member of the Democratic Central Committee for the Fifty-First Assembly District. "As there were few Democratic businessmen in my community," Holifield later noted, "my fellow Democratic townspeople came to me." Holifield's colleagues "wanted someone of standing in the business community to represent them." Holifield was 31 years old and had operated his haberdashery for several years. He threw his hat into the ring.

Holifield did not forget his socialist roots. One of the townspeople who urged him to run for the committeeman post in 1934 and offered to pay the filing fee was a Socialist. In fact, much of Roosevelt's social programs, including Social Security, was socialistic in origin. It was not surprising, therefore, that Holifield stumped for Upton Sinclair for California governor in 1934 at the same time he ran for his own office. He threw his enthusiastic support to Sinclair and his EPIC (End Poverty in California) Program, even though Sinclair himself was an openly-declared Socialist and had registered as a Democrat only in order to capture the Democratic nomination. Sinclair's campaign failed by a thin margin, but Holifield won by the largest plurality of any candidate. He thus began his long journey into politics. As a result of his large win, Holifield became not merely a member, but chairman of the Democratic Central Committee for the Fifty-First Assembly District.[36]

Once into politics, Holifield came into contact with many politicians, but none for whom he had more respect than Jerry Voorhis. Interestingly, Voorhis had registered as a Socialist as a young man, but had finally joined the Democrats. "One night I went to [a meeting of] the Los Angeles County Democratic Committeemen's Association and heard a speech by someone named Jerry Voorhis," Holifield remembered. He "went home and told Cam, 'the ideas expressed by that young man remind me of some of Lincoln's speeches.'" Holifield was "tremendously impressed by his [Voorhis'] sincerity, idealism, and political philosophy." Before long, the two men were close friends. In 1936, Holifield was co-director of the 40 Democratic State and County Central Committeemen who managed the Voorhis campaign for Congress. Voorhis won, and appointed Holifield as chairman of the State Democratic Central Committee for the Twelfth Congressional District.[37]

It was only a matter of time before Holifield took another political step inspired by Voorhis. In 1938, Voorhis told Holifield that he was planning to run for the U.S. Senate in 1940. Voorhis encouraged him to run for Los Angeles County supervisor. The race was open because the incumbent had declared himself as a candidate for governor against Culbert Olson. Voorhis made it clear that it was very unlikely that he would win, but that the race would give Holifield campaign experience, since if Voorhis won in 1940, Holifield could run for Voorhis' vacated congressional seat.

Even though he knew he probably would not win, Holifield threw himself wholeheartedly into the County supervisor's race. A total of 17 candidates filed for the position. "The only money I had," Holifield remarked later, "was $500 which I had set aside for an education fund for my two little girls." Holifield used his small fund "for gasoline and quarter cards to nail on telephone poles." There was no money left for newspaper ads. Nonetheless, Holifield finished "among the top three or four in number of votes received," but not enough to get the nomination. "I wasn't bitter at all," Holifield recalled, because "I hadn't expected to win; and Jerry agreed, but said the experience had widened my belt." But Holifield had "a lot of explaining to do" when Cam discovered that the $500 education fund had been spent![38]

Holifield Becomes a United States Congressman

Voorhis decided not to run for Senator in 1940 due to insufficient funding, so there was no congressional race for Holifield. But events continued to be favorable. In 1940 the California congressional districts were reapportioned, with three new districts created due to the state's phenomenal population growth. Two of these were partly in Holifield's business area, meaning that he could run in 1942. His friends urged him to run. The Holifields had just reconstructed their business, and were doing well at about $7,500 a year. Congress paid $10,000 per year, so Holifield decided to run.

In his bid for Congress, Holifield recalled that he "had seven opponents" in the new, heavily-Democratic 19th Congressional District. Capturing the Democratic nomination would essentially mean victory. His chief opponent in the Democratic primary was "a man named Wheeler, editor of the Bell, California newspaper." He won the primary handily and faced Republican Max Ward in the November election. "We were both Lions Club members and knew each other," Holifield said later, "so it was a clean campaign." Holifield won with 65 percent of the vote.[39]

Holifield was elected from a "safe" district. He proved to be the first and only congressman who served in the 19th Congressional District as constructed in 1940, since he won 16 consecutive elections, usually with over 70 percent of the vote. When he entered Congress, the Republicans controlled the State Legislature, and gerrymandered districts to ensure their continued control. Holifield benefitted from their actions, since his district contained a large Democratic majority. At one point, he represented 800,000 people, while the three adjoining congressional districts contained an average of 250,000 people each! This was not gerrymandering at its worst, however. State Senator (later Congressman) Tom Rees once represented seven million residents in Los Angeles County because the state constitution at the time stipulated that each county was entitled to one state senator. The senator in Modoc County, a northern California county, represented 18,000 people during this same period! When the Supreme Court decided on "one man, one vote," Los Angeles County gained 14 state senators almost overnight.[40]

After 32 years, it was Holifield's decision to retire that ended his congressional career, not the opposition. He faced one tenuous challenge in 1948, but was able to fend off his opponent. In some later elections, Holifield even cross-filed and won the nomination of both the Democrats and the Republicans, as permitted under California law. In later terms he became unbeatable, a fact that even his political enemies appreciated. The 19th Congressional District changed in later reapportionments and the 1970 reapportionment did prove to be damaging, but members of his delegation like Jim Corman were convinced that he would win by a 10 to 1 margin if he ran again in 1974. Holifield, though, believed that it was time to retire.[41]

Once in Congress, Holifield encountered the atomic energy field through happenstance. Because of his leg injury, he could not serve in a military capacity during World War II, but he was interested in a position on the Military Affairs Committee. Holifield gained a bottom-rung seat due to a California member's death. Thus, he was on the committee when it considered the May-Johnson bill in 1946, and was able to embark upon an essentially nonpartisan career in atomic energy due to his "safe" district.

To his constituents, Holifield remained an unusual combination of idealist and pragmatist. On the sensitive subject of Vietnam in the late 1960s, he was direct in replies to inquiring constituents, even when he did not agree with them. If he seemed overly idealistic to some, he knew the pitfalls of politics--he could not be bought. When he ran for Los Angeles County supervisor, big oil companies sought him out. He knew that they would give him funds for his campaign, with no demands. But he knew if he took the money, he would be obligated, so he refused. The money went elsewhere and he lost. From then on, he remained his own man. Even upon his retirement, he declined to become a lobbyist for narrow or self-interested viewpoints.[42]

To some who knew him, Haberdasher Holifield seemed very much like the classical Roman leader Cincinnatus, who left his plow to answer the call of defending the *res publica* in time of grave public danger and who then turned his back on public glory and prestige to till the soil again. Holifield never ended his lifelong love of haberdashery as a congressman. He often went upstairs in his store while home at Christmas to help out with the extra volume of alterations. In Congress, he made a point of always carrying a sharp knife with him, true to his tailoring profession. One of his sons-in-law,

Bob Feldmann, recalled being fitted in 1948 for his wedding "going-away" suit in Holifield's office on Capitol Hill! Several leading political and business figures also had their suits pressed by him at his store in Norwalk, some when they delivered highly classified information to the JCAE chairman.

On one break, Holifield was visited by his friend Jim Ramey. "I had him take off his coat so that I could show him how I got started as a presser," Holifield mused. Ramey reciprocated by giving a speech in Montebello. "After he had said some nice things about me," Chet recalled, "he recounted the story of my pressing his coat." Later some of his constituents told him that "they were surprised at the impression this had made on my friend!"[43]

Holifield's career as a haberdasher was often compared to that of President Truman, also a haberdasher. At a large public banquet during his career, the master of ceremonies was moved by Holifield's success as a haberdasher to compare him with Truman. "Both men had two things in common and one great difference," the speaker quipped. "They were both elected to Congress, both married women from Missouri, but Holifield succeeded as a haberdasher and Truman failed!" Truman himself often enjoyed hearing this comparison.

The personal tie between Holifield and Truman was always close. When Holifield's daughter, Betty, and her Foreign Service husband, Bob Feldmann were sent to Vienna in 1958, they traveled on the ocean liner *Independence*. Also on board was the former president and Judge Samuel Rosenman and their wives. Betty's father had sent a note to Truman, and to their surprise, the Feldmanns were invited by Truman to visit with him in his stateroom. According to State Department protocol, junior Foreign Service officers were to spend only 15 minutes at such visits, but the Trumans insisted that the Feldmanns stay for over an hour! Truman spoke enthusiastically of his daughter Margaret's first child. "But," Truman added, "Chet's got me way beat when it comes to grandkids!" Truman never forgot that when almost all leading politicians began to attack him personally between 1950 and 1952, Holifield had gone on radio to defend him, saying, "We had the New Deal before, now we've got the Tru-Deal!" In a letter handwritten on board, Truman wrote to Chet that the visit with the Feldmanns was "most pleasant from our viewpoint." He added that Chet had "way yonder the advantage on the grandchild basis . . . Believe I've got something on you! But it's good!"[44]

A large part of Holifield's success was his winning personality and his ability to get along with a wide variety of people. He became the master of the "give and take" of personal ties and relationships. One-time Senate Majority Leader Alben Barkley, also Truman's vice president, probably put it best in a jesting comment on Holifield, his distant relative: "Chet Holifield's a relative of mine. He's close enough so if he does anything good, we both can take credit; and distant enough so that when he does anything bad I don't have to take any responsibility!"[45]

California's Legislative Dean

The basic characteristics Holifield exhibited during his developmental years as a person and politician stayed with him over the years. This is nowhere more true than in his years as California's legislative dean, a position Holifield gained as the longest-serving representative in the California delegation from the late 1960s through 1974. Prior to Holifield, the House's largest state delegation had rarely worked together in the overall interests of the state. The previous dean, Representative Harry Shephard, an amiable legislator, had let each member go his or her own way. Cecil King, Shephard's successor, briefly held the post and initiated some moves toward coordination, but not with the intensity that Holifield mustered when he assumed the office. Under Holifield, Republicans and Democrats began working together, as the *Los Angeles Times* reported, with "muscle and harmony." Holifield organized weekly breakfast meetings to discuss issues affecting California. He also consulted with the ranking Republican, William S. Mailliard, to encourage bipartisan efforts, with joint meetings where unified efforts were possible. The *Los Angeles Times*, which did not support Holifield for most of his career, credited him with making the delegation more effective, noting "Perhaps most important of all is the considerable bipartisan harmony and goodwill that exist among California's 38 representatives." The delegation grew to 43 members before Holifield retired.[46]

Holifield's seniority assured him the position of California's dean and thus gave him time to exert significant influence on the office. Determined to be fair-minded, as always, he sought accommodation with the state's senior Republican legislators. Under an unwritten agreement he developed, the entire delegation met frequently, taking no votes on any issue, and allowing all members to vote afterwards as their consciences dictated on any specific issue. Holifield allowed any California industry or organization to express its views and be questioned before the entire delegation, as long as the matter at hand was not highly emotional or controversial. Partisan politics was to have no part in the delegation's deliberations, with dedication to California's welfare serving as the cement for coordinated activities.

Holifield's bipartisanship as dean did not imply that he would forego measures to strengthen the power of California Democrats in the House. Nor did he hesitate to oppose fellow Democrats who attempted to violate the delegation's unwritten customs. A case in point was that of the late Philip Burton, a brilliant, hardworking, but sometimes abrasive envoy from Northern California who asked Holifield in 1968 to help him get a vacant seat on the House Appropriations Committee. Unfortunately, by custom it was the turn of a Southern Californian to be on the committee, so Holifield advised Burton he could not have the post. Burton mounted an aggressive campaign to overturn this decision. Having grown up in Arkansas, however, Holifield had formed a previous alliance with Arkansas' Wilbur Mills, chairman of the Ways and Means Committee, the "Committee on Committees" that acted in conjunction with the Speaker in assigning committee memberships. Holifield explained the situation to Mills, and Burton's effort was readily repulsed.[47]

Holifield's attempt to maintain a Northern-Southern balance in assigning House posts was not easy. Sometimes he had to press unwilling representatives into committee slots. During the Burton episode, Holifield ironically found he had to coax a Southern Californian into the Appropriations Committee vacancy. Holifield's choice was not interested since he already had an assignment on Foreign Affairs, and would have to resign that position to serve on Appropriations. Agreement finally came when Holifield pointed out that in the forthcoming election, voters would turn against the congressman when word leaked out that he had rejected the Appropriations post. Holifield's clinching argument was that once the congressman joined Appropriations, he would always have campaign funding because political action committees would not want to see him replaced.[48]

As the California dean, Holifield worked hard. He recalled his response to a phone call from William Ketchum, then a freshman Republican, as illustrative of his political style as dean. Ketchum had requested time for the delegation to hear from three California growers who were concerned about the state of their industry. Holifield's response went something like this:

> Bill, this is Chet. I bet you're calling me on that letter you sent. You want me to convene a meeting of the delegation; but I want to ask you who these people are and what the meeting is for? Let me explain, Bill. We have a rule in our delegation. On controversial matters, like Caesar Chavez and the grape pickers, some Democrats represent union areas. Now you've also got congressmen like you and Bernie Sisk who represent growers. On things which we can work together on, for instance, when the American Legion puts in a plea for more hospitals--projects that pertain to the whole state--we stay together. But if a problem just pertains to Northern California, or to the South, like mass transit in Los Angeles, we can't burden representatives from San Francisco. When we have ideological differences, we listen to all sides. But we don't take action. We all go our separate ways; then when the matter comes up, in Congress, we vote on our consciences. That keeps us from one another's throats.[49]

"While Ketchum was speaking," Holifield recalled, "I grabbed my coat on the chair to pull his letter out of my pocket." After rereading the letter while Ketchum talked, Holifield realized the pitfalls possible in such a presentation. Ketchum was a new member, so Holifield frankly told Ketchum "I was afraid some of these businessmen would criticize Caesar Chavez." "Then," Holifield added, "members who supported labor would not attend the delegation's meeting to support Bill Ketchum, who represents a conservative agricultural district." Ketchum agreed with Holifield's assessment and made arrangements to take the matter up before the Republican caucus, while Holifield agreed to bring the matter up before the Democrats. Such were the everyday compromises which Holifield engineered as dean. His formula worked.[50]

Holifield's personal concern for California's long-range interests was evidenced in his protracted battle to use heat generated by nuclear power to provide desalinated ocean water as an additional water source for California. Historically, riparian rights fueled heated controversies and even wars among states, counties, and even individual farmers as the West was won. Many a rancher and farmer lost his life when he tapped water supplies or dammed up water flows that others further downstream believed belonged rightfully to them. With rainfall in parts of Southern California averaging only eight to eleven inches per year, Californians discovered early, as did others in states of the Southwest, that their economic fortunes hinged on federal assistance.[51] Over his legislative career, Holifield was not particularly identified in the public mind with the constant skirmishing over water rights. Yet parallel to his interest in advancing the future of nuclear power was his underlying concern for effective use of California's water. He believed that nuclear power could be used to pump water over California's mountain ranges into Los Angeles, to provide improved planning of watershed resources in the Pacific Northwest, and also, as he often proposed, to desalinate ocean water.

Beginning in 1964, JCAE Chairman Holifield and AEC Commissioner Ramey put forth a complicated proposal under which several federal, state and local agencies would collaborate to use nuclear power to desalinate ocean water at the average rate of 100 million gallons a day. An artificial island would be built off the California coastline at Huntington Beach where Southern California Edison would construct a dual-purpose, nuclear-powered desalinization plant. The Southern California Metropolitan Water District would install pipelines and distribute the water, and the Department of Interior and the AEC would be involved in R&D and other aspects of the venture. Financing would be authorized by the JCAE and other federal and state legislative bodies. This dual-purpose plant would also generate between 150,000 and 750,000 kilowatts of electric power to be sold by Edison to the private and public utilities in the Southern California area.[52] This large-scale desalting plant would have been by far the largest ever built. It would produce between 50 and 150 million gallons of water a day, enough to meet the needs of a population of 250,000 to 750,000. In contrast, a plant that was moved from San Diego to Guantanamo Bay had a capacity of only one million gallons, and the world's largest plant at the time, on the island of Aruba in the Caribbean, produced only three and one-half million gallons. Today, larger, oil-fired desalting plants operate reliably throughout the world.

To support the desalting project and similar sea water conversion ventures, Holifield pushed through Congress the Desalinization Act of 1967. With considerable foresight, Holifield hoped to assist California in confronting its number one need: water for irrigation of food crops in the great valleys between Arizona and Southern California, and water to meet the needs of people who inhabited the former desert of Southern California.[53] On this particular battle, Holifield eventually lost and the desalinization plant was never built in the face of mounting opposition from the growing antinuclear movement and eventual loss of interest by the involved private utilities.

Holifield's youthful journey to the West and his Southern roots enabled him to move easily among many other delegations in the House. He was close to the Texas delegation during much of his career. In 1960 he supported Lyndon B. Johnson of Texas over John F. Kennedy for the presidency. When Jim Wright, another Texan, entered Congress in the 1950s, he sensed that fellow Texan and Speaker Sam Rayburn had special confidence in some non-Southern liberal Democrats, particularly John Blatnik (D-Minnesota) and Holifield. Holifield and Blatnik were then leaders of efforts to make the Rules Committee more amenable to the will of the House. Rayburn trusted Holifield and Blatnik, Wright noted, because they insisted that the reformers neither work behind the Speaker's back nor seek to undermine his authority.[54]

Holifield and the Rules of the House

Speaker Wright himself liked to tell stories about Holifield's experiences with the House rules. In one story, Holifield's integrity was unjustly impugned, a practice forbidden by House rules. In 1955, Cleveland Bailey (D-West Virginia) claimed a point of order against an alleged late vote cast by Holifield in the well of the House. Bailey believed Holifield was not in the chamber when his name was called, and therefore "the member is not entitled to vote." Speaker Rayburn was personally infuriated by Bailey's effort to question the honor of another member, and chastised Bailey. Several members informed Bailey that Holifield had been in the well, but the clerk had overlooked his response. Bailey went forward and issued a tearful public apology. He had been so caught up in the debate, he said, that he had not realized what he did. Wright pointed to this episode to emphasize that the key to effective legislating is trust for the word of one's colleagues.[55]

Although Holifield had a solid reputation for sticking to the rules, one incident showed that even conscientious legislators such as he could run afoul legislative etiquette. As told by Wright, Holifield's avid defense of civil liberties during one debate in the late 1940s or early 1950s caused him to refer to the House Committee on Un-American Activities inadvertently as "the Un-American Activities Committee." Because the latter designation was a derisive term often used by the committee's critics, John Rankin, a powerful committee member, rose to a point of order against Holifield's offending remark. Rankin asked that the words be "taken down," that is, stricken from the record. By a somewhat lengthy process, Holifield was censured by his peers. Upon Rankin's rise to a point of order, the chairman pro tempore

banged the gavel and told Holifield to take his seat. The Sergeant-at-Arms
was sent to get the Speaker. Rayburn appeared, banged the gavel, and asked
that the alleged objectionable words be read. Rayburn realized that Holifield
had made an unintentional error, but he had to apply the penalty nonetheless.
Despite Holifield's protestations and much to his embarrassment, he was
denied any voice on the floor for the remainder of the day other than a "yea"
or "nay" when a vote was taken. Jim Trimble, an older member from the
Arkansas district where Holifield had lived between the ages of eight and
fifteen, went over to Holifield, put his hand on his friend's shoulder, and said:
"Chet, let this be a lesson to you. Never get into a [urinating] contest with a
skunk!" This was homely but sage advice that Holifield never forgot.
Ironically, the 1963 Congressional Directory, using a new format to list
committees, listed the first one as "Un-American Activities!"[56]

A New Invention: the Local District Office

At first preoccupied with atomic energy and other national and
international issues, Holifield initially evidenced a tendency to overlook
specific concerns of his legislative district. But early in his career he sensed
that neglect of those who had sent him to Congress would be self-defeating.
He thus came up with another "invention" on the California political scene:
the first local congressional district office where constituents could bring their
concerns. Holifield staffed his local office with two capable associates, Harold
Lane and Florence Odemar, both of whom had been active in youth
employment work during Governor Culbert Olson's administration and active
with Holifield in the "Young Democrats" club. Lane was an extension of the
congressman's capacity to communicate with his constituents rapidly and
effectively. He also kept Holifield informed of the political temper of the
district. Near the end of Holifield's career, William O'Donnell, a young lawyer
in his district, whom Holifield had helped and encouraged through law school,
succeeded to Lane's post after Lane's death. "Ode" Odemar, considered by
the Holifields to be a member of their family, continued to be the mainstay
of the office and retired in 1974 along with Chet. Opening a local office had
a very positive impact on Holifield's future, as his office aides and a cadre of
volunteers provided him with a formidable local presence unmatched for some
years by other California representatives.[57]

For his constituents in California, Holifield always had a ready ear. Since
he had no nuclear enterprises nor large defense installations in his district, his
approach to politics and reorganization was unusually objective. "The only
time he would complain to the president," commented Harold Seidman, a
long-term federal career official, "was if a reorganization threatened to harm
him politically back home." Seidman also noted that "Chet was responsible
for the establishment of various federal agencies and several cabinet-level

departments, including Housing and Urban Development and Transportation"
and "He was fair-minded in what he did." Holifield also tended to give fair
warning to his opponents. According to Seidman, when Labor and the Bureau
of the Budget tried to close a small office in East Los Angeles that was
helping Vietnam veterans, Holifield arranged to keep it open. Seidman
related that Holifield warned the Bureau of the Budget: "Don't harm me
politically on minor issues, . . . and then I can help you on the major issues."[58]

Holifield had important enemies, as well as friends, in his local area during
much of his career. The *Los Angeles Times*, the largest newspaper in his
district, was notoriously anti-labor and anti-Democratic during much of
Holifield's first twenty years in Congress. The *Time's* pages were often filled
with paid political advertisements which emphasized name-calling rather than
discussion of public issues. In Holifield's 1950 campaign, for example, one
full-page ad assailed Holifield and other Democrats as "political stooges" of
labor bosses. From the 1960s on, however, the *Times* finally endorsed him,
much to Holifield's astonishment. "About that time," Holifield remembered,

> I met Otis Chandler, the publisher. The AEC had just built a two-mile-long, $114
> million linear accelerator for Stanford. Chandler said to me, "the scientists at
> Stanford where I went to school, think a lot of you and I want to thank you for that
> accelerator." He never mentioned his paper's endorsement.[59]

Politics and Friendships

Although Holifield lost many battles he wanted to win, he did not lose
heart. The brighter sides of politics that he always enjoyed were the
friendships he made that in part helped to sustain him in difficult times.
During his long tenure in California and national politics, Holifield forged
close political and personal relationships with many California legislators.
Probably his strongest ties were with Jerry Voorhis. Voorhis was, in many
respects, Holifield's mentor in political ideals. Both Voorhis and Holifield
shared a similar philosophy on the linkages which should exist between the
public and private sectors. When Holifield followed Voorhis to Congress in
1943, Congressman Voorhis asked a young aide, Ben O'Brien, to help the
Holifields rent a home in the Capitol. O'Brien became a trusted, life-long
friend of the Holifields, as did so many of Holifield's staff members. In
wartime Washington, heating fuel was scarce, and after moving to their first
Washington home, the Holifields discovered that their oil rationing coupons
had been lost by the owner and none were available. A photo showing Chet,
Cam, and the two younger daughters, Willa Mae and Jo Ann, bundled in
heavy winter clothing and blankets at their kitchen table appeared in
newspapers all across the country, generating much attention among
constituents and friends.[60]

Several of Holifield's other close friends from his early days as a member of the "Young Democrats" included William Mosely Jones, Elizabeth Snyder, and Susie Clifton. Jones, who became Speaker of the Assembly in California and then founder of Pacific Savings and Loan, received considerable advice and help from Holifield. So did Elizabeth Snyder, a publicist and former teacher, who garnered Holifield's strong support in becoming the first woman to be elected as a chairperson of the Democratic Party of California. Nationally, she was the first woman to be elected to head a state political party. Susie Clifton was his long-time campaign treasurer and trusted friend. She was later appointed by Governor Pat Brown as Chief of the Industrial Welfare Division for the State of California, which promulgated the minimum wage, maximum hours, and working conditions for women and minors.[61]

Once he forged friendships with others, Holifield was always available with a helping hand. Whenever any of his close associates got into serious difficulties, both he and Cam remained in close contact with them and their families. When a former House colleague was sent to prison during the Korean War, for example, Holifield wrote to him regularly. That was the kind of friendship that endeared him to many back home in his district.[62]

Holifield was somewhat known outside the halls of Congress and his local congressional district, but a lead story in *Life* magazine in June 1952 brought him widespread national attention. The story told of Holifield's unusual service to two of his constituents, Mr. and Mrs. Paul Craig. The story was about a two-year-old Catholic German girl, an orphan named Blanka Sylvia Schoenhammer. The Craigs had adopted Blanka through their church, and "They wanted to get Blanka from New York, where she was brought from Germany, to California," Holifield remembered. Holifield told them he was planning a trip to California and could save the Craigs the air fare. Holifield detoured to Idylwild (now John F. Kennedy) Airport, picked up Blanka, and spent the night in a local hotel to await a flight to California:

> Since I already helped raise five girls of my own, I knew what I was doing, even to caring for a cold! I fixed her curls in the morning; My German wasn't very good. I said something like "Drinken zee milch, liebchen." But it worked and she drank up. The hardest thing was getting her to part from me when I delivered her to the Craigs.[63]

Holifield remembered that "I wasn't smart enough to put out a press release then--but *Life* got wind of it and sent a photographer and reporter to meet with us." Holifield's private generosity thus became public information. Ironically, the California congressman received more complimentary mail on this incident than for anything he ever did in public life, which is perhaps testimony to what Holifield's constituents and other Americans saw in Holifield: here was a good man as well as a good politician.

4

Ideas Have Consequences

A Very Liberal Democrat

Holifield's singular upbringing, his early years as a businessman in Montebello, and his personal traits prepared him well for a life in politics. He was comfortable with and acceptable to a wide variety of people. He was also able to understand a wide range of political and economic philosophies. More importantly, however, his early experiences imbued him with a unique world view with important consequences for his own political philosophy. Holifield's ideas, rooted as they were in his unique life experiences, eventually would have national and even international repercussions.

From his hard upbringing in the rural South, Holifield acquired a large measure of self-reliance, developed at least partly from his successful adventures away from home as a young man. Yet his self-reliance was tempered by his Christian faith, which told him that not all persons had the same opportunities and potentials that he had. His close ties to his family, despite intermittent friction with his father, also provided practical lessons about the give and take of relationships and working together for the good of all. Thus, he came to possess a compassion for the less fortunate and a willingness to work together with other individuals to achieve common goals.

If his early life experiences in small towns like Paragould, Pryorsburg, and Enid helped shape the way Holifield felt about himself and society, his catastrophic accident on Catalina Island in 1931, while very painful, ironically gave him much-needed time to read widely on many subjects, to reflect on public issues, and particularly, to concentrate his thoughts on the devastating effects of the Great Depression. This period of reflection proved to be the catalyst for his entry into politics and extended his horizons from the Great Depression onward into still other issues in California and national politics.

Having left high school at age 15, Holifield never formally earned a high school diploma. Yet he possessed a natural curiosity and thirst for knowledge not usual for a person in such a position. This self-styled "non-scholar" not only drank heavy draughts from the well of hard life experiences, but he also seized every opportunity to widen his horizons in public affairs and his own personal treasury of information. So aggressive and far-ranging did his pursuit of knowledge become in Congress that he impressed colleagues and congressional staff alike as unusually vigorous in learning all aspects of issues he believed to be germane to his work. A case in point is that of atomic energy. In 1945, Holifield virtually cornered the market on atomic energy information when the atom burst upon an astonished world. Little wonder that he became the foremost congressional authority on atomic energy![1]

The upshot of Holifield's life experiences and personal traits was that he became a committed liberal Democrat of the Roosevelt/Truman variety. His backing of Upton Sinclair's 1934 campaign for California governor showed his support for far-reaching social and economic reforms. His consistent backing of Franklin D. Roosevelt (FDR) forshadowed his equally avid support of Truman after FDR's death. As a liberal Democrat, he found himself often in the minority, even during the Democratic Congresses of the 1940s and 1950s. Eventually, his ideas and those of like-minded Democrats came to prevail during the 1960s and 1970s. Most of his ideas remained constant from his early years as "a voice in the wilderness" to his latter years as a senior statesman.

FDR, the New Deal, and the Cold War

Like the Great Depression, World War II proved to be another of the cataclysmic events of the twentieth century, and it was no less so for Holifield than for others. His views on whether the U.S. should enter the war changed after Pearl Harbor, but his support for FDR and his domestic programs did not waver. In April 1940, one month before Hitler's troops poured into the Netherlands and Belgium on their way to France, he and other California Democrats launched a campaign to draft FDR for an unprecedented third term. Both Holifield and his political mentor, H. Jerry Voorhis, were delegates in the newly formed "California for Roosevelt" delegation.[2]

Although World War II had begun in September 1939, Holifield and other California "New Dealers" were still primarily concerned with domestic issues. In their campaign newspaper, *The California New Dealer*, they avowed their support for FDR's domestic revolution, the New Deal. Governor Culbert Olson set the tone by stressing that the two great challenges in the state were to reduce unemployment and to provide water and power at low cost. He called for public ownership of every phase of the "conservation, diversion, storage, and distribution of water" and "generation and distribution of electric power."[3] Holifield thus would gain his public power spurs long before he was sent to Congress, but he was never a complete partisan of public power.

Holifield support of the New Deal was predictable, with its assistance programs to business, farmers, labor, and most importantly, the working man.

He believed that government had a strategic role to play in achieving social and economic justice. It could not do everything, of course, and he opposed monopoly power of any kind, whether public or private. His common sense told him that too much government power to intervene in people's lives and private business affairs was dangerous. His shattering experiences during the Depression convinced him that citizens could not be allowed to twist slowly and eventually choke in an unjust economic wind, especially as in the 1930s, when they tried to help themselves but did not have the wherewithal to do so. His other practical conclusions were that trade unions were needed to extend social rights into the marketplace and that the Social Security Program, health care, and other basic social programs should become available to all.[4]

Neither Holifield nor his allies in 1940 foresaw Pearl Harbor. He and other California New Dealers were worried about the European conflict, but like FDR, they attempted to steer clear of the Charybdis of isolationism and the Scylla of interventionism, preferring neutrality. California Democrats did, however, support Roosevelt's efforts to prevent, as they argued, "any creation of a bloc in the nation dependent for profit on the European conflict." As sincere democrats, they were deeply conscious that "this government by its very nature cannot be a silent partner, as is Russia, to the systematic despoiling of small nations." On the other hand, they were sure that "this government cannot allow its citizens to be driven into war by a small group of profit-makers." The California Democrats believed their party should stand with Roosevelt in favoring neither the Allies nor the Germans and Russians.[5]

World War II profoundly affected Chet's international views. Initially, he was an idealist, hopeful that something good would come out of the horrors of war. Both world wars, he believed, had occurred chiefly because of human greed. Humanity had moved progressively beyond the family into the tribe, the city, and the nation state, and the next step had to be evolution into a world community. This step was absolutely necessary because of the advent of the nuclear age. Any retreat backward would spell peril, since humanity now faced a nuclear trip-wire. Holifield thus became an avid U.N. supporter:

> The next step is the formation of an international order which by mutual consent of the nations of the world shall be empowered to settle by law (an international code of laws) the irritating and conflicting interests which arise in their international contacts. This is the next evolutionary step in human relations. . . . . The hope of mankind for the elimination of the new type of destructive Atomic conflict between nations lies in the delegation of power from each nation to an international authority which will formulate and enforce a code of international law for the peaceful settlement of disputes and conflicts in the international field.
>
> The next step must be taken now. The time is shorter than you think! The sand in the Atomic hour glass is running out.[6]

Holifield's support of the U.N. was so heartfelt in 1947 that he actually criticized the Truman Doctrine. Truman's pronouncement was aimed at Turkey and Greece and declared that the U.S. would provide aid to any government facing a Communist assault from within or without. Chet's initial reaction was that the doctrine would undermine the authority of the U.N. He termed it "an undeclared declaration of war," and "a drastic departure from our foreign policy." He feared that it was a "return to the unilateral relationship between nations." It appeared to be "a betrayal of the principles enunciated in the United Nations' Charter, which clearly indicates that collective security of the nations of the world depends upon a multilateral approach to the problems between nations."[7]

In time, however, the ever-practical Holifield began to recognize the U.N.'s underlying weakness--it could only become what its members wished it to be. With the USSR flexing its military muscle on Western Europe's borders and refusing to pull its armies out of Eastern Europe, political realism required Holifield to set aside his hopes. Almost as fast as he chastised the Truman Doctrine, Chet embraced the Marshall Plan for restoring Western Europe's economies. As long as Moscow maintained its aggressive stance, Chet felt there was little prospect for normal relations between the two countries.

Holifield's hope for a new world order was eventually replaced by a preoccupation with America's antagonists. Like most of his countrymen, he viewed the next forty or so years within the context of an East-West conflict. The "Cold War," as this struggle was known, pitted America and the "Free World" against a seemingly monolithic Communist order that took its orders from the Kremlin, and later perhaps, from either the Kremlin or Peking. The Soviet Union (and later Red China) became the archenemy, to be fought against at every turn in a long road of inconclusive skirmishes. Holifield became something of an archetypical Cold War Warrior, perhaps more committed than many because of the atheism that communists espoused. He supported every postwar U.S. president, regardless of party affiliation, in defending America's interests and allies. In the 1960s, when many began to question the Vietnam War, he was undaunted. He was convinced that the U.S. had to be strong against communist aggression, wherever it occurred.[8]

Civil Libertarian

Once in Congress, Holifield became a leading civil libertarian. His Christianity, exposure to nondoctrinaire socialist ideas, and strong ties to family naturally led him to support democratic principles and fair play, and influenced his beliefs that one should be fair-minded and tolerant of others. His defense of civil liberties brought impassioned criticism in the early postwar era. Journalist Ralph de Toledano, for example, noted that Holifield had a "pinko image," chiefly because of his stance on civil liberties.[9]

In his first full month on Capitol Hill in February 1943, Holifield displayed his civil libertarian tendencies with a vengeance. Not only did he vote against continuation of Martin Dies' House Committee on Un-American Activities, but he inserted into the *Congressional Record* a statement chastising the committee and demanding that "the Dies committee should die!" He was crystal clear on why: "This committee had prostituted every decent law of evidence and procedure in its investigative actions and had usurped the functions of investigation, trial, condemnation and punishment, which ran contrary to America's principles of civil liberties toward the accused."

After this broadside, Holifield put another, more sedate, statement in the *Record* on the proper role of Congress in times of war hysteria. Congress should display mature judgment, he noted, in order to preserve civil liberties. If Congress "bowed to that hysteria or yielded to the passions of hate and persecution," he asserted, "we would . . . become the 'blind leaders of the blind' and cease to act as the guardians of our Constitutional liberties."[10]

In his second statement in the *Record*, Holifield had in mind an action by the Kerr Subcommittee on Appropriations regarding three federal civil servants, Goodwin E. Watson, Robert Lovett, and William E. Dodd, Jr. The subcommittee had investigated the three's alleged disloyalty and had played the role of judges without any trial, in Chet's view. Based on their findings, the subcommittee recommended a rider to an appropriations bill to deny the three their salaries. Holifield found this hard to believe. "You can't ram this through," he thought to himself, "It's a Bill of Attainder." But the House majority thought otherwise, much to Holifield's surprise and chagrin:

> I studied high school civics only. But this was protection wrung from King John at Runymede. For the first time, I realized what the Constitution meant. There were 267 lawyers in the House at that time. But the Kerr amendment carried; Jerry Voorhis, myself, and a minority were voted down.[11]

Chet did not remain silent as the Kerr amendment was considered in House debate. He provocatively asked whether Thomas Jefferson had been a subversive, like Watson, when he wrote to James Madison in 1787 that "I hold it that a little Rebellion, now and then, is a good thing, and as necessary to the political world as storms are in the physical." He did not know whether the three were loyal Americans or not, but he emphasized, "I do not believe that such a determination is the prerogative of a Member of Congress or a committee thereof." In his opinion, "any legislation passed by Congress should be general in its impact and not directed either for or against an individual," and moreover, "The civil and Federal courts are the proper places to determine the punishment of an individual." "In this time of war hysteria,"

Holifield noted, "it is the solemn duty of every representative of the people to defend the civil liberties of our citizens." He warned that "we should be on guard for the first attack on the Bill of Rights, even if that attack is instituted and authorized by a congressional resolution."[12] His position proved to be correct. In 1946, the Supreme Court ruled that the Kerr amendment was in fact a Bill of Attainder and that it was unconstitutional to hold up the three men's salaries through a discriminatory piece of legislation.

Holifield's concern for civil liberties extended also to the nation's minorities, including the Japanese-Americans who were being interned in camps during World War II. In 1972, Holifield was honored by the Japanese-American community for cosponsoring a bill with Congressman "Sparky" Matsunaga to repeal Title II of the Internal Security Act of 1950. "I was reminded not only of the wartime evacuation and internment of Japanese-Americans," Holifield commented, "but also of the fear of those who dissent and who question, that they too might be placed in concentration camps."[13]

Fair-minded as always, Holifield also would not be stampeded into railroading the administrator of the internment camps, Dillon Meyer. Prejudice against Japanese-Americans was particularly high at the time, and more so when they protested against General John L. DeWitt, commander of the West Coast Military District, for arresting them without due process after Pearl Harbor under an order of California Governor Earl Warren. As Chet recalled, "The Sons of the Golden West, the American Legion, the Hearst *Examiner* in Los Angeles and San Francisco and Earl Warren were all talking about 'the Yellow Peril'." Dillon Meyer, an FDR appointee, was criticized in a "particular crusade" by the *Los Angeles Examiner*. The *Examiner* claimed that "camps at Tule Lake and the former Santa Anita racetrack had received red meat coupons, chocolate candy, and nylon stockings," all of which "were hard to get during wartime." The *Examiner's* editors "demanded that Dillon Meyer be fired and handed such a resolution to the California delegation." Holifield was not about to support such a resolution without a hearing.[14]

Reflecting on Holifield's defense of relocated Japanese-Americans, Mike Masaoka, Washington representative of the Japanese Americans Citizens League, wrote in 1972 that "during the World War II period, when persons of Japanese ancestry were most unpopular, Chet Holifield was among the very few, *about five in number*, who consistently advocated fair play and justice for Japanese-Americans in the halls of Congress." Masaoka noted that Holifield "fought against repressive and racist bills directed against those of our ancestry" and "took advantage of every possible opportunity to use his good offices with the Administration to promote our welfare and civil rights." Masaoka praised Holifield for being "always willing to stake his political and business life on his belief in Japanese-Americans."[15]

In 1946, Holifield's penchant for defending unpopular causes led him to assist Hollywood actors maligned by J. Parnell Thomas' (R-New Jersey) House

Committee on Un-American Activities. As Holifield remembered the incident, "A group of actors chartered a DC-3 and came to Washington to protest, but they didn't know what to do when they got here." Among the group were Jane Wyatt, Humphrey Bogart, Lauren Bacall, Danny Kaye, Charlie Dunne, "and maybe Dashiell Hammett and Dalton Trumbo." The actors realized they could not change the opposition arrayed against them, but "they wanted to do something and protest the House Un-American Activities Committee." Holifield met with them and suggested, "Why not file a petition for a redress of grievance?" When the group asked for details, Holifield explained that it was a Constitutional privilege; whenever a group of citizens have a grievance, they have the right to petition Congress for a redress of the grievance. He remembered that "Late that night a petition was drafted and I gave some advice and filed it with the Clerk of the House." "Nothing came of it," he lamented, "But at least it gave them satisfaction as citizens."[16]

This protest was only the tip of the iceberg in Holifield's defense of citizens against Thomas' committee and others caught up in anti-Communist hysteria. Into the early 1950s, Chet pummeled legislators who relied on congressional immunity to smear reputations. He believed there was a wide gulf between ideas and actions; he defended the right of every citizen to his beliefs, no matter how obtuse. While he went along with the decision that communists should not have access to the nation's educational institutions to indoctrinate others, he strenuously objected when Thomas' Committee sought to conduct in-depth reviews of the loyalty of American universities and colleges. This time, he contended that Congress should abolish the Committee because it had no definition for "Un-American." He believed that the Committee was an inappropriate organization to have in the House.[17]

Holifield proved to be a balancing force on the issue of alleged disloyalty by employees of the AEC. Joseph Volpe, a lawyer who met Holifield during World War II when Volpe worked on the Manhattan Project, considered Chet and his close associate Mel Price to be allies on civil liberties. Of Holifield and Price on the JCAE, Volpe noted that "They had judicious and easy-going temperaments." "Neither could be genuinely vindictive if they tried," Volpe continued, "and both were staunch civil libertarians."[18]

While Chief Counsel at the AEC, Volpe was particularly thankful for Holifield, Price, and their JCAE allies. In 1949, he was on an AEC "hot seat" when Senator Bourke B. Hickenlooper (R-Iowa) charged that "security risks" were holding responsible AEC positions. Hickenlooper also chastised the AEC and AEC Chairman David Lilienthal for "incredible mismanagement." Using the JCAE's authority to be kept "fully and currently informed," Hickenlooper demanded access to all personnel files and open hearings to publicize them. With Chet's and other JCAE members' tactic approval, the AEC refused to turn the files over, responding that innocent citizens had no way to defend their reputations in open hearings. This did not satisfy

Hickenlooper, who then suggested closed executive sessions where three or four cases would be considered. Reluctantly, the AEC agreed.[19]

Hickenlooper's investigation turned up nothing of importance and damaged his own credibility more than the AEC's. When the JCAE weighed the so-called "security risk" cases, members found that the derogatory information in some files was mostly gossip and hearsay. Chet, Volpe noted, "didn't hesitate to take on Hickenlooper or anybody else." Incensed by the waste of time "at taxpayers' expense," Holifield called the investigation a "fiasco" and Hickenlooper's charges "rash and unwarranted." Even Republican members were unhappy. Senator Ralph Milliken (R-Colorado) grew exasperated and finally told Hickenlooper that he knew what "credible mismanagement and incredible management" were, but the hearings had taught him what "incredible mismanagement" was and where it existed--at the JCAE rather than at the AEC! Democrats and Republicans alike joined Milliken's protest on the grounds that the JCAE was usurping the rights and privileges of the Executive Branch, and Hickenlooper's investigation came to naught.[20]

Nonpartisanship on the JCAE, as with the Hickenlooper investigation, was not unusual. Attempts to politicize both the AEC and the JCAE usually failed due to sensitivity of members about the importance of this strategic enterprise. Another such case involved Volpe while he was in the "hot seat" at the AEC. Volpe remembered that a major flap occurred when Senator McMahon's former law partner, Gordon Dean, was nominated to succeed Lilienthal. Another AEC commissioner, Sumner Pike, commented that he hoped there would be no more politics on the commission. Incensed by Pike's statement, McMahon deliberately delayed Pike's renomination hearing. As AEC Counsel, Volpe went to see Holifield and Price. According to Volpe, "Chet Holifield told me, 'Don't worry about Senator McMahon, we'll work out matters with him.'" Holifield felt that Pike was a fine commissioner and deserved a prompt hearing. True to his word, he and Price interceded, McMahon was eventually brought around, and Pike was reconfirmed.[21]

In 1947, Holifield found it necessary to come to the defense of his friend, scientist Edward U. Condon, whom he had met at the 1946 Bikini tests. Condon, then Director of the Bureau of Standards and earlier an advisor to McMahon's Senate Special Committee on Atomic Energy, was accused publicly of being disloyal by Thomas. Thomas publicized his accusation in the press, supporting his claim primarily by the fact that Condon had visited the Soviet Union at the invitation of the Russian Academy of Science.

In view of the postwar anti-communist hysteria, Holifield lost no time in giving a scathing public rebuttal. He said that he was witnessing a "renewal of attempts to discredit the scientists who worked on the atomic bomb." He proclaimed on the House floor that such efforts had "exploded" in the face of the perpetrators, noting that Thomas' earlier attempts to suggest AEC bungling in the handling of uranium and security "leaks" had ultimately resulted in discoveries of misdeeds by the Army. Not to be outdone by the fingering of Condon, he then pointed to General Groves, former head of the Manhattan Project, as the "prime source for unwarranted insinuations about Dr. Condon." Groves, he charged, was out to indirectly discredit civilian control of atomic energy. "If there is anyone in America who has any serious evidence to present against him [Condon]," he charged further, "that person is almost guilty of treason in not having come forward in a responsible way to the President or to the Congress of the United States."[22] With such a vigorous defense, Thomas' forces were unable to muster a meaningful offense. No creditable evidence was forthcoming, and Condon's security clearance was continued after an investigation by the FBI and the AEC.

The J. Robert Oppenheimer Case

Holifield's defense of civil liberties also surfaced, this time unsuccessfully, in his response to the charges made in 1954 against the loyalty of a brighter scientific luminary, the "father of the atomic bomb," J. Robert Oppenheimer. Oppenheimer had forged the team that built the atomic bomb. Possessing a brilliant, wide-ranging, and cultured mind, Oppenheimer was learned in fields beyond science and had few peers among American atomic physicists. He headed several strategic scientific bodies, like the AEC's General Advisory Committee (GAC), which had overwhelmingly opposed the hydrogen bomb.

William Borden, JCAE Executive Director, initiated the effort to revoke Oppenheimer's security clearance in 1954, at the height of the anti-communist hysteria of the 1950s. Holifield felt Borden was motivated by a sincere belief that Oppenheimer was a danger to U.S. security because of the almost hypnotic spell he cast over his colleagues and his open associations with known Communists. Borden, an ardent weapons advocate, also blamed Oppenheimer at least in part for the disarray at the AEC, lack of work on the "super," and the failure to stockpile atomic weapons immediately after the war. Borden and others pointed to Oppenheimer because they believed he should have warned Congress about this apparently desperate situation.

Most serious in Borden's view, however, was Oppenheimer's association with known communists. Oppenheimer's brother Frank was a member of the Communist party and a woman friend was also a communist, as were many of his close scientific associates, including a French Communist, Haakon Chevalier, who was close to French scientist Joliot-Curie, head of the French atomic fraternity and the son-in-law of Madame Curie.[23] Holifield was not convinced of Oppenheimer's alleged disloyalty. He "had spoken to many scientists and realized they tended to have very free ideas about religion and politics." He found "In their search for truth they respected a person for his scientific ability; his religious, moral, or political convictions and habits were not as important as they would be to non-scientists." He also understood Borden's position, however, and did not find politics at the heart of it.[24]

The Oppenheimer case represented something of a moral dilemma for Holifield and other JCAE members. Anxious to give him the benefit of doubt, they wondered why he, unlike other scientists and public figures, had not dropped his associations with Communists when the Russo-German nonaggression pact was signed in 1939, or at least when American politics was not tolerating such associations. Holifield admitted that Oppenheimer "did have a cloud over his head" in view of his continuing relationships.[25]

Holifield was sure that Oppenheimer was not wise, but he continued to believe in the scientist's basic patriotism. "Although the case didn't come before the JCAE," Chet noted, "I defended Oppenheimer and wrote him a letter." In the letter, he noted that "I expressed my personal confidence in Oppenheimer as an American citizen, recognizing that he had very strong feelings about the hydrogen bomb." "His views were different from mine," Chet observed, "but I accorded him the right to have his own opinions. That was not a popular action on my part."

In fact, Chet believed that he came under close scrutiny during his limited defense of Oppenheimer. "When I defended Oppenheimer's patriotism," he noted, "I became suspect to the witch-hunters and extremists on the right; maybe that's why unknown parties were rifling my files at night." He became suspicious "that my files were being looked into . . . during the night when I wasn't in my office." In a characteristic act of defiance against such activities, Chet said "I took a copy of the [Oppenheimer] letter and I filed it under the letter "O" in my personal files. To this letter I pinned a hand-written note: ~To Whom It May Concern--This letter is made available to you in order that you may understand how I feel about Dr. Oppenheimer.~"[26]

Eventually, the AEC decided to revoke Oppenheimer's security clearance. Holifield had remained in the background and could do little about the AEC's action, especially since the JCAE was split over the issue. When he became JCAE chairman, however, Chet helped to add a final footnote. Senator Anderson, working closely with him, AEC Chairman Seaborg and Commissioner Ramey, urged President Kennedy to give Oppenheimer the prestigious Enrico Fermi Award. Action was awhile in coming and the death of President Kennedy intervened, but Oppenheimer ultimately received this honor shortly before his death from President Johnson.[27]

A Genuine Free-Enterpriser and Supporter of Labor

Holifield was as concerned about abuses by big business as he was about excesses of government in stifling individual creativity and initiative. He was "a sincere believer in responsible free enterprise," as he told a congressional audience in the mid 1940s, "the kind of free enterprise which has been the backbone of our Nation, until recently." In his view, "the environment of early American business," which "rested entirely upon the personal participation and ownership of the individual," no longer existed in its purest form. He charged that there was "a well-financed campaign, traceable directly to the centers of big finance and big business, to sell the American people a bill of goods under the banner of 'free enterprise.'" Chet was not convinced that big meant either better or free. He asked rhetorically, "Was not the 'free enterprise' of big business in control, without government interference, preceding the crash of 1929 to 1932?"[28] He worried that monopolistic trends in business would lead to "some form of economic or political fascism," or possibly class war, if left unchecked. As the best defense, "I believe that 'little people' should own little farms and little businesses, and that 'big people,' as they are commonly called, should be kept to those fields in which they do the best job toward making this a better life for everybody." For him, "The perpetuation of democracy depends upon the protection of 'little people.'"[29]

If Holifield seemed hostile to big business, he was not always so. Especially where survival of big business meant survival of jobs for the "little people," he was inclined to be practical rather than ideological. A case in point was his support in 1971 for the "bail-out" of the Lockheed Company. In dire financial straits, they asked the government for a loan guarantee to allow the company to meet its financial obligations and prevent its collapse.

Holifield faced this issue on the practical level. He voted for the loan guarantee "because of the serious blow which would be delivered to the national economy, and the economy of our area, the suffering which would occur to unemployed workers and their families, and the potential great financial loss to the federal government." He pointed out that collapse of Lockheed and its government-supported L-1011 aircraft program would mean unemployment for 30,000 workers, with about half of the affected jobs in Southern California, which already had a higher unemployment rate than the national rate. There was also the possibility of an overall increase of 60,000 welfare cases. With so much at stake, he was willing to put ideology, even politics, aside, and vote to solve the crisis. He also pointed out that "the loans should not result in a loss to the Federal Treasury" since "The proposed legislation authorizing these loans provides ample protection against losses."[30]

Holifield's support of labor and labor unions was a natural spin-off of his attitude toward big business in particular. Eminently practical, he realized that big businesses were here to stay, whether he liked them or not. Labor unions were one method of protecting the "little people" against the excesses of the new giant industries. Chet believed, like most New Dealers, that labor unions were essential to the nation's welfare. He supported labor unions at every juncture he could and vigorously opposed any legislative efforts to introduce punitive and destructive antilabor laws. Still, he was willing to curb union abuses, as when he supported President Truman's takeover of the nation's railroads when U.S. security seemed at stake in 1946.

The immediate postwar period was not an auspicious time for trade unions. Despite Truman's stand in defense of trade unions, Congress seemed bent on cutting labor's power "down to size." Public sentiment was also against unions due to the numerous strikes during the late 1940s. Everyone had forgotten, it seemed to labor's supporters such as Holifield, that labor unions had been an important component in U.S. victory in World War II.

Holifield was particularly incensed by the Smith-Arends bill of 1946. He wondered publicly whether the bill would "slyly cut the heart of free collective bargaining out of the breast of labor and obtain the same result Hitler and his storm troopers accomplished with gun and club." For Holifield, the bill was "the most dangerous antilabor bill brought before this House since the Smith-Connally bill," and he believed it portended ill for labor.[31]

Despite Holifield's and others' efforts, little could be done to stave off a spate of antilabor laws that enjoyed tacit public approval in the late 1940s. Among these was the Taft-Hartley Act of 1947, which passed under enormous pressure from big business and a public alarmed by postwar strikes. Like Truman, Holifield was opposed to Taft-Hartley and believed that it should never have become law. In 1948, he called for repeal on the grounds that it "superimposes a prefabricated labor relations policy tailored to much of the worst in labor relations and little of the best."[32] He remained a firm supporter and enduring favorite of unions throughout his career. In 1967, *Labor Outlook* noted that his record over the previous 18 years consisted of 67 "good" votes and only two "bad" votes on issues affecting the AFL-CIO.[33]

Religion, Politics and Theology

Holifield did not believe that religion and politics could, or should, be separate. A central desire of his life was to see religious principles applied to politics, an outlook which probably had its genesis in the juxtaposition of Christian fundamentalism and socialism in his upbringing.[34] He stressed was that "certainly it is true that Christianity has flourished most in countries dedicated to the democratic principle, freedom of religious choice." He probably had Communism and atheism as his perspective when he elaborated:

> The great spiritual principles that bulwark and protect the dignity of the individual soul grow and expand most in an atmosphere of political liberty such as exists in the democracies. Therefore it seems to me that the virility of religion and its growth depends upon the extension of democracy. If this statement be true, and it is my opinion that few would deny it, there is every reason for religious people to interest themselves in the political activities within the democratic structure.[35]

Another focal point for his thoughts about the interrelationships between religion and politics dealt with Christ's admonition to "Render unto Caesar the things that are Caesar's and unto God the things that are God's." He felt that citizens in a democracy had a "dual obligation" to participate in both the spiritual and political progress of their country. There was "little or no conflict between spiritual and political progress" in a democracy because "the prime duty of members of religious groups is to participate in political activity as individuals with free and independent choice of political preference." Chet would, of course, "oppose as vigorously as anyone the unity of church and state," since "political activity should be free and independent of any control by . . . ecclesiastical leaders." This link was a necessary and crucial one:

> Practical people realize that social reforms are accomplished by political action. The motive force behind the demand for social reform usually stems from a sense of moral indignation caused by evidence of the violation of spiritual principles. Unless that moral indignation is activated toward practical social reform, it becomes sterile. Once activated, it becomes fruitful and our society becomes a better place for spiritual expansion. The removal of slums, the eradication of vice, the improvement of health, and the solving of economic ills through political action will provide an environment for our people that will be conducive to real spiritual growth. I am glad, therefore, to see signs of cooperation between individuals interested in both political and spiritual progress.[36]

Clearly there were non sequiturs in his arguments about the relationships between religion and politics. He was hardly setting forth a broad or cohesive theology or philosophy of political life, for such was neither his bent nor intent. He was, rather, articulating some practical ideas concerning the way that religion and political action could be related realistically and practically in a democratic society. To some, his basic perceptions are sound and instructive. In a democracy, there are no intrinsic nor extrinsic barriers to apply religious principles to the challenge of social and economic reform. As evidenced in the U.S. civil rights revolution that welled up in the 1960s, religious and moral convictions had observable and concrete consequences in the political arena. No less a figure than President Kennedy, in the spring of 1963, urged all Americans to grant full rights to African-Americans and minorities, not because this would benefit society economically or engender good will, but simply because "it was right." Fired up by this moral imperative, black Baptist and evangelical ministers, aided by their mainstream white counterparts, took to the streets to desegregate the nation and achieve other measures of social justice that were, in Holifield's moral/civic lexicon, "directly traceable to fundamental spiritual laws."

On a personal religious level, Chet Holifield grew up deeply imbued with fundamentalist Christian ideas, but neither he nor his wife Cam attended church frequently. In fact, both often spent weekends working in his congressional office, responding personally to the needs of his constituents. He was never far from religion, however; he maintained a lively interest in religion and religious ideas, an interest that increased after he left Congress.

In his later years, Holifield held more and more to what might be termed a natural theology. In 1977, as his closest associate and colleague in public life, Herbert Roback, lay dying of cancer, Chet wrote him a letter on his religious beliefs. In the letter, Holifield expressed some of the guiding religious principles which he believed had sustained him through the course of his life and had "given strength more times than I could tell." "Always in the recesses of my soul and mind," Holifield wrote,

> There has been a belief that there must be a Supreme Power with a capability for planning and direction of the universe and the Galaxy around us. It has seemed to me that the order in the natural world, the process of death and regeneration we see in every plant and seed and flower could not have occurred or persisted without a power which goes beyond the human mind to conceive or perpetuate. Certainly when we observe the wonders of nature and the mountain peaks or human creativeness in art, music, intellectuality, and the nobility of human love and sacrifice for others that has occurred and is still occurring, we can not believe really that we are the same as the lower forms of life in the world around us.
>
> We are forced by logic to believe that human beings have within them something more noble than the beast of the field. We do not know and we can not prove that there is something within us that places us in a different category than the animal. Neither can we reject the intuitive belief that we are different.
>
> Could that difference be a quality of nobility which yearns for immortality, not of the body--but perhaps of what we have termed a Soul or Spirit?
>
> Here again we have the area of knowledge--of provability, and we find ourselves entering an area perhaps of hope--perhaps an unwillingness to believe that we must perish as does the beast of the field without prospect of continuance into a life of some type which goes beyond mortal death. Perhaps it is an area of Faith that there must be a Divine plan. There must be some part of us, something within us that we call immortality of the Spirit.
>
> I have never had what is called generally a religious experience. I have never received a supernatural message or instant rebirth of the Spirit. So I can only say that the experiences of life and the observation of death of loved ones including our two daughters, our parents, and so many of our dear friends, causes me to believe, to have faith that somewhere, somehow there is a divine creator of the order that obtains in the universe and the nobility and creativeness that can and often does obtain in people like you and me and millions that have gone before us, and will live after we are gone.[37]

One feature of Holifield's long dedication to public service proved troubling to him: the hardships on his family due to his unrelenting dedication to his work. His younger daughters found his frequent absences from home hard to bear. For years, the family had only one car, and Cam would regularly make the long trip from home by bus to meet Chet on Capitol Hill after work. Several years before Holifield retired and the anti-nepotism rule went into effect, Cam joined Chet's staff as receptionist and official greeter of visiting citizens from his District. A factor in Chet's retirement was his desire to spend more time with his family, which good health enabled him to enjoy.[38]

Holifield and Foreign Affairs

For the most part, Holifield was not known for his views on U.S. foreign policy, except those issues related to atomic energy. His JCAE and Government Operations assignments made his work crucial in atomic foreign policy areas. He was instrumental in assisting in the creation of the International Atomic Energy Agency and its international nuclear "Safeguards" Program. His leadership position on Government Operations in the late 1950s also allowed him to assist in creating the U.S. Agency for Arms Control and Disarmament. His support for these two important agencies flowed from his belief that there must never be another world war. The discovery of the atomic bomb had "forced mankind to chose between harmonious cooperation and universal destruction."[39] He could never again get out of his mind the destructive wreckage at Bikini. Yet, the atomic bomb was only a primitive first step in the science of destruction. He never once forgot that while the atomic bomb dropped on Hiroshima was equivalent to 20,000 tons of TNT, the hydrogen bomb tests in the Pacific were equivalent to 10,400,000 tons. In nuclear war, human survival would be impossible.[40]

One important, fixed idea on international affairs that Holifield took with him to Congress was his deep concern for a national homeland for the world's Jews. By 1938 or 1939, Holifield recalled, he had become convinced, chiefly due to his religious upbringing, that a Jewish state had to come into existence. During World War II, he was appalled by the suffering of Europe's Jews, fortifying his conviction. Once the modern state of Israel came into being, he became a firm supporter. To his support he added the fact that as the only democratic state in the Middle East, Israel deserved full U.S. backing.[41]

In March 1948, Holifield spoke in the House in favor of the partitioning of Palestine. He insisted that the partition must be enforced by the U.N. and the U.S. The religious basis for his support was clear. "Believing as I do," he told his colleagues, "that God will again restore the land of Moses, Solomon, and David to Israel, I have sought to harmonize my actions with this purpose," i.e., establishment of "a National Jewish state." Not only did he speak regularly in Congress on this issue, but during the U.N. debate on the partitioning of Palestine, he repeated this theme at a gathering of one million people in New York City, and then flew to Los Angeles where he gave the same address the next day at City Hall before an audience of about 200,000. Among other concrete measures of support he urged was that the U.S. lift its embargo on munitions to Israel on the premise that otherwise the Jews would be unable to defend themselves against Arab attack.[42]

A Local, State, and National Democrat

Holifield was somewhat unique among the several hundred congressmen who served in the House during his career. Almost from the beginning, his advice was sought by national, state, and district officials in his party. His national influence was apparent during passage of the first Atomic Energy Act. Part of his influence at the state and local level derived from his strong standing in his district. His political views, service to constituents, and style of campaigning ensured him easy reelection. He usually won 65 to 70 percent of the vote, and was proud of the fact that the most he ever had to spend for reelection was $14,000. As he gained seniority and stature in Congress, his secure election base enabled him to play a strategic role in the Democratic Party both within California and nationally. In California politics, he was mentioned as a possible candidate for the Senate. Nationally, he became an early supporter of Senator Lyndon B. Johnson's presidential bid, speaking on Johnson's behalf at the 1960 Democratic National Convention.[43]

As a politician and person, Holifield had a relaxed approach to other human beings, but no one ever considered him a pushover. When he made up his mind, it was almost impossible to dissuade him. Only new evidence could get him to change a decision that he believed appropriate and correct. Especially near the end of his career, when adversaries tried to embarrass him publicly, he fought back with "no holds barred." When convinced he was right, he would hold his ground tenaciously, firmly believing that fellow Democrats would support his position--and they did.

An example of Holifield's rock-like convictions as a politician and Democratic stalwart can be seen in his relationship with Jesse Unruh in the election of 1968. During that election, Unruh and another of California's leading Democrats, Senator Alan Cranston, supported Senator Robert F. Kennedy for president, while Holifield backed Vice President Hubert H. Humphrey. After Kennedy's assassination at the Ambassador Hotel in Los Angeles, Unruh and Cranston, according to Holifield, refused to work vigorously for Humphrey. "We could have elected Humphrey president had they and other Democrats been willing to help us," Holifield claimed, "but the only thing they did during the campaign was to ride in an open car one Saturday to the State Democratic Convention." Incensed, Holifield told Jesse:

Jess, I know how grieved you are at the loss of Bobby Kennedy--and so am I. Still, we now have a party nominee, Hubert Humphrey, who has spent 30 years fighting for the liberal principles you and I believe in. Let's get behind him.[44]

Holifield remembered that Unruh stared right through him and replied, "Chet, I could care less who is president of the United States." Holifield responded, "Jess, I'm sorry you feel that way," and turned and walked away.[45]

Two years later, the political shoe was on the other foot. By then, Holifield was dean of the California delegation and Unruh was running for governor. Unruh called him and said, "Chet, I'm going to the National Press Club to announce my candidacy; I'd really like you to sit by my side." Unable to forget Unruh's remarks during Humphrey's campaign, Holifield remembered that he replied: "Jess, I could care less who is governor of California." Taking a cue from their dean, most California Democratic congressmen "refused to turn their hands for Unruh and he lost. Had they all got behind him, he'd have won, and no doubt become a first-rate governor."[46]

A Common-Sense Approach

It is hard to overemphasize Holifield's common-sense approach to everyday problems. He often lent his practical bent toward solving the nation's problems, sometimes on a mundane, but critically needed level. In 1944, for instance, he visited a fighter base in Great Britain as a member of the Military Affairs Committee. The British operated the base, he later remembered, "but we had American pilots working with the Royal Air Force making runs across the Channel and engaging in dogfights with German fighters." Once he was on the runway, he noticed "a big white circle stretching around the camp." He thought, "That's what you would do if you wanted to outline the camp." Mystified, especially in view of the munitions dumps around the airfield, he inquired about the circle, but no one seemed to have an explanation. Determined to find out, he asked the commanding officer after finishing their formal briefing. He recalled their exchange:

"We don't have gravel here, so we grind up mussel shells for the roads used by patrol jeeps both night and day. The jeeps go around the wire fence."

"That's fine," I [Holifield] noted, "but German bombers undoubtedly know where this base is because of their intelligence. If they wanted to bomb it, all they'd have to do would be to come over at night, use moonlight for guidance, follow the white circle around the base and drop bombs inside the circle. That would not only destroy the planes and your men, but result in blowing up the ammunition dumps."

There was dead silence from the military staff, so I inquired: "Had this thought ever occurred to you? . . . That's the first thought that occurred to me, and I'm not a military-trained man, but just common sense should tell you that."[47]

Having made his point, Holifield suggested a practical solution. Noting that he was sure the base had wagons with some type of sprinklers on them, Holifield suggested to the commanding officer that "maybe you could sprinkle that road with green dye, making it look like the grass-covered ground surrounded by and within the camp."[48]

Another telling example of Holifield's concrete approach to his legislative obligations occurred in 1960 when he was on a JCAE mission to Europe to evaluate the readiness of North Atlantic Treaty Organization (NATO) bases. JCAE concern about rapid transformations in nuclear weapons technology was the primary reason for Holifield's trip. Prior to the launching of the Soviet satellite *Sputnik* in 1957, the fissile material for U.S. thermonuclear weapons was kept under AEC control. The material was maintained separately from the rest of the mechanism on the theory that Americans would have sufficient time to assemble atomic devices once war was declared. *Sputnik* and other improvements in Soviet missiles, however, dramatically reduced warning times. In addition, new designs and manufacturing methods had produced devices in which the bomb became an integral part of the delivery vehicle and could not be separated from it. In view of these changes, the JCAE was concerned about the safety and custody of nuclear weapons within NATO. Under existing arrangements, the delivery vehicle, whether missile, gun, or aircraft, was owned by a NATO ally. The bomb itself was owned by the U.S. and was supposedly in U.S. "custody."

Whether U.S. "custody" was as firm as the Pentagon believed became the touchstone for JCAE concern. The Pentagon argued that the arrangements were foolproof; the JCAE was convinced otherwise. As Senator Clinton Anderson (D-New Mexico) charged later in 1962, "in 1958 and 1959 we found that the Defense Department had been concealing some 'custody' arrangements which raised grave questions as to their legality under the Atomic Energy Act, as well as serious problems of possible unauthorized use or accidental detonation." In the summer of 1960, JCAE Chairman Anderson had therefore authorized a staff study of the problems and approved an inspection trip to NATO bases by an ad hoc subcommittee chaired by Holifield. President-Elect Kennedy also supported the mission, and in November and December of 1960, Holifield and his subcommittee went to eight European countries for visits to fifteen nuclear weapons installations. In October 1960, the JCAE had visited Los Alamos, and JCAE Director James Ramey had urged scientists to look into devices "to prevent accidental or unauthorized use in the NATO nuclear system," i.e., devices to improve U.S. custody electronically. Anderson later remembered that the Pentagon set up a Committee on Weapons Safety to examine the problem when it became aware of the JCAE's interest. The Pentagon thus provided the name for the new electronic "custody" devices: "Permissive Action Links" (PALS).[49]

During their tour, Holifield's subcommittee became disturbed by problems with the key-lock system used to assure that the weapons were not detonated without authorization. Under the existing system, the U.S. president's authorization to use a weapon would be conveyed in code by telephone or electronic means to military officers in charge of assembling the weapons. For NATO weapons, a message had to be sent to the U.S. officer with custody of the nuclear device, and another message had to be sent to the NATO ally with control over the delivery vehicle. An elaborate system of keys was used to activate the assembled weapon jointly. Two weak links appeared obvious to Holifield's subcommittee. They found that the communications system was not foolproof and could be tampered with in several ways. Secondly, the subcommittee determined that the key system could also fail if, for instance, a revolt occurred within a NATO country such as Turkey. U.S. officers might be overpowered and their keys used to detonate nuclear devices without authorization from the American president.[50]

The findings were controversial. The Pentagon considered the revolt hypothesis highly improbable, and regarded the JCAE's investigation as a political attack on its integrity. Respected scientists such as Harold Agnew of Los Alamos, the technical advisor on the Holifield mission, however, considered the possibilities to be real. When the Defense Department continued to oppose the use of the so-called PALS, Agnew and others spoke to Kennedy's scientific advisor, Jerome Weisner, who talked to Kennedy. Kennedy then formally instructed the military to develop the PALS.[51]

Aside from the subcommittee's findings, Chet again evidenced his practical mind-set on this 1960 mission. When the subcommittee visited Bari, Italy, where the U.S. had a Hercules missile, he had two practical recommendations for the local NATO commander. Landing at the airstrip, Chet spotted smoke plumes coming out of the forest on each side of the runway, and asked the commander about them. "The farmers cut wood here as a crop," was the reply. "Those are woodcutters' cottages out there--they cut wood and sell it. That's the way they raise wood in Italy. They don't cut down primeval forest; they must raise the wood used for timber or firewood."

Holifield's first recommendation concerned the Hercules missile itself. He knew that such missiles stretched one hundred feet into the sky when ready for launch and also that this type of missile had a very thin shell. Turning to the local NATO commander, he pointed out that saboteurs (about half of the Italian Chamber of Deputies at the time were avowed Communists) posing as woodcutters could hide in the woods with a rifle and easily shoot the missile and perforate its shell. Then it would never get off the ground. "If you must have it in the glen," Chet instructed, "you should protect it, like we do missile launch sites at home." The commander replied that he had not thought about the missile's vulnerability as described by Holifield.[52]

His second practical suggestion dealt with the installation's communications system. Later in the tour, he inquired: "How do you communicate with NATO headquarters, with Paris?" The reply was "by telephone." "You mean that telephone line strung from your camp toward that little village next?" he asked. The answer was yes. Chet then responded: "Suppose you're waiting for a message from General Norstadt [then the overall NATO commander] and someone climbs the telephone post with a pair of lineman's spurs and two-bit pliers and cuts the line. Isn't that the end of your communication with NATO military headquarters? Don't you have auxiliary ways of communicating?" Holifield thereafter saw to it that all U.S. bases were outfitted with short-wave or long-wave communications.[53]

Holifield's motives in making recommendations on this tour were simply practical, to improve American defense and weapons systems. He was not simply trying to meddle in Defense Department policy matters. In this instance, his subcommittee made important contributions to the system of command and control imposed upon nuclear weapons, particularly on land-based missiles and on large bombers where nuclear weapons use is under tight presidential control. An ancillary result of Holifield's mission was that the military communications system was also tightened. Kennedy, acting on his recommendations, ordered that telecommunications on nuclear weapons be made secure from potential saboteurs and possible mishaps.

Nuclear Power for Space Use

On the issue of nuclear power for space use, Holifield again stepped into the breech to keep the government's commitment strong. In 1961 the U.S. was preparing to lift into space the world's first nuclear-powered satellite. The satellite was a navigational device using an isotopic power supply weighing about 42 pounds that produced 72 watts of continuous power. Two weeks before the launch date, however, the State Department canceled the mission, chiefly on the socio-political grounds that nuclear satellites in space were a potential source of danger if they re-entered the atmosphere without burning. Holifield found this argument unconvincing and took the position that the only way to test nuclear satellites effectively was to test them in space. With Vice President Johnson's help, he persuaded President Kennedy to override the State Department's decision, and the satellite was sent into space. The first isotopic power supply unit was expected to operate effectively for one year, but amazed its designers by lasting for ten years![54]

In 1964, Holifield was again in a similar battle, this time to launch the first nuclear power reactor in space, the so-called SNAP-10A device (System for Nuclear Auxiliary Power). Administration opponents were determined to delay or cancel the launch, arguing that it could be tested on the ground and posed a serious threat to U.S. relations with Cuba if it failed in orbit and fell on the island nation. In such a situation, they argued, the Cubans would gain a great propaganda boon. By this time, Holifield was JCAE chairman, and he joined forces with Senator John O. Pastore (D-Rhode Island), then JCAE vice chairman. The two believed that nuclear power was the best way to gain long-term rocket propulsion for space exploration and that such devices providing power and propulsion needed to be tested in space. They persuaded President Johnson to reverse the decision and launch the reactor.[55]

Holifield and his JCAE allies were ultimately unsuccessful in persuading the American government to use nuclear power for space propulsion. For economic and political reasons, the U.S. adopted chemical, rather than nuclear, propulsion for its space programs. Holifield was not convinced that the right decision had been made. He continued to believe that nuclear rocketry would become the key to future interplanetary travel, including safe returns to earth for astronauts. He and most of the JCAE foresaw nuclear-powered rockets putting large payloads into outer space, and they contended that the failure to use nuclear power as propulsion for exploration would build obsolescence into the U.S. space venture. The solar system, they argued to no avail, was essentially run on nuclear energy, not chemical energy.[56]

If the issue of nuclear or chemical power for space propulsion was at least temporarily settled during Holifield's career, the congressman's role in promoting nuclear propulsion was not forgotten. In 1970, astronauts Alan L. Bean and Charles Conrad presented Holifield with an unusual plaque for his role in ensuring the continuance of the SNAP program during the 1960s despite determined opposition. The plaque shows one astronaut standing on the moon after placing a SNAP device near his feet on the lunar surface at the area known as the "Ocean of Storms." Above and behind the astronaut is a crudely-drawn sketch of the adjacent territory on the moon. Bean and Conrad planted SNAP-27 on the moon on November 19, 1969.[57]

A Legislator's Role

Holifield's oversight of government activities went well beyond nuclear programs. For him, Congress was the eyes and ears of the American public on all aspects of the government, at home and abroad. Congress might not always initiate foreign policy, but it should attempt, he believed, to see that public funds were spent wisely. Holifield believed that congressmen should bring a great deal of common sense rather than specific technical expertise to the process of governance. His concept of the proper role of a legislator in representative government emphasized the responsibility of a legislator to keep in touch with his constituents and understand their concerns:

Every congressman has the job of going home continuously to keep in touch with his people. He has to find out--is he leading the people or is he going down a side street,

while his constituents are moving down the main path. When he does take the side
road too often, then people replace him with somebody more in touch with their
ideas. That's the basis of our representative form of government.[58]

Holifield was emphatic, however, that a good legislator does not always
support popular sentiment. His own career was testimony to this, as he
adopted many unpopular positions over his 32-year career. A legislator should
always seek, he believed, to represent the people of his district *in good
conscience* to the best of his ability. The legislator must know what people
think, but vote consistent with his oath to uphold and defend the Constitution:

This doesn't mean doing what the majority may want done at a particular time. A
legislator has access to more information than they have. He has inputs into his
judgment which they don't have. Then comes the tough question: Should the
representative give his best judgment to the people or should he be a slavish reflector
or a mirror to reflect their ignorance and lack of knowledge?

Or does he see the real problem and its solution, selling this to his constituents? A
genuine representative does that. . . Service in the House . . . goes far beyond
parochial interests, parochial prejudices. Thus, there comes times in every
Representative's life when he or she has to walk the plank, so to speak. One either
remains true to his convictions because of the extra knowledge he possesses, or else
he has to subordinate his conscience to popular feelings. However, uninformed
popular feelings cannot always be depended upon to be right.[59]

When asked by a constituent whether he sometimes opposed the
sentiments of a majority, Chet was fond of reciting a famous line in Edmund
Burke's well-known treatise on a representative's duties. Burke, an English
orator and historian, told the electors of Bristol: "Your representative owes
you, not his industry only, but his judgment, and he betrays instead of serving
you if he sacrifices it to your opinion." Holifield would add that he voted
"according to my conscience and to my best knowledge as to what I thought
was right for you and for the country." His perspective on his duties meant
that he sometimes took chances. He always went to his constituents and
explained why he voted as he did, and responded to letters of constituents
hostile to his viewpoint. He realized that if a majority of voters no longer
wanted him as their representative, they could register such a decision at the
polls.

As a legislator, Holifield maintained a reputation for objectivity and fair-
mindedness. As a Democrat, he could be highly partisan, but when
conducting legislative business he generally strove to be reasonable. The
committee structure from 1943 to 1971 did not provide a very good role
model for objectivity, in comparison to the reforms mandated by the House
Democratic Caucus in 1971 and 1973. Prior to 1971, the chairman of each
committee possessed rigid control and unbridled authority over its operations,

its subcommittees, and its entire staff. After the 1971 reforms, subcommittees were given more autonomy, and their numbers and staff proliferated. Prior to the reforms, chairmen could be autocratic. Carl Vinson (D-Georgia), for example, controlled all aspects of his Armed Services Committee. Vinson allowed freshmen legislators to ask only one question in hearings![60]

The rigid committee system of the postwar period was maintained for decades through the determination of the South's long-serving Democratic representatives. For most of the postwar period, the Democrats controlled the House, and southern chairmen, immune from challenges in their largely-Democratic districts, dominated the House. They usually cooperated with northern Republicans to control the flow of legislation. Until reforms imposed during the 1960s through the efforts of Holifield and other liberal Democrats, the House Committee on Rules was the most notorious example of this system. Without a rule, a bill could not be sent to the House floor, and if the Rules Committee did not like the bill, it did not get a rule. Similar autocratic arrangements marked many other committees. Junior legislators in both parties found that their voices did not count.[61]

Nonpartisanship and Partisanship

Within the earlier postwar system, Holifield was regarded by his peers as among legislators determined to make congressional activities and committee work proceed in an objective and generally fair-minded way. This was particularly evident in the JCAE when he was chairman. He established such a close working relationship with Craig Hosmer (R-California) that atomic energy issues took on a genuinely bipartisan quality. He also worked closely with his fellow Democrats, but insisted that the staff's loyalty be connected to the committee, rather than to any partisan posturing or policies. This attitude helped to bolster the cohesiveness of the JCAE, and during this period, the JCAE was at times superior in authority and judgment to the AEC. "From a statutory viewpoint, it was uncertain as to whether the AEC was actually under the authority of the executive branch of government or of the JCAE," observed Jack Newman, the committee's lawyer in the early 1960s. "In practice, though, there was no question: the JCAE exercised greater authority and power over the AEC than did the executive branch."[62]

For both Newman and Jim Graham, a bio-radiology expert who advised the JCAE during 1961-1964 and 1969-1976, service on the JCAE involved overt efforts to avoid partisanship. In the "N" reactor controversy, Newman found himself assigned to help Republican Hosmer shape his arguments to counter Holifield's arguments in favor, but Newman knew that he could just as easily have been assigned to the opposite task.[63]

Holifield was consistent in his nonpartisan approach with Government Operations as well. While at the helm of this committee, he established a close relationship with Representative Frank Horton (R-New York), the ranking minority member. Both Holifield and Horton worked together with little friction, and both believed that the committee staff, especially during Herbert Roback's long tenure as director, was totally responsive to their mutual interests and their opposing views and concerns.[64]

Although Holifield attempted to work in harmony, there were occasional serious disagreements that broke the spirit of nonpartisanship he sought. On the issue of establishing specific minority party staffing for standing committees that arose in the 1970s, he was unyielding. Republicans demanded a greater number of staff members who would work directly for Republican efforts. Holifield angered them when he opposed this reform on grounds that just as the president can select all of his own advisors, so too can the majority party in Congress. That did not mean, he argued, that the committee staff should serve partisan interests; rather, the staff should serve the entire committee's interests and should be legislating in the national interest. In theory, this argument had merit, although most Democrats probably did not practice it. In attempting to achieve a spirit of nonpartisanship, Holifield was at least practicing what he preached.[65]

Holifield and His Committee Staff

Chairman Holifield's friendship with most members of his staff was legendary on Capitol Hill and continued long after his retirement. In his eighth decade, some 30 to 40 associates would still gather with him whenever he returned to Washington. Before Chet's retirement, Jack Newman remembered meeting him in 1961 in New York for an overseas trip to Europe. Ever the haberdasher, he wondered why Newman was not wearing a hat, saying he looked half-dressed. Following their meetings in Vienna, the two men were walking down a street late one night. All of the shops were closed, but Chet spotted a hat in a store window and insisted that it was the perfect one for his aide. The next morning as they arrived at the airport for the flight home, they discovered a three-hour delay, just enough time for Chet to race back and purchase the hat. Newman wore it as a treasure afterwards.[66]

On a regular basis, when committee work was done each afternoon, Holifield usually returned to his office for what he termed a "sip and sign" session. "He kept a small bar in his office," Graham recalled, "and while he signed letters, he invited his principal aides for a drink at the end of the day." Graham felt that the sessions had a two-fold purpose: to promote "a free exchange of ideas while plotting legislative strategy for next day," and to ensure that the JCAE staff stayed out of bars after work. "Chet warned us constantly that public officials should never enter a bar unless an aide were also present, since they might be placed in compromising situations," Graham noted. Holifield was concerned about preserving reputations and national secrets, Graham explained, so "he worked to create an atmosphere of harmony within his staff so that no one would place the nation in jeopardy by some strange action after work." Informed scientific writers such as physicist Ralph Lapp wrote that the technical competence of Holifield's staff on the JCAE should have served as an impressive model for the entire Congress.[67]

Mostly, Holifield tended to extend a cordial hand to friends, political enemies, and to constituents of every stripe. This accounted, no doubt, for the way that most Democratic members supported him in 1973 when Benjamin S. Rosenthal, angered at his stance on consumer affairs legislation, mounted a drive within the Democratic Caucus to oust him as chairman of Government Operations. Holifield generally buried the hatchet with political adversaries once the din of political battle died down. Although hardly a pushover, Chet was generally reasonable with everyone, regardless of their political persuasion or even the status of their relationships, good or bad, with some of his closest associates and colleagues.[68]

As JCAE chairman, Holifield was aware that ideas had consequences as he endeavored to set the general tone of the JCAE by example. He periodically pressed Jim Graham, for example, to pose difficult questions to witnesses in hearings, including star witnesses such as the U.S. Surgeon General. Graham was fully aware of Holifield's own example. "His questions reflected the immense homework he did beforehand," Graham noted. "Chet knew, for instance, the amount of radiation dosage by millirems that a person could pick up in any area of the country." He "liked to direct questions toward hard areas where the scientists and public officials sometimes found themselves in a technical quagmire." His goal was not to embarrass these witnesses, Graham explained, "but merely to get at the truth." Holifield wanted to understand the complicated aspects of atomic energy questions. "He felt that if he didn't understand something," Graham commented, "then he couldn't help Congress or the public comprehend what was at stake."[69]

Sometimes Holifield took his quest for knowledge to unusual lengths to meet the public need for information. Graham recalled a trip to Portland, Oregon where Holifield was scheduled to give several speeches. According to Graham, "early in the morning before he gave any speeches, Chet personally drove around the city with a geiger counter making radiation dosage calculations at different locations." When the time came for his speeches and answering questions, Holifield thus was armed with practical knowledge the public wanted to hear. In response to the inevitable question about whether there was too much radiation from nuclear power plants, Chet would ask the questioner where their children went to school, and then give the *natural* radiation dosage near the school, along with a comparison of dosage near a nuclear plant. Sometimes, he revealed that the radiation dosage was higher near the school than near the plant![70]

With so technical a subject and the logistics of coordinating and responding to relevant testimony, it was only natural that Holifield occasionally erred. At times, his efforts to plunge ahead and get answers to questions created confusion. Sometimes, he would shift his line of questioning before technical experts like Graham had finished their explanations. Had the hearing record been printed with Graham's incomplete answers, readers could not have made "heads nor tails" of the proceedings. Graham recalled one instance in which he took the extraordinary step of "banging" Chet on the leg under the table, whispering that he had not completed his technical explanation.

Holifield was nonplussed by Graham's blow. Recognizing that the partial explanation would have confused those studying the record, he immediately gave Graham time to complete his response. "Had it been another committee member, I might not have done it since some might even have struck back at me!" Graham noted. "But Chet was even-tempered with his staff," Graham continued, "He looked after them personally and never criticized them unless they made the serious mistake of not briefing him completely beforehand, even to the point of criticizing his own lack of knowledge."[71]

On occasion, particularly as he grew older, Holifield could be rough on frivolous or politically antagonistic witnesses who appeared before his committee. The "public interest" lobby, Common Cause, complained in 1976 after Holifield's retirement that the JCAE had rarely paid attention to "public interest" groups during the previous 23 years. This was a gross overstatement, since no one could deny that Holifield, in particular, would bend over backwards to assure a fair hearing when serious, qualified, and informed experts desired to testify before the JCAE. He did on occasion, however, remind them that the issues were probably covered previously.

A case in point about Holifield's open forum practices concerned the testimony of Dr. Barry Smernoff of the Hudson Institute at JCAE hearings on the Liquid Metal Fast Breeder Reactor in late 1972. As usual, the number of people desiring to present oral testimony exceeded the time available, and JCAE staff was asked to determine which papers should receive priority for oral presentation and which should be included in the record. Ed Bauser and Jim Graham met with Smernoff and reviewed his proposed testimony, which dealt with placing nuclear power plants underground. Bauser and Graham advised Smernoff that, although his paper was excellent, they believed that the JCAE had received sufficient oral testimony on this subject. Due to time limitations, they indicated they might recommend that his statement be accepted for the hearing record only. Smernoff replied that he was very pleased to have received an understanding review and agreed that oral testimony was probably not justified. He then confided that he had met with various Senate committee staff and was advised not to contact the JCAE staff, since they would be unlikely to give him a fair and considerate reception. He added that he found his meeting with JCAE staff, to the contrary, very gratifying and on a highly professional level.   He expressed sincere appreciation and departed.

Later, Bauser and Graham met with the Chairman and presented their recommendations. Relative to Smernoff, they presented the basic aspects of his proposed testimony and recommended that Smernoff be allowed to make an oral presentation. Bauser and Graham noted that while oral testimony was not justified under committee guidelines, they believed that an exception should be made in light of Smernoff's very candid and forthright discussion with them. Holifield assented without comment.[72]

During the hearing, just as Smernoff was called to the witness table, Holifield indicated he wanted to speak. Bauser and Graham were very apprehensive about what might transpire. They did not know what he was going to say, mindful of their somewhat confidential discussion with both him and Smernoff. Their fear was unjustified, however, as Holifield proceeded:

> Before you begin, I feel I must tell you this story: There was a fellow who was in the Johnstown flood and ever after that, he delighted, any time he could get two or three people together, in telling them the story of the Johnstown flood. He died and went to heaven. Peter met him at the gate and said, "Is there anything we can do for you?" He said, "Yes, I would like to tell the Heavenly Hosts about the Johnstown flood." St. Peter replied, "Well, we can accommodate you on that. We always try to give the first request of a newcomer some consideration, and so," he said, "you be at the amphitheater in the morning and we will let you tell the story about the Johnstown flood."

> So the newcomer was there and all of the Heavenly Hosts were sitting around on the logs preening their feathers and tuning up their harps and a few little things like that, understand, they do up there. And when St. Peter introduced him, he said, "Our friend here is from Pennsylvania and he was in the Johnstown flood and he wants to tell us about it." But he turned to him and said, "Before you start, now, I want you to know that Noah is in the crowd."

> Now I tell this story to sort of indicate that underground siting of reactors is not a new concept to this committee, but we know you've spent an appreciable amount of time on it, and we are allowing you to give your testimony this morning.[73]

Dr. Smernoff smiled good-naturedly and gave an excellent presentation.

Holifield was well-known for injecting humor into what might otherwise be mundane proceedings. Even in his eighth decade he was a master. In 1986, Norman Augustine, Chief Executive Officer of Martin-Marietta, enjoyed telling Holifield's story to a national assembly about the time that Holifield's broker had called Holifield with an offering of high-yield bonds that would mature in the year 2010. "Young man," Holifield responded: "at my stage in life, I don't even buy green bananas, let alone bonds for the year 2010!"[74]

The Political Infighter

Although Holifield was knowledgeable and had a sense of humor, he could be dead serious in an important confrontation and was not immune from trading blow for blow in political infighting. This was particularly true between 1970 and 1974 when environmental and consumer activists often turned their political guns publicly on him. Much of his response is lost because it occurred in unrecorded sessions of congressional committees. Over the course of his career, Holifield had stormy rows not only with environmental and consumer groups, but with AEC chairmen and fellow members. His quarrels were more political than personal, however, and were short-lived. He could never hold a grudge and he later patched up his fragile relationships with most of his political opponents, even to the point of visiting his nemesis, former AEC Chairman Lewis L. Strauss, for example, on his Virginia farm, and working with Rosenthal, as another example, to pass consumer affairs legislation.[75] At heart, Holifield was not a political hater, and while he disagreed fiercely at times with other public figures over specific courses of action, he usually did so on the basis of a carefully considered rationale and a general attempt to be objective. Once his mind was made up, he continued relentlessly on course to pursue his goals, demonstrating a certain brusqueness in his appearance as he did so. It was this confidence in his own judgment, perhaps more than any other factor, that appeared to draw the ire of environmentalists determined to "bury" the nuclear power industry.[76]

A small-town businessman with fiercely-held liberal principles when he arrived in Washington, Holifield pressed his way into the political maelstroms of Congress, pushing hard along the way to force through legislation in which he believed. At the end of his career, his former liberal outlook, critics charged, had been tossed aside as he rose upwards in seniority and esteem in congressional ranks, turning him, they alleged, into a conservative out to block progress. Whatever the appropriateness of such charges, Holifield's public record indicates that neither he nor his ideas and the principles he brought to Congress ever changed significantly. What did change, however, were the circumstances and conditions within which he found himself. As he matured, these circumstances and conditions did come to color, although not transform, the way that he would unfailingly look at life and politics. In his own time, Holifield was undeniably a liberal reformer. Those younger and less patient than him, without his perspective, sometimes put another interpretation on his career and principles.

5

Towards Mastery of the House

A Legislator of Distinction

Holifield was among perhaps two dozen or so House members during his time who earned a special, if unofficial, distinction. These few were recognized as true masters of the legislative process, with their influence extending well beyond their single vote in Congress. Holifield became a master legislator more by study and hard work than by connections. His longevity in office also figured in his success.[1] He was a formidable leader by his retirement. For a time, he held the unusual distinction of being chairman of two committees, attesting to the respect he had earned from his colleagues.

Holifield began modestly enough, as a freshman member of a relatively minor committee, the Committee on Post Offices and Post Roads. In 1944, he won a chance appointment to the Military Affairs Committee. Then, in 1946, he joined the Committee on Expenditures in the Executive Departments (Executive Expenditures). From these humble beginnings, he launched a significant legislative career. From his vantage point on Military Affairs, he influenced the content of the Atomic Energy Act of 1946 and was appointed to the new JCAE. This won him distinction enough, since he became JCAE chairman by 1961. Yet his seemingly boundless energy and attention to duty brought him still other important assignments. On Executive Expenditures (known as the Committee on Government Operations after 1946), he became a subcommittee chairman almost immediately, acting chairman of the full committee by the late 1960s, and formal chairman in 1970. In these roles, he was instrumental in reorganizing many facets of the U.S. government, including creation of the three cabinet-level departments of Defense, Housing and Urban Development, and Transportation, and other major federal agencies. He also helped implement recommendations of the First Hoover Commission, and served as a member of the Second Hoover Commission.[2]

As a liberal Democrat, Holifield was also a significant legislative reformer. This was one of his more unlikely roles, since during his first two decades in Congress, he was regarded as a political anomaly, if not a maverick. His detractors considered him a radical, left-wing Democrat, whose major objectives included overturning the free enterprise system and ignoring inroads of Communism in the federal government. These were caricatures of his positions on public issues, but the left-wing label stuck to him for a long time. Republicans, in particular, saw him as a protegee of California politicians like Jerry Voorhis and Helen Gahagan Douglas, both of whom had been shoved out of political office by a tough-minded Richard M. Nixon in bruising campaigns in 1946 and 1948. During his 1948 California senatorial race against Douglas, Nixon called her "the pink lady."[3]

Anti-Communist hysteria largely disappeared in the late 1950s, and Holifield finally enjoyed his place in the political sun. He helped to lead the Democratic Study Group (DSG), a group of liberal House Democrats. Among other things, the DSG ended the decades-old stranglehold that the House Committee on Rules held over legislation it considered offensive. The DSG also helped to elect more liberals, so that before he retired, Holifield was in the majority wing of the Democratic party.[4]

The Executive Expenditures Committee

When Holifield was asked in 1946 to serve on Executive Expenditures, he scarcely realized that he would play a continuing role and eventually become its chairman. This committee had been created in December 1927 by consolidation of eleven Committees on Expenditures overseeing many federal departments. It was an investigative committee, with no authority to propose legislation. Its purpose was to ensure efficient administration of federal programs by investigating broadly how funds are expended by federal departments and agencies, with a focus on evaluating execution of policies rather than the policies themselves.[5] This broad oversight authority is distinct from the "legislative oversight" performed routinely by standing committees, where the emphasis is on specific policy and program areas, not improving efficient administration. Thus, misfeasance or broad program failures are rarely identified until after serious losses to the program and the treasury.

Membership on Executive Expenditures would not have been a member's first choice, since members can rarely forge a public reputation working there. Holifield was creative enough to fashion a significant role for himself partly because he saw the enormous possibilities in such a body. He knew that the committee's unlimited investigative charter could be wielded to serve as one of the important "checks and balances." This made his role as broad as he chose to make it. With policy initiation as much the preserve of the executive branch as the legislative in the twentieth century, he knew that strong congressional oversight could be an effective counterweight.

Holifield's view of oversight colored his participation on Executive Expenditures and its successor, Government Operations. To him, Congress was primarily a legislative, not an administrative, body. Thus, he preferred that it provide mechanisms to curb abuses rather than attempt to do the job itself. He wanted departmental "watchdog" units, not his committee, to uncover wrongdoing or administrative mistakes. Congress could keep a wary eye on agency "watchdog" units, of course, and he was also willing to investigate specific problem areas.[6] Periodically, he was attacked by partisan critics, who castigated his view as too restrictive on Congress's capacities to investigate wrongdoing. This was his answer to such critics:

> I just believe that when the Congress of the United States takes upon itself the burden of specific administration of the laws which it has passed, it weakens itself from a legislative standpoint. Our position in the Congress is to legislate and to investigate, and hold accountable the administrative agencies . . . . Secondly, when we become a party to an act, we remove ourselves from the objective which we have. We nullify our ability to objectively criticize the activities of the department, because we have been participants in the administration of the act.[7]

Holifield fully agreed with Elmer Henderson, the long-time subcommittee staff director of Government Operations under Chairman Dawson (D-Illinois) from the 1950s to the late 1960s. Henderson noted, "Congress can move this [oversight] process along through its ability to raise problems and issues up from bureaucratic holes and dungeons into the glare of public light," adding, that Government Operations "is particularly good in fulfilling this role."[8]

"Oversight" soon became an even more powerful word in Holifield's lexicon through the Legislative Reorganization Act of 1946. Committee reformers Senator Robert LaFollette of Wisconsin and Congressman Mike Monroney of Oklahoma focused heavily on oversight. They decided that Congress should have full oversight committees and remove oversight functions from standing committees. To them, standing committees did not possess the time or energy to study economy and efficiency of federal programs. Some committee had to assure the public that the bureaucracy was not running amok. Thus, the limited-oversight committees in each house, Executive Expenditures, were chosen to become full oversight committees.[9]

The LaFollette-Monroney Act, as the 1946 act was also known, thus expanded the mandate of Executive Expenditures in each house. Each committee was renamed the "Committee on Government Operations" in 1952 by House and Senate resolutions. The 1946 act empowered the committee in the House to study "the operation of Government activities at all levels with a view to determining its economy and efficiency." Under their legislative charters, the Government Operations committees were largely limited to reviewing policy execution rather than policy itself. They could not propose legislation as could the other standing committees. The new committee in the House did possess, however, an important and unique procedural power: the power to subpoena witnesses and documents.[10]

Looking in retrospect at the 1946 act, Holifield knew why reform was needed. While the act's authors "contended that every committee should continuously oversee those agencies for which they were legislating," he felt that "few committees do it adequately." As he saw it, "Committees are so busy passing legislation that they don't have time to examine what they have done." He pointed to Armed Services as an example. "It would have been impossible for me, when I was not on the Armed Services Committee," he noted, "to grasp the meaning of an eighty-billion-dollar Defense budget." Most committees, according to Chet, "are specialist committees" for "one particular agency or department." Government Operations, on the other hand, inherited the more general function of "investigating all departments."[11]

The Government Operations Committee

As a small businessman concerned with market efficiency, Holifield also possessed an unbounded passion for improving government efficiency. He joined Executive Expenditures in 1946, and was made a chairman of its Subcommittee on Executive and Legislative Reorganization by 1949. A short time later, he became chairman of the Subcommittee on Military Operations. He thus became a powerful influence in government reorganization and military affairs, eventually handling more than sixty presidential reorganization plans. In addition to the three cabinet-level departments of Defense, Housing and Urban Development, and Transportation, he assisted in creating the General Services Administration, the Federal Energy Administration, the Energy Research and Development Administration, the Nuclear Regulatory Commission, the Government Procurement Commission, the Federal Catalog System, the Drug Enforcement Administration, and many others. Over the years, he became an expert in the activities necessary to vote on a reorganization plan. As he described it:

> The Reorganization Act of 1946 said that if the president sent up a plan, Congress either had to accept it or reject it within sixty days. The vote was simply up or down on the plan. Many members of Congress openly resented this procedure. But the president knew and the act recognized that if you tried to pursue the regular legislative course, which would include amending suggested plans by the president, you'd never get anything done.

> Government Operations tried to be fair-minded in exercising its role. If the reorganization plan affected something in the Department of Commerce, we would notify the chairman of the Committee on Interstate and Foreign Commerce about it. We'd send him an analysis of the plan, then invite him to come over and testify either for or against it. On the basis of hearings we would develop a printed record to give to all members of Congress. When the time came for House debate, there was a specified time limit. Then the vote would be up or down on the plan, without amendment.[12]

While the 1946 act established the committee's overall mission, the committee's specific goals were unclear. Thus, it had to define its own role precisely in order not to interfere with legislative committees' oversight functions. Under Dawson and himself, Chet noted that "Government Operations was careful to watch its subcommittees and to see that their investigations did not get into the policy field." He continued:

> In other words, we'd look at crop subsidies if we heard that there had been violation of the Commodity Corporation Act, which holds an immense amount of wheat or cotton. But we didn't investigate whether these *should* make subsidies or not. That's the standing committee's jurisdiction.[13]

As implied above, the investigative role of Government Operations had virtually no limits, and it routinely probed into many matters. Each investigation assumed a methodology appropriate to the problem. In some instances, hearings were not held, but reports were issued to correct problems. In other cases, full-scale hearings and field investigations were used to uncover the facts. Congress and the public were regularly informed of the results of its probes, and the committee often recommended changes in law.[14]

Holifield often discovered that standing committees were, ironically enough, responsible for the problems Government Operations identified. "It's almost impossible for a congressional committee not to become paternalistic, or maternalistic over the agencies for which it legislates," he noted. Since a standing committee naturally wants its agency to do well, "It's therefore more inclined to be too lenient with it than to be too tough." Thus, in many investigations, "we found that our work would have been unnecessary if the committee of legislative jurisdiction had really dealt at arms length with their agencies." There was a relatively simple solution:

> Each legislative committee should also possess an oversight function with strict lines of jurisdiction. It should be warned to operate at arms length from agencies and to bring to the chairman any information it has. It should have the power to get necessary information through subpoena issued by the chairman.

> If the chairman of the committee exercises this subpoena power judiciously, it can be of tremendous value. If it is exercised for publicity purposes or unwisely, it can be a very dangerous thing. I've always felt that the power of subpoena, which my committees (both the Joint Committee on Atomic Energy and the House Committee on Government Operations) had, should be exercised with extreme caution. We don't need government running wild among our citizens.[15]

First Efforts: General Services Administration and Department of Defense

Holifield honed his legislative skills during the Truman era while he served on Executive Expenditures. The committee investigated the War Assets

Administration and concluded, in his words, that "Much skulduggery had occurred," and that administration of federal properties could be improved by creating a central organization with experts in procurement and the selling of government surplus. Thus, they called for a General Services Administration (GSA), as did the First Hoover Commission, and Congress created it.[16]

"GSA had growing pains," Holifield observed, "but it gradually became an invaluable arm of government." As an illustration, Holifield noted:

> In my own district, the Department of Agriculture and the Navy were seeking space. Both wanted warehouses. There was a lot of space in Vernon. Both agencies were bidding against each other for the same space. Astute owners, with the agencies bidding for their property, would keep playing off one against the other; the rental price would quickly become 50 or 100 percent more than what the owners should have received.

> Our solution was to make the GSA the buyer of space. It then went to the suppliers and said: "We need 10,000 feet of warehouse space." Owners would reply: "We'll lease for a dollar a square foot." But the GSA knew that the standard leasing price in Los Angeles was sixty cents a square foot. So it wouldn't pay the high price. If no one else was bidding for vacant space in the area, the federal government wound up getting space for the going rate.[17]

About the same time that he was assisting in creating the GSA, Holifield was instrumental in implementing an important recommendation of the First Hoover Commission. Specifically, he managed the floor legislation to establish a new U.S. Department of Defense (DOD). This new department unified the nation's armed forces under a single administrative structure.

The first Commission on Organization of the Executive Branch of the Government was named for former President Herbert C. Hoover, who was appointed by President Truman to head the commission. The commission was a bipartisan body composed of twelve members, with four members each appointed respectively by the President, the President *pro tempore* of the Senate, and the Speaker of the House. It enlisted the aid of outstanding consultants and citizens from many fields, and issued a series of 18 subject-matter reports, plus a summary report with about 300 recommendations. Within a year after its final report, about one-fourth of the recommendations had been put into effect by administrative order or congressional action. By 1958, about 72 percent of the recommendations had been implemented.[18]

DOD was a central recommendation of the commission. Truman and others had found the separate departments of War and Navy too cumbersome during World War II to conduct an effective war effort. "After the war," observed Holifield, "President Truman decided that we had to have a unified Defense Department." Hoover's commission agreed with Truman, but the military services were vehemently opposed. "Nobody wanted unification," Holifield observed, "[who was] in the Army, the Navy, or the Air Force."[19]

Hoover's DOD plan also faced determined opponents on Capitol Hill, particularly in the House. Naval Affairs Committee chairman Carl Vinson (D-Georgia) was openly against it, believing that it would not work. On Government Operations, soon-to-be-chairman William Dawson and ranking Republican Clair Hoffman of Michigan, were also opposed. According to Holifield, "Dawson feared that unification might result in a German general staff type for the U.S. military." Hoffman was "particularly antagonistic to the military" and he "objected to strengthening any military agency."[20]

By circumstance, Holifield became instrumental in passage of the bill. He knew that although Dawson was opposed, "he loved Truman," and would vote for DOD, but did not want to fight for it since Dawson thought the proposal was a mistake. Instead, Dawson gave Holifield the go-ahead to manage the bill, a good choice since Chet had "studied the proposal carefully." Chet believed the proposal "should eliminate unnecessary, competitive rivalries and empire building" and "the security of the nation will be better protected." Despite the opposition, the DOD bill passed and became effective on August 10, 1949. It not only unified the armed forces into a single administrative entity, but made the Joint Chiefs of Staff a permanent body.[21]

In 1950 assisting with GSA and DOD, Holifield almost became chairman of Government Operations, except for an unusual twist of fate. When the chairmanship became vacant in 1950, both Holifield and Dawson were next in line under seniority rules, having entered Congress on the same day. Ultimately, Dawson got the post because his name was alphabetically first!

Dawson's selection created a minor flap. Some southern Democrats were upset at the possibility of serving under an African-American. Holifield was simply upset because Dawson had not attended many committee meetings, whereas Holifield had been one of the committee's most active members. Holifield refused, however, to be part of what became a movement to replace Dawson with himself, based upon race. Instead, Holifield went to Speaker Rayburn and without naming names, assured Rayburn that he would not oppose Dawson. Rayburn, Chet observed, seemed fully understanding, and both agreed that Dawson should be chairman. He then visited Dawson, who acknowledged that he had not been a faithful member, but would be so in the future. Both men agreed to work together closely on the committee. For the next two decades, this bargain held fast, as Dawson relied upon Chet to handle important matters, especially military oversight.[22]

The chairmanship episode showed Holifield to be more interested in the committee's work than in personal gain. According to Elmer Henderson, "Dawson relied heavily on Holifield because Chet was always sound on civil liberties and civil rights." He added: "While Chet opposed human oppression or racial discrimination of any kind, he [also] just knew how to get things done without raising up a storm. If all else failed and if people got in his way while he was trying to do the right thing, he would just bowl them over."[23]

Holifield and the Second Hoover Commission

Although he worked tirelessly on several subcommittees of Government Operations, Chet's reputation was forged as much outside as inside the committee. Especially notable was his participation on the Second Hoover Commission. This second commission headed by Hoover was also composed of twelve individuals, with four members each appointed by the President, the President *pro tempore* of the Senate, and the Speaker of the House. In view of Holifield's work on reorganization plans by 1955, Speaker Rayburn appointed him as one of the four House members on the commission.

Unlike the first commission, the second commission was created jointly by President Eisenhower and Congress. In its final report in June 1955, the commission also saw itself as separate from the first commission. It differed with the first commission, whose "proposals were directed to removing the roadblocks to more effective organization and the reduction of expenditures." The commission felt it had "dealt more extensively with the organization of the executive branch and with questions of policy than the first commission."[24]

To carry out its directives, the commission relied on nineteen "task forces" to examine such subjects as medical services, military procurement, real property management, overseas economic operations, and water resources and power. The federal agencies examined by the task forces covered some 95 percent of the expenditures in the executive branch. Recommendations to the Congress included 50 for presidential decision, 145 which fell within the purview of various federal agencies, and 167 for congressional consideration.[25]

Although participating intensively, Holifield became perturbed by the commission's actions. To his seasoned legislative eye, it was usurping some congressional prerogatives. It was issuing sweeping policy statements, he believed, about which neither it as a whole nor its task forces had any real political or legislative understanding. He was primarily concerned that the commission had assumed a partisan, rather than bipartisan, stance on important policy questions. By the time the commission had finished its work, Holifield was forcefully opposed to many of its recommendations.[26]

Holifield registered his concerns by issuing separate dissents on the commission's various reports. On the report on *Federal Medical Services*, he was livid at the recommendation to do away with Public Health Service hospitals. "This Hoover report," he charged, "has as its 'whole passport' to close up Public Health Service hospitals which are now in existence, to close out military hospitals and veterans hospitals in the name of economy." Chet was appalled, especially "because of the danger of radioactive fallout which would occur if we have an enemy attack on this country." He warned that "the facts that have recently been released warn us against closing up any hospital facility." If there were an assault, he charged that the U.S. would not only need existing hospitals, but "probably a great many more."[27]

Holifield also took umbrage with two other task force reports. He considered the report on *Lending Agencies* an attack on the New Deal policies of the Roosevelt and Truman years. He charged that the recommendations "if fully carried out, would make it harder for American citizens to buy homes or to get loans for their farms or businesses."[28] It was against the commission's *Water Resources and Power* report, however, that Holifield weighed in most heavily. He was so incensed that he provided an separate 85-page report, charging that the findings were "based on the investigations of a Task Force mainly inspired by preconceived ideas and personal predilections." The report, he felt, had "facts which are distorted, findings which are unwarranted, conclusions which are inconsistent, and recommendations which are prejudiced." And, the "earlier recommendations on power which were criticized by members of the First Hoover Commission as biased, are reflected in reports of this Commission and Task Force!"

Holifield's major concern with *Water Resources and Power* was that it favored one side of the public versus private power issue then being debated nationally. These findings, he charged, "follow the private utility line" and "would destroy present benefits of low-cost Federal power development and leave future development in the main to private interests." The findings were "useless if not dangerous in the face of national defense needs for energy."

In addition to overall comments, Holifield ripped into the findings on a line-by-line basis. At one point, he argued that "within the space of a single page, the Task Force completely dropped out and lost the general welfare clause of the United States Constitution, in both a literal and a figurative sense." He also found a significant omission: there was no recommendation on nuclear power, which was "a new and promising field of energy supply." The commission had ignored the fact that "in the decade or so since atomic energy was discovered, the public has invested about $14 billion in the field," an amount "roughly equal to the total of Federal government expenditures for all water resources developed since the nation was founded!"[29]

On the commission's overall report, Holifield argued that "to a 'significant extent,'" precisely because the commission overstepped the bounds of its mandate, "it placed itself in the anomalous role of sitting in judgment on the wisdom of any and all enactments of the legislature which created it." It thereby set itself an "impossible task." With such spirited opposition from a Democrat of Holifield's stature, the recommendations of the commission were not warmly received by House Democrats. Only four of 26 recommendations in *Water Resources and Power* were implemented in whole or in part by 1958.[30]

The Rules Committee Controversy

As America moved into the 1950s, Holifield and others were dismayed that the Eisenhower administration had stymied much of the earlier spirit of reform spawned by the New Deal and the Fair Deal. Democratic proposals to develop cities, clean up the environment, advance educational opportunities, improve Americans' health, and promote civil rights ran into continuous roadblocks. The main roadblock on any liberal agenda was the conservative Committee on Rules which had acquired, over time, almost dictatorial power over the flow of legislation.[31]

For legislation going to the floor, the Rules Committee became a gateway to opportunity or the end of the line. It allowed noncontroversial legislation to proceed expeditiously, by placement on the Consent Calendar or sometimes even by suspension of the rules. For controversial legislation or legislation it opposed, the result was often death or delay. During the postwar period, this committee could keep legislation reported by standing committees from floor consideration. It could also ignore Senate-passed legislation and preclude House-Senate conferences needed on legislation both houses had passed. It worked its will either by a majority vote or a tie vote, or sometimes by delays due to the chairman's spur-of-the-moment decisions to take a rest at his farm! The chairman, Virginia's aging Howard Smith, thus thwarted liberal legislation and civil rights measures from reaching the floor. The Rules Committee had become, in effect, the "Third House" of Congress.[32]

The reason the Rules Committee was so powerful was because of the rigid seniority system in the House. Under this system, the posts of committee chairmen (and long-standing committee assignments) were gained solely on the basis of seniority. Thus, southern Democrats, who tended to be elected for much longer periods than their counterparts elsewhere, acquired the most committee chairmanships. In cooperation with conservative Republican members, these leaders, including Howard Smith on Rules, were able to maintain their power in each Congress. The result was that between 1937 and 1960, the Rules Committee, controlled by this coalition, was able to keep liberal legislation it deemed undesirable from reaching the floor for a vote.[33]

The seniority system in existence until 1974 had both positive features and negative side effects. It did allow legislators to become quite knowledgeable about their primary subject areas during their long tenures on committees. On the other hand, the system had the effect of ossifying the judgment of younger members, who were unable to make serious contributions. Under Chairman Carl Vinson of Georgia, freshmen members on Armed Services were limited to asking one question during a hearing, second-term members were limited two questions, and even a four-term congressman could ask only four questions. Such rigidity finally produced a reaction. One Democrat on Armed Services, for example, got the chairman's attention by voting several times with the Republicans. Vinson relented and extended the olive branch.[34]

Under the seniority system, liberal Democrats such as Holifield were harassed at every turn if they attempted to initiate action to fulfill more of FDR's socially-oriented New Deal objectives. During Roosevelt's tenure, these Democrats had confronted obstacles from other blocs, such as the farm and labor blocs, but they had learned to work out compromises and then coalesce their forces. As Holifield pointed out in a 1960 letter to his colleagues, he himself had belonged to many ad hoc blocs over the course of his career. But for Holifield, the Rules Committee "block" was something different. There seemed to be no political accommodation to be had with it.[35]

As early as 1949, Holifield was one of the first to seek to curb the power of Rules. In the Eighty-first Congress, he and his allies got the House Democratic Caucus to accept the 21-day rule. Under this rule, if the Rules Committee did not act on legislation reported by a committee, the chairman could then use the second or fourth Monday of the month to call up the bill for consideration on the floor. The 21-day rule reform was short-lived; in the next Congress, the conservative coalition eliminated it. During its brief existence, however, several important laws, including statehood for Hawaii and Alaska, were passed.[36] In 1952, Holifield again complained:

> In practice, the Rules Committee over a period of years developed what I believe to be a pernicious habit of blocking legislation to which a majority of its members objected, instead of facilitating the consideration of legislation in the House. ... No seven men can sit in judgment upon the merits of every bill that is reported by every legislative committee of the House. It is beyond the scope of any seven men's (a majority) mental ability to sit in judgment on the merits or demerits of legislative proposals.[37]

After Democratic increases in the 1956 elections, Holifield and other liberal House Democrats again grew increasingly restive. Despite growing numbers of liberal Democrats, they believed, the House leadership was unable to provide effective direction to advance the party's platform. Unhappy with repeated defeats, a number of House Democrats returned to Washington late in 1956 determined to improve communications among themselves.

The "Liberal Manifesto," the "M Group," and the Democratic Study Group

The upshot of liberal Democratic dissatisfaction was issuance in early 1957 of the "Liberal Manifesto." An informal group of House Democrats, led by Eugene J. McCarthy (D-Minnesota) and also including Holifield, formulated what they envisioned as the liberal Democratic platform for action. This document contained the liberal Democratic position on various subjects, such as natural resources, education, civil rights, economic development, public works, and atomic energy (which Holifield authored). After discussions with Speaker Rayburn, the Manifesto was released to the press by its 80 cosigners before Eisenhower could deliver his 1957 State of the Union address. If the Manifesto had a weakness, it was that many more congressmen were unable to commit themselves to limited portions and thus could not endorse it.[38]

Over the next year, this informal body became known as "McCarthy's Marauders," and then simply as the "M Group." Holifield was a member of the inner circle that ran, in a very loose fashion, the group's operations. The early objective of the Group was to increase the number of liberal Democrats. He and his peers were successful in the elections of 1958 in helping to add 47 new representatives.[39] With this sweep, the Group concentrated on reforming the Rules Committee. In January 1959, the group sent Chet and John Blatnik (D-Minnesota) to discuss the matter with Speaker Rayburn. Chet pushed for increasing the committee's size, but Rayburn did not like this alternative. Instead, he agreed not to permit the Rules Committee to bottle up legislation indefinitely; if he could not fulfill his promise, he would support procedural reforms. To cement their agreement, Chet and his cohorts drafted and issued a press release. They expressed confidence in "Mr. Sam" and the Speaker's support "for such procedural steps as may become necessary to obtain House consideration of reported bills from legislative committees." The reform step became necessary, ironically enough, because a conservative Republican militant, Charles Halleck (R-Indiana), ousted Joseph Martin (R-Massachusetts), a moderate GOP leader, and Rules became a more vigorous opponent. Chet and the Group knew that something would have to be done.[40]

To build support, Holifield decided to carry the fight beyond the halls to the highest reaches of the party: proceedings of the national convention. Along with Chester Bowles (D-Connecticut) and others, Chet served on the platform committee at the 1960 convention and was instrumental in producing the *Rights of Man* platform that served as their trumpet in the Kennedy-Johnson era. It urged that "the rules of the House of Representatives . . . be so amended as to make sure that bills reported by legislative committees reach the floor for consideration without undue delay."[41]

Prior to taking on the Rules Committee directly, the M Group underwent a name change. Indicative of his growing stature in the group, Holifield suggested the name change to broaden the group's horizons and membership. Holifield wanted a more formal and less controversial title: the Democratic Study Group (DSG). After all, he told his M Group colleagues, "no one can condemn you for studying." He also insisted that the group remain informal and not publish a membership list. He feared that the group would be viewed as "Communist" or "ultra-liberal," and would thus be damaged. By 1960, he replaced Lee Metcalf, (D-Montana) as DSG chairman.[42]

True to its new name, the DSG became, according to Holifield, a "solid research source for moderate and liberal Democrats." As he explained, "we began by analyzing bills that would be voted on the following week, sending out a section-by-section analysis to our associates." Soon, "non-members of the DSG would ask for this analysis and we'd mail it to them." Such activities limited controversy about the DSG, since the House leadership did not object to members banding together to study subjects of mutual interest. To ensure the group's continued effectiveness, Holifield insisted on rotating the DSG chairmanship, board of directors approval of all press statements, and shared financing of the DSG office staff. Sensitive to congressional traditions, he also urged that the House leadership be kept informed about DSG activities, since a tenuous alliance between some Democrats and Republicans had begun to move some bills. Rayburn thus did not get unpleasant surprises from the DSG that would have led him to openly oppose the group.[43]

During Holifield's DSG chairmanship, the DSG finally destroyed the Rules Committee's control. Their hard work began to pay off. Discussions with the Speaker produced a strategy to enlarge Rules to 15 members. The fight was hard and victory uncertain, but this reform measure narrowly passed and spelled the end of conservative blocks to liberal legislation. Chet's leadership in this struggle was part of his career-long interest in removing roadblocks to sound legislation, and was a major, if hidden, factor in the ultimate success of the Kennedy and Johnson social reform programs. Without this trailblazing, the New Frontier and the Great Society would have been stillborn.[44]

Following the 1964 presidential elections when two southern Democrats defected and campaigned openly for Goldwater, Chet helped spearhead the caucus efforts to strip the defectors of their committee seniority. New initiatives were also proposed to strengthen the role of the new Speaker, John McCormack, over the Rules Committee and to make other reforms. Again, the DSG dispatched Holifield and Blatnik for meetings, this time with McCormack, which were held between Christmas and the New Year. The Speaker agreed to several features of the DSG reform package, including a provision for caucus review of committee assignments. This proposal helped to give the Democratic Caucus tighter control over committee assignments.[45]

A Reformer--But a Party Regular, Too

Holifield was one of those rare combinations: he was a congressional reformer, but also a party regular and loyalist. His efforts to oust the two Democrats for supporting Goldwater in 1964 showed that he was no renegade. He only rebelled when good sense indicated to him that something was amiss, as with the Rules Committee. As a party loyalist, he was mainly concerned that the party lacked sufficient cohesiveness. Chet felt that both within and outside, the sense of party lacked the discipline of the Republicans.[46]

Holifield was not always, of course, on the side of the Democratic Party. If this was true with regard to the Rules Committee, it was also true with the Tidelands Oil Bill. Introduced at the request of the Truman administration, the bill intended to take away the oil rights of states bordering on the Atlantic and Pacific oceans. Specifically, the bill removed these states' rights to oil deposits in the water within three miles off shore. Chet's hitch was practical:

When Culbert Olson was governor of California, he established a principle of leasing by bid on royalties for the state-owned tidelands' oil. California was receiving some 50 percent royalty from the oil companies on oil produced from the wells off Huntington Beach and Long Beach. Nationally, this royalty was a low 8 percent on any federal lands; major oil companies acquired leaseholds on federal lands by making high "bonus" cash payments. California had earmarked its higher royalties for purchases of ocean beach frontiers.[47]

Then, too, what was wrong with ocean-front states profiting in the same way that states having forests or other natural resources benefitted from their location? Holifield thus voted against the Tidelands Oil Bill. It was better, in his judgment, for the citizens of California to receive a 50 percent royalty on this strategically-located natural resource than to receive a mere 8 percent.

Oil proved to be the "sticking point" in another of Chet's rare divergences from the Democratic party norm. Although he got along well with the House leadership, Holifield showed he could resist even the pressures of the Speaker. Such was the case when he voted against a natural gas regulation bill sorely desired by Rayburn after advising him that the bill would raise the natural gas price in Chet's "district by an average of $2 a month or more":

"It'll do no such thing," Rayburn said. It wasn't hard for me to stand up for my own district. But it was hard to turn down the Speaker. I told him I had to vote against the gas bill on principle. Red-faced and angry, his eyes glowered right through me.[48]

If Mr. Sam was periodically unhappy with Holifield, he nonetheless recognized the Californian's sense of party regularity. Although Holifield was a reformer, too, he was perceived even by the reformers themselves as a stabilizing link to the House leadership as well as a cohort. Given his status on the JCAE and yet his opposition to the "unfair" House Rules Committee, neither traditionalists nor reformers considered him an extremist. Conscious of the prerogatives of the Speaker, Holifield insisted, under both Rayburn and McCormack, that "all we want to do is give more effective assistance to the Speaker and the program." He insisted that "We don't want to dictate policy or take away any of the Speaker's power."[49] Not every DSG member was as cautious in approaching the issue of enlarging power-sharing in the House. But Holifield's view that precipitous action might doom reform made sense.

Assisting Former President Truman

Holifield's party loyalties were put to the test particularly during the 1958 initiative to grant a pension and staff assistance to former presidents. Deep-seated feelings were aroused by this. Historically, Congress had objected to giving former presidents status similar to that found in England, where former prime ministers belong to the House of Lords. As Chet observed, all federal judges, including those on the Supreme Court, "are entitled to full salaries for life after retirement or upon disability before retirement age, so we have recognized that in the public interest these considerations should be made and Congress has approved them." Also, "five-star" generals and admirals were accorded not only pensions, but funds for staff assistance. Majority Leader McCormack and GOP leader Martin favored such assistance. They pointed out that citizens continue to place enormous demands upon them and their time. Former President Truman, for instance, was receiving 100 to 400 letters a day for advice, but he lacked the financial resources to respond.[50]

Despite Democratic and some Republican support for a presidential pension, the problem was not a simple one. For one thing, the only former Republican president still living, Herbert Hoover, was wealthy and did not need extra help. This meant that the primary beneficiary would be Truman. Along with Joseph Martin and other Republican leaders, Hoover publicly supported proposals to grant pensions to ex-presidents, with a view to aiding Truman. But many Republicans, still bearing rancor against the Truman presidency and Truman himself--"that little man in the White House," they termed him with disdain--were not prepared to grant him a pension. Still other legislators thought the national committees of each party, rather than the public treasury, should provide any benefits needed by an ex-president.

The battle to aid Truman proved to be long. The Senate favored the bill from the start, but it languished in the House for three years because Tom Murray (D-Tennessee), chairman of the Committee on Post Office and Civil Service, adamantly refused to report the bill. Murray was only the hub of the opposition, which remained fierce until July 1958. Ultimately, Speaker Rayburn devised a solution; he asked Holifield to return to Murray's committee as a low-ranking member to help Jimmy Morrison get the bill reported. Holifield agreed because he wanted to help Truman, but indicated that he wanted off the committee as soon as the task was done.[51]

Holifield immediately set to work to fulfill his goal, and accomplished it in a relatively short time. "By a series of parliamentary maneuvers," he noted, "including holding a committee meeting on a day when we knew that Murray would be late, we finally got the bill through." Ironically, when the bill was finally voted out of committee and reached the House floor, Murray did an about-face and graciously acceded to the legislation. Chet was not so lucky, however, in obtaining his wish to get off the committee. He explained that "it took me several years to get off the committee" because "Rayburn said a 'bad fellow' wanted to replace me and he couldn't allow that."[52]

Holifield Becomes Government Operations Committee Chairman

Few could deny that Holifield was a major legislative leader by the time he helped to engineer the pension bill for Truman. His career blossomed further when he took the helm as head of the JCAE in January 1961, after almost 18 years in Congress. His second chairmanship followed on Government Operations after Dawson's death in November 1970 and surprised no one, since he had been *de facto* chairman long before that. Very few congressmen in history have headed two major committees in Congress.

If Holifield's early image had been that of a vigorous liberal, his handling of his assignments from the House leadership was ultimately interpreted by most as even-handed and fair-minded. Moderate Republicans like George Meader noted that Chet's practical, non-ideological approach, and especially his sense of fair play, continued when he became chairman of Government Operations. "Ordinarily, Chet didn't try to step on the toes of other committees or subcommittee chairmen," Meader remarked. "We both agreed on one key issue that angered some Republicans: committee staff should serve all committee members on a nonpartisan basis." Meader explained that he had experienced the nonpartisan staff approach "as a wartime counsel on the Truman Committee, so it was not novel for me." Other Republicans, including Minority Leader Gerald Ford, did not buy Chet's argument, opting to increase the GOP's staffing on the Hill. Holifield was unmoved, according to Meader, and "ran his committee on that [nonpartisan] principle."[53]

To moderate Republicans like Meader and Frank Horton (R-New York), Holifield's long-range vision was to improve government economy and efficiency. The work was performed without much fanfare and publicity and sometimes moved very slowly, but Holifield did not lose sight of his vision. In 1959, Meader told his House colleagues that the committee was successful, even from his standpoint as a Republican under Democratic leadership. He enunciated a number of reasons that he would later feel still held true under Holifield's regime, including the facts that "the committee has avoided partisan political controversy" and that it had "exercised restraint and has confined itself to its proper role--that of . . . determining whether the execution of congressional policy is economical and efficient." Meader also believed that the committee had "acquired a small but able staff selected on the basis of merit, not political patronage." The committee had also "never undertaken hearings without preliminary staff work and advance preparation." Mirroring Holifield's civil libertarian views, Meader also averred that Government Operations had been "assiduous in protecting the rights of witnesses and persons both in Government and in private life whose conduct has been subjected to committee scrutiny." Finally, the committee's reports had been "carefully prepared with full documentation for its findings and with judicious restraining in its inferences and conclusions."[54]

Holifield could not have asked for a better apologist than Meader nor a more judicious summary of his work, even from his Democratic colleagues. Meader's overall assessment was not shared by hard-line Republicans. John Erlenborn, for example, regarded Chet as a Democrat who would never try to embarrass his president nor his party by pursuing bureaucratic wrong-doings. On the other hand, moderate Republicans like Meader and Horton did not share Erlenborn's view, and in fact, were sometimes chastised by conservative Republicans for working too closely with Chet. If these opinions showed anything, it was that Holifield was at least minimally acceptable as a committee chairman to most congressmen, Democrat and Republican alike.[55]

Meader's apt assessment left out one small period of significant unrest on the committee that was not of Holifield's making and not during his chairmanship. For most of the period from 1946 to 1974, the Democrats controlled the committee, as they did the Congress. During that period, two Democrats, Dawson (1950-1970) and Holifield (1970-1974) were the formal chairmen, with two significant exceptions. During the Eightieth Congress (1947-1948) and the Eighty-Third Congress (1953-1954), the Republicans were in control and chose Clair Hoffman (R-Michigan) as their standard bearer. During these periods, members were at loggerheads, more as a consequence of Hoffman's curmudgeonly behavior than because of partisan wrangling. This point was demonstrated when Republican members, supported by the Democrats, led a successful revolt that curbed Hoffman's powers.[56]

Aside from his tempestuous chairmanships, Hoffman often tangled with Holifield. A widely-known conservative and an obstreperous personality, Hoffman charged up against Republican and Democrat alike. Holifield recalled that on his first day in Congress, another member leaned over and whispered in his ear: "See that man over there [Hoffman]? He is the most consistent man I have ever known; he is sore all the time!"[57] Holifield and Hoffman often jousted while serving together on subcommittees. They were often embroiled in debates over such matters as granting presidential emergency powers in wartime, depoliticizing the Federal Home Loan Bank Board, and proposing a Fair Employment Practices Commission. During one House colloquium, Hoffman found Holifield unwilling to yield. "The gentleman distrusts him," Holifield remarked, "because the gentleman does not talk to the issue; he goes back into long rambling discourses about his grandparents and things like that." Hoffman retorted testily, "Like Christianity, of which we need a little!" On another occasion, Hoffman complained that he thought "as most of your committee do, with the exception of my friend from California and those who think as he does, that there should be some restriction on spending!" Once Hoffman asked whether Holifield believed that "we must have a law in order to make the Democrats behave and go along with what is good for the country!"[58]

Holifield and Herbert Roback: The Age of the Giants

Without question, Herbert Roback was Holifield's most valuable advisor and confidant in virtually all committee activities from the time he first joined

Holifield soon after World War II. By the late 1960s he was staff director of Holifield's Military Operations Subcommittee, and was later elevated to the post of staff director of the entire committee when Holifield became chairman of Government Operations. Among many other assignments, Roback served side by side with him on special assignments, including special subcommittees. More than just close professional associates, Herb and his wife Arline were personal friends of both Chet and Cam Holifield up to Herb's death in 1977.

A key to any representative's success is the capacity to attract competent and politically-savvy staff who share his or her aspirations. In Holifield's case, this individual was indisputably Roback, in whose memory a national award is presented each year to an outstanding public servant by the National Contract Management Association. Roback represented the best tradition of staff advisors. He was extremely loyal, although even moderate Republican Meader acknowledged that Roback "served us all."[59]   At the same time, Roback defended, sometimes abrasively, Holifield's turf on committees he chaired. Possessing a no-nonsense attitude at work, Roback also tended to try to keep other staff at bay, away from Chet. Some staff ignored this tactic, since they found easy access, anyway, to the very approachable Holifield.

Roback, who had escaped from imprisonment by German troops while serving as a U.S. soldier in Europe, first came to Holifield's attention after the war. Holifield found himself staring with dismay at books given him by the Congressional Research Service staff.   Wrestling with a government reorganization problem, he had asked the service for help. Several weeks later, he received a large pile of books with relevant pages simply tagged by markers.   Sally Thompson, on his staff, suggested that Holifield hire a legislative expert, Roback, to tackle such major issues. Roback was available and pressed into service; he thereafter became Holifield's alter ego.[60]

With his mentor, Roback shared two rules of behavior: do not step on the toes of other committees and keep tight control over attempts by government to intrude on the lives of individuals or the affairs of corporations. What eventually became clear, contrary to Holifield's liberal image, is that he and Roback were constitutional conservatives. Their philosophy colored nearly everything they did. Close observers like Harold Seidman of the Brookings Institution still refer to the Holifield-Roback impact on military affairs and defense procurement as the "Age of the Giants."[61]

With dedicated, competent staff such as Roback by his side, Holifield was able to face the turbulent 1960s and early 1970s with assurance. This period brought many challenges, but also fulfillment to his career in many ways. As leader of the JCAE and later head of the Government Operations Committee, he was at the forefront of legislative activity.[62] Two Democratic presidents in the White House--John Fitzgerald Kennedy and Lyndon Baines Johnson-- meant also that he had friends, rather than opponents, in the highest office in the land, and his advice was listened to. This period was one of great change and challenges to the American political system, and very unlike World War II and the immediate postwar era. Then, the nation's economy had been harnessed by price controls, rationing, and other measures necessary to concentrate on the war effort and restrain domestic consumption. After the war, constraints were removed, pent-up consumer demand was unleashed, the civilian economy re-ignited, and a prolonged national expansion began. During the Eisenhower years, though, there were still some constraints. Civil rights momentum was held in check; federal spending for health, education, job creation, manpower development, and welfare remained at reduced levels; and cities were ignored. After Eisenhower, the nation was galvanized into taking action on a broad social agenda. American society faced a plethora of unresolved problems: urban sprawl and congestion, air and water pollution, clogged transportation arteries, lack of educational opportunities, decaying inner cities, widespread consumer complaints about shoddy or even dangerous goods, unprecedented housing shortages, a lack of social justice and economic opportunities for minorities, and a new, undeclared war in Indochina.

Holifield and the New Department Initiatives

At one important helm in the eye of the growing storm was Holifield and his Government Operations Committee. When Congress and the president decided in the 1960s to establish new cabinet-level departments to respond to specific societal problems, Holifield figured prominently and continually until his retirement in the mid 1970's.

In 1962, President Kennedy sent to Congress a reorganization plan to establish HUD. The proposal was taken up by the full Committee on Government Operations, rather than by a subcommittee, and approved. But the plan was rejected by the House in February 1962. Holifield believed that the defeat was due to two factors: "broad opposition to it and Kennedy's inexperience in congressional legislation." As he saw it, "Kennedy was an inspiring and effective president and we tried to get his plan through," but "all of the vested interests were comfortable where they were." That explained the broad opposition. Chet was frank in assessing Kennedy's inexperience:

One problem which led to my failure to get a bill passed was that Kennedy announced beforehand that he was appointing a Negro to head HUD--a highly capable man by the name of Robert Weaver. Later he became the Administrator. But in 1962-1963 there were riots and race troubles in the South and the Administration was embroiled in these racial difficulties, just like President Nixon became embroiled in Watergate. As a result, Kennedy lost influence in the Congress.

Instead of pre-announcing his selection of Weaver, the President should have said that he was going to get the best man possible for the job. That way he would have had the organization first before he brought in the racial factor.[63]

After Kennedy's assassination in Dallas in November 1963, Lyndon B. Johnson succeeded to the presidency. Soon after he was sworn in, Johnson assembled congressional leaders, including Holifield, at the White House. By then, Holifield was a member of the Executive and Legislative Reorganization Subcommittee as well as chairman of Military Operations, and was in an influential position to affect legislation. At the meeting, Johnson announced his intention to enact Kennedy's programs and gave specific instructions to various leaders on what he wanted done. He told Chet, his long-time friend, that he wanted him to "head the Housing and Urban Development effort." He also indicated that "With the growth of mass populations in our cities, we've got to pay more attention to this area than we've done in the time where we were an agrarian society." He informed Chet: "I want you to bring that bill up again, hold hearings on it, and report it to the floor." To Chet's recollection, Johnson added that "I can promise you that you'll have my help in getting it passed." He stressed "If you get into trouble, let me know."[64]

LBJ was a man after Holifield's own heart. As he pointed out, "Johnson was a member of the House, later a Senator, and finally Vice President." In fact, Johnson had served with him on the JCAE. Unlike Kennedy, who had not cultivated legislators, Johnson was a master of congressional process and politics. "As president," Holifield added, "he [Johnson] put this background and knowledge together to work on Congress." He "knew many of us by our first names." Johnson would often call Holifield to find out about the status of legislative matters. It was not uncommon for Johnson to ask, "Chet, how about getting out this bill?" or "Do you need my help in any way?"[65]

Following up on Johnson's HUD request proved much easier than working with the Kennedy administration. Chet needed and received Johnson's personal help. The bill was reported out of his subcommittee with little opposition, in no small measure due to additional practical help from the administration. Holifield remembered how Johnson had helped:

> We started the hearings. Suddenly a committee member began raising obstacles. Joseph Califano, a White House aide, called to inquire how I was getting along. I replied: "I'm having trouble with one congressman." "In what way?" he asked. I explained what the difficulty was and why he was opposing us. President Johnson then called the erring congressman personally and said, "Listen, John, why are you opposing this bill? It's one that Kennedy came out for. It's a good bill. Why don't you get behind it and help Chet rush this bill through?" About a week later, this gentleman came over to me and said, "Chet, I've been thinking over my opposition to this bill and I'm kind of changing my mind." He added, "I may not argue for the bill on the floor, but I think I can vote for it. I'll vote to get it out of committee." Right then, I knew Johnson had twisted his arm.[66]

Later on, Holifield found out the *quid pro quo* of this congressman's sudden change of heart: a post office that this southern congressman had desired for ten years suddenly appeared in the federal budget!

Holifield also had some trouble with the Rules Committee. As he put it, "some of this former opposition was still around." "But President Johnson was smart enough not to say whom he would appoint to the department," he noted. "A practical man, he knew how to get legislation done and also how to ruin it." Holifield had done his job well. The task of floor manager fell to Dante Fascell (D-Florida), in order to draw in a broad range of support. The tactic was successful. The HUD bill passed and was signed by Johnson. Then Johnson did something that Kennedy had intended, but did not have the power to do: he appointed Robert Weaver as the first Secretary of HUD.[67]

When proposals for a new Department of Transportation (DOT) were sent to the Hill by President Johnson in 1966, Holifield was acting chairman of Government Operations. By giving deference to other committees affected by the bill, Holifield hoped his committee could assure relatively smooth passage in the House. Although he brushed aside complaints of individual transportation agencies worried about the new department, he remained fair-minded as always. He agreed to transfer agencies as complete organizations into DOT, thereby retaining existing responsibilities and functions and alleviating fears of organizational annihilation.[68]

Holifield's hopes for an noncontroversial bill were soon dashed. When the bill reached the House floor, a basic weakness of Government Operations became apparent. As an investigating rather than legislative body, Government Operations tends to be relatively immune to the interest groups which normally surround, and indeed, at times envelop, federal agencies. After eleven days of subcommittee hearings, Holifield's committee had approved the bill almost as submitted. On the floor, however, opposition groups redeployed their forces and attacked the bill through the legislative committees with which they were on friendlier terms. As a consequence, important changes were made in Holifield's DOT bill by the full House.

From the moment the bill was introduced, Holifield knew that a floor fight was in store over certain provisions, mainly those including the Maritime Commission from Commerce. Chet was nonplussed, however. His bill included Maritime in DOT, but Holifield realized that it might be thrown out on the floor. As an acting chairman, he was not about to capitulate to any of the interest groups concerned with DOT; he believed that such a decision should be made by the full House. As he viewed the matter:

> The transportation interests were quite comfortable with existing arrangements. No one likes to be disturbed when he's comfortable. We all enjoy the warmth of our bed and look with suspicion on getting out of bed into what may be a cold part of the house. The involved interests were apprehensive about losing their status.

> We worked out a bill acceptable to aviation, highway, and railroad groups. But we
> never could convince the maritime interests--the greatest example of government
> subsidization in existence. About 75 percent of their operating expenses--that is, of
> the American Merchant Marine and the private shipping interests--are paid for by the
> public. Their argument was that we must have a merchant marine in case of war.
> That's not true. The Merchant Marine's not going to be needed if we have a world
> war involving nuclear weapons.[69]

As Holifield re-examined the DOT battle, he was proud overall that DOT
was created as an umbrella agency for the transportation agencies. The only
significant omission, in Holifield's eyes, was the exclusion of Maritime from
DOT. "We defeated all opposition but the maritime lobby," Chet noted. "The
maritime unions and shipping interests wanted an independent agency so they
could control their agreements. Their opposition was political: they wanted
increased maritime subsidies."[70] Chet's stand proved to be correct. Seven
years after he retired, the industry, the Maritime Union, and Congress
concurred with his judgment; Maritime was shifted into DOT.

The Procurement Commission and the Federal Catalog System

Holifield had scarcely finished with the DOT bill when he became the
leader in another of a series of government-wide efforts to improve the
efficiency of the federal contracting system. In 1967 in the *Journal of the
National Contract Management Association*, he described the many problems
in the federal government's procurement of goods and services by contract:

> Hardly a day goes by without a complaint conveyed to the Military Operations
> Subcommittee by members of Congress who, I am sure, have desk drawers full of
> complaints from subcontractors who can't get paid by their primes, patent holders
> who believe that Government procurement agencies are infringing upon them, small
> businessmen who are lost in the maze of Government procurement regulations, big
> business contractors who feel hemmed in by the many Government restrictions, civil
> servants who believe there is too much contracting out, and outside organizations who
> believe there is too much in-house work.[71]

As acting chairman of Government Operations, Holifield was concerned
that the system needed overhauling both to avoid waste and to decrease
overall costs of doing business. Federal purchasing was already big business
in 1967 and increasing by leaps and bounds. The government found itself
dealing with every type of private organization, including businesses,
individuals, universities, and consulting firms, to mention a few. Chet's
concern was not that there were no mechanisms for controlling contractors,
since each federal agency had its investigative arm, and his and the Senate's
Government Operations committees investigated problems and oversaw the
procurement process. Moreover, the GAO annually issued dozens of reports

that reviewed contracting activities. His major point was, rather, that no intensive inquiry had been made since the First Hoover Commission in 1949. He was sure that by 1967 much of the system was outdated.[72]

As a remedy, in early 1969 Holifield introduced Resolution No. 474 to establish a national Commission on Government Procurement. Its purpose would be to make a broad inquiry into all aspects of the federal procurement system and make recommendations for improvements. Despite his ill-fated experience with the Second Hoover Commission, he opted for a presidential commission rather than a congressional body. Chet contended such commissions could play a less-inhibited role, whereas congressional bodies were apt to become bogged down in disputes over jurisdiction and other problems. To buttress his case, he cited a similar initiative decades earlier which had illustrated "the awkward situation when expertise and participation are required from several committees at a given point in time." For Chet, "A commission could more easily and expertly draw together relevant information, analyze the statutory and procedural interrelationships, and recommend appropriate solutions to serious problems."[73]

Congress agreed with his position. There were only the details to be worked out, which took a while. In 1969, by act of Congress in cooperation with the president, a 12-member commission was created. In recognition of his authorship of the legislation, House members chose Holifield as vice-chairman of the commission. E. Perkins McGuire was named chairman.[74]

The work of the new Commission on Government Procurement took about three years. In December 1972, it issued its final report, comprised of four volumes with 149 formal recommendations, many of which have since been put into effect by the president or Congress. In addition, the commission's study groups made dozens of recommendations to separate federal agencies, with many accepted and implemented. Unlike the Second Hoover Commission, the commissioners concurred on most suggestions. Dissenting statements tended to be limited in scope, due in large part to the way that Holifield and Senator Henry Jackson crafted the final legislation.[75]

Among its findings, the commission discovered that even though some 80,000 federal employees were then involved in some form of procurement activities, it did not find that "blanket criticisms" of the procurement system were in order. Rather, it pointed out that piecemeal operations then existing could be improved, with substantial savings to the government.[76]

Holifield's work on procurement gave rise to another of his creations to promote increased government efficiency: the consolidated federal catalog system. In surveying the government's procurement system, Holifield observed duplicate purchasing of the same products by different agencies. As he put it, "There was no central inventory from which to order." In each separate department's catalog, identical products were, in Holifield's words, "identified by each agency under a different serial number."[77]

For Holifield, separate purchasing catalogues also "meant duplicate inventories." He and his fellow commissioners "estimated there were twenty-seven billion dollars worth of items in inventory." Because of separate catalogs, there was actually much more inventory on hand than was needed at any one time. Holifield noted that "If you would eliminate the duplication, you would cut that [twenty-seven billion dollar figure] in half."[78]

There was much opposition to a single inventory system. Each federal agency sought to protect its own interests by claiming that its own needs were unique. This was particularly true of the military, the government's biggest purchaser, which "didn't like" the idea. Holifield and the Procurement Commission, however, had the support of Congress; in Chet's words, "Congress also wanted to establish a uniform federal catalogue for purchasing goods." Given the cost savings both from eliminating separate pricing and consolidation of existing inventories, Holifield and the commission felt strongly about their recommendation. "We concluded," he explained, "that there should be one government inventory located in the General Services Administration with a uniform identification system." They got their way.[79]

Holifield was not content with his Procurement Commission achievements in reducing federal costs. He began to look into the subject of reducing unnecessary and duplicative federal paperwork. In 1974, he pushed legislation through Congress creating the President's Commission on Federal Paperwork. This body was chaired in 1975 and 1976 by his long-time Republican ally on Government Operations, Frank Horton. This group eventually made over 150 recommendations, many of which were implemented.[80]

The Legislator's Legislator

Not every student of Congress would share Holifield's enthusiastic judgment about the value of presidential commissions as vehicles for improving efficiency. Nor would every congressman agree with his ideas on how to achieve legislative goals. He once told northern California journalist Leo Rennert half-jokingly that "If you keep breathing long enough under this system, you get there eventually."[81] On a more serious note, however, Holifield explained some ingredients of legislative mastery that he had picked up over the years through his experience as a legislator:

> I knew the temper of the House. I could count the votes. That's a feeling one gets by being around a long time. You have to do whatever is possible to get a good bill through. Extremists who wanted more than I could accomplish criticized me. But our system of legislation depends a whole lot on the manager of the bill and his motives.
>
> Success in Congress becomes a matter of judgment on every legislative issue that goes onto the floor. There's a difference between desiring to get something through and

failing. Once a bill manager gets a reputation for defeat, his effectiveness goes right down the tube. Wilbur Mills and I wouldn't handle a bill we couldn't pass, unless the national interest demanded that you take a desperate gamble. There were times I moved out on a limb.[82]

Key elements in Holifield's legislative skills were compromise and getting along. He realized the value of compromise very early in his career and explains its importance in Congress this way:

. . . If you come to the floor with something reasonably acceptable to both sides, the bill can pass. Otherwise, your bill will be replaced by substitute bills, or cut to pieces by substitute amendments. In Congress, you've got to accept these realities or adjust to them; it's far better to pass 80 percent of your bill than zero. Maybe a year or two later you can come back and get another 10 percent.[83]

In a similar, but more expansive, discussion, Chet stressed that politics is the art of the possible and emphasized the practical concept that half a loaf is better than none. He also pointed to the practical limitation that any congressman, no matter how experienced, has only one vote himself:

The idealist can butt his head against a brick wall until he knocks himself out, and come up with zero. But the pragmatist, the realist, realizes the kind of a world we live in where a half a loaf is better than none. He gets the half a loaf, then adds slices to it. Legislation is a living, breathing entity. It's not a dead letter, unless you let it become dead. It's subject to growth, just like a tree. Branches are pruned off and then grafted on. It's subject to being fertilized with funds so it will grow, or, having fertilization kept away from it, thereby letting it die. The legislative process includes living with people who have the same vote you have.

That's what businessmen don't understand. Particularly those who control a corporation's destiny, if they own a controlling block of stock. They don't need the other eight votes. They vote the weight of their own stock. Their vote is evaluated in relation to the number of proxies they have or the numbers of shares of stock they own or control.

But in the House of Representatives, your vote is one. The newcomer who was sworn in yesterday can vote "no" and kill your "yes" vote. Of necessity, you soon realize that it's a composite body that has to be worked with and cultivated. As a legislator, you must do things for others and they will do things for you. It comes back to the adage that Speaker Sam Rayburn used: "To get along, go along." Not against your conscience, of course.[84]

Probably as important as his ability to compromise was Holifield's knack of getting along with a wide variety of people and legislators. He was friend to Democrat and Republican, liberal and moderate. His alliances crossed regional lines to include Northerners, Westerners and Mid-Westerners, and Southerners. About the only people with whom Holifield did not share much common ground were those he referred to as the "extremists," including the very liberal, the very conservative, and "single-issue" advocates. For his part, he tolerated them and even worked well with them on specific issues, but he failed to understand their unrealistic approach to politics.[85]

As a practical legislator, Chet moved in circles that encompassed more than liberal Democrats. Beyond the liberal ranks, he formed other alliances, notably with the more centrist Texas, Arkansas, Louisiana, and Oklahoma Democrats who would eventually support liberal reforms, including those on civil rights. These Democrats, legislators such as Sam Rayburn, Carl Albert, Hale Boggs, Wilbur Mills and Jim Wright, would also eventually hold principal House leadership posts. What brought Holifield together in regular alliance with them--alliances which made some consider him a moderate, rather than a liberal, Democrat--was his belief that, like himself, they were populists at heart. While some northern and mid-western Democrats were not so certain of their convictions on this score, Chet was. In his mind, the liberal views he had carried with him in his youth from Arkansas to California were not too different from those of centrist Democrats from the more open-minded southern states.[86]

In turn, the moderate southern leaders--including the Texans and their principal leader, Lyndon Johnson--came to repose great confidence in Chet's judgment. Like him, they believed that the U.S. should have the strongest possible military and defense policies and programs. With footholds in the northern and western liberal camps and the southern populist camp, Holifield would gradually play a strategic role, together with John Blatnik, as a principal balancing force between Democratic House reformers and the House leadership. Both men shared one common view: liberal reforms had to be pursued, but there was no reason to embarrass the House leadership.

Another quality of his legislative mastery involved his instinctive grasp of how to get along with the House leadership, particularly Speaker Rayburn. Although Holifield never became close personal friends with Rayburn, the two worked well together. Of Rayburn, Holifield remembered:

> Mr. Sam had a motto: "If you want to get along, you go along." Both of us worked extremely hard. We actually never took a shine to each other. There was never intimacy. Sam never pulled me in with his cronies to the "Board of Education," the bourbon cabinet in his private office. But, there was friendliness and respect. In 1946, when the Senate bill on atomic energy adopted principles which Mel Price and I alone stood for in the House, I am sure that Rayburn said to himself: "Mel and Chet were right," and therefore appointed us to the Joint Committee on Atomic Energy.[87]

Legislative mastery also can not be had without hard work and considerable knowledge. As a subcommittee chairman under Holifield, Dante

Fascell had first-hand knowledge of Chet's intensive efforts and tireless work habits:

> Chet carried his personal style of operation into the committee hearing room. He wanted to know all matters in detail and not merely pro forma. When I served as a subcommittee chairman under him on Government Operations, he let me run hearings any way I wanted. The only caveat was that he required us to produce legislation he could live with. That meant that I had to become thoroughly familiar with all aspects of issues before my subcommittee. In turn, he expected me to educate him so completely that the legislative process would produce results and not mere posturing.

> Few people in Congress could work as tirelessly as he did. On one occasion, he was so sick that he couldn't get off the couch; he was white and perspiring profusely with a raging fever. Yet he insisted on personally finishing our report. The more complicated the subject, the more he seemed to dig into it.[88]

Fascell was not exaggerating about Holifield's intense dedication to his duties. In August 1974, Holifield was presiding as head of the Military Operations Subcommittee over a meeting of about one dozen officials. The officials present included subcommittee members, senior Defense Department officials, and committee staff. During the meeting, Holifield suddenly was called out of the room to receive an urgent message. On his return, there were tears in his eyes, participants later recalled; he had been advised of the death of his daughter, Willa Mae, from a long bout with cancer. Accepting that there was nothing for him to do except catch the next plane to California that evening to be with his family, he returned to the business at hand, rather than cancel the meeting. The meeting continued on improvements needed in the procurement practices of the Defense Department to correct newly-uncovered abuses. Only after the meeting concluded did Chet share with his colleagues the tragic news of his daughter's death.[89]

Holifield was an excellent legislative strategist, one of the best in the House. As a prelude to developing a strategy, after each hearing or meeting Holifield would summarize the discussion on long, yellow sheets of paper, slowly and methodically, in his large handwriting. This was a practice he followed steadfastly during his 32 years in Congress. He used this process because he wanted to know personally, and then be able to explain to others, the substance of any meeting, legislation, or other matter. A careful listener in meetings, it might take him twenty minutes afterward to summarize the discussion. Once he clearly understood the matter, he developed practical steps for action. Others remained silent until Holifield had plotted out a course. On one occasion, Miles Q. Romney, a staff aide who served on Holifield's subcommittee, recalled that Chet turned to the group and said, "You've provided me with everything except a strategy to get this legislation passed!" Romney added that legislative strategy "was Chet's 'forte' and he personally outlined what needed to be done."[90]

Holifield's mastery made him one of the most influential members of the House. His modish attire and gentlemanly air belied the fact that he was a very hard-working and effective legislator. Little known in the northern California, he had nonetheless become--in the view of Leo Rennert, writing in the *Sacramento Bee, Modesto Bee*, and *Fresno Bee* in 1968--California's premier politician in Congress, with power surpassing even that of the state's two senators. "By far the most influential Californian on Capitol Hill," Rennert wrote, "is a 65-year-old Los Angeles congressman little known in Northern California who first entered the House in 1943--Chet Holifield." In view of Holifield's "more than a quarter century of seniority and close behind-the-scenes working relationships with key congressional leaders," Rennert declared that "Holifield readily qualifies as one of the towering figures of the new Congress." Rennert ticked off Chet's considerable achievements: chairman of the JCAE; "de facto head" of Government Operations, "which has power to investigate every executive agency"; chairman of the 21-member Democratic delegation from Southern California; and chairman of the entire 40-member California delegation. "Yet visible rank fails to tell the whole story," Rennert continued. "In an institution where unseen power often is decisive, Holifield packs perhaps a bigger wallop in the shadows than in the open." Clearly right on that point, Rennert also allowed that "A freshman might be awed by such concentration of power in a single legislator." But, Rennert concluded, "as an old hand, Holifield takes it all in stride."[91]

Holifield's skill in achieving legislative goals is evident during his last term. Of fourteen measures reported from his subcommittee, all but one became law. The exception was a bill to establish a Consumer Protection Agency, which passed the House but failed in the Senate due to a filibuster.[92]

Government Operations staff person Miles Romney probably provided the best overall assessment of Holifield's mastery of the legislative process. His remarks show that certain, almost indiscernible character traits are necessary:

Only a few House members have the tenacity and patience needed to really become legislative masters. Genius of this kind has little to do with one's I.Q. It's not merely an instinctive legislative understanding, either; rather, it means having your agenda, sticking to it--win or lose, learning the procedural ropes in the House, lining up your support, and then figuring out how to drive the legislation to passage. Maybe ten percent of the people elected to Congress really do get to the top as premier legislators; they are the ones who stay long enough, apply themselves to study and then learn how to use the process. Holifield devoted all his waking hours to the subject. Once he mastered it, he had few peers.[93]

6

In The Eye Of Legislative Storms

Achievement and Controversy

Although Holifield had become a master legislator by the 1960s, his achievement did not mean that he was immune to trials and tribulations. It was true that he had achieved considerable stature and prominence within Congress. His legislative skills brought him enormous respect among his congressional peers and from presidential administrations. In large part due to his practical, non-ideological outlook, he was seen as and used as a principal mediator to forge legislative agreements on controversial issues, especially related to energy policy. Not all of his activities met with warm responses, however. Indeed, from the early 1960s to the end of his career in 1974, Holifield found himself in the eye of many a legislative storm, and there was not always a bright and sunny day following each. But Holifield knew there would not always be sunshine, even though there was sure to be heat. In this regard, he followed President Truman's lead in quoting a time-honored adage: "If you can't stand the heat, get out of the kitchen."

Holifield could stand the heat, and got a lot of it in the 1960s. He became involved in several pitched battles where his legislative judgments and positions were sharply questioned and on occasion vehemently opposed. But he stood his ground and in some cases managed to bring something good out of the controversy. This was true of his contributions to the Hanford N-reactor initiative and to the interstate-federal agreement for the Pacific Electrical Intertie. Results were less conclusive in other legislative storms, including Holifield's attempt to rein in the Government Accounting Office, and his stand against minority party staffing on Capitol Hill. Yet reasonable people would have to conclude that Holifield had substantial reasons for the positions he took, whether or not they agreed with him, and most would agree that his solutions were oriented toward either practicality or the public interest.

The Hanford N-Reactor: Converting Heat to Electricity

From 1944 to 1962, most of the American public were unaware that vast amounts of waste heat from eight nuclear reactors were being absorbed by the Columbia River at Hanford, Washington. Hanford had been a top-secret site during World War II. It was one of the key facilities for the Manhattan Project, the super-secret weapons project which developed the atomic bomb. These Hanford reactors were solely used for producing weapons-grade plutonium. After World War II, these facilities continued to expand to help rebuild the nation's weapons arsenal as the Cold War developed.

That so much heat from the reactors' cooling water was wasted in the Columbia would probably have drawn a collective yawn from Americans in the 1940s and 1950s. The fact that its immense heat energy was being wasted would have mattered little to most, as would heat rejected from other sources such as the drains in bath tubs, and heat from automobile and aircraft engines. Not so for a poor farm boy from Arkansas like Chet Holifield. "Waste not, want not" had been drilled into him from an early age. Lacking shoes in summer, he learned as a boy not to scuff his boots in winter. Although generous to a fault with his own personal time and money, he disliked waste of any kind, especially of the magnitude occurring at Hanford.[1]

From his JCAE perspective, Holifield had several reasons for advocating development of a dual-purpose (plutonium *and* electricity production) reactor. He knew that steam turbines added to such plants could produce electricity using the heat from the reactors. Testing such a concept seemed appropriate. Another reason was that in the event of a moratorium on plutonium production, a dual-purpose reactor could continue to be operated to produce electricity and, therefore, would be available for plutonium production if necessary. Holifield also knew that the Russians were building dual-purpose reactors. The dual-purpose reactor did have its liabilities, of course. Holifield was aware that relatively high steam temperatures are needed to produce electricity efficiently and that some plutonium production would have to be compromised to have a single reactor serve both needs.[2]

The dilemma at Hanford was not only one of design and cost for converting a plutonium-production reactor to power production. At stake was a hotly-contested issue: should the federal government be involved in the production of thermal power? All across the U.S., the federal government and state and municipal utilities were producing hydroelectric power. The Tennessee Valley Authority (TVA), created in 1933 as a part of Roosevelt's New Deal, was producing thermal as well as hydroelectric power by burning coal. TVA was not popular with businesses. Private utilities feared its encroachment on their service areas and viewed TVA as the opening wedge for a socialized power system. The utilities fought against every TVA expansion attempt, and warned Congress continually to reduce TVA's size or maintain it at current levels. Private utilities also reasoned that if a dual-purpose reactor were built at Hanford, a new TVA-type power facility would operate in the West, and would provide another opening wedge in hastening the end of private power.[3]

The Hanford question was one of a series of public versus private power confrontations in the 1950s. In 1953, the Eisenhower administration fired perhaps the opening shot in the overall conflict through its heavy-handedness in insisting that the Atomic Energy Act of 1946 be amended. Using their 1953-1954 majority in Congress, the Republicans forced through the Atomic Energy Act of 1954, greatly expanding the role of private business in atomic energy development. Holifield complained to no avail of the Republican "give-away" of the multi-billion-dollar enterprise to business interests, which he believed were ill-equipped to accept such a sensitive responsibility.[4]

When industry did not respond immediately to develop atomic power under the new act, Holifield became the primary House sponsor in 1956 of a Democratic alternative. The so-called Gore-Holifield bill called for an expanded government program of reactor R&D and construction at isolated government sites. Under intense Republican opposition, the bill did not pass, but Holifield got piecemeal authorizations over the next couple of years for additional government research on various reactor types, including the dual-purpose reactor. He was anxious to develop the new reactors ahead of the Russians. In 1958, together with Republican JCAE leader Craig Hosmer (R-California), he proposed and Congress approved construction of a dual-purpose reactor at Hanford. The reactor, also known as the New Production Reactor or N-reactor, was thus born in a period of fierce conflicts.[5]

When President Kennedy proposed in 1961 that a power-generating facility be added to the N-reactor, the battle was on again in earnest. While Senators Henry Jackson (D-Washington) and Clinton Anderson (D-New Mexico) encountered little difficulty in obtaining Senate approval, the N-reactor's opponents, including private utilities and most Republicans in the House, were adamant that the proposed steam plant was unacceptable because it would put the AEC in the power business. Even some Democrats, especially those from coal regions, fought against the N-reactor because they feared it would hurt the coal industry. Northeast congressmen feared that cheaper West Coast power would induce industries to head west. Others opposed it on technical grounds; they believed a dual-purpose reactor was not good for power production alone nor a good model for more widespread use.[6]

Holifield attempted to reason with the opposition by pointing out, first and foremost, that most Russian reactors were dual-purpose, which gave the Russians not only the technological lead, but a propaganda boon by demonstrating Soviet commitment to peaceful applications. He also warned that failure to create dual-purpose reactors could leave the nation with billions of dollars of idle plants if a future disarmament agreement obviated the need for producing plutonium. There was also the practical need for more power in the rapidly growing Pacific Northwest. The area needed this new power because coal was unavailable and there was no room for more hydroelectric plants on its rivers. He also noted that one-half of the power would go through the Bonneville Power Administration (BPA) to private utilities. Thus, the plant posed no competitive threat. Finally, he lamented the waste of this heat source, which was intolerable to him personally.[7]

The N-reactor's opponents were unmoved by Holifield's reasoning. They had opposed the N-reactor and saw no reason to support a steam plant for it. Republicans, including Eisenhower, were determined to safeguard private enterprise against the "forces of socialism" at any price. Even Hosmer, frequently Chet's ally, joined the opposition, contending that it was unclear whether the government would get a proper return on the $95 million cost. Parliamentary wrangling became intense in the House. James Van Zandt (R-Pennsylvania) led the opposition, and won adoption of an unprecedented motion in 1961 to instruct House conferees how to vote in their conference with the Senate on a compromise bill. Van Zandt's motion incensed Holifield, who warned to no avail that it was a dangerous precedent, since such a motion had never passed the House in his two decades of service.[8]

The fight over the N-reactor was probably one of the most frustrating disputes of Holifield's career. His proposal was defeated a total of seven times before it finally passed in greatly-amended form. In 1961 alone, the House rejected it three different times by very large margins. The House was the critical vote on Hanford, since Anderson and Jackson had put the Senate firmly in Holifield's camp. In view of the many rebuffs, Chet knew that it would be pointless to bring up the same proposal in 1962. He seemed willing to accept the House's decision and let the matter rest, at least for awhile.[9]

Unbeknownst to Holifield, a compromise proposal was in the making. Realizing that Holifield and other N-reactor supporters had done all they could, sixteen public utilities in the Pacific Northwest joined together to develop a new proposal. Charles F. Luce, head of BPA, was the primary mover, along with others such as Byron Price from Eugene, Oregon, and Eugene Star from BPA. The new idea was to privately finance construction of the steam plant through the sale of bonds, get an agreement with the AEC for purchase of the steam, and make the power available through BPA. The utilities, organized as the Washington Public Power Supply System (WPPSS), also proposed to make one-half of the power available on a nondiscriminatory basis to private utilities. Under the arrangement, the government would not have to spend the $95 million for the steam plant, and would, moreover, receive an estimated net benefit of $125 million over the plant's life from purchase of the steam, at rates to be set by the Federal Power Commission.[10]

The WPPSS believed it had devised an acceptable plan, and began discussions with the AEC. Holifield was kept abreast of their dealings, but he did not become involved until the General Accounting Office informed the AEC that congressional authorization would be necessary for any contract with WPPSS. Holifield then announced he would hold hearings on the WPPSS proposal and what congressional action would be necessary.[11]

"Holifield jumped somewhat reluctantly into this final battle," according to Alex Radin, former long-term head of the American Public Power Association (APPA). "He had borne the brunt of the legislative struggle, and the several previous defeats in 1961 left him dispirited." When Holifield was informed that the new initiative could not be passed without his enthusiastic backing, he "agreed to give it one more try, and pitched into the fray." His appetite was further whetted when Van Zandt announced plans to kill the Hanford proposal once and for all. Holifield was determined not to let that happen.[12]

Holifield's first Hanford battle in 1962 was not encouraging. His admonition that the N-reactor's steam could be wasted or used to the government's benefit was no match for Van Zandt's charges that the 1962 proposal was essentially the same as the 1961 plan. The House rejected the 1962 proposal by approximately the same margin as the 1961 proposal.[13]

Although the House was unmoved, it was clear to Holifield that the WPPSS plan still had a chance because of a new groundswell of support. Support from the local area chambers of commerce, utilities, and several newspapers, particularly the small *Tri-City Herald* published by Glenn C. Lee, was soon followed by national organizations and newspapers. The new proposal even intrigued Hosmer. He now believed that the WPPSS plan would benefit everyone. As he told his colleagues, "last year the money was being put up by the federal taxpayers." The 1961 proposal had "created a large block of federal power and the assumption of this large expenditure and heavy risks by the taxpayers for no gain." Hosmer was now willing to let WPPSS build the steam plant, since the government would make a profit from waste steam sales. He influenced many wary, conservative legislators. Since Hosmer was viewed on both sides of the aisle as a nuclear authority, his switch indicated to many congressmen that a formula for compromise had been found.[14]

In addition to Hosmer, Holifield gained the votes of every Republican JCAE member except Van Zandt. This proved to be a great boon when he marshaled his forces for the next battle. With Van Zandt isolated on the JCAE, House members began to get a clearer picture of the plan. But Holifield left nothing to chance; he sent out extensive literature, carefully explaining the differences between the 1961 and 1962 plans and including the major documents his committee had amassed. Holifield also had many of the documents reprinted in the *Record*, along with a repeat of his arguments.[15]

Van Zandt's and other advocates' unyielding opposition proved worrisome to Holifield as he strove to erect a legislative strategy. He was plainly mystified at the reaction of the business interests. After all, the nation's nuclear system had been built with taxpayers' money, from which private industry had benefitted. Private utilities could also benefit from the WPPSS proposal. Holifield pondered long and hard over a solution, and ultimately came up with what he believed was the answer. He had observed previously that a JCAE attorney, George Norris, had invariably inserted an "escape clause" in legislation to give administrators some leeway. "Why shouldn't the president have the same authority?" Chet thought, as he awoke in the middle of the night, mulling over the problem. It made no sense to give leeway to lesser public officials and not to the president under whom they served.[16]

For Jack Newman, the JCAE's then-youthful counsel, Holifield's solution at first seemed preposterous. The legislation had gone to the floor previously in that session as well as in other sessions, and had been soundly rejected. "Most legislators," Newman remarked, "bring legislation forward once during a session and drop it if it's defeated. Yet here was Holifield still plunging ahead in the same Congress." Newman remembered the Sunday call to give him the new wording which Holifield enthusiastically believed would break the deadlock. Grabbing pen and paper, Newman wrote down Holifield's wording and agreed to turn it into a legally-acceptable amendment. "At that stage, no one in the Capitol thought the legislation would pass," Newman added, "but Chet knew the temper of the House and the ways to get action."[17]

In 1962, Holifield thus saw a new legislative opening. He used Van Zandt's own amendment, including all of Van Zandt's prohibitive language dating back to 1958. Holifield merely inserted a short clause which, in effect, wiped out the purposes of Van Zandt's initiative, essentially allowing a "presidential decision" to override Van Zandt's prohibitions if the president found it to be in the national interest! Holifield did not call attention to this wording, which was lost in the voluminous printed language of the amendment.[18]

Holifield's strategy did not end here. He used every opportunity to praise Van Zandt's sterling record in war, in peace, and in the Congress. Holifield sensed that Van Zandt would have less success in opposing a decision made in the national interest by the president. The Hanford issue was still confusing when Holifield introduced his amendment as part of the AEC authorization bill. He, along with Hosmer and the JCAE Republicans, thus rallied around the compromise and persuaded the House to vote down Van Zandt's renewed effort to instruct conferees. Most members were satisfied that the compromise was a solution to a very wearing three-year battle.[19]

When the Hanford legislation was considered by the Senate, it went through still other changes. The House-Senate conference report contained further language to assure that power production would not receive priority over plutonium production. Since weapons stockpile needs were already known, this was not a problem. Van Zandt staged a last-ditch effort to ward off the proposal, but to no avail. As Holifield had foreseen, his provision, modified by the conferees, left the door open for the presidential decision that ensued. President Kennedy responded by finding that adding the steam plant at Hanford was in the national interest. Construction began almost immediately through the use of $125 million in revenue bonds, and was completed in late 1966. Through much of the 1970s, the N-reactor remained the largest dual-purpose reactor in the world, and supplied a significant amount of electricity for Northwest residents. When plutonium production was suspended in 1971, as Holifield had foreseen, the N-reactor continued to produce electricity until February, 1988, when it was placed on cold standby.[20]

According to Morgan Dubrow, then manager for BPA, "Chet Holifield stood out in this legislative melee because he had a long-range, but a practical, vision of an energy future for the Pacific Northwest and was willing to put his neck on the political block." Dubrow noted that "The main problem with BPA then was that it provided large amounts of secondary, unfirm power (sold at low prices), but was weak on responding to firm power commitments." Due to the uneven flow of the Columbia River system, its dams were unable to guarantee an adequate flow of "firm" electricity when and where required. Dubrow explained that "Once the power supply was firm, BPA received higher prices." Dubrow was emphatic that "Chet's persistence enabled this legislation to pass." He was "liked by both Republicans and Democrats . . . [and] had absolutely no personal political stake in the outcome; he saw a concept and made it work."[21]

The Pacific Intertie

Holifield scarcely had time to bask in the sunlight of his hard-won Hanford victory when he became involved unexpectedly in July 1964 in another critical power issue. The issue was creation of the Pacific Electric Intertie, or Northwest-Southwest Intertie, as it was also known. The intertie was a proposed electrical transmission linkage among the states of Washington, Oregon, California, Nevada, and Arizona, using the hydroelectric power of the BPA's dams as the source. The idea for an intertie was sound, and disarmingly simple: transmit excess power created by BPA to other states with growing power needs, thereby benefitting both. Anytime, day or night, excess energy was available in the Pacific Northwest, often on an intermittent basis. Instead of being dumped, this surplus power could be used in the Southwest by shutting down thermal plants utilizing high-cost, low-sulfur fuels.

Implementation of the intertie idea, simple on paper, was far from simple in reality. Completing this venture meant resolving long-term and sharply-conflicting claims and counterclaims over rights to water and electricity among a plethora of organizations and agencies. There were international disputes to settle between the U.S. and Canada, and agreements to work out among the western state governments and federal agencies. Conflicts also had to be resolved with municipally-owned and private utilities whose distribution areas would be affected by the new high-voltage intertie lines to be built. Local utilities also feared any intrusions--public or private--into their territories.[22]

Holifield hardly expected to be involved in working out an agreement for an intertie. This proposal, after all, did not involve nuclear power, and was within the preserve of committees other than his. But he agreed to serve as chairman of an ad hoc committee on the project at the request of his close friend, President Johnson. Holifield's intense work on this ad hoc committee brought about the agreement, which had been sought for many years. In forging the agreement, Chet displayed not only attention to details, perseverance, and ability to work with people of many persuasions, but also the keen legislative skills he had developed in two decades in Congress.

The need for a Northwest-Southwest intertie arose after World War II. During the war, an aluminum production plant using large amounts of electricity was built at the Dalles River Dam in Oregon. BPA spent heavily to meet this need. At war's end, this and other defense plants fed by BPA shut down. BPA found itself with expensive power plants to operate, not enough customers, and problems in meeting its bonded indebtedness. Fortunately, by 1945, it became apparent that the rapidly-growing population of California would require much more electricity. Hydroelectric power was much cheaper than power produced from fossil fuels. As a consequence, both California and BPA determined that California's use of cheaper BPA power would be helpful to both. The chief stumbling blocks were California's private power companies, which resisted distribution of BPA power through their areas. The dispute on the intertie thus had been simmering, with various flash points, since 1961, with little prospect for agreement in sight.[23]

Thankfully, for those who advocated the intertie, there was an important precedent for transmitting excess power interstate from low-population regions to highly populated areas. It was the federally financed Hoover Dam (then Boulder Dam), which was built in sparsely populated Arizona on the Colorado River, which ran through sparsely populated Nevada and also bordered rapidly growing California, where the population was exploding. After years of fighting, these three neighboring states agreed to share Arizona's and Nevada's overabundance of water and electrical power. The resulting interstate-federal agreement included non-federal participation by California's Metropolitan Water District, a state-authorized, bond-issuing entity with a huge water aqueduct from Lake Meade to Los Angeles and San Diego. Distributive power lines also were funded by non-federal agencies.[24]

What made the intertie issue ripe for agreement in the 1960s was the subtle, but decisive, victory of the public power philosophy at the national level, a victory in which Holifield participated. In 1961, President Kennedy helped Holifield in championing the N-reactor proposal. The president also appointed Stewart Udall as Secretary of the Interior, Holifield's former House colleague and a firm supporter of Hoover Dam and other federal irrigation projects. With his new jurisdiction over all federal hydroelectric power production facilities, Udall was now in a position to make himself felt.[25]

Another important factor was the new man in the White House in 1963. "LBJ" was a personal friend of Chet. In fact, Holifield had supported Johnson over Kennedy in the election of 1960. More so than Kennedy, Johnson believed in vigorous federal action to meet local needs. LBJ's "Great Society" reforms mirrored this view, as would his intertie efforts.[26]

As Holifield remembered it, in July 1964 several northern California Democratic congressmen, including Harold Johnson, Bernie Sisk, and John Moss, visited Holifield and asked him to join them in a meeting with Johnson and Udall. They wanted help in untangling the numerous snags that prevented creation of the intertie. The congressmen hoped that Holifield's friendship with Johnson and Udall would help them get action.

At the meeting, Holifield was a silent observer as the three congressmen made their case. The discussions in the Oval Office went back and forth. According to Holifield, Johnson discovered that there were disagreements both among the congressmen and between them and Udall. Holifield recalled that Johnson suddenly interrupted the discussion and said: "You're all friends of mine. But you apparently have different viewpoints. If you think I am going to get in a position of being shot down by both sides, you are mistaken." Then, turning to Holifield, the president pointed his finger at him and said: "Chet, I am appointing you as chairman of an ad hoc committee composed of all interested senators and representatives and other involved entities. Get everybody together and develop a unified position by all of the parties. I want you to report back to me in 30 days." Johnson added for emphasis: "Let me know if there is a unified position. If not, I want you to report back to me and tell me *why* and *who* is responsible for any lack of unity."[27]

Startled by Johnson's forceful request, Holifield recalled telling Johnson: "Mr. President, I'm not an expert in this field. My district has long ago solved its public versus private power problems." Johnson was sure his statement was true, but "you have had a lot of experience in holding hearings and negotiating compromises, and I have confidence in you." As far as Holifield was concerned, that ended the matter. When any president asked something, for him it was a command, so he responded: "Mr. President, I'll do my best."

Once Johnson had Holifield's full assent, Johnson explained to Holifield that the matter was urgent if Congress were to consider the overall agreement before it adjourned. The imminent adjournment is why Johnson wanted Holifield to report back in 30 days. While Johnson showed his full support for Chet's month of heavy work ahead, the president left him with one admonition: "Remember the budget is 'locked up' for the coming year, 1965. Don't ask for any money [for the transmission lines] until fiscal year 1966."[28]

Typical of his work habits, Holifield went all out to do a thorough job. After thorough study, he scheduled hearings to amass additional data. His ad hoc committee meetings, which included informal consultations as well as testimony, were held in a public hearing room on the Senate side of the Capitol. Because this committee was created by the president rather than by Congress, it had no recording secretaries to take down the proceedings. Still, there was substantial attendance by House and Senate members and the affected utilities. With Holifield forcefully urging compromise, House and Senate members from the five states solved their major disagreements.[29]

Problems in California were somewhat more difficult to resolve. The major problem was that the utilities had been purchasing constant megawatt power from BPA. This power was cheaper than they could generate themselves. The purchasers had avoided the capital costs of building their own plants, so they were not ready to change their system overnight, especially when change meant higher costs and intrusions into their distribution areas. Holifield, was able, however, to allay most fears and erect a workable agreement.

By the last week of July, Holifield had narrowed the major obstacles down to two. First was the funding for transmission line construction. He knew the government would have to share in these costs. Johnson's instruction not to propose any more funding for fiscal year 1965 loomed as a large limitation on sewing up an agreement and was always at the back of Holifield's mind. Once again, Chet suddenly woke up one night with a solution. He recalled an earlier $35 million federal budget authorization for part of San Francisco's network of federal-state freeways. In working on this project, he had found that a prior budget authorization which for any reason was unused could be used elsewhere for a similar purpose if approved by the president, the affected executive department, and the House Committee on Appropriations. Using this approach, Holifield had successfully obtained funds for the Century Boulevard freeway link in Los Angeles. He now had a funding strategy: was there any unused funding which had been intended for a similar purpose?[30]

The next morning, Holifield quickly found what he wanted. The intertie called for the government to fund a transmission line from the BPA system south across the state of Oregon to the Pacific Gas and Electric Company's (PG&E's) Round Mountain transmission center, not far inside the California-Oregon border. In the Hoover Dam model, Holifield found authorizations for three transmission lines to Southern California. The third line was never constructed because of decline in the water flow of the Colorado River!

Elated, Holifield called Udall and informed him of the discovery, explaining the possibilities for using the third line's funding for the intertie. Udall seemed excited, and immediately got Interior's lawyers to investigate. In a few hours, Udall called Holifield to say that his lawyers had found the third line's funding authorization, approximately $60 million, sufficient to build the transmission line. Approvals by the Interior Secretary, the president, and the House Appropriations Committee were easy to obtain since Chet began with Udall and Johnson already in his court. The transmission line could be built without any funding delays, an important bargaining chip in the negotiations.[31]

Only one dilemma remained: PG&E's resistance. For decades, PG&E had fiercely fought intrusions into its distribution area. The utility did have interchange agreements with Southern California Edison and San Diego Light and Power Company. The three utilities' service areas extended from northern California south almost the entire length of California's coast.

Holifield felt he needed to meet the senior executive of the company, Robert Gerdes, who had been briefed on Holifield's hearings through a Washington aide, Herman Kruse. Since he had never met Gerdes, Holifield asked his colleague Bernie Sisk to come to his office and introduce Gerdes over the phone. Gerdes then took a night flight to meet with Holifield the next morning.[32] Holifield later recalled the gist of his comments to Gerdes:

> Mr. Gerdes, I'm aware of the opposition by your company to a public transmission line intruding into its distributive area to compete for customers. But in this case, the federal transmission line will bring cheap kilowatts to the PG&E to distribute to its own customers. The power will be cheaper than your company can generate in plants demanding large-scale capital investment. It will provide needed additional source power both for private, investor-owned electric utilities such as PG&E, Southern California Edison, and public power companies like the Sacramento Utility District, and the Los Angeles Department of Water and Power. [33]

Holifield's meeting with Gerdes lasted for about 40 minutes, with Holifield explaining the main features of the intertie and underlining for Gerdes the urgency of obtaining agreement. Afterwards, Gerdes inquired: "If we should agree to the tentative agreement you have outlined, what additional requests will be made, other than the present tentative accord?" Cautious as always, Holifield replied that he could not answer that question. Instead, he invited Gerdes to attend the ad hoc committee meeting that afternoon so that they might together report on their morning meeting and pose Gerdes' question to the northern California members. Holifield indicated he would poll each legislator individually so that Gerdes could make his decision and give answers publicly on the basis of each legislator's views.[34]

The afternoon meeting turned out to be the concluding session of the ad hoc committee. Holifield made a brief statement on progress and then introduced Gerdes. Holifield put Gerdes' question to the congressional members, asking each to respond personally. They were unanimous in stating that they were satisfied with the compromise agreement and would not ask for any new or additional concessions. For his part, Gerdes stated that on the basis of the members' answers, he would recommend favorable action to

PG&E's board of directors and urge them to direct their lawyers to convene with counsel of the other companies and public entities to draw up the legal documents necessary to effect the intertie agreement.[35]

After the meeting with Gerdes, a triumphant Holifield was able to report to Johnson that agreement had been reached on the intertie. Dozens of state and national leaders, including Johnson and Udall, publicly praised Holifield for a job well done. They recognized that Holifield had been instrumental in turning a long-held dream for the Northwest and California into a practical reality. Within a four-month period, the intertie became a legal reality. Attention was then directed to completing the transmission lines. Physically, the intertie was to be made up of two alternating-current (AC) lines delivering a total constant capacity of 2500 megawatts, plus a direct-current (DC) line with a constant capacity of 1560 megawatts, stretching 800 miles from the Dalles River Dam in Oregon to the Los Angeles Department of Water and Power's transmission center near Sylmar, California. The lines were completed in two years, allowing formal operations to begin in 1969.[36]

Engineers consider the Pacific Intertie to be one of the greatest electrical transmission achievements of the twentieth century. In 1969, this was the longest distance over which commercial electrical transmission had ever extended in the U.S. and the largest volume that long-distance transmission had ever attained on the planet. The DC line, the longest in the world at the time, was developed on the theory that transmission of DC would be more energy efficient than AC. Since DC incurs a transmission loss of about 5 percent whereas AC's loss is about 8 percent, this 3 percent saving, amounting to millions of dollars per year, justified the costs of the DC line. Under the intertie agreement, the non-federal agencies contributed the cost of the DC transmission equipment to accept the AC at the Dalles River generators and transmit it to the Sylmar center. The DC line was constructed over difficult terrain despite skeptics who argued that the technology would not work.[37]

In 1964, a congressional report forecast benefits to the Northwest at $1 billion over the anticipated 50-year life of the intertie. Due to much higher oil prices after the 1973 Arab Oil Embargo, benefits increased dramatically. California consumers enjoyed obtaining a substantial portion of their electricity at the cost of about one cent per kilowatt hour, instead of the minimum of five cents they would have had to pay for electricity generated by coal, oil, or nuclear power. Pacific Northwest consumers also benefitted, but less so due to lower population growth and WPPSS nuclear plant costs.[38]

Holifield rightfully considered the breaking of the deadlock on the intertie as a major highlight of his career. However he is judged, it is clear that he found himself playing a central role in a very important political dilemma that was solved, thus opening up new sources of power in the West and bringing together private and public power in a form long presumed impossible.

The General Accounting Office (GAO) Controversy

In the Hanford and intertie struggles, Holifield found himself not only winning, but coming out on the side of the angels politically.   In these controversies, he was the mediator who welded together conflicting claims to produce an overall consensus beneficial to the participants, the public, and the government.   These results did not benefit him in his own district, but they increased his stature as a legislative master in the House.

The GAO controversy, which erupted in 1965, proved to be a legislative storm of a different kind.   It caused hard feelings against Holifield and gave rise to questions about the impartiality of his legislative judgment.   Even some of his colleagues on his Military Operations Subcommittee deserted his positions.   Holifield, however, remained firm in his convictions.   He had substantial reasons for his actions, and in this case the reasons involved civil liberties, a sensitive subject with him from his earliest days in Congress.

Holifield launched the controversy as chairman of the Military Operations Subcommittee.   In 1965 during oversight hearings, he chastised the GAO for some of its determinations and auditing practices.   His major objection was the GAO's practice of widely publicizing the names of private companies and individuals as wrongdoers without even the most rudimentary due process of affording the employers and individuals an opportunity to reply before airing the charges in public.   He was especially concerned because, as he pointed out, the GAO's audits were the only ones given press release prominence, even though other agencies also referred findings to the Justice Department for action.   "In most cases," Holifield charged, "the subcommittee was given to understand [that] the Justice Department found insufficient evidence or insufficient grounds upon which to prosecute."[39]   He implied that the GAO was rushing to judgment without sufficient legal justification.

Holifield's unexpected GAO criticisms and subsequent subcommittee report created a furor on Capitol Hill.   What led to his actions became a matter of press and political speculation.   Some congressmen charged that Holifield was unwisely seeking to muzzle the GAO, which was acting responsibly by issuing public reports on alleged wrongdoing by federal contractors.   Other critics complained that this congressional wrist-slapping was, in effect, a power grab by the Pentagon and a demotion of the GAO itself, approved, at least implicitly, by the full Committee on Government Operations.[40]

Sensitivity about the Pentagon was particularly intense during 1965, with the Vietnam War then in progress.   Some legislators, even some subcommittee members, considered Holifield's chief aide, Herbert Roback, "too sympathetic to the Pentagon."   Having survived and then escaped German imprisonment in World War II, Roback had been rescued by U.S. troops after he had lived for awhile on frozen vegetables which he dug up by hand.   Roback thus had sound personal cause to trust the military. Legislators hostile to the Vietnam conflict disliked Roback's attitudes, but Roback was not singled out. Holifield's detractors suggested that Holifield was out to protect California's defense and aerospace industries, a charge that angered Holifield.[41]

Holifield was obviously stung by the outcry and was also dismayed that his subcommittee had received undesirable notoriety. His critics failed to see an important historical thread that ran through his and Roback's thinking. Although neither were lawyers, they both had been and still were staunch civil libertarians. As such, they objected to the penchant of some governmental agencies to go off half-cocked after some alleged malfeasance, whether corporate or individual. Holifield had always contended that the subpoena power of Government Operations should be used only in a limited way. He feared that some legislators would use any instrument at their disposal to curb what they perceived as wrongdoing. Their intentions might be laudable, but the end result could be dangerous to the rights of individuals.[42]

When the subcommittee's findings were in draft form, James A. Lanigan, associate counsel for Government Operations, read the galley proofs. His first impression was that "as the first draft stood, the report would have had a devastating impact on the GAO." So Lanigan went to Chairman Dawson, who referred him to Porter Hardy, a member of the subcommittee and also of the Armed Services Committee. Hardy agreed that the report would harm the GAO and had Lanigan send it to the GAO for review; thus, the GAO "saw it before Chairman Dawson returned it to the subcommittee for approval." As Lanigan explained, "Ordinarily, we don't let an agency see such a draft before it was published, but in this case Frank Weitzel and Bob Keller of the GAO met with me and gave us their comments." There was no way to stop the GAO report, but it was toned down. "And the GAO did say," Lanigan noted, "they'd stop pillorying individuals in public, a tactic that Holifield believed was an infringement on their rights."[43]

Holifield proved to be even-handed in his opening statement on the GAO report. He noted that although the GAO, as an arm of Congress, performed "necessary and useful work in pinpointing illegal, improper, or unnecessary expenditures," his hearings "had demonstrated that at the same time it must be recognized that the audited agencies and GAO are not always in agreement." Contractors, Holifield continued, "often believe the GAO reports invade their privacy" and "[the reports] place the companies in a derogatory position which they believe is unjustified." Chet felt that a particular problem area was that GAO judgments that prices charged were too high were often contested by the defense agencies as well as the contractors. These agencies often had been "unwilling or unable to effect recovery because agency officials believed there was no basis in law or equity to effect such recoveries."[44]

As a result of his subcommittee hearings, Holifield announced in his report that the GAO had agreed to improve its handling of defense contract audits. First and foremost, in the interest of fairness, the GAO would discontinue "disclosing the names of individuals immediately responsible for actions or operations under criticism and no longer make public any recommendations for disciplinary or other personnel actions." Perhaps as important, the names of contractors would be omitted from the titles of reports, thereby not automatically subjecting businesses, individuals, and universities to public attacks on their reputations before final decisions were made by the defense agencies involved. Defense agencies and contractors would also be afforded an opportunity to attach their comments on draft GAO reports as appendices. Holifield also recommended other improvements. The "style, format, and contents of its reports referenced to Congress" would be changed in order not to "overstate findings in their negative aspect," i.e., the reports would become more businesslike in tone. The GAO would also delve more deeply in the future into the "basic cause of repeated deficiencies," thereby reducing the volume, but increasing the value, of its reports. GAO would also provide more effective safeguards over "confidential business data" and assure better legal review of policy issues which arise in audits. Finally, the GAO would also not uniformly recommend "voluntary refunds by contractors," except under limited circumstances where the facts clearly warranted such a step.[45]

Within the subcommittee, dissent to Holifield's recommendations was forceful. The tone of the dissent was set by Jack Brooks (D-Texas), who would succeed Holifield as chairman in 1975. Brooks declared that "many of the recommendations contained in the report, in my opinion, will deter rather than encourage improvement in GAO audit procedures." The report, Brooks felt, "contains little discussion, cites only three examples, and contains no evaluation or classification of deficiencies found in specific GAO audit reports." Moreover, "the testimony did not adversely reflect upon GAO audit procedures or the action the GAO took." Overall, Brooks believed that "The defense industry, as well as all government agencies over which GAO has audit jurisdiction, in evaluating this report, may well react in a manner adverse to the interests of the government." Republican members, including Robert Dole (R-Kansas) and Donald Rumsfeld (R-Illinois), contended that while the report was sound overall, certain aspects would derogate "from the people's right to know." They disassociated themselves from those portions.[46]

Holifield chose to be conciliatory toward the GAO and amicable to his critics. In appending other views to the report, he emphasized the value of the proceedings, granting that the inquiry had not been exhaustive:

> The value of the inquiry has been attested to by all parties affected, including the GAO, and the beneficial results reflected and summarized in this report. As we made plain in the body of the report, this is in the nature of a progress report and not an analysis of each and every case.

A few points are made in the Acting Comptroller General's behalf and in the report with respect to information to be made available to the press. These changes relate to (1) the announcement in the established report of the referral of a case to the Justice Department in the naming of individual contracting officers by the GAO as being responsible for negligence or malfeasance; and (2) the handling of confidential business data. I believe in a free press and open debate of public transactions, and I do not believe that this report on the changed procedures in the GAO transgresses these principles.[47]

Holifield's reference to the Acting Comptroller General showed the depth of the crisis experienced within the GAO over Holifield's report. As the GAO prepared to respond to the findings, Comptroller General Campbell resigned, reportedly due to "ill health." An Eisenhower appointee, Campbell had been business manager of Columbia University where Eisenhower was president. Once elected, "Ike" had brought Campbell to Washington, appointing him as an AEC commissioner. Shortly thereafter Campbell resigned to accept the post of Comptroller General. While at the AEC, Campbell supported the Dixon-Yates contract and voted with Chairman Lewis Strauss against the three Democratic commissioners. Campbell's relationship to the Dixon-Yates contract undoubtedly must have crossed Chet's mind when Campbell crossed Holifield's path again, this time in his position as Comptroller General.[48]

Elmer B. Staats Becomes the New Comptroller General

With Campbell's resignation, President Johnson named Elmer B. Staats, then Deputy Director of the Bureau of the Budget, as the new Comptroller General. Staats realized that he was stepping into a potential mine field; when the GAO asked him to sign its reply to the subcommittee's conclusions, Staats declined on the grounds that he was unfamiliar with the issues. Visiting Holifield, he explained that he "had not had an opportunity to review the committee's hearings carefully, and would, therefore, reserve judgment on the letter which had been filed with the committee by the acting Comptroller General, Frank Weitzel." However, Staats "was willing to give the committee's recommendations full consideration," and indicated that he would be willing to meet with Holifield "from time to time as any steps are taken to modify the GAO's procedures in audits of the Defense Department."[49]

Staats proved to be a wise choice for Comptroller General. He served for fifteen years, working closely with Holifield for the rest of Holifield's tenure. "I had great confidence in Chet," Staats recalled, "and knew that he was committed to keeping the GAO as an independent agency in keeping with its long-standing tradition of nonpartisanship and objectivity. We both recognized that credibility was one of GAO's greatest assets . . . ." Staats did not believe that Holifield was trying to protect California's aerospace and defense industries. As Staats saw it, "Chet was concerned with the method by which the GAO conducted its audits, the tone of its reports, and the titles of its reports rather than the extent to which GAO placed priority on auditing of the Defense Department or defense contractors." In fact, Staats informed Holifield without incident shortly after his appointment that he was increasing the amount of GAO resources assigned to defense audits![50]

Holifield found Staats to be a fellow traveler on many issues. Staats fully agreed with Holifield, for example, that "the GAO had overstepped its bounds in terms of the 'headline' type titles which it placed on its reports." Staats observed that "these [titles] seemed to be more nearly designed to attract publicity than to reflect the substance of the report." The new Comptroller General believed that "we would not seek--or need--publicity to be effective." Staats thus ensured that future titles to GAO reports would be "designed to be descriptive, but not accusatory of the actions of the agencies." As Holifield had already experienced, Staats similarly found it difficult, but not impossible, to remain objective during the Vietnam War era when "tempers were short and strong passions and emotions were present on all sides." On the one hand, "attention was heightened with respect to GAO reports as to whether our reports were sufficiently critical," and on the other, some congressmen and journalists "wanted the GAO to rip into the Defense Department and contract firms, pillorying them in public even when the facts did not support doing this." Staats was adept at steering a middle course, although he allowed that "There was simply no way to avoid our work from becoming involved in the political controversy surrounding the Vietnam War."[51]

Another major factor cementing the Holifield-Staats relationship was Staats' willingness to meet the needs of Congress. In his first meeting with Holifield, Staats said that he was aware "of certain views that the GAO's work needed to be made more relevant to congressional needs and interests," and he intended "to see what I could do to meet this concern in line with . . . the legislation [establishing the GAO]." Staats was pleased that by the end of his tenure "the share of GAO's effort initiated by Congress had increased from 8 percent to approximately 45 percent." Staats was "satisfied that this had been done without losing any of GAO's independence."[52]

With the appointment of Staats, the controversy surrounding the GAO began to diminish and was soon gone. Holifield had done what he thought was best, sticking to his guns because he was genuinely concerned with civil liberties, particularly those of individuals. Operating from a philosophy of constitutional conservatism, Holifield was invariably conscious of the need to protect such rights. He was simply ultra-cautious when it came to the question of federal powers invading individual rights or privacy. That perspective was one from which he rarely, if ever, departed.

The other reasons attributed to Holifield's attack on the GAO hurt Holifield and, moreover, had little truth to them. It was true that Holifield did not like Campbell's administration of the GAO. Also, his concern for

California probably intruded into his judgment at some point, and his support for Vietnam made him a natural adversary with some anti-Pentagon viewpoints.[53] Protecting the Pentagon, however, probably never entered his mind. Subcommittee member Dante Fascell (D-Florida), also chairman of the House Foreign Affairs Committee, thought that such a view was ludicrous:

> During the Eisenhower years, his [Holifield's] pursuit of defense spending questions was unceasing. He was determined to streamline defense operational and contracting procedures and impose standardization and cataloging of materials and resources on military purchasing.

> Chet's unflinching insistence on standardizing and cataloging military procurement and supplies was to have a long-range payoff. Even today, many of the changes he instituted 30 years ago influence the way the military does business.

> Chet knew that the Defense Department was too vast an enterprise for Congress to keep on top of all its operations. So he went after individual contractors to search for wrongdoing. His idea was to hold them up as an example. We once spent two years getting to the bottom of one contract until we could expose the wrongdoing involved.

> There's only one way to describe his attitude toward the Defense Department: he was not a "watchdog" on Government Operations, but a ferocious "bulldog." The military's job is to defend the country, he said, but the role of Congress is to worry about costs to the taxpayer.[54]

Holifield and Changes in the Congressional Committee System

By the 1960s, Holifield was beginning to acquire the accolades of a long legislative career, especially committee chairmanships. He had worked unceasingly for about 18 years before he became chairman of the JCAE in 1961. While acting chairman of Government Operations during much of the 1960s, he did not gain the formal mantle until 1970. With these legislative posts now his for the duration of his career, it would have been unthinkable for him to give them up easily. Such an issue would be hard to characterize as conservative or liberal on his part--it was merely healthy self-interest![55]

Yet, by the time Holifield made it to the top of the congressional committee system, change was in the wind. A large influx of freshmen were determined to change Congress' hallowed committee system, and make entry into the highest posts easier. As early as 1964, Senator Mike Monroney (D-Oklahoma) indicated that he intended to introduce a resolution to establish a successor to the LaFollette-Monroney committee that had reorganized Congress in 1946. Monroney's resolution passed and a joint committee on reorganization was set up. This committee produced 15 volumes of printed testimony based on public hearings and made 66 legislative recommendations, most of which were minor ones. While the proposals sailed through the

Senate, they were blocked for several years in the House, primarily because they would upset procedures long used by the lower chamber to buttress the power of committees when committees brought legislation to the floor.[56]

"Mostly, Holifield was neither a proponent nor opponent of the Monroney-Madden reorganization efforts," remarked Nicholas Masters, at that time a House consultant and professor at Southern Illinois University. "Like most senior members of the House then, he was satisfied with the status quo." Actually, Masters noted that the Monroney-Madden changes, "while having a positive, long-range effect on the operations of Congress, were not unduly disruptive of the committee system." According to Masters, the changes "didn't affect the power of committee chairmen."[57]

With the Monroney-Madden efforts stymied at least until 1970, other calls for change emerged. In the Eighty-ninth Congress, a resolution was adopted to create a Joint Committee on the Organization of Congress. In 1965, it was passed unanimously by both houses. As House Minority Leader Gerald R. Ford (R-Michigan) pointed out, however, the new joint committee had as its two co-chairmen legislators who were from the same (majority) party.[58]

As the minority party in Congress during most of the postwar era, the Republicans were highly sensitive to their lack of power under the Democratic-controlled committee system. To offset the imbalance on the new joint committee, GOP leaders created the Republican Task Force on Congressional Reform and Minority Staffing. Its purpose was to assure that Republican concerns were aired before the joint committee. A member on the joint committee, Thomas Curtis (R-Missouri), also became task force chairman. The task force's reforms focused on increased minority staffing, the seniority system, and the overlapping jurisdiction of committees.[59]

Holifield led a group of Democrats who had met informally with Curtis and other Republicans during the mid-1960s to seek constructive bipartisan solutions. He, however, opposed the concept of minority staffing. Nor did he approve of another conspicuous Republican proposal. Robert H. Michel, then a member of Government Operations and later House Minority Leader, wanted the majority on Government Operations to be from a different party than the one to which the president belonged. Pointing out that the Speaker gave control of some committees to the minority party until the Civil War, Michel contended that minority control of Government Operations would ensure greater objectivity in the committee's investigative functions.[60]

Congressional reform efforts finally coalesced in the Legislative Reorganization Act of 1970 (Public Law No. 91-510), which had been initiated six years before in the Monroney-Madden resolution. This act was the beginning of limitations on the power of committee chairmen; a teller vote provision in effect reduced the power of chairmen to control legislation on the floor, since chairmen would no longer know how committee members voted.

More importantly, the 1970 law contained a provision allotting one-third of committee investigative funds for hiring minority staff members.[61]

Of all of the provisions of the Legislative Reorganization Act, Holifield was most unhappy with the minority staffing provision. To him, the idea of hiring one-third of the staff by the minority was injurious to a well-run committee. He believed that since the majority party was responsible for the legislative program, it had to control the committee staff, while also assuring that the staff worked in a nonpartisan manner, as he had always stressed. He insisted that they all worked for Congress, not a party.[62]

Based on his practical consideration that committee staff should not be split into political factions, Holifield worked to defeat the minority staffing plan. In January 1971, he successfully pressed the House Democratic Caucus to approve a binding resolution. The resolution essentially rescinded the minority staffing plan contemplated in the Legislative Reorganization Act.

The Holifield-led rejection of staffing for the minority party angered the Republicans. House Minority Leader Ford, disappointed at the outcome, termed it a "setback" to hopes for real reform. Most Republicans concluded that Chet was being ultra-partisan. Yet, Holifield was a committed Democrat and his entire history as a congressman and committee chairman belied the charge that he was only a heavy-handed Democrat in this affair.[63]

Lyndon Johnson's "Place" Horse

Jack Newman, a former staff counsel to the JCAE, recalled with amusement one of Lyndon Johnson's comparisons before the senator from Texas made it to the White House. "When Lyndon B. Johnson was Senate Majority Leader," Newman observed, "he often claimed that Congress was composed of 'show' and 'place' horses." Newman explained further: "'The show horses predominate' was then Johnson's punch line."[64]

Johnson's analogy had truth as well as humor. When they first arrive, congressmen, like the citizens who send them off to the Capitol, have mixed purposes. Some seem bent to use the legislative chambers as a springboard to other roles in various sectors. Others want to learn the ropes, but eventually find themselves worn down by the daily legislative grind. Only a few emerge to become genuine legislative craftsmen behind them. These few are Lyndon Johnson's "place" horses who gain opportunities to make exceptional and long-range contributions through political and legislative leadership. In the 1960s--indeed, for his entire career--Holifield was one of Lyndon Johnson's place horses. Johnson had great confidence in him and used him personally to solve major problems. Chet thus won unique openings to contribute to the nation. He braved many a legislative storm--not all of them were to his liking nor brought him personal success--but they all gave him experience to become the proficient master legislator he became.

7

Who Shall Live?

A Student and Teacher of Atomic Energy

If Holifield had contributed to the field of atomic energy only through his work on the Atomic Energy Act of 1946, the hydrogen bomb decision, and the Hanford N-reactor controversy, his role would have been considerable enough. Holifield's role did not end, however, with these controversies. The California congressman proved to be a continuous, influential force in atomic energy affairs from 1945 until his retirement in 1974, and indeed, even beyond. He had to respond to changing political winds as the issues changed over time, but he did this with aplomb, staying at the forefront in atomic energy issues perhaps more than any other congressman or senator. He stayed active not out of political necessity nor for political advantage, but because he personally wanted the new atomic field to be managed effectively.

The atomic field was not quiet between the hydrogen bomb decision and the Hanford controversy. During the 1950s, atomic energy was of acute interest to many Americans, largely as a result of the deepening Cold War with the Soviet Union and the growing knowledge of what nuclear weapons would mean in future conflicts. Initially concerned with atomic energy as an international issue, Holifield favored strong international controls that would allow development of nuclear power, but avoid nuclear weapons proliferation. He was later than most to concede the limited capabilities of such controls.

From the mid-1950s, one of Holifield's primary roles was that of an educator. He became without a doubt the nation's most active and influential civil defense educator. He held the most extensive hearings ever conducted on the nation's civil defense systems and warned the public of the limited possibilities of survival against a nuclear attack. Holifield also became the chief Democratic critic of the Eisenhower administration's civil defense plans, showing how they would be ineffective in a nuclear confrontation. As public attention increasingly became riveted upon nuclear fallout resulting from weapons testing, Holifield considered this problem in hearings in 1957 and 1959, providing Americans with their first, in-depth knowledge of the effects of fallout. As a result of this work, Holifield answered a question on many Americans' minds: who would survive if there were a nuclear war?

The Atom: For War or Peace?

As he wrestled with the enormous dimensions of the nation's nuclear enterprise, Holifield wanted the atom to become the servant of humanity, rather than its master. This meant developing safe, atomic technologies for the marketplace. He wanted the atom to be used for producing energy, curing illnesses, and helping to feed a burgeoning world population.[1]

However worthy an ideal in theory, the peaceful atom was overshadowed by the atom that had been used first for destruction. In the postwar world, with the growing conflict between the U.S. and the Soviets, the atom's military and defense features remained paramount. At least half of the AEC's budget continued to be used for military applications during the first 35 years of the postwar period despite the peaceful initiatives in the 1954 amendments. If there was any silver lining to this military cloud, it was that constant improvement of weapons yielded some important peacetime applications.[2]

Aside from the Soviet threat, part of the military atom's resurgence was due to the state of the U.S. weapons arsenal. Large numbers of scientists left the weapons laboratories soon after Japan's defeat and the atomic bomb arsenal was empty when the AEC took over in 1947. Operating in stringent secrecy, the AEC and the JCAE worked hard to rebuild the stockpile. Thus, weapons production and improvement received the highest national priority, especially after the "atomic spy scares" of 1949. The number of weapons and improvements increased multiplied dramatically, increasing destructive force per weapon while reducing size.[3]

Holifield, ever mindful of the need for U.S. superiority, was a strong supporter of the military atom as a deterrent to a third world war. From his experience at the Bikini Atoll tests in 1946, Holifield was convinced that real defense did not exist against the terrors of nuclear war, especially given the state of technical knowledge. Perhaps the human mind might some day also conceive of a defense against nuclear war. But history seemed to suggest, Holifield contended, that military offense had outpaced military defense over the last century, a gap that had been greatly widened by nuclear weaponry. In consequence, nuclear weapons had one purpose for Holifield: to deter war. Their actual use in a major confrontation would, in his judgment, prove horrible beyond human calculation, because nations with the capability could not be expected to forego the use of such powerful weapons.[4]

From his World War II and Bikini perspectives, Holifield arrived at two goals for the military atom, from which he never wavered. His first goal was to assure U.S. atomic weapons superiority and maximum safeguards in the international arena. His second goal concerned the public's "right to know" about atomic energy. Holifield resolved to help guarantee that the public was fully aware of the dangers posed by the nuclear age, and that they were protected as fully as possible from its disastrous effects.[5]

In partial fulfillment of his first goal, Holifield wanted to be sure that the increased dispersion of nuclear materials did not result in proliferation of bomb-wielding nations and other risks to peace. In the 1954 debate to amend the original Act, Holifield cautioned against what he believed would become an uncontrolled, pell-mell rush to privatization of atomic power. He did not believe that industry in the U.S. or the world was ready to assume the burden of developing nuclear power and of making it available on the world stage.[6]

Just as Holifield had dissented against the May-Johnson bill as the major precursor to the 1946 act, so he found himself opposing the Cole-Hickenlooper bill, which would become the 1954 amendments. As in 1946, Holifield persuaded Mel Price to join with him in filing a minority report. In their report, Holifield and Price warned of adverse repercussions on international control if the government's exclusive control of fissionable material were given to private enterprise. They observed that "international matters relating to atomic energy would be better treated in legislation separate from that which seeks to open the atomic field to domestic private enterprise and profit-making opportunities." The two men favored a two-package (international and domestic) approach. In Holifield's thinking, the two arenas required separate considerations, and the international proposal should have first priority.[7]

As with their dissent to the May-Johnson bill nine years earlier, Holifield and Price found themselves again in a small minority, only this time their minority status did not change. Most Republicans and many Democrats in Congress, sensitively attuned to the views of the Eisenhower administration, were ready to dismantle the nuclear enterprise so that it did not remain as an "island of socialism" in the economy. This majority was anxious to pry the "dead hand" of government controls off of the newly-emerging industry. This might be detrimental to international control, but many viewed such liberalization as inevitable if the U.S. and the world were to benefit.[8]

On the international control question, Senator John O. Pastore's (D-Rhode Island) views expressed during Senate debate were widely accepted. Pastore emphasized that in 1946 "our Nation was the sole possessor of atomic weapons," and so "it was only prudent to make our atomic-energy program a governmental monopoly and subject the control and dissemination of classified atomic information to the strictest possible safeguards." Pastore declared, however, that "today [in 1954], both the British and the Soviet Union have mastered the art of producing fission weapons," and the Soviet Union had "also achieved a thermonuclear explosion." With more nations becoming familiar with the technology, Pastore predicted that "the prospect of useful atomic power which would be used in lighting cities and turning the wheels of factories . . . in all probability . . . will be a reality within the next decade." Pastore had concluded that "changing perspectives in atomic energy now suggest that the time has come to revise our original law, wherever the practical experience of a decade has shown that revision would speed desirable developments, both on the peacetime and military sides."[9] Faced with Soviet opposition to international control, Pastore considered the quest lost, and sought to open up the field of atomic energy to augment the free world's military strength and promote U.S. commercial interests.

Contrary to the Holifield-Price position, the advocates of the new 1954 act indicated that it was unwise to worry excessively about proliferation in view of the urgent need to introduce U.S. private enterprise and U.S. allies to the nuclear field. The nation's primary objective, then, would be to increase free world military might and develop a domestic nuclear industry within the free enterprise system. Other concerns became secondary, perhaps to the later detriment of the JCAE. Less than two decades later, competing and suddenly-aggressive congressional committees would overtake the JCAE on non-proliferation by dramatizing the need for action on nuclear proliferation.

Holifield was down, but not out. He was able to do very little as the 1954 act produced "agreements for cooperation" between the U.S. and its allies for sharing nuclear technology. Holifield held out for international controls longer than most, but the course of events was against him. He worked to achieve the other portion of his goal, i.e., that U.S. nuclear weapons would be second to none. He also supported the Treaty on the Nonproliferation of Nuclear Weapons approved during the Johnson administration. Although he had lost some of his youthful idealism on forging an effective international community, he remained convinced that an effective world organization was a prerequisite to international peace and effective control of atomic energy.[10]

Prelude to Civil Defense

Holifield's second goal, to make the American public fully aware of the atom's dangers and protect them as much as possible from its disastrous effects, brought him quite naturally to the subject of civil defense. Since the Hiroshima explosion, Holifield had been awed by the power of the atomic bomb. As a JCAE member, he advocated that the public be told as much as possible about the effects of radiation and nuclear war. In February 1949, in a speech entitled "Atomic Warfare Leaves Mankind Nowhere to Hide," he took to the air waves to demand that the public be given the opportunity to know more about nuclear weaponry. Holifield was not talking about defense secrets, but practical information, such as what a nuclear war could do "to our children" and to "American civilization."[11]

Holifield came by his "civil defense wings" in two of the optimal theaters of catastrophe in his time: war-torn Europe and the Bikini Atoll tests of 1946.

In 1945, the California legislator toured Europe as a member of the House Military Affairs Committee. Some impressions gleaned from this trip helped to shape his perspective on defense against war in the nuclear age, even though this study mission was made prior to the dropping of the first atomic bomb. What this World War II destruction made clear to Holifield is that civil defense would be difficult henceforth even in conventional wars.

Holifield's trip included a visit to an underground factory that had made Germany's V1 and V2 rockets. On June 7, 1945 at Nordhausen some 300 to 800 feet beneath a fir-covered mountain, he viewed the factory's thirty-one miles of tunnels, complete with railways and auto lanes and sophisticated machinery, and barracks for 25,000 forced laborers. Holifield and his congressional colleagues rode through the tunnels in cars, and then through nearby Buchenwald, where many of the former laborers still awaited transportation back to their countries.[12]

Like his colleagues, Holifield was horrified at the evidence he saw of the Nazi atrocities. He was also amazed that Nazi Germany was able to produce 900 "V bombs" per day. Holifield noted that rocket warfare "presages the most revolutionary change in future wars." Military experts said that "the principles and development by German scientists of this type of warfare had already assumed terrifying and serious proportions." The V-rocket factory was built late in the war, and "had we not stopped them at this stage, it is almost certain that another year or two would have endangered our victory."[13]

Holifield came away from his trip with several solid convictions. For one, political evil had to be stopped in its tracks before rampant militarism could turn into rampant barbarism. The appalling destruction of European Jewry reinforced his longstanding religious conviction that a Jewish homeland had to be created in the postwar world. His populist antipathy toward unbridled business monopolies was also reaffirmed. "Many people are unaware of the connection between the industries of Germany and the German war machine," Holifield later commented. "Without aid from the chemical trust of I. G. Farben and cartel agreements with American and Allied firms, it would have been impossible for Hitler to have produced his war machine." The German war enterprise had been "based on strategic synthetics such as rubber, gasoline, plastics, etc." Agreements with American and Allied firms excluded these firms "from developing and marketing competitive synthetics in the rest of the world," and thus, "Hitler built an independence from imports in strategic fields." By preventing development of "vital substitutes for natural products" elsewhere, Hitler "weakened us almost fatally in our hour of peril."[14]

Most important for civil defense issues, Holifield reached an important conclusion from his first-hand review of the V-rocket. This new information convinced him that future wars would be very different. In the age of rocketry, advance warnings of military attacks would be shorter, if not impossible. Civil defense would have a new array of challenges to meet.

Protecting civilians would be more difficult than ever. Holifield wanted to ensure that "such a condition of unpreparedness" by America in many aspects of military defense, as occurred in World War II, would never happen again.[15]

The atomic blast at Hiroshima and more particularly, his 1946 trip to the Bikini Atoll tests in the Marshall Islands and a side-trip to Japan also brought a major departure in Holifield's thinking on civil defense. The tests reinforced his view gained in Europe that the nature of human warfare had changed dramatically and that the parameters of civil defense were now in uncharted territory. In Japan, he witnessed first-hand the bombed-out remains of Hiroshima and Nagasaki in a tour arranged by General Douglas MacArthur.[16] As in Europe, Holifield again became convinced that America should never be as unprepared as in World War II. He foresaw no easy way to contain the destructive force of atomic warfare other than through an evolution of humanity's political systems, which he knew was nowhere near at hand. As he wrote on returning from the Pacific in June 1946:

> It is unlikely that an effective defense against atomic missiles or bombs will ever be developed, because that defense to be effective must be a "total defense." . . . Previously, no offensive weapon had been developed which could in one application destroy a city, kill the greatest part of its population, and completely eliminate such a city, military [base] or naval base as a war-making factor.[17]

When Holifield returned from Bikini, he had new perspectives from which to consider civil defense. He was confronted, however, with an American public uninterested in such topics. Having experienced few attacks, Americans have tended to be apathetic to measures protecting civilians against disasters, and this has remained the norm. During World War II, civil defense was given short shrift in federal planning and spending. President Truman gave some priority to this area, and with the outbreak of the Korean War, the administration hurried planning for civilian and industrial protection. Until about 1950, however, the country did little in civil defense, relying instead on massive nuclear deterrence by fleets of bombers.[18]

The mood toward civil defense began to change in 1949, with news of the first Soviet detonation of a nuclear device. In 1950, the government issued its first overall assessment of the impact of a nuclear weapons exchange on the civilian population. The first editions of the report, entitled *The Effects of Atomic Weapons*, gave guidance concerning blast, thermal, and radiation consequences of nuclear weapons. The report scarcely considered, however, the longer-term fallout hazards borne on wind currents.[19]

Prior to report, Holifield was already busy with his campaign to educate the American people. He was among a number of JCAE Democrats who felt that the public should be given more information about the dangers of an atomic confrontation. In a House speech in early 1949, he called on the AEC to give the public more data on the military atom, and threatened an investigation if the information was not forthcoming. In practical terms, he asked that the AEC divulge solid information about the 1946 Bikini blasts, to make the public more aware of the dangers of this new warfare. "The truth about atomic warfare is perhaps the only real defense we have," he said. Holifield clearly felt that civil defense efforts were inadequate.[20]

In 1950 and 1951, Holifield continued to focus on civilian defense. He introduced legislative resolutions to establish a commission to examine ways for assuring continuous operation of the government in case of an all-out nuclear attack. He also attended the 1950 civil defense hearings that led to passage of the federal Civil Defense Act of 1950. Holifield believed that act was an important step forward, but inadequate overall due to its dependence on local initiatives to protect the population. Holifield continued to believe that more vigorous action at the federal level would be necessary to provide for an effective civil defense system.[21]

Although Holifield's and other JCAE members' urgings led to some actions, they were able to do very little, especially after passage of the Civil Defense Act and the 1952 election of Eisenhower to the presidency. Civil defense advocates were lonely voices in the early 1950s as they sought to gain an optimum allocation of resources under the nation's defense efforts. During the 1950s, some theorists, including Henry A. Kissinger and Thomas E. Murray, thought that limited forms of nuclear war were plausible, an argument abandoned soon by Kissinger and most nuclear theorists. The emphasis soon came to be placed upon deterrence, which required a full-fledged build-up of nuclear arsenals by the U.S. and Russia to make nuclear war an inconceivable option. This was active defense, based on preserving the nation's war-making capacity and its ability to retaliate against enemies.[22] Civil defense was the flip side of active defense, a passive defense that focused upon minimizing civilian deaths and damage to critical facilities.

The Eisenhower administration soon issued recommendations for urban evacuation, but these were accomplished by national study teams and some federal agencies rather than through a broad-based civil defense initiative. With massive retaliation as the basic national defense posture, the administration, Congress and the public saw no need for evacuation programs and shelters. When *Sputnik I* demonstrated Soviet capabilities in 1957, it became clear that evacuation was a chimera. By then, of course, Holifield was also educating the public on the futility of mass evacuation plans.[23]

The Civil Defense Act and the administration proved to be an unbeatable team for thwarting significant civil defense efforts until 1954, when a nuclear mishap shook the world community. The AEC's CASTLE tests in the Marshall Islands proved to be troublesome and forced the evacuation of thousands from the islands nearest the blast. Japanese fishermen working outside the restricted ocean area were exposed to nuclear fallout carried on wind currents and suffered severe radiation poisoning and some deaths. This "radiation scare" caused great public concern in the U.S. and elsewhere, and led to increased awareness of the dangers of the military atom.

Holifield's worst fears were confirmed by the CASTLE test accidents: the U.S., like all other nations, was ill-prepared to cope with the dangers of widespread nuclear fallout. He did not lose any time in pressing his concerns and was in fact preoccupied the next eight years with campaigning for a heightened civil defense effort. Holifield was not completely certain that even a strengthened civil defense program would provide sufficient protection, but he was sure that a complete national system should be developed with a total seriousness of purpose, which had not been the case up to 1954.[24]

One of the first things Holifield did was to call for increased federal spending on civil defense, development of a full-time corps, and a national system for civil defense training. His strategy for creating the corps was simple: recruit men judged unfit for military service. Holifield fervently believed that a civil defense corps was necessary implement programs to protect the public against a nuclear attack.[25]

As chairman of the Subcommittee on Military Operations of the Government Operations Committee, Holifield soon also directed his staff to plan hearings on civil defense to investigate the subject in detail. He wanted to know specifically what more could be done. He was sure that lack of information on atomic blast effects would be one area of concern. Holifield also urged the administration to let the American public know more of the facts about fallout and the other hazards of nuclear war. After he had been stymied for four years in expanding civil defense, Holifield was sure that he would find that Eisenhower had been remiss in planning for this area.[26]

Holifield's Hearings on "Civil Defense for National Survival"

By January 1956, Holifield was ready with his hearings, which opened in Washington, D.C., but were also held in other cities probably targeted for attack. In his opening remarks, Holifield stated that "There is a widespread belief in this country that civil defense is either futile against sudden massive assaults with nuclear weapons, or is hopelessly inadequate under present arrangements." Holifield felt that "effective civil-defense measures can be taken if the need for them is sufficiently understood by the public, if they are financially supported by the Congress, and if they are courageously administered by the Executive."[27] The hearings received considerable publicity because they were timely and comprehensive; the public was anxious to know what was being done to protect them. The committee heard over 200 witnesses, including the military and other officials, scientists, political leaders, and civil defense officials. The record ultimately filled seven volumes.[28]

One surreal, if not morbid, facet of the hearings was a colloquy between Congressman Dante Fascell and Admiral Arthur Radford, Chairman of the

Joint Chiefs of Staff. In discussing a hypothetical situation where some fifty population centers in the U.S. had been "completely annihilated," Fascell asked whether the Army would then have to "take over control of the United States." Admiral Radford replied that martial law was possible, but he contended that "it would be better if we could avoid it, certainly from the military standpoint." Fascell agreed that "one way of doing it would be to have an effective federal civil defense separate and apart from the military."[29]

In reporting on his hearings to the House, Holifield did not mince words. He summarized the Military Operations Subcommittee's work by stating that it had been "sternly critical of the existing civil defense program." The Eisenhower administration's program had relied heavily on mass evacuations of civilians from urban areas. According to Holifield, such a program "is weak and ineffective, and, indeed, dangerously shortsighted."[30] To buttress his point, he explained that "As a civil defense policy for the Los Angeles area, evacuation is absurd," and averred that earlier federal plans to evacuate urban populations were outmoded and should be replaced by shelter construction. His committee's report suggested "a program of group shelter construction to protect people from the direct blast and heat effects of atomic-hydrogen bombs and the lethal fallout radiation which persists after the explosion."[31]

The Holifield subcommittee findings boiled down to simple, but important recommendations not then being followed: replace evacuation plans with group shelters, and coordinate military and civil defense programs. Holifield estimated that the group bomb shelters he contemplated would cost about $19 to $20 billion, but would be well worth the cost in terms of human lives saved. To coordinate military and civil defense efforts effectively, Holifield recommended a new cabinet-level Department of Civil Defense, into which would be merged existing federal civil defense functions and agencies. Holifield and his committee believed this organizational change was absolutely necessary for civil defense to achieve the importance it deserved.[32]

Holifield's contribution to national civil defense policy through his subcommittee's hearings was undeniable, especially when the administration decided to drop its strategy of mass evacuation from urban areas. Even the *Los Angeles Times*, normally hostile and antagonistic to Holifield, concurred that Holifield's hearings had substantially shifted the nature of the debate over civil defense. In an editorial about a month after publication of Holifield's findings, the newspaper commented that "Legionnaires had an unusual opportunity to hear opposite views on civil defense from leading exponents of evacuation and digging in." The *Times* did not have very kind words for Holifield, describing him as a "big-government Democrat," but conceded that his report "seems to have been unanimous; the three Republican members went along with the rest." It also noted that proposals "for evacuating cities for nuclear bomb attacks has been shot at from both sides of the political fence since he brought it forth about two years ago."[33]

As a result of Holifield's efforts, the national debate over whether "to run, dig or hide" was over. He had clearly shown that there was not time to run. But to move from debate to action on construction of public shelters was very difficult. The cost-conscious Eisenhower administration was not given to supporting adventurous propositions or large-scale budgetary increases, let alone those proposed by a Democratic-controlled subcommittee. Civil defense had a limited "on again, off again" constituency. Holifield could only continue his annual hearings and call for group shelter construction.[34]

Determined to achieve the upper hand, the Eisenhower administration proposed a new, cost-conscious civil defense package, in keeping with Republican views on public spending. Essentially, the package encouraged the construction of private, rather than public, bomb shelters. As a substitute, the administration chose instead a limited program of identifying space in existing public buildings for use as shelters. Holifield was not to be put off so easily. He charged that Eisenhower's measures provided only an "illusion of security." He noted that most urban structures could not withstand the blast and thermal pressures of a nuclear bomb.[35]

New Hope for Civil Defense: The Kennedy Administration

In January 1961 when John F. Kennedy became president, Holifield hoped for a turnaround in civil defense policies. As the new JCAE chairman, Holifield also had some additional leverage for eliciting a positive response, but his first civil defense contacts with the administration proved to be awkward. Matters quickly improved in the summer of 1961, however, when Kennedy proposed transferring civil defense to the Defense Department and tripling the funds in the pending Eisenhower budget requests. Holifield wrote thanking the president, but called his attention to some terminology in the president's proposal that Holifield believed might hurt civil defense efforts.[36]

Holifield continued to hope for more emphasis on civil defense, although he remained cautious. He was pleased that the new administration was more open-minded. Holifield was especially encouraged when Secretary of Defense Robert McNamara testified before Holifield's subcommittee that although 50 million citizens might be killed by a massive hydrogen bomb attack, a "comparatively modest" civil defense program could save millions of lives. McNamara wanted to concentrate on protecting people from nuclear fallout, rather than blast or heat injuries. What Holifield did not like was Kennedy's reference to civil defense as mere "survival insurance." He wrote speech writer Ted Sorenson that this was too narrow a justification.[37]

By mid-1961, the Kennedy administration began to distance itself from civil defense, and this seemed to gain more momentum as time went by. In the fall, Kennedy inadvertently created public hysteria during the Berlin Wall Crisis by implying that nuclear war was a serious and immediate danger. This set off a veritable wave of private shelter construction that would have made the Eisenhower administration proud. Neither the Kennedy administration's positive stands on civil defense nor the Cuban Missile Crisis of 1962 changed general congressional feelings about civil defense. Carl Vinson and Albert Thomas, House chairmen of the Armed Services Committee and the Appropriations Committee's Subcommittee on Defense, continued to chop Kennedy's funding proposals with little resistance from the administration. Though complaining loudly, Holifield could do little to stem the tide. Finally, in March 1963, Kennedy himself downgraded civil defense as an administration priority, thus backing away from his previous commitments.[38]

While Holifield persisted personally in battling for civil defense, his subcommittee support began to erode. Porter Hardy, Jr. (D-Virginia), who served on Armed Services as well as Holifield's subcommittee, complained in 1962 that Holifield's civil defense report "too strongly injects the Committee on Government Operations into the policy-making field." Hardy contended the subcommittee "should present its facts and suggestions to the appropriate legislative committee for further study and evaluation and for the reporting of legislation which it deems appropriate."[39]   In 1962, other subcommittee members also criticized the subcommittee's recommendations for civil defense programs as warmed-over propositions. "The majority seems to feel," they charged, "[that] mere repetitions of its proposal will make the same case for its $20 billion federally-financed shelter program." They complained that "We are being offered the same arguments for the sixth time--twice in this Congress--in support of a proposal first presented in 1956," and "We could not in good conscience support it then and we cannot now."[40]

Civil Defense Loses to the Nuclear Test Ban Treaty

Holifield did not foresee that a Nuclear Test Ban Treaty, concluded by Kennedy with the Russians in 1963, would spell the end of active civil defense efforts in the U.S. In the wake of the treaty, which Holifield supported, public interest in civil defense dissolved quickly.   Civil defense has thereafter remained a perennial orphan under national defense planning. It continues to be mentioned with respect, but is generally ignored.   In 1961, Defense Secretary McNamara declared that Kennedy's civil defense commitment of about $270 million would triple, but this pledge proved to be evanescent. President Johnson subsequently gave pro forma support to civil defense[41] and later administrations followed suit. In 1982, President Ronald Reagan, also pledging to protect civilians from nuclear attack, launched what was slated to be a seven-year, $4.2 billion program to provide shelters and evacuate people to rural areas in the event of nuclear war. Three years later, the White House abandoned this effort. The Office of Management and Budget then slashed the proposed 1986 funding request from the Federal Emergency Management

Agency from $345 million to $119 million, which was half the sum requested by Kennedy in 1962. Administration opponents complained that it was the lowest figure since 1967, when $60 million was budgeted.[42]

Holifield was deeply disturbed by the public inattention to civil defense, and by late 1963 he was pessimistic that an effective civil defense program would ever be developed.[43] He felt that the government should do more than it was doing to prepare for a nuclear attack. As a politician, however, Holifield saw the handwriting on the wall and was obliged to accept overall congressional judgment. Busy with so many other assignments, he could no longer devote time to pressing a reluctant America toward further civil defense efforts. He emphasized in his remaining years in Congress that a nuclear war among the major powers was unthinkable in terms of the civilian casualties that would result, and the U.S. and the Soviets appeared to agree with this judgment.

Holifield and the Radiation Issue

When the radiation issue began to "heat up" in 1956, Holifield was in the middle of his civil defense hearings. Already he had learned much from the testimony that had pertinence for the nuclear testing and fallout issue. Sensing considerable public interest (and anxiety), Holifield saw to it that the 1956 Democratic platform contained a provision calling for "a comprehensive survey of radiation hazards from bomb tests." He then requested that JCAE Chairman Carl Durham (D-North Carolina) hold hearings on the radiation hazards from nuclear bombs and testing. Holifield hoped to alleviate some anxiety over the radiation issue by considering from a scientific standpoint the probable effects of such testing.[44]

Durham agreed with Holifield, naturally wanting to be sure that the problem of fallout and radiation would be assessed comprehensively. In view of Holifield's background and specific request, Durham appointed Holifield chairman of a Special Subcommittee on Radiation. Holifield moved quickly to prepare for the upcoming hearings scheduled for 1957. He directed his staff to accumulate and analyze as much material on radiation as possible, and to develop potential witness lists. Holifield intended to develop a "textbook" on radiation from the scholarly testimony at the hearings.[45]

Holifield's Special Subcommittee convened in the Senate Caucus Room in May of 1957 amid much publicity and fanfare. In opening the hearings, Holifield insisted that his primary purpose would be to "get the facts" about the effects of fallout from a scientific viewpoint. For purposes of the hearings, he was not interested in the moral, religious, or philosophical implications of fallout.[46] He believed that this radiation issue should be discussed without resorting to emotional diatribes against testing. In one sense, Holifield's view was questionable, because a number of scientific assumptions from both sides of the argument on testing could not be proven. Yet, in terms of potential importance, it was highly expansive, directed as it was to the very heart of the administration's broadly suspect and arguably irrational policy of massive retaliation. In another sense, his approach was the best one, since the world community also needed objective consideration of the issues to make informed policy judgments.

The radiation hearings covered several major subject areas, including the origin and distribution of fallout, the probable impacts of a nuclear war, the biological effects and tolerance levels of radiation exposure, the effects of past testing and the potential impact of future tests. Approximately fifty witnesses, testified. The witnesses included scientists and AEC officials, among others.[47]

In summarizing the hearings, Holifield emphasized their scientific nature and the reality that radioactivity was a natural part of the environment. As he told his colleagues, "The subcommittee hearings were not a forum for discussion of public policies." He said they were, instead, "a scientific seminar to lay a basic groundwork of knowledge for discussion by the public and for policy decisions by the responsible agencies of government." He emphasized that "Our world is radioactive. The air we breathe, the water we drink, and the food we eat contain minute bits of radioactivity." The "new and most fundamental problem" confronting the world was that of "evaluation and control of the new hazard of man-made radioactivity."[48]

The 1957 hearings produced important conclusions. First, the subcommittee learned that fallout was a product of all nuclear bomb tests and explosions. It was highly unlikely that a "clean" bomb (one devoid of radiation) would ever be developed, despite statements to the contrary. The subcommittee was also startled to learn that the AEC knew far more about fallout hazards, even before the 1954 tests, than it was willing to share with the public. Also, on the distribution of fallout, the subcommittee learned that the patterns were uneven; most fallout from nuclear testing was concentrated in the Northern Temperate Zone. With regard to biological effects, high exposure levels could be dangerous. Human beings receiving high levels of exposure could and did experience serious biological mutations.[49]

Although Holifield's subcommittee could confirm some definite biological effects on human beings resulting from acute exposure to radiation, tolerance levels were difficult to pin down. Experts, while agreeing that some levels of exposure were safe, could not agree on exact tolerance levels. The exact impacts of nuclear war were also unclear because they depended upon sizes and types of nuclear weapons used.. Experts did agree "the amount of bomb testing which one could do safely in one year." They projected "that somewhere between 2 and 10 megatons of split atoms could be injected into the stratosphere each year without undue biological risk on a global basis." They noted that the 1954 Marshall Islands test had approximated the 10 megaton upper limit, and that "It is possible to fabricate a single bomb with five times this explosiveness." Holifield's conclusion was that "unless some element of control is introduced into the testing of nuclear weapons, it is possible for a single bomb to overshoot the worry limit."[50]

Beyond general conclusions, Holifield's subcommittee also educated the public on the make-up of nuclear fallout. Experts identified strontium 90 and cesium 137 as principal radioactive ingredients, although attention tended to center on strontium. In his summary of the hearings, Holifield attempted to trace the route of the strontium and assess its significance:

> Once locked in plants, the strontium is on its way into the food supply. Dairy cattle, grazing in Wisconsin, or in the New York milk shed, for example, take in the strontium that happens to be in the grass or feed. Fortunately, only a fraction of this strontium finds its way into the cow's milk. Due to the cow's physiological mechanism, much of the strontium is blocked out of the milk.[51]

The real question was the effect of strontium on human beings, and on this score, Holifield could not be exact. The data had shown that just as the cow manages to block out much of the strontium in its feed, so did humans discriminate against strontium. He felt that "what we really need are some standards against which we can measure whether or not a given amount of strontium will be harmful." In simpler terms, Holifield averred that "We need some worry limits." He noted that "Experts differ on what the worry limit should be, but it was interesting to note that they do not disagree too much."[52]

Physicist and scientific writer Dr. Ralph E. Lapp followed Holifield's 1957 hearings in depth. In retrospect, Lapp seemed most taken by the conclusions on effects on the human food chain that nuclear war and fission products of nuclear testing could produce. According to Lapp, "These open hearings developed the technical basis for understanding the phenomena of radioactive fallout associated with the detonation of nuclear weapons." Lapp pointed out that the hearings established "that very large areas could be contaminated with the fallout from megaton-class weapons." Lapp explained that "one kiloton of fission products per square mile" could be "very serious in its lethal effects on anyone exposed above the surface of the earth," and that a 20-megaton nuclear bomb "could under proper conditions contaminate 10,000 square miles" at the one-kiloton level. Lapp was even more impressed that fission byproducts from nuclear weapons "represent a persistent source of radiation sufficient to deny a contaminated area to occupation." As such, "This phenomenon introduces a wholly new 'denial' character to warfare, since the fission product radioactivity dies off slowly, forming a persistent hazard."[53]

Lapp knew that Holifield had accomplished an important public service with the hearings. They had revealed that "These three phenomena--the huge area subject to lethal effect on man, the denial of this land to occupation, and the uptake of strontium 90 in the food supply--constitute a true revolution in warfare." By merely sticking to the "facts," Holifield's subcommittee had shown to a wide public audience that war in the atomic age would no longer be the creature that it had been for thousands of years of recorded history.[54]

Holifield's hearings had an important political effect precisely because they were a scientific landmark. They helped to publicize information that was previously held very closely within the government, information sorely desired by some anxious citizens who wanted to understand it earlier. After the 1957 hearings, the Eisenhower administration was forced to justify further weapons testing in light of national security needs. Holifield's subcommittee had succeeded in putting the Republican administration on the defensive. Most unfortunately and hardly unexpected, the subcommittee's work did not lead to a reduction in testing. Shortly before the U.S. and the Soviets declared in October 1958 a joint one-year moratorium on testing, both countries engaged in unprecedented levels of testing, leading to a "fallout scare" in the U.S. in early 1959.[55]

Holifield's 1959 Hearings on Radiation

Holifield's 1959 hearings were held in a much more rarified environment than in 1957, and tempers were sharper due to the fallout scare. Also, test ban advocates had organized for political action after the 1957 hearings, most notably in the National Committee for a Sane Nuclear Policy (SANE). In such an environment, Holifield's attempts to educate the public through updating his 1957 hearings were less appreciated. He was also under severe time constraints, since the JCAE allowed him only four days for the hearings. His objective of getting "only the facts" and not conducting forays into the moral and other implications of testing would not work as well in 1959. He consulted scientists as before, but his greatly-truncated witness list, which excluded test ban advocate Linus Pauling and others, was heavily criticized.[56]

In some important aspects, the 1959 hearings were different from those in 1957. The 1959 hearings focused much more pointedly on scientific findings on radiation hazards from nuclear testing, and not on nuclear war. Holifield decided that the hazards of a nuclear war should be considered in a separate set of hearings scheduled for mid-1959. While nuclear war was eliminated as a subject, two new subject areas were added: scientific testing alternatives to atmospheric testing, and government efforts to monitor and evaluate fallout.[57]

The 1959 hearings demonstrated the increased amount of scientific research conducted since 1957. Witnesses identified new radioactive ingredients in fallout, including carbon 14, strontium 89, barium 140, and iodine 131. They also confirmed that fallout was unevenly distributed around the globe, and that perhaps two-thirds of the fallout had landed in the Northern Temperate Zone. Scientists also posited that past weapons testing had brought human strontium 90 contamination to about ten percent of an agreed-upon safe level of exposure. If testing at the same intensity were to continue for two more generations, the experts surmised that humanity would definitely be at risk. Scientists were still unable to agree upon precise safety thresholds for each radioactive chemical despite the attention given to defining "worry limits."[58]

In the new subject areas of the 1959 hearings, the public was apprised of some good news. Underground testing was seen as a viable alternative to atmospheric testing and largely radiation-free. Testing in outer space was also considered, but its effects were not known well since such testing had not been conducted nor were conditions in space adequately known. The public was also informed that the Public Health Service (PHS) had been conducting tests of radioactive (strontium 90) contamination of the milk supply and found that contamination had reached a pinnacle, and was now declining. The PHS was credited with performing a valuable public service on a tight budget.[59]

Despite the fact that the hearings highlighted important new facts, Holifield was heavily criticized in the press. This time, his attempt to get "only the facts" apart from moral, political, and other considerations was greeted with widespread skepticism and anger. Editorials in liberal periodicals accused him of conducting a "whitewash" of the potential risks and hazards. His style of handling the hearings was also chastised as high-handed and inappropriate. Critics saw sinister meanings behind his cutting off of emotional reactions or political recommendations. SANE demanded new hearings.[60]

Holifield was personally hurt by these reactions because he sincerely believed he had been objective. When the hearing record was published, it was clear that Holifield had aimed for objectivity. He had not adhered to any particular political viewpoint. Even though he did not allow scientist and test ban advocate Pauling to testify, for example, Holifield did give serious attention to Pauling's "discovery," carbon 14, and emphasized its problems. In fact, the hearing record concluded that "carbon 14 from past weapons tests could constitute a genetic hazard to the world's population."[61]

If anything, the 1959 hearings heightened awareness of nuclear testing hazards and the biological effects of large-scale nuclear warfare, and greatly intensified public and world pressure for a test-ban treaty. Also, the hearings helped to quell public fears about radiation from past weapons testing. The hearings demonstrated that strontium 90 levels would be short-lived.[62] Although critics assailed Holifield for not recommending whether or not the U.S. should sign a test-ban agreement, that had not been Holifield's concern during the hearings. With his usual practical perspective, he had been in favor of a "talk and test" strategy,[63] and did not want to hem in the administration or weaken its negotiating position with the Russians. If some critics charged that Holifield was not fulfilling his legislative role, from his perspective, he knew that legislators sometimes had to withhold judgment in the international arena so as not to damage the interests and policy positions of the government. Holifield was wisely, but subtly, working in the same direction as the test ban advocates.

Holifield Advises President Kennedy on Nuclear Testing

In 1960, Kennedy had declared during his race for the presidential nomination that he would do everything possible to negotiate a test-ban agreement with the Soviets. While the test-ban moratorium was in effect, the Kennedy administration undertook strenuous efforts at Geneva to negotiate a test-ban pact. The Soviets proved to be intransigent on the question of inspections. They were unwilling to permit a large number of on-site inspections which scientists needed to ensure compliance.

In early 1961, JCAE Chairman Holifield became, in effect, Kennedy's top atomic energy advisor in the Congress. Faced with renewed obstructionism in negotiations and threats from Khrushchev to detonate a 100-megaton bomb, he advised Kennedy to renew atmospheric weapons testing while still continuing to negotiate. Chet sensed that this was the best way for the U.S. to improve its weapons and safety features while prodding the Soviets toward an agreement. In August, the issue became moot when the USSR announced it was renewing tests unilaterally and re-initiated a series of weapons tests of unprecedented size and volume. The Kennedy administration followed suit.[64]

Holifield's advice to Kennedy had been sound. Unlike many Americans, Holifield was not fooled by the wavering Soviet attitudes toward atmospheric testing. Holifield lectured both AEC and Department of Defense (DOD) personnel many times on the dangers of being sandbagged by the Soviets, and with very good reason. He was greatly disturbed by the U.S. loss of weapons testing initiative both during and following the moratorium. During the moratorium, the Soviets worked diligently to prepare for a new atmospheric testing program. The U.S., on the other hand, made no such significant effort. In fact, U.S. weapons laboratories apparently believed that weapons development and atmospheric testing had ended for good. As a consequence, laboratory capabilities--including both physical and personnel resources--were greatly attenuated. Thus, when the Soviets unilaterally rescinded the moratorium, they were able to proceed immediately with a major test program which yielded very significant data. The U.S., with completely inadequate preparation, was unable to conduct significant tests. In fact, most of the U.S. test launches had to be destroyed without obtaining any nuclear data because launching vehicles did not perform satisfactorily and data-recording systems failed. Before the U.S. could get its atmospheric test program back on track, the Soviets again called for termination of tests, to which the U.S. assented. The Soviets, therefore, completed a very successful test program and the U.S. made little progress in this last series of tests.[65]

Holifield was thankful, of course, that there was ultimately a good outcome from the U.S.-Soviet sparring in atmospheric testing policy. This did not occur, however, before the two superpowers came close to nuclear war. The U.S. and the USSR sized each other up during the remaining months of 1961 and most of 1962, coming very close to a nuclear confrontation in the Cuban Missile Crisis of October 1962. Soon after, both heavily-armored sides began to realize the dangers inherent in direct confrontation, and agreed on a limited Test Ban Treaty in 1963. Under terms of the agreement, both nations forswore any future atmospheric testing of nuclear weapons. In large measure, the test ban agreement depended on both nations' recognition that strontium 90 presented a global threat to all of humanity. This had been a major finding of both sets of Holifield hearings. Like most Americans, Holifield was strongly in favor of the Test Ban Treaty.[66]

For the rest of 1959 and during 1960, Holifield continued to keep the specter of nuclear war before the American public with his nuclear war and civil defense hearings. His approach was to bring out the technical aspects of a nuclear confrontation, as opposed to emotional opinions that nuclear war was "unthinkable" or would destroy civilization. The major effect was to convince many associates, the public, and at least portions of the world community that all-out nuclear war would be extremely costly and devastating, regardless of the civil defense measures taken. Holifield also showed that it would prove disastrous to believe that populations could be protected through effective military means, other than through massive nuclear deterrence.[67]

In retrospect, Holifield believed that only "universal fear of universal death" has kept humanity from going over the brink of destruction. To the end of his life he remained an optimist that humanity will ultimately master the nuclear challenge. Providence, he contended, has given human beings both the intellect and the will to enter the atomic age. With these will come one day the capacity to find a reasonable way out of the nuclear trap imposed by the power and proliferation of nuclear weapons.[68]

Yet, Holifield emphasized that the issue of international proliferation still demands more serious attention. He noted that the legislative branch, with partial exception of the JCAE, has not aggressively pursued these matters. Indeed, both Congress and the public continue to engage in an "on-again, off-again" pattern. Johnson and subsequent presidents have highlighted the issue with signing of treaties, but such agreements only bind the signatories, rather than the entire world community. Aside from his enthusiastic support for such efforts, Holifield realized that he and others were unable to solve the thorny issue, which is more a political problem than a technical one. This has been confirmed again and again in many domestic and international studies, particularly the comprehensive, multi-volume International Nuclear Fuel Cycle Evaluation (INFCE) in 1978.[69]

8

The Atom At Sea

The Nuclear Navy: A Career-Long Involvement

During the late 1940s and early 1950s, as the Cold War with the Soviets grew, Holifield and the JCAE focused on the military atom--rebuilding the nation's nuclear arsenal, developing the hydrogen bomb, and perfecting other U.S. nuclear weapons. Once it was clear that atomic energy was not to be placed under international agreements, the ever-practical Holifield and the JCAE worked hard to ensure that the U.S. would remain ahead of the Soviet Union in what became an almost inevitable nuclear arms race. Although Holifield became increasingly engrossed in the late 1950s with civilian nuclear power R&D and other peaceful uses of the atom, he remained mindful of national defense needs. In addition to civil defense as a primary emphasis (at least through 1963), Holifield carried one particular military interest to the end of his career: building the "nuclear navy."

Holifield's interest in building a nuclear-powered and nuclear-armed navy extended back to his earliest JCAE days. There he encountered the dynamic personality of Navy Captain Hyman G. Rickover, and eventually cemented a relationship that was to last his entire career, in fact, until Rickover died in 1986. Rickover was the prime mover in forcing the U.S. Navy into the nuclear age. In addition to talent and drive, Rickover had the political savvy to enlist the aid of Holifield and other JCAE members in supporting the first nuclear propulsion concept for a naval submarine. In only four years, Rickover's teams built the world's first reactor to produce nuclear power in useful amounts and soon demonstrated reliable plant performance in two technologically-different propulsion plant prototypes on land. Two years later, the Navy successfully tested the first nuclear-driven submarine, and the second one shortly thereafter. From these initial successes, Holifield and other JCAE members assisted Rickover in expanding the nuclear navy to include the first nuclear-powered surface ships. Concurrently, they helped Rickover and Admiral William F. Raborn, head of the Polaris program, establish perhaps the world's most effective deterrent to nuclear war: nuclear submarines carrying strategic missiles. Holifield was enthusiastic about nuclear-powered and nuclear-armed submarines, but less so about surface ships, which he considered obsolete in the nuclear age. Soon, however, as he had with civil defense, Holifield accommodated widespread congressional sentiment for surface ships that ran counter to his own initial inclinations, and modified his position. He and other JCAE members later supported combatant ships also, insisting that all new ones should be nuclear-powered.

No stranger to conflict, Holifield found himself at odds with the Eisenhower administration and the Kennedy and Johnson administrations over nuclear propulsion for U.S. merchant marine ships. During Eisenhower's presidency, one major dispute centered on the world's first nuclear-powered merchant ship, *Savannah*. In this confrontation, Holifield sided with Captain Rickover and his key assistant Milton Shaw, who was ordered to evaluate the ship's status. Shaw shocked those responsible by finding that *Savannah* had serious planning, technical, and contractual problems and was in no position to soon set sail as a symbol of America's peaceful atom. During the Kennedy and Johnson administrations, Holifield feuded with Secretary of Defense Robert S. McNamara over nuclear propulsion for USS *John F. Kennedy*, the nation's newest aircraft carrier, which McNamara insisted should be conventionally-powered despite the proven successes with USS *Enterprise* and USS *Long Beach*. In these disputes, Holifield and the JCAE failed to gain their initial goals, although they advanced the cause of nuclear propulsion for ships and the critical need for superior management and engineering practices. In JCAE hearings and reports in the 1960s they also emphasized the fallacies in McNamara's early arguments against nuclear propulsion.

Throughout his career, Holifield remained a loyal champion of Rickover. The two men became acquainted in the late 1940s and early 1950s because Holifield was on the JCAE, but by the late 1950s they were solid allies and friends. Holifield and other Rickover allies on the JCAE saw to it that Rickover remained head of the Naval Reactors (NR) organization and that he obtained the requisite promotions to stay in charge of the naval propulsion program. The JCAE's actions enabled Rickover to remain on active duty through the Nixon, Ford, and Carter administrations. Rickover was eventually sent into retirement by the Reagan administration, but not before he had effected the revolutionary transition from oil to nuclear power for naval propulsion. He also established and validated the fundamental imperatives for others, here and abroad, for producing safe, successful commercial nuclear plants. Holifield's close experience with Rickover's activities, like his engineering and safety criteria, his high standards and rigorous discipline, and his management and personnel selection and training skills, left an indelible mark on the Montebello congressman. For him, Rickover's example was not only a remarkable success story, but a large part of the vantage point from which Holifield guided and promoted the development of civilian nuclear power and other energy related issues affecting national well-being.

Rickover, the Navy, and the Submarine in World War II (WWII)

The Holifield-Rickover relationship eventually grew out of Rickover's career in the navy and his quest to improve the submarine. Rickover was a submariner and electrical engineer who had a superb wartime management record as the iron-fisted, tireless, and highly practical head of the electrical section of the Bureau of Ships. Rickover's determination to achieve technical excellence and his refusal to compromise, coupled with an abrasive and controversial personality, had made him a naval legend. Single-minded, he alienated many of his peers, but some of his superiors saw his commitment and attention to duty as critical for achieving important results for the Navy.[1]

Rickover's singular view of the submarine, as the most critical element in the Navy's arsenal, challenged the consensus view for its future which had emerged from the experience in WWII. He did not question the fact that the Navy had fulfilled a vital role then, nor disagree with naval strategists that the balanced mix of weaponry had contributed to success, mainly in the Pacific theater. Rickover's concern emerged over applying the WWII balanced fleet idea to the future. Most Navy strategists believed that the balanced fleet concept had to be taken into account during postwar planning. Because of the Navy's time-honored link to the sea, the underlying implication was that surface ships would continue to be as valuable as aircraft and submarines in the future as in the past. While Rickover appreciated the concept, he realized that the nature of warfare had changed with the advent of the nuclear age. To him, the nuclear submarine was the Navy's most important future asset.[2]

While most strategists did not agree with Rickover's views, they considered submarines to be an important component of their concept. Developed at the turn of the century, submarines were another variety of small, oil-dependent surface ships that had the ability to submerge for relatively brief periods. Submarines had been critical in both WWI and WWII as destroyers of enemy shipping. In WWI, the "U-boat" (*Unterseeboot*) proved to be valuable to Germany by hiding beneath the surface and attacking Allied warships and merchant ships, contributing to U.S. entry into WWI. In WWII, U.S. submarines achieved greater success by destroying over 5 million tons of Japanese merchant shipping and over one-half million tons of warships.[3]

Despite the successes, Rickover was perhaps more appreciative than many of the Navy brass of the WWII their limitations and suitability for future warfare in terms of speed, flexibility, and endurance. Powered by diesels, they could travel at the moderate speed of 20 knots on the surface and depended upon frequent refueling. When forced to submerge to hide or more covertly attack enemy shipping, these submarines depended upon battery-powered motors. They could travel silently, but only a few hours at slow speed (about 10 knots). Since the endurance of battery power was short, the diesel submarines had to surface or snorkel for recharging their batteries and for renewing their oxygen tanks. The increasing sophistication of radar and sonar systems during the war made detection of snorkeling submarines easier, and thus, even the most modern versions became susceptible to destruction. Into the early 1950s, the average submergence time and speed of U.S. submarines were not much greater than those of some thirty years earlier.[4]

Although the Navy appreciated the effect of atomic weapons on ships, it failed to fully comprehend that the nature of war had changed. The tests provided the Navy many insights on requirements for the future, but the Navy tacitly assumed that ships would continue to be dependent upon oil.[5] Rickover did not share this assumption and set out to design future submarines for the exigencies of future warfare.

Rickover Courts Holifield and the New AEC

Neither Holifield nor Rickover was privy to the first stirring of nuclear research by the Navy. Before the war, a handful of naval scientists recognized that nuclear propulsion might offer a new direction for the fleet. Beginning in 1939, researchers at the Naval Research Laboratory undertook small-scale initiatives toward the goal of nuclear propulsion on the theory that a controlled nuclear chain reaction could produce heat which could be converted to mechanical energy. Yet, experts were virtually isolated from the highly-classified wartime information whose control rested with the Army. Also, the Navy's relatively-small amount of nuclear research was largely unknown and unappreciated by most of the service's top officers.[6]

About a year after the end of the war, a chain of circumstances led the Navy's Bureau of Ships to assign a group of three civilians and five naval officers, led by Rickover, to the Oak Ridge Laboratory in Tennessee. The group's assignment was to learn the fundamentals of nuclear reactor technology and examine the possibilities for naval applications. A few of Rickover's superiors undoubtedly sensed that he would improve the potential for bringing the atom into the Navy's orbit.[7] During the rest of 1946 and 1947, his team worked hard to fill in the enormous gaps in their knowledge. This was Rickover's first exposure to the AEC and the JCAE. By and large, the focus of most activities was on weapons, not on nuclear reactor development.[8]

Within a year, Rickover's team had concluded that a nuclear-powered submarine could be built within a few years. But the group also concluded that many of the scientific, engineering, and operational information and processes, and health and safety parameters were then outside of the body of existing knowledge associated with nuclear technology. Building a steam propulsion plant inside a submarine would be difficult, since the plant and the crew would be in a hermetically-sealed environment, and had to be shielded from steam leaks and other accidents. This challenge would be made even more difficult by the stringent naval standards and requirements for personnel safety, and power plant and ship survival during combat.[9]

While at Oak Ridge, Rickover began to build the necessary political connections and other essential relationships which enabled him to become the premier force in moving the Navy into the atomic age. Despite constant attacks and setbacks, he became the national focal point for transforming the rapidly-developing nuclear theories into practical engineering designs. He also worked constantly on political connections including key congressmen and senators in a position to help him. They included, for example, Clarence Cannon (D-Missouri), the dominant power on House Appropriations with whom he maintained a constant personal liaison. The cornerstone of his support, however, was the JCAE. Holifield was a charter JCAE member. He recalled that Rickover actively promoted his ideas with most committee members. As Rickover explained his ideas to Holifield and the committee, they began to appreciate the nuclear submarine's advantages.[10]

In mid-1947, Rickover's team returned to Washington only to be dispersed. He was assigned to Rear Admiral Earle W. Mills, Chief of the Bureau of Ships, where he did not let the matter of the nuclear submarine rest. Without a national commitment, Rickover worked diligently (aided by some of his former team) with Holifield, the JCAE, and other influential policy makers. He argued that the Navy should pioneer nuclear propulsion in parallel with the AEC's role for nuclear R&D. Rickover fought tenaciously to put the program in the AEC, rather than in the massive Department of Defense (DOD), where it could be subsumed or pigeon-holed.[11]

In July 1948, Rickover was named the Bureau of Ships' liaison officer with the AEC. In early 1949, he was ordered to duty with the AEC's new Division of Reactor Development, with commensurate responsibilities in the bureau. This was the beginning of the Naval Nuclear Propulsion Program and the basis for Rickover's acquisition of two hats in directing work in the single NR organization.[12] Rickover's plan was to use AEC's research-oriented, multi-purpose laboratories, such as Argonne National Laboratory (ANL) and Oak Ridge National Laboratory (ORNL), for some R&D and other limited aspects of the program, while employing two strong, mission-oriented engineering organizations, General Electric (GE) and Westinghouse, to take the lead roles. To help ensure success, Rickover sought and obtained the sustained help of Chet and the JCAE.[13] GE, which had been working on the breeder reactor program for the AEC, was operating the Knolls Atomic Power Laboratory (KAPL) at Schenectady. Westinghouse, which had signed a letter contract with the AEC in December 1948, was assigned to be the operating contractor for the newly-purchased Bettis Laboratory near Pittsburgh for the PWR program. Both were expected to work closely with the ongoing R&D activities at ANL and ORNL. Over the next several years, Knolls and Bettis laboratories became solely dedicated to NR's programs.[14]

Holifield was simply amazed at the Navy's response when Rickover proposed to build the first nuclear-powered submarine. The Navy, supported by key congressional leaders, opposed the move largely because of cost! Their rationale was that it could buy two regular submarines for $50 million, the estimated cost of one nuclear.[15] The Navy then got its surprise; Rickover had done his homework, with Holifield and the JCAE solidly behind him.

The JCAE worked diligently to get the Navy to agree to a compromise and the Navy finally obliged. The JCAE would provide funds in the AEC budget to develop and demonstrate two prototype plants, as well as the money for the two submarines' power plants. The Navy would build the rest of the two submarines, *Nautilus* and *Seawolf*. Rickover contracted with Westinghouse at Bettis for the prototype, and a PWR plant for *Nautilus*. GE got contracts at Knolls for the prototype and a sodium-cooled reactor plant for *Seawolf*.[16]

Holifield Supports Rickover's Engineering Approach

Although Holifield and Rickover were not yet close associates, Holifield was among a group of about four or five JCAE members who stayed abreast of the difficulties Rickover faced. Chet fully supported Rickover's conservative engineering approach and agreed that no effort should be spared to carry out his mission. He endorsed Rickover's position that national security came first and should not be compromised by interesting, but not absolutely essential, R&D initiatives when conservative solutions were already available.[17]

From the beginning, the R&D presented a tremendous, unprecedented challenge in nuclear power generation history and far more difficult to achieve than anticipated. Yet Rickover proved to be especially decisive at critical moments. When ANL encountered strong criticisms just as Bettis became better equipped to handle engineering, Rickover reacted firmly and transferred more of the this effort to Bettis. He soon had full control over the programs, an outcome supported by the JCAE. As Holifield saw matters, such hard-headed, customer-oriented management involvement by Rickover was essential for success. Holifield believed that Rickover had handled with aplomb a very demanding, complex technology while too many other AEC R&D reactor projects were unsuccessful due to the absence of such strong management, engineering leadership, and solid performance criteria.[18]

Construction on the first, full-scale PWR prototype, reactor plant and propulsion machinery for *Nautilus* began in August 1950 at the AEC's Idaho desert site. These components were enclosed in a real submarine hull surrounded by a 300,000-gallon tank simulating the ocean. In June 1953, an all-navy crew performed a successful 96-hour, full-design power run, simulating a submerged crossing of the Atlantic Ocean. This was the first time in history that significant quantities of useful nuclear power had been sustained. The prototype power plant for *Seawolf*, also in a submarine hull section surrounded by a water tank, was at an AEC site in West Milton, New York. The reactor plant portion was encased in the first high-integrity containment structure ever used for a nuclear power plant. *Seawolf*, with its all-navy crew, successfully completed its full-design power run in 1955.[19]

Holifield, among many others, was deeply impressed with Rickover's scientific and engineering approaches, which left very little to chance. It was evident that his approaches were holistic, encompassing the long-term validation of far broader and more vital functions than those normally associated with even advanced machinery development. The prototypes were constructed and designed to validate not only Rickover's specific scientific, engineering, construction, and safety objectives, the processes, and operating and maintenance procedures, but management and personnel performance and the training of the teams of officers and engineering crews, also.[20]

Holifield, Rickover, the PWR and *Nautilus*

Holifield was amazed at Rickover's success and with the remarkably short schedule. In August 1949, the Chief of Naval Operations had signed an operational plan to develop a submarine nuclear propulsion plant, including a "ready-for-sea" date of January 1955! Six years later, right on schedule with its tight deadline, *Nautilus* underwent its sea trials including sustained, full-power operations as well as completion of all tests. On its fully-equipped "shake-down cruise" in May 1955, *Nautilus* steamed totally submerged from New London, Connecticut to San Juan, Puerto Rico in 84 hours. The total distance it traveled was over 1,300 miles--a distance greater than ten times that previously traveled continuously by any submerged submarine!

Although he had supported Rickover from the beginning, Holifield was filled with excitement and confidence with the success of *Nautilus*, as were the other JCAE members and many in the submarine Navy. The performance of the nation's first nuclear-powered submarine was clearly superior to any other non-nuclear ship propulsion system. Holifield, among others, grasped the significance of this first-time performance: A submarine was no longer bound to the earth's atmosphere; it could remain silent and submerged for months and even years, and was generally immune from naval and air attack with its new silent propulsion system. Those close to NR could hardly contain their enthusiasm over the magnitude and significance of the *Nautilus* achievement. Rickover had transformed an unproven concept to a reality in a very brief time period during peacetime. Little wonder that his stock soared with the JCAE and among knowledgeable professionals.[21]

When the time came to pick the best reactor concept to replicate in future submarines, Holifield and the JCAE supported Rickover's choice of the PWR, instead of the liquid metal reactor. The years of thorough research and testing proved that both concepts were highly successful in their respective prototypes and submarines, and it was clear that either concept would suffice. Despite protests by many and the PWR's limited potential for improvements in nuclear and thermal efficiencies, Rickover chose the PWR. Holifield and the JCAE agreed with Rickover that only one concept should go into future production and that by concentrating on and setting tight standards for the PWR, Rickover could focus all resources on maximizing performance. The sodium-cooled reactor program was not a loser, either, since it later contributed significantly to the liquid metal breeder R&D program.[22]

The JCAE Pushes for More and Gets More

Urged on especially by JCAE members Holifield, Melvin Price (D-Illinois), and Senator Clinton Anderson (D-New Mexico), Rickover used his Navy and AEC hats to design and build still other advanced nuclear power plants for submarines. One success quickly followed another. In just *two* years after conception, a smaller submarine, *Skate*, was completed and successfully operating at full power at sea. In 1960, *Triton*, the only submarine powered by two nuclear plants, traveled around the world underwater, covering almost 42,000 miles in 84 days. Another smaller submarine, *Seadragon*, made the first underwater trip through the Northwest Passage, traveling from the Atlantic to the Pacific through the Canadian archipelago.[23]

In his last retrospective on the naval program, even with the "Cold War" gone and dramatic changes taking place from the break-up of the USSR, Holifield was proud of the program and expressed intense admiration for the leadership and exacting work of the NR Program Directors, including Rickover, from 1948 to 1982; Admiral Kinnaird R. McKee, 1982 to 1988; and Admiral Bruce DeMars, 1988 to the present (1995). In comments to the authors, he summarized the submarine program's success:

As we in Congress had hoped, eventually the submarine program was supported by the Secretary of the Navy and the Joint Chiefs of Staff. Despite varied and intense opposition over the years, and the large cutback underway in the armed forces, today our Navy is operating over 130 nuclear submarines and ships in oceans around the world. By the middle of 1994, these submarines and ships had steamed over 100 million miles! Most significant is that with all the operating experience not one serious nuclear accident has occurred. The Navy lost *Thresher* in 1963 and *Scorpion* five years later, but in-depth investigations determined that neither loss was due to reactor plant failure.

We know about the excellent training of the crews and how careful and professional they really are, individually and as tightly-knit shipboard teams. We also know how much care has been taken to protect them in these potentially-dangerous jobs, particularly in the subs. I could go into a sub with my watch and the amount of radium on the dial would set off the alarms. That's why they don't allow the sailors to wear radium-dial watches. That's how meticulously Rickover built those power plants and the Navy designed the subs to run faster, quieter, longer, and safer.[24]

Holifield, Rickover, and Murray

Although Holifield was one of Captain Rickover's most vocal and loyal supporters on the JCAE, the two men were not close associates until the late 1950s when they were brought together by a mutual friend, Thomas E. Murray, an AEC commissioner from 1950 to 1957. Like Holifield, Murray was a liberal Democrat who disagreed with many of the Eisenhower administration's nuclear policies and shared similar views about the need for development of nuclear power. Murray, an electrical engineering industrialist, shared this professional link with Rickover. As the three leaders with vastly-different backgrounds worked with each other, their mutual respect increased. They spoke the same language and wanted the same type of practical and reproducible results. Both Holifield and Murray appreciated the longer-term significance of Rickover's attempts to revolutionize and strengthen the Navy by using the propulsion plant route to bring the Navy into the nuclear age. Both hoped that with help from others, Rickover's initiatives would increase the potential of this option to strengthen energy security, and provide an excellent example and a strong foundation for the commercial sector. They hoped that each of Rickover's repeated successes would help attract favorable attention and reinforce the incentives of naval and utility customers to use the highest standards to all of their nuclear R&D and production commitments.[25]

Holifield was so impressed by Rickover's leadership and decisive approach to nuclear R&D that he was willing to support Murray's 1955 proposal to have Rickover appointed as head of AEC's Division of Reactor Development. Both agreed that this was the best solution to strengthen AEC in-house capabilities. Murray's proposal was controversial, encountered opposition in the nuclear industry, and was rejected by a majority of AEC commissioners.[26]

Holifield's relationship with Rickover continued to grow after Murray left the AEC in 1957. So close did the relationship become that Holifield did not hesitate to defend Rickover against the DOD, the AEC and the private sector. A clear instance where Holifield's support was crucial arose in July 1958, when AEC Chairman McCone confronted sudden DOD resolve to assume exclusive responsibility for the safety aspects of nuclear weapons in its custody. The

01954 act mandated that the AEC, not the military, was to have ultimate authority over nuclear weapons, but the provisions of the act were somewhat unclear on this point. McCone feared that the AEC could not exercise adequate control over the growing array of nuclear weapons. Rickover sensed almost immediately that the DOD initiative posed a threat to the Navy's nuclear program and to the formal relationship of dual responsibility between the Navy and the AEC for ensuring nuclear safety. In April 1959, Rickover put the matter before the JCAE in a hearing held deep in the ocean aboard the *Skipjack*. Rickover instantly had Holifield's support. The veteran congressman flatly informed the AEC that the 1954 act had given reactor safety authority to the AEC, not to the military.[27]

Despite Holifield's vigorous stand, McCone was not satisfied with Chet's interpretation. He persuaded some JCAE members to introduce amendments to the 1954 act that would allow the president to transfer these reactor safety activities to DOD. This set off a hot debate within the JCAE and national policy circles. Holifield remained adamant against transferring nuclear safety authority, and his view ultimately prevailed, with the result that McCone abandoned his efforts. With Holifield's aggressive stand, NR's control over nuclear safety in the Navy's plants was actually strengthened. In a September 1961 directive, President Kennedy reinforced Holifield's and Rickover's preference for dual responsibility by the AEC and Defense.[28]

Even beyond the JCAE, Holifield seized any legislative opening to set Rickover's approach before Congress and the public. In March 1959, Holifield's Subcommittee on Military Operations held detailed hearings on the organization and management of missile programs in all three military services. These were the first such hearings to examine missile programs from a comparative perspective. What particularly drew Holifield's attention was Rickover's determination to keep national political and industrial factors from interfering with the high engineering discipline he had imposed on the Navy's nuclear program. Holifield was also attentive to Rickover's insistence that the Navy's personnel system (as well as many contractors' personnel systems), was outmoded in a technological age, with frequent rotations continuing to be interpreted as a major factor in the promotion of officers. Rickover argued that the performance, safety, and security of nuclear systems depended upon long-term commitments by highly competent officials, whether civilian or military. Promotions should go to those most qualified, rather than to officers or civilians transferred routinely in and out to enhance their careers.[29]

Despite Holifield's agreement with Rickover's views on the Navy's personnel system, Rickover did not succeed in curtailing rotation as a criterion of promotion, even for many outstanding senior engineering officers in his own organization. Mostly, NR's officers did not rotate, and they paid a dear price with far fewer promotional opportunities. In fact, only one NR engineering officer advanced beyond the rank of captain in forty years! That officer had to rotate through a period of non-nuclear duty before being promoted to admiral. The most practical option for most affected officers was to resign their commissions and leave the naval service prematurely while in their early forties; the signals were clear that each one would be passed over for admiral. Most who left remained dedicated to federal service, continuing productive careers in the AEC or elsewhere. Even Rickover would have been passed over for admiral without decisive action by Holifield and the JCAE.[30]

Strategic Nuclear Missiles for Nuclear Submarines

With nuclear propulsion for submarines a reality, Holifield and other JCAE members now moved in a new direction. They supported efforts to arm new nuclear-powered submarines with strategic nuclear missiles. Holifield's own ideas about nuclear missiles germinated from a series of circumstances, the main ones being his trip to Bikini Atoll in 1946 and his personal experiences in wartime London during 1944. He was also influenced, however, by William L. Borden, the JCAE's first staff director and the first pilot of a B-54 Liberator bomber in 1944. By chance, Borden was a family friend of Senator Brien McMahon (D-Connecticut), the first JCAE chairman, who invited Borden to become the JCAE's first staff director.

Holifield made trips to several other places during his 1946 journey to witness the ABLE and BAKER tests at Bikini Atoll. His visits to Corregidor, Hiroshima, and Nagasaki left an indelible imprint and he came away convinced that America must be prepared to meet all military challenges in the postwar world. Holifield did not like war, but he believed that preparedness was one avenue to ensure peace in the world community. The Cold War with the Soviet Union after the war reinforced this conviction.[31]

Holifield's visits in wartime London gave him his first experience with missiles. As a member of the House Military Affairs Committee, Holifield visited London in 1944, when the Nazi V-1 rockets were roaring nightly across the English Channel. With Congressman Walter Horan (D-Washington), he lodged at the Savoy Hotel, which had dark blinds drawn down over the windows at night. Holifield recalled that the first rocket he heard "clattered like an old Ford engine about to throw its connecting rods." Traveling just below the speed of an airplane, the V-1 crashed about a mile away from his hotel, setting the building on fire. Holifield and Horan walked to the bomb site as the Home Guards pulled injured people from the flaming building.[32]

The later V-2 rocket was launched into the stratosphere and had more destructive potential. Flying a Liberator back to England from Holland in 1944, JCAE Staff Director Bill Borden said that he suddenly saw his cockpit light up with the fiery streak of a V-2 headed for London. His plane would make the trip in two and one-half hours, yet the V-2 rocket, traveling like a meteor, would cover the same distance in five minutes! Borden became convinced that the age of the bomber had passed, just as the horse and buggy had passed into history with the advent of the automobile. Upon returning to law school in 1946, he wrote a dramatic book entitled *There Will Be No Time: The Revolution in Strategy.* In graphic, but coldly analytical terms, Borden propounded as his major thesis that the advent of the rocket had effectively made human beings nowhere on earth safe from biological or atomic warfare. Instant war would be the world of the future and humanity no longer had any choice but to create a world constitution and a world parliament as the only way to secure human survival. This view paralleled Holifield's ideas upon his return from Bikini Atoll in July 1946.[33]

One year later, in 1947, Holifield and Borden met. Over the next seven years or so, Holifield would work closely with the new JCAE staff director. The two men discussed their determination to see that the U.S. became the first nation to mate atomic weapons with the rocket, especially on the nuclear-powered submarine. Their different, but parallel, personal experiences during wartime in England drove them both to the inescapable conclusion that the U.S. had to be prepared as much as possible to deter attacks on world peace.

Holifield was not the major player in the missile arena, even on the JCAE. Between 1946 and 1955, as a member of the JCAE and also of the House Military Affairs Committee for part of the period, Holifield did have many opportunities to monitor progress of the nation's missile systems. Within the JCAE, Holifield tended to support his close associate Mel Price's more direct participation. Following the congressional reorganization of 1946-1947, Holifield lost his seat on the House Military Affairs Committee (now the House Armed Services Committee), the position from which he had launched his successful dissent in 1945 against military control of the atom. In the postwar legislative shuffle, he preferred to maintain his seniority on the Government Operations Committee. Price, on the other hand, returned to Armed Services, staying and becoming its chairman during the 1970s and early 1980s. Since both legislators were consistently together in their political outlook, Holifield tended mostly to support Price's leadership in the military area, aside from specific nuclear issues. Holifield's and Price's integration of their outlook and legislative activities made them a formidable team within Congress as they gained seniority and stature after the mid-1950s.[34]

By 1955, the stage was set for national efforts to mate guided and intercontinental missiles with the nuclear submarine. Holifield, Price and others on the JCAE leaned heavily towards insisting that DOD establish a crash venture under Rickover to place strategic nuclear weapons on the Navy's new submarines. For their part, neither DOD nor the Navy wanted to give Rickover that control. Rather, to expedite the introduction of such a submarine launching system, the Navy created a new program organization headed by Rear Admiral William F. Raborn. Raborn's selection was not unanticipated by Holifield, who would have preferred Rickover. Despite

Holifield's preference, other JCAE members did not believe that Rickover was the logical person to run this program under the Bureau of Ordnance.[35]

Once Raborn was selected, Chet was quick to admit that the Navy had made a sound choice. The Navy was urging both the JCAE and the House and Senate Armed Services committees to accelerate national commitments toward the nuclear fleet. Raborn's decisive and competent administrative actions satisfied Holifield that Raborn was equipped to get his job done well.[36]

The Polaris Program was the responsibility of the Armed Services Committee in each house. In the early years of the program, JCAE Chairman Anderson and Price were the members most deeply involved in adding nuclear warheads to submarines. Holifield, Price, Craig Hosmer (R-California) and others in the JCAE and AEC still had critical roles to play, however, since ingenious modifications of the submarine were required. Because the addition of nuclear warheads to the submarines was an urgent matter, the new additions were expedited by using the proven S5W nuclear plant in the advanced cigar-shaped, *Skipjack*-class attack submarine and by actually cutting the partially-constructed hull in half and adding a 130-feet missile section amidships. The first such submarine was redesignated *George Washington* and commissioned in December 1959. Six months later, two 1,200-nautical-mile Polaris A-1 missiles were fired successfully from *George Washington*, the first such firing ever. More advanced missiles and submarines have been designed since then and built for the follow-on Poseidon and Trident missile programs.[37]

Holifield and the *Savannah* Episode

At about the same time, Eisenhower moved to seize the initiative in maritime nuclear propulsion. As part of Eisenhower's "Atoms for Peace" plan, the administration wanted to build the world's first nuclear-powered merchant ship as a symbol of world peace. Seeking to bypass Rickover, they insisted that the AEC's Reactor Development Division, rather than the Navy, develop the new ship's plant with Maritime building and operating the ship.[38]

The president's ship, to be named *Savannah*, found itself in a political storm from the very beginning. Both Holifield and Rickover were opposed to building the ship. Holifield "called the President's proposed ship a floating 'showboat'" and "argued that the plan would do little to advance atomic knowledge since the ship would use a submarine reactor that has already been developed." On Eisenhower's side, AEC Chairman Admiral Lewis S. Strauss "conceded that if time were taken to develop a 'completely new design' there would be a greater chance of producing a more advanced ship," but Strauss was worried in light of other countries' development efforts that "it would be an error for the United States to take second or third place both from a 'military standpoint as well as a propaganda standpoint.'" Finally, the

Eisenhower administration decided to proceed on the basis of a new light water reactor plant designed by Babcock and Wilcox in Lynchburg, Virginia.[39]

For Holifield, *Savannah* demonstrated the contrast between Rickover's system and the approaches typical in the AEC's civilian program. As a result of Holifield's and other member's opposition, the JCAE refused to authorize funds for *Savannah*. Refusing to accept defeat, the Eisenhower administration sought and obtained funding from the House Merchant Marine Committee.[40]

Dwight Ink, who was Assistant General Manager of the AEC during 1957-1961, was also sure, from his vantage point, that *Savannah* was not on firm ground. He later noted that "The success of Rickover's management and engineering system was evidenced in an oblique way when this 'peace ship,' *Savannah*, was developed." According to Ink, "the Strauss proposal was to put *Savannah* on a timetable much too short to permit the far more rigorous Rickover approach." In fact, propulsion systems intended for the commercial arena were susceptible to budget and other trouble.[41]

Several days before *Savannah*'s launching at New York Shipbuilding Corporation yard in Camden, New Jersey, John McCone, a tough and highly competent engineer-turned-businessman who had just succeeded Admiral Strauss and shared Holifield's respect for Rickover's talents, decided that Rickover should inspect *Savannah* before it "hit the waves." Dwight Ink was assigned the sensitive task of advising Rickover. According to Ink, when Ink broached the subject, Rickover bellowed, "Absolutely not, the Navy won't have any part in looking after this ship." Rickover continued: "That program is not managed worth a damn, and I will not have my busy people wasting their time getting involved in any way." Ink wrung a reluctant acceptance from Rickover only after dropping his trump card: "I said that McCone was not making a request, but was giving an order as AEC chairman."[42]

Once ordered, Rickover lost no time in complying. He called for Milton Shaw, widely regarded by his peers as the embodiment of the Rickover management and engineering approach, who was on sea trials and required two days to reach port. Arriving in Camden the day before the ship was to be christened by First Lady Mamie Eisenhower, Shaw spent six hours reviewing, with shipyard and AEC personnel, the technical and construction status of *Savannah*'s plant and the management-organizational arrangements, including schedule.[43] Ink remembered that Shaw's report was a bombshell:

> McCone and I then flew to New York the following morning where we met with Shaw, the AEC's project manager, and the shipbuilder's top management while the crowd was gathering for the launching ceremony. McCone asked Milt his opinion about the engineering status of the plant and the readiness of the ship for operation. Shaw stunned the entire group by stating flatly that there were serious planning, technical, and contractual problems at this stage which would jeopardize seriously its schedule and timely successful operation, and its intended mission as an international showpiece for demonstrating American nuclear merchant ship capabilities.

Shaw's judgment drew loud rebuttals from those in charge of the project and the shipyard. They complained bitterly and gave a series of reasons why his conclusions, based on only a few hours' review, were wrong. In an amazing display of in-depth knowledge of design, construction, operation, contractual arrangements, and management, Shaw's reply devastated their protests, argument-by-argument and point-by-point. New York Ship nor the AEC project officer had any real answers to Shaw's basic points, and *Savannah* was launched with McCone and I knowing that the ship's schedule and contract arrangements for delivery were in trouble.[44]

Ink later recalled that McCone briefed Holifield and Senator Anderson immediately upon his return to Washington on the serious problems facing *Savannah*. He asked the JCAE for additional time and funds to correct the problems, and the JCAE obliged. *Savannah* eventually went to sea, but according to Ink, "it never became the success that Eisenhower and Strauss had wanted." Ink believed *Savannah* suffered to a large extent "because the AEC tried to demonstrate both technical and economic feasibility in one step, a fundamental mistake caused in part by budgetary considerations." More telling was Ink's belief that *Savannah's* failures were "due to the absence of the rigorous management leadership, planning, technical judgment, and quality control measures typically obtained by Rickover and his capable staff."[45]

The effective life of *Savannah* proved to be relatively short. After a number of goodwill tours, *Savannah* was retired and mothballed. The ship's relatively high cost, low operating levels, and intensive personnel training requirements, as compared with oil-fired merchant ships, left little doubt that Holifield and Rickover had solid and legitimate reasons when they opposed the Eisenhower administration's development of the merchant ship.[46]

Holifield's Views on the Navy's Nuclear Surface Ships

Holifield was not an early proponent of the nuclear surface fleet. In fact, through the late 1950s, the congressman seemed to be of two minds on the future of the surface fleet. Holifield was convinced that the day of conventional surface ships for war purposes was over; the atomic and missile age, especially the new submarines, had rendered them obsolete. Moreover, even though the JCAE nuclear surface ship effort was underway, Holifield was not certain that such ships should be built. He did not reverse his position until shortly after 1960 when a series of events, including the Cuban Missile Crisis, convinced him that his judgment had been too sweeping.[47]

Holifield's basic conviction about the nuclear surface fleet was formed at Bikini Atoll in 1946. Amid the destruction that he witnessed, Holifield concluded that war had become unthinkable because, as he wrote in his notebook, "the horrible results of this type of warfare between two or more great industrial nations would be cataclysmic," and would in effect "mean the end of civilization as we know it." The nature of warfare itself had changed.

Holifield believed that "the warfare of the future undoubtedly will continue to develop along the line of radar-controlled, rocket-propelled missiles." Effective defense against atomic bombs and missiles was probably impossible because "[such] defense to be effective must be a total defense." The California congressman was even less optimistic about naval defense:

> As to the possibility of naval defense, this is even more fantastic. This first aerial atomic bomb explosion at Bikini sunk more tonnage, immobilized more ships through destruction of radar, radio, fire power, and other topside ship paraphernalia than would happen, except in a major engagement heretofore. The second underwater atomic bomb explosion sunk three times the tonnage as compared to the first. Let us assume that through dispersal such a fleet would avoid the danger of concentration and thereby avoid massed losses. Capital ships costing approximately 100 million dollars would be economical prey for a single atomic missile costing much less than a million dollars.

> A still greater hazard to naval vessels, however, and a more probable target would exist in the elimination of their maintenance, repair, and supply bases, which cannot be dispersed, hidden, or defended against atomic missile attack.[48]

One decade after he wrote about naval defenses, the advent of the nuclear-powered submarine made Holifield more convinced than ever that a nuclear surface fleet was untenable. Writing in *Western World* in May 1958, Holifield drew a seemingly logical conclusion. He was sure that "The day of the great surface ship is ending." His 1958 arguments seem jarring:

> We are in the middle of a weapons development revolution. Yesterday's arms are inadequate to meet the weapon of today. . . . The real issue is whether the four years required for launching another large carrier and the billion dollars for the aircraft carrier and its complement of planes shall be used in a sacrifice to naval tradition or should the time and money be used to produce modern hunter-killer and missile-launching submarines to meet the number one naval threat of the Soviet Union.

> All of these weapons can carry nuclear warheads so powerful that direct hits are unnecessary. Any of these weapon systems can achieve destruction of a billion dollar surface ship with one hit or near hit.

> I believe that the era of the aircraft carrier is drawing to an end. It is vulnerable to supersonic missiles guided into its bowels from supersonic aircraft.[49]

History has not been kind to Holifield's 1958 position expressing doubts about the nuclear surface fleet. His support of nuclear submarines over nuclear aircraft carriers was reasonable: in the face of an all-out nuclear war, a surface fleet, given the ongoing militarization of space through satellites and effective guided missiles, could not hide. Yet, from the 1950s until recently, the U.S. turned increasingly toward building nuclear-powered capital ships.[50]

Holifield was convinced that these ships were obsolete, but he hedged somewhat on his apparent opposition to nuclear-powered vessels. Certainly his support of Rickover should be taken into consideration in assessing his overall view toward surface vessels and their value in future wars. But Holifield's views did not mirror simple blind faith in Rickover; Holifield was his own man and he knew Rickover's limitations well.

Although Holifield's fundamental ideas about total war were sound, he did not always consider in depth the subordinate propositions about war, national power, and deterrence that had a bearing on the continuing importance of a surface fleet. They would be an important strategic military component, for example, in crises with non-nuclear nations, and also could project national power at critical moments, "show the flag," and even land and provide logistical support for American troops and equipment on foreign soil. The fleet could be valuable in demonstrating America's national will in non-nuclear disputes, for establishing blockades and controlling sea lanes, and even for engaging in limited naval warfare. Put simply, Chet was more worried about conflicts with large powers, especially the Soviet Union, than with small nations, a position on which he would refocus by the 1960s.

Political factors were very important in Holifield's change in focus on the nuclear fleet. Holifield was seldom unwilling to admit that he had been wrong or to adopt a new or modified position if facts and developments so dictated. Although on the surface Holifield appeared to be setting aside subordinate propositions on the value of a surface fleet in his 1958 complaint on the aircraft carrier, eventually he did reassess his reasoning. He realized his posture placed him at loggerheads with traditional Navy loyalists in Congress like Carl Vinson, James Van Zandt, and Mendel Rivers, all of whom simply wanted more ships, nuclear or non-nuclear. Holifield realized he would gain nothing by attacks on colleagues who had more power than him to effect changes in the Navy. Ultimately, he accepted that if there was to be a surface fleet, it had to be nuclear-powered and nuclear-armed. This was a compromise that he could support.[51]

Developing the Nuclear Surface Fleet

Using a similar pattern of operations of about five years earlier, the DOD agreed to the AEC's development, under Rickover's direction, of a Large Ship Reactor (LSR) project. This design effort developed into the world's first nuclear-powered surface warship, USS *Long Beach* (CGN9), authorized in the FY 1957 shipbuilding program, with two reactors and two steam plants driving two shafts. *Long Beach* was over 700 feet long and displaced approximately 17,000 tons.[52] This design effort was adapted also to serve as the nuclear power propulsion plant for a large aircraft carrier then being designed. The carrier, later named the USS *Enterprise*, would have eight reactor plants, two per steam plant for driving each of four shafts, and would be over 1,100 feet long and displace over 92,000 tons. There were some major differences in the power plants for *Long Beach* and *Enterprise*, but these could be tested in the same prototype facility. There were also R&D efforts underway for these unique power plants for other applications of intense interest to the AEC.[53]

The LSR project activities were assigned to the AEC's Bettis Laboratory. Construction of the land-based prototype plant (A1W) began in April 1956 at the National Reactor Test Station (NRTS) in Idaho. It consisted of two physically similar, first-of-a-kind reactors and associated steam-generating equipment necessary to drive one shaft of an aircraft carrier and to demonstrate steam catapult operations for launching aircraft. Both PWR plants operated at full power for the first time in September 1959. Soon thereafter, this prototype facility had the flexibility to test the higher power level and other objectives for one shaft of *Long Beach*. Two years later, in late 1961, these first two ships were commissioned and in operation, *Long Beach* first in early fall, and the larger *Enterprise* a few months later. Like *Long Beach*, the carrier *Enterprise* successfully completed its full-design power test and all other plant tests. The nuclear surface fleet had become a reality.[54]

The third ship of the original nuclear surface fleet was USS *Bainbridge*, a destroyer over 560 feet long, displacing about 9,000 tons. Due to the R&D nature of *Bainbridge's* nuclear propulsion plant, a land prototype (D1G) was built in West Milton, New York, with the reactor and machinery for one of the destroyer's two shafts. AEC's Knolls Laboratory managed the project, using the containment sphere that previously housed the *Seawolf* prototype. This plant for *Bainbridge* operated successfully at full power on May 9, 1962, about five years after the Navy had requested that the AEC develop as rapidly as possible a PWR plant for a new nuclear-powered destroyer![55]

Although the nuclear surface navy got off to a good start, budgetary considerations began to bog down further progress. The Kennedy and Johnson administrations imposed constraints that made additional ships untenable. From January 1961 and midway through Johnson's term in 1966, only one other nuclear ship was authorized. This was USS *Truxton*, a duplicate of *Bainbridge*, authorized in the FY 1962 program.[56]

In early 1964 Holifield and his colleagues were considering whether another nuclear carrier should be built to join *Enterprise*. Having become a convert, Holifield advised his colleagues in a House floor speech that the JCAE had held hearings and had issued a unanimous report stating that "we should have nuclear propulsion in an aircraft carrier if we are going to have an aircraft carrier." Holifield noted that "We did not pass judgment on whether we should have a carrier or not, but if we are going to have one, we should have it [nuclear-powered] on the basis of expert testimony."[57]

Chet was taking on one of the most powerful members of Kennedy's and Johnson's cabinet, Secretary of Defense Robert S. McNamara. He was known for his "whiz kids," systems analysts who boiled military and defense policies down to a complex numerical matrix from which he issued his judgments. The McNamara team's argument against a nuclear carrier was that while *Enterprise* had proven that nuclear power was feasible, the costs of building and operating nuclear carriers were too high to permit their use. McNamara had decided that the next carrier should be a conventional, oil-fired one.[58]

Holifield did not agree, based on his experience with nuclear-powered ships, and tours and briefings on the *Enterprise*, as part of a JCAE field trip during naval exercises off Guantanamo Bay. Captain V. P. DePoix advised JCAE members that a primary feature of *Enterprise* was its "tremendous acceleration" and further, "also the deceleration which we can gain with this ship." DePoix explained that these capabilities were "particularly useful to an aircraft carrier--because we do so much maneuvering in connection with the operation of aircraft." He stressed that the carrier could be dispatched to any spot in the world and "arrive at station--at destination, ready to go, and not with our oil reserves depleted, and with the requirement at that point to slow down and take on a considerable amount of black oil." Since it did not need to burn oil or refuel, DePoix also noted that this carrier did not have to face the problem associated with stack gasses that corrode airplanes. To be sure, there were a few drawbacks to the nuclear carrier. Nuclear carriers were more costly and had to be larger to accommodate the propulsion plant. Also, such carriers required a higher level of training for the plant operators. Still, Holifield was convinced that the next carrier should be nuclear-powered.[59]

The 1963 and Later JCAE Hearings on the Nuclear Surface Fleet

Another contributing factor to Holifield's conclusion were JCAE hearings in 1963, with John O. Pastore (D-Rhode Island) as chairman, for a complete look at nuclear propulsion for the surface fleet. The JCAE's target was DOD, where McNamara had no plans to expand the nuclear navy beyond the ships and submarines previously authorized. The JCAE did not pretend to answer the question of "whether aircraft carriers or any other types of naval ships should or should not be built," since this decision belonged to DOD and other congressional committees. Despite this limitation, though, the JCAE did highlight the conventional, oil-fired CVA-67 carrier then under construction. With Vice-Chairman Holifield clearly at the forefront with Chairman Pastore, they charged that the nation's newest carrier, to be named USS *John F. Kennedy*, would be obsolete before it was launched. Many felt that an obsolete warship was an inappropriate way to honor the fallen president. The JCAE published a report in 1963 refuting all of McNamara's arguments.[60]

The JCAE was not the only committee which found McNamara's reasoning hard to bear. Senator Richard B. Russell (D-Georgia), a JCAE member and also House Armed Services Committee Chairman who was unable to be present at the 1963 hearings, did not think highly of McNamara and his ideas. Russell referred to McNamara as a small man with very little vision. Due to his key role on Armed Services, fellow senators as well as two JCAE senior staff persons, John Conway and Edward Bauser, briefed Russell about the hearings. When informed of McNamara's position, Russell volunteered that he had found McNamara at times "lacking in depth of understanding or appreciation of issues before him" and that he was "not shocked by the tenor of the Defense Secretary's testimony. . . ."[61]

During the 1963 hearings, McNamara made his position clear that cost-effectiveness comparisons demonstrated that the advantages of nuclear warships did not appear to make them particularly better than oil-fired ships. Whether the Secretary really understood the political and technical quagmire into which he was heading by advocating an end to building more nuclear ships seems uncertain. Eventually, he would give in to the JCAE and other proponents.[62] The domestic struggle waged back and forth between the JCAE and other committees, while McNamara sat supreme in his seat like no Defense secretary before or since. He remained undaunted, once he had made his decisions, and his capabilities enabled him to dominate not only his department, but in fact, the entire cabinet. Yet he had not been that far removed from the JCAE's viewpoint on nuclear carriers, and eventually, at a JCAE hearing in early 1966, he yielded to congressional pressure by announcing for nuclear power on the nation's *next* carrier. Holifield's and the JCAE's victory, therefore, was only partial since McNamara continued to insist that the *John F. Kennedy* remain a conventional, oil-fired carrier.[63]

Results from Vietnam with the nation's nuclear-powered ships helped to bring about McNamara's change of heart and the end of the JCAE's battle with his systems analysts. Successes in the waters off Indochina with *Enterprise, Long Beach,* and *Bainbridge* were too self-evident even for McNamara and his associates. While McNamara agreed that all carriers after *John F. Kennedy* would be nuclear, the same provision was not made for escort vessels. Most of the escort vessels would continue to be non-nuclear, another limitation on Holifield's and the JCAE's push for the nuclear navy.[64]

Holifield did his part to make sure that McNamara's policy change would be given wide circulation. In releasing the January 1966 JCAE hearings which dealt with nuclear warships, JCAE Chairman Holifield observed with satisfaction that McNamara had called for a second nuclear carrier. Ever on the offensive, Holifield now also pushed for nuclear-powered escort vessels:

> The Joint Committee was pleased to be informed by Secretary of Defense McNamara that he has requested both authorization and appropriation for a second nuclear propelled aircraft carrier. . . . The Committee strongly supports the provision of nuclear propulsion for escort warships as it did in the case of submarines and aircraft carriers. It is obvious that, in order to maintain our Navy's present superior position, we must have nuclear propulsion in our first line warships.[65]

Holifield used the testimonial of an influential JCAE member to buttress his case, referring to a fact-finding mission by Senator Henry M. Jackson (D-Washington) aboard *Enterprise* during its operations off the coast of Vietnam:

> Senator Jackson told us that the *Enterprise* and *Bainbridge* are proving their military superiority daily under the rigors of combat. He told us the time has come to stop futile studies and get on with filling the Navy's needs for nuclear propulsion for its warships.[66]

Holifield took the opportunity of the May 27, 1967 launching of *John F. Kennedy* to emphasize again the need for more nuclear-powered aircraft carriers. As McNamara and the Kennedy family assembled at Newport News, Virginia, for the formal launching ceremonies, Holifield remained in Washington where he told the House that it was "unfortunate" that the new carrier was not nuclear-powered. He felt that the new warship was something of a discredit to the nation's slain president because the ship represented "the end of an era" rather than being a forward-looking symbol of national progress. As McNamara addressed the assembled guests, including President Johnson, he faltered near the end of his speech and had to cut his remarks short. Perhaps the specter of John Kennedy's untimely death was too much for him, but for whatever reason, McNamara's behavior added a further pall over the event. McNamara's announcement one year earlier that the next carrier would be nuclear-powered, while insisting that *John F. Kennedy* should remain oil-fired, created a historical anomaly: a carrier that was, as Holifield lamented in Washington, "obsolete before ever going to sea."[67]

The JCAE Keeps Rickover on Duty--Again and Again

From the 1950s into the 1970s, the JCAE had to fight to keep Rickover afloat in the Navy. Far from enhancing his status by his spectacular successes, Rickover gained ever more enemies among his peers. Holifield recalled:

> Rickover was a highly abrasive individual, a constant gadfly and not a member of the club. What was worse, he had gone over the heads of his superiors and demonstrated conclusively to Congress that they [his superiors] were wrong. The Navy brass continued to attack him in countless ways. Even the White House snubbed him. It didn't even invite him to the 1958 ceremony that celebrated the historic voyage under the North Pole! *Nautilus's* captain, William Anderson, was so embarrassed that he left the White House and went directly to Rickover's office to apologize. Senator Jackson then had President Eisenhower appoint Rickover as his personal emissary to *Nautilus* ceremonies in New York. Had that not been done, Rickover might never have been promoted to vice admiral.[68]

A barrier that almost blocked Rickover from completing his mission was the Navy's insistence that an officer retire after 30 years of service if not advanced from the rank of captain. In 1953, an Admiralty Selection Board passed over him twice, refusing to recommend him for rear admiral. Retirement was therefore automatic, but under powerful pressure from Congress, the Navy relented and gave Rickover his promotion. Senator Jackson and Congressman Sidney Yates (D-Illinois) were in the forefront of this fight, although Holifield and other JCAE members were also called upon to champion the Rickover cause, which they did enthusiastically.[69]

Holifield realized that Rickover did not become more popular in the Navy after his promotion to rear admiral. The White House snub of Rear Admiral Rickover at the 1958 *Nautilus* celebration was only one manifestation of the continuing attacks on the "father of the nuclear navy." Rickover's promotion to vice admiral also had to be forced upon a mulish Navy by a determined JCAE. Holifield and JCAE Chairman Senator Clinton Anderson were particularly instrumental in obtaining this promotion to vice admiral. Holifield remembered that Anderson called Secretary of the Navy Thomas S. Gates to the JCAE's inner meeting room:

> We sat for two or three hours, arguing with Gates about making Rickover a vice admiral. Gates had a management expert with him, who showed us a personnel chart. The Navy explained that in order to give Rickover this rank, you had to have an organizational structure to support him! They had several hundred admirals at the time, but no pyramid for Rickover. It was obvious that they really didn't want to push him further; they wanted to get rid of him. Rickover was Jewish and I always felt there was a certain amount of anti-Semitism involved.

> After we had heard enough of Secretary Gates' arguments, Senator Anderson said: "The appropriations bill is going through the Senate in a few weeks and it will contain an amendment making Rickover a vice admiral!" He asked me would it pass in the House and I replied it would. Then he pounded the gavel and got up and walked out. The rest of us followed. Gates was left sitting there, stunned. The next morning, Secretary Gates telephoned to say he was convening the Admirals' Selection Board at 10:00 a. m. to consider the elevation of Rickover from rear admiral to vice admiral. One hour later, he phoned to say it had just acted favorably. That's the way Rickover got to be vice admiral.[70]

Four years after he had attained the rank of vice admiral, Rickover was again faced with forced retirement, this time due to his age. On January 27, 1962, Rickover became 62 years old, the statutory retirement age for Navy officers. Knowing that the president had the statutory authority to retain Rickover for an additional two years, Holifield and other JCAE members lobbied Kennedy with a veritable barrage of entreaties to keep him on duty. Kennedy obliged, acknowledging the power this group enjoyed in Congress.[71]

The question remained of what to do when the two additional years were up, on February 1, 1964. Holifield and the JCAE decided not to leave anything to chance. They prepared well in advance, meeting with President

Johnson in December 1963 on the issue. Holifield recalled that Johnson was at a loss. "How can I keep him?" Johnson asked. Johnson knew "I can't make him Chief of Naval Operations," since Rickover would not be able to remain with the Naval Nuclear Propulsion Program in such an event. Since the JCAE had already researched the matter, Holifield provided the solution. "An admiral or a general can be called back into active service by the Commander-in-Chief," Holifield told Johnson. "You can retire him on Friday and call him back into active service on Monday to serve at your pleasure!"

Johnson accepted Holifield's JCAE-supported recommendation and was willing to keep Rickover on board. But several anti-Rickover industrial cliques fought pitched political battles to oust the admiral, and Secretary of the Navy Paul Nitze seemed determined to retire Rickover. When Nitze went to Johnson about the matter, Johnson did not tell him about his meeting with the JCAE. He simply advised Nitze that he could go ahead on his own, if he wanted to, and "sound out the waters," but he warned Nitze not to offend the JCAE. Upon arriving on Capitol Hill for a meeting with Senator Anderson, Nitze found himself also facing both Rickover and a determined Holifield. Realizing that prudence is the greater part of valor, Nitze dropped his efforts and agreed to have the President bring Rickover back on permanent duty.[72]

Rickover's continuance in NR was thus assured. According to a December 17, 1963 United Press dispatch, President Johnson announced (somewhat wryly) that "In view of Admiral Rickover's unique qualifications and his long experience in the field of nuclear reactor development, the Secretary of the Navy Paul H. Nitze plans to retain him on active duty after his name is placed on the Retirement List." Despite sustained pressures from the anti-Rickover forces, Presidents Johnson, Nixon, and Ford all accepted the JCAE's method of keeping Admiral Rickover in service, although usually not without some skirmishing between the JCAE and the Navy.[73]

Why was Rickover so Successful?

Holifield's opinion of Rickover's amazing successes in nuclear propulsion are the product of over 30 years of exposure to Rickover and his programs. Holifield's own desire to know, his need to understand, and his eagerness to learn from others about the broader implications, as well as the technical aspects, of atomic energy brought him to a fuller and deeper appreciation of Admiral Rickover's multi-faceted talents than most persons inside or outside of Congress. Holifield, along with Price, Hosmer, Pastore, Anderson, and other active members of the JCAE, sought answers to their questions about details as well as philosophy related to nuclear affairs. Hundreds of JCAE meetings and hearing records attest to these facts.

In Holifield's eyes, Rickover was an excellent team-builder and a consummate manager of his teams. Rickover was capable of delegating, but not in the usual sense. Rickover did delegate authority and responsibility to hand-picked subordinates, but constantly--day and night, weekends and holidays--demanded and got full accountability, while retaining ultimate authority and responsibility and some oversight himself. What Holifield admired particularly about Rickover's handling of subordinates was that he did not automatically accept any aspect of a subordinate's performance. As Holifield saw it:

> Rickover wasn't an engineering genius, but he had a kind of sixth sense: he knew what it took to make people, organizations, technology, engineering and other things work. Just because others he trusted recommended a course of action to him wasn't enough; he would reflect on a specific matter, check it out, and then do what he thought was right. If he saw a path was wrong, he was not too proud to stop and take another one. This capacity to admit uncertainties and his errors allowed him to cut his losses and move in a sounder direction to make things come out right.[74]

A politician himself, Holifield saw in Rickover some of the qualities that Holifield valued in himself. Holifield especially praised Rickover as a consummate, practical politician. He was politically adroit beyond most military traditions to the point where Congress and succeeding administrations had the highest possible confidence in him, and supported him against persistent critics within the government, in industry, and from parts of the scientific community. Yet, congressional support was critical to Rickover's success, and he acknowledged this himself. Indeed, whenever Admiral Rickover testified before Congress, he invariably pointed out that without its support, "I would not have done the job I have done," and that he was, in effect, "appearing before members of the same family." Rickover's assessment was correct, since in the entire postwar period, no other public official received the kind of legislative backing that he did. Congress was convinced that he was open and honest with its members, and if his manner was occasionally extreme, that was likely all to the good.[75]

Holifield appreciated, and indeed shared, the legendary capability of Rickover to sustain his fierce independence from influence by contractors and even from the Joint Committee. The JCAE would generally support the projects he proposed and would hold him accountable. In turn, JCAE members were not permitted to interfere in his work. Rickover's constant review and rejection of most of the defense contractors' claims for more money following delays and "cost overruns" was also regarded favorably by JCAE members and other members of Congress. Holifield knew many stories about the admiral, including the one about Rickover's refusal to meet corporate heads at the Newport News Country Club to discuss business. Instead, he would show up unexpectedly for personal inspection tours of work in progress and instruct his highly competent on-site Newport News representative, Captain Jack Crawford, to arrange meetings with shipyard officials at places like a small diner on the edge of the city.[76]

When Rickover delegated authority to subordinates like Crawford, he expected and got thorough and detailed attention to effective management and high engineering standards without regard to contractors' opinions or desires. For example, when Crawford first arrived at the Newport News Shipyard, he noted there was no independent quality assurance organization for work being done on naval ships. Believing such an organization was then mandatory, Crawford urged the executive vice president of the shipyard to establish one. The shipyard dragged its feet at first, but when it became clear that Crawford had Rickover's backing, a strong quality assurance organization was established. Under the outstanding leadership of Richard S. Broad, the new organization contributed immensely to the timely and economic success of the Navy's first nuclear-powered aircraft carrier, *Enterprise*, in 1961 and to the follow-on nuclear shipbuilding programs for both naval nuclear-powered surface ships and submarines at Newport News.[77]

Two in Tandem: Holifield and Rickover

Holifield's support of Rickover was constantly challenged. One complaint registered frequently with Holifield against the admiral by the legion of Rickover's opponents was that Rickover appeared to be an extremely vain individual who often set himself up as a principal authority in fields other than nuclear engineering. To the chagrin of his critics, Rickover's views often made sense to Holifield and others who were not automatically subscribing to the "most popular" views. Opponents added another more serious charge, however; they claimed that Rickover rarely expressed a judgment or opinion that did not somehow benefit him personally or the programs he supervised.[78]

Holifield rejected most of the negative views and opinions about Rickover. The California congressman respected tangible results. He was largely unconcerned about style or personality, although he believed that Rickover often was much too opinionated for his own political good. On the positive side, however, Holifield also recognized that Rickover's judgment was politically sound when Rickover insisted that he himself "had to serve as the flag" for the good of his program. Based on experience, Holifield was convinced that when it came to situations where Rickover had to put the good of the nation ahead of his own good, Rickover invariably put aside his own interests in an enlightened and patriotic manner. Those who knew Holifield well and were aware of his many activities, were convinced that Holifield's characterization of Rickover was unquestionably true for Holifield as well.[79]

On some issues, the two men found themselves supporting each other. For example, when DOD and much of the Kennedy administration supported the concept of a multilateral nuclear force for the North Atlantic Treaty

Organization (NATO), Rickover bucked them completely and took his opposing arguments directly to the president. His basic thesis, one shared openly by Holifield, was that the U.S. should not entrust or give away its nuclear technology to other nations. In the end, President Kennedy agreed. Rickover told his closest associates, even before he made his position clear to Kennedy, that he knew his opposition might well cost him his job. Not unlike Holifield, even on more mundane issues, the admiral often fought for the sake of principles or standards.[80]

As with Rickover, it would have been difficult for anyone to accuse Holifield of using his position to benefit himself personally; his actions proved otherwise. When he was dean of the California delegation, Holifield became directly concerned with the welfare of the entire state. No action or position he took on the naval nuclear fleet or on civilian nuclear power could help him with voters in his legislative district, nor did any local industries or firms benefit in his congressional district. To work so unreservedly and persistently for controversial issues, or on Rickover's or another's behalf was, in effect, to set himself up as a political foil for many well-organized and well-funded opposition groups who intensely opposed some well-publicized issues that Chet favored or simply disliked him for other reasons.

Still, Chet Holifield never withheld his support for issues or individuals simply because they were unpopular or controversial. He fought openly and resolutely for what he believed was right. Although the courage he displayed on many controversial issues gained him respect and sometimes grudging admiration from opponents, the opposition would nonetheless often paint him with the same broad brush strokes that they used on Rickover and other unpopular persons that Chet defended. He knew this, but he refused to take stands based simply on what others might write, think, or presume. The nuclear option was a new and risky force, and nothing in Chet's experience showed him that most nuclear scientists, persons in industry, or even most members of the engineering profession were prepared to cope with it, much less oversee its proper development as an instrument of war and peace. Rickover, he had realized early on, was different and one of the few creative leaders who could be relied on to produce desired results; thus, he gave Rickover his unstinting support throughout his JCAE tenure, even when opponents of Rickover believed such support to be in error. Holifield never regretted his decision. "Of all of the men I dealt with during my public service," he noted shortly after he retired, "at least one will go down in history: Admiral Hyman G. Rickover, the father of the nuclear navy."[81]

The "gun barrel" house -- with one long room and a small lean-to kitchen on the back -- built by his father and in which Chet Holifield was born in 1903. Pictured are Holifield's Uncle George, Aunt Lula and cousin Clyde who moved into the house after Holifield's family moved to Arkansas.

Bessie Lee Brady Holifield displays her six-month-old son, Chester Earl. *1904.*

Chet Holifield at 17. *1920.*

Wedding portrait of Chet and Cam Holifield, both 18 years old. *September 14, 1922.*

Holifield, 24, and his haberdashery store, Montebello, California. *1927.*

Business owner Holifield at Pioneer Days' celebration, Montebello, California. *Early 1930s.*

Holifield and wife, Cam, with daughters Willa Mae and Jo Ann, wait for oil ration card at rented Alexandria, Virginia, home. *Winter, 1943.*

Second-term Congressman Holifield and family in Alexandria, Virginia. From left, Jo Ann, Willa Mae, Betty, Lois, Cam and Chet. *1945.*

Political campaign for 1942 election to Congress.

Movie stars confer with Holifield about their persecution by the Dies Committee Un-American Activities. From left, Lauren Bacall, Humphrey Bogart, Holifield and Marsh Hunt. *1940s.*

General Dwight D. Eisenhower and Holifield. *1945.*

Democratic legislative strategists gather at signing of original federal Full Employment Act of 1946. From left, Wright Patman (D-Texas), Andrew Biemiller (D-Wisconsin), President Harry Truman, George Outland (D-California), Walter Granger (D-Utah) and Holifield.

Chet and Cam Holifield visit with Eleanor Roosevelt on one of her trips to Los Angeles. *Mid-1940s.*

Holifield comforts a German child he brought from New York to her adoptive parents in Montebello, California. *June 1952.*

Swearing-in at the White House of the second Hoover Commission by Supreme Court Justice Harold Burton, far right. President Dwight D. Eisenhower is second from the right, Herbert Hoover third from the right and Holifield is fifth from the left. *September 29, 1953.*

Holifield congratulates Adm. Hyman Rickover c receiving a special congressional medal for h outstanding work on atomic submarines. *1959.*

Adm. Hyman Rickover shows Holifie the diving controls aboard *USS Triton.*

Speaker John McCormack of Massachusetts, seated, confers with, from left, Majority Whip Hale Boggs (D-Louisiana), Holifield and Majority Leader Carl Albert (D-Oklahoma). *1962.*

Cam Holifield, seated left, attends dedication ceremonies at the site of Holifield Park in Montebello, California. *December 1963.*

Holifield with President John F. Kennedy and Vice President Lyndon Johnson. *1962.*

Alongside *USS Triton*, Holifield and Adm. Hyman Rickover with JCAE members and staff.

Recipients of American Political Science Award from left: Sen. Jacob Javits (R-New York), Holifield, Sen. Edmund Muskie (D-Maine), Sen. Karl Mundt (R-South Dakota). *1967.*

Holifield addresses banquet in Montebello, California, after the completion of the Pacific Electric Intertie that brought approximately 5,000 kilowatts of electric power through Oregon to the Southwest. The Intertie established national long distance and international volume records for commercial electrical transmission. *October 22, 1966.*

Chet and Cam Holifield at 50th anniversary celebration of their hometown, Montebello, California. *October 1970.*

Holifield travels to California with President Richard Nixon aboard the presidential plane and wins his commitment to the Liquid Metal Fast Breeder Reactor. *March 29, 1971.*

With Sen. Hubert Humphrey (D-Minnesota), family and other friends, Cam and Cha Holifield celebrate their 50th wedding anniversary in Washington, D.C. *September 1972.*

Gathering to lay the keel of *USS Los Angeles* i Newport News, Virginia, are, from left, AEC Chairman James Schlesinger, Cam Holifield Holifield and Adm. Hyman Rickover. Cam Holifield authenticated the keel-laying at th ceremony. *January 1972.*

As he did many times, Holifield sits as Speaker Pro Tem of the House of Representatives during consideration of a legislative bill.

Holifield with congressional allies, Hous Speaker Tip O'Neill (D-Massachusetts) an Majority Leader Carl Albert (D-Oklahoma

Key nuclear power advocates, from left, AEC Commissioner James Ramey, JCAE staffers John Conway and Ed Bauser, Holifield and ranking minority JCAE member Rep. Craig Hosmer, (R-California). *1973.*

Holifield visits with former nuclear power associates in Washington, D.C. From left, Francis Cotter, Milton Shaw, James Ramey and John Reich. *May 16, 1987.*

Following his retirement, Holifield meets in Palm Springs, California, with former President Gerald Ford.

Holifield Heavy Ion Research Facility, Oak Ridge National Laboratory, Tennessee. Dedication ceremonies at the facility December 8, 1980, honored the California congressman for his years of dedicated service in the nuclear power field.

9

Swords Into Plowshares

Holifield and the Course of Atomic Development in the 1950s

By the mid-1950s, Holifield had acquired considerable knowledge about the complexities of nuclear technology. He gained this education through relentless self-study, sustained discussions with leading experts, in-depth JCAE hearings, and on-site visits to weapons facilities and AEC laboratories. He also had many competent advisors and associates. With the knowledge he amassed, he was more convinced than ever that atomic energy had infinite possibilities for civilian uses as well as for war. He recognized that the time was not far off for turning at least some of the atomic swords into plowshares. What concerned him most was the specific path that the U.S. would take.

Holifield became a central, although not always successful, figure in the 1954 effort to amend the Atomic Energy Act of 1946. As industry clamored for more participation, Congress decided, with prodding from the Eisenhower administration, to loosen restrictions in the 1946 act. Although Holifield was not opposed to revision *per se*, he felt that the time was not ripe for commercial applications. His policy concerns ranged from basic safety issues to public interest safeguards. He did not think the private sector could build safe nuclear plants without heavy government supervision. He had witnessed Rickover's successes and the strenuous managerial and technological demands that Rickover had placed on the best suppliers. From his perspective, much of private industry, including the utilities, was traditional in its operations and not yet qualified nor philosophically oriented to respond effectively to the managerial and technical imperatives involved in developing nuclear power.

Holifield was also very concerned about fairness in opening up atomic energy and distributing its multi-billion-dollar benefits to private enterprise. He was adamant throughout debates on the 1954 act that the government's investment be protected against the acquisitive tendencies of powerful corporations. Holifield viewed the patent provisions of the 1946 act as central to preserving public control. He feared that the Eisenhower administration was preparing to give away the establishment at wholesale prices to the biggest and wealthiest bidders. As a California populist, he found this prospect repugnant. On the basis on fairness, he argued that either all or none of American business should share in the atomic energy programs.

Holifield's voice proved to be one of the few urging restraint and caution in amending the 1946 act. He could not stop the Eisenhower steamroller, but he succeeded in slowing its momentum. His view that industry was unready to shoulder nuclear power development turned out to be correct. In the years after the 1954 act, industry conducted very few development activities without government assistance. Holifield's lack of confidence in industry's ability and his wariness of atomic monopoly by large corporations hardly made him a darling of the business community. This did not, of course, bother him very much. His innate California populism, which he shared with Jerry Voorhis and partisans of California's Governor Culbert Olson, set him naturally at loggerheads not only with big business, but the Grand Old Party (GOP) as well. It was not anathema to Republican dogma that motivated him, however. His view about the best way to develop peaceful atomic applications was mainly grounded in his increasingly sophisticated grasp of the complexity and business risks of nuclear technology itself. To him, few business leaders fully appreciated the requirements that had to be mastered to develop this technology in an economically sound and technologically safe form.

Holifield's worst fears about the Republicans' real intentions materialized in the Dixon-Yates contract of 1954. Although the contract was billed simply as a power exchange agreement to supply the AEC with electricity at a Kentucky AEC installation, Holifield concluded that the contract's real purpose was to reduce the Tennessee Valley Authority's (TVA's) electrical service area and thereby damage this public power giant. Holifield was the first congressman to express opposition to the contract, and he fought hard to end the contract before permanent damage could be done.

First the Swords, Then the Plowshares

Holifield's and others' growing interest in nuclear power and other civilian atomic uses did not mean that military applications were ignored. Weapons development continued to occupy center stage, as the "Iron Curtain" descended across Europe and the U.S. and the Soviets entered the Cold War. Under darkening international horizons, the U.S. attempted to move in two primary directions: to achieve international control, an effort which ran aground, and second, to improve atomic weapons so they might serve as a deterrent to global war. During 1946-1952, Holifield actively supported the military atom as the U.S. concentrated on fulfilling the second objective. The AEC focused on replenishing the weapons stockpile, reducing bomb size while increasing destructive power, and on developing the hydrogen bomb. It was necessary to rebuild the atomic arsenal because, as the late JCAE Chairman

Sterling Cole noted, "shortly after our committee began operations, both we and the AEC discovered, much to our mutual surprise, that the U.S. effort on nuclear weapons development had fallen off sharply once the war ended."[1]

After McMahon's death in November 1952, Holifield continued to support weapons development as well as Rickover's naval program. He and the JCAE pushed a reluctant Navy brass to develop nuclear-powered submarines and warships. In so doing, they also assisted civilian atomic uses, especially by developing additional sources of uranium. After the war, uranium was available only in limited quantities, and increasing supplies above military requirements meant that this important substance soon would be available for civilian-related research. In 1952, the JCAE also greatly increased military spending, enabling the AEC to open a new uranium enrichment facility in Portsmouth, Ohio. The AEC thus set the stage for civilian-oriented R&D when the military atom became a less pressing issue.[2]

Holifield was most ardent about the peaceful atom. As early as his 1945 report on the May-Johnson bill, he noted that the "constructive possibilities of the use of atomic energy in our civilian life far exceeds [sic] the importance of atomic energy for military purposes." Holifield foresaw the use of atomic energy in myriad ways to "ease the daily burdens of each of us." He was confident that the peaceful atom would eventually be used to produce electricity, preserve food (through irradiation), attack human cancers and other diseases, and perform a host of other functions. Even the AEC soon obliged with Plowshare, a civilian program replacing common explosives with atomic blasts powerful enough to move earth, dig canals, and make tunnels.[3]

The Atomic Energy Act of 1946, surely influenced by Holifield, was the first written U.S. policy on the atom. Its peaceful uses were seen as second in importance only to the nation's defense. The 1946 act provided that "the development and utilization of atomic energy shall, so far as practicable, be directed toward improving the public welfare, increasing the standard of living, strengthening free competition in private enterprise, and promoting world peace." The peaceful atom would be, of course, "subject at all times to the paramount objective of assuring the common defense and security."[4]

The JCAE Splits on Nuclear Power Policy

Early on, the JCAE became divided over the specific path that nuclear power development should take. Some members wanted to go faster than others in testing various concepts for nuclear power plants. Many Democrats wanted the public interest priorities of the 1946 act not only maintained, but expanded. Liberal Democrats such as Holifield and Melvin Price believed industry was not ready, and thought the government should direct and finance R&D, with industry cast in a supporting role. These Democrats split from the committee Republicans, who favored giving private industry the major role.

Holifield had good reasons to worry about industry's readiness. The AEC had begun a reactor development study program in 1951 with four industrial teams, and there were only ten teams by 1953. Holifield felt that industry did not yet fully grasp the magnitude of the requirements.[5] John Reich, a highly competent and respected AEC pioneer and legal consultant, agreed with Holifield's assessment. According to Reich, "By the end of 1952, there was a strong, general confidence that atomic power for civilian purposes was technically feasible if cost was not a factor." Reich also pointed out, however, that "the most advantageous route to take to advance the technology further and to improve the cost picture remained indistinct and debatable." In reviewing the four study group findings available to the JCAE before the 1954 act, Reich noted that industrial leaders were unsure about how to proceed:

> One industry study group proposed that the Government build a pilot plant to produce both power and plutonium. Private industry might decide if it would be worthwhile to construct a full-scale plant at its own expense. Another argued that private companies should continue to do further research at their expense, and then, at some future time, build a full-scale power plant without waiting for any pilot plant. Still another group asked the Government to build a reactor to produce both power and plutonium, with private companies hooking up their own generating equipment to convert the power to electricity. The AEC received other suggestions, including an opinion that it should build the first-of-a-kind nuclear power reactors, using the electricity in its own programs.[6]

Thus, the AEC and the JCAE wrestled with a basic question: How far should the government proceed on its own to build first-of-a-kind nuclear power plants, as opposed to waiting for and encouraging the private sector to take the lead and commit resources? Both entities recognized, of course, that the 1946 act did not allow private ownership and operation of nuclear plants.

The year 1952 was not opportune for a drastic change in the atomic energy law. The JCAE was preoccupied with a $3 billion supplemental increase in the AEC's military budget. The House Appropriations Committee slashed this figure in half, forcing JCAE members to carry the battle to floors of the House and Senate, where they restored most of the money.[7] Then too, since a new president would likely succeed Truman in 1953, conservatives in both parties preferred not to make changes in law until after the election.

The JCAE's hearings on "Atomic Power Development and Private Enterprise," held in June and July of 1953, presaged the course that the new Eisenhower administration would take. In fact, the hearings were hailed by Representative Sterling Cole (R-New York) and Senator Bourke B. Hickenlooper (R-Iowa), the new Republican leaders of the JCAE, as the prelude to changes in the act. They wanted the hearings to clarify how private industry could have a major role in atomic power development, so that appropriate legislation could follow in 1954.[8] Ironically, the hearings had been planned by the JCAE Democratic majority a year earlier. In August 1952, acting JCAE Chairman Carl Durham (D-North Carolina) had informed the AEC of the upcoming hearings and asked for a review of policy positions. The Republicans expanded on the Democratic idea and turned the hearings into a major event. There were over twenty sessions, with testimony coming from business leaders, utility executives, public and private power advocates, scientists, and government officials. Many witnesses criticized the government monopoly as holding back atomic progress. Even Eisenhower supported this view, calling for freer exchange of atomic information with other nations. Witnesses advocated reforms, including private ownership of reactors, fewer constraints on possession of nuclear materials, and fewer patent restrictions.[9]

Holifield Challenges the Republican Leadership

With a Republican president and Republican majorities in both houses, Holifield faced a veritable "private enterprise" tide that seemed to engulf the hearings. Holifield read "private enterprise" as "private monopolies," and put his point across in some sharp-edged colloquies with AEC Chairman Gordon Dean and scientist Isidor Rabi. He was particularly concerned about patents, because he knew they were at the heart of the U.S. industrial system. In his exchange with Dean, Holifield surmised that potential monopolies over patent rights might ensue from amending the 1946 act. He saw a difference in patents of a nuclear industry built with federal dollars, and those of industries developed with private funds. Dean responded that he wanted to "correct one impression that some people may have," namely that "somehow it is proposed by the Commission or by someone else that an industrial concern could come in, walk off with a patent, and somehow the public, the Commission, or the other branches of government, would lose rights under that patent." Dean insisted that "No one anywhere has ever proposed this, even in industry."[10]

Holifield was not impressed with Dean's seeming attempt to erect a strawman argument. He replied, "No, but you have been silent on the subject [of patents] under consideration in your legislative draft, and you have left that responsibility to this committee." Holifield then added: "And it is a responsibility that this committee cannot meet if it follows the other points of your legislative proposals. . . ." Dean followed Holifield's comments by insisting that private industry "demand not any change in the law; they do demand some liberalization of the patent rights," and then he admitted that "We have not spelled those out." An angered Holifield responded heatedly:

> Well, I will say we have not. And that is the thing that I want spelled out before you start changing the law . . . . I want it spelled out as to what incentive is going to be necessary to give them, and what field of private interest they are going to stake out in this project that has cost the taxpayers $12 billion. . . ."[11]

Holifield was worried that corporations would create patent monopolies. In his debate with Rabi, Holifield commented that he did not want to get "into the whole philosophy of patents," since he realized that they were "a part of our economy and necessarily so." He pointed out that "patents in the automobile industry and other industries were in the majority of cases not built upon an expenditure of many billions of dollars of the taxpayers' money in that particular field." Rabi rejoined that most of the atomic expenditures were for war purposes. Holifield was not satisfied with his reply:

> Now, I am certainly not against private industry taking out patents, but I am against letting a few people come into this program when it is on the verge of accomplishments, let us say, and in the last few hours of the day collecting an unreasonable or restrictive benefit over other people. It seems to me that we should draw the line, and put everybody on the line at the same time, and let them go forward; and then such additional inventions as they acquire, let them patent them.[12]

As they geared up for legislative battle, Holifield and Price were convinced that the Republicans were out to gut the public interest sections of the 1946 law, especially the patent provisions. Even Southern Democrats on the JCAE like Carl Durham were complaining about the "socialized" state of the atomic enterprise,[13] and this played into the hands of other legislators who wanted government out of the nuclear business. Holifield was alarmed by the Republican assumption that private industry was ready to build safe, low-cost, reactors. Nothing in his experience supported this view.[14]

From mid-1953 onward, both Holifield and Price plunged into the national debate over revamping the 1946 act. Price emphasized that "the distribution of future civilian benefits of atomic energy must be done in a widespread, fair, and equitable manner." He insisted that "all companies, large or small, should have equal access to the future benefits."[15] Holifield warned Congress and the country that the rush to industry was premature. He also charged that a few corporations were maneuvering to steal this government-financed program for themselves:

> The science and technology of atomic energy are progressing rapidly and legislative changes may well be needed at a later date. Indeed, the Atomic Energy Act expressly contemplated that the need might arise. But the need has not yet arisen, except in the minds of a few enterprising men who are maneuvering to get into the atom-bomb business as a means of building privately-owned atomic power plants with government subsidy.[16]

Holifield was equally concerned about the view enunciated in the hearings that industry stood ready to develop nuclear power immediately. Speaking in the House, he told his colleagues that if they carefully examined the AEC's proposals to amend the 1946 act, "they will find that the possibilities of atomic power have been greatly exaggerated for self-serving ends." He continued:

The policy statements nowhere touch upon the exact relationship of fissionable material for weapons and fissionable material for atomic power. The Commission knows full well that nuclear reactors are too costly to be built now and for many years to come. In other words, atomic power cannot pay its own way. All proposals to date made by private utility or industrial companies for the development of atomic power offer only one avenue of feasibility--dual-purpose reactors producing plutonium for atomic weapons and byproduct power from the energy released in the fission process. These private companies want the law changed so that they can produce the plutonium in their own facilities, sell it profitably to the Government at set prices in a guaranteed market, and use this assured source of income to bring atomic power within economic reach.[17]

In Holifield's eyes, the AEC was about to hand over the atomic program:

Why the sudden rush to formulate a new policy and to propose far-reaching changes in the legislation when economically-feasible atomic power is still a fancy and not a fact? The blunt truth is that the Atomic Energy Commission is capitulating to the overzealous demands of industrial and utility spokesmen who seek special concessions to private industry in atomic affairs.[18]

Holifield did not object to private industry playing a leading role. What he resisted were efforts to change the act prematurely, solely to benefit private industry.[19] Instead of rushing into unwarranted legislative changes, he insisted that when atomic power came to the point of proving its practical use, there would be time enough to decide what new legislation was needed.

Holifield Warns of a "Give-away"

As JCAE hearings on changes to the act neared, Holifield's criticism of the Republican initiative became more strident. He used every opportunity to warn of what he believed was an impending "give-away" of the atomic enterprise.[20] In April 1954, just before the hearings, he argued on the House floor against government give-aways to private businesses. He felt the new proposals were vague and "government responsibilities in the production and distribution of atomic power are not spelled out." He continued:

. . . such legislation should impose upon the Atomic Energy Commission an affirmative duty to pursue atomic-power developments, not only in the experimental sense, but into full-fledged operation of facilities for the production of atomic power for use in the atomic plants. . . . New multiple-purpose reactors might well reduce the present electrical energy costs by furnishing auxiliary power on a byproduct basis. The original McMahon Act provided for this contingency. It has never been utilized nor does the pending legislation provide affirmatively for such use.[21]

As the inevitable became clear, Holifield became very upset at what he believed was a fabricated reason for handing atomic power over to private industry. He did not believe, as proponents charged, that the heavy hand of government was holding back progress. To the contrary, Holifield argued that the government's monopoly was actually an important factor in the success:

> The blunt fact is that existing atomic energy legislation--Government monopoly and all--has provided the framework for great progress in this field.
>
> It will be necessary to examine carefully the proposed legislation to determine the nature and extent of the subsidies demanded. I believe that private atomic industry should not expect to live and grow on the largess of the taxpayer. If those who say that what atomic energy needs is more private enterprise are sincere, then they should be prepared to make good on their own, to stand on their own feet and to be self-supporting.[22]

Despite his best attempts to educate Congress and the public, Holifield was unable to stymie Republican efforts. He protested in vain at the hearings and was ultimately outgunned by the JCAE Republican majority. Although Eisenhower also "got into the act" by proposing fifteen changes in the law through a special atomic energy message to Congress, JCAE Chairman Cole and Vice-Chairman Hickenlooper composed the final bill themselves by the end of June. It was a slightly modified version of the administration's bill.[23]

The Cole-Hickenlooper bill called for significant changes. It provided for private ownership of reactors and production facilities, and widened the definition of fissionable materials, now called "special materials." The bill provided for leasing, rather than outright ownership of these materials. Immediate normal patent rights were also extended to American businesses for civilian applications. Finally, the bill included Eisenhower's international proposal--the "Atoms for Peace" Program, which proposed an international atomic energy agency to promote the peaceful uses of atomic energy and provided for sharing information and materials with U.S. allies.[24]

Holifield and his JCAE allies managed to wrest three important concessions even before the proposed legislation left the JCAE. They obtained a "public power preference" clause, giving preference to public bodies for any excess power generated by the AEC. They also managed to obtain a five-year waiting period for normal patents, as also called for by Eisenhower. On a more philosophical level, they exacted wording giving equal station to public and private concerns in nuclear power development.[25]

Although the changes pleased Holifield, he was still very much opposed to the Republican bill. Thus, just as he did on the May-Johnson bill in 1945, Holifield filed an extensive written dissent in cooperation with his friend and JCAE associate Price. In their minority report, the two men argued against linking Ike's international proposal in a "single package" with granting private ownership, patent rights, and other domestic proposals. Holifield and Price preferred, for obvious reasons, that the international package be considered separately, *before* the domestic package. They also charged that the Cole-Hickenlooper bill was premature since the AEC had not yet issued a finding that atomic developments had "practical value," as required by the 1946 act.[26]

Both men also challenged the dual status of AEC Chairman Admiral Lewis Strauss, who was also serving as special nuclear advisor to the president. They argued that this diminished the role of the AEC. In addition, a JCAE report, bowing to Strauss's wishes, had proposed making him the commission's "principal officer." Such a position, the two charged, would in effect destroy the organizational structure which Congress had set up in the 1946 act. Strauss's proposed role would undermine the "collective judgment of a five-member commission on crucial matters in the atomic energy program." AEC Commissioner Thomas E. Murray also vigorously opposed this idea, and the "principal officer" proposal failed in Congress.[27]

Holifield and Price also hammered away at the "unpleasant spectacle" of the Dixon-Yates contract. Eisenhower had forced the AEC, in the two men's views, to enter into a 25-year contract with a group of private utilities. They charged that this contract was, among other things, "alien" to the purposes of the 1946 law. They opposed Dixon-Yates as a separate issue in itself, but also railed against it in their report because it was authorized by the bill.[28]

Of even more critical importance to Holifield and Price was the issue of patents, an issue they considered to be "one of the most controversial in the atomic energy field." In their minority report, they traced the patent issue:

> It [the patent issue] arose in the very beginning, when the drafters of the McMahon Act decided to make an outright ban on patents for inventions or discoveries which concerned the production of fissionable material or the utilization of such material in atomic weapons. In the nonmilitary field, patents could be granted, but were subject to a "public interest" declaration under stated conditions, in which case the Atomic Energy Commission and its licensees automatically were entitled to their use, with reasonable compensation to the owner. This constituted a form of compulsory patent licensing.

> Since the licensing provisions of the McMahon Act were never utilized and the Commission acquired practically all of its patents through arrangements with its contractors, who were operating with public funds, the "public interest" provision remained a dead letter. It is this feature which H.R. 9757 adopts with modifications, broadening the permissible area of private patenting and authorizing others to have access to the patented inventions or discoveries under certain conditions.[29]

Holifield and Price called for a minimum ten-year transition period before normal patenting could be extended to inventions. This was much longer than Cole's immediate patent provision and twice as long as Eisenhower's, but it showed the importance that Holifield (especially) attached to patents.[30]

To give civilian applications equal footing with the military atom, Holifield and Price also proposed reorganizing the AEC. They called for a Division of

Civilian Power Application and an Electric Power Liaison Committee to correspond to the existing Division of Military Applications and the Military Liaison Committee, but they were unsuccessful. From the 1960s on, they would get the focus on civilian applications that they had called for in 1954.[31]

The Cole-Hickenlooper bill went through many changes before it finally passed. In the House debate, Cole managed to reinsert his "immediate patents" provision in the bill over Holifield's objections, only to have the Senate place Holifield's ten-year provision in its version of the bill. The Senate version also authorized the AEC to produce power and added the "public power preference clause" to govern distribution of the power.[32]

At the first conference on the bill, despite fierce opposition from Holifield and other Democratic conferees, Cole watered down the public power preference clause by inserting the phrase "insofar as practicable" as a qualifier. Cole also regained his "immediate patents" provision. The conferees also agreed that employees or contractors involved in association with the government had to turn over any patent rights; otherwise, atomic patents would acquire the same status as normal patents. Cole also made sure that while the AEC could build a reactor that was a byproduct of its research efforts, it could not build one to generate electricity commercially.[33]

Holifield indicated he would not support the conference bill and made his feelings plentifully known both at the conference and afterwards. In his view, the bill opened the door to more contracts of the Dixon-Yates variety, precluded the AEC from supplying atomic power to municipal and rural cooperative electrical systems, and gave the AEC universal discretion to allow private patents on inventions and discoveries made under AEC contracts. The conference version was a "thoroughly bad bill from the standpoint of farm, labor, rural electric co-op, public power, and consumer organizations."[34]

On August 9, 1954, Cole brought the conference report to the House floor for what he thought would be final confirmation. With Republicans still the majority, he obtained passage of the conference version. The Senate, however, voted down the conference bill and called for a second conference. Democrats and Republicans in both houses completely disagreed over certain provisions, particularly those related to questions affecting public power and patent rights. In the Senate, the debate centered more around political issues dividing the parties than it did around the proposed law itself. These problems brought the Cole-Hickenlooper bill into a second conference.[35]

In the second conference, Cole also had to compromise, with Holifield and other Democratic conferees exacting two concessions. They obtained a minimum five-year transition period for patents, and also managed to expunge the "insofar as practicable" phrase from the public power preference clause. With these changes, the second conference version of the Cole-Hickenlooper bill was approved by the Senate and then by the House. Eisenhower then signed the bill, which became known as the Atomic Energy Act of 1954.[36]

In 1975, Holifield looked back on what he had attempted to do in 1954 to protect the public interest:

[Congress] has been willing to let private industry do almost anything it wanted, as long as it didn't interfere with security or the safety of the people. Because under the law the Atomic Energy Act makes the AEC responsible for the safety of this very dangerous substance [radioactive material], from beginning until it is safely disposed of, even though it is called waste. And any time a private manufacturer utilizes it, he utilizes it under a license, and that license has certain safety features in it that they have to comply with. And if they don't comply with it, the AEC withdraws the license. . . . [T]he ultimate control is in the hands of the government because of its obligation of safety for the people and because of its obligation in the weapon field to protect the security of the nation. And so we were not adverse to allowing this to be done under licenses, but we didn't want it to be done to the point where we lost [final] control of it . . . .

. . . [T]here were some laudable purposes in [the 1954 act], but . . . included in that was also the allowing of private enterprise to patent research and development devices which were made with government money. . . . Now they do that all the time under the Defense contracts.

. . . And billions of dollars of patents have been stolen from the government and given as a bonus to the Defense contractors who are making a device. Why, they would have patented the atomic submarine if we would have let them.

. . . Up to a point I had some success in this patent struggle because I fought for a basic principle of American law. He who pays for the research and development is entitled to the fruits thereof.[37]

Many public power advocates and others openly praised Holifield's active role in the battles over the 1954 act. Clay L. Cochran of the National Rural Electric Cooperative Association, in particular, credited Holifield personally with blocking some of the more far-reaching Republican proposals.[38]

Dixon-Yates: A Public Versus Private Power Controversy

The Dixon-Yates contract, which Holifield fought vigorously during passage of the 1954 act, was part of a larger public versus private power controversy that had been waged since Thomas Edison and George Westinghouse first pioneered the generation and transmission of commercial electricity in the late 1800s. As with the Hanford N-reactor dispute, at issue was whether public or private bodies would provide electricity to the public. Due to the scarcity of water for hydroelectric projects (particularly in the West and Southwest), growing populations, and other factors, the federal and state governments eventually became involved in producing electricity to meet the needs of some areas. In the 1930s this trend became more pronounced, as

the Franklin Roosevelt administration created the Tennessee Valley Authority
(TVA) to provide flood control projects (and later, electrification) in an
impoverished seven-state area. In the early 1940s and into the 1950s, TVA
built additional hydroelectric dams and coal- and oil-burning power plants to
satisfy the urgent demands of the Manhattan District's new uranium
enrichment facilities in Oak Ridge (Tennessee) and Paducah (Kentucky).
TVA's growth during and following World War II, combined with heavy
growth of public power in many areas, became a threat and drew the ire of
private utilities. By the 1950s, public power had taken over almost one
quarter of the U.S. electrical market and by 1955, coal accounted for nearly
70 percent of TVA's power production. As TVA prospered, anger mounted
in Congress, which was footing the bill for its expansion.[39]

Dixon-Yates resulted from the City of Memphis's need for more power.
TVA had an exclusive contract with Memphis to supply power for the city's
growing electricity needs. To provide this power, TVA asked Congress for an
appropriation to build a coal-fired steam plant at nearby Fulton, Tennessee.
Enraged, private utilities mounted a national campaign against it. The
campaign gained stature when President Eisenhower gave it a warm reception.
Budget-conscious as always, Ike hoped to avoid Fulton, and in fact dropped
it from the budget. To avoid the plant permanently, Ike announced that he
would allow TVA to supply Memphis by reducing TVA's commitments to the
AEC's Paducah facility, and would direct the AEC to purchase private power
to make up any shortfall at Paducah. He promised to request the Fulton
plant if necessary. The president's plan sounded good, but suffered in the
implementation stage. Local utilities refused to build a plant near Paducah
since they feared the AEC's power needs might change and they would be left
in a remote location with few other customers.

The president was now in a bind. He either had to acquiesce in the
Fulton plant or devise a creative plan for Paducah. He chose the latter
course. Knowing he would get no help from the Truman appointees on the
TVA board, he decided to use the more friendly AEC, where his appointee
Strauss was chairman. Under the new arrangement, Edgar Dixon of Middle
South Utilities and Eugene A. Yates of the Southern Company agreed to form
the Mississippi Valley Generating Company (MVGC). The MVGC signed a
contract with AEC to provide for the shortfall of power at Paducah, but here
was the rub. Since the TVA would not accept private power, the TVA would
continue providing power to Paducah, and MVGC would provide its
replacement power for Paducah at Memphis! Eisenhower thought he had
solved the problem: power would be supplied to both Paducah and Memphis
without a new Fulton plant. The president ordered the Bureau of the Budget
and the AEC to quickly consummate the Dixon-Yates contract.[40]

The administration's actions against TVA did not stop at Dixon-Yates.
Joseph M. Dodge, Director of the Bureau of the Budget, conducted a financial

study of TVA. Democrats would charge later that the hidden aim was to destroy public power. The study's author was Adolphe H. Wenzell, a vice president of the First Boston Corporation, a securities-underwriting firm for the utility industry. Neither Dodge nor Wenzell, both men insisted later, saw Wenzell's role as a conflict of interest. TVA was not advised of Wenzell's study, however, and Bureau of the Budget employees were warned not to reveal Wenzell's presence. Wenzell, who spent half of his time in Washington, forged a plan to sell TVA's power system intact to a new private firm, although TVA would retain its water and navigation operations.[41]

Holifield Attacks the Dixon-Yates Contract

Dixon-Yates and Wenzell's scheme might have succeeded had there not also been a struggle over amending the 1946 act. Senate Democrats, including Clinton Anderson (D-New Mexico), Lister Hill (D-Alabama), and Albert Gore, Sr. (D-Tennessee), attacked the contract, which was included in the proposed changes. Gore led the charge, declaring that the contract was an attempt to destroy once and for all the Fulton proposal, and moreover, to lay claim by private utilities to the TVA's Memphis service area. The issue of further support to TVA was so volatile, however, that Senate Democrats as a whole announced that they would not take a formal stand on Dixon-Yates. TVA supporters, however, argued that Eisenhower's order to the AEC was destroying the AEC's independence. The AEC was not a willing handmaiden; a majority of commissioners opposed the contract.[42]

Leading the Democratic charge in the House was none other than Holifield, who knew of Gore's comments, and set to work studying the contract. He concluded that the proposal was a malicious attack on public power and an underhanded, if not illegal, attempt by the president to use the AEC for purposes not intended by the 1946 act. Holifield was aided by public accusations from Commissioner Murray that Strauss was using Dixon-Yates as one weapon to impose one-man rule on the five-member commission. As Eisenhower's nuclear advisor and AEC chairman, Strauss supported the president's efforts to force the agreement on the AEC majority, who contended that the AEC was an R&D agency, not a public power agency.[43]

On the House floor Holifield detailed his reasons against Dixon-Yates:

> . . . [T]he President of the United States has been ill-advised and misinformed when he was persuaded or advised to recommend that the Atomic Energy Commission, because of the fact that it had a 25-year contracting privilege, should be used to become in effect a power broker to contract with a private-utility company to supply electrical energy--not to its [the AEC's] own facilities--not one kilowatt to its own facilities--but to the Tennessee Valley Authority grid, in the southwest area of the Tennessee Valley grid, for commercial, residential, and industrial uses. . . . .

> The Atomic Energy Commission is an independent agency of the Government. It
> operates under the law, the McMahon Act . . . . It does not operate under the
> direction of the President of the United States . . . . So it is my considered judgment
> that the President has gone beyond the power and authority given to the Atomic
> Energy Commission in its basic authorizing legislation. . . .[44]

On the practical level, Holifield also complained that the government was
picking up the Federal income and other taxes to be owed by the combine:

> Mr. Speaker, do you realize the impact of what I am saying? The Atomic Energy
> Commission is going to pay $820,000 Federal income taxes for a private utility
> corporation. This is the most amazing thing I ever heard of. Will the Government
> pay the private corporation income taxes of other corporations in the future? Will
> they pay your Federal income tax and mine in the future?[45]

In addition to speaking out, Holifield and other JCAE Democrats decided
to investigate the contract and other Republican forays against public power.
Despite Dodge's news blackout of Wenzell's study, JCAE members heard
rumors of the financier's secret presence both at the Bureau of the Budget
and at the AEC. This information and the overzealous attempts on the
contract aroused their suspicions of collusive wrong-doing by senior officials
of the administration, including Strauss, and certain businessmen. The JCAE
assigned respected JCAE staff member Francis J. Cotter to investigate.[46]

According to Cotter, a former FBI agent who later became JCAE Staff
Director, "The core of the [Wenzell] rumor was that someone linked to Dixon-
Yates was working in the Bureau of the Budget, trying to cut TVA's annual
appropriation, but that he was also visiting the AEC." Cotter felt this situation
"was a piece of cake" and took a taxicab to AEC headquarters, where Bryan
LaPlante was head of security affairs. Relying on a calculated bluff, Cotter
told LaPlante that "We've learned that the AEC's security is so sloppy that
anyone can march in and out of the AEC's headquarters without being
noticed." LaPlante protested, "Nonsense, there's no way they'll pin that charge
on me." LaPlante then showed Cotter the book containing the names of all
visitors. Wenzell's name was listed with his First Boston affiliation. "We had
the evidence we needed on his dual role," Cotter remarked. Upon closer
inspection, Cotter found that Wenzell was signing his name "half of the time
with First Boston and half with the Bureau of the Budget." It appeared that
Wenzell had tainted the contract through his conflict of interest.[47]

Cotter's bluff had worked. LaPlante really had no choice, since he knew
that the JCAE had a legal right to be kept "fully and currently informed" of
all AEC activities. LaPlante also knew that he, rather than Strauss, would
have been blamed for security violations. The next day, Cotter, accompanied
by three typists, went to the AEC and sifted through 30,000 cards, checking
all references to Wenzell. Strauss discovered the card checking and now

knew, thanks to his own security officer, that trouble was not far off. "When I told Senator Clinton Anderson of New Mexico what I had uncovered," Cotter remarked, "he danced around the Senate cloakroom in great spirits."[48]

Although the Eisenhower administration was in trouble with the Dixon-Yates contract, it moved doggedly to complete work on it, despite the increasing opposition. In 1954, the AEC initiated action, consistent with specific provisions for the contract under the 1954 act and the president's order to wheel private power through federal facilities.[49]

The Dixon-Yates contract finally collapsed rather precipitously in mid-1955. Since it was part of the 1954 act, JCAE Democrats chose not to try to kill it by legislation because of a certain Eisenhower veto and insufficient votes to override. Other events proved to be its undoing. In February 1955, the Wenzell episode came to light and the JCAE began investigating this possible conflict of interest. In March, the Tennessee legislature barred construction of the necessary lines to implement the arrangement. If this was not enough, Memphis decided to build its own municipal power plant rather than accept Dixon-Yates power. By July 1955, Eisenhower realized that the contract was not tenable, and canceled it abruptly. The Dixon-Yates combine sued for termination costs, but Holifield and others urged appeal of an initial court decision favoring the utility. In 1961, the Supreme Court ruled that no costs were owed due to Wenzell's conflict of interest.[50]

The Dixon-Yates struggle was a high point in Holifield's career as a public interest stalwart. For liberals like him, the TVA symbolized the value of public power as a yardstick for fair pricing for electricity. The TVA had been very beneficial in improving the economy of the Tennessee River Valley. It was a poor area whose timber lands had been cut, creating a disaster area second perhaps only to the Appalachian coal regions. Holifield heartily approved of the economic development spurred by the TVA's flood control, electrification, and other activities, and often pointed to the Muscle Shoals plant, which made nitrogen for agriculture as well as for weapons during World War II. Overall, though, he felt that Dixon-Yates was about fairness:

> I wasn't a 100 percent pro-public power nor was I a 100 percent pro-private power [advocate]. I felt it was a good thing to have public power, and if the people wanted it, why, they could get it in any city or any state that they wanted to. And I thought it was good from a yardstick standpoint that it allowed the people to know that they were being charged legitimate rates, including the profit and the expenses necessary, of course, for any operation of any business.

> So I was pro-TVA in the TVA area and I thought that private investors had their rights also in other areas.[51]

Dixon-Yates was costly to some officials, notably Murray and Strauss. Murray lost his AEC seat at renomination time partly because Strauss disliked his opinions and close alignment with JCAE Democrats. Strauss's losses came later in 1959 from the Senate's refusal to accept him as Eisenhower's nominee for Secretary of Commerce. Strauss received harsh criticism from JCAE Chairman Anderson and others. Holifield agreed that Strauss should not be confirmed. In Holifield's eyes, Strauss had tried to cripple the AEC, flouted the will of Congress, and ended the AEC career of Murray.[52]

Probably the most important aftermath to this acrimonious issue was that JCAE Democrats became more aggressive about government continuing its position of leadership. Holifield and his JCAE colleagues rejected accusations that they were out to destroy private power, as private power had attempted to do to public power. They were adamant that the government should continue to develop civilian nuclear power. Simply put, Holifield and most JCAE Democrats felt that the federal government could provide the best leadership for getting nuclear power off to a quicker and stronger start.

By the mid-1950s, Holifield believed that the private sector had promised too much. Few commercial nuclear plants were on the drawing boards, let alone producing reliable power. Other JCAE Democrats joined Holifield in expressing alarm that the Soviets would soon outdistance the U.S. in nuclear R&D and production. Disturbed by the slow pace of the AEC's new Power Demonstration Reactor Program, Holifield and other JCAE Democrats called on the government to construct, operate, and test nuclear reactors on federal lands. On this issue, Murray again broke ranks with other AEC commissioners and joined Holifield in urging the AEC to undertake a large-scale demonstration program. Potential major designers and manufacturers of nuclear plants also approached JCAE and AEC staff members privately in support of government R&D programs to prompt the private sector to develop these plants more quickly and stave off government encroachment.[53]

Holifield was not alone in his ideas. In 1957, a special committee of the business-oriented National Planning Association urged a similar course. The committee argued that "the reliability, operating performance, and cost prospects of United States designs must be demonstrated soon if they are to help meet the requirements of industrial countries over the next decade." The committee agreed with Holifield: "The prospect for commercial profit from power reactor construction or operation . . . is too remote to justify a national policy relying exclusively on the current pace of private investment."[54]

Along with other JCAE Democrats, Holifield wanted action on what he believed was the best path for nuclear power development. In the late 1950s, a major controversy in Congress would erupt around a bill that would bear his name. Holifield would attempt to chart a more practical and ambitious, and ultimately successful, course for nuclear power development than the 1954 act did. He and his allies would also acquire additional power for the JCAE to ensure that they had the capabilities for marshalling America's resources down the path that they believed had the best potential for success.

10

The Atom Goes Into The Market

JCAE Leadership and the Peaceful Atom

By the early 1950s, the atom was proving as difficult to contain in the political arena as it had been in early scientific environments. Ironically, the administration of Dwight David Eisenhower, the former war general, seemed determined to open the field of peaceful atomic development, particularly nuclear power, to private enterprise. Holifield was thus able to concentrate at last on his long-time goal of developing the peaceful uses of the atom, but not entirely in the way he had anticipated. The 1950s, a watershed in atomic energy legislation and the decade that set the U.S. on the course of nuclear power development, proved to be a battleground for the California politician.

From 1953 to 1958, Holifield unsuccessfully opposed efforts to open nuclear power development to private business. As noted earlier, during 1953-1954 he challenged Republican efforts to amend the 1946 act to give the development role to private industry. He could not prevent passage of the 1954 act, but was correct that business was not yet prepared to assume the major development role. Thus, in 1956 he and other JCAE Democrats produced a counterproposal in the so-called Gore-Holifield bill, which proposed an expedited government reactor R&D program. The bill failed, but Holifield and the JCAE persisted in their efforts. Gradually they gained the upper hand through increased powers over the AEC budget. Starting in 1957--with expert guidance from successive JCAE executive directors James Ramey, John Conway, and Edward Bauser--they began to direct that specific development efforts be undertaken. By this time, the JCAE was the most powerful energy body in the government, more powerful than the AEC, which now took its direction, and even more powerful than the president.

By the 1960s, Holifield was House leader and chairman of the JCAE (vice-chairman in alternate congresses, since the Senate shared the chairmanship). His leadership was pivotal in guiding the massive effort to produce economic and safe electricity from the atom. Together with Ramey, Conway, Bauser, and his Senate counterpart, John O. Pastore (D-Rhode Island), Holifield actively promoted development of nuclear power by prodding both the AEC and private industry. From the AEC, Holifield demanded and obtained long-term policy goals and development plans. He wanted the AEC to have the primary development role, because he still believed that business alone was unequal to the task. He knew that private enterprise would have to play a very important role, but he made it clear that he expected the same commitment to managerial and technical excellence that Rickover had displayed in the Shippingport and naval propulsion programs. He pushed hard in the early 1960s (and later) to centralize and coordinate the AEC's laboratories and contractors to bring them in line with Rickover's principles. As the light water reactor (LWR) technology matured, he made hard decisions to eliminate R&D on other many reactor concepts.

Although he sometimes approached nuclear power development with a single-minded intensity, Holifield remained level-headed and actually quite cautious. In fact, by the mid-1960s, he was already worried about industry's lack of appreciation for the complexity of the technology. He was also concerned about much of industry's lack of strong commitments to disciplined engineering and strong quality assurance, and its seeming inability to benefit from practical experience and proven standards. He proved correct in his view that there would be trouble if utilities bypassed essential technical and managerial preparations prior to undertaking difficult nuclear commitments.

Shippingport: The Real Beginning

Practically speaking, civilian nuclear power originated in the AEC's 1953 project at Shippingport, Pennsylvania. According to Holifield:

> The genuine father of this power source was the R&D work going on in our country on what was then considered large nuclear plants, namely, the first land-based PWR demonstration plant for generating electricity. What became Shippingport was an offshoot of Rickover's Naval Nuclear Propulsion Program at the AEC's Bettis Laboratory, and first intended to develop one shaft's worth of the main propulsion plant for a very large aircraft carrier. Prior to this, we had experiments in labs but no viable civilian power program, nor was one planned.

> Under the direction and control of the-then Captain Rickover and his Naval Reactors staff, Shippingport truly became the centerpiece of the U.S. civilian power program. This plant and all other Rickover prototypes for the Navy have operated over their estimated design lifetimes; some have operated as long as thirty years. They have been combination engineering test beds, for reactor development and personnel training, and for providing experienced personnel in all managerial, professional, and technical categories, directly and indirectly for the primary benefit of the Navy and civilian power programs here and abroad.[1]

The Shippingport demonstration plant was an impressive achievement. It partly reflected the vision of AEC Commissioner Thomas E. Murray, who recognized the need for a nuclear power breakthrough and engineered--with Holifield's and the JCAE's help--President Eisenhower's approval of the project.[2] Shippingport's success was also a reward for Holifield and other JCAE supporters who had taken political risks to support Rickover's LWR technology. Holifield was pleased that the plant proved to be a vital R&D and training facility for leaders in U.S. industry and abroad.

Shippingport's remarkable performance led a few prudent utilities and suppliers to adopt Rickover's disciplined standards and methodologies. They later contributed notably to building the LWR industry. Those who used these businesses provided a stark contrast later with those who did not.[3]

The Cooperative Power Demonstration Reactor Program

The overall purpose of the 1954 act was to open the field of atomic power to private industry. Accordingly, the AEC announced the first round of a new Cooperative Power Demonstration Reactor Program in January 1955 and noted its intent to work with utilities and industry to construct and operate large-scale, experimental power reactors. The AEC hoped to advance beyond its initial five-year plan and select a development approach different from Shippingport. Thus, the AEC would not own nor be responsible for plants developed under "Round One." Rather, industry would be given modest R&D support and the chance to own, design, build, and operate the reactors.

Four plants were authorized. They included a General Electric BWR to be built near Chicago by Commonwealth Edison; the Enrico Fermi breeder reactor to be built near Detroit by Detroit Edison Company; a Westinghouse PWR to be constructed in western Massachusetts by Yankee Atomic Electric Company; and Atomic International's sodium graphite reactor to be built by Consumer's Public Power District of Columbus, Nebraska.[4]

To expand developments further, the AEC announced Round Two of the demonstration program in September 1955. This time, the agency stressed the need for developing small experimental reactors and encouraged, for the first time, participation by public power groups. The AEC took title to those portions of the reactor plants built with government funds, thus returning to the partnership used for the Shippingport project.[5]

In this initial period, there proved to be some genuine interchange of personnel between government and industry, as former AEC experts accepted industry positions. These efforts were gratifying to the AEC but they left Holifield and others more dissatisfied than ever with the government's slow progress. Private industry would not or could not seize the initiative. There were still no contracts signed for Rounds One and Two by April 1956, almost a year and a half after Round One was announced and seven months after

Round Two began. Holifield and his allies felt that the AEC's program lacked leadership and focus, and these concerns led to a JCAE initiative.[6]

The Gore-Holifield Bill

Holifield's decision to prod the AEC was not reached alone and did not emerge overnight. Senator Albert Gore, Sr. (D-Tennessee) first introduced the future Gore-Holifield bill in July 1955 because he was unhappy with the slow pace of development. Holifield had beat the drums even earlier, calling for a billion-dollar crash development program in his conference minority report on the 1954 act.[7] He also laid the groundwork with Senator Clinton Anderson (D-New Mexico) in the 1956 Democratic platform:

> Clint Anderson and I began working on the ideas to overcome these concerns within the Democratic party at the 1956 presidential convention. We wanted the party platform to contain serious provisions endorsing civilian atomic power. . . .
>
> These platform hearings lay [part of] the groundwork for the Gore-Holifield bill. This sought to guarantee active participation and federal funding of demonstration reactor plants to produce electric power. Senator Anderson played a key role in this fight, but he didn't want his name used; by then, he was such a controversial figure, he felt his advocacy might hamper passage. In the event the bill didn't pass, Clint, a shrewd politician, moreover didn't want his name associated with it.[8]

In the spring of 1956, Holifield introduced Gore's 1955 Senate bill in the House. The Gore-Holifield bill "authorized and directed" the AEC to build six large-scale nuclear power reactors in different regions of the country. As eventually revised, the bill called for an expenditure of $400 million for accelerated development of large-scale and small-scale government-built reactors, but left up to the AEC the exact number and types of reactors to be built. The Gore-Holifield R&D program was intended as a supplement to, rather than a replacement for, the Cooperative Power Demonstration Reactor Program. As an enticement to Eisenhower and the Republicans, the final bill also proposed accelerating development of reactors in the international arena in furtherance of the "Atoms for Peace" Plan. The bill also reflected Holifield's concern that the U.S. should remain in the lead internationally.[9]

The Gore-Holifield bill had many enemies from the start. It was repugnant to AEC Chairman Strauss, who complained that the phrase "authorized and directed" was "the kind of expression you use to your valet!" He indicated that the AEC was more than willing to go ahead, but that "we hate to be flogged as tardy schoolboys for not having done a better job."[10] Eisenhower and the Republicans were even less enthusiastic. Eisenhower quietly lobbied against the bill, and congressional Republicans openly opposed it as another means to expand public power. Holifield himself noted that some opposition also came from "many Southern Democrats and coal and oil representatives." He noted that "twenty-eight [opposition] votes . . . came from West Virginia, Pennsylvania, Kentucky, and the Ohio Valley." Private utilities also opposed Gore-Holifield for the same reason as most Republicans. In Holifield's words: "Private utilities fought our proposals, of course, as they saw them as another government grab for power."[11]

Holifield's most formidable opponent was Sterling Cole (R-New York), the former JCAE chairman who had engineered the 1954 act. The Senate passed Gore-Holifield by a vote of 49-41, but Cole and his allies eventually defeated it in the House. Holifield knew Cole was out to emasculate the bill:

> I was pretty annoyed with my colleague, Congressman Cole. I thought we had it worked out together in the Joint Committee and made the necessary compromises so that we would have a unified position when the legislation came to the floor. Instead, Stub Cole immediately started proposing amendments to the bill to cancel out his concessions.[12]

Arguing on the House floor, Holifield charged that private industry could not do--were not doing--the job, and it was time for Congress to act:

> Where do we go from here? I do not think that we will get ahead by setting up some more task forces and study groups. We have all of the information needed to decide whether we want to coast along with a modest research and development program financed by the AEC and the planned projects of the utility industry or whether we want to launch a vigorous program with some positive goals.

> . . . But this industry cannot get to work on the formidable technical problems involved until and unless somebody gives it some contracts to build atomic power plants. These have to be full-scale plants or we will never learn how to design, build, and operate plants that will produce cheap atomic power. AEC has abdicated to the private utility industry the responsibility for deciding whether the equipment manufacturers are to get any opportunities to build plants, what types of plants will be built, and when they will be built. These first plants are very costly; their performance is uncertain, and their useful life is unknown. They entail risks and hazards of uncertain dimensions. It is totally unrealistic to expect the private utilities to be able to proceed with such undertakings with anything like the dispatch which the Government, with its larger resources, could do.[13]

Despite Holifield's urging, the House rejected the bill on a recommittal motion by James E. Van Zandt (R-Pennsylvania). Holifield was angry about the defeat and laid the blame on Eisenhower and Strauss. He reiterated that "the Federal Government must proceed boldly and constructively" if atomic power were to be developed anytime soon and warned that the bill would be "a crucial item on the agenda of the next Congress."[14]

The defeat of Gore-Holifield had an immediate impact on the Price-Anderson bill. Introduced by JCAE members Melvin Price (D-Illinois) and

Clinton Anderson, this bill would have provided $500 million in government indemnification to supplement private industry's liability insurance for nuclear accidents. In deference to Gore and Holifield, the JCAE Democratic majority decided that this bill should die along with Gore-Holifield, at least in the Eighty-fourth Congress. This brought remonstrances from the JCAE Republicans and even from President Eisenhower, but to no avail.[15]

When the Price-Anderson bill was reintroduced in the Eighty-fifth Congress, Holifield continued what proved to be a lone opposition to the bill. He pointed out that "hard-headed insurance companies" refused to provide full-coverage insurance to nuclear projects because there was insufficient operating experience to assess the risks involved. In place of the bill, he suggested that "the quickest and safest way to progress is to build reactors at present, Government-owned isolated sites." Despite his opposition, the Price-Anderson bill was supported by all other JCAE members, passed both houses of Congress, and was signed by Eisenhower on September 2, 1957.[16]

Although Gore-Holifield was not resurrected in the Eighty-fifth Congress as Holifield had predicted, the issue of accelerating development did not go away. The AEC sought to appease the JCAE by issuing Round Three of the Cooperative Power Demonstration Reactor Program on January 7, 1957. Round Three appeared strikingly similar to Gore-Holifield. It placed no limitation on reactor sizes, and in fact, the AEC later (in 1962) insisted upon large-scale reactors. Holifield still was not satisfied. He did not hide his preference for the sure-fire method of direct government R&D, since industry traditionally had not been willing to take large risks in untried fields.[17]

After Gore-Holifield, the JCAE Democratic majority changed their overall strategy. Instead of a broad program of government reactor R&D, they sought the more limited goal of promoting specific projects. This was accomplished in 1957, when House Appropriations Committee chairman, Clarence Cannon (D-Missouri), suddenly announced that the AEC could no longer receive most of its funds as "operating expenses"; rather, funding for specific projects would have to be authorized by the JCAE, or Cannon implied he would refuse to approve the appropriations. This put Holifield back into the driver's seat, since he was the responsible JCAE subcommittee chairman. He did not let the AEC forget that it had fought him on the Gore-Holifield bill. He announced brusquely that the AEC had lost the "high estate" it had previously enjoyed, and was now "face to face with the grim fact" that it was "going to be treated like the Agriculture Department and the rest of the [federal] agencies from here on out."[18] Under the 1957 legislation pushed through Congress by the Democrats, the AEC had to seek specific authorization for funds for the Cooperative Power Demonstration Reactor Program and for nonmilitary reactors over 10,000 kilowatts. Related contractual arrangements and other important AEC actions were also made subject to JCAE review for 45 days prior to their effective dates.[19]

Holifield and the JCAE lost no time in using their new 1957 authorization powers. In 1957, they authorized funding for various levels of R&D on three new reactor concepts: a gas-cooled, graphite-moderated reactor, a plutonium-recycle reactor, and a dual-purpose (electricity and plutonium production) reactor. In 1958, they authorized development of a heavy-water reactor, and more than doubled AEC's total authorization.

In 1963, under Holifield's and Pastore's leadership, the JCAE completed its mastery over AEC expenditures by gaining control over the operating budget. Ironically, some AEC programs and activities benefitted from JCAE control because they could be assured of continuing support if viewed positively by the JCAE.[20] With these new powers, Holifield offered in-depth counsel to the AEC, including guidelines each year on what the JCAE wanted the AEC to do regarding the president's proposed AEC programs and budget. In one instance, for example, Holifield suggested that a particular reactor concept should be developed by the AEC rather than by private industry:

> It seems to me it would be better to put this type of a preliminary experimental reactor, making it as wide as possible in its scope for the whole fast breeder art, into a national laboratory . . . . You have people there that are going to drift away if they are not given a function to perform . . . . GE [General Electric] has just about got the market pretty well covered at this time. . . . I think this is a project that ought to go to the national laboratory.[21]

The import of Holifield's advice was clear: cooperate or else. The AEC could ill afford to go against the suggestions of the JCAE, especially given the unanimity among its ranks by the 1960s. Partisan wrangling had given way to nonpartisanship by the end of Holifield's first term as JCAE chairman. John T. Conway, a former JCAE Staff Director and later Executive Vice President of Consolidated Edison of New York, described the JCAE's unanimity:

> Within the private councils of executive hearings, the JCAE ordinarily handled difficult questions in a non-partisan manner. Midwest Republicans like Bourke Hickenlooper and John Bricker mostly saw eye to eye with liberal Democrats like Chet Holifield and Senator John Pastore. In 1961, a public storm erupted over using the Hanford facilities for both military and civilian uses. A compromise was worked out whereby power produced was split evenly between the public and private utilities. Otherwise, the Committee had a common front on most nuclear projects.[22]

With its new authorization powers, the JCAE became easily the most important atomic energy entity in the government. The AEC's flexibility was severely circumscribed, and even a few presidents discovered that they were not as powerful in atomic energy as the JCAE. Not content with budget controls, Holifield, Ramey, and their JCAE allies also pushed the AEC for long-term policy goals consistent with the JCAE's expansion of their programs. They wanted confirmation that the AEC correctly understood its role and expanded responsibilities. JCAE leaders were still dissatisfied with the AEC's performance, particularly its five-year plan, which they found not to be ambitious enough.[23]

As a spur to action, the JCAE drafted and published its own *Proposed Expanded Civilian Nuclear Power Program* in 1958. It concluded that nuclear power could one day supplement dwindling supplies of fossil fuels, envisioning the construction of twenty-one reactors of various types in the next five to seven years. The JCAE report also called upon the AEC to provide the leadership necessary to maintain America's international lead in peaceful applications. The JCAE noted that the government viewed the objectives of the program "of great importance from a national and international standpoint" and that the JCAE intended "to provide positive leadership to make certain the objectives are achieved in terms of practical results." As specific objectives, the report called for effective demonstration by 1970 of competitive nuclear power in the U.S. and in "high-cost free world nations" by 1968.[24]

In 1986, looking back at the nation's nuclear power record, Holifield was pleased that the JCAE's 1958 long-range objectives had been realized:

> By 1970, the U.S. had pretty well achieved some significant parts of the JCAE's 1958 objectives in terms of operating civilian power reactor plants. As of 1 January 1970, we had: 15 central station plants, ranging from 22 to 525 megawatts, with 48 others licensed and being built; four smaller experimental power reactors; one large dual-purpose reactor plant; one civilian maritime propulsion plant; in addition to 10 civilian power reactor plants sold abroad. The naval program had 120 reactors operating at sea and seven land-based prototypes in operation.[25]

In early 1960, the AEC responded to the JCAE's 1958 report with its own similar Ten-Year Plan. It concluded that nuclear power would be competitive with fossil fuels by 1968 and would help maintain U.S. leadership abroad by assisting other nations to reduce nuclear power costs. A part of the AEC's international program included the Euratom bill, enacted in 1958. This bill authorized cooperation with the European Economic Community, and noted the need for developing the breeder reactor. The AEC also hoped to move LWR technology toward economic self-sufficiency by 1968.[26]

The AEC's 1962 Report to the President

The JCAE's 1958 report and the AEC's Ten-Year Plan were not the last words in defining America's future in nuclear power. President John F. Kennedy urged the AEC in March 1962 to "take a new and hard look at the role of nuclear power in our economy." Kennedy was apparently trying to seize the initiative from the JCAE. For different reasons, Holifield was equally concerned. With plenty of input from Ramey, he was disturbed about vacillations in the civilian nuclear power program and the lack of public awareness of the need for nuclear power. Like Kennedy, he wanted to clarify the need for a new energy source and the part nuclear power should play. He was also disturbed because Kennedy's FY 1963 AEC budget proposal contained no new program funds and no new starts for prototype plants.[27]

Holifield and Anderson may have unwittingly prompted Kennedy's request. These JCAE Democrats had been urging Kennedy and the AEC to develop a "genuinely nonpartisan and vigorous administration of the atomic energy program." During the 1960 campaign, they inserted a plank into the Democratic party's platform calling for heavy federal commitments to atomic power.[28] When Holifield became JCAE chairman, he also sent notes to Kennedy decrying lack of action by the AEC. "Until the Strauss-McCone resistance to a vigorous federal atomic program were reversed," Holifield recalled writing to Kennedy, "the decline would continue." Yet, space and defense received the largest priorities in Kennedy's first budgets. Nuclear reactors were treated like scientific waifs, to Holifield's alarm. In February 1962, he wrote Kennedy again, stressing that he would be politically vulnerable for de-emphasizing nuclear power even more than Eisenhower had.[29]

Holifield's concern helped to alarm Kennedy into directing Dr. Glenn Seaborg, the new AEC chairman, to review nuclear power. Seaborg had earlier urged Kennedy to take the "new and hard look" that Kennedy now directed toward him. Seaborg was caught amid conflicting pressures from government budget cutters, his own commitment to atomic power, and Holifield's and the JCAE's alarm. If Kennedy was seeking to diffuse the JCAE's criticisms, his order to Seaborg backfired. Holifield wanted action, not words; he termed the study unnecessary and led a bipartisan assault on the atomic power portion of the FY 1963 budget. Even before the study was issued, the administration gave in to his demands for one prototype reactor, some reactor R&D studies, and more funding for Round Three.[30]

Reeling from the intense pressure, Seaborg set his own directives for the study. Taking cues from Holifield and Ramey, he insisted that AEC staff should investigate "the immediate short-range objectives of breeder reactors together with the long-term utilization of nuclear fuels in breeder reactors." The report thus opened the door to the breeder development program, including its demonstration as a commercial option. The report called for "vigorous development and timely introduction of improved converters" and breeders "essential to long-range major use of nuclear energy."[31]

Kennedy released the 1962 report without his personal endorsement. As an AEC document, the 1962 report naturally placed emphasis on the AEC's vigorous leadership in achieving technical goals and assuring growing participation by equipment suppliers and utilities as nuclear power became economical.[32] Historians and energy experts agree generally that the AEC's *Civilian Nuclear Power--A Report to the President--1962* was an important and strategic driving force for accelerating federal-industrial commitments to a long-term, mission-oriented nuclear power program.[33] It found that nuclear power would become increasingly important by the turn of the century and might soon be accounting for "the total increase in electrical-energy production." The AEC viewed nuclear power--with agreement from Interior, the Federal Power Commission, and the National Academy of Sciences--as the only practical supplement to fossil fuels in meeting national needs by the year 2000. By the twenty-first century, the AEC envisioned nuclear power's share as about half of all power production and achieving competitiveness was a primary national goal. The AEC urged that nuclear power be pursued vigorously along with coal as the two key elements for a healthy energy mix.[34]

Holifield held public hearings on the report and gave interested parties--government agencies, industry, the academic community, and the public--a chance to present their views. Surprisingly, no one disagreed with the AEC's conclusion that new energy sources were needed and that nuclear power could meet a large part of the need.[35] Holifield was generally pleased with the report; at last, the federal government had included nuclear power within the context of the nation's overall energy strategy. Also, the report implicitly approved of the direction that Holifield and the JCAE had taken in nuclear power affairs. Holifield commented, however, that the report would remain "worthless" unless specific measures were adopted to act on it. As JCAE chairman, he continued to insist that the Kennedy and Johnson administrations live up to the impressive goals outlined in the report.[36]

In 1966, Holifield encouraged the AEC to update its findings. The AEC obliged with a 1967 supplemental report that reflected the impact of Holifield and other JCAE members, such as Melvin Price and Craig Hosmer. It also included the views of Chairman Seaborg, Commissioner Ramey, AEC General Manager Robert Hollingsworth, and RDT Director Shaw. The new report called for focusing stronger attention on expanding knowledge in nuclear technologies through the AEC's laboratories and in-house contractors. It also recommended augmenting planning and management strength and obtaining centralized direction of reactor development. Only through these changes, according to the report, could exemplary results like Shippingport be achieved with the breeder demonstration program. The report also stressed that LWRs would become a moving target for any advanced reactor concept, since they would have to compete on their total economic features.[37]

The New JCAE Chairman

When he first became JCAE chairman in January 1961, Holifield brought to the office over fifteen years of experience and an intense determination to make the economic and safe nuclear kilowatt a reality. Holifield's JCAE approach both compared and contrasted with his management style on

Governmental Operations. On both committees, he took his duties very seriously when it came to overseeing programs of the Executive Branch. At the same time, Holifield recognized that federal programs, such as the area of defense, were so vast that Congress could not hope to review all transactions individually. Rather, it had to establish overall guidelines and policies to ensure that mistakes and excesses were to be kept to a minimum. Beyond this view, Holifield also sensed that Congress had to be sufficiently ruthless to stop funding of obsolescent or unproductive programs. It was not always easy or even possible to pursue this objective, at least partly because "pork-barrels" and "horse trading" are, after all, seemingly intrinsic to the legislative process.

Beyond these similarities, the line between the two committees was distinct. The mission of Government Operations was oversight, while the goal of the JCAE was to facilitate development of new technology.   On Government Operations, Holifield's tendency, as his long-time colleague Dante Fascell observed, was to set down guidelines for military procurement and purchasing patterns.   There was no better way in Holifield's view, especially given the immense size of the Defense budget.[38] Holifield took a different tack on the JCAE vis-a-vis the AEC. Here, Holifield was a leader in full command, formulating rather than reviewing government policy. Possessing an in-depth knowledge of the industry he was overseeing, he was a formidable public guardian. Together with (alternating Chairman) Pastore, he ensured that taxpayers received the highest returns on expenditures.

In most hearings as JCAE leader, Holifield reiterated three basic principles. Together with JCAE Director John Conway, he insisted that AEC should (1) have a major, if not the primary, role in developing nuclear power; (2) have a strong in-house capability to develop nuclear power and provide guidance for its laboratories and contractors; and (3) use its capabilities to ensure that its laboratories and contractors met stipulated requirements.[39]

Holifield's first principle was in evidence by the time he introduced the Gore-Holifield bill. His second evolved naturally from his support of the "Rickover system." Holifield's third flowed from his basic distrust of putting too much faith in contractors to do what was in the government's best interest. He explained himself at 1966 JCAE hearings:

> I certainly am in favor of subcontracting those areas where competence is sought, that we do not have in-house. But, my own judgment is that unless we retain control we can run wild in the field of, let us say free enterprise contracting, because we must always remember that the free enterprise contractor has the selfish interest of getting business.
>
> There is nothing wrong about it, but he has that drive to obtain a contract and then to perpetuate that contract. We run into this pressure time and time again. To them it is business, it is employment, all of which we are, of course, in favor of. But they

carry it and have carried it to the point of advocating the continuation of an obsolescent program.

We have had to step in, the committee has stepped in some instances, and overruled the recommendations of the Commission.

Now maybe we were right, maybe we were wrong, but I think that this is something that we both must work at because you are more susceptible to this pressure being in constant administration of these programs and scrutiny of it than we are.[40]

The Age of Prosperity

During Holifield's tenure as JCAE chairman, the boom period for nuclear power began. Some early plants in the AEC's demonstration program started to show promise, including Yankee Atomic's plant near Rowe, Massachusetts and Commonwealth Edison's Dresden I. As projections for electrical demand rose at about seven percent per year, utilities began to look at the nuclear option. Both General Electric (GE) and Westinghouse prepared to scale up their next plant sizes: GE to 515 megawatts at the Oyster Creek plant in New Jersey, and Westinghouse to 430 megawatts at San Onofre in California. GE and Westinghouse persuaded the JCAE that nuclear power could win against coal through larger plant sizes. Many engineering extrapolations would be required and the AEC agreed to pick up some of the development costs.

Holifield's determination to expand nuclear power, like many of his decisions, received little fanfare but was widely felt. "That was the crucial turning point," according to John W. Simpson, "where the Joint Committee, especially with Holifield's leadership during the 1960s, played a mostly unsung role in pushing the civilian industry off the ground." Simpson knew whereof he spoke; he was involved from the beginning, having worked with Rickover during World War II while head of the Switchgear Division at Westinghouse. After the war, Simpson was sent to Oak Ridge to study reactor technology and encountered Rickover again. When the AEC and the Navy embarked on the first submarine plant, Simpson became Westinghouse's project director of *Nautilus'* prototype, later sea-going plants, and then Shippingport.[41]

From this experience, Simpson acknowledged that "we felt there would be few serious technical problems to overcome in making the transition to civilian nuclear power." As he saw it, "what problems we found could be handled properly." Still, extrapolations proved to be difficult:

On the reactor plant side where large extrapolations of size of components and systems were being committed, General Electric had to work doubly hard to iron out some problems with its boiling water reactors; these problems were abetted somewhat by their direct relationship to turbine and other steam plant systems. Even we at Westinghouse, as well as Combustion Engineering and Babcock and Wilcox, faced persistent steam generator, water chemistry and other pressurized water reactor plant problems; these had to be corrected on a plant by plant basis.[42]

Above all, however, the "major barrier" for Simpson and others was "the uncertain cost." This was the reason why "after the 1954 amendments to the Act industry moved [very] slowly into the nuclear field." The principal acceleration factor proved to be Holifield and the JCAE. According to Simpson, "From 1958 onward with its rapidly increasing power and influence, the Joint Committee under Holifield pushed industry."[43] Holifield used the "carrot and stick" approach. The expanded market opportunities for utilities and the help from the AEC's R&D program were the "carrots," and the "stick" was reconsideration of the Gore-Holifield bill. According to Simpson:

That threat hanging over our head was a powerful incentive for us to get going. Beyond this, the Committee helped us in positive ways, of course. . . . When we faced a problem, we only had to talk it over with the JCAE. We didn't have to deal with a half dozen committees in Congress, many of whose members wouldn't have had the knowledge or time to comprehend fully the issues involved. If we needed extra money to overcome unforeseen emergency difficulties as we greatly scaled up the initial plants, Chet always listened. He usually found ways to help.

We all knew--those of us in industry and in government--that the key to success would lie in getting the best management to do the job. Our first real success at Westinghouse came after 1958 at Yankee Power when a group of utilities in New England and the Joint Committee provided perhaps one-fifth of the funds required to finish the project.[44]

In the mid-1950s, one approach of reactor manufacturers, often together with architect engineers and construction contractors, was to offer "turnkey" plants. By taking the lead role in design and management, including licensing and training of utility management and staff, reactor manufacturers encouraged utilities to commit to nuclear plants. As Holifield described it, "At first Westinghouse and GE built 'turnkey plants,' that is, plants in which all the utility customer had to do was 'turn the key.'" He continued:

The companies then sold the whole plant, both reactor and steam plant or only the reactor plant portion and associated services, to the utilities on a "fixed-price basis." While some utilities got very involved, all the utilities really had to do was to learn to operate and take care of them afterwards. In most cases, there were no contractual provisions to retain the expertise in these supplier organizations for follow-up maintenance, consultation and continuing oversight and service, as was done with the main turbines and generators. Two new suppliers, Babcox & Wilcox and Combustion Engineering, also became major suppliers.[45]

The "turnkey" period was short and enhanced the prospects for progress even though the firm price commitments, some with guarantees, became very costly for the suppliers. By the mid-1960s, when the "turnkey" era was ending, the more traditional fossil-fuel practices reappeared with utilities satisfied to accept delivery of hardware and paper support from the reactor plant and major component suppliers. Such practices soon led to regulatory concerns about quality of workmanship during construction and operation.

The nuclear power market continued to grow markedly. By early 1969, 94 U.S. power reactors, or about 64,800 megawatts (Mwe) of capacity, had been sold in the U.S., and 20 (6,650 Mwe) had been sold abroad. The 64,800 Mwe total equaled the total installed U.S. electric generating capacity from all sources (e.g., steam, hydro, diesel, etc.) twenty years earlier![46]

Holifield was understandably excited with nuclear power's success. He termed the year 1965 as "the year of the breakthrough," since the total kilowatts of plants ordered that year were greater than the total of all previous orders. Yet he remained cautious. "Many people tended to forget that we were in the Model T stage of nuclear power generation," he commented. "We had a lot to learn and there was no reason not to suspect that in the year 2025 people would look back at the early days of nuclear power and wonder how companies managed with such primitive, and so much different, equipment on just about every plant."[47] He began to worry about industry's lack of appreciation of the complexity and uniqueness of the technology, the public health and safety issues involved, and related matters.

Holifield and the San Onofre Nuclear Power Plant

The San Onofre nuclear power plant near San Clemente, California, was one of the crowning achievements of Holifield's promotion of nuclear power in the early 1960s. He proved to be pivotal in development of the first San Onofre Unit. He obtained the land for the plant and also assisted development of what then became one of the world's largest nuclear plants.

The San Onofre plant needed a push from the beginning, and Holifield supplied it. San Diego Gas and Electric Company and Southern California Edison offered to build a nuclear plant in Holifield's home state under Round Three of the AEC's program, but needed a suitable plant site. Part of the Marine Corps base at Camp Pendleton appeared favorable due to its proximity to ocean water and its isolation from populated areas, but the Marines refused to grant an easement. Holifield fought a hard and long battle. He solicited help directly from President Kennedy and finally obtained passage of a bill granting an easement. Speaking in 1964 at ground-breaking ceremonies for the plant, Holifield humorously reminded his listeners that he had helped change the wording of the stirring Marine anthem to read:

> We will fight our country's battles; On the land and on the sea;
> From the halls of our Congress; To the shores of San Onofre![48]

Holifield noted that he was using poetic license "because these shores--just about where we stand today--were the terrain for one of the greatest legislative battles in modern Marine history."[49]

Holifield's San Onofre troubles had not ended with procuring the site. John W. Simpson, a nuclear power pioneer who served as Westinghouse's project manager at Shippingport, commented that "What the chairman did not mention to his audience at San Onofre were the practical steps he himself took to assure that the plant was actually built." Simpson added:

> The story about his [Holifield's] personal siege on the Marine Corps to get the land in the first place is now well known to anybody familiar with the nuclear industry. However, I was present when he also bucked up wavering officials of Southern California Edison. Several feared that the risk of doubling the reactor size beyond that of Yankee Rowe was too great a hazard for the company to choose. Chet informed them bluntly that if they didn't get on the team and build the reactor--which has worked well ever since--they needn't bother to darken his doorstep so long as he remained in Congress! The message was convincing . . . to say the least.[50]

Into Troubled Waters: Unprepared Utilities and Suppliers

By the mid-1960s, Holifield was becoming increasingly concerned. He and his JCAE allies sensed that the nation was headed for trouble. Many utilities were unable to fulfill basic ownership requirements, including the capabilities to license, build, operate, and maintain safe plants. Qualified leaders and trained personnel were in short supply, and the lead times to find and train others were long. Some utilities had limited or no experience with large, conventional steam plants, let alone any nuclear facilities. Many owners signed contracts without realizing that they would get little help from suppliers in recruiting and training their in-house managers and personnel.[51]

Holifield found it virtually impossible to convince executives of many utilities of the magnitude of managerial and technical gaps in their tradition-laden organizations. In his view, the few examples of successful utilities had actually led many executives to assume that nuclear power could be managed easily in traditional ways. "Put simply," Holifield commented, "they didn't realize that if they weren't good, knowledgeable customers, they were not going to get good, reliable suppliers and in-house capabilities." Holifield was also concerned about "the traditional operating mode in most utilities of 'calling in the plumber after something breaks.'" He was also especially critical of most utilities' failure to take basic precautions, and particularly, to adopt the methodologies and lessons learned by the few successful owners:

> In most cases, utilities were not developing contractual provisions to retain the expertise in these experienced nuclear power plant supplier organizations. Rickover and some other owners, including the utilities in Japan, were more than willing to pay for continuing oversight and services from the original suppliers; they knew they were

dependent on well-managed expertise that possessed detailed design and statistically meaningful operational knowledge about plants and equipment from other comparable installations.

The Joint Committee had its hands full in trying to assess these utility management and development problems. There was no shortage of differing opinions or in-depth insight and information on these matters in the extensive series of hearings we held or in our reports on authorizations and appropriations. There was also a series of special studies conducted by many sectors of the industry and organizations in government on readiness to commit plants, nuclear power, energy options, and energy security.[52]

Holifield was as concerned about suppliers, architect-engineers, and construction organizations as he was with the utility customers. Many lacked in-depth experience and strong training. All were marketing hardware and services "off the shelf," promising increased economic benefits from plants significantly larger in size. In fact, "In general, in the late '60s and early '70s, some supplier organizations really didn't mind slipping away from their utility customers, since they were being overloaded by mounting orders and delays."[53]

If the nuclear industry seemed chaotic by the mid-1960s, especially to its critics, it actually was to an alarming degree. Holifield and Ramey were concerned with increasing breakdowns in quality assurance from rashes of engineering and construction problems. As in other industries, these problems were basically the result of major shortages of qualified management, skilled professionals, and craftsmen. These also led to delays and cost escalations in an increasingly inflationary economy and expanding regulatory environment. Some of the most persistent difficulties were quite similar to traditional problems associated with conventional power plants. Nevertheless, the persistence of the nuclear plant problems had a higher adverse effect on the public image of the nuclear power and utility industries.

Holifield's and Ramey's detailed involvement in these matters contributed to critics viewing them as nuclear power promoters and part of the "nuclear establishment." The JCAE and AEC were, in fact by law, promoters as well as regulators of nuclear power and even more so under Holifield's leadership. Yet Holifield had solid practical reasons for his intensive involvement:

In my mind, the JCAE had no option but to try to help as much as we could. In a large-scale undertaking such as this, we knew that there would be plenty of engineering and construction problems at the plant sites, and we also knew that they had to be overcome on other plants before they became national issues. But, many more problems emerged even before 1970 when both federal and state regulatory requirements were increasing and media attention became intensive. In most areas of the country these trends were spurred onward, in part, by more errors and deficiencies at too many plant sites.[54]

Holifield stayed abreast of these problems because he and his staff were intimately familiar with the industry and the key executives. The JCAE was involved in prolonged discussions and formal hearings where they reviewed program assessments and recommendations of AEC staff and others. By open discussion, Holifield was aware that he was providing ammunition for his critics. "The critics became pretty good at taking these problems and playing them back through widespread media coverage as they tried to cripple nuclear power," he acknowledged. He believed that he had to air legitimate concerns:

> Our role was to fight to help make nuclear power come out right. But, we had no choice but to talk publicly about nuclear power plant problems. That was the best way to focus attention on the legitimate concerns of both proponents and critics in this new industry.

> In our hearings, we spelled out many of the root-causes of the problems in the AEC's R&D programs and the industrial sector; we sensed the nation lacked the will, the commitment, and the capability to bring about extensive changes needed to address the basic characteristics of the industry at that state.[55]

Ramey, Milton Shaw, Jack Crawford, Angie Giambusso, Dick Kosiba, Ed Kintner, Mel Rosen and others in the AEC were as committed to high standards, engineering excellence, and strong quality assurance as Holifield and the JCAE were. In early 1966 during JCAE hearings, Shaw summarized the major factors jeopardizing the success of some 20 commitments for start of construction of new large commercial nuclear plants in 1969 and 1970. As often done in JCAE hearings, Shaw identified twelve major considerations:

> An emphasis on the need for quality assurance in the technical sense, the unprecedented backlog of commitments, the large financial outlays required, the non-turnkey approach, the new participants in all aspects, the extensive engineering extrapolations to be required, regulatory requirements and involvements, siting considerations, fuel cycle considerations, long lead times, the need for experienced personnel and skilled labor, and the increasing costs and uncertainties of R&D.[56]

As pioneers and former key members of Rickover's NR, Crawford and Shaw were particularly attentive to high standards and disciplined quality assurance as basic technical activities and philosophical imperatives. They also agreed with Holifield on most aspects of nuclear power development. In assessing the factors affecting the sudden growth in the nuclear industry, Shaw often described the positive actions that the AEC and others were taking:

> We know that there are many actions that the nuclear community--which includes the utilities, the industry, and the Atomic Energy Commission--can take, should be taking, and are taking, to improve the likelihood that nuclear power will perform in a predictable manner. This includes strengthening the engineering and the management capability in all sectors of the community. It also includes accelerating efforts on the

development and implementation of quality assurance practices, codes and standards, and it includes increasing developmental support to, and proof-testing of, the first-of-a-kind components.[57]

Applying Rickover's Principles to Nuclear Power

As JCAE chairman, Holifield encouraged application of the Rickover system to all nuclear R&D activities. His interest in centralized direction and coordination of R&D by AEC headquarters, along with systematic and disciplined management, technical excellence, and clear lines of programmatic accountability, continued unabated and even increased as the years wore on. He promoted these principles not only in the AEC, but more broadly into government operations and energy security issues. He was influenced not only by Rickover himself, but also through his close association with Shaw and other RDT and industrial associates who had helped to develop, apply, and validate these principles in the NR and RDT programs since 1950.

Holifield's confidence in the uniqueness of the Rickover approach was not shared by everyone. Some senior officials at Westinghouse and GE, even some who worked hand-in-glove under the direction of the two-hatted AEC/Navy NR organization, would contend that they, not Rickover, developed the standards, technology, and engineering and safety systems for the industry. In their view, these were simply part of the process. Nuclear engineers, they would assert, would imbibe this lesson like "mother's milk" whenever they worked with the potentially dangerous atom. For them, it was sound industrial engineering practices, not a system. Whatever the facts may be, the reality is that Holifield and most JCAE members were convinced that the Rickover system brought many things new and different to nuclear power engineering that have yet to be matched, much less surpassed.

Conway, Crawford, Shaw, and other Holifield associates, along with Holifield and Ramey, clearly understood the need to continually recruit and strengthen managerial and technical personnel, in-house and elsewhere, to ensure effective use of the AEC's laboratories. They considered some of these laboratories as critical to the success of RDT's programs as the Bettis and Knolls laboratories had been to NR programs. The prestigious interagency Cambel report of 1965, entitled *Energy R&D and National Progress*, essentially mirrored their opinions. The report declared that "no matter how heavily the Government relies on private contractors, it should never lose a strong internal competence in research and development." Also, "there must be sufficient technical competence within the Government so that outside technical advice does not become de facto technical decision-making." The report also noted that it was "highly important for the Government to be able to turn to technical advice from its own establishment as well as from outside sources," and that "one major source of this technical knowledge is the Government-operated laboratory research installations."[58]

In a colloquy with Holifield and Hosmer during a 1966 JCAE hearing, Shaw discussed the Cambel report findings. When Holifield asked point blank if "the complement of scientific people that we have in the laboratories and the function of the national laboratories provide the training ground and the testing ground for these [the Cambel] proposals," Shaw responded cautiously, noting that expertise was sometimes not available and even when available, was not always focused on priority programs. He saw enormous potential for competence and was determined to correct this situation:

> It is in this area that we have been working in an attempt to get these laboratory resources aligned more specifically to our high priority commitments. At the same time we must be careful not to stifle the basic and applied research, the applied development and the exploratory development that are necessary and can be carried forward most effectively in these laboratories.[59]

In his discussion with Shaw, Holifield was also concerned about the need for the AEC to maintain a high level of in-house competence to manage and effectively oversee nuclear power R&D:

Holifield: Is there danger in having a vested interest grow in permanent Government employees in a laboratory, and is there a possibility that this vested interest will result in either mediocre judgments or in a stagnated concept of technology, of the development of technology?

In other words, can technology develop outside of the laboratories which goes beyond the knowledge of the Government employee in the laboratories and beyond their competence to evaluate?

Shaw: I think so, very definitely, Mr. Holifield. But here is where we have to accept our responsibilities to insure that this does not happen....

Holifield: In other words, the top management should prevent a vested interest from growing in the laboratory which would make it either blind or incompetent to evaluate other discovery and development outside of the laboratory?[60]

Holifield Pushes for Responsiveness and Accountability

Holifield's attempts to incorporate Rickover's principles was not limited to JCAE hearings and persistent admonitions to AEC management. With Shaw and Bauser, Holifield visited AEC laboratories and sites to encourage improved responsiveness and accountability. Both he and Shaw believed that nuclear power R&D should be managed like the earlier NR programs, with centralized direction and coordination under an overall mission-oriented umbrella (Shaw's RDT) to assure timely success of R&D commitments.[61]

In trying to bring the AEC field offices, laboratories and other facilities more in line with these principles, Holifield and Shaw faced resistance at least equal to that which the JCAE had encountered in the utility industry. The institutions were different, but the problems were the same. The struggle hinged on the capability and willingness of senior AEC management to commit themselves quickly. Holifield wanted Shaw to change traditional ways of thinking, which included the assumption that the AEC's major role was to "send money and keep hands-off" the field offices, laboratories and contractors. Holifield expected the R&D entities to develop, if necessary, but certainly adopt the leadership style, standards, and methods of the NR programs. Yet he was realistic; he knew it would be difficult to penetrate long-established attitudes, ethics, and structures in nearly every RDT activity, much less gain acceptance of the need for new experienced leadership to bring about such changes. While some changes had already occurred due to AEC and JCAE pressure, even these had been limited by deeply ingrained attitudes and reluctance to accept AEC and JCAE guidance.

As Holifield's point man at the AEC, Shaw insisted that programs had to be managed, scheduled, and coordinated from his office since RDT had the overall responsibility to AEC commissioners and Congress. This basic reform was discussed routinely at JCAE hearings for almost a decade. Almost every major field office, R&D laboratory, contractor, reactor concept, and R&D program was caught up in this centralization struggle. During the early 1960s, there were over twenty reactor concepts being developed concurrently, with facilities spread around the U.S. and in Puerto Rico. By the end of the 1960s, partly as a result of this conflict, RDT (with concurrence of the JCAE and the AEC) had reduced the reactor concepts to six, and later, to three.[62]

RDT's struggle with most field participants began over AEC and JCAE dissatisfaction with the general ethic of top management, particularly as it related to discipline, nuclear safety and reactor reliability, and resources versus achievement. Holifield and Shaw were convinced that AEC entities were more capable than their performance showed. Shaw also believed that many of the "project managers" did not have the nuclear engineering qualifications, authority, or capability to convert from general R&D to a strong mission-oriented engineering mode. At first, when Shaw and his associates made these views known and provided factual support for their position, the responses of field offices, laboratories, and contractors ranged from denial to unwillingness to consider the problems important enough to discuss. Most entities insisted that they had capable, in-house engineering teams and that AEC headquarters prior to the Shaw era must have agreed, in view of the continual increases in their program funds. Some complained to the JCAE that RDT's attempts to centralize management had undercut efforts far more than they had helped.[63]

Despite the resistance, Shaw and his key personnel pushed ahead. They visited sites and met with field management to address concerns and achieve necessary upgrading. Frequently, RDT management dispatched memoranda detailing AEC's expectations on project funding, management, staffing, and project direction. At first, R&D entities considered such directives to be "overmanagement" and disruptive to their activities, even though the directives were issued pursuant to specific JCAE and AEC requirements. Shaw was nonplussed by the criticism; he concentrated on technical realities and facts, rather than personalities and politics. In some cases, he documented clear signs of inadequate performance. He also noted failures to use conservative nuclear engineering techniques and reluctance to use existing hardware, systems, instrumentation, and most importantly, lessons learned elsewhere.[64]

Because RDT had the facts to support its positions, Shaw was strongly supported by Holifield, Ramey, and AEC headquarters. Holifield was especially pleased with the direction of RDT in concentrating on nuclear power R&D rather than general R&D. "There is no doubt that many of the scientific results obtained in the national labs have been interesting and even valuable in the field of general scientific accomplishments," he noted. "However, the principal mission of the labs should have been to develop all phases of peacetime applications of atomic energy, with the major mission the development of [economic and safe] electric-generating reactors."[65]

By the end of the 1960s, Holifield and Shaw had either worked out mutually satisfactory arrangements with affected entities, or in some cases, discontinued those they judged incapable of being upgraded. Their reform efforts did not go unnoticed. Observers of the nuclear power scene reported on the power struggle within the AEC over centralization and noted that the struggle had ended in victory for Holifield, Shaw, and their allies.[66]

The New Sense of Mission

From the mid-1960s onward, Holifield and other JCAE members scrutinized the AEC's R&D programs. They often visited laboratories and plant sites to assess performance. For example, on one Saturday in mid-June 1970, at a critical period for aligning the AEC's financial resources with hard commitments in the laboratories, Holifield visited Argonne National Laboratory (ANL), along with Price, Bauser, and Shaw. The men came to discuss Argonne's investments in facilities and people, particularly for the Experimental Breeder Reactor (EBR II). The most important topic of discussion, however, was the shift in national priorities toward breeder R&D, which dictated prompt, responsive action by ANL. Holifield confirmed this in his follow-up letter to Dr. R. B. Duffield, ANL's new director:

As I indicated in our conversation, the Committee is cognizant of budget restrictions which have been imposed in the funding of this and other important work in the atomic energy program. Accordingly, our efforts must be planned and executed as efficiently as possible in order that we obtain maximum benefits from the available funds. I fully realize that difficult changes must be made in many cases to assure the needed talents are devoted to the priority breeder program. . . . I am sure you and your colleagues view the importance of the effort in the same way the Committee does and will do what is necessary to assure the success of the program.[67]

By 1972, both Holifield and Shaw realized that the AEC had a new sense of mission that did not exist in 1965. They confirmed this in an exchange at a JCAE hearing. Shaw was looking ahead to refinements for greater success:

Holifield: Do you feel there is an increased sense of mission on the part of these laboratories today with respect to the development of the LMFBR?

Shaw: Yes, sir. There is definitely an increased sense of mission. But there is also the problem we have of trying to get this feeling at all levels.

             . . . Once you get the management agreement, and once the philosophy is established, you have to get these down to every man working on the job throughout the industry. Actually, until you get that commitment, you have not solved your problem. A very, very difficult problem is to get this all the way down through the echelons that one has to go through to achieve success in these plants.[68]

With Holifield's unflagging support, much was accomplished in nuclear power's beginning years. The LWR technology was brought to at least its adolescence, if not maturity, and reactor R&D was reduced to the most promising and practical concepts for the future. RDT brought about many of the changes that Holifield considered long overdue in the AEC's relationships with its laboratories, contractors, and others. But the costs were high. Unhappy laboratories and the backlash to RDT pressure to implement the disciplined approach eventually sapped the strength and momentum of Holifield, Ramey, Shaw, and others, and, more importantly, of promising R&D programs they felt essential for America's energy security. Despite the downsides to success, however, Holifield and others were pleased with the progress that nuclear power achieved in the 1950s and early 1960s. Holifield had few regrets about his trumpeting the NR system as a symbol and operating philosophy and his efforts to centralize the R&D efforts. Whether or not one agrees that there was a "Rickover system" and a need to centralize these activities, it can not be denied that it was Holifield's particular vision, genius, and contribution to deploy nuclear power under, if nothing else, a very demanding label.

11

Refining The Nuclear Enterprise

Challenge and Response

Getting the atom into the market had been a big task in itself for Chet Holifield, Jim Ramey, John Conway, and their allies in the 1950s and early 1960s, but they faced new challenges as they moved to refine the nuclear enterprise in the late 1960s and early 1970s. Commercial nuclear power faced a series of complex problems which undercut its maturation and potential to compete with fossil-fueled plants. While it had benefitted from the Navy's experience and the successes of some well-managed utilities, it suffered the woes of other new industries, including engineering problems, inadequate quality assurance programs, growing instances of plant reliability problems, and lack of standardization, all resulting in a poor public image. Its problems were exacerbated by the political milieu of the late 1960s and early 1970s. Increases in the need for electricity, compounded by the Arab Oil Embargo, stimulated a veritable rush by utilities to own nuclear power plants. The Vietnam War and the birth of the environmental movement added still more dimensions to the industry's problems. Vietnam brought home the fact that America could not have all the guns *and* the butter it wanted at the same time, while environmentalism threatened to halt development altogether.

Despite the problems, Holifield marched onward with determination, both as nuclear power's advocate and as one of its most severe in-house critics. As in earlier years, he continued to prod both the AEC and industry to bring commercial nuclear power to a technologically sound and safe maturity. He gained new strength by two important AEC appointments in the early and mid-1960s. Jim Ramey became one of the five AEC commissioners in 1962 and in December 1964, Milton Shaw, one of Rickover's best engineering managers, was brought back to the AEC to head the Division of Reactor Development and Technology (RDT). With these allies, Holifield intensified his ongoing call for management and engineering excellence.

Defying conventional wisdom, Holifield held open JCAE hearings on the potential of nuclear power to augment fossil-fueled power. Year after year, his hearings emphasized both the serious problems and efforts to solve them. He was critical of the AEC, industry, environmental activists, and those blocking or inhibiting R&D programs on the nuclear fuel cycle, including safe storage of radioactive wastes.[1] He knew that the private sector could not do the job alone; he stressed that even the AEC and the few qualified utilities must improve their personnel and engineering systems to inspire greater public confidence. If he had harsh words for environmental extremists, Holifield also considered himself an environmentalist and promoted nuclear power as good for the environment, energy security, and national defense. Although sympathetic to public power, he was never reticent to bluntly apprise rural and small municipal cooperatives and other public power advocates that nuclear development, particularly with experimental reactors, was too big a job for them. Yet he later fought to give public power the option to benefit from nuclear power generation by private utilities.

An important touchstone of Holifield's success in providing some refinements to commercial nuclear power was the AEC's standardization policy. He, Ramey, Shaw, and others encouraged the AEC to issue its first formal policy on commercial LWRs in 1972. The new policy reduced the scope and enhanced the value of RDT's earlier, separate initiatives for strengthening standards, disciplined engineering, and quality assurance practices. The policy was intended to cover not only LWR technology, but also the non-nuclear "balance of plant." Although the policy was too late to accrue significant benefits for existing plants, it restrained further increases in plant size beyond 1,300 Mwe, and alerted the industry to prepare for the costly consequences of not having insisted earlier on standardization.

The Growing Complexities of Baseload Electric Power Plants

Holifield believed that one of the important reasons that most of U.S. industry was unprepared for nuclear power had to do with the nature and development of the utility industry itself. Power engineering (and fossil-fueled generation of electricity) is largely a twentieth-century art, relatively simple in concept and easily adapted for a highly dispersed industry. The early, small baseload plants fueled by coal, oil, or gas required only simple technology and a few major components, which were purchased from suppliers and assembled and tested at plant sites by craftsmen. Although utilities were mostly privately owned, each company operated as a regulated monopoly in its geographical region. Some have suggested that this situation discouraged innovation and the testing of new technologies, such as control of flue gas and particulates. In the early days, the utilities also made little attempt to address environmental problems associated with the plants.[2] Within the industry, the various professionals--engineers, operators, and technicians--advanced in rank and income as much through seniority as through management competence.

The relatively simple pattern of fossil-fueled power served the needs of utility customers for decades. As demands for power increased, suppliers and utilities remained conservative in their design, manufacturing, and operating practices. Thus, there was only moderate growth in the sizes of major components and plants. From 1882, when the first central generating station opened in New York, until the late 1930s, the largest electric generator gradually grew to about 100 megawatts. Generator sizes increased to about 200 megawatts after World War II and only up to 300 megawatts by 1960.

Nuclear power began to thrive after 1960, at a time when utilities were seeking improved and larger steam plants. As was routinely discussed in JCAE hearings, increasing power demands fueled a push to improve fossil-fuel efficiencies by exploiting higher steam pressures and higher temperatures, even into the supercritical range, for both commercial power plants and large naval ships. This was due primarily to the Navy's support of innovative R&D in its boiler, turbine, and steam plant programs with U.S. suppliers. There was also a simultaneous drive to develop much larger plants to improve economic performance and overall operations. After 1960, plant size thus surged dramatically, from about 300 megawatts to over 1,000 megawatts for the first time in a coal-burning plant in 1965. Even so, the overall power reserve deteriorated rapidly in some areas, highlighted by the "Northeast blackout" of 1965.[3] Thus, designers of nuclear plants found themselves "leap-frogging" what were no longer traditionally conservative growth patterns of power equipment and technology. Added to this problem was the geographical dispersion and fragmentation of the utility sector itself, with over 300 investor-owned utilities and thousands of municipal distributors and rural electric cooperatives possessing highly variable capabilities to operate even large fossil plants, much less nuclear ones.

By the mid-1960s, although utilities had chosen the LWR as the dominant reactor type for commercialization, there were few efforts to standardize. Nearly every plant was custom-designed and custom-built according to each owner's desires and circumstances, just as most fossil plants were. There were no practical means to prevent any utility from negotiating with its suppliers, experienced or not, for a "new and different" nuclear power or fossil-fired plant, especially when such agreements were approved by the state public utility commission (PUCs), financial institution, and other affected parties.

Holifield's Early Warnings on the Risks of Nuclear Power

With the situation chaotic even in the fossil-fueled sector, most of the growing pains of nuclear power did not come as a surprise to Holifield. From his earliest JCAE days, he had studied nuclear power's special difficulties and risks. He knew that containment and control of radioactive materials was the price to be paid for taming the atom, which was much more serious than the price of air pollution from fossil-fueled electricity. In JCAE hearings and frequent contacts with industry, the utilities, and the public, he regularly outlined the new obligations that came with nuclear power. In February 1957 at an AFL-CIO Conference on Radiation Hazards, he emphasized that both unions and the public were face-to-face with "the dangerous environment of reactor technology, with its complicated shielding apparatus, radiation measuring devices, protective clothing, and sanitation measures." In this unprecedented environment, he declared that "new work habits must be learned, new industrial disciplines observed."[4] He continued to amplify this sentiment after becoming JCAE chairman. On nuclear safety, he declared:

> There are also stringent safety requirements to be met. The nature of the nuclear technology and the magnitude of the hazards require a much greater degree of technical competence and a far higher level of public responsibility by both government and industry than have earlier industrial technologies.[5]

A continuing, primary concern of Holifield was whether the private sector was equal to the task. He posed the question many times, and directly in his speech before the AFL-CIO. "As the government relaxes its hold on atomic energy development and transfers an increasing burden of responsibility to private enterprise," he asked rhetorically, "will it be able to enforce the high safety standards in industry that it boasts for government-sponsored operations?"[6] He was hardly sure. In the early 1950s when nuclear power was introduced, many industry spokesmen responded with what might be described as plain boosterism. They declared that industry could "do the job" and develop nuclear power if government would let them. They predicted that nuclear power would rapidly become a reality. Such predictions proved naive and misleading about the complexities involved, and completely wrong on the pace of development. As Holifield had recognized early, the basic problem was the inexperience and traditional attitudes of utilities and their suppliers, architect-engineers, constructors, and component and instrumentation companies. These entities were far from prepared for the growth in demand for their services. The few exceptions were Duke Power, Commonwealth Edison of Chicago, and Wisconsin Electric.[7]

Ramey and Then Shaw Join the Commission

Despite nuclear power's problems, Holifield had some cause for optimism soon after he became JCAE chairman. Partly through the JCAE's influence, he was able to obtain the appointment of Jim Ramey as one of the five AEC commissioners. In fighting for Ramey's nomination, Holifield made personal contacts with President Kennedy to ensure that the chief executive was fully aware of Ramey's outstanding background and qualifications. He emphasized Ramey's extensive legal and contracting experience in the TVA and AEC, the military and civilian sectors, and his service as JCAE Staff Director since 1956. He also stressed Ramey's adeptness in working closely with other JCAE members, such as Price and Hosmer, and Senators Anderson and Jackson. Ultimately, Kennedy accepted the advice, and Ramey was appointed in 1962.[8] John Conway replaced Ramey as JCAE Staff Director.

Holifield now had a strategic ally to assist him and the JCAE in nuclear development. Ramey was in complete accord with Holifield regarding the need for management and engineering excellence. In Ramey's eyes, Holifield was among the first politicians to grasp the importance of disciplined quality assurance for strengthening engineering management practices. "He [Holifield] had carefully monitored the Rickover system for the Navy, and with Hosmer and Price, and Jackson and Anderson, insisted on its application to the civilian nuclear industry," Ramey recalled. "However, Chet was also anxious to press forward with invoking standardization on the utility sector so as to improve power plant performance." Holifield "seemed to feel this would propel the industry towards adopting more efficient and economic practices needed to improve design, construction, licensing, and safety features, as well as more uniform personnel selection and training programs." He too believed, Ramey said, that "Standardization would also enhance performance and public confidence in the power plant industry."[9]

Beyond their belief in the Rickover system, Holifield, Ramey, and Conway also wanted the AEC to set a concrete management and engineering example. They were keenly aware of the contrast between the problems plaguing the civilian sector and the exemplary performance in the naval programs, even though both sectors used the same LWR technology and most of the same methodologies and suppliers. For them, the difference was in leadership. The Navy had a single, knowledgeable, long-term customer in Rickover, who strove to learn everything possible about nuclear power in order to demand accountability and achieve success. He fought hard for a national priority to recruit outstanding engineers and scientists and the brightest technical graduates. On the other hand, the civilian leadership consisted of numerous AEC R&D and industry executives acting as customers. Each operated in a different traditional environment, with widely varying managerial and technical capabilities, disparate experience, and differing industrial systems. A few utility leaders hired a young "graduate" or two, either from the Oak Ridge Reactor School or (later) from universities, in anticipation of the need for such expertise. In the first decade of nuclear R&D and often beyond, however, very few utilities, even those working with the AEC, accepted the need to develop standards for joint R&D projects with the AEC and others.

As a solution, Holifield, Ramey, and Conway decided that the AEC's R&D leadership had to be upgraded significantly. They envisioned a strengthened AEC as an example for nuclear power R&D in the U.S. and abroad, with a level of performance comparable to NR and the best-managed utilities.[10]   The three thus became insistent that the AEC recruit a knowledgeable, experienced leader in reactor R&D who could encourage and demand technical excellence and exemplary performance. With Holifield and the JCAE solidly behind Ramey, the AEC acquiesced in December 1964 and brought on board one of Rickover's pioneers and best engineering managers, Milton Shaw, as Director of the new Reactor Development and Technology Division (RDT). At the time, Shaw was serving as the first civilian technical assistant to his third Secretary of the Navy.[11] He had transferred from NR to the Pentagon in 1961 after the highly successful sea trials of *Enterprise*.

Knowing that Shaw shared their philosophy, Holifield and Ramey viewed his appointment as a harbinger of major changes to come. Shaw did not disappoint them. With Shaw, RDT began to strengthen, centralize, and coordinate the AEC's vast R&D programs. JCAE hearings, well attended even by the press, were filled increasingly with Shaw's (as well as Rickover's) in-depth status reports and special reports on progress and key problem areas. There were often raucous discussions of scientific and engineering issues, both managerial and technical in nature. Shaw believed firmly that most plant deficiencies were caused either by the lack of qualified management and personnel or failure to demand disciplined use of proven engineering standards and procedures. Holifield backed Shaw's assessment, declaring that it was intolerable when customer management did not address these issues decisively. Frequently, during and after he became RDT director, Shaw (and his key associates) emphasized the need for management and engineering excellence, especially in the field of nuclear safety. Shaw's 1966 speech before the American Nuclear Society is a hard-hitting and unequivocal example:

> Safety is a paramount concern demanding a higher order of attention to standards, performance, methods, and use. The imperative to control radioactivity is the price of harnessing nuclear energy. For nuclear power plants, materials and processes of construction must be carefully and conservatively chosen, tested, controlled, and checked. Dependability is demanded, performance in service difficult to monitor, and costs of repairing and redoing exceedingly high. Public safety demands that exacting engineering standards be established and met, recognizing that the design and use are a less direct approach than sound, preventive measures. This principle is not unique to nuclear power.[12]

In one regard, Shaw was very much like his mentor Rickover--he could be blunt to a fault. He did not mince words nor attempt to mislead the JCAE or AEC commission when unfavorable information came to light or was even suspected. When queried about safety problems or his continuing efforts to upgrade the AEC's management and programs, Shaw answered forthrightly and to the point. When asked, for example, about the faulty components he inherited in taking over Rickover's light water Advanced Test Reactor (ATR) in Idaho, under construction and in deep trouble, he replied:

The ATR situation is deplorable. . . . Of course, we had a strike out there which did hurt some. But the fact remains that too many of the components weren't built right in the first place. . . . We found that the people who apparently inspected and certified suitability of many of the components must have been blind.[13]

Blunt talk like this delighted JCAE members. Holifield, Hosmer, Pastore, Conway, and others liked to draw Shaw out on R&D issues and problems affecting both nuclear and non-nuclear power plants because they got straight, honest answers, reinforced by charts. Some areas were not his responsibility, but he was expected to stay abreast of these subjects and advise them about lessons learned in all areas of energy R&D, production and energy security.

Improving Management and Engineering Performance

Holifield, Ramey, and Shaw--joined by highly motivated JCAE staff professionals led by John Conway and later, Captain Edward Bauser--had their work cut out for them in improving management and engineering performance.   Holifield was among the first to warn the engineering community that a bleak outlook loomed for U.S. nuclear power unless major improvements were made.   In a December 1965 address at the University of California, he called for nuclear engineering improvements as a top priority:

I would like to suggest something which to my mind ought to be placed near or at the top of the agenda of items to be given early consideration by the National Academy of Engineering.   The subject concerns professional ethics and standards in the field of engineering.

During the Joint Committee's continuing reviews of technical projects under the Atomic Energy Commission, I have been struck by what appears to be an increasing frequency of problems occurring with equipment that has been designed inadequately. One recent case brought the problem into acute focus. The spotlight was turned on this rather appalling case by Admiral Rickover, who on more than a few occasions has spoken out for higher standards of excellence.[14]

Holifield also wanted engineering excellence in the non-nuclear "balance of plant." He cited the case of the nuclear submarine *USS Thresher*, lost at sea in 1963, where the balance of plant was found to have serious flaws:

Take, for example, the tragic loss of the nuclear submarine *Thresher*, lost at sea with 129 persons aboard. In our review of the incident which preceded [sic] this disaster, it was found, among other things, that the design of the deballisting system was inadequate to meet the emergency requirements of the higher-performance nuclear submarines.

I would like to mention a few of the lessons learned as a result of our look into the *Thresher* tragedy. Basically, we found that *Thresher* was built to two standards. The standards of design and construction for the nuclear power plant were far more stringent than the rest of the ship. We also found that one of the reasons for this was the lack of continuity of technical management in the design and construction of the conventional portion of the ship.

We are, of course, speaking of the situation in the military, but as you know, the problem of continuity of professional engineering management in civilian endeavors is no different. If responsibilities for engineering are not assigned on the basis of carrying a project through to completion, we lose a basic factor in getting and keeping high standards in the engineering profession.[15]

Even as some plants succeeded by the early 1970s, Holifield continued to insist on improving management and engineering performance. Wallace Behnke, later Vice-Chairman of Commonwealth Edison of Chicago, noted that Holifield and Shaw were two of the premier voices in this regard:

Holifield was pounding on the utilities to wake up to the problems looming before us. Most of his work was done in executive session in one back office behind the hearing room. Chet would call us in and at times he would tear us apart for failing to adopt tougher engineering standards. Both publicly and privately, he kept telling us that we were bound to run into trouble. Milt Shaw was also a forceful voice at the Commission driving home the same message while citing the details of lessons learned to achieve more timely success.[16]

Strong quality assurance and improvement of industry's performance and safety standards were also at the top of Holifield's list. He declared in 1964 that "It is of prime importance to the nuclear industry, as it is in any relatively new industry, that the highest quality of workmanship be maintained in all projects." He warned of danger if *any* problems were not addressed:

When a nuclear reactor is shut down because of difficulties, the layman does not differentiate between what may be a defect in an individual piece of equipment-- nuclear or non-nuclear--and the fundamental soundness of the project. When one project suffers because of poor workmanship or failure to meet technical standards, other projects may suffer. It causes people to lose confidence in the dependability of nuclear reactors.

Each project owes a responsibility and a duty to the entire industry. To assure a continually-growing, viable industry, extra attention must be given to meeting high standards of quality in the nuclear and non-nuclear portions of reactor projects.[17]

Holifield continued, regarding the related need for high safety standards:

It is of prime importance that in the decade ahead and in the years following that there be no lowering of safety standards. Scientists and engineers must continuously be on guard that competitive pressures to cut costs do not result in any lowering of this high safety standard. The AEC particularly has a duty and responsibility to the industry and the public at large to help set and maintain these standards.[18]

Holifield argued that it was far better to overreact to safety issues than to ignore minor problems. He felt that utilities had not paid enough attention to the lessons learned from Shippingport and other early projects. New firms after the mid-1960s were not educated adequately, nor versed even in the achievements of highly successful projects, such as the "turnkey" projects. In his mind, most turnkey projects had demonstrated their efficacy repeatedly.[19]

Holifield would often refer back to the conclusions of the AEC's 1967 supplemental report. One particular paragraph drew his attention:

> During the intervening years, there has been a growing recognition of a matter crucial to the successful development of nuclear power plants, yet not specifically emphasized in the 1962 Report--the achievement of demonstrated reliability through strong engineering and through growing experience. Delays, increased costs, and in some cases cancellation of experimental and demonstration reactor projects have been at least partly due to inadequate depth in reactor design and engineering efforts. Such inadequacies can result in an inability to demonstrate the worth of the concept under study. Careful and high standards of design, construction, inspection, and operation of nuclear power plants are necessary to provide the reliability and safety needed for utility operation.[20]

In pushing for more uniform plant reliability, Holifield emphasized that achievement of reliability was possible only in the best-managed LWR plants. As a practical matter, Holifield agreed with the finding of the 1967 report that "The high state of development and production of the light water reactors clearly will make the development of competing systems difficult." Just as "fossil fuel was a moving target for the light water reactors," Holifield also agreed with the report that "light water reactors, as well as fossil fuel, will be a moving target for the advanced reactors." On this score, Holifield undoubtedly had the Liquid Metal Fast Breeder Reactor in mind.[21]

Although he was always urging improvements, Holifield was also proud of the U.S. nuclear safety and performance record. In late 1993, he noted:

> The experience that we have with over 1,900 reactor-years of operation in the civilian arena and over 4,200 reactor-years in the Navy program established the potential worth of our design and safety philosophy with our light water reactors. It also established the potential political and financial dangers we face if even a single owner or operator refuses or is unable to follow this proven road to success in terms of reliability, economics, and assurance of safety.[22]

An Industry Perspective

Holifield, Ramey, and Shaw were not solitary, irrelevant voices crying in the wilderness. Their criticisms and calls for improvements in the nuclear power art were valid, as early utility leaders will attest. A good example is Wallace Behnke, later Vice-Chairman of Commonwealth Edison of Chicago, one of the nation's major nuclear power utilities. Behnke agrees that most utilities were unprepared for nuclear power's complexities. The need for new, specialized staff and retraining of existing staff was obvious. "We had to hire and train new staff for our nuclear activities," Behnke noted. "It was not only our own management and engineering staffs that needed redirection and retraining," Behnke commented, "but also the outside architectural and engineering firms which do much of the industry's basic planning."[23]

Behnke also remembers the reorganization activities that were necessary. Commonwealth, a firm which many utility leaders and bankers then regarded as among the best-managed firms, decided to go the nuclear route in the early 1950s. Then, its primary sources to fire boilers were coal and oil. "Federal and state regulations to operate these boilers were few and the technology was relatively simple and widely understood," Behnke noted. "What was required with the move to atomic power was a major cultural change in the approach to engineering design, construction, and plant operation." Behnke found that "the most difficult group to deal with were the engineers." According to Behnke, "They were accustomed to working within one engineering mode and their careers within a specific company were tied up with this." Engineers often failed to appreciate the unique characteristics of nuclear power. Behnke believed that "Many engineers were unwilling to accept that even though much of the existing power technology could be adopted to nuclear use, the basic engineering discipline was entirely different."

Commonwealth had the foresight to plan. "As a first step," Behnke noted, "the company sent teams to Argonne and Oak Ridge for extended learning periods." The first concrete result was Dresden I, the nation's first privately financed nuclear plant, which went into service in 1960. Operated apart from the company's fossil plants, it produced power safely, economically, and reliably. It also served as a training facility for the engineers and operators who headed up the company's full-scale commitment to nuclear power in the mid-1960s. By the early 1970s, the company had created a separate nuclear division and initiated intensive training that included the first full-scale nuclear power plant simulator. Probably more significantly, the company "did something that other utilities [and even the Navy!] failed to do--it opened up the corporate promotion path so that those entering the nuclear area within the company could use that path for career advancement." This career path became so important that today, "almost all of the Commonwealth senior managers have been involved with some aspect of nuclear power."

Like all utilities, Commonwealth had start-up problems, but now boasts eleven other large nuclear plants. Commonwealth did not initially have a strong in-house quality assurance system. "In some ways we didn't understand how much we would need this in the beginning," Behnke noted. "This was true because General Electric provided our first five nuclear units on a turnkey basis which meant that they were responsible totally for designing and building the plants." Thus, "when GE turned its boiling water plant over to us, all we had to do was 'operate it safely.'" According to Behnke, GE "had a disciplined engineering culture and QA systems from beginning to end, chiefly because they were pressed into this mold by Admiral Rickover and the Navy." "The Navy's watchword," Behnke explained, "was that nuclear submarines and the Shippingport demonstration plant which it built to help bring utilities into the nuclear era should neither leak nor malfunction in any way." Behnke continued: "Even so, we had our share of difficulties."

The end of the turnkey era exposed the inadequacies of Commonwealth's in-house engineering and quality assurance programs. "Chet Holifield could see what was coming, as did AEC Commissioner Ramey," Behnke noted. The turnkey plants proved to be "loss leaders." "Both companies used the 'turnkeys' to drum up business, but they lost millions of dollars on this approach," Behnke explained. After 1966, Westinghouse and GE "began to sell their reactor components, systems, and services off the shelf, so to speak, to interested utilities, and it was up to the utilities to arrange separately for the design and construction of their plants." This brought a moment of reckoning. "Suddenly, our company and others were faced with finding an experienced architect-engineering firm, buying all the various components, and then organizing ourselves to manage the construction." At the same time, "we were also faced with formalizing and strengthening our quality assurance program." During the 1960s, Commonwealth had been introduced to Aerojet General Corporation and the Air Force's quality assurance system. "Our formal QA program was drafted with the aid of a young engineer who had been associated with the Naval Reactors Program," Behnke remembered, "and we retained the arm of GE responsible for overseeing the NASA program to review our plan." Behnke added that "Milt Shaw was helpful, particularly in referring us to the Newport News Shipbuilding Corporation, where we gained further insight into nuclear QA management."[24]

The Gap Widens Between Utility Commitments and Capabilities

By the early 1970s, Holifield began to prepare himself and others for what seemed almost an inevitable crisis in nuclear power's future, due to both new problems and escalating problems of the mid-1960s. Overlaying the industry's general lack of preparedness was a new headlong rush by utilities to get into the market, intensified by the Arab Oil Embargo of 1973. Late-entry utilities, unable to contract with the more experienced, but overloaded suppliers, encouraged inexperienced firms to design and build custom-designed plants. These novices proceeded expeditiously but with a very limited understanding of their capabilities to meet licensing, construction, and other requirements.[25]

These serious problems impacted most segments of the nation's widely-dispersed commercial nuclear power front. Adverse consequences were evident in many plant commitments, and were discussed routinely by Holifield, Hosmer, and other JCAE members in frequent hearings. Orders for new plants had simply outstripped the nation's capabilities to provide qualified leadership and personnel to meet commitments. The cumulative delays and devastating financial effects sure to follow were unanticipated by the utilities. Maintenance and operating problems forcing shutdowns at both new and old plants also led to increasing public concerns about safety and the adequacy of utility management and the nation's engineering and construction resources. Many plants were scheduled for start-up with great fanfare but then delayed or shut down, naturally with unanticipated cost increases. Holifield was among the few experts who understood the serious implications, longer-term consequences, and the cumulative effect on all participants.

Holifield's Open JCAE Hearings

Holifield's concerns about the industry's problems did not deter him from more detailed public airing of such issues in open JCAE hearings, even though many felt this was contrary to conventional political wisdom. Holifield was convinced that such problems required the systematic attention that such JCAE hearings gave them. He wanted nuclear power to grow to a healthy maturity, but he also wanted it to be developed both safely and in a disciplined manner. He felt that the public had a right to know how the twin goals of safety and disciplined development were being implemented.

Holifield was fully aware of the risks that the well-attended, open hearings posed. A national debate about the shape and directions of nuclear R&D slowly rose to a crescendo during his chairmanship. The JCAE, the AEC and its national laboratories, the nuclear industry, consumer and environmental advocates, and the Bureau of the Budget all came to play a part in the hearings. The JCAE found itself in the eye of a growing storm where the winds of political rhetoric and scientific and technological expertise clashed relentlessly. Environmentalists attacked the safety of nuclear power, sometimes on the exotic theories of individual scientists and often used the hearings as weapons to magnify health and safety concerns. The Bureau of the Budget, pressed to finance President Johnson's Great Society programs and the Vietnam War too, stood ready to choose between "guns and butter" and eliminate nuclear activities that seemed unpromising or too expensive. The open hearings also attracted increased media attention and public debate, which sometimes had the unintended effect of eroding public confidence. Still, Holifield was convinced that the benefits outweighed the risks, and that wide-open discussion was the best way to deal with problems.[26]

At the same time he criticized and allowed criticisms of the industry, Holifield also strongly defended nuclear power from the standpoints of national defense and security, environmental protection, and national well-being, even before the Arab Oil Embargo of 1973. Beyond minimizing America's dependence on foreign oil, he pointed to nuclear power's role in maintaining U.S. world leadership. As he observed, "We had many friends from overseas who were continually learning from our experience and applying the best of what they saw to move ahead with their nuclear power programs." He turned environmentalist arguments inside out, arguing that nuclear power was an ally in the fight for clean air and water. He often noted that nuclear power provided "a clean air plant and the only long-range option we have other than coal for generating electric power in the future."[27]

As nuclear power continued to grow during Holifield's leadership years, the nature of the industry changed. Commercial nuclear power became, by circumstance rather than by design, a "blue chip game,"[28] as Holifield put it, one which required large managerial and technological resources, as well as ample risk capital. It became affordable primarily by the well-managed, larger utilities and a few well-managed, smaller ones, like Wisconsin Electric and Pennsylvania Power and Light. Some believed that this was due mainly to costs incurred during shutdowns. Yet, all nuclear plants had additional costs for maintenance, repairs, new fuel, and for supplying adequate replacement power, if required. In general, such economic considerations tended to favor the larger utilities, which had integrated utility systems with access to reserve power to pick up the load lost during shutdowns. Only a very few of the smaller companies could compete under such circumstances.

The Edison Electric Institute (EEI) pointed out in testimony before the JCAE in the 1960s that "a nuclear unit cannot be looked upon in isolation as providing a reliable power supply for a utility system." EEI noted that "it is important to distinguish between a power supply from a single unit and supply from a power system." According to EEI, "Power systems are designed and operated so that reserves of generation are available to take care of outages, both scheduled and unforeseen." Thus, "A single unit is not expected to supply continuous power; a power system is." A system should have, at a minimum, enough "spinning reserves," or instantaneous back-up capability, to compensate for the failure of its largest single unit.[29]

Holifield and Public Power

Holifield was quick to realize the implications for public power in the increasingly "blue chip" industry. As with most issues, he trod on both sides of the public power question. His view was practical rather than ideological, although he believed unwaveringly that the federal government had to play an important oversight role in nuclear power R&D and regulation.[30]

Holifield eventually came to the practical conclusion that small utilities, such as municipal utilities and rural cooperatives, should not enter the race for nuclear plant ownership. He shared his view with his public power allies, many of whom had participated in early R&D efforts with varying reactor coolants, fuels and moderators. In fact, many public power entities with limited or no experience in nuclear technology were participating in these one-of-a-kind concepts. As early as 1961, he warned the American Public Power Association that few of its members would be able to build such plants:

> . . . the costs and economic uncertainties involved probably mean that a relatively limited number of your utilities can or should participate directly in these developmental plants.
>
> During this developmental period, I suggest that you prepare for the future use of atomic power by planning now for interconnection of your public and co-op systems. The economics of atomic power favor large plants even more strongly than those of conventional plants. . .[31]

Municipal utilities and rural cooperatives were somewhat incensed by Holifield's suggestion that they should back away from trying to build nuclear plants. Rivalry between investor-owned utilities and the small public power utilities was strong. Once he had warned them, however, Holifield was not overly sympathetic when the small firms experienced losses. As he remarked, "these small cooperatives have been warned time and time again that they were getting into a game that, at the time they signed the contract, was experimental, and that there was no guarantee of its being an economic operation." On one troubled "co-op" plant, he averred that "as far as I am concerned, if the operator wants to close down the reactor, the Government has its value out of it, whatever it might be, and I see no reason why he should not close it down."[32] If he seemed unsympathetic, he was prescient: all but a few small firms who tried ran into insurmountable difficulties.

Holifield supported the participation of public power in nuclear plant commitments wherever feasible. One case in point was his support for the 1970 amendments to the Atomic Energy Act. In this effort, he joined forces with Senator Philip A. Hart (D-Michigan), chairman of the Senate Judiciary Subcommittee on Antitrust and Monopoly, and Senator George D. Aiken (R-Vermont), a distinguished senior member of the JCAE. Their combined efforts resulted in legislation which required pre-licensing antitrust review of nuclear power plants before the plants could be licensed as commercial projects. The new measure subjected virtually all plants to review by the AEC, assisted by the Attorney General, to determine whether the activities under the proposed licenses would tend to create or maintain a situation inconsistent with the antitrust laws.[33] This gave some consideration to continued participation of public power entities. Public power remains an important part of the nuclear power community. Local, state, and federal public power systems currently own over 20,000 Mwe of nuclear plant capacity or approximately 20 percent of the total U.S. nuclear generating capacity.[34]

Holifield and His "Weeping Chair"

As the Vietnam conflict dried up federal monies available for nuclear power, Holifield faced increasing opposition not only from consumer and environmental groups, but from the Bureau of the Budget, which was determined to restrain nuclear power and other federal spending. He recalled the JCAE's problems in supporting long-term, costly R&D during this period:

> We had the responsibility for both enhancing the development of nuclear power and protecting our energy security for future generations. The U.S. had limited resources available to meet the mounting commitments to increased dependence on electric power.   In the JCAE, we became increasingly concerned about the need for perspective.   We said, "Let's focus on the highest priorities and conservative approaches, avoiding technological "pied-pipers" and "leap-froggers," other diversions, and complacency.   "Let's practice restraints and standardization to the maximum degree possible across the board." Whoever takes time to browse through the JCAE hearing records of the 1960s and early 1970s can readily see how these concerns were laid on the table and how they were acted on within the Committee's jurisdiction and within that of other governmental agencies and by the private sector.[35]

Thus, in his office next to his desk, JCAE Chairman Holifield had a "weeping chair" that came into increasing use in the mid-1960s and beyond. Many people in the laboratories ended up in the "weeping chair" after decisions to terminate projects that were judged less promising than others. According to Holifield:

> After the utilities made their move to build increasing numbers of LWRs, the JCAE decided in the mid-60s to go full speed ahead on the R&D and demonstration of the breeder. These decisions gave us compelling reasons to have the AEC reexamine the incentives and costs for pursuing other reactor concepts, including other potentially promising breeder concepts. Someday, some few of these concepts, at the most, might be worth looking at again for some special purposes. But that was not so evident then or now. At the early stage, even if they could have been well engineered, which few were, none of these other concepts appeared to offer many incentives, if any, for experienced nuclear utilities. They, and most others, had concluded that greater efficiencies and other incentives could only come from more uniform success with the LWRs and the LMFBR.[36]

When the JCAE was forced to make hard termination decisions, political howling broke out on all sides by the aggrieved. Sometimes the reactions were dramatic. In one case, Holifield felt compelled to cancel a multi-million-dollar project and a senior AEC official went to the West Coast to inform the affected company. The chief executive responded at the meeting by jumping up on his coffee table and giving a "war whoop" while loudly insisting that Holifield was wrong and had no authority to make such a judgment! When Holifield heard about the reaction, he observed:

Maybe we were ignorant amateurs in the Congress. But on these matters, scientists were developing, testing, and probing the unknown even though there were no longer significant incentives. As congressmen, our job was to help them. But also to call a halt whenever they were going nowhere fast or when others had achieved the goals.

The JCAE had to be tough on these issues. Scientists in their own laboratories, and some of the commissioners wanted desperately to keep going ahead with these unique concepts like the "molten salt" reactor. This particular one was developed at the Oak Ridge lab and there was little legitimate interest and support for it or for most of the other concepts in the other labs by potential customers, or from industry or the scientific community. I felt this concept was not working even in the lab's test program under ideal conditions. We had already spent a lot of money on it and on too many others. No one else seemed interested and we needed the money and the best scientific talent for the breeder. It would be needed sooner or later.[37]

Holifield also used his "weeping chair" to lecture those he felt had stepped out of line. Holifield once lectured a prominent JCAE member without the benefit, but very much in keeping with the spirit, of his "weeping chair." The person was his close friend and unfailing ally, the late Senator Henry Jackson (D-Washington). Jackson experienced something of a loss of enthusiasm for JCAE work in the 1960s. "Space" had become the new glamour word, and senators, much fewer in number than congressmen, spread themselves ever more thinly as they looked to space and other subjects to make their mark. Holifield believed that senators Clinton Anderson and Albert Gore remained committed to the JCAE, especially since they had to look out for the Los Alamos and Oak Ridge laboratories in their respective states. Senator Pastore also continued to work hard. What brought Holifield's wrath was Jackson's inattention to an important Hanford project, not that his interests had shifted. Holifield found himself handling a project Jackson should have handled. While Jackson did not do the work, he issued press releases to his constituents about the latest funds for Hanford. Holifield was more than a little miffed. He told Jackson that he would hold the authorization until Jackson showed up for the next "mark-up session," where a final vote would be taken. Jackson came to the session, voted, and asked to be excused. Holifield's reply was curt: "The gentleman from Washington is excused!"[38]

Even so prominent a figure as Admiral Rickover was not immune from sitting in Holifield's "weeping chair." The admiral found this out when he participated in the controversy over the breeder demonstration plant on the Clinch River in Tennessee. Rickover, the major proponent of his own LWR thermal breeder plant earlier at Shippingport and Shaw's former boss in NR, had been unrelenting in chiding RDT Director Shaw as often as possible about Shaw's and others' difficulties with liquid metal plants, as compared to their many, mutual successes in earlier years. Now the admiral seemed to regenerate his, Holifield's and Shaw's earlier opposition to the Enrico Fermi Liquid Metal Plant and superimpose it on the Clinch River breeder program.

It was not surprising that there was controversy on the first breeder plant. In contrast to the siting of the Fast Flux Test Facility (FFTF) at Hanford a few years earlier, siting for the breeder plant provoked heated debate primarily because the plant held promise for bringing huge benefits to the region selected. Even some JCAE members were at loggerheads: Hosmer wanted to build the plant in California, while other members wanted it in Texas and New York. Holifield remained impartial, arguing that the AEC should propose the location that could best serve the R&D program for the long term. "Mel Price didn't try to get it for Illinois, nor did I for California," Holifield explained. "We only wanted to have it built away from large population centers and from partisan politics."[39] Ultimately, the decision was left up to the AEC. "The people of Oak Ridge and of Tennessee were for locating the breeder on a government site near Clinch River as recommended by the AEC," Holifield later remarked, and that site was eventually selected.[40]

Holifield was incensed at Rickover's periodic negative comments to members of Congress on breeder siting and related issues. He decided to do something about it. After all, Rickover had been advised frequently that AEC was attempting to invoke the discipline and conservatism of the NR, EBR, Fermi, and other liquid metal programs and that the R&D was patterned after Rickover's and Shaw's work on the LWRs and *Seawolf* plants.

Since the admiral owed much to Holifield, Holifield invited Rickover to his office for a sit in the "weeping chair." "Rick," Holifield remembered beginning, "you know who supported you on the building of the nuclear submarine." "I sure do," the admiral replied, "Jackson, Anderson, Price, and Holifield." "We got that one done," Holifield rejoined, but he added: "Rick, you're bad-mouthing our decisions on the breeder. I want you to pull back. We believed in the thing you believed in, so you believe in what we do now." Rickover got the message. "You're right, Mr. Chairman," came the reply, and Rickover kept his word. After the discussion, the admiral muted his open opposition to the breeder, but never relented until his death in 1986 on his constant chiding and "giving free advice" to Shaw.[41]

As the Rickover episode showed, Holifield did not let allies and friends come between him and his perception of the best interests of the country. According to friend and foe alike, Holifield set a very high ethical standard for the JCAE, notably so during the 1960s. On many occasions, Edward Bauser, a former Navy captain and JCAE Executive Director from 1967 to the committee's demise in 1977, witnessed Holifield's approach:

> Chet shot from the shoulder . . . he expected his associates to do likewise. "Tell me where I'm wrong, Ed, not where I'm right," he would insist. "I want to know everything I should know so there are no surprises." If we failed on this score, he'd let us know loud and clear.

But it was not just his staff and the AEC management from whom he expected straight talk and hard facts. He would also demand such from nuclear experts like Alvin Weinberg of the Oak Ridge National Laboratory and Chauncey Starr, then with Atomics International. Many scientists and engineers were far more knowledgeable about atomic energy than Chet was. So he would listen to them. If he thought their proposals were sound, he'd push the Joint Committee and the AEC to back them fully. But if our reviews of their programs showed that their theoretical concepts were not being engineered right and standards of excellence were not being applied as required for success, or if they turned out to be impractical in terms of realistically demonstrating the potential for producing competitive reliable power safely, then he would slash or eliminate their budgets. He was as ruthless with the concepts pushed by persons he knew as he was with the projects of individuals and organizations for which he had low regard in the first place.[42]

Holifield's impartiality extended even to the purse strings that affected his state, even though by the 1960s he was dean of the California delegation and was expected to look out for his state. As Bauser observed, "Even though the Joint Committee tried to operate in a non-partisan manner, that didn't mean some of its members weren't interested in seeing that nuclear projects, test facilities, and reactor plants were channelled to their own states or legislative districts." Such facilities were "'big ticket' items," and Bauser pointed out that "During the 1950s when Senator Clinton Anderson was chairman, for instance, JCAE appropriations leaned heavily in the direction of New Mexico."[43] Holifield, however, did not show any particular favoritism toward California. After careful reviews, he excised troubled or unpromising projects from the AEC's plans without regard to location. Holifield axed the developmental Mobile Compact Reactor Project, for example, even though part of the program was located in his own district. In another action, Holifield pulled the plug on the Hallam sodium-cooled and graphite-moderated reactor in Nebraska, even though Senator Carl Curtis was a JCAE member, Holifield's friend Chauncey Starr of Atomics International was the major contractor, and Atomics International was based in California.[44]

Standardization: Holifield Embraces Henry Ford

Holifield, along with cohorts Ramey, Shaw, and others, proved to be a major player in standardization, one of the most significant steps to be taken in nuclear power in the late 1960s and early 1970s. Holifield was a powerful JCAE voice already in the 1960s calling for more standardization. "Build nuclear plants like Henry Ford did the automobile" was Holifield's slogan; he advocated building only one kind of plant with one technology. "I always thought we should put a stop to the custom designs and standardize nuclear plants like Henry Ford did his first cars," Holifield explained. "Ford gave every customer the car he wanted, provided it used his engine and its body was standard size and black!"[45]   At the inception of the RDT standards program in 1966 for AEC reactors and test facilities, Holifield realized that the ultimate success of commercial nuclear power hinged on standardization, along with strong quality assurance. The step was critical to coalescing the field into a definable discipline, as had been done in NR programs.[46]

Holifield's and his allies' overall reason for pushing the private sector to standardize LWR and balance-of-plant designs was practical. Accumulating evidence suggested that many costs, delays, and other liabilities could be attributed to one-of-a-kind problems, or the failure to standardize. Holifield also believed the process was necessary to obtain improvements in future plant performance and economics. Holifield did not, of course, view standardization as a panacea and the process itself could not solve many of the problems in existing plants. However, he believed that standardization of future LWRs would help restore sagging public confidence in nuclear power.[47]

Holifield was equally concerned about standardization of balance-of-plant components in order to achieve successful interfacing with the reactor plant. He pointed out that the non-nuclear, electricity-generating part was still too much like those in fossil-fueled plants and that significant upgrading was needed to prevent serious undercutting of nuclear plant performance. He bemoaned the fact that standardization had not been forthcoming for many years despite mounting evidence about licensing, costs, and other drawbacks:

> When a utility makes a decision to build a nuclear plant, a reactor vendor is selected and, in general, an architect-engineering firm is retained to design and sometimes supervise the construction of the balance-of-plant. The trend toward standardization, I regret to say, has not been pursued as vigorously by the utilities and architect-engineering firms as I would have hoped. To date, only one such firm has made a firm commitment to the AEC to prepare and submit a standard design for a balance-of-plant.[48]

Holifield's ideas about standardization were not well received in all quarters. "Many leaders in the AEC, its laboratories, and industrial contractors objected loudly to my viewpoint," he explained. "They felt they should experiment with their reactor concepts, changing designs, and testing them out as they went along."[49] Some JCAE members, AEC commissioners, and others felt the same way. They had collectively promoted for years, with AEC support, a variety of reactor and fuel cycle concepts. Nonetheless, Holifield knew that the best-managed utilities, buttressed by their suppliers, ultimately selected LWR technology for the near term,[50] along with the fast breeder for the long term, based partly on the Navy's success with LWRs:

> American industry has long been a great believer in the advantages of standardization. Why shouldn't this principle have applied also as a first-order priority to the large numbers of reactor concepts and fuel cycles? Admiral Rickover provided us with a

model for making hard decisions when he had the guts to set aside the excellent performance of his sodium-cooled reactor on *Seawolf* in favor of concentrating all of his program resources on the pressurized water reactor concept. To him, even with his string of successes with both reactor concepts, it was simply a matter of assuring that all of the resources would be applied to making sure what we knew would work. That way he could most efficiently develop its full potential.

Likewise, the Joint Committee came to believe that we had to apply most of the talent in the AEC laboratories and contractors, as well as all the money we could pull together, to concentrate on the high-temperature breeder and the mixed-oxide fuel cycle. After all, this breeder type is significantly more efficient than any of the other concepts, and can be operated with the "once-through" fuel cycle if that was really preferred by the utilities before commercial reprocessing becomes economically attractive and available in our country.[51]

Holifield had no better success with the utility industry. At every opportunity, Holifield continued to urge, with little effect, conservatism and caution on changes and extrapolations affecting plant sizes and designs:

Suppliers were selling them [nuclear plants] at 1,000 [megawatts] and were shooting for 1,500 and even up to 2,000 Mwe. So I said, "You're going too fast. Why don't you standardize the size at 750 or 1,000 Mwe?" They [General Electric and Westinghouse] and other companies were introducing new features and models to increase each's nuclear plants competitive edge in the market as well as their competition with fossil-fired plants.[52]

Holifield did not sway GE and Westinghouse or their competitors. The companies responded by "claiming they had to follow the path they were on to make the plants more efficient, economical, and attractive to the utilities." Holifield continued to feel "they should have standardized their models and restrained their appetite for new features and for selling to any utility whose management made up their mind to buy a nuclear plant." Holifield fervently believed that "had the utilities and industry restrained theirselves, the nuclear business might still be thriving now," rather than "just limping along."[53]

The issue of standardization became more acute by the early 1970s primarily because of the increasing demand for electricity. Growing electricity demand, the public's concern over blackouts and brownouts around the country, and the dangers of dependence on imported oil all made nuclear power more attractive and caused it to grow precipitously. These factors brought many new and untrained utilities, suppliers, engineers, and craftsmen to fill the heightened demand. Common sense often seemed overridden by the veritable waves of new plant orders that flooded in on top of the existing overload from the late 1960s. Plant numbers and sizes skyrocketed. By the start of 1970, the AEC's licensing bodies, including the Advisory Committee on Reactor Safety (ACRS), had approved about 70 civilian plant construction permits, with only 17 plants operational and another 48 under construction.

The operating plants ranged from 22 to 575 megawatts, with five plants over 400 Mwe having accumulated only seven reactor years of operation. This situation drastically worsened by 1974, when over 50 mainly inexperienced and highly decentralized utilities proposed an additional 155 large nuclear plants, to be custom-designed and custom-built at over 80 sites![54]

Neither Holifield nor others could do much to stem the tide that appeared to be engulfing nuclear power. There was no practical way within the free enterprise system to prevent trained or untrained suppliers from "selling bigger and better reactors like hot-cakes" to both knowledgeable and unqualified utilities. Holifield faced enormous problems in just trying to obtain reliable data from suppliers, utilities, PUCs, financial institutions, and others on the growing crisis. He knew that most inexperienced utility converts naively expected to buy proven plants off the shelf which could be readily licensed and built and would then produce power quickly and efficiently.

As Holifield feared, rapid growth in plant sizes and their wide dispersal cast the public spotlight on both large nuclear and large conventional plants. JCAE and public interest focused on big mistakes, delays, cost overruns, and cases of poor management. Public attention also converged on pollution problems, especially from the larger, coal-fired plants. These problems led to stronger public reactions and more involvement from state and federal regulatory agencies and, more importantly, led to the passage of the National Environmental Policy Act of 1969 (NEPA). After NEPA, public debates on environmental and radiological safety standards intensified, and a number of individuals and groups became "intervenors" in the complex and controversial plant licensing processes. A rash of books and articles highly critical of nuclear power also appeared.[55] Nuclear power's problems were also sensationalized in newspapers, the pulp press, television, and movies.

The nuclear industry had financial and technical problems aside from a poor public image. Many industrial leaders acknowledged that they could not meet the schedules and budgets of most individual utility owners. Then there were the ever-changing technical and economic criteria, including safety and environmental standards, that were increasingly more volatile and stringent. These problems resulted in many required changes to plants on the drawing board, under construction, and even those already completed, but shut down. Such changes were often environmental, such as those for the discharge and disposal of stack gas, condenser cooling water, and waste, or for safety, such as those involving retrofitting newer safety devices and systems. Custom-built plants also had other built-in problems. Virtually all modifications required different engineering and equipment considerations on the wide variety of custom plants. Critics and the media interpreted the changes and other problems as *prima facie* evidence of the utility industry's inability to operate safe, reliable, and economical nuclear plants. The excellent performance and safety record of the majority of plants was ignored.

Given the impending crisis, Holifield focused his own spotlight on the need for standardization. He used the JCAE hearing process, speeches, and other means to warn about the seriousness of the problem and need for a solution. It was painfully clear that standardization would not apply to plants already purchased and built, or to those in the new wave of orders.[56]

Holifield's frustration and discouragement extended beyond the standardization issue to the general state of disarray in the nuclear industry. The JCAE hearing records of the period are replete with data on the disarray in the industry--the warnings, the overcommitments, the shortages, and other problems. At times, it seemed to him as if the utilities were demanding that nuclear suppliers sell them a reactor system, or else (another competitor would). Despite his frustration, Holifield was convinced that standardization could ameliorate at least some of the growing problems with nuclear power. In 1974 he once again spoke on standardization to his House colleagues:

> The merits of standardization of reactor design have been recognized for some time. As a matter of fact, the Joint Committee on Atomic Energy over recent years has urged manufacturers to develop standardized reactor designs and has urged the AEC to give consideration to defining the technical information required of the licensee for the safety review of such designs.
>
> It has been the Committee's belief, and I believe the Commission's belief as well, that if standardization of nuclear plant design and power level could be achieved, then reactor licensing time could be appreciably reduced. The attention of the reviewers would focus principally on the site considerations, including, of course, all the environmental impact considerations now required by the National Environmental Policy Act.[57]

One potentially thorny aspect of standardization involved legal restraints on the AEC. Ironically, although Holifield's JCAE and the AEC agreed that standardization was necessary, federal anti-monopoly laws appeared to indicate that standardization could be interpreted as an antitrust violation. In fact, some legal interpretations appeared to preclude imposing a single reactor design on industry. Nonetheless, other experts in engineering felt that standardization could be achieved through selective specification and procurement options appropriately arranged to obtain industrial competition.

In recalling the AEC's standardization efforts, AEC commissioner Ramey confirmed that the antitrust laws were a hindrance. He noted that the AEC issued its first policy "to help industry stop its race to larger and different designs, and to focus instead on the depth of the problems related to their commitments to power plants as well as their capabilities to complete and operate them in an efficient manner." "We were aware of some other countries which had licensed U.S. designs," he added. "They were following advice [on standardization] they had garnered here ." Ramey recalled that

"France, in particular, was prepared to push forward with standardization, basing itself on our experience with Westinghouse's PWR." In the U.S., however, "both government and industry" had to "tread warily in giving an impression of violating these [anti-monopoly laws], even when a sophisticated technology like nuclear power could benefit from standardizing approaches."[58]

Holifield's JCAE and AEC efforts to encourage standardization began to influence designers and customers. In the early 1970s, most of the suppliers, in cooperation with the utilities, accepted "AEC-imposed" limitations on plant size of 1,300 megawatts. Some suppliers also began to standardize key plant equipment and hardware to the extent that utilities would purchase them.[59]

Westinghouse was a leader in the trend toward standardization. The company spearheaded two initiatives by negotiating multi-plant purchases with several large, rapidly-growing utilities. One of these was the Offshore Power Systems (OPS) commitment for several, complete 940-megawatt plants with Public Service of New Jersey and the Newport News Shipbuilding Company in Jacksonville, Florida. This program, directed by Al Zechella, a tough Westinghouse executive for NR's surface ship program, envisioned floating, offshore power plants as a creative application of lessons learned in NR. Zachella's experience included Shippingport, two large A1W prototype plants in Idaho and also (with some adjustments for ship configurations) two reactors for *Long Beach*, and eight reactors for *Enterprise*. Zechella's management team developed an exciting, promising approach for standardized large-scale, high-quality production of reactor plants. Unfortunately, this "shipbuilding approach" suffered many delays in the intensified regulatory and recessionary turmoil of the mid-1970s and 1980s, since construction permits were required for both this first-of-a-kind factory and for each reactor plant and its location. The OPS facility was eventually completed in Jacksonville, Florida, but actual production of floating power plants was delayed and then terminated as the 1980 recession dramatically reduced projected electricity demands in New Jersey. The other initiative was the Standardized Nuclear Utility Power Plant System (SNUPPS). The SNUPPS project involved the purchase of six large plants by a group of five utilities which combined to support this effort in cooperation with Bechtel. Only two of the plants were eventually completed, but their performance continues to be good.[60]

Holifield Gets a Standardization Policy

By 1972, the AEC had completed a standardization policy acceptable to Holifield. It was an imperfect policy, but an important start. By 1974, the AEC's regulatory body accepted separate reactor designs from the four major suppliers and also approved balance-of-plant plans from construction firms like Bechtel and Stone & Webster. The balance-of-plant standardization was adaptable to all but GE's BWR design and it was in place as a policy by 1976.[61]

Ironically, standardization did not get a real test run in this country once the first policies were promulgated. The recession led to heavy reductions in new plant orders and numerous cancellations of proposed plants. The nuclear industry came virtually to a standstill, except for the completion of existing commitments and services for reactor plant fuel, maintenance and repair. The utilities' avoidance of commitments to large baseload power plants, both nuclear and fossil-fueled (in effect, a moratorium), has continued into 1996. At present, utilities can not afford such large financial risks.[62]

Holifield often noted regretfully that little credit was given to the efforts of the experienced utilities to improve already good performance. Just as most of the U.S. utility newcomers were encountering difficulties, the experienced utility leaders discovered that the public was judging nuclear power by its weakest performers. Moreover, the newcomers seriously diluted the experienced body of talent from the better utilities, indirectly encouraging regulatory bodies to impose new criteria and more requirements on all utilities, thus further undercutting the well-managed utilities.

The experiences of other countries in nuclear power could not have been more different. While some learned the hard way, most accepted U.S. leadership and profitted from the U.S. standardization initiative and other U.S. government and industry efforts. Some countries, like France and the United Kingdom, started their commercial programs with gas-cooled, graphite-moderated reactors for combined military and civilian power applications. These countries eventually shifted to the mature U.S.-designed LWR through licensing arrangements. Others, like Japan, South Korea, and Taiwan, started their programs just as U.S. technology became readily available and joined in the initial benefits from standardization on plant schedules, costs, and performance. Holifield noted that most of the countries standardized their civilian nuclear power programs consistent with the 1,300 Mwe size limitations imposed on U.S. LWR technology. Most countries have settled on standard plant sizes ranging from 900 to 1,300 Mwe.[63]

Besides standardization, Holifield had other major concerns pertinent to strategic nuclear planning. The very large number of LWR commitments in such a short time reinforced his decision to develop the breeder. Although he had serious doubts about the ability of industry to bring more than 100 LWRs on line in a timely fashion, the utility leadership believed otherwise. Holifield knew that without success with the LWRs there would be a loss of public support for nuclear power. Moreover, without uniform success with the LWR, there would be no role to play in the national energy strategy for the highly efficient breeder or any other advanced reactor concept. He understood better than most the technical, financial, and political synergism between the LWR and the breeder, and the potential long-term benefits of the breeder R&D and demonstration plant programs. He was determined to promote the breeder as the last major project of his JCAE career.[64]

12

Toward Distant Horizons

The "Breeder": America's Best Hope for an Inexhaustible Energy Supply

Even as he pushed the utilities to improve the performance and safety of their LWR plants in the late 1960s and early 1970s, Holifield also had his eye on more distant horizons. On the JCAE, he had become acutely aware of the larger national energy picture, especially the heightened demand for electricity. He thus became increasingly concerned about the nation's energy security, including the potential perils of dependence on foreign oil. Aside from the fact that gas and oil supplies could be denied by rising costs or unfriendly governments, these fossil fuels (and coal, too) were exhaustible energy sources. He sensed that the country should be developing longer-term, environmentally safe, and more efficient methods for producing power. Of the few viable alternatives for a domestic source--solar energy, fusion, and fission--Holifield naturally leaned toward fission, and the breeder reactor concept in particular, as the logical choice for clean and safe baseload energy in the future. It could provide a virtually inexhaustible supply of power and would, moreover, complement the existing LWRs by utilizing their waste products for fuel. The breeder concept also had already been cited by many scientists and engineers here and abroad as an effective, long-term solution.

With the need clearly defined and anticipated support from the AEC commissioners, Holifield provided the JCAE advocacy for demonstration of the breeder. With his characteristic vision, zeal, and enthusiasm, he envisioned a national effort similar to Rickover's intensive efforts to develop civilian nuclear power. In his quest, Holifield knew he would have RDT Director Shaw's expertise and leadership to help face the formidable managerial and technical obstacles. He knew that the AEC's complex of laboratories and contractors did not yet operate on those principles, but he was hopeful that Shaw's continuing centralization and coordination efforts would eventually bring them into line with the breeder's mission-oriented requirements. Due to Shaw's close association with Rickover, he expected that there would be determined opposition from some of the AEC's civilian

R&D community, and he was correct. Yet, with his, the JCAE's and the AEC's backing, RDT was able to harness the best of the AEC's resources, achieve uniform discipline, engineering excellence, and accountability, and develop a solid R&D base for demonstrating the breeder, including the world's largest, most flexible, high-temperature breeder test facility, the Fast Flux Test Facility (FFTF), and other key support facilities.

Until his retirement, Holifield worked hard to push the LWR, breeder, and other R&D programs. Because of his views on the looming energy crisis, he worked diligently even with Nixon's Republican administration. His efforts were instrumental in making the breeder the centerpiece of Nixon's June 4, 1971 energy message, which designated the breeder as the nation's highest priority energy R&D program. With this, success seemed assured. JCAE, AEC, and industry-utility cooperation produced significant results in a relatively short time, despite many difficulties and delays. By the end of his career, Holifield could take pride in results of the FFTF and other facilities, although full scale demonstration of the breeder would prove elusive.

U.S. Leadership and the Need for the Breeder

The U.S. had been the leader in developing breeder reactor technology since the 1940s. The possibilities for a breeder were already evident in the days of the Manhattan Engineering District. During World War II, the Los Alamos Scientific Laboratory built the first experimental reactor to explore the breeding concept, using plutonium fuel and mercury as the metal coolant.[1] By 1946, tests indicated that a breeder was technically feasible. In 1947, the Argonne National Laboratory (ANL) started a small "test bed" in Idaho known as EBR-I; in 1951, it was the first reactor to produce enough electricity to illuminate a few light bulbs. Also in 1951, the AEC's Naval Reactor Division began building the sodium-cooled reactor prototype and a seagoing propulsion plant for *Seawolf*, the second nuclear submarine; both became operational by the mid-1950s. These power plants (not breeders), along with that of the *Nautilus* LWR plants, led to confidence worldwide in the potential of liquid metal steam plants for commercial applications.[2] In 1958, ANL built a larger facility in Idaho, EBR-II, a 62.5-megawatt, sodium-cooled reactor with steam-electric generation capabilities with an integral experimental metal fuel reprocessing and recycling plant. This reactor went critical in 1964 and provided important technical information on fuel and small plant performance until shut down in 1994. In 1967, General Electric (GE) built the 20-megawatt Southwest Experimental Fast Oxide Reactor (SEFOR) in Arkansas, sponsored by several U.S. utilities and suppliers, the AEC, West Germany, and others in Europe. Holifield was the main speaker at the dedication of this unique test facility, operable from 1969 to 1972. SEFOR was shut down after validating the inherent safety aspects of using mixed-oxide fuel.[3]

Like reactors in general, there are many breeder concepts possible, and the JCAE provided long-term support to several projects in the 1960s and 1970s. The only concepts that proved feasible were the Liquid Metal Fast Breeder Reactor (LMFBR), which eventually became the favored concept, and a light water thermal breeder which used uranium-233 as the fissionable material and thorium-232 as the fertile isotope. Rickover was a strong proponent of this low-gain breeder and successfully demonstrated it in the AEC's Shippingport plant in the 1970s. Scientists Edward Teller and Alvin Weinberg also favored the use of thorium as a fertile material with low-gain thermal breeders, and the AEC financed further experimental work in this area.[4] During the late 1960s, the AEC also supported pre-conceptual research on a steam-cooled fast breeder of interest to GE and on a gas-cooled fast breeder by General Atomics. Most concepts were not of interest to the utilities since they could not match the efficiency of the LMFBR. Its efficiency potential translates into a thirty-fold increase in fuel utilization over the LWR and vastly improved environmental advantages over fossil plants.[5]

Holifield was an enthusiastic supporter of early breeder tests, except for one. In 1956, the AEC granted Detroit Edison a permit for the Enrico Fermi Nuclear Power Plant, an experimental breeder plant. Owned by Detroit Edison and the Power Reactor Development Company, Fermi was essentially a commercial venture, but it was plagued with technical problems and controversy. AEC Commissioner Thomas Murray warned Holifield and others about locating a breeder near a populated area, about twenty miles outside Detroit.[6] Holifield and other JCAE Democrats joined the United Auto Workers in opposing the plant. Attacking AEC Chairman Lewis Strauss for "overruling the grave warnings" of the AEC's Advisory Committee on Reactor Safeguards and for "proceeding in a reckless and arrogant manner," Holifield charged that use of breeder technology in commercial plants at that time was premature and dangerous. After a much-publicized accident in 1966 when some fuel melted (no one was hurt), the plant was repaired over a four-year period through the persistence of the chairman of Detroit Edison, Walker Cisler. In late 1970, it resumed operation for two years before shutting down permanently after AEC rejected it for use as a test facility.[7]

Holifield, always concerned about U.S. nuclear leadership, stayed abreast of breeder R&D also underway from the 1950s in the United Kingdom, France, and the Soviet Union. Later, these nations were joined by Japan, West Germany, India, Belgium, Luxembourg, Italy, and the Netherlands. In general, these earlier programs were directed towards building experimental facilities, as the U.S. had been doing since the 1940s. Russia was the most aggressive, moving quickly to increase plant sizes in its R&D program. France moved somewhat slower toward larger-scale plants.[8]

In view of the notable breeder efforts in other countries, Holifield was displeased by the 1960s by the comparative lack of U.S. commitment:

I didn't necessarily agree with everything other countries were doing by the early 1960s. But the French, the Soviets, and other nations were moving ahead with their national energy policies, and we weren't. With some exceptions, most of us were satisfied with the mixed results from early experimental facilities; however, some of these were started before the AEC had a formal reactor development program. Each lab and contractor was proud of what they were doing and so were we with those research-oriented results with this novel technology. But as the 1960s approached and Rickover's centralized management program produced far more consistent and remarkable results, I became convinced that the foreign programs were moving ahead of us. Looking at this situation and the potential for success in the commercial programs led me to believe we should get going with our breeder R&D program with our best laboratories and contractors, like other nations were doing.[9]

For Holifield, validation of the breeder's major characteristics here and abroad figured prominently in his support for the concept. He and other experts argued that unless the breeder became a reality, the large-scale LWR commitments by the utilities ultimately might not be worthwhile because of the limited supply of economic fuel. Most experts believed that without a very efficient breeder, the amount of useful energy stored in the known quantities of natural uranium would not be much more than that found in projected supplies of natural gas. As the demands for uranium grew in the 1950s, the costs did rise, but other pressures were building toward keeping uranium fuel more economic. In 1964, the JCAE encouraged Congress to pass legislation ending an 18-year government monopoly on ownership of special nuclear materials. This, along with industry's marketing success with the "turnkey" plants, contributed to a huge increase in plant orders, which led to mounting pressures to increase the supplies of economic fuels. These pressures also led quite naturally to increased interest in breeder reactors.[10]

Holifield knew that the breeder concept was controversial. Opponents have contended that the breeder would be too costly to develop and build, would never be safe even if built, and that it generates large quantities of plutonium, a dangerous, man-made element. Supporters argue that no nation can afford to waste the immense energy potential contained in the spent nuclear fuel in storage throughout the world and in the tailings from the enrichment process. Given an effective breeder with a complete fuel cycle, the energy potential of these currently unusable sources alone is far greater than the energy capacity of all the known oil and coal reserves in the world![11]

Holifield Decides to Push the Breeder

In the mid-1960s, Holifield felt that the time was ripe for development and demonstration of the breeder as a complement to the LWRs. He wanted to validate the potential benefits of the synergistic relationship between the LWRs and the breeder, using the uranium-plutonium cycle. He felt that--

sooner or later--uniform success with the LWRs would exert pressures here and abroad for developing the more-efficient breeder as an energy option.

The overall complementary concept was simple but Holifield knew that the development and demonstration path would be long and difficult. Breeder development would require enthusiastic and strong scientific and engineering leadership at the AEC. Development would be complicated and very different from the naval program, however, involving in-depth consideration of entirely different engineering criteria and realities, fuel utilization, safety, economics, and even public confidence. A strong and capable AEC, moreover, was only the beginning. A successful program would need politically strong, stable, and technically knowledgeable leadership in Congress, consistent support from a series of presidential administrations, significant and timely commitments by industry and the scientific community, and an objective attitude from the media. Sustaining an already precarious public confidence in the safety of LWR technology, while focusing on both LWR improvements and the most promising breeder concept, would be especially critical. The final hurdles would include a lengthy demonstration program and obtaining utility acceptance of the breeder as an option for electricity production.

Holifield and the JCAE's foremost task was to strengthen the AEC. Milton Shaw had been brought aboard RDT in 1964 to establish mission-oriented, dynamic leadership first at headquarters and then within each of the laboratories and industrial contractors. Although Shaw was making some progress, Holifield knew the obstacles were enormous. The major question was the extent to which the laboratories and contractors could be transformed to do the job. From lessons learned by NR in earlier years, would it be practical to carry out a long-term, top-priority, mission-oriented breeder program under these well-funded, but decentralized, research-oriented, multi-program organizations? Some of the AEC's R&D entities seemed to Holifield to be imbued with a traditional philosophy that scientists and their research need not be concerned with disciplined engineering nor be held to firm commitments for projects requiring their use.[12] In addition, a second major aspect of the problem was that the AEC and its R&D entities did not exactly fit within the same program parameters as NR's projects had. On paper, NR was an integral part of the AEC's Reactor Development Division, with Shippingport as its star achievement. However, Rickover's organization was virtually independent of the AEC's decentralized R&D network. Rickover made use of the AEC's formal structures to help him work his will, but he did not waste his time in trying to change their basic nature nor their way of doing business. In reality, NR was set up as a virtually autonomous technical organization possessing its own tightly-interrelated reactor development and production discipline, mostly *outside* of the AEC's traditional headquarters and field offices.[13]

Holifield Goes to Work with Seaborg, Ramey, and Shaw

Encouraged and pushed hard by Holifield, the AEC was prepared by late 1965 to strengthen its reactor R&D programs. Holifield lent his assistance mainly to Chairman Seaborg, Ramey, and Shaw, who were at the operational forefront. Together, the JCAE and AEC began the complex tasks of redirecting program activities, reprioritizing programs, imposing disciplined engineering approaches, and making other changes. During hearings and meetings, Holifield and other JCAE members encouraged implementation of Shaw's agenda for a strengthened RDT. They applauded the commission's decision to recruit experienced professionals and the best of the nation's college technical graduates as interns for RDT. This was in keeping with the goals of centralizing management of the civilian, Army, Air Force, and maritime (but not naval) R&D programs under Shaw. AEC's new orientation entailed a redefinition of the roles of many multi-program laboratories and defining objectives for maximum utilization of industry in applied R&D.[14]

Holifield was under no illusions about these new initiatives. He fully recognized that the changes would lead to opposition, both emotional and professional, from some senior headquarters personnel, field managers, laboratories, and contractors. He had experienced such opposition before. During the early 1950s, when Rickover's assignment was broadened to include the civilian power demonstration project at Shippingport, laboratory resistance was formidable. In 1955, Holifield was aware of even stronger reactions when he and AEC commissioners considered centralizing management of all reactor R&D programs under Rickover. Holifield saw similarly strong opposition when Shaw was brought back to the AEC in 1964 based on strong recommendations by Rickover and others. Shaw's agenda for centralizing and strengthening line management also led to strong negative reactions.[15] Despite the opposition, Holifield wanted to address what he believed to be the "root-cause" of the AEC's unexceptional R&D performance when compared to Rickover's achievements: the traditional methods of the AEC's laboratories and contractors were simply not producing meaningful technical successes. Holifield underestimated the fierce, if not always open, resistance by some laboratories and a few key industrial contractors. The proposals of Holifield and his allies soon elicited general agreement, but only so long as they remained general. Holifield concluded that many senior AEC field office and contractor officials were making common cause together to prevent any sweeping changes. Shaw's determination to fulfill his agenda did, however, create serious difficulties for his opponents. Many AEC officials and contractors began to complain openly that the management methods forged under NR programs were not applicable to their R&D programs. Others argued that no changes were needed, since their R&D approaches had been accepted for over two decades by AEC staffs and their field offices and, moreover, AEC commissioners, the budgeteers, successive presidents, and even the JCAE and Congress had approved ever-increasing budgets.[16]

For Holifield, Melvin Price and Craig Hosmer, as well as their key associates John Conway and Edward Bauser, these arguments no longer "held water". Holifield emphasized that the criteria for accepting results from the field had changed; simply achieving "advances in technology" was no longer sufficient. The new criteria, Holifield contended, focused on excellence in responses to written requirements and to fulfilling engineering and safety standards, including quality and safety assurance programs and demonstration of exemplary facility performance. While the JCAE would support some other promising R&D ventures, the highest R&D priorities were to be improvements in LWR safety and breeder technology, in that order, since the fates of these two concepts were intertwined.[17]

RDT's Recruiting and Intern Programs

At AEC headquarters, Shaw made RDT a show case for the AEC's new orientation. In strengthening RDT, nothing rated higher on Shaw's agenda than recruiting top talent. His initial call for help went to former Navy Captain Jack W. Crawford, who was working in the private sector with former AEC Commissioner Murray in New York. For most of their careers since 1950, Shaw and Crawford had worked closely, each reporting directly to Rickover, on NR's challenging managerial, technical, and recruiting activities involving first-of-a-kind submarine and surface ship projects, including the eight-reactor *Enterprise*. Shaw's admiration for Crawford's integrity, insight, and other personal and professional attributes were matched only by Crawford's command of the technical and political "know-how" in naval and nuclear power development and plant production activities. Those who knew this pair well were not surprised when Crawford responded immediately to Shaw's call and soon became an RDT Assistant Director with responsibility for projects, personnel matters, and special assignments. Holifield also knew Crawford, having worked closely with Crawford and Murray during Murray's AEC term and later when Murray became a JCAE consultant. Holifield also knew that Crawford and Shaw had been named by Rickover as those qualified to take his position if and when such a need should arise.[18]

In rounding out his top management cadre, Shaw chose Angie Giambusso, Ed Kintner, Melvin Rosen, Dick Kosiba, and Woody Cunningham as his other key assistant managers. All were highly capable and dedicated nuclear managers with many years of experience. Giambusso and Rosen were former Army nuclear power engineering officers assigned to the AEC. Kintner and Kosiba, like Crawford, had been Navy engineering officers who had come to NR after completing intensive nuclear engineering graduate courses at MIT. Both had worked closely with Shaw and Crawford and were recruited for

RDT after leaving NR. Cunningham, a talented metallurgist and manager with experience at the AEC's Oak Ridge Laboratory, was recruited after receiving his doctorate from the University of Tennessee.[19]

All of Shaw's appointments and others in RDT and the AEC, particularly John Vinciguerra, Assistant General Manager for Administration, were determined to help attract outstanding personnel. The AEC and Dr. Charles L. Shultze, the Director of the Bureau of the Budget, supported RDT's efforts to recruit experienced nuclear managers and engineers as well as the most outstanding technical graduates. According to Holifield:

> Commissioner Ramey, Bob Hollingsworth [General Manager], John Vinciguerra, Milt Shaw, and Jack Crawford were increasing the pressure on the laboratories and contractors to recruit and train better engineering managers and professionals. No one was working any harder than Milt to accomplish the same goals within his own organization and his field offices. Just about everyone knew that nothing had a higher priority on his agenda than recruiting such competent personnel and promising interns; this was fundamental in AEC's commitment to excellence for the long term.[20]

Holifield knew that RDT's intern program was similar to the NR approach. In recruiting, Shaw and Crawford did not, of course, have the naval sources to help supply candidates. RDT personnel, even the secretaries and administrative experts, seemed dedicated to attracting and investing in young, outstanding engineering and science graduates. One key to getting top-notch graduates was RDT's promise that each intern would work closely with carefully selected highly qualified "technical mentors" in the AEC.[21]

Breeder Program Objectives and Activities

Developing overall programmatic objectives that would mirror both the JCAE's and the AEC's criteria for breeder R&D was another important step. The breeder objectives were two in number but multifaceted. The first was "To achieve through R&D, the technology necessary to design, construct and safely, reliably, and economically operate a fast breeder reactor power plant in the utility environment." The second was "To assure maximum development and use of a competitive self-sustaining industrial capability in the development program." These objectives provided the framework for discussions at the Bureau of the Budget and JCAE hearings, which covered all breeder aspects, including definitive technical requirements, cost data, and action plans. Holifield, Hosmer, Pastore, and key JCAE staff Conway, Bauser, and Jim Graham studied the objectives in depth at JCAE hearings.[22]

Holifield made sure that the AEC concentrated primarily on only the proven reactor concepts and the highest-priority needs of the breeder. He knew that long lead times would be needed for developing the most critical elements, such as fuel, reactor control and safety systems, and primary plant hardware and systems. Most elements were handled by ANL, then starting its EBR-II test program in Idaho. Years earlier, the JCAE had authorized ANL to build another small fuels test reactor (known as FARET) there, also.

With ANL at center stage, it seemed natural that the Program Plan would be developed there. Holifield was apprehensive about Shaw's desire to use ANL for the plan, but agreed as long as it was under Shaw's personal direction. Shaw chose A. N. (Bud) Tardiff, a pioneer in the Army Reactors program, to serve as manager of the planning and liaison within RDT, ANL, and other entities. At ANL, the formal planning effort was managed by Dr. Al Amorosi, who had extensive breeder experience, including the Fermi plant. Amorosi's group was charged with outlining technical requirements, state of knowledge and options, and courses of action (including test and validation facilities). The completed ten-volume Plan became one of the most productive, unheralded efforts in the breeder program and a solid road map. It was updated regularly for many years and distributed widely to both U.S. and overseas program contributors, including breeder participants in government, industry, universities, R&D organizations, and electric utilities.[23]

In view of the extensive AEC investments in ANL's Chicago and Idaho facilities, Holifield and the AEC urged ANL's top management to recruit appropriate technical leadership and qualified engineers for the project. RDT wanted ANL to focus on the problems in the leading-candidate breeder fuels, fuel cycle concepts, and critical high-temperature materials and components. Both the JCAE and AEC were deeply concerned about ANL's capabilities to analyze and validate (in test facilities) the developmental fuel and materials characteristics. Holifield realized that extensive investments would be needed for ANL's program activities to be effective.

To ensure breeder success, Holifield insisted that the JCAE conduct frequent, in-depth public hearings on all aspects of the program. As JCAE chairman, he supported the AEC's dictate that laboratories restructure to set up effective management and engineering groups for each major commitment instead of relying upon traditional alignments. This would provide improved methods for accountability for costs, schedules, and other requirements. Affected laboratories were urged to establish strong quality assurance and safety oversight activities. ANL was required to assign it highest priority to EBR-II and related safety and physics facilities. These were unique and vital program elements, and higher performance was the key to success.[24]

The Ordeal of Change

In the RDT's early years, over twenty small experimental reactor facilities were terminated after reviews of their performance and future potential. The need to choose the most cost-effective test facilities led to the termination of others, including ANL's FARET program in 1967. This resulted from an

RDT review by Jack Crawford and John Yevick, a pioneering, engineer-scientist from NR's *Seawolf* programs at AEC's Knolls Laboratory and later at Fermi. The two men concluded that without significant and costly changes in plant features, neither FARET nor EBR-II could provide the fuels and materials information essential for the breeder and other high-temperature programs. The AEC argued--with Holifield's support--that EBR-II, with effective management, could contribute more than FARET. Holifield noted that "We had no choice but to not fund FARET any longer even though a few million had been spent on research for the project."[25]

This decision provoked vehement protests from other laboratories, contractors, and even some congressmen, who had long looked favorably on ANL's breeder activities. For Holifield, the decision was practical, involving ANL top management's attitude and clear lack of responsiveness to commitments. The outcry caused Holifield and his allies to question whether laboratories could improve their attitudes and responses to the AEC's redefined mission. Some scientists openly resented the changes and minced no words. Holifield was equally blunt in JCAE hearings, doubting whether some labs would upgrade their professionals and facilities to respond to program needs in a timely manner even if the JCAE increased funding. Many knew that AEC's vast investments, mainly at ANL and Idaho, precluded a major move. After intense reviews and negotiations, including a Saturday visit by Holifield, Price, Bauser, and Shaw for a face-to-face discussion with ANL's Dr. William Cannon (management sponsor at the University of Chicago), the JCAE and the AEC obtained agreement that major changes would be made. Similar actions followed at the AEC's other laboratories and facilities.[26]

Many more major differences of opinion developed as the AEC attempted to bring about dramatic changes. The AEC's actions were generally endorsed by Holifield, Hosmer, the JCAE majority, and senior administration officials, such as Dr. Charles L. Schultze, Director, and Fred Schult of the Bureau of the Budget. One major issue involved the extent to which laboratory management should staff project commitments with research-oriented professionals on the basis of their tenure and availability. RDT insisted on identifying necessary qualifications and conducting intensive recruiting for managers and engineers. Other problems arose when RDT attempted to assure disciplined application of quality assurance standards and practices. Assigning RDT site personnel was challenged by some laboratories, as was RDT's order to obtain reports on critical items and potential problem areas for high-priority commitments.[27]

With so much at stake, Holifield's "weeping chair" sessions increased more than ever before. But so did successes and smoother operations as AEC headquarters and stronger field leadership made their influence felt. Holifield knew that he had finally gotten the attention of the key field management and was determined to hold his position. In fact, his and the JCAE's support became critical to enforcement of RDT requirements. He continued to subject its programs to intense scrutiny in JCAE hearings where he, Hosmer, and other JCAE members clearly supported RDT. Despite some hard debates, problems were eased through recruitment of experienced managers, scientists, and engineers, which seemed to reinforce RDT's intern program.[28]

As momentum increased, so did appreciation of the enormous challenges that had to be overcome. Holifield, Ramey, Conway, Bauser, and Shaw began to feel greater support from government and industry for the breeder. They believed that RDT's centralization effort was working, but still needed improvements. With exceptions, RDT's R&D units seemed to evidence more creativity and accountability in meeting goals and requirements.

The Fast Flux Test Facility (FFTF)

One of the most difficult and critical challenges in the revitalized breeder program was the planning and construction of a large, flexible, and well-instrumented fuels and materials test reactor. Pre-conceptual design work was begun on the FFTF in 1965 by Battelle Northwest after it was proposed by the AEC and authorized by Holifield and the JCAE, with Ramey's help. Battelle was a division of the Battelle Memorial Institute and the major operating contractor for the AEC's Pacific Northwest Laboratory (PNL).

This unique, 330-megawatt, high-temperature, sodium-cooled reactor plant, was designed to be the AEC's highest-priority, multi-purpose test facility. It was to be used primarily for testing fast reactor safety, physics, fuel, and materials. As such, it was to be the major focus of the breeder R&D program. Among other things, it was designed to test full-size breeder fuel and safety-control elements, as well as most other materials, hardware, and system features that could be used in the breeder and future high-temperature R&D programs, nuclear and otherwise. It was also designed to validate the managerial and technological aspects for all associated safety, licensing, construction, operation, maintenance, and recovery processes and procedures for high-temperature machinery, plants, and facilities.[29]

From the beginning, the AEC and Battelle management were divided over the personnel needed by PNL for the FFTF. Holifield shared RDT's concern about Battelle's seemingly unbridled confidence that they could design and build the FFTF quickly and efficiently *if left alone*. While he shared Battelle's enthusiasm about its pre-conceptual design, he was also aware of Battelle's relative isolation from ongoing R&D on fast reactors and liquid metal designs. Thus, the JCAE and AEC insisted on an immediate, aggressive strengthening of management and engineering personnel for the two-year conceptual design effort. Battelle management agreed and began on the basis that strengthening could be enhanced with a JCAE-authorized project.[30]

Early on, Battelle's conceptual design effort began encountering serious difficulties and delays. Holifield and Shaw perceived that the problems emanated largely from Battelle's failure to have its personnel work in consort with specialized reactor plant experts of other laboratories and industry as a demanding "owner and customer." This checks and balances set-up was frustrating, although anticipated to a degree. Both Holifield and Shaw realized that PNL was not an AEC national laboratory, but they believed that its major contractors definitely had similar traditional characteristics. After all, for over two decades the Hanford site had operated on a decentralized basis with only limited oversight by AEC field offices and headquarters. Holifield knew that it had been devoted to defense weapons material production, reprocessing, and waste disposal activities since the 1940s. GE had been the long-term operating contractor until diversification in early 1960 led to three new contractors, with Battelle assuming the R&D role.

In addressing the issues with Battelle, Holifield, Ramey and Shaw relied in part on their experience with Rickover. They believed that nuclear plant technical decisions, like design details and standards, had to be made by qualified engineers, not by scientists or administrators, or even by politicians. Thus, the JCAE and the AEC fully supported RDT's efforts to monitor and guide PNL. Holifield and Ramey championed Shaw's policy of requiring satisfactory completion of each developmental phase before authorizing the next phase, particularly construction and testing activities. Holifield agreed with Shaw that the FFTF delays and cost increases were getting serious, but far less than if Battelle were permitted to continue along their traditional course, as they seemed determined to do. Battelle did not appear to be mollified by the fact that Holifield and Shaw were similarly pressuring other laboratories and contractors. In fact, some laboratories had responded well in obtaining qualified personnel and addressing their most serious challenges.[31]

Holifield and Ramey were very upset that such major problems were already occurring in the early breeder phases. It appeared to them that many serious problems were not being recognized and aggressively addressed at the engineering level. These problems appeared to reflect PNL's failure to accept AEC requirements and the necessity of working with RDT and other R&D entities. This was unacceptable. While still giving Battelle credit for doing a credible job at first, they were incensed that it had taken nearly four years for Battelle to recruit even a few top-echelon nuclear managers and experienced engineers, much less adequate numbers. Holifield remembered:

> Battelle's acceptable performance and experienced personnel in some scientific fields proved that there were plenty of good people at their laboratory. But none had ever tackled a major project like the FFTF. Battelle's management claimed that it had made serious efforts to recruit an engineering team capable of managing this project but were unable to understand why they could not hire highly qualified key engineering management personnel. We all knew about the shortages of capabilities

throughout the rapidly-expanding civilian power business at that time, but this project should have been a relatively attractive one for creative and capable leaders. In 1969, they were finally able to attract an outstanding nuclear engineering manager, Dr. Bertram Wolfe, with excellent experience as General Electric's top man on the SEFOR project. In turn, he attracted a few others. But the AEC multi-purpose laboratories had a questionable reputation for attracting, much less wanting, help from senior experienced engineering leadership from the outside.[32]

The solution to the FFTF problems was disarmingly clear to Holifield, Ramey and Shaw, but obviously easier said than done in the existing political environment. The action required would be similar to those finally taken on almost every successful nuclear plant and facility commitment since the early 1950s. It was necessary to recruit more competent managers and engineers.

Some Rays of Hope

Although there were serious problems, significant technical progress was achieved by the industrial contractors and by selected groups within the other key laboratories, including ANL, PNL and Oak Ridge National Laboratory (ORNL). Most laboratory division managers proved technically competent in responding to the AEC's new rigorous requirements. Solid industrial participation also became a reality. In response to an AEC solicitation, Westinghouse was selected early in 1968 for the pivotal role of designer, and Bechtel was chosen as the architect-engineer and construction manager for the FFTF. The Westinghouse team was managed by John J. Taylor, who reported to Corporate Vice President John W. Simpson. Like Simpson, Taylor had served in the Bettis NR operations before he became Manager of Engineering for Westinghouse's commercial nuclear business. The Bechtel team reported to D. W. Halligan under Corporate Vice President Harry Reinsch. These two men were also respected engineering managers.[33]

As observers of the industrial efforts, Holifield and the JCAE majority were pleased with the effectiveness of these experienced managers. Through site visits, hearings, and close contacts with RDT, they were satisfied with Westinghouse's and Bechtel's aggressive attempts to obtain realistic perspectives on breeder technology, engineering, manufacturing and safety, and the gaps and processes that had to be addressed. They were satisfied that RDT had disciplined industrial contractors moving the program forward.

There were also many notable accomplishments in the laboratories that were vital to success with the FFTF and the breeder program. At ANL, Dr. Milton Levenson, a highly competent, disciplined, and aggressive chemical engineering manager, had taken over as EBR-II project manager after RDT ordered it shut down because of major, basic deficiencies during the start-up program. In working closely with RDT's Assistant Director Jack Crawford and ANL's recently recruited Associate Director Robert V. Laney--both

Rickover protégés and pioneer project managers--Levenson proved to be very effective in restructuring the redefined EBR-II program. His achievements contributed much to the FFTF and other breeder programs.[34]

Many Battelle professionals also contributed notable accomplishments. Dr. Ersal Evans, a creative metallurgist, managed Battelle's mixed-oxide breeder fuel and cladding developments. His cadre of scientists and engineers worked closely with the RDT's reactor and fuels engineering organization managed by Assistant Director Edwin E. Kintner, another well-qualified pioneer leader from NR. Together, Evans and Kintner demonstrated, among other innovative fuel design and fabrication features, an effective process for handling mixed oxide-plutonium fuel production under stringent but practical guidelines and with strict accountability. Their program established milestones in working safely with plutonium and easing concerns about employee and public health and safety and about proliferation and theft of valuable fissionable materials from fuel cycles. The combined results from ANL's EBR-II program and PNL's plutonium fuel production program helped thrust the U.S. into a world leadership role in fuel and cladding R&D, automated, high-quality, fuel-manufacturing processes, and fuel performance.[35]

As this type of leadership became stronger, shortages of experienced engineering leadership eased, but there were still serious weaknesses in some activities. Despite pressure from many sides and his own desire to move ahead, Shaw was unwilling to recommend the start of the more costly design phases for the FFTF without satisfactory completion of the conceptual design phase. Holifield agreed and continued his JCAE hearings and meetings, even more concerned about AEC laboratory capability to meet deadlines:

Holifield: You need this facility now and it won't be ready for 5 or 6 years.

Shaw: Yes, sir. . . . We are doing it as quickly as we know how. We must do it right. I wish we had it today, but we do not.

Holifield: How are you going to solve some of these problems that you need to solve in the breeder without this?

Shaw: We are using the EBR-II. As you recall, EBR-II was designed not as a test facility, but as an experimental power plant. We have shifted the EBR-II over to be a test facility and are using it as such. We are getting enough information from EBR-II . . . . in order to support the first cores, the first fuel we put into the FFTF. We will build from that--sort of building by our bootstraps--in order to achieve the overall objective we are after.

               We recognize that this is a pioneering effort in terms of the way we are doing the job. As you indicate, it would have been better if we had the FFTF now, but we don't. We have to make the most of it as we can.[36]

To Holifield, Battelle's problems seemed embedded and intractable as a "way of life" from the "top" down. Holifield, RDT, and key JCAE staff were increasingly concerned that Battelle's problems were costly and undercutting other efforts. RDT stressed that the design effort was not acceptable without Battelle and PNL first complying internally with AEC requirements and then monitoring and enforcing these by working with all other entities.[37]

Battelle did not see things in the same light. Battelle continued to complain to the AEC commissioners and to Congress that Shaw's activities undercut efforts to get the project underway. Holifield strongly supported Shaw, who stood his ground while continuing to meet with Battelle's management with Holifield's blessing.[38] Shaw had little choice but to dispatch an increasing number of memoranda detailing requirements and project management expectations. Battelle continued to see Shaw's directives as "overmanagement" and disruptive. A frustrated Shaw finally sent a "white paper" to the commissioners explaining the problems and his unwillingness to work further with Battelle. He bluntly told the commissioners that the FFTF project was doomed to failure under existing conditions and that he would resign if he were not given total control of the FFTF and the breeder program. Shaw's conclusion after months of wrangling was that a highly qualified plant designer should replace Battelle for the FFTF project.[39]

Pressed by Shaw on one side and Holifield on the other, the AEC backed away from support of Battelle. Within months, Battelle asked the AEC to exclude the FFTF and related activities from its contract extension due in January 1970. Battelle's stated reason was that changes in its "not-for-profit" tax-exempt status might be jeopardized under a new 1969 tax reform law. The AEC commissioners granted the request and transferred the FFTF and related activities to Westinghouse. This move provoked an uproar and Holifield again placed his own prestige on the line by openly supporting Shaw.

After four years of trying to upgrade Battelle, Holifield and Shaw were able to get the FFTF project on what they believed to be the right track for moving ahead.[40] Their efforts to upgrade RDT activities had precipitated fierce administrative and political struggles. Holifield and Shaw were able to take the heat and succeeded in bringing about increased centralization and coordination of breeder R&D by AEC headquarters, as well as the R&D strengthening actions they sought. It was clearly evident to outside observers that the struggle had ended and they were the victors.[41]

Moving Toward Mission-Oriented Commitments

Holifield knew that the Battelle decision was unsettling to some RDT entities, but it had the very positive effect of symbolizing the enforcement of mission-oriented standards and commitments. RDT's solid authority led to enhanced program momentum, enthusiasm and confidence by almost all RDT participants. Holifield's JCAE and the AEC could now concentrate on the next phase: a conceptual design for a hypothetical 1,000 Mwe breeder plant. This study enjoyed participation and across-the-board representation from all of RDT's R&D entities and experienced utility advisory teams.[42]

Holifield was pleased with the completed conceptual design study. It provided guidance on future R&D priorities, safety factors, and funding levels for the FFTF and other breeder efforts, and also an appreciation of the long lead-times, standardization, and costs that a commercial breeder would require. Holifield agreed with the overlapping accounting for R&D and with integrating the FFTF with other breeder engineering efforts. RDT moved to organize and realign R&D support, standardization, and safety-related efforts.

As RDT assumed routine management of the program, Holifield and the JCAE concentrated on the plans for the first of three anticipated demonstration breeders. Virtually every JCAE discussion and hearing focused on RDT's problems and progress in the EBR-II and FFTF programs and meeting other planned R&D objectives. These hearings also had to address the serious problems of the commercial LWRs, including the problems of LWR safety R&D and the vast overcommitments by the utilities. Holifield was stunned at the proliferation of problems in the LWR industry as the number of plants ordered appeared to spiral out of control.[43]

In frequent discussions, Holifield and AEC spokesmen routinely emphasized the limiting factors of the first demonstration plants. First, the plants would be part of the R&D program, *not economically attractive commercial ventures*. No utility was expected to build commercial breeders until demonstration plant results and comparative data on fossil plants was closely evaluated, including fuel cycles and waste disposal. Breeders were also not intended nor likely to replace the less-efficient LWRs. Instead, breeders would augment these "burners" to accrue extensions on the use of available supplies of uranium over the long term. While other features might appear attractive, Holifield stressed that the benefits of increased nuclear (from the breeding) and thermal (from the high temperature) efficiencies would influence utilities to select the breeder. Still other practical and financial factors would figure in utility-PUC decisions on a commercial breeder.[44]

With active support from government and the private sector, the JCAE and the AEC were ready to proceed with the demonstration plant program. The major suppliers and utilities were encouraged to initiate meaningful multi-year personnel and financial commitments and other preparations for entering a cooperative arrangement with the AEC for the first breeder plant. For his part, Holifield made sure that the FY 1969 (in 1968) *AEC Authorizing Legislation* hearings, along with future annual and other special hearings, pursued in-depth discussions of virtually every aspect of the demonstration plants and other R&D activities. The first of the three plants was to be authorized in FY 1970.[45]

The Breeder Demonstration Program

During his last years in Congress, Holifield was deeply involved in the plans for the breeder program. The AEC's plans included a two-phased Project Definition Phase (PDP) approach. The first phase defined the entire project in sufficient detail to give an assessment of the scope of the project, including the technical and economic risks. The second phase, the "definitive cooperative arrangement," consisted of contracts with a utility or a group of utilities, the reactor supplier(s), and the AEC to conduct the detailed design, R&D, testing, construction, and operation of the three consecutive demonstration plants. RDT's base R&D program, including the FFTF, would be utilized for the demonstration project.[46]

Shortly after the PDP solicitation was announced, Holifield was not surprised to learn that each of the three major suppliers--Atomics International, General Electric, and Westinghouse--had been working with separate utility teams to develop an alternative. At the 1966 annual "Section 202" JCAE hearings, the senior executives of the teams advanced proposals to build breeders concurrently. They argued that they could provide a "faster and less costly" program than the AEC's approach. The three teams each requested $25 million in AEC funding and R&D to build their three plants.[47]

As Holifield studied the industry proposals in the hearings, he wondered how well the utilities understood their role in LWRs, much less breeders. He was restrained in his initial comments even though he knew that almost every utility and supplier was already overcommitted on LWRs, with cost overruns from building, start-up problems, and delays from personnel shortages. His concerns did not subside after reviewing the industry proposals in detail after the hearings. Nor did his doubts diminish about the uncertainties of in-depth involvement of the utilities. He wondered if waiting for utility and industrial cooperation and involvement in the breeder program was advisable at all.

After discussions following the hearings, Holifield firmly rejected the new proposals in favor of the conservative PDP approach. He expressed earnest hope that R&D on the first breeder would be patterned on the Shippingport precedent. He insisted that industry work closely with the AEC to gain familiarity with the challenges ahead. He found it hard to understand how experienced industrial managers failed to appreciate the magnitude of the LWR and gas reactor problems. He was especially distressed about industry's attempt to "leap-frog" and "scale up" high-temperature breeder technology without a solid R&D base and high reliability with LWRs. As he often did, he reminded the utilities and suppliers that they were still falling short on their LWR commitments and should realize that unproven R&D concepts, including the breeder, would be even more difficult than they assumed.[48]

In the ensuing years, Holifield used every opportunity to emphasize the importance of success with LWRs, breeder development, and energy security.

As the key speaker at the Atomic Industrial Forum/American Nuclear Society meeting in San Francisco in 1969, he summarized the national imperative of developing the breeder.[49] The following year, as key speaker again at the meeting in Washington, D.C., he felt that the national situation had worsened:

> Despite clear indications for at least half a decade that this Nation would be facing serious power shortages if reasonable provision was not made for our clearly foreseeable needs, this country is now confronted with an energy crisis of serious proportions. The old adage "forewarned is forearmed," which I have always particularly liked because it is an acknowledgment of man's reasoning faculties, is apparently no longer operative.[50]

Energy Security, Blackouts, and a New President

The great Northeast blackout of 1965 and later brown-outs undoubtedly did more than Holifield to call attention to the nation's need for more, cleaner, better-engineered, and more reliable electric power. To sustain interest in long-term energy security, Holifield linked the breeder initiative with current power issues in JCAE hearings of the late 1960s and after. By then, consequences of the blackout had eased, but experts remained anxious about reliability of the power supply. Holifield continued to conduct hearings on various topics concerning the national power industry. In his 1969 and 1970 hearings on the "Environmental Effects of Producing Electric Power" and thereafter, he emphasized the comparative advantages of nuclear power and called the breeder "the solution to our long-term electrical needs."[51]

In January 1969, when President Nixon took office, Holifield was unsure of what his administration would mean for nuclear power. As Californians, Holifield and Nixon had, despite basic antipathies, come to know and respect each other as politicians and legislators. Nixon had helped generate public support for President Eisenhower's "Atoms for Peace" plan while vice president in the 1950s. Holifield saw Nixon as neither a vigorous devotee nor a politician sensitive to the role of the breeder in future energy security. Moreover, Nixon's plans for the AEC's enrichment plants troubled Holifield:

> Mr. Nixon came in with a private pledge to the oil industry: he had a plan to sell the AEC's three enrichment plants to private industry. And he began the moment he entered the White House. Once the oil companies saw atomic energy coming on stream, they started buying up mines, separation plants and fuel fabrication plants. The one thing left which they wanted to control was the enrichment plants; these were like their refineries which gave them vertical control of oil. That was behind the President's plan to reorganize the AEC. I saw what was happening; when Nixon entered office I knew I had to switch from being Chairman of the Joint Committee on Atomic Energy to Chairman of the Government Operations Committee. From that spot, the President would need me; I would have a position of strength from which to bargain.[52]

Uncertainty about Nixon's breeder stance was troublesome for Holifield. Still, he was not going to let his opposition to Nixon's views interfere with his respect for the office of the president. "I had a policy of never attacking presidents personally because there may come a day when you might need their help in getting through some legislation," he explained. "That held true for Mr. Nixon also. The people chose him to head the Executive Branch. I thought they made a terrible mistake. But he had the right of veto, [the right] to appoint his Cabinet, and they served at his pleasure."[53]

Nixon Takes on the Energy Issue

With energy security at the forefront, it was expected that Nixon would have to address the issue. In mid-1969, Holifield and others received news that Dr. Paul McCracken, chairman of Nixon's Council of Economic Advisors, had been charged by the president's Domestic Council with gathering information on the domestic energy supply and long-term requirements and options for addressing projected energy supply shortages. To this end, McCracken had developed plans to solicit proposals for a national energy program from various agencies and institutions.[54] Holifield, for one, was glad the administration was addressing the domestic energy security issue:

At first, the concern was not directed at nuclear power as an issue. But there were plenty of people who wanted to blame nuclear power for the problems when electrical power shortages developed because demands were increasing so fast. The nation was in deep trouble from complacency about energy adequacy. I knew that it would get much worse in the longer term, even if our utilities could start meeting their nuclear plant commitments. Our hearings and outside efforts had tried to get others to recognize the seriousness of the absence of a meaningful national energy policy and the sustained neglect of top political focus on the major issues. Signs of serious national and international troubles were plentiful with the most serious volatility in the Mid East because of our dependence on importing their oil.

The winter of 1969-70 was the coldest in thirty years, and heating oil and natural gas were in short supply. Large-scale shifts to electrical heating and other uses in new homes had been subtle and growing. These demands plus normal growth had adversely affected reliability of electricity and there were plenty of "brownouts" in the late 1960s and in certain regions like the East Coast in the summer of 1970.

I had felt that we were doing our part in openly discussing status on the most serious nuclear plant problems in every JCAE hearing since 1965. We were trying to urge the utilities to understand what they could do to upgrade their nuclear plant commitments significantly. I was convinced then that there was absolutely no excuse for not achieving uniformly excellent performance from every commercial plant. But, more and more weak utilities were getting into deeper and deeper trouble by then. Too many utilities were listening to the reactor salesmen and placing orders without understanding and addressing the limitations and consequences of a heavily overcommitted industrial base. Public concern and opposition were rising from widespread construction problems, schedule delays, cost increases, plant reliability problems, and other inadequacies of too many utilities who did not have to be qualified before placing orders for their plants. Of course, no one could realistically separate so many widespread incidents and inadequacies from potentially real safety problems or environmental concerns if the plants were operating or being tested.

I thought it was timely that the president get more involved, and McCracken appeared to have the job to get some things moving.[55]

As part of his survey, McCracken wrote to AEC Chairman Glenn Seaborg regarding the AEC's view that the breeder was the major long-term answer to the power supply problem. He asked Seaborg for proposals on "a program that would establish and implement a national goal of completing a successful demonstration of a commercial size fast breeder reactor in this decade."[56]

AEC Chairman Seaborg Proposes the Breeder

Holifield fully agreed with Dr. Seaborg's response on October 30, 1970, which stated "the need to begin at once the vital task of dealing with the longer term aspects of the energy supply problem." Seaborg declared that "the development of the breeder reactor on an urgent basis is essential to assure an adequate supply of energy--the very lifeblood of our national strength and well being." This was because "the breeder reactor holds the key to providing the world . . . with an abundant and economic source of useful energy for a thousand years or more." In urging the president to promote the breeder as a high-priority national goal, Seaborg emphasized that such an action would be "the most decisive single step that could be taken now toward assuring an essentially unlimited energy supply, free from problems of fuel resources and atmospheric contamination." Seaborg also noted the greater urgency due to dwindling fossil supplies and dependence on foreign sources.[57]

Although he supported Seaborg, Holifield knew that while such written exchanges are impressive, they are usually not very effective. As a long-term congressman, he had learned the value of forceful personal contacts to make sure that one's views were understood. Such contacts were invaluable with an extremely busy president and other key officials. He also worried about just how forceful Seaborg could be in advocating such a costly, long-term program, not only in view of the well-organized nuclear opposition, but because the breeder's budget might force cutbacks in other AEC programs. Such reductions would require, at least annually, tough budgetary discussions face-to-face with the president. Holifield was also aware of other pressures from McCracken's requests, particularly from the coal, oil, and gas industries, and from the R&D community promoting other energy programs. The JCAE chairman thus concluded that he had a lot more to do to help Seaborg.[58]

Holifield Meets With President Nixon

Holifield got his chance to help Seaborg when Nixon invited the California congressman to fly to California with him on *Air Force One* in March 1971. Nixon wanted to talk about his massive reorganization plans:

The president invited me to ride along on *Air Force One* to California on March 29, 1971. I knew he wanted something from me, most probably my help on getting through his ultra-ambitious plans for federal reorganization. After the flight began, the President sent for me. That was what he wanted. I told him that it was a Herculean job; it was unrealistic that you could transform seven departments into four, a plan put forth by Roy Ash. Ash was a corporate executive who chaired a presidential commission on reorganizing the government. But I promised Mr. Nixon that I would hold hearings; and the president replied that was all that he expected.[59]

Referring to charts he had, Holifield brought up the breeder reactor:

Appealing to the President's Taft-Hartley anti-union mentality, I told him that strikes could interrupt conventional coal burning power plants, and added, "You can supply new leadership for the people. President Eisenhower had his 'Atoms for Peace.' Kennedy placed men in space. Both have a secure place in history. Mr. President: you, too, can secure your place in history, not at $50 billion, which was the cost to go into space, but at $2 billion now and maybe $3 billion eventually by promoting three breeder demonstration plants. And the 'breeder' reactor for generating more electricity is one major solution to our air pollution concerns!"[60]

Holifield, wanting to sell the breeder on its potential value over the next several centuries, knew his comments had to be memorable to be effective:

But I also knew I had to appeal to the president's vanity or ambitions and his sense of history. I knew what I was doing. In selling, one uses the tools of salesmanship. As Matthew's Gospel says: "Again the devil taketh him up to an exceeding high mountain and showeth him all the kingdoms of the world and the glory of them." I never forgot that lesson from Sunday School in Paragould.[61]

After his visit, Holifield noted that "The president said he wanted to think about this and would talk it over with his assistant, John Erlichman." When nearing California Nixon said: "Chet, when we go down the steps, and the press meets me, I will say we talked about the governmental reorganization plan. Is that alright?" Holifield answered affirmatively, adding that he would say nothing about the breeder program to the press. He kept his word.[62]

Holifield's meeting turned out to be pivotal. Erlichman arranged on April 13, 1971 for Holifield's team, including Pastore, Seaborg, Ramey, and Shaw, to make its presentation in the Cabinet Room before Nixon, his Cabinet, and key leaders of Congress. Holifield had decided upon simplicity and clarity. He asked Seaborg, a Nobel Laureate, to keep his part simple enough for a high school graduate. He asked Senator Pastore to cover possible oil and gas shortages, which Holifield felt were real, even at this early date (1971).[63]

Another result of Holifield's meeting with Nixon was an invitation to discuss the breeder with former AEC Chairman John McCone, who was vacationing in the Bahamas. Holifield went. The two agreed that Nixon needed a major energy issue and the breeder could be it, but McCone said that the White House was worried about political fallout. Holifield was prepared; he gave McCone some notes to pass on to the president. Mr. Nixon, he argued, would have to be subtle in supporting the breeder.[64]

Holifield sprang into action when the White House advised him that Nixon would deliver a major energy address soon. Holifield dredged up an October 5, 1968 speech in which Nixon declared that the nation had to strengthen the AEC's breeder program. To give the speech the greatest chance of reaching Nixon and his writers, he passed a copy to McCone. Holifield noted that "One month later, on May 24, I met with George Schultz, later Secretary of State for President Reagan. . . . Schultz said the administration would commit itself to the fast 'breeder' reactor as part of a general appeal for the need for all fuels. His sympathetic response was a surprise, as was his request that I review a draft of the President's speech."[65]

Nixon's speech on June 4, 1971 was the first comprehensive energy message ever delivered by a president to Congress. Holifield was very pleased by Nixon's attention to the nation's future energy supply, and that the breeder demonstration program was the centerpiece of the message. Nixon announced a national commitment "to complete the successful demonstration of the liquid metal fast breeder reactor by 1980," and recommended more funds for the first demonstration plant. As the nation's "best hope" for economical clean energy, Nixon assigned it the highest priority in the national R&D program. The breeder had reached the height of its political support.[66]

The Breeder Takes a Giant Step Forward

Shortly after Nixon's energy message, with Holifield's concurrence, the AEC and utility leadership agreed to proceed on the basis of the AEC's PDP approach, with the extent of utility involvement to be determined later. Holifield was pleased but was still concerned about utility participation:

> This left me with the question of whether we are going to be able to go ahead as a cooperative program or whether this demonstration breeder, if it is built, is going to have to be built on a Government reservation and . . . with Government funds. I am aware of the many problems that are involved in this sort of thing. You take the solicitation of utility participation, for example; utility interest is based to some extent on being able to get on-line power. . . . it seems to me that there may be a fundamental weakness in expecting the utilities to put money in on the basis they are buying into on-line power supply.[67]

Also in 1971, the AEC created an effective method for strengthening and coordinating breeder activities.   After conferring with the leadership of the investor-owned, public power, and rural cooperative sectors of the utility industry, the AEC established two advisory committees: the Senior Utility Steering Committee and the Senior Utility Technical Advisory Panel. They consisted of twenty-six experienced senior management and engineering executive utility officers and two senior AEC executives, all known and respected by Holifield and his staff.[68]

Wallace B. Behnke is an excellent example of the highly qualified executives chosen to serve on the Senior Utility Technical Advisory Panel. Then, Behnke served as Vice President of Engineering for Commonwealth Edison Corporation, one of the nation's pioneering, largest, and most successful nuclear utilities headquartered in Chicago. Later, when he became vice-chairman of Commonwealth's board of directors, he was thrust into a technical leadership position in the national breeder R&D and demonstration programs.   From the mid-1960s on, Behnke had an active engineering leadership role with the development, licensing, building, and operation of Commonwealth's large group of commercial LWRs. He also served in an advisory capacity in the boiling LWR and liquid metal breeder research programs.   Behnke, along with Thomas G. Ayers and James O'Connor, successive Commonwealth chairmen, all contributed to the breeder program.[69]

The advisory committees got beyond briefings to the important role of advising the AEC on the specific needs of the demonstration plant. Subcommittees of the Technical Panel were charged with evaluating and recommending utility-preferred features, such as fuel type, steam and primary coolant temperatures and pressures, refueling and fuel handling, materials, etc. The AEC as well as the Panel wanted simplicity, standardization, design margins, and conservative engineering practices. The AEC and Holifield intended that margins be provided to facilitate the plant's use for testing and validating improved versions of major components (e.g., steam generators, pumps, fuel, valves, special instrumentation). The plant was also to be used for testing and validating systems in the base R&D program.

The advisory groups were not only helpful to Holifield and the AEC, but were also productive learning experiences for utility leaders. In fact, these leaders often noted in meetings with AEC commissioners that such exposure and in-depth technical involvement could have been extremely beneficial to every senior utility executive considering any nuclear commitment. Holifield agreed, noting that such intensified exposure could have led to a more orderly introduction of the LWRs by the utilities and suppliers.[70]

In keeping with Holifield's concerns about involving utilities directly in the breeder, the Senior Utility Steering Committee was charged with a second major mandate. The AEC wanted the committee to garner financial support from the utilities for construction of the breeder plant. By the end of 1971 the committee, led by Thomas G. Ayers, had obtained conditional pledges for over $250 million from over 700 utilities. This is still, by far, the largest financial contribution ever pledged by the utilities to a single R&D project.[71]

Holifield agreed with the AEC that a valuable result of the cooperation between utility and AEC leaders was the high quality of the three responses at the end of 1971 to the AEC's request for proposals under Phase Two of the PDP. These included proposed Definitive Cooperative Agreements for the plant. The AEC selected the joint proposal from the Tennessee Valley Authority (TVA) and Commonwealth Edison that became the Clinch River Breeder Reactor (CRBR) Project. The two utilities represented almost one-fifth of the nation's orders for commercial nuclear power plants at that time.[72]

To maximize benefits from the TVA-Commonwealth proposal, utility leaders created two nonprofit, tax-exempt organizations: the Breeder Reactor Corporation (BRC) and the Project Management Corporation (PMC). BRC, whose board was chaired by Ayers, was formed to provide project advice by senior utility executives on behalf of the utility industry, and serve as the mechanism for collecting utility pledges for the plant. PMC, whose board was chaired by Behnke, was to oversee the design, construction, and operation of the plant in liaison with the AEC; the AEC remained solely responsible for the base R&D programs. Central to the line management and technical direction of the overall project was the Project Steering Committee (PSC), composed of Behnke, Shaw, and James Watson, TVA's Manager of Power.[73]

Neither Holifield nor the other participants were satisfied with the time and effort it took to reach the four-party CRBR agreement. A final contract covering the definitive details and contractual obligations of the AEC, TVA, Commonwealth, and the PMC was not submitted to the JCAE for review until early 1973. Meanwhile, the roles and responsibilities of the four parties were hashed and rehashed in JCAE hearings and other meetings with Holifield, who was still deeply worried about the utilities' role.

The final agreement showed the depth of the issues encountered and Holifield's insistence on the details. All issues were resolved, and the contract received required approvals by the Bureau of the Budget and the AEC. The final agreement provided that the plant would be built on land owned by the TVA near Oak Ridge, and the power would go into the TVA's network. All parties would bring a broad spectrum of expertise and resources to the project. The AEC agreed to accept the open-ended financial risks beyond the utility pledges (estimated at $253 million over ten years) and make best efforts to obtain any additional legal authority and funds required.[74]

Holifield's Concerns

Holifield was not pleased with the proposed contract. His most serious reservations concerned the AEC's sharing of overall project control with the two utilities and other participants who were in serious trouble with their LWRs because of shortages of qualified personnel. The AEC, he stated, already had highly qualified, experienced leaders and equally strong scientific and engineering teams. RDT had direct access to most of the nation's technical and engineering competence in the breeder field. Yet, Holifield observed, the AEC was not to be fully in charge of its highest-priority, most difficult, multi-billion-dollar R&D program! He was also unhappy with the financial provisions, since these were a factor in project control. The government would be funding 100 percent of the sizeable R&D program, and 75 percent of the estimated construction costs. The utilities would be contributing less than 25 percent, with the government obligated to pick up cost overruns and open-ended R&D costs. Holifield was not satisfied with only AEC control of the R&D and AEC required approval of all designs.[75]

Holifield was worried even more so about protecting the taxpayers' money, as he had been in many instances during his career:

> We need a contract that we can go to the Congress, and say we have protected the taxpayers' money, which is going to be at least 75 percent of this property. If there is any way of clarifying it and improving it, (the contract) I want it improved. There is no one who wants the fast breeder reactor any more than the man now speaking. We have worked on it for many, many years, and we want it done.[76]

Unfortunately, Holifield was unable to register the depth of his concern to the other political circles leading the fight for the breeder.[77] His intense review of the contract and search for acceptable options in key areas in various hearings and meetings led to delays of about six months, and won for him some of the same criticisms he had leveled at the utilities regarding their slowness to move. His concerns and willingness to fight for changes did, however, have a salubrious effect for contractual changes on project control:

> I thought I was doing the right thing to insist on a stronger control of the project by the AEC even when others accused me of delaying the project just to get my way. In April 1973, I finally gave in when the major participants came up with revised provisions in the Project Steering and Project Management Committees. New language further qualified all lead role assignments by stressing that lead role actions would be subject to review and approval pursuant to procedures adopted by the three-member steering committee that would direct the project. Other changes tightened up means for resolving disputes. By reading through the volumes of those JCAE hearings it is easy now to discover that I was not very happy with this arrangement. I was getting lots of pressure from the administration about the role of government and fiscal responsibilities; the utilities were also pressuring me and there appeared to be no other acceptable alternative at that stage. So, I was willing to try a joint scheme with gerry-built financing under which industry constituted some $270 million--a sum that proved to be only a small share of the total costs. But, I told my close friends I would not live long enough to see this breeder demo plant built under such a joint public-private scheme.[78]

Suddenly--Stalemate

After a series of compromises worked out by the group, Holifield accepted the imperfect realities and the JCAE approved the final four-party agreement. With high confidence in the arrangement's management and technical aspects, the AEC signed contracts for the full-scale design, development, and licensing activities related to the CRBR.[79] Sadly, just at the point when it appeared that the program could make headway, the CRBR project became mired in serious and divisive, non-managerial and non-technical issues that threatened its very existence. Politics became the culprit jeopardizing further progress.

The CRBR had begun to generate criticism from a number of quarters, including elements at AEC headquarters, the laboratories, some contractors, other federal agencies, outside anti-nuclear organizations eager to halt nuclear power, and a growing group of anti-nuclear congressmen and senators who were responding to environmentalists' concerns. Clearly, some of the opposition was natural and predictable as a result of the breeder's high priority, visibility, and most importantly, its projected annual costs in future years. For his part, Holifield took all reasonable measures to prevent the opposition from delaying the program and thereby further increasing costs.

The primary cause of the stalemate, however, was a new kind of friction between the JCAE and the AEC. The amicable political relationship between the two bodies that had existed during the long months of program planning and contract negotiations--in fact, since Lewis Strauss had left the AEC in 1958--eroded suddenly in 1973. The swelling hostile environment engendered by a new, antagonistic AEC chairperson and a number of other factors would soon prove to be very inhospitable, not only to the breeder and RDT as an organization, but to key figures in the JCAE and the AEC, including Holifield, Ramey, and Shaw. Soon, all three highly respected professionals and many of their key associates--and even the AEC as a centralized, effective organization--would be gone from government, braking program momentum and leaving large voids at the top of the government's leadership role in the breeder and other civilian nuclear power R&D programs. The heavy damage to these R&D programs left Holifield with serious questions, even as he retired, on how long the nation would be able to sustain the nuclear option as an effective, long-term counterweight to inordinate dependence on foreign oil and gas, and domestic coal. As he reviewed the troubled nuclear option and the geopolitical, national security, environmental, and economic disadvantages of dependence on mostly foreign fuels, Holifield was sure that the nation would be facing difficult times ahead.

13

The Pitfalls of Politics

Trouble on the Domestic Energy Front

Holifield did not anticipate the magnitude of the problems that he would encounter in the last years of his career. From about 1969 to his retirement, it seemed that most aspects of atomic energy were fraught with controversy and seemingly endless trouble. Many problems were political rather than technical, but they touched most AEC programs and nearly every nuclear power plant. The result was endless strife for Holifield and the beginning of the end of his and the AEC's centralized R&D and breeder initiatives.

One set of problems centered around the pell-mell expansion of nuclear power and the concomitant growth of its opposition. Real electric growth rates, coupled with public concerns over adequacy of electric power supplies, plus fears of environmental degradation and inordinate dependence on imported oil, were largely responsible for the rapid and haphazard growth of nuclear power. The overcommitments by inexperienced utilities to custom-designed and custom-built plants and the resulting mistakes, delays, and start-up problems brought unwanted media attention. At the same time, the isolated and disorganized opposition to some troubled plants in the 1960s mushroomed into an increasingly organized and effective anti-nuclear lobby by the early 1970s. Holifield and others who openly discussed problems and sought solutions found themselves targeted by the media and anti-nuclear opponents, who sometimes misinterpreted or sensationalized incidents and ignited widespread fears about nuclear safety, deteriorating public confidence.

Another major source of discord was the Nixon administration. As the quintessential Democrat, Holifield expected some difficulties. Although he enjoyed personal rapport with Nixon, Holifield had to fight repeated administration attempts to sell the AEC's uranium enrichment plants to private enterprise, an action he vehemently opposed. In 1973 and 1974, his greatest obstacle was a new, inexperienced, and combative AEC chairman, Dixy Lee Ray. As Watergate slowly sapped Nixon's political strength, the virtually unchecked Ray wreaked calculated havoc by leveraging nuclear safety

R&D and other contrived issues to defy the JCAE and eliminate Ramey, Shaw, and other top-level AEC officials. In less than two years, Ray largely destroyed the JCAE-AEC working relationship that had propelled the nation's nuclear power programs the previous two decades. Having lost much of its leadership and momentum, the breeder program never really recovered. The AEC also did not survive the onslaught. Due to the nation's energy crisis, environmentalist complaints, antagonism within Congress, and other pressures, Holifield replaced the AEC with the Energy Research and Development Administration (ERDA) and the Nuclear Regulatory Commission (NRC). This coincided with his retirement from Congress.

Nixon and the Uranium Enrichment Plants

The enrichment plant controversy which began in 1969 proved to be a long, pitched battle fought by two equally determined sides. As chairman of the JCAE, Holifield worked hard to prevent the Nixon administration from transferring the nation's uranium enrichment plants from the government to the private sector. Remembering the Dixon-Yates controversy of the 1950s, he feared a "giveaway" of this expensive, taxpayer-financed technology.[1]

Gaseous diffusion was the most successful uranium enrichment process developed in World War II. The U.S. eventually built and owned three large enrichment plants at Oak Ridge, Tennessee; Paducah, Kentucky; and Portsmouth, Ohio. All were operated for the U.S. by private contractors. From the late 1960s, experts believed that U.S. enrichment capacity had to be expanded. Some experts, here and abroad, responded with proposals on new enrichment methods, including the gas centrifuge and advanced laser beam methods. Still, gaseous diffusion remained the U.S. technology of choice.[2]

In November 1969, when Nixon announced plans for the AEC to operate the enrichment plants as a separate commercial entity, Holifield was alarmed. He had been hearing rumors that the administration planned to sell the plants to private industry. He immediately threw up warning signals, noting publicly that not even one member of the JCAE would agree to sell the plants.[3] Chet believed that what the Nixon administration had in mind "was to build up a parallel commercial-like cadre to replace the regular AEC managers, and then give it to those people to run, when they sold the enrichment plants."[4]

The Nixon administration felt it had a firm rationale; it wanted to run this enterprise as a separate business entity, much like the TVA. Thus, the plants would not be subject to the limitations of annual funding cycles. Holifield did not buy the argument; he called it a "red herring," since any TVA-type venture had always been anathema to Republicans and industry.[5] Nor did he sit idly by and hope for the best. He trumpeted his misgivings to Warren Unna of the *Washington Post*, arguing that the administration was preparing an eventual giveaway of the enrichment plants for cents on the dollar.[6]

Holifield feared most the concentration of energy in a few companies' hands since the utilities lacked capital to bid for the enrichment plants. Only the oil companies--through their tax advantages--had the money required. "If they are going to control basic energy in the United States," he contended, "they will be controlling power across the board." He claimed that "the big steal can come in selling them at book value or something less." Although the taxpayers' $2.3 billion investment had been reduced by depreciated use to $1.2 billion, "the plants are not obsolete, or worn out, or poorly maintained. They are the only plants of their kind in the world and still worth $2.3 billion from a production standpoint." Under the "Atoms for Peace" program, the U.S. was then committed to assuring foreign users of at least a 30-year supply of enriched fuel; thus, whoever owned the plants would also have overwhelming influence as the free world came to depend more heavily on nuclear power.[7]

Holifield's media blitz and other JCAE opposition led the administration to back away from its proposal but he was not able to dissuade it. Over the next few years, it pushed the utilities in this direction. Utility supply contracts, for instance, were put on a 10-year basis, ostensibly precluding companies from getting more uranium. Previously, if firms gave six months' notice, more enriched uranium was readily available. The JCAE's view was that the utilities might have to plan further ahead than they did before.[8]

The controversy continued as a protracted battle long after Holifield's retirement and enrichment remained in public hands until the 1990s. Erratic government decisions limiting the amount of enriched fuel available to foreign nations eventually backfired. During the Carter administration, the AEC placed a three-month embargo on shipments to Europe. Reprocessing and recycling fuel were also banned.[9] This led Europe to build its own facilities and to rely on the Soviets as back-up supplier. The new European plants by the late 1970s ended the U.S. monopoly. So obtuse did the world market become that France and other nations could sell a U.S.-designed PWR to China, while U.S. suppliers were forbidden by law to make such a sale! U.S. policies thus destroyed a formerly secure export market and undermined confidence in U.S. nuclear policies and suppliers. By 1993, the U.S. supplied only about half of the world demand. Under the National Energy Policy Act of 1992, the U.S. Enrichment Corporation (USEC) was established initially as a government corporation and has been operating as a commercial business with domestic and foreign utility customers.

Holifield and AEC Chairmen

With the enrichment plants, Holifield was dealing with a predictable opposition. In 1973 and 1974, however, he was quite suddenly faced with a political and personal problem of unexpected proportions in Nixon's appointment of Dixy Lee Ray to the AEC chairmanship. Thus, for the first time, he found himself without solutions in dealing with the new chairperson. He had experienced friction with some AEC chairmen before, but now he reached what was for him the nadir of the JCAE-AEC relationship.

During the 29 years of the JCAE-AEC relationship, Holifield had varying working relationships with each of the seven AEC chairmen. These chairmen included David E. Lilienthal (1946-1950), Gordon Dean (1950-1953), Lewis L. Strauss (1953-1958), John McCone (1958-1961), Glenn T. Seaborg (1961-1971), James R. Schlesinger (1971-1973), and Dixy Lee Ray (1973-1974). From the start, Holifield (and other JCAE members) expected a privileged relationship with the AEC. The basic reason was the AEC's statutory responsibility to keep the JCAE "fully and currently informed" on all of its activities. Some observers have claimed that this provision and other JCAE controls virtually turned the AEC into a creature of the committee. That judgment, however, oversimplifies the complex relationship between the two bodies. One less-than-efficient feature was that the commission, as intended by Congress, was a body of five independent and equal commissioners. The AEC was able to perform adequately within this framework, however, because the AEC chairman was also intended as a first-among-equals to coordinate activities with both the JCAE and the administration. JCAE members' relations with AEC chairmen were thus central to effective cooperation.

During the Lilienthal and Dean years, Holifield was a junior member of the JCAE. The JCAE was preoccupied with the new AEC commissioners and such issues as secrecy, security, and weapons development. During Lilienthal's term, the JCAE did not aggressively use its public forum either to address urgent issues facing the AEC or to educate the public. The Dean chairmanship was something of a continuation of the Lilienthal years, a bridge between the weapons-dominated period and the advent of nuclear power.[10]

Holifield's relationship with the third AEC chairman, Admiral Lewis Strauss, was stormy to say the least. "We had terrible rows," Holifield remembered, "mainly over the Dixon-Yates power contract. Strauss foolishly involved the AEC in this. We also fought over radiation effects, fallout from nuclear tests, and potential nuclear war." So abrasive did this relationship become that when the AEC dedicated a reactor at Fort Belvoir, Virginia, Strauss deliberately left out Holifield's name when introducing the JCAE. Later though, after Strauss left the AEC, they buried the hatchet, exchanged correspondence, and even visited together at Strauss' Virginia farm.[11]

Holifield was also involved in two of the most acrimonious disputes between Strauss and Commissioner Thomas E. Murray, who opposed Strauss's efforts to become "principal officer" of the commission. Holifield and the JCAE supported Murray effectively. For his part, Strauss successfully kept an in-depth study of the biological effects of all-out nuclear warfare, urged by Murray, from being conducted by the AEC, even if highly classified. So Murray convinced Holifield that the JCAE should do the study. Chet was one of the few members with the courage to address this issue in the face of hints that it was somehow disloyal to do so. When Strauss urged Eisenhower not to reappoint Murray, Holifield had Murray appointed as a JCAE consultant.[12]

After Strauss became interim Secretary of Commerce, John McCone became AEC chairman. "McCone was much more straight-forward, a person I could get along with," Holifield observed. "During the Nixon administration when he had retired to private life, I called on him for help, since he shared my interest in moving forward on the fast breeder reactor."[13]

Ironically, McCone's 1958 confirmation hearing before the JCAE did not portend well for his relationship with Holifield. McCone became visibly upset when he observed Holifield quoting from a document that the AEC had not yet released publicly. McCone was not yet aware of the "fully and currently informed" provision. When Holifield reportedly told McCone that if he couldn't stand the heat, he should get out of the kitchen, a new political feud seemed at hand. However, this inauspicious beginning was corrected when it became apparent that Chet's remark was directed more at the AEC's dilatory behavior at the time than at McCone personally. While he and McCone were always cordial and friendly, Holifield did object to McCone's adherence to one aspect of Lewis Strauss's behavior. He felt that McCone, like Strauss earlier, did not aggressively pursue a powerful role for the AEC in atomic power.[14]

Holifield had excellent relations with Nobel laureate Seaborg, who served twice as long as any other AEC chairman. Seaborg's era witnessed great strides in nuclear affairs. His links to the JCAE tended to be productive and on an even keel, even though there was some strife between President Kennedy and Holifield's JCAE. When Seaborg first took office, Holifield was mounting a blistering attack on the administration and the AEC for their collective reluctance to concentrate greater resources on nuclear power. This attack paid off with the landmark report of 1962, and the supplemental report of 1967. Seaborg handled this and other political skirmishing adroitly, so that his relations with Holifield remained friendly for over a decade.[15]

Holifield's productive relationship with Seaborg was matched only by his relatively brief association with James R. Schlesinger, the sixth AEC chairman. With the rising public interest in bomb testing, environmental concerns, ever larger coal and nuclear plants, and new safety issues, many nuclear power proponents assumed that it would be difficult for Schlesinger to become an effective spokesman for nuclear power. Many were worried about his tenure at the Rand Corporation and his involvement in AEC programs while at the Office of Management and Budget (OMB). Despite his brief chairmanship, however, Schlesinger was regarded highly by Holifield and other JCAE members. Schlesinger, Holifield, and Ramey were very much of the same mind. They all strongly supported centralization of R&D, and stronger quality assurance and standardization for nuclear power plants. Schlesinger's chairmanship also proved to be a watershed of support for nuclear safety and the breeder. He understood AEC programs well from his OMB tenure, and assisted Holifield in getting Congress to promptly approve the priority programs outlined in Nixon's energy message. Schlesinger was anxious to understand all of the complexities of the nuclear energy field.[16]

Schlesinger abruptly left the AEC in January 1973 to become head of the Central Intelligence Agency (CIA). In early 1977, President Carter named him as White House Energy Czar, and in October appointed him as the first Department of Energy (DOE) Secretary. Holifield recalled later that "many of us were happy when Schlesinger accepted the Czar role, since we admired and respected him for his contributions at the AEC" and "moreover, few people appeared as well qualified as Jim was." Holifield noted, however, that "Carter--bending to the advice of members of his domestic policy staff-- overrode Schlesinger's support of nuclear power-- saying nuclear power should be used only as 'a last resort.'" Holifield was dismayed at this position, and Schlesinger himself privately expressed frustration. In Holifield's opinion, Schlesinger "did his best at 'damage control,' but with limited success":

> I had retired before Carter was elected, and was very upset by his decision to wipe out the word "Plutonium" from the U.S. energy initiatives. The fact was muted that about 30 percent of the power from LWRs is produced by plutonium converted from uranium-238 in every commercial LWR in the world. Actually, there's nothing that he could do about that law of physics except to shut down all of the plants in the country, as many of his key decision-makers and anti-nukes around him in the White House probably wanted him to do. However, he and they didn't hesitate to try to impose a ban on plutonium, as well as on reprocessing and recycle of spent fuel on this country and on the rest of the free world. Carter also tried his best to kill Clinch River, offering instead "a bigger and better" breeder R&D program. But, Congress wisely rejected that proposal. Clearly, Carter and those around him opposed to nuclear power and their allies did what they could to frustrate the DOE and our nuclear policies.

> Many of us felt that Schlesinger was caught in a bad situation and probably did as much as anyone could do with President Carter and the strong anti-nuclear crowd around him. One day I'll just have to ask Jim what his real position was then before I give up my highly favorable impressions of him. Until then, I'll continue to thank him for all the good he did in those 18 months that he chaired the Commission.[17]

Holifield's Problems Become More Serious

Holifield's problems with all other AEC chairmen and commissioners combined were small when compared to those with AEC Chairman Dixy Lee Ray. He probably would have been very surprised if he had been told that he would have a destructive relationship with the AEC near the end of his career. He quickly discovered that his disputes with an often hostile Ray, more personal and political than philosophical or technical, had much wider ramifications for effective functioning of the JCAE-AEC relationship than any other issue. Holifield's years of developing a close working relationship with the AEC were ruined by what can only be described as "politics."

During his career, Holifield found himself twice at loggerheads with AEC chairmen: with Lewis Strauss from 1953 to 1958, and with Dixy Ray during 1973 and 1974. Holifield was impressed by the similarities and differences between the two. Both attempted to challenge the JCAE's authority and to elevate the chairman's role into one of plenary authority. In both cases there was a heavy-handed "politicizing" of the AEC. With Strauss, this was largely due to an experienced financier and politician who evidenced a forceful philosophy to "let the private sector do it." Ray's case involved an articulate but isolated associate professor of marine biology, who was inexperienced in management and unfamiliar with the nation's nuclear programs. Holifield and others noted Ray's fervid concerns about personal prerogatives, especially in interactions with experienced managers and congressmen.[18]

Holifield was not the only person to experience trouble with Strauss and Ray. Their unilateral actions drew the ire of the other commissioners, as well as JCAE members and government officials both inside and outside of the AEC. Many felt that the two chairmen's actions were designed to wipe out or circumvent important involvement by others, or to set aside what others believed to be vital legislative and technical considerations. Ray also openly ignored the JCAE's wishes and jurisdiction. Holifield and the JCAE found it cumbersome to work with five commissioners instead of one administrator, yet they supported the structures of the Atomic Energy Act. They had always been able to work with the general manager, division directors, and their staffs to get the job done even during disputes with the commissioners--at least up until 1973. Then, Ray turned the JCAE-AEC relationship into an utter shambles by driving out AEC officials friendly to the JCAE.

The Ray AEC only compounded problems in what was becoming a period of uncertainty. The Watergate Crisis began to balloon and would have repercussions for the nation and nuclear power. Within government, the budget strain from nuclear programs was less acceptable than before, especially as resources were diverted for the Vietnam conflict. The utilities and industry, despite the sudden jump in *orders* for nuclear plants from seven in 1965 to twenty in 1966 and then thirty in 1967, were becoming more unsettled and finding nuclear power a costly enterprise. Utilities were especially aroused as the AEC, backed by Holifield, pressed them in and out of JCAE hearings to recognize the liabilities of engineering limitations, inexperienced personnel, overcommitments, and extrapolated hardware. He repeatedly urged them to become more aware and demanding customers.

Despite Holifield's and others' admonitions, the uncertainties of nuclear power's risks and costs were set aside in favor of a powerful wave of public pressures for the theoretical benefits "inherent in commercial nuclear power."

These pressures included high demands for electricity, a cleaner environment, and far less dependence on imported oil. By 1974 over 50 new, relatively inexperienced utilities entered the nuclear field--all with approvals from their state public utility commissions (PUCs) and financial support from Wall Street. In the hands of inexperienced utilities, the impressive growth of nuclear power belied its significant weaknesses. Some well-managed utilities built successful plants, but their achievements were ignored. The troubled utilities quite naturally elicited critical reviews from Holifield and the JCAE, the AEC, and suppliers, and garnered plenty of unfavorable media attention. These concerns also carried over into other issues, such as the shipment and disposal of radioactive wastes. Holifield felt that the opposition was exploiting media coverage to the fullest in attempts to convert virtually all weaknesses, costly delays, and mistakes into potential "safety problems." These "safety problems" were springboards for more intensified opposition.[19]

Proof that this "safety issue" had become a major concern already by 1971 was evident at Schlesinger's first meeting with the JCAE during the Geneva Conference on Nuclear Power in September 1971. Holifield, Hosmer, Price, Congresswoman Julia Butler Hansen (D-Washington), Senator Wallace F. Bennett (R-Utah), Ramey and Shaw gathered to greet the new AEC chairman and discuss pressing issues. Discussion centered on growing public concerns of reactor safety fueled by media coverage of the utilities' problems. Holifield agreed with the others that industry must address the widening gap between utility commitments and capabilities. It appeared to him that neither the media nor the public were aware (or were ignoring the fact) that there were many ways to assure safety in addition to the costly corrective actions on troubled plants. He wanted to be sure the public understood that the industry's problems, as prevalent and costly as they were, were carefully monitored by regulatory agencies and were not going to result automatically in major "safety problems." For him, every problem was a costly problem, but not necessarily a "safety problem," as the nuclear opposition declared.[20]

Holifield wanted to deal with the growing public concerns about nuclear safety promptly and in a straight-forward manner. He and other JCAE members urged Schlesinger to undertake a comprehensive review of LWR safety for Congress, industry, and the public. The overall objective would be "to place before the public, hopefully in a manner understandable to the reasonably informed layman, a fairly comprehensive statement of fact, along with some history and policy considerations, regarding the safety and environmental aspects of nuclear power reactors and their support facilities."[21]

In the following months as the annual JCAE hearings drew near, Holifield and other JCAE members were pressed for increases in LWR safety R&D funding by the AEC's laboratories. The JCAE knew that some of these "safety advocates" had held special briefings and distributed material to the media and anti-nuclear groups to trumpet an urgent need for increased LWR safety R&D spending. Much of the material was concocted and misleading, and clearly lacking in disciplined analysis, credible peer review, and applicability to real safety concerns. Holifield's assessment was that the curiously uniform character of the misleading information was damaging to public understanding of reactor safety issues. It appeared that the lobbyists wanted to convert nuclear plant mistakes, malfunctions, and other problems into major "safety problems" and "accidents" that could be solved *only* through large funding increases in safety R&D for the laboratories.[22]

While Holifield was not naive about lobbying, he was especially dismayed by the misrepresentations. He was upset that some laboratory managements evidently did not care or were unwilling to clarify the technical and legal issues. At the heart of LWR safety R&D was the fundamental fact that the safe design, construction, and operation of each nuclear plant was and always had been the sole responsibility of the utility that owned the plant. The JCAE, the AEC, and industry understood this. Holifield often reminded utilities that this requirement encompassed all safety-related activities, including the R&D programs necessary to obtain and sustain an AEC license. It seemed that the dissidents and the media were deliberately failing to disclose that the safety obligations of owner-utilities could not be assumed by the AEC nor its advisory committees, nor be contingent upon accomplishment of any of the AEC's past, ongoing, or future safety R&D activities![23]

Holifield, the AEC, and utility leaders were surprised that some AEC laboratories and industrial contractors would seek common ground with the anti-nuclear opposition and the more extreme environmentalists on LWR safety R&D issues. This is understandable, however, when examined in the light of the weakening status felt by AEC laboratories and contractors. These field entities had come to a crossroads by the late 1960s, after years of success and a relatively free rein in R&D.   The push for centralized reactor R&D comprised only the tip of the iceberg of changes that several laboratories--Argonne, Oak Ridge, Hanford, the National Reactor Testing Station (NRTS), and others--found unsettling.   They resented not being wanted in the expanding naval and commercial LWR industries. They also faced increased competition among themselves, as well as competition from contractors qualified to build space and other small power sources.[24]

If this were not enough, AEC laboratories also experienced losses in their diversified reactor R&D programs and felt constrained to venture into new areas. As industry moved toward LWRs and the mixed-oxide fuel cycle as a standard, serious utility interest in alternative reactors and fuel cycles virtually disappeared.   The JCAE, with Holifield in the vanguard, responded to budgetary pressures from the Johnson and Nixon administrations and terminated many less-promising concepts. Laboratories, like Oak Ridge and Argonne, thus ventured into non-nuclear energy concepts, and environmental research, including studies on removing sulphur from coal, controlling water and air pollution, and minimizing acid rain problems. However, these activities, along with the breeder, carried no assurances for continued laboratory health. While there were plans to utilize two or perhaps three laboratories for the breeder, the AEC could not define more precisely future laboratory roles in other reactor R&D arenas.[25]

Holifield, Hosmer, the JCAE staff and OMB had reached an informed consensus that RDT's safety activities were already on the right track by strengthening generic safety R&D. They expected that higher confidence in commercial reactors would ensue from further generic testing using the AEC's two new, special-purpose safety test facilities in Idaho: the Loss of Fluid Test (LOFT) Facility and the Power Burst Facility (PBF). These facilities were built to obtain a better understanding of normal and abnormal reactor operations common to all LWRs such as complete loss of coolant and melting of fuel and structures that might cause the worst postulated reactor accidents.

With these and other AEC test facilities already integrated into cooperative government-industry safety R&D activities, Holifield fully supported RDT's strengthening of these newer programs more in the context of improvements in laboratory technical standards, discipline, quality assurance, and overall engineering than in annual increases in funding. A realist, Holifield knew that funding increases for safety R&D were not the answer to most problems. The "body of knowledge" would never be complete, any more than it is in any sphere of activity. Funding for safety R&D would never be enough to cover every real and conceivable problem. Nor would information gained from R&D programs continue to be only one of many considerations in licensing approvals. In addition, Chet realized that safety issues would be ongoing and would affect licensing bodies and regulators before, during, and after the life of each nuclear plant.[26]

However logical and constructive his reasoning, Holifield found it difficult to get the media to even listen. He believed that the media lacked the motivation to address the complexities of most public safety concerns. After all, the JCAE held frequent, documented public discussions and there was an overwhelming amount of written information available from the AEC and elsewhere about problems and proven solutions. Instead of investigating, the press seemed to favor more emotionally appealing, fear-mongering stories or simple answers to complex problems. On the safety issue, the media and laboratories failed to provide Holifield or anyone else with meaningful examples where more safety R&D funding would reduce environmental and accident risks of commercial LWRs or enhance public confidence. Nor did they show how additional R&D would mollify or allay public fears about nuclear safety spawned by troubled utilities and highlighted by the media.

In Holifield's view, the media and the laboratories had not only distorted the relevance of funding increases to actual nuclear plant safety, but had also obscured many real efforts by the AEC and industry to help ensure safety.

He knew that constantly upgrading staff qualifications and training was essential for assuring safe plant performance and for taking maximum advantage of plant safety features. The AEC also required use of independent containment structures, multiple engineered barriers, and other engineered-safety systems, plus the application of Price-Anderson indemnity coverage, just in case. Each utility's role, including safety R&D, was well defined in AEC regulations. These requirements should have been well understood by commercial participants. However, as Holifield observed, "Obviously, we'll always keep discovering that they aren't." He stressed that "several years ago we declared that these water reactors were commercial reactors and that the utilities themselves should take over part of the burden of the continuing safety research and development." He was not willing for the government to assume responsibility for the adequacy of any part of a utility's commercial power plant. To do so would be a step backward.[27]

Holifield and Schlesinger Defend Shaw

Holifield realized that the laboratories would not be deterred from their lobbying and assaults. Thus, Holifield was not surprised when he heard that they had shifted their strategy. They now had revived an earlier initiative to get rid of Shaw, or alternately, to have LWR safety R&D placed in a separate organization reporting to the AEC's General Manager.[28]

Holifield had heard in some of his "weeping chair" sessions and from a few of his JCAE associates some of the same criticisms about RDT stewardship of safety R&D that continued to appear mostly in local media. He felt that many of the initiatives to get rid of Shaw or break up RDT were similar to, but not as frequent and intense, as in earlier years. Even before Shaw took office, most AEC laboratories and contractors had collectively objected to his appointment. Some of these critics never gave up on their efforts to oust him, just as some Navy brass and lobbyists never gave up trying to get Rickover fired. Shaw's critics, mainly from NRTS, Oak Ridge, and the media, charged that Shaw's "abrasive and single-minded promotion of the nuclear breeder reactor" as the highest priority R&D program had adversely affected other promising reactor concepts, particularly the gas and molten salt reactors. His interference in safety R&D, these critics charged, had created the serious public safety problems of nuclear plants. Holifield was not swayed by these arguments. He had faced the same types of criticisms as Shaw had, and even so, neither he nor Shaw could match Rickover's record of accumulating and sustaining critics (even after Rickover's death in 1986)!

As he did with Rickover's critics, Holifield disagreed strongly with Shaw's detractors. He contended that the nation had embarked on the breeder program in the 1940s, decades before Shaw joined RDT. In his view, Shaw was carrying out the JCAE's and the administration's directions. As for

Shaw's supposed "meddling" in safety R&D, Holifield pointed out that RDT was looking hard at the standards, discipline, and quality assurance practices. Shaw was requiring the same type of management attention, quality, and timely reporting from laboratories as the JCAE required from AEC officials.[29]

Persistent pressure on Holifield, Price, and Pastore by a few, relatively new members of the JCAE was soon followed by a proposal from them to have safety R&D placed directly under the AEC General Manager. This was discussed at a April 24, 1972 special JCAE executive session only with the AEC commissioners.[30] The next day, Schlesinger wrote to JCAE Vice Chairman Price addressing the issue directly. "Since so many issues were covered in the session yesterday," Schlesinger began, "I thought it might be useful to set down what I consider to be the most significant points regarding the proposal that safety research and development be separated from other reactor research and development." He stressed the integral nature of safety questions in reactor R&D, and expressed AEC opposition to any change.[31] Schlesinger closed by adding that "the Commission is unanimous regarding these points and in the views which I expressed during the hearing yesterday." Due to his letter, open attacks on Shaw did not recur while he was chairman.

The *Science* Articles

The same supposedly "substantive" criticisms of the LWR safety R&D program (and Shaw) persisted in the pulp press, and finally made their way into a series in the scientific journal *Science* in September 1972. Robert Gillette homed in on the AEC's safety R&D record, based upon his visits to laboratories conducting LWR safety R&D.[32] Holifield was certainly not impressed with Gillette's work. His writing appeared to Holifield to be simply another version of an unconvincing thesis, but also careless with commentary, pointedly biased, anti-nuclear, and anti-Shaw. Yet, Gillette acknowledged Shaw's forceful management direction of the safety R&D program, and his notable strengthening of laboratory and contractor management. One of Gillette's major theses appeared to be that the AEC, with Shaw in the vanguard, had down-played LWR safety R&D in favor of the breeder, and thus, all LWRs were potentially dangerous. It was clear to Holifield that Gillette, whether intentionally or not, had been used by the laboratories seeking larger funding increases. For Holifield, the articles were just more careless media output which hampered, rather than helped, better public understanding of the causes of nuclear power's problems.[33]

In early October, Congressman Orval Hansen (R-Idaho), a new JCAE member, requested the AEC's position on the articles.[34] AEC General Manager Hollingsworth did not have to search very far for the problems the AEC found. In his response, Hollingsworth posited that Gillette presented "a distorted view" of the AEC's safety R&D program. He noted that "many of the comments contained in the *Science* stories so transgress the bounds of objectivity and accuracy as to mislead the public and to have a disruptive effect on a program of great national importance." Gillette showed "a total lack of understanding of how decisions are made on the conduct of programs within the Commission, and who makes them." He also abused the concept of nuclear safety because he did not differentiate between the media's and public's perception of reactor safety and the concept of engineered safety, nor demonstrate how it was provided. Hollingsworth also faulted the implication that reactor safety depended on unfinished research. Finally, he disputed Gillette's view that LWR safety R&D had been upstaged by the breeder, calling such a view was "totally without foundation."[35]

In his systematic rebuttal, Hollingsworth charged that Gillette displayed "ignorance of the responsibilities and roles of the various participants in the civilian nuclear power programs, including those who are contributing to the check and balance system to assure safety." He had also erred grievously "by concentrating so heavily on research not yet done and by placing the AEC's generic LWR safety research program in the context of a unique and pivotal matter on which safety of commercial plants hinges."[36]

Gillette's provocative suggestion that the AEC had tailored its LWR safety R&D program to win more utility support for the breeder was dismissed by Hollingsworth as one of the most unfounded charges of all. He noted that the AEC's decisions were "based on priorities established by the Commission." Moreover, the decisions were discussed in open JCAE hearings. Thus, "the misrepresentations with respect to specific issues raised in the *Science* articles are effectively refuted" by the JCAE hearing records.[37]

Holifield was satisfied with the AEC's response, but he knew that the media and the public did not understand the weaknesses of Gillette's articles any more than those of other anti-nuclear writers. Holifield felt that the value of nuclear power was becoming obscured by clouds of political rhetoric. He realized that this would have ramifications on public acceptance of complex developments in future technological fields. This incident suggested that if a scientific journal could so badly misinterpret the nature of the AEC's work, what could be expected from less-informed segments of the media?

In addition to the facts in the safety R&D controversy, Holifield found other good reasons to remain a strong supporter of Shaw. Aside from his impeccable credentials, including several national civil service awards, Shaw's colorful and forceful presence appealed highly to Holifield, Price, Hosmer, Pastore, and other experienced JCAE leaders and staff. They trusted him and his top-level cadre of highly competent managers. As far as they were concerned, Shaw's AEC leadership and accomplishments were consistent with what they had learned from those who worked closely with him since 1950 and recommended him for RDT, including Rickover and three successive Secretaries of the Navy: John Connally, Fred Korth, and Paul Nitze.[38]

Holifield and other supporters of Shaw knew that Shaw created strong waves of opposition when his personal characteristics were coupled with his persistent demands for excellence and integrity in "first-of-a-kind" national R&D programs. As a supporter of the "Rickover precedent" for more than two decades, Holifield knew that Shaw would be a natural target for AEC laboratories. He also realized that Shaw, like Rickover, rankled many in the utilities, in the industry, and in the AEC by his candid, in-depth testimony and responsiveness to the commission, the OMB, and congressional committees. He and others who Shaw worked directly for knew that they could count on him to do what he was hired and urged to do.[39]

During the Seaborg and Schlesinger chairmanships, Holifield was unaware of any other efforts to oust Shaw. Despite the understanding of some to the contrary, Schlesinger strongly supported Shaw and reinforced Holifield's defense of him. This was especially so during Schlesinger's last meeting with the JCAE. Responding to media charges that safety R&D delays by Shaw were detrimental to reactor safety, Schlesinger reacted strongly. "There have been delays in that program," he allowed, "but the delays do not cause concern of a major nature about the safety of reactors." Schlesinger was even more emphatic in what amounted to a spirited defense of the RDT director:

> I underscore for the record that Milt has fought for these programs, that the survival of some of these programs is directly attributable to Milt, and I think that it is an injustice to scapegoat Milt for decisions of the Commission or decisions of the Bureau of the Budget or, if I may say so in the room, decisions of the Joint Committee on Atomic Energy.[40]

Earlier in the same JCAE hearing, Schlesinger had declared that "The LOFT program would not exist at this point in time if it were not for Milt Shaw. Milt fought for that program desperately and he fought for the overall funding of the R&D program."[41]

Schlesinger Departs: Some Parting Words on Safety

In early January of 1973, Holifield and others were surprised to learn that Schlesinger had been nominated by President Nixon to be CIA director and would very soon leave the AEC. Holifield, Hosmer, and others on the JCAE were deeply concerned about the implications of this dramatic change. They moved quickly to advance the public hearings on the reactor safety program, even though the comprehensive LWR safety report was not yet complete.[42]

In his opening remarks at the special JCAE hearing, Schlesinger noted that "there is nothing absolutely riskless in society," noting that even simple actions such as walking across a street or opening a file cabinet posed some risks. He maintained that "if one wants to look at statistical probabilities of one in a hundred million or one in 10 million," then "one can always say that there is no absolute certainty of anything." What the AEC had attempted to do "within a statistical framework of reasoning" was "to reduce risks to a very low level, levels that are tolerable." American society was faced with "adapting to these changes in technologies with a due appreciation of risk."[43]

Schlesinger admitted that "the nuclear area is one that lends itself to sensationalism" because of its complexities as a source of heat for steam power. He believed "we should view it primarily as an alternative source of heat to be compared with such heat sources as come from fossil fuels." He conceded that "I have been a skeptic about nuclear power in the past because I did not think in the 1960s that it was cost-effective, and I thought that it was coming on too fast," but "I have changed with regard to my personal perspective for three reasons." These were the growing dependence on foreign oil, and economic competitiveness and environmental advantages of nuclear power. On environmental advantages, he asserted that "almost anyone will agree" that "a properly operating nuclear reactor is the most desirable form or the least undesirable form of power production, recognizing that all power production will have a degrading effect on the environment."[44]

Holifield and other JCAE members were impressed and pleased by Schlesinger's comments. He essentially amplified what Holifield had been saying all along: safety is relative, and the only reasonable approach to nuclear safety is to reduce risks to acceptable levels. Assurance of absolute safety with nuclear power--or any other technology--simply is not possible.

Dramatic Changes at the AEC

Schlesinger's departure marked the end of an era for the JCAE-AEC relationship. Quite suddenly, relations between the two bodies soured. Holifield was as surprised as he was concerned, since the breach came from unexpectedly from the new AEC chairman, Dixy Lee Ray. Almost at once after Nixon appointed her, Holifield discerned a decidedly different attitude at the AEC. The change proved to be without remedy; Holifield did not have good relations with the AEC for his last two years in Congress.

Ray became a member of the commission a few months prior to becoming chairman, mainly because of the administration's desire to appoint a woman scientist. Her qualifications were thin; she was a former associate professor of marine biology without experience in nuclear activities or in government administration. It was primarily Ray's personal traits and her political maneuvering, however, that created lasting enmity between the AEC and the JCAE during her tenure.[45]

Ray began her tenure inauspiciously by engaging in open political warfare with the JCAE and Holifield personally. She apparently took, if she did not come with it, an almost instantaneous disliking to Holifield and those in the AEC whom she knew were close to him. Often, Ray appeared reluctant, and sometimes even refused, to communicate directly with Holifield and with Ramey, Shaw, and some other senior AEC officials. Ray's inattention to Holifield's concerns was soon manifested in some AEC organizations. It appeared to Holifield and the JCAE staff that some top-level AEC managers were no longer responsive, nor driving to remove bottlenecks and delays. Fear and politics appeared to have replaced cooperation at the AEC, and Holifield perceived these factors to be at the heart of the AEC's new stance.[46]

Like many who tried to work productively with Ray, Holifield was nothing short of astounded. He had rarely encountered such a change in attitude, or such opposition to his requests to have AEC staff at meetings and hearings. Her reclusive, authoritarian, and rude manner was unlike any he had known. Some officials who had to communicate with her perceived that her decisions were predetermined and based more upon personalities than substance.

While Ray eventually became an effective spokesperson for nuclear power and even the breeder (she expanded on this role later as governor of the state of Washington), Holifield did not hold a high opinion of her qualifications or capabilities. He concluded that she was determined to operate as Strauss had done, as a one-person show rather than, as Congress intended, the first among five equal commissioners. She cowed the other commissioners into submission; like Strauss, she used the chairmanship to control and withhold information, and appeared to work hard to isolate and destroy commissioners who would not pay homage. In Holifield's opinion, Ray did not appear to know or accept the requirement that the AEC keep the JCAE "fully and currently informed." Nor did she, along with some commissioners during her tenure, appear to have the capability to work productively with the JCAE and other organizations to keep the AEC's programs moving forward.[47]

Holifield knew Ray had equally unflattering views of him and the JCAE. She appeared convinced that Holifield, through his allegedly arbitrary and unbridled power over the JCAE and also the AEC, constituted a danger to the republic. His alter-egos at the AEC ranked not too far behind in her estimation of national menaces, and she seemed to be out to redress the imbalance single-handedly. In opposing the JCAE leadership, Ray picked up some recently appointed allies on the JCAE, including Senator Stuart Symington (R-Missouri) and others, who seemed to be boring from within to undermine and eliminate the committee.[48] So long as she was chairman, negative relations between the JCAE and AEC leaders contined unabatted.

Ray's antagonism toward Holifield--feelings he would soon reciprocate--did not heavily concern Holifield. Having engaged in prolonged polemics with a few others, Holifield was accustomed to the hard knocks that came with all bruising political fights. However, his conflict with Ray filled him with far more foreboding because of the nature of the conflict, its timing, and import. This fight was not philosophical or about whether there should be a breeder or other program; it was about Ray's unwillingness to work with the JCAE to achieve results in AEC programs, and ultimately, about Ray's perception of her personal power and prerogatives. To make matters worse, the disputes occurred just as utilities were facing growing overcommitments, the opponents of nuclear power were gaining a wider audience, and Nixon and Congress were becoming preoccupied with Watergate. The AEC was left to fend essentially for itself. Holifield's disputes with Ray thus had implications for all of the AEC's activities, particularly R&D and its statutory roles in regulation, licensing, and safety.

Ray Sets Her Sights on Shaw and Ramey

The new chairman set out almost at once to change the AEC to her liking and get rid of AEC allies of Holifield and the JCAE. Ray homed in almost immediately on Shaw and his division.[49] While completely avoiding direct contact with Shaw, Ray seemed determined to get rid of him and RDT's obviously large role and influence at the AEC and elsewhere in energy affairs. According to some she met even before she met Shaw, Ray seemed interested in soliciting stories and other ammunition against Shaw as she drove her motor home across the country to join the commission. During this trip, she visited several AEC facilities, particularly those laboratories involved with high-priority RDT programs. Ray listened as some managers and scientists voiced their complaint that "much of the autonomy the laboratories had enjoyed for decades had been replaced by a forceful new style of management from Washington." As one safety R&D manager at NRTS often told visitors, "historically, Washington was content to let us tell them what their designs didn't cover, and then to make research proposals." Because reactor safety was "such an extremely complicated area," the manager averred that "in effect, they let us tell them what we should be doing in reactor safety."[50]

Holifield was convinced that Ray had parleyed dissident desires in the safety R&D controversy to serve her political objective of "taking care of Holifield, Ramey, and Shaw." To some disaffected laboratories, eliminating Shaw appeared to be the surest way of reverting back to the previous, decentralized "good old days." Others in the safety R&D program wanted autonomy and more funds for safety R&D and to be completely apart from RDT. Holifield realized that Ray was sympathetic to arguments of environmentalists, disaffected AEC personnel and others concerned about safety R&D, without even considering the views of adherents of the other side on the matter, including other commissioners. He knew that activists in the contrived safety R&D controversy had thus leveraged their arguments for a rather singular and personal destructive purpose, totally without regard for technical or program considerations or adverse national consequences.[51]

The Watergate tragedy that was bringing down the Nixon administration was also key in blackening the national political horizon for nuclear power development. Taking advantage of the state of disarray in the administration and Congress, Ray in a surprise move soon after her appointment apparently "convinced" the AEC commissioners to reverse their previous decision and support her reorganization of RDT. She then announced to an astonished Holifield and JCAE her "Solomon-like" solution to the friction between Shaw and some of the laboratories: separation of RDT into a Division of Reactor Research and Development (RRD) for reactor R&D and a new organization to conduct LWR safety R&D, with both reporting to the General Manager.

Ray's hasty decision rocked the nuclear community, since it not only defied the JCAE majority, but overturned previous AEC decisions. The separation of safety and reactor R&D also ran counter to the decades-old philosophy and practices of most, if not all, R&D practitioners in the AEC's R&D divisions, including NR, Space Reactors, and Defense and Research, not to mention the similar traditions of the nuclear industry. The decision also seemed to ignore the role of the AEC's independent safety and licensing organization, under the Director of Regulation and later the Nuclear Regulatory Commission (NRC), which reviewed for approval all RDT safety R&D proposals and licensing-equivalent actions required of commercial applicants. If this were not enough, Ray's action, which would lead to decentralization, clashed directly with the spirit of Nixon's reorganization initiatives. Nonplussed, Ray had Hollingsworth request a prompt reply from Shaw to an "offer of the position of Director of the newly created RRD."

Recognizing what lay behind this manipulation and bracing himself for what would follow, Holifield realized the depth to which "the politics of destruction" had begun to dominate most of the AEC. He had been through enough JCAE hearings and "weeping chair" sessions to know that "there was nobody neutral on Shaw" any more than they were on Holifield, Rickover, Ramey, or many other leaders. Shaw had served in the AEC's R&D director job longer than all of his predecessors combined. Holifield knew that Ray's attack on Shaw was also a personal assault on him and Ramey. He wanted to seek Nixon's personal intervention, but Shaw urged that this not be done. Holifield, Hosmer, and Price insisted that Shaw discuss the situation in a special JCAE executive session even though nothing more could be done.[52]

Shaw had difficulty evaluating the strange "offer" from the General Manager, since he could not obtain from him, commissioners, or other key officials any specifics about what was expected in managing RRD. Rather than continue to embarrass these officials by raising reasonable questions in face to face discussions, Shaw prepared a memorandum laying out necessary actions to enable his management of RRD to be effective. Holifield knew that no one in the Ray commission and staff could respond or clarify such a disingenuous offer. Hollingsworth and most commissioners privately extended their regrets to Shaw about "what happened to RDT." Without any other response to his memorandum, Shaw retired on June 30, 1973.[53]

On the same day, most unfortuitously for Holifield, the JCAE, and the AEC, Ramey also retired, as his second five-year term expired. With Ray as chairman, Ramey could not have hoped for reappointment, as Ray later confirmed to her biographer. Other scientific and engineering career professionals soon also began encountering hostility and encouragement to transfer out of RDT or leave the AEC. Such actions substantially reduced the effectiveness of what had once been a highly respected and qualified line management technical organization at AEC headquarters. Incredible as it seemed, even RDT's scientific and engineering intern program was canceled![54]

The Ripple Effect

The effects of Ray's reorganization, together with the encouraged departure of some key leaders, led to many problems, including confusion, low morale, longer delays, and larger cost increases on programs and major facilities targeted for construction, such as the LOFT, FFTF, and CRBR. Safety reviews, licensing, and major, long-lead-time items under procurement, such as CRBR's reactor vessel, head, and other primary system components, were also seriously affected. Approved by the Congress, these components were technically and contractually ready for release for fabrication, but formal approval was not forthcoming from Ray's commission, increasingly in disarray. Thus, CRBR delays and cost overruns became highly visible to Congress, and significantly undercut program momentum as well as political support.

Holifield was appalled by the costly, if not yet fatal, set-backs to breeder projects and momentum being wrought largely by the Ray AEC itself. He had trouble accepting the insensitivity of his associates on Capitol Hill and in the administration to the eradication of RDT. For Holifield, the very existence of the JCAE, the breeder, and the health of nuclear power seemed to be at stake. Yet with Watergate engulfing the administration, no officials were willing to challenge the destructive trends in the AEC and elsewhere.[55]

By 1974, the organizational losses and dislocations in the Ray AEC began to undercut the breeder program beyond delays and cost increases, The AEC responded to its dwindling resources by significantly down-sizing the original R&D program. Operating experience would be gained from a government program of testing components in a new non-nuclear, liquid metal facility.[56]

Remembering such extrapolations of size with LWRs, Holifield sensed that history was repeating itself. Now it was the government, rather than industry, that was ignoring the step-by-step technical successes in favor of attractive political and budgetary considerations. Holifield knew that this approach could not sustain a long-term energy program as important as the breeder. He knew the new plan's promoters were not aware of the costly and sometimes fatal engineering and licensing liabilities incurred with the LWRs and HTGRs in attempting large extrapolations and other high-risk efforts."[57]

From a practical standpoint, there was little Chet could do. He had announced that he would not run for a seventeenth term; Craig Hosmer, Republican JCAE leader, was also retiring. Both were thankful that the JCAE, other energy leaders in Congress, and most experienced utility leaders continued to support the breeder. While many capable and knowledgeable professionals had left, there were still many experienced and dedicated leaders and teams at headquarters, at key sites and laboratories, and among the AEC's and industry's contractors and utility participants. These included, among others, the AEC's Jack Crawford, Ed Kintner, Tom Nemzek, Bob Furgeson, Woody Cunningham, and Loch Caffey, and Westinghouse's John Taylor, George Hardigg, John Yasinsky, and Ersal Evans. Also, due to efforts by Wallace Behnke and James O'Connor (the two chief executives at Commonwealth Edison) and other utility leaders, almost all of the utility executives remained as active members of the BRC and the PMC. Those remaining continued to do their best to reinforce the standards of excellence, while hoping for a more opportune time to restore what had been lost. There was still optimism, because a solid R&D base had been developed and successes had been achieved. Holifield wondered, of course, how much longer the breeder coalitions could sustain momentum in the face of intensified attacks on funding nuclear R&D activities.[58]

Holifield Remains Influential

Even as Holifield watched the loss of his friends, mounting delays, and confusion at the AEC, he was down, but not out. During the last 18 months or so of his career, Holifield remained very much at the forefront of atomic energy--in the area of government reorganization. As chairman of the House Government Operations Committee, he presided over a reorganization of the AEC in a way that his nemesis Ray could only fathom. His work grew out of growing concerns since the mid-1960s about the nation's broader energy security dilemmas and his awareness that commercial nuclear power eventually had to be integrated into the overall U.S. energy supply system. Holifield was also aware that nuclear firms were being merged into larger energy industries, a signpost of newer economic tides. In addition, the environmental movement had come of age, and by the early 1970s was insisting upon separation of the AEC's promotional activities from its regulatory functions to assure appropriate licensing and nuclear plant safety.[59]

The increasingly stormy issue of whether the AEC could properly both promote and regulate was not novel. As early as 1961, Holifield had told the California Bar Association that he had an open mind on the AEC's future and the degree to which difficulties might develop from the AEC providing financial assistance in many forms to the same companies which, under the law, it was required to regulate. The "strain" on AEC's objectivity, he said, "is apparent and the policy question is squarely posed: 'Shall the policeman of an industry also be charged with the responsibility for its promotion and development?'" Holifield knew that there were no easy answers to this question, but already by 1961 he had proposed legislation to establish an Atomic Safety and Licensing Board while giving more thought to " a more definitive separation of promotional and regulatory functions." [60]

Like other JCAE members, Holifield was concerned about nuclear safety, energy security and a clean environment. Unlike many legislators, though, he refused to cave in to unreasonable demands made by some groups from the mid-1960s onward. In his view, the nation required two things to maintain its domestic and industrial systems: an adequate and a growing supply of clean energy and effective governmental policies to support this growing supply. By the late 1960s and early 1970s, Holifield was among the few forecasting an imminent energy crisis. He argued that the nation's growing dependence on imported oil, the diminishing supply of economic domestic oil and gas, and continuing low production of coal would lead to an energy shortage. In 1971 he told the National Rural Electric Cooperative Association:

... Without electrical power industrial and human activities are paralyzed. It is essential to industrial, economic and social progress in our society and in the society of the foreseeable future. . . .

And I am in complete agreement with those who take the position that wasteful uses of electricity should be eliminated. The fact that two-thirds of our electric power is used in industrial and commercial activities involving the basic necessities of our society leads to only one inescapable conclusion--there very clearly will not be much power margin left to tamper with during the next 30 years. . . .

. . . The public has the impression that our power shortages can be cured simply and easily by cutting down the voltage, and if problems increase, all we have to do is reduce the voltage further. This inaccurate portrayal has in fact been used and widely publicized; but the public is not told power shortages cannot be corrected by voltage reductions, that any further voltage reduction may result in damage to electric motors; and the true fact that the next step in voltage reduction is interruption of service and no electricity.[61]

What incensed Holifield about some environmentalists was their thesis that alternative fuels--solar, wind, tidal power, and fusion energy--would soon become energy sources to replace dwindling fossil fuels and nuclear power. He advocated including these sources in planning R&D while cautioning that they would not be ready until well into the twenty-first century or later.[62]

Years before the Arab Oil Embargo in 1973 dramatized the dangers of excessive dependence on foreign oil, Holifield was considering how an AEC reorganization and his predictions of an energy crisis would fit together. He had alerted Congress to a looming energy crisis, but he had not yet fit the

AEC into the puzzle. This was done for him by Nixon's reorganization plan issued in January 1971. Under this plan, four new departments were to replace seven existing agencies. One agency was to be the Department of Natural Resources (DNR), into which the Energy and Minerals Resource Administration, some AEC units, and other agencies were to be placed. Nixon envisioned DNR as the nation's "single energy authority."[63]

Holifield held hearings on Nixon's proposals, keeping the personal bargain he had with Nixon in 1971 on *Air Force One.* Nixon's DNR and other plans did not, however, reach the floor of either house during the Ninety-second Congress. As energy conditions worsened in 1973, the plans were superseded by a plethora of new proposals. Holifield and others folded in plans for reorganizing the AEC. They proposed creation of an independent Energy Research and Development Administration (ERDA) which would absorb all functions of the AEC, except for licensing and regulation. Licensing and regulatory functions would go to a new Nuclear Energy Commission (NEC). When the energy crisis erupted suddenly in October 1973, action on ERDA was accelerated because its mission included R&D on all forms of energy.[64]

Holifield's last major role in his public career was to devise the legislative strategy to reorganize the AEC into ERDA and the NRC. He proposed the NRC in his committee's bill, calling it the NEC until it was renamed. By carefully preparing the structure of ERDA, he also influenced creation of the Department of Energy (DOE), which absorbed ERDA in 1975. James Schlesinger became the first Secretary of Energy.[65]

An End to the Ray AEC

The AEC chairman was left without a post as Holifield entered retirement and his two new creations replaced the AEC. For Holifield, it was hardly a victory. In less than two years, Ray had, in Holifield's opinion, done irreparable damage to the AEC. Ray, by her own admissions, started out her AEC career by relying on destructive political moves rather than constructive technical activities. With similar political guidance from the White House, she never took the time or the risks of learning how to work constructively with technical experts in the AEC and the JCAE, as Seaborg and Schlesinger had done. Nor did she appear to recognize that Holifield had earned his reputation for leadership, vision, and constructive relationships with agencies based on high standards of accomplishment rather than aspirations to control.

While some may disagree, there are those besides Holifield who now realize that Ray's activities in her short tenure have had far-reaching, adverse consequences. It was evident that the Ray AEC attracted few, if any, exceptional, experienced managerial and technical leaders. Those proven professionals she eliminated certainly were not replaced. The losses in leadership, capability, and morale set the stage for a future of continuing and costly degradation of managerial talent, technical activities, and material conditions. Since then and in more recent years, the deterioration in conditions at weapons complexes has come to public attention at various sites, including Hanford in Washington, Savannah River in South Carolina, and Rocky Flats in Colorado. It is important to observe, however, that DOE leaders and congressional committees overseeing DOE also failed to insist that DOE be converted back to a strong, technically oriented agency in order to carry out its important missions. Instead, corrective actions were left to Secretary James Watkins, who took over the stewardship of DOE early in 1989. Unfortunately, Watkins was able to attract only a few qualified personnel and most of these professionals left when he did.[66]

Downward Slide of the Breeder and Energy R&D

The Ray AEC was not immediately fatal to parts of the breeder program. Clinch River managed to stay alive until early 1983, in part due to careful groundwork laid by Holifield and his associates, and the efforts of committed industrial teams and utilities. Holifield and his allies spent over six years getting congressional clearances for the CRBR arrangement finally signed by the AEC and the other principals in late 1973. After this step, it took another year for approval of a "reference design," providing the initial cost estimate of $1.7 billion for the first, firm plant-design concept. This took into account new environmental and licensing requirements which were then being retrofitted on commercial plants, the back-loading of certain large R&D costs to the project, heavy cost escalation caused by schedule and funding delays and other anticipated factors. Before retiring, Holifield and Hosmer worked hard to obtain new authority for a revised cost estimate which permitted continuing the ongoing activities.[67]

Still, the downward slide of support for the breeder and other promising R&D programs continued after Holifield's retirement. The breeder still enjoyed some strong support under President Ford (1974-1976), but necessary strengthening of the program was not forthcoming. Soon, the CRBR became one of the two last, large demonstration projects remaining among the nation's once abundant, advanced nuclear and non-nuclear energy R&D projects. With the advent of the Carter administration in 1976, the nation had elected a president who considered nuclear power as an option of "last resort" and who actively sought, but failed, during his entire presidency to kill the Clinch River project.[68] The CRBR was finally killed by Congress when it declined to appropriate further funding for the project. By this time, the CRBR was the last of a few advanced energy projects managed by DOE. In the debate in the Senate, the anti-nuclear congressional opposition managed to obscure the CRBR's pivotal role as the nation's highest-priority energy R&D program and led uninformed and anti-nuclear members of Congress to believe that it was primarily a commercial venture. President Reagan, who had been a firm supporter of nuclear power as governor of California and as president, declined to use his influence to complete the mission of this decade-old project, the "best hope" and only remaining R&D plant in the government's stable of promising energy options.[69]

An Unfinished Story

Holifield was correct when he publicly doubted toward the end of his career that he would live to see the breeder demonstration plant become a reality.[70]   A generation has passed--over *two decades*--and the U.S. has forgotten about its unfulfilled commitments to future energy security and to demonstrating the breeder. No new baseload energy R&D plant has been developed in the past three decades in the U.S. Even now, Holifield and others would no longer find any national forum, such as the JCAE once was, in which vital national energy security matters are discussed, much less acted on. Holifield suspected when he retired that the Ray AEC and the anti-nuclear and anti-JCAE group in Congress had likely triggered an irrevocable loss of national energy R&D leadership and consensus. He was right when he sensed that it was just a matter of time before many of the laboratories and contractors would fall back into their traditional, decentralized modes of operation and that funding promising R&D activities would become more difficult to sustain. A saddened Holifield knew then that his opposition's victory was a Pyrrhic one; no one had won anything and everyone had lost something important. The real losers were primarily the breeder, nuclear power, and most importantly, the future generations of Americans.

14

A Revolutionary Upheaval on Capitol Hill

Political Ferment and Change

During the last few years of his career, Chet Holifield was confronted with changes in just about every aspect of his work. Many of the changes were due to transformations occurring in American society. Capitol Hill was beset by demands from several of the reform movements spawned in the late 1960s. The civil rights movement, feminists, anti-war protesters, environmental interest groups, and consumer advocates all sought political solutions for what they perceived as society's major ills. Ironically, just as Holifield reached the zenith of his personal power and prestige, he found himself under intense fire from some of these groups. The liberal Holifield now found himself labeled as a conservative, primarily because of his support for nuclear power and the Vietnam War, and his approach toward consumer protection legislation.

Even within the legislative confines of the House, Holifield found neither stability nor refuge. His committee chairmanships were challenged during his last five years in office--not by one, but by two separate congressional reorganization efforts. A reformer in the past, Holifield now found himself a target of reform. His work as a committee chairman came under more intense scrutiny, as junior House members jockeyed for more power. with help from new interest groups. The 1971 Hansen reforms forced him to choose between the chairmanships of the JCAE and Government Operations. Holifield chose the latter as his primary power base, while he remained a ranking member of the JCAE. This enabled him to create the Energy Research and Development Administration (ERDA) and the Nuclear Regulatory Commission (NRC) to replace the AEC, but the loss of his forceful leadership on the JCAE lessened the committee's power and authority. By 1974, Richard Bolling (D-Missouri) sought to eliminate the JCAE in a reorganization move, but was unable to do so as long as Holifield remained in the House. Bolling got his way soon after Holifield's retirement.

In the controversies of his last years, Holifield characteristically fought for realistic and practical solutions. In doing so, he accrued the ire of single-issue interest groups, House rules reformers and legislators unhappy with his particular brand of liberalism. He did not always win, but he usually exacted a price from his opponents that left him with at least a modicum of success. He retired as a senior statesman and master legislator with a record of impressive accomplishments that would be hard to equal in any era.

Holifield's Liberalism and Civil Rights

It is more than a little ironic that Holifield was viewed as a conservative by the 1960s. On domestic issues, his critics would have found a thorough-going liberal if they had cared to investigate. In the early 1960s, Holifield helped lead the fight to force the House Rules Committee to release its hold on liberal reform and civil rights legislation. In the later 1960s, he fervently supported President Johnson's Great Society and helped to shepherd some of the legislation to passage. As a small businessman, he fiercely fought against all attempts at monopoly. He was hardly a darling of big business, believing that economic opportunity must be unfettered and enlarged from time to time to accommodate newcomers to the market place.[1]

Holifield staunchly defended individual and civil rights throughout his career. When he first entered Congress during World War II, he had argued that the nation should treat its Japanese citizens with respect and dignity. He was one of very few congressmen willing to make such views known. He manifested the same tolerance and cultural sensitivity in his Montebello business by learning Spanish to deal equitably with his Hispanic neighbors. Later he helped get established a Cabinet Committee on Opportunities for Spanish-speaking People to focus on this growing population.[2]

On civil rights for African-Americans, Holifield was equally sensitive. Although born in a southern state at a time when African-American fortunes were at their lowest ebb since the Civil War, he learned racial tolerance. The lot of blacks was hard during his childhood. He recalled that "when a Negro came to town, he would go to the back door of a restaurant to buy a hamburger. Also, he couldn't stay overnight in the town. He went out and camped outside the town somewhere along the road." His father believed that Lincoln was right in the War Between the States, emphasizing to young Chet that "no man has a right to enslave another man's body, mind, or soul." Thus, as Holifield explained, "I wasn't a red-hot southerner, by any means."[3]

As much as any liberal, Holifield tried in his dealings with minorities to uphold the egalitarian philosophy of the Constitution. He did, however, draw a practical line at admitting floods of illegal immigrants and providing them with public amenities. Thus, he insisted that Nixon's 1971 reorganization plans strengthen the Border Patrol.[4] Another practical limit involved violence. As one urban center after another was burned between 1965 and 1970, he insisted upon law and order as well as redressing of grievances:

If the Negro protests again with his feet, joining the rioters in the streets, we can understand at least that this is one of the ghetto techniques of survival. Rioting is violent and dangerous, but it is also a desperate effort to communicate--seeking to put an end, for better or worse, to indifference and neglect by the larger community. . . What is the answer to the riot problem? Putting first things first, law and order will be, *must* be, maintained. That is a requisite of any civilized society. . . . Beyond maintaining law and order, beyond improving its law enforcement agencies, America . . . must broaden opportunities in every field of human endeavor.[5]

Holifield and Nuclear Power Safety Issues

Holifield had some of his stormiest controversies with environmentalists, despite his frequent attempts to seek common ground with them. In the last years of his career, the environmental movement displayed its increasing power around the country in organized protests, in reactor licensing hearings, at JCAE meetings, and ultimately, in Congress. Even the National Environmental Policy Act of 1969 (NEPA) failed to mollify the more avid activists. They continued to work for the complete demise of nuclear power.

Even before NEPA, in 1967, Holifield found himself under attack on the issue of uranium mine safety. New research indicated that approximately 1,000 uranium miners would die from lung cancer from inhaling radon gas. In May 1967, the JCAE held hearings on this hazard and the Labor Department's uranium mine safety standards. A few critics declared that they were ready to shut down the nuclear industry completely because they believed the health risks too great. Holifield faced the issue squarely, pointing out that public safety issues are always sensitive by their very nature:

In the 1940s it was finally concluded that radon gas was escaping from exposed rock surfaces, and ultimately the short half-life radon "daughters" were deposited in the miners' lungs. Obviously, improved ventilation to remove the radon, or filtering to remove the daughter products, would be part of the solution. How to provide suitable protection posed many technical problems, some of which are still not resolved. . . . Because we did not have valid technical data in time, much confusion and anguish will be generated before we can develop the instruments, gather the data, and design and develop a solution to this problem.[6]

Holifield was correct; the issue was sensitive. Adverse publicity on radon "daughters" led one hostile political foe to suggest that radon gas poisoning should be measured in units called "Holifields." Columnists also chastised him as a one-time liberal who had turned his back on mine workers.[7]

After 1967, instead of narrowly focused criticisms, the JCAE endured environmentalist attacks on broader issues connected with nuclear plants. A recurring complaint was that the plants produced intolerable amounts of radioactivity, especially for persons living near the plants. Holifield used basic and irrefutable scientific findings to set the record straight:

The levels of allowable radioactivity in the operation of a nuclear reactor for the production of electric power is five milliroentgens, five one-thousandths of a roentgen a year to each person in the population. Yet you get six one-thousandths of a roentgen going from California to Washington and back in an airplane. Those are the levels that we're talking about: the same levels that the scare-mongers--the Naders, the Concerned Scientists, the Friends of the Earth, and the Sierra Club--are referring to.

A person gets a roentgen when he or she has a fluoroscopic chest examination. When you have your jaw teeth x-rayed you may get perhaps a hundred or more milliroentgens in one sitting. That's as much radioactivity as you'd get in twenty years if you sat on the fence outside of a nuclear plant 365 days a year, twenty-four hours a day.[8]

The most vigorous arguments against nuclear power had to do with nuclear plant accidents. Holifield respected these views, but he also urged that the possibility of deaths from radiation and plant accidents be put into perspective with the negative results of other man-made inventions. He often cited facts about people injured and killed each year from accidents involving electricity, automobiles, aircraft, swimming pools, and other developments.[9] He felt that critics were too ready to allege that nuclear energy was too dangerous at any cost. He especially frowned on the use of scare tactics:

Can the U.S.-designed commercial light water nuclear power plants explode like an atom bomb? No. It is impossible for these nuclear power plants to explode like a nuclear weapon. The laws of physics do not permit this, because the fuel in these U.S. plants contains only a small fraction of the fissionable material needed for weapons.[10]

When public attention focused on nuclear fuel "meltdown," Holifield also addressed this issue openly. He noted that "meltdowns" had occurred in small experiments and in a few test and power reactors, but that no member of the public was ever killed or even hurt by the resulting radiation releases. He stressed that the major environmental problem was not the "meltdown" itself, but the possible hazards of the resultant fission releases. After all, he pointed out that some early experimental reactors used liquid and even molten fuel! He emphasized that major costly test facilities, like LOFT, were built to study the processes and consequences of meltdown and plant protection systems had been developed to avoid both the causes and results of fuel meltdown.[11]

Holifield believed that more full-scale proof of the basic safety of U.S. LWR power plants occurred ironically in the full-scale meltdown of Three Mile Island Unit No. 2 (TMI-II) in 1979. No planned test program could have validated as well the extremely low probability of escape of fission products into the environment from severe meltdown in a large U.S. LWR. Although the TMI-II incident was scrutinized by the media and scientific experts for its negative effects, the event (and many lesser plant incidents) also confirmed that U.S. power reactors, with their multiple safety systems, were safe and worthy of strong public confidence when properly managed.[12]

As Holifield's career moved toward its conclusion, the battle lines between the JCAE and AEC and the environmental movement hardened. For some activists, the struggle became almost a religious movement, as they sought to overcome the "Nuclear Power Establishment" by any means. The JCAE, along with the AEC and industry, was accused of making a "calculated effort . . . to minimize and conceal the risks inherent in nuclear power." Holifield and Hosmer were assailed personally by spokesmen like Ralph Nader, who alleged that they had "condemned, bullied or ridiculed citizens" who were trying to "point out the risks and hazards."[13] Holifield and the JCAE did find it hard to maintain objectivity, since they viewed some JCAE critics as fanatics speaking only for themselves. Both Holifield and Hosmer dismissed many critics as naive when they failed to understand scientific findings. They felt that some anti-nuclear forces were actually arrayed not only against them, but against most technological aspects of modern society.[14]

Although the JCAE allowed many citizens to testify, it was not easy prey for unprepared critics. For example, David Comey, head of a Cayuga Lake environmental coalition, received harsh criticism when he testified in 1970 JCAE hearings that discharge of waste water into a lake made the water dangerous. His major point was that over a 6-year period, sufficient amounts of cesium-137 would be discharged into the lake so that a person consuming about three pounds of lake trout would receive the total permissible tolerance level. Hosmer disputed Comey's calculation, demonstrating that a person would have to eat *30,000 pounds* of trout to reach the tolerance level![15]

By the late 1960s, some independent, qualified observers like physicist-writer Ralph Lapp attempted to "separate the wheat from the chaff" in assessing the JCAE apart from the environmentalist view. Lapp credited the JCAE with solid foundations on which it made judgments. He acknowledged the widely-accepted competence and long years of service of Holifield and other leading House members. Lapp also praised the JCAE's technical staff as an excellent model for handling science and technology issues. In his view, critics tended to overlook the JCAE's long-standing concerns for the Atomic Energy Act's "due regard of the health and safety of the public." Not all JCAE critics shared Lapp's view, of course, including some nationally-known scientists previously linked to the AEC's laboratories. But Lapp and many others felt that JCAE criticisms had to be weighed against accomplishments.[16]

Holifield, Consumer Rights, and Civil Liberties

Holifield was something of a forerunner of the consumer advocates of the 1960s. His very first bill was on consumer protection and he had introduced over 165 such bills by the 1960s, mostly on public health and safety.[17] Despite this record, he was at loggerheads with consumer activist Ralph Nader after 1969. Nader's allies included Benjamin S. Rosenthal (D-New York), a subcommittee chairman of Chet's Government Operations Committee. Holifield had problems with Rosenthal, and felt that Rosenthal was often unwilling to admit when he was wrong. He remembered that Rosenthal, for example, once placed a statement in the *Congressional Record* that nuclear power plants were unique in that they heated up their condenser cooling water. When informed that all thermal power plants warmed up the water, both he and his staff continued to insist that only nuclear plants did so.[18]

At the heart of Holifield's dispute with Nader and Rosenthal was their vehement disagreement over consumer legislation introduced by Rosenthal. In 1969, Rosenthal cosponsored a bill to establish a cabinet-level Department of Consumer Affairs to unify the scattered consumer-related functions in the executive branch. When he could not obtain enough support, he advanced instead an independent consumer agency with the power of subpoena. His new proposal would not have consolidated all consumer-related programs.[19]

As the acting chairman of Government Operations, Holifield opposed Rosenthal's proposal on several counts, but most firmly on granting subpoena power. Having been in Congress much longer than his colleague, Holifield had seen the havoc that had been wreaked unfairly in people's lives through the use of subpoenas. As a devoted civilian libertarian, he was unwilling to countenance any broad subpoena power for an independent agency.[20]

Although Chet thought the bill "essentially had been drafted by Ralph Nader," he went before the Rules Committee in 1970 for a rule. He was publicly embarrassed there because Rosenthal apparently had not done his homework and a rule was refused.[21] As a legislator seldom criticized on completed bills, Holifield was not about to be embarrassed again. His notes from the Rules Committee hearing indicated that "there were 16 different objections to the bill, or demands for clarification." In the following year he held hearings on it, and came up with a bill that met every one of the objections." He did not always include Rosenthal, because he believed Rosenthal was leaking information to the consumer lobby.[22]

"When my bill prevailed in the committee," Holifield remembered, "I took it back to the Rules Committee and asked for a rule . . ." He made sure that the Rules Committee was clear on the bill and was behind him this time. Not wanting to appear arbitrary, Holifield asked for and was granted an open rule on the bill, which would provide others with an opportunity to offer amendments. The bill was then sent to the House floor, where allies of Nader and others predictably insisted on amending it to include the subpoena power. A floor fight ensued and the amendment was finally defeated, 218-164. Holifield's bill passed 344-44 and was sent to the Senate which killed the bill.[23]

In view of the problems they had given him, Holifield was unforgiving upon the bill's demise. He issued a public statement, declaring that the bill had been killed by Rosenthal and Nader. In turn, the Naderites picketed Holifield's California office, Ralph Nader attacked him verbally, and Rosenthal called a protest meeting.[24]

Intracommittee wrangling at one point led Holifield to reorganize the Government Operations Committee, removing consumer affairs from the jurisdiction of Rosenthal's subcommittee. Despite Nader's request that he reconsider his decision, he refused, making it clear that he, and not Nader or Rosenthal, was in charge of Government Operations. Holifield told newsmen: "Ralph Nader is not going to run the House Government Operations Committee. Let him run his own damned affairs."[25]

When Congress reconvened in January 1973, Rosenthal decided to move his feud with Holifield to another forum--the Democratic Caucus--in an attempt to use the 1971 Hansen reforms to unseat Holifield. Making his best case, Rosenthal charged that Holifield had performed poorly, as evidenced by a decline in formal investigative reports issued by the committee.[26]

Rosenthal had again apparently not done his homework. He failed to note the committee's legislative as well as investigative work. In 1972, in fact, the committee had considered numerous bills. Ten, Holifield would note in his rebuttal, had been enacted in the Ninety-second Congress. Others were reported out or had been acted on by the House, but not by the Senate. Rosenthal's charges plainly wilted before the facts marshalled by Holifield.[27] Insiders knew the source of Rosenthal's irritation, and most were unwilling to allow single issues to decide a chairman's fate.[28]

Although a secret ballot was used, Rosenthal's effort was very unsuccessful. Holifield garnered nearly 80 percent of the votes. The *New York Times* noted he gained a standing ovation from the caucus.[29]

Before Holifield retired, a Consumer Protection Agency was created. While he did not rush the legislation, Holifield scheduled new hearings after Rosenthal dropped his insistence on subpoena power. Success was also partly attributable to Holifield's work with the Nixon administration. When Nixon sought Holifield's help on his reorganization bills, Holifield agreed to hold hearings, provided that Nixon would also back Holifield's new consumer protection bill. Nixon's consumer affairs adviser, Virginia Knauer, publicly agreed, thus opening the way for congressional passage and administration acceptance of the new U.S. Consumer Protection Agency.[30]

Stirrings of Congressional Unrest and The "Hansen Reforms"

Holifield could take the heat associated with controversies, since he did not worry excessively about being viewed as liberal or conservative. He also was unafraid of the political fire of his opponents if he believed he was right--

that is, provided the shootings were purely metaphorical. He had one genuine scare from a real shooting in 1950, when Puerto Rican terrorists opened fire in the House chamber. He had just spoken on a bill to bar undocumented aliens from crossing the Mexican border and taking American jobs. Sitting down at his table, he heard a popping noise that sounded like firecrackers. Glancing up, he saw one figure in the gallery with a Luger which spouted flame. "Actually," he remembered, "there were three people up in the gallery, two men and a woman, waving a flag and shouting, 'Viva Libertad Puerto Rico.'" He "hit the deck," explaining that "I was on the aisle seat and went right to the floor." Later, he "found a split in the carpet where a bullet hit." He helped put a tourniquet on an Alabama member whose leg artery was spurting blood. Another member from Michigan was shot in the chest. It was the roughest day he would see as a legislator.[31]

Just as Holifield became formal chairman of Government Operations and reached the peak of his career, two major House reorganization efforts from 1970 to 1974 challenged the committee structure and seniority system. Many members believed reform necessary to respond more effectively to issues such as the technology explosion and the prolonged war in Asia. Junior members were also impatient for their place in the sun; they wanted the committee structure "streamlined." This meant assuring that members did not serve on too many committees, reducing jurisdictional overlapping, and most important, adding more leadership posts. The reforms were much more radical than in 1946; they would lead to abolition of seniority as the basis of committee leadership and creation of a multiplicity of subcommittees.

Holifield, like his legislative peers with extensive experience and vested interests, did not favor the reforms. He had come to appreciate the importance of committees and the seniority system as a school for channelling experience and wisdom into legislation. For him, the inner workings of committees could be learned only through experience. He argued that "there's no perfect way to do it, but through the principle of seniority, which is pretty well grounded in merit." He noted that "seniority obtains in every line of work, whether it's teaching, union membership, or the professions."[32]

The first reforms Holifield faced were the 1971 Hansen reforms, named after Julia Butler Hansen (D-Washington), who headed the Committee on Organization, Study, and Review created to recommend reforms. The most important of the changes reducing committee chairmen's powers was that the Democratic Committee on Committees could nominate chairmen without any adherence to seniority, thus allowing the caucus to reject a nomination. Other reforms reduced chairmen's control over staff and limited members to only one committee or subcommittee chairmanship.[33]

These reforms obliged Holifield to choose between chairing the JCAE and Government Operations. He chose Government Operations since it was continuous, while the JCAE chairmanship rotated between the House and the

Senate in alternate congresses. It also had the important power of subpoena, just like the JCAE. He felt he could be more effective in Government Operations, where Nixon's proposals for energy program reorganization would be directed. Finally, he felt that the time had come for his close associate Mel Price to assume JCAE leadership, in view of his long service there.[34]

A New Reform Tide: Bolling's Reforms

In 1974, Holifield faced a more far-reaching reform movement spearheaded by Richard Bolling, chairman of the House Select Committee on Committees. Bolling's committee advanced a number of ambitious, novel, and even revolutionary proposals to reorganize committees. The reforms provoked heated resistance from Holifield and many other legislators.[35]

Holifield found much to dislike about the reforms even though he would not be around for them in 1975. Like others, he felt that Bolling, who had been close to Speaker Rayburn, was manipulating reform as a stepping stone to the speakership. "Reform is often the cloak of ambitious men," he noted, "and I disliked seeing those 1974 reforms go through simply because of Dick Bolling's ambitions to be Speaker." As he recalled, "Before that time, he had wanted my support in his original attempt to become Speaker instead of Carl Albert." Holifield had declined and still felt the same way, explaining that "Although I was retiring from Congress, I still felt Bolling's accession to this post would be destructive of the Democratic party." Part of his hesitance involved Bolling's attempted concessions to the Republicans, such as including them in the reform process and his support for minority party committee staffing.[36] Holifield would have preferred Hansen's committee to Bolling's.[37]

Despite Holifield's preference, Bolling took charge of reorganization. At its May-June 1973 hearings, his committee heard some problems, but also some compliments about committee leadership. Frank Horton (R-New York), the ranking Republican on Government Operations, praised Holifield's objectivity and capabilities.[38]

Holifield believed that many of Bolling's recommendations were based on pure politics. In his own testimony before Bolling's committee, however, he emphasized the positive, especially the need for an energy committee, perhaps fearing that Bolling might be doing away with the JCAE. His testimony was based heavily on data and charts supplied by energy consultant Jack Bridges. Concentrating on a primary subject of his career, the nation's energy security, he reviewed the situation between 1960 and the year 2000, providing an in-depth assessment of the prospects for fuel options, conservation, and alternative energy sources. He said that he had written to President Nixon in 1971 about the impending crisis in energy. Noting that he had given this briefing to some 130 legislators and planned more, Holifield declared that "it is inevitable" that Congress should "create a committee on energy."[39]

A few months later, Holifield addressed the full House about the negative aspects of the Bolling reforms while wondering aloud whether the challenge was one of "Committee Reform or Committee Confusion." He charged that the proposals would lead to a swollen legislative bureaucracy, and insisted that "the greater the staff of that bureaucracy, the less independent the member." Holifield was also unhappy with the so-called "single-track" system intended to guarantee members that they would eventually chair a committee. He also opposed the recommendation that each committee should set up an oversight subcommittee, since the LaFollette-Monroney reforms had already urged this. He did not like the idea that Government Operations be in the impossible position of overseeing all committees and thus into direct confrontation with every chairman![40] As before, he objected to Bolling's proposal on separate committee staffing.[41]

Another, somewhat disguised, feature of the proposed reforms concerned Holifield. He was suspicious that Bolling's real motive was to transfer the energy function to some of his friends.[42] Aside from the practicality and advisability of some of Bolling's reforms, Holifield was also concerned about the proposed strengthening of the Rules Committee by giving it the right of refusing a rule on a bill and also the right of referral. Its members could select committees to which to send bills while knowing if they were *for* or *against* the measure. This ploy would have given Rules great power. Having fought hard during 1958-1963 to reform Rules, Holifield did not relish the thought of giving such powers to this committee.[43]

Holifield eventually became embroiled in a head-to-head debate with Bolling over the reforms. In October 1974, they engaged in a sharp exchange of correspondence about the possible results. Bolling finally let Holifield and Hosmer know that he intended to abolish the JCAE. Holifield was not surprised; he surmised that Bolling believed that if he was able to divide the JCAE into several committees, he would then have some heavy political debts to call in for his bid for Speaker. Bolling was astute enough to recognize that the JCAE was safe as long as Holifield and Hosmer were in Congress.[44]

Holifield argued forcefully that the Bolling committee had no jurisdiction over joint committees, because they were the "joint creations of the House and the Senate, usually by law."[45] But his argument that the Bolling reforms would specifically undermine the JCAE fell on a growing number of deaf ears. The JCAE's prestige had reached its zenith during the 1950s and in the Holifield and Pastore chairmanships of the 1960s. By then, as much as 80 percent of the work was done by House members; senators simply had too many committee assignments and were focused (with the exception of Senator Pastore) on space and other issues. The loss of Chet Holifield as JCAE chairman under the Hansen reforms also figured in the JCAE's downward trend. Although he continued as a ranking member to faithfully attend meetings, Holifield had to focus much of his attention on Government

Operations when he became its chairman in 1970. After 1970 the JCAE seemed to lose more of its influence when the issue of non-proliferation burst onto the legislative scene. Outside members, such as Congressman Jonathan Bingham (D-New York) and Senator Abraham Ribicoff (D-Connecticut) took the lead in grappling with this emerging issue.[46] This probably would not have occurred under Chet's leadership. But, it was clear that the air was slowly going out of the committee's once impressive bubble of legislative prestige.

When Hosmer and Holifield retired at the end of 1974, the JCAE came to a precipitous end in the House. In January 1975, Bolling was able to stifle the JCAE by refusing to appoint members to the body and by spreading its jurisdiction to other committees through changes in House rules. The Senate's appointed members continued their participation. A statute passed by both houses of Congress in 1977 was necessary to formally abolish the JCAE, since federal law had brought it into existence. Such was the long and labored end to what had been in Holifield's time and under his leadership one of the most powerful and productive committees on Capitol Hill.[47]

Holifield Leaves Congress

Holifield would have preferred to leave Congress under more auspicious circumstances, since his retirement marked the end of an era in atomic energy affairs. The JCAE's demise in January 1975 through Bolling's designs coincided with the dissolution of the AEC into ERDA and the NRC. Without Holifield, atomic energy lost the central focus and cohesion that it had known since 1945. It became almost imperceptible as a field of endeavor among the many congressional committees that soon divided its activities among them. This reorganization, first in the House and then in the Senate, would have widespread ramifications for the nation's nuclear option.

Politics aside, Holifield's personal standing in the House by the end of 1974 was never higher. Colleagues on both sides of the aisle celebrated his long and varied career on December 20, 1974 in more than an hour of tributes on the House floor. Congressmen Horton and John Moss were the managers of the proceedings, with Horton pointing to the hallmarks of Holifield's career. Horton declared early in his remarks that "One title Chet has earned is that of 'Mr. Atomic Energy,'" and that his dedication had "made him one of the experts and prophets in the field of energy." Horton also pointed to his service in Government Operations and his varied and significant contributions. Other members took up the list from there, noting their personal losses at his retirement and referring to Holifield as "a Congressman's Congressman," "a skilled legislator and an outstanding leader," and an exemplary member of the House Committee on Standards of Official Conduct. Still others called Holifield "a giant of the Congress," "a great American," and "one of the [House's] brightest lights of this generation."

Benjamin Rosenthal, with whom Holifield had often clashed, joined the tribute, characterizing him as "one of this Nation's most influential public servants," and indicating that he would remember Holifield as "a 'doer,' an 'innovator,' and a 'builder.'" Future House Speaker Tip O'Neill called him "a real master in the areas of organization, atomic power, and Government procurement." Chet's career-long associate, Mel Price, noted that "It will not be easy for me to get accustomed to work in committee without Chet at my side." The Speaker of the House, the Honorable Carl Albert, was retiring, too, and was appropriately the last speaker. In his final tribute he noted that "the House of Representatives and the Nation will miss Chet Holifield," but Albert probably did not fully appreciate his prescience when he continued, "He has established a record that will go down in history."[48] Holifield had established a rich and varied record in his 32 years in the House. He was a man of energy and energy security, of atomic energy, of government operations and organization, one of a dozen or so master legislators with the opportunity and will to powerfully impact many aspects of American government and society. He would indeed be missed.

Epilogue

Until early in his 92nd year when he died, Holifield often reflected on his 32 years of achievements and influence in Congress. He readily acknowledged the inspiration and support of others, including his wife "Cam" and their daughters, and also the large number of mentors, associates, and talented professionals who increasingly looked to him for leadership. His growing influence and achievements did not come easily; he earned his leadership role through years of plain hard work, growth as a master legislator, and intense dedication to the public interest. The result was that he became one of a few Representatives of his era to achieve enduring national stature, especially in his work in atomic energy and government reorganization. His leadership style, effectiveness, and remarkable accomplishments are his everlasting legacy.

Even before he retired, it was clear even to Holifield that the Congress in which he had exercised significant leadership had begun to lose its focus and effectiveness. In this era of bloated Federal agencies, one looks in vain for the "Holifields" who have the wisdom, the authority, and the will to initiate effective action or to induce federal agencies to acquire and retain qualified leadership with the technical and management capabilities to meet vital national commitments. The principal interests of today's Congress seem aimed more toward short-term, political activities and raising funds for re-election, rather than setting and achieving national goals. The short-term focus and possibilities for "gridlock" in Congress seem further heightened by the effects of continuing "congressional reforms" and other changes that have minimized the influence of individual congressmen. Partly as a consequence, the nation has increased, or at least allowed by default, reliance on potentially dangerous policies, such as increased dependence upon imported oil, and has failed to deal effectively with interest groups that have destroyed institutions such as the JCAE without providing realistic policy and program alternatives.

Continuing to follow atomic energy matters closely in his retirement as he had while in Congress, Holifield believed that nuclear power is a prominent example of the way the current American political system has mismanaged science and technology. Many of the major, disciplined measures he sought-- had they been fully implemented by the nuclear industry--might well have prevented the costly accident in 1979 at Three Mile Island. For him, the most important lesson of TMI was embodied in the conclusion of Dr. John G. Kemeny, who headed the commission which investigated the accident. It was "for our nation to recognize that the present system does not work" and "the only way to save American Democracy is to change the fundamental decision making process, at the federal level, so that it can come to grips with the enormous and complex issues that face this nation." Also, Kemeny noted that ". . . even when the hard evidence is overwhelming, if the issue is sufficiently emotional you can always get an expert to dispute it and thereby help throw all of science into national dispute." Holifield was concerned that this generation and those to follow may be denied the full benefit of technological advancements due to the government's failure to address this central problem.

Almost two decades later, Kemeny's warnings have gone largely unheeded in their larger dimensions despite overwhelming evidence of the need to address them. Shocked by TMI, at least the nuclear industry, utilities and contractors regrouped and attempted to solve most problems. They established new, strong technologically oriented organizations, including the Nuclear Power Oversight Committee and Institute of Nuclear Power Operations. They also systematically assessed the "root-causes" of nuclear power's problems and proceeded to use the new organizations to put remedial measures in place, starting with the most serious managerial and operational deficiencies in the commercial plants. These actions, consistent with the views and recommendations advanced earlier by Holifield and others, have led to significantly improved performance in many plants. While some utilities lagged in responding, Holifield was proud of the significant improvements and maturation in the nuclear industry as a whole, a success demonstrated by the fact that in 1993 twenty of the twenty five current top plants in the world in terms of performance were U.S. plants! But, while billions are being spent, the federal government and industry have done little to address other relevant, important problems directly, resulting in much wasted effort. For example, Holifield recently expressed regrets that DOE has become so weakened in technical leadership and qualified management that it is no longer able to exercise the roles that its predecessor, the AEC, did during his career. It has become especially low, in his estimation, in those technical management capabilities he and others worked so hard to urge the AEC to establish.

Holifield's criticisms should be taken as they were always intended--as constructive rather than destructive. To the end, he remained optimistic for the future. He had too large a belief in the American people, too extensive a knowledge of its history, and too profound a faith in its fundamental system of government and its resiliency not to believe that current difficulties can be overcome. Chet felt a sense of justifiable pride that he had remained the master of the situation while he was in Congress and was able to retire with that large sense of satisfaction which Robert E. Lee once described as "consciousness of duty, faithfully performed." Men of vision and statesmanship like Holifield have always arisen in times of national difficulty and peril to summon the American nation to rise to the challenges confronting them. They will yet do so again, taking confidence from the example which he and others like him have so courageously and selflessly provided.

Carl Albert
Federal Building
Third and Carl Albert Parkway
McAlester, Oklahoma 74501

Afterword

The daily life of a congressman is often unknown territory, even to his closest friends and associates, let alone to the citizens he represents. Much of the business of Congress takes place in committees and subcommittees, all of which have both open and closed hearings. Then there are long debates on the floor of the House of Representatives before a bill finally becomes a law. Years may elapse before a fine idea becomes a statute.

In the course of a legislative year, a representative must become familiar with an almost incredible range of legislation.   Thousands of bills are introduced each year--so many, in fact, that it is impossible for any one legislator to become familiar with many of them, their purposes, and contents. The Congress, fortunately, has developed its own winnowing process whereby many of these bills are properly considered but do not become law.

To help it conduct its business in an orderly manner Congress has developed its own legislative system and rules of procedure. Those legislators who rise to the top must invariably learn how to make this system and its procedures work smoothly. Not every person who goes to Congress possesses either the talent or the energy to devote to this formidable task. But those who succeed at this task-- their numbers are few--must often labor in obscurity as their work is rarely known to the public.

Yet such legislators are among the genuine heroes of our democracy. Aside from the constituents they represent, few citizens may even know their names. They labor in the legislative trenches, so to speak, where the only reward they enjoy is knowing that thousands and millions of citizens will benefit from their handiwork.

Chet Holifield's name will long be listed among such legislative giants. Not only did he chair one of the extraordinary and most powerful committees in the history of our republic, the Joint Committee on Atomic Energy, but through his service on the House Government Operations Committee, which seeks to improve efficiency and economy in the entire Federal government, he showed that an ordinary citizen, once elected to Congress, can help assure that our institutions serve the public good rather than their own fortunes.

The Joint Committee on Atomic Energy was a committee whose work was filled with public drama, high prestige, and extremely serious work. Senators and Congressmen fought hard to serve on that Committee. Legislators often approached me and asked my help in getting on the JCAE. That Chet Holifield would become the principal leader on the Joint Committee for both Houses of Congress attests to the remarkable initiative and sense of public duty that were the hallmarks of his career. Chet Holifield's name should be stamped in capital letters on every atomic energy program of the nation. In the legislative area, he, more than any other, has been Mr. Atomic Energy.

On the other hand, work on the House Government Operations Committee was less prized. The results of its work were not always visible and its daily operations had to be carried on in an objective and, at times, grindingly slow manner. In consequence, it was rarely the first choice of Congressmen. Yet Chet Holifield saw the importance and value of this committee for the effective workings of our democratic system. Year in and year out, he became the corner-stone for much of its work. That fact alone testifies to the integrity and love of country that shone through everything to which Chet set his legislative hand.

On the basis of his work on Government Operations and his leadership on the Joint Committee on Atomic Energy, Chairman Holifield gained the unwavering respect of his legislative peers. Even those who were opposed to his views found that he did his homework thoroughly and put the public interest before all private interests. This often led him into heavy political thickets and legislative battles. But his fair-minded spirit and respect for the rules of the House gained him friends on all sides of the political aisles.

If the United States is today a better and more just community than when Chet Holifield first went to Congress--and I firmly believe it is--then he is among the visionary few who have helped to bring us this far. In Gladstone's famous words, the American Constitution is the finest instrument ever struck off by the mind of man at one time. But for the Constitution to prosper in our day as it did two centuries ago, we need men and women ever vigilant in support of its principles. Chet Holifield was precisely such a legislator. During all my years in the leadership of the House, he was my wise counselor. Equally important to Mary and me is the fact that he and Cam will always be numbered among the finest, dearest friends we have ever had.

Carl Albert

Carl Albert, Retired Speaker
U.S. House of Representatives

Notes

Introduction To Endnotes: These notes have been drastically limited due to space considerations, and are not intended to be a comprehensive listing of sources. The principal manuscript collections used were the National Archives and the Library of Congress in Washington (for the JCAE and other papers) and the Holifield Papers in the Regional Cultural History Collection of the Department of Special Collections in the Edward L. Doheny, Jr. Memorial Library at the University of Southern California (USC). Enid Douglass' three volumes of typed 1975 interviews were available exclusively in the Special Collections Room of the Honnold-Mudd Library at the Claremont Colleges in Claremont, California. Other collections in the USC libraries, the University Research Library at the University of California, Los Angeles (UCLA), the Robert A. Millikan Library at the California Institute of Technology, and Holifield's own extensive home library in Balboa, California also yielded important information. Much material used by Gannon (1983-1988) and Dyke (1990-1995) included both formal/informal and verbal/written--and often undated--recollections of Holifield and close associates who comprise the Holifield Book Associates. For brevity, the following abbreviations are used:

CH	Chet Holifield	**HP**	Holifield Papers
CH-HBA	Chet Holifield and the Holifield Book Associates	**JTR**	James T. Ramey
FXG	Francis X. Gannon	**MS**	Milton Shaw
HBA	Holifield Book Associates [See Acknowledgments]	**RWD**	Richard W. Dyke

Terms with a slash such as CH/FXG; CH/RWD; CH, MS, and Jack Crawford/FXG; CH/Douglass; and MS/RWD indicate interviews, and/or less formal contributions of the person(s) to the left of slash mark conducted by or with the person to the right of the mark, followed by any other specific data known/available, such as date, or volume and page (e.g., CH/Douglass; see n. 3 below). "CH/FXG, CH-HBA input to RWD" formats are often used, denoting further input to RWD to clarify ideas/facts.

Chapter 1: The Meaning of Bikini

1. CH/FXG; CH/RWD, 20 Feb. 1984.

2. For samples of CH's warnings about fossil fuels, see JCAE, *Environmental Effects of Producing Electric Power--Part 1*, hearings, 28 Oct. - 7 Nov. 1969, 91st Cong., 1st sess. (Washington, D.C.: GPO, 1969); *Environmental Effects of Producing Electric Power--Part 2 (Vols. I and II)*, hearings, 27 Jan. - 26 Feb. 1970, 91st Cong., 2nd sess. (Washington, D.C.: GPO, 1970); and JCAE Report, *Nuclear Power and Related Energy Problems--1968 through 1970*, (Washington, D.C.: GPO, December 1971).

3. CH/FXG; CH/RWD, 20 Feb. 1984. CH also discusses the LMFBR in CH/Douglass, i.e., *Chet Holifield, United States Congressman*, typed transcripts of interviews by Enid H. Douglass, Oral History Program, Claremont Graduate School, Claremont, California, 1975, vol. 3, 55-56.

4. CH/FXG. CH also provided written, often undated notes to FXG, RWD, and MS.

5. CH/FXG, with subsequent CH-HBA input to RWD.

6. Ibid.

7. Ibid. CH provided almost identical details in CH/Douglass, vol. 2, 145-154.

8. A copy of Nixon's June 1971 message is in Box 26 (Presidential Energy Message June 4, 1971), HP. The phrase in parentheses following the box number denotes the file name within the box.

9. JCAE, *AEC Authorizing Legislation, FY 1972--Part 2*, hearing, 4 Mar. 1971, 92nd Cong., 1st sess. (Washington, D.C.: GPO, 1971), 509.

10. CH/FXG, with subsequent CH-HBA input to RWD.

11. Michael McGinn/FXG, 20 Sept. 1984.

12. Committee on Military Affairs, *Atomic Energy Act of 1945*, 79th Cong., 1st sess., 5 Nov. 1945, H. Rept. 1186, 16-18.

13. CH, "Atomic Bomb Tests: Bikini, July 1st and 25th, 1946; also 'Conditions in the Far East,' as observed by Chet Holifield, Congressman, 19th District, California," pamphlet, [1947], Box 41 (Bikini Atom Tests), HP; Warren Unna, "Atomic Energy," unpublished typescript CH gave to RWD. [dated 1 May 1974], 6. Former *Washington Post* reporter Unna completed a 9-chapter draft autobiography.

14. See Dyke, *Mr. Atomic Energy*, 309 n.1; and Harold P. Green and Alan Rosenthal, *Government of the Atom: The Integration of Powers* (New York: Atherton Press, 1963), 127.

15. CH/FXG.

16. Claremont McKenna College, *A Report of the California Congressional Program, 1990*.

17. Unna, "Legislating," unpublished typescript [1 May 1974].

18. Dwight Ink/FXG, 15 Sept. 1985. In 1985, Ink was Acting Director of the GSA.

19. Memorandum, Edward J. Bauser to MS, 23 Sept. 1991, and MS discussions with RWD.

20. Notes, Adam Klein to Betty H. Feldmann, 25 Oct. 1991, and MS discussions with RWD.

21. Ibid.

22. Ibid.

23. H. Res. 593, 79th Cong., 2nd sess., 13 Apr. 1946, Box 51 (H. Res. 593), HP.

24. Dwight Ink/FXG, 15 Sept. 1985.

25. Committee on Military Affairs, *Atomic Energy Act of 1945*, 5 Nov. 1945, H. Rept. 1186, 17.

26. CH/FXG.

27. Quotations are taken from CH, "Atomic Bomb Tests: Bikini."

28. CH, "Atomic Bomb Tests: Bikini"; CH/FXG, CH-HBA input to RWD.

29. CH/FXG, CH-HBA input to RWD.

30. Nixon's letters to CH (11 May 1972 and 24 Jan. 1973) are in Box 62 (White House, 1972) and Box 63 (President Richard Nixon 1971-1974), HP.

31. See Chapter VII of Richard G. Hewlett and Francis Duncan, *Nuclear Navy, 1946-1962* (Chicago: The University of Chicago Press, 1974). On safety record, see U.S. DOE and U.S. DOD, *A Review of the United States Naval Nuclear Propulsion Program*, June 1991.

32. CH/FXG.

33. Green and Rosenthal note, for example, that CH nearly doubled the FY 1959 AEC authorization, from $193,379,000 to $386,679,000. (*Government of the Atom*, 189-190.)

34. MS/RWD, 29 March 1990; Dyke, *Mr. Atomic Energy*, 265-66.)

35. Dyke, *Mr. Atomic Energy*, 365 n. 2, cites sources calling CH part of the "Atomic Establishment."

36. CH/FXG, CH-HBA input to RWD.

Chapter 2: Mr. Atom Goes Critical

1. Richard G. Hewlett and Oscar E. Anderson, *The New World, 1939/1946*, vol. 1 of *A History of the United States Atomic Energy Commission* (University Park, Pennsylvania: Pennsylvania State University Press, 1962), 7-11; Frank G. Dawson, *Nuclear Power: Development and Management of a Technology* (Seattle: University of Washington Press, 1976), 12-14.

2. See Hewlett and Anderson, *The New World*, 408-427.

3. See Committee on Military Affairs, *Atomic Energy: Hearings on H.R. 4280*, 9 Oct. 1945 and 18 Oct. 1945, 79th Cong., 1st sess. (Washington, D.C.: GPO, 1945).

4. Unna, "Atomic Energy," 1-2.

5. Committee on Military Affairs, *Atomic Energy: Hearings on H.R. 4280*.

6. CH/RWD, 7 Mar. 1981; CH/FXG; Warren Unna, "Holifield of California," *Atlantic Monthly* 205 (April 1960), 80; Paul Houston, "Holifield: A 32-Year Flashback on His Congress Career," *Los Angeles Times*, 21 Feb. 1974, Part II, 1. There was also a copy found loose (no file) in Box 1, HP.

7. Hewlett and Anderson, *The New World*, 433, 436, 482.

8. *Atomic Energy: Hearings on H.R. 4280*, 49, 76-77, 109-111, 119, 121, 129-29, 130-31.

9. Ibid.

10. Ibid.

11. CH objected to the 1954 patent provisions. See Dawson, *Nuclear Power*, 68-70.

12. Unna, "Atomic Energy," 2.

13. CH discusses his 1945 dissenting report in Unna, "Atomic Energy," 3. The report, entitled "Dissenting Views of Members of the Military Affairs Committee on H.R. 4566," may be found in *Atomic Energy Act of 1945*, 79th Cong., 1st sess., 5 Nov. 1945, H. Rept. 1186, 16-18.

14. *Atomic Energy Act of 1945*, 79th Cong., 1st sess., 5 Nov. 1945, H. Rept. 1186, 16-18.

15. Ibid.

16. Ibid.

17. Ibid.

18. See Hewlett and Anderson, *The New World*, 436, 443-54, 483-86, 491-92, 505-507, 512-13, 516. See also Dyke, *Mr. Atomic Energy*, 30-37, and Byron S. Miller, "A Law is Passed--the Atomic Energy Act of 1946," *University of Chicago Law Review* 15 (Summer 1948):811.

19. Hewlett and Anderson, *The New World*, 421-23, 431-35, 445-48.

20. Alice Kimball Smith, *A Peril and a Hope: The Scientists' Movement in America: 1945-1947* (Chicago: University of Chicago Press, 1965), 397-98; Unna, "Atomic Energy," 4-5.

21. CH/RWD, 7 Mar. 1981; CH/Douglass, vol. 2, 91-94; Smith, *A Peril and A Hope*, 400-402.

22. See Hewlett and Anderson, *The New World*, 483, 507, 512-13, 529-30.

23. CH/FXG, CH-HBA input to RWD.

24. Ibid.; Unna, "Atomic Energy," 9.

25. Unna, "Atomic Energy," 6.

26. CH/FXG, CH-HBA input to RWD. For CH's defense of Condon, see "Smearing the Scientists: Attempts to Discredit Civilian Atomic-Energy Control," reprint of CH House speech, 22 July 1947, and "Sabotage of American Science: The Full Meaning of Attacks on Dr. Condon," reprint of CH House speech, 9 Mar. 1948, both in Box 50 (Dr. E. U. Condon/Civil Liberties), HP.

27. 11 Mar. 1946, *Congressional Record*, 79th Cong., 2nd sess., vol. 92, 2127-2129.

28. CH, "Atomic Bomb Tests: Bikini."

29. Ibid.

30. CH/FXG, CH-HBA input to RWD; CH, "Atomic Bomb Tests: Bikini."

31. CH, "Atomic Bomb Tests: Bikini."

32. See Dyke, *Mr. Atomic Energy*, 81-83, for the CH-inspired fight to gain parity with the Senate.

33. Hewlett and Duncan, *Atomic Shield, 1947/1952*, vol. 2 of *A History of the Atomic Energy Commission* (University Park, Pennsylvania: Pennsylvania State University Press, 1969), 89-95, 328-31, 352, 355-58; Dyke, *Mr. Atomic Energy*, 47-56.

34. CH/FXG, CH-HBA input to RWD.

35. CH mentions Klaus Fuch's treachery in Unna, "Atomic Energy," 7-8.

36. CH/RWD, 7 Mar. 1981; Unna, "Atomic Energy," 8. CH describes the meeting with McMahon in CH/Douglass, vol. 3, 4-7.

37. CH/FXG; CH/RWD, 7 Mar. 1981. See also Robert Gilpin, *American Scientists and Nuclear Weapons Policy* (Princeton, New Jersey: Princeton University Press, 1962), 80-110, and also a two-volume, 1969 JCAE draft report initiated by JCAE Chairman CH, *The Influence of the Joint Committee on Atomic Energy on the Decision to Build the Hydrogen Bomb*, Part I, 3-5, 49-53, Box 44 (Decision to Build the Hydrogen Bomb), HP, **hereafter cited as** *JCAE Hydrogen Bomb History*.

38. The AEC memo to Truman on the 3-2 commission vote was sent on 9 Nov. 1949 and is at the National Archives. (NND-862005, Record Group (RG) 128, JCAE Subject Files, Bar 60, Tab 4.)

39. William L. Borden/FXG, 20 Sept. 1984.

40. Ibid.

41. A declassified version of Hamilton's 15-page report, "Inquiry into Aspects of a Superweapon Program," 8 Nov. 1949, was provided to Gannon in April 1986 through the auspices of Senator Robert Byrd (D-West Virginia). The 5,000-word letter is now in the National Archives. (NND-82005, RG 128, JCAE Subject Files.) *JCAE Hydrogen Bomb History*, Part II, 39-45, 70-76, quotes from these documents.

42. *JCAE Hydrogen Bomb History*, Part II, 39-43.

43. Ibid.

44. Ibid., 43-44.

45. Ibid., 44-45.

46. Borden/FXG, 20 Sept. 1984.

47. CH/FXG, CH-HBA input to RWD. Unna, "Atomic Energy," 10, has similar quote.

48. Borden/FXG, 20 Sept. 1984.

49. "Smearing the Scientists: Attempts to Discredit Civilian Atomic-Energy Control," 22 July 1947, and "Sabotage of American Science: The Full Meaning of Attacks on Dr. Condon," 9 Mar. 1948.

50. Unna, "Atomic Energy," 9.

51. David E. Lilienthal, *The Atomic Energy Years, 1945-1950*, vol. 2 of *The Journals of David E. Lilienthal* (New York: Harper and Row, 1966), 582.

52. CH/FXG, CH-HBA input to RWD.

53. CH/RWD, 7 Mar. 1981; CH/FXG.

54. See *JCAE Hydrogen Bomb History*, Part II, 68-69.

55. *JCAE Hydrogen Bomb History*, Part II, 70-76, contains quotations from McMahon's letter.

56. David Alan Rosenberg, "American Atomic Strategy and the Hydrogen Bomb Decision," *Journal of American History* 66 (June 1979):86.

57. Ibid.

58. CH/RWD, 7 Mar. 1981; Unna, "Atomic Energy," 10.

59. Unna, "Atomic Energy," 10.

60. CH, "Item for Reader's Digest Article, Submitted by Congressman Chet Holifield of California" [1957], Box 41 (Atomic Energy 1956-60 Misc.), HP.

61. "The Day I was Proudest to be an American," *New York Times*, 25 Aug. 1959.

62. CH/FXG, CH-HBA input to RWD.

63. See H.R. 4641, 80th Cong., 1st sess., Box 50 (Dr. E. U. Condon/Civil Liberties); CH to [*Los Angeles Sentinel* publisher] Leon H. Washington, Jr., 8 Dec. 1947, Box 51 (Chet's Bill H.R. 4641), HP.

Chapter 3: A Haberdasher Presses into Politics

1. CH to G. P. Wachtell, Secretary, Princeton Association of Scientists, 22 June 1949, Box 50 (1950 David Lilienthal), HP.

2. Unna, "Boyhood, My Own Family, and My Own Business," unpublished typescript, 1-2.

3. Unna, "Boyhood," 2.

4. CH/FXG, CH-HBA input to RWD; Unna, "Boyhood," 1.

5. Unna, "Boyhood," 5; CH to Roy L. Holifield, 12 Sept. 1969, and CH to Robb Hicks, Special Rep. for Alumni Affairs, Loma Linda University, 13 Aug. 1971, both in Box 1 (Relatives), HP.

6. Unna, "Boyhood," 5.

7. Ibid., 3-4.

8. Ibid., 4.

9. Ibid., 4-5.

10. Ibid., 6.

11. Ibid., 6-7.

12. CH/Douglass, vol. 1, 10-17; Unna, "Holifield of California," *Atlantic Monthly*; Unna, "Boyhood," 7-8; CH/FXG; CH/RWD, 19 Feb. 1980; CH to John Reich, 18 Dec. 1970, Box 47 (JCAE Outgoing Letters 1970 [Blue Copies]), HP; FXG, RWD interviews with CH's family members.

13. CH/FXG, CH-HBA input to RWD.

14. CH/Douglass, vol. 1, 20; Unna, "Boyhood," 10; Houston, "Holifield: A 32-Year Flashback."

15. CH/FXG; CH/RWD, 19 Feb. 1980; "Boyhood," 10.

16. Unna, "Boyhood," 8-9; CH/FXG.

17. Unna, "Boyhood," 8.

18. CH/RWD, 19 Feb. 1980; Unna, "Boyhood," 9.

19. CH/FXG, CH-HBA input to RWD.

20. Unna, "Boyhood," 10; CH/RWD, 19 Feb. 1980.

21. Unna, "Boyhood," 10; CH/RWD, 19 Feb. 1980.

22. Unna, "Boyhood," 10.

23. CH/FXG; CH/RWD, 19 Feb. 1980; Unna, "Boyhood," 11-13.

24. CH/RWD, 19 Feb. 1980; Unna, "Boyhood," 11.

25. Unna, "Boyhood," 12.

26. Ibid., 11.

27. CH/FXG; CH/RWD, 19 Feb. 1980. See also a biographical fact sheet requested by *Congressional Quarterly*, 30 Jan. 1968, and a "Candidates Biographical Fact Sheet," requested by the *East Whittier Review*, 1 Aug. 1968, both in Box 1 (Biographical Material), HP.

28. Unna, "Boyhood," 13-14; CH/FXG.

29. CH/FXG, CH-HBA input to RWD; CH/RWD, 19 Feb. 1980; Unna, "Boyhood," 12.

30. Cam Holifield/RWD, [20 Dec. 1980].

31. Unna, "Boyhood," 13-14.

32. CH/RWD, 19 Feb. 1980.

33. Unna, "Boyhood," 13-16; CH to Mr./Mrs. Clyde Holifield, 6 Aug. 1971, Box 1 (Relatives), HP.

34. Unna, "Boyhood," 14-15.

35. Unna, "Politics," unpublished typescript [1 May 1974], 1.

36. CH/RWD, 19 Feb. 1980; Dyke, *Mr. Atomic Energy*, 11-12; Unna, "Boyhood," 1-2.

37. Unna, "Politics," 1-2; CH/FXG; CH/RWD, 19 Feb. 1980.

38. Unna, "Politics," 2-3; CH/FXG.

39. Unna, "Politics," 3.

40. Ibid., 4.

41. CH/FXG; CH/RWD, 19 Feb. 1980. See also Box 14 (I.P.P.), HP.

42. CH's daughter, Betty Holifield Feldmann, described her father as "a very odd combination of an idealist and a pragmatist." (Unna, "Boyhood," 15, and "Politics," 4.) Samples of CH's Vietnam views are CH to John D. Coty, 14 Jan. 1970, and CH to Harry A. Lindsay, 17 Mar. 1970, both in Box 22 (Vietnam - 1970), HP; Unna, "Holifield Biography Outline," 14, and "Vietnam," 1-3.

43. Unna, "Boyhood," 16-17; Robert Feldmann/FXG.

44. Betty and Robert Feldmann provided FXG the story of their visit with the Trumans aboard the *Independence*. Truman's letter is Truman to CH [1958], private communication.

45. Alben Barkley's comments are in Unna, "Boyhood," 8.

46. Paul Houston, "The California Group--Muscle and Harmony," *L.A. Times*, 1 Oct. 1972, 1, 14.

47. Unna, "Politics," 5-6; CH/FXG.

48. Unna, "Politics," 5-7; CH/FXG; CH/RWD.

49. Unna, "Politics," 5-6.

50. Ibid., 7.

51. Editorial, *Washington Post*, 7 Nov. 1985.

52. See H.R. 17558, 89th Cong., 2d sess., Box 56 (H.R. 17558), HP; "Holifield Hails Desalting Program," *Montebello Messenger*, 27 Apr. 1967, 3, Box 45 (Desalting); and Box 45 (Bolsa Island 1968).

53. Box 7, HP, among the boxes (2-7) devoted to California/district issues, is devoted to "Water."

54. Jim Wright (Speaker of the House of Representatives)/FXG.

55. Ibid.

56. Ibid.; CH/RWD, 19 Feb. 1980.

57. CH/FXG; CH/RWD, 19 Feb. 1980. Boxes 14-24, HP, are the local district office files.

58. Harold Seidman/FXG, 20 June 1986.

59. Unna, "Politics," 8-9; CH/FXG; CH/RWD.

60. *New York Sunday News*, 10 Jan. 1943, loose in Box 1, HP.

61. In a September 1991 telephone interview with Betty Holifield Feldmann, Ms. Clifton considered that her work over the years was a typical example of CH's influence on the lives of his close associates.

62. CH/FXG.

63. Unna, "Politics," 7-8, and transcript, n. d., dictated by CH and transcribed for FXG, n. d.

Chapter 4: Ideas Have Consequences

1. Warren Unna, "Holifield of California," *Atlantic Monthly* 205 (April 1960):79.

NOTES

2. CH/FXG, CH-HBA input to RWD.

3. The quotations are from *The California New Dealer*, April 1940.

4. See CH to Ralph Jacques, 11 Feb. 1974, Box 1 (Relatives); CH to Andrew J. Biemiller, 15 Dec. 1969, Box 22 (Voting - 1970); and typescript [1965], Box 44 (Holifield Speech Material), HP.

5. *California New Dealer*, April 1940.

6. CH, "Atomic Bomb Tests: Bikini." Sample of CH's UN views is "The Truth About National Affairs," typescript [1948], Box 79 (1948 [Undated] Speech, "The Truth About National Affairs"), HP.

7. 1 Apr. 1947, *Congressional Record*, 80th Cong., 1st sess., vol. 93, 2964.

8. See esp. CH to Harry A. Lindsay, 17 Mar. 1970, Box 22 (Vietnam - 1970), HP.

9. CH/FXG. See also JCAE, *Hearings*, 93rd Cong., 2d sess., March 1974. For common-sense exceptions, see *Montebello Messenger*, 27 Aug. 1970 and "New Bill to Control Pornography Passes House," 5 Aug. 1970, Box 83 (Press Release--"New Bill to Control Pornography Passes House"), HP.

10. See "The Dies Committee Should Die," 10 Feb. 1943, *Congressional Record*, 78th Cong., 1st sess., vol. 89, A525, and "Protest Against ... the Goodwin B. Watson Case," 11 May 1943, A2317.

11. Unna, "Civil Liberties," unpublished typescript, [1 May 1974], 1-2.

12. CH/FXG; 18 May 1943, *Congressional Record*, 78th Cong., 1st sess., vol. 89, 4592

13. Unna, "Civil Liberties," 2.

14. Quoted in Unna, "Civil Liberties," 3.

15. Mike Masaoka, *Pacific Citizen*, 2 June 1972.

16. Unna, "Civil Liberties," 3-4.

17. CH to Leon H. Washington, Jr., 8 Dec. 1947 and H.R. 4641, 80th Cong., 1st sess., Box 50 (Dr. E. U. Condon/Civil Liberties), HP. Speaker McCormack once told CH: "Chet, you're too good a legislator to waste your time fighting the Un-American Activities Committee." CH replied: "I didn't come here to do what's popular." (Unna, "Civil Liberties," 5.)

18. Joseph Volpe, Jr./FXG, 15 Feb. 1985.

19. Ibid.; Unna, "Atomic Energy," 17.

20. See Dyke, *Mr. Atomic Energy*, 55.

21. Volpe/FXG, 15 Feb. 1985.

22. Ibid.

23. Borden/FXG, 25 Sept. 1985.

24. CH/FXG, CH-HBA input to RWD. See also untitled press release in Box 79 (April 13, 1954, Press Release Re: Dr. J. Robert Oppenheimer), HP.

25. CH/FXG, CH-HBA input to RWD.

26. Ibid. CH to Oppenheimer, 6 Jan. 1955, is in Box 50 (Robert J. Oppenheimer [*sic*]). Unna, "Holifield Biography Outline," 6, and "Civil Liberties," 4, note that CH was the only JCAE member to publicly praise Oppenheimer after his clearance had been lifted.

27. Unna, "Civil Liberties," 4-5.

28. 31 Mar. 1944, *Congressional Record*, 78th Cong., 2nd sess., vol. 90, A1720.

29. Ibid.

30. "60,000 More on Welfare Seen by Holifield if Lockheed Fails," *Antelope Valley Press* (northern Los Angeles County newspaper), 10 June 1971.

31. 11 Dec. 1945, *Congressional Record*, 79th Cong., 1st sess., vol. 91, 11837.

32. "Protection of Labor Rights is the Basic Foundation of Prosperity," 11 June 1948, typescript, Box 79 (Speech - Floor, "Protection of Labor Rights is the Basic Foundation of Prosperity"), HP.

33. *Labor Outlook* (a publication of Oxford Industries, Los Angeles, California), August 1967, 4.

34. CH notes his "Christian principles" in politics/voting in CH/Ralph Jacques, 11 Feb. 1974.

35. CH, "Can Religion and Political Objectives be Harmonious in a Democracy?" 13 Sept. 1944, *Congressional Record*, 78th Cong., 2nd sess., vol. 90, A4018.

36. Ibid.

37. Quote is from CH to Herbert Roback, [1977], made available to FXG by Mrs. Roback.

38. CH/RWD, 19 Feb. 1980; Cam Holifield/RWD, 20 Dec. 1980.

39. CH, "Atom Bomb Tests: Bikini."

40. CH/FXG, CH-HBA input to RWD.

41. For example, see 16 Oct. 1945, *Congressional Record*, 79th Cong., 1st sess., vol. 91, 9685.

42. Quotations are from "Palestine Partitions Must be Enforced," 17 Mar. 1948, *Congressional Record,* 80th Cong., 2nd sess., vol. 94, 3117.

43. CH/RWD, 19 Feb. 1980 and 8 Feb. 1982.

44. Box 62 (Humphrey Campaign 1972 Correspondence), HP, contains letters from Humphrey and CH's 28 Jan. 1972 acceptance as 1972 California chairman. See CH to Thomas P. ("Tip") O'Neill, 22 Apr. 1972, Box 62 [1972 Democratic National Convention], HP, for CH comments on 1968 convention.

45. CH/FXG; CH/RWD.

46. CH/FXG, CH-HBA input to RWD.

47. Ibid.

48. Ibid.

49. CH notes his upcoming trip to NATO installations in CH to President-Elect John F. Kennedy, 26 Nov. 1960, Box 45 (Nuclear Weapons 1960-1968), HP, and offers to make the findings available.

50. CH/FXG, CH-HBA input to RWD. A 3-page report, Harold Agnew (Los Alamos scientist/advisor on the trip) to Major General A.D. Starbird, 5 Jan. 1961, declassified, was also helpful.

51. CH/FXG, CH-HBA input to RWD. For the debate on PALs for nuclear submarines, see Desmond Ball, "Nuclear War at Sea," *International Security,* 10 (Winter 1985/86):3-31. See also an article by Aleson, Carnesale, and Nye in *Washington Quarterly* (Summer 1986):54.

52. CH/FXG, CH-HBA input to RWD.

53. Ibid.

54. See Dyke, *Mr. Atomic Energy,* 266, 391 n. 16.

55. Unna, "Atomic Energy," 28-29; CH/FXG, CH-HBA input to RWD.

56. "The Atomic-Powered Committee," *Nuclear News* (February 1968), 34-35; JCAE hearings, e.g., *Nuclear Energy for Space Propulsion and Auxiliary Power,* 87th Cong., 1st sess., 28-29 Aug. 1961.

57. The plaque was displayed prominently at CH's home in Balboa, California until his death.

58. CH/FXG, CH-HBA input to RWD.

59. Ibid.

60. Ibid.

61. Box 13, HP, contains numerous materials on congressional and Rules Committee reform. Unna, "Holifield Biography Outline," 2, 4, 12, and "Legislating," 2-4, provides discussions.

62. Jack Newman/FXG, 18 Feb. 1986. CH describes the start of his relationship with Hosmer in Unna, "Atomic Energy," 13-14, and CH/FXG and CH/RWD.

63. Newman/FXG, 18 Feb. 1986; Graham/FXG, 25 Feb. 1986.

64. CH/FXG.

65. CH/FXG, CH-HBA input to RWD; Newman/FXG, 18 Feb. 1986.

66. Newman/FXG, 18 Feb. 1986.

67. Graham/FXG, 25 Feb. 1986.

68. CH/RWD, 8 Feb. 1982; CH/FXG, CH-HBA input to RWD.

69. Graham/FXG, 25 Feb. 1986.

70. Ibid.

71. Ibid.

72. Ibid.

73. JCAE, *Liquid Metal Fast Breeder Reactor,* 92nd Cong., 2nd sess., 7, 8, 12 Sept. 1972, 130-131.

74. Norman Augustine/FXG.

75. Ibid.; Unna, "Holifield Biography Outline," 11.

76. CH/FXG, CH-HBA input to RWD.

Chapter 5: Towards Mastery of the House

1. CH to Ralph Jacques, 11 Feb. 1974; "Updating Hon. Chet Holifield's Public Service Record," 26 Nov. 1974, *Congressional Record,* 93rd Cong., 2nd sess., vol. 120, reprint (CH gave to RWD).

2. CH/FXG; CH/RWD, 7 Mar. 1981; Unna, "Government Operations Committee," 1.

3. Unna, "Politics," 2-3; Unna, "Nixon," 1-2; CH to Mr. Mark Gladstone, 19 June 1974, Box 63 [President Richard Nixon, 1971-1974], HP.

4. CH/FXG; CH/RWD; Unna, "Legislating," 3-6. A 1977 paper (the first to make use of HP) also provides factual background. (RWD, "The Fight for the Third House, 1958-1961: The Importance of Chet Holifield," presented before the Phi Alpha Theta Student History Conference at Loyola-Marymount University, Los Angeles, California, Apr. 1977, 24 pp.)

5. House Committee on Government Operations, *Notes on the Jurisdiction of the House Committee on Government Operations*, 86th Cong., 1st sess. (Washington, D.C.: GPO, 1959).

6. CH/FXG, CH-HBA input to RWD. On Government Operations oversight, see Thomas A. Henderson, *Congressional Oversight of Executive Agencies: A Study of the House Committee on Government Operations* (Gainsville, Florida: University of Florida Press, 1970).

7. 28 Apr. 1952, *Congressional Record*, 82nd Cong., 2nd sess., vol. 98, 4516.

8. Elmer Henderson/FXG, 23 Jan. 1985. See also *Cannon's Precedents of the House of Representatives*, vol. 7 (Washington, D.C.: GPO, 1935), 831, Section 2041.

9. On accountability, see Bruce L. R. Smith and D. C. Hague, eds., *The Dilemma of Accountability in Modern Government: Independence Versus Control* (New York: St. Martin Press, 1981).

10. 1946 act is 60 Stat. 832. Subpoena power in Unna, "Government Operations Committee," 3.

11. CH/FXG, CH-HBA input to RWD.

12. Ibid.; Unna, "Government Operations Committee," 12.

13. CH/FXG, CH-HBA input to RWD.

14. Ibid.

15. Ibid.

16. Ibid.; Unna, "Government Operations Committee," 4. See also 28 July 1949, *Congressional Record*, 81st Cong., 1st sess., vol. 95, 10389; 18 Oct. 1949, *Congressional Record*, A6435.

17. CH/Douglass, vol. 1, 8-14; CH/FXG.

18. CH describes commission in 18 Oct. 1949, *Congressional Record*, A6435.

19. CH/Douglass, vol. 2, 26-29; CH/FXG, CH-HBA input to RWD.

20. CH/Douglass, vol. 2, 26-29; CH/FXG, CH-HBA input to RWD.

21. CH/Douglass, vol. 2, 26-29; For DOD opposition, see Robert J. Donovan, *Conflict and Crisis: The Presidency of Harry S Truman* (New York: W. W. Norton & Co., Inc., 1977), 138-140, 200-201, 265.

22. CH/FXG, CH-HBA input to RWD.

23. Henderson/FXG, 23 Jan. 1985.

24. The Second (2nd) Hoover Commission's final report is *Final Report to the Congress by the Commission on the Organization of the Executive Branch of Government* (Washington: GPO, 1955).

25. Ibid., for a discussion of the 2nd Hoover Commission's work and recommendations.

26. Ibid., 25-31, contains CH's dissenting statement.

27. See 2nd Hoover Commission, *Federal Medical Services* (June 1955) for CH's dissent.

28. See 2nd Hoover Commission, *Lending Guaranteeing and Insurance Agencies*, for another dissent.

29. See 2nd Hoover Commission, *Water Resources and Power*, 10-94. In Unna, "Government Operations Committee," 1, CH notes that this task force wanted "to rid the nation of public power."

30. *Final Report to the Congress from the Commission on the Organization of the Executive Branch of Government*, 25-31, contains CH's overall dissent to the Second Hoover Commission's report.

31. CH/FXG, CH-HBA input to RWD. For Rules' restrictive nature, see *A History of the Committee on Rules*, congressional print, 97th Cong., 2nd sess. (Washington, D.C.: GPO, 1983).

32. CH/FXG; CH/RWD, 7 Mar. 1981; Unna, "Legislating," 3-6. William Phillips, long-time DSG staff director, gave FXG some DSG materials and 10th Anniversary booklet (4 Dec. 1969). FXG also interviewed DSG members John Blatnik (D-Minnesota) and James M. Quigley (D-Pennsylvania).

33. CH/FXG, CH-HBA input to RWD; RWD, "Fight for the Third House," 1-2.

34. CH/FXG, CH-HBA input to RWD.

35. See two CH to "Dear Colleague" letters (14 and 20 Dec. 1960) in Box 13 (The DSG), HP.

36. Richard Bolling, *Power in the House* (New York: E. P. Dutton, 1968), 178-80; Dyke, "Fight for the Third House," 4-5.

37. "Organization and Operation of Congress"--Hearings before the Committee on Expenditures in the Executive Departments, U.S. Senate ... on Evaluation of the Effects of Laws Enacted to Reorganize the Legislative Branch ..." Box 13 (Holifield's Public Statements on the Rules Comm.), HP.   38. CH/FXG. See 30 Jan. 1957, *Congressional Record*, 85th Cong., 1st sess., vol. 103, 1324-26.

38. CH to RWD.

39. CH/FXG, CH-HBA input to RWD.

40. CH/FXG, CH-HBA input to RWD; RWD, "Fight for the Third House," 8. See press release, 3 Jan. 1959, in Box 13 (Sam Rayburn's Role in the Rules Fight), HP.

41. CH/FXG, CH-HBA input to RWD. Dyke, *Mr. Atomic Energy*, 194, 294 for CH's 1956/68 roles.

42. CH/FXG, CH-HBA input to RWD; Unna, "Holifield Biog. Outline," 6, 12; "Legislating," 4-5.

43. CH/FXG; CH/RWD, 7 Mar. 1981.

44. Dyke, "Fight for the Third House," 2-3, 15.

45. CH/FXG, CH-HBA input to RWD.

46. Ibid. See Unna, "Holifield Biography Outline," 14.

47. CH/FXG, CH-HBA input to RWD; CH/Douglass, vol. 1, 145.

48. Unna, "Legislating," 5.

49. CH/FXG, CH-HBA input to RWD.

50. Ibid.; The rationale ultimately for the Truman pension is found in House Committee on Post Office and Civil Service, H. Rept. 2200, 85th Cong., 2nd sess. (Washington, D.C.; GPO, 17 July 1958).

51. CH discusses the proposed Truman pension in Unna, "Legislating,"4-5.

52. CH/FXG, CH-HBA input to RWD; Unna, "Legislating," 5; Public Law 85-745, 25 Aug. 1958.

53. George Meader/FXG, 18 Apr. 1985.

54. Meader's statement is in Henderson, *Congressional Oversight of Executive Agencies.*

55. Meader/FXG, 18 Apr. 1985.

56. Donald E. Walker [Hoffmann's biographer] to FXG, [1985], notes that CH "led the charge ... against the chairman's behavior." The vote was 23-1 against Hoffman.

57. CH/FXG.

58. Ibid.

59. Meader/FXG, 18 Apr. 1985.

60. CH/FXG, CH-HBA input to RWD.

61. Harold Seidman/FXG, 20 June 1986.

62. CH became JCAE chairman in January 1961. (Dyke, *Mr. Atomic Energy*, 257.)

63. CH/FXG; CH/RWD, 8 Feb. 1982.

64. CH/FXG; CH/RWD, 8 Feb. 1982.

65. CH's close ties to Johnson are described in Dyke, *Mr. Atomic Energy*, 274-276.

66. CH/FXG, CH-HBA input to RWD; CH/RWD, 8 Feb. 1982.

67. Unna, "Legislating," 6-7.

68. CH/FXG, CH-HBA input to RWD. Box 30, HP, contains several files on DOT.

69. Ibid.

70. Unna, "Legislating," 4-6, notes "I was so tired after that fight I ended up in the hospital." (6)

71. CH, "Statement on H.R. 157," reprint from *Congressional Record*, in *Journal of the National Contract Management Association*, I (February 1967):18-20. Box 56, HP, has three files on H.R. 157.

72. CH/FXG, CH-HBA input to RWD; Unna, "Government Operations Committee," 4.

73. CH/FXG, CH-HBA input to RWD.

74. Ibid.

75. Summary and full *Report of the Commission on Procurement*, 4 vols. (Wash., D.C.: GPO, 1972).

76. Ibid. CH followed up with H.R. 14494. See Box 61 (H.R. 14494), HP.

77. CH/FXG, CH-HBA input to RWD.

78. Ibid. Many of CH's ideas are from the *Report of the Commission on Procurement.*

79. CH/FXG.

80. See H.R. 16424 and H.R. 16550, 93rd Cong., 2d sess., in files with same names, in Box 61, HP.

81. Leo Rennert, "Public Power Loses Fight for Nuclear Power Plants," *Sacramento Bee*, 3 July 1968, Box 45 (1968 Atomic Energy Commission), HP.

82. The essence of CH's comment is in Unna, "Legislating," 1, with further elaboration by CH.

83. CH/FXG; CH/RWD. Unna, "Legislating," 1.

84. CH/FXG, CH-HBA input to RWD.

85. Unna, "Legislating," 1, calls Bella Abzug/Ben Rosenthal "100 percent idealist[s]."

86. CH/FXG, CH-HBA input to RWD.

87. Unna, "Legislating," 2-3.
88. Dante Fascell/FXG.
89. Ibid.
90. Miles Q. Romney/FXG, 18 Jan. 1985.
91. CH/FXG; CH/RWD.
92. Committee on Government Operations, *Activities of the House Committee on Government Operations, Ninety-Third Congress* (Washington, D.C.: GPO, 1974), H. Rept. No. 93-1659, 129-136.
93. Romney/FXG, 18 Jan. 1985.

Chapter 6: In the Eye of Legislative Storms

1. On Hanford, see Hewlett and Anderson, *The New World, 1939/1946*, 7; Dawson, *Nuclear Power*, 12-14. Also CH/FXG; CH/RWD, 19 Feb. 1980.
2. CH/FXG; CH/RWD; HBA input to RWD. Per MS notes to RWD, 18 Oct. 1991, U.S. has not had timely success with dual-purpose plants (viz., Hanford N-reactor, Bolsa Island, and Midland).
3. CH/FXG; CH/RWD; HBA input to RWD.
4. CH/FXG.
5. Bonnie Baack Pendergrass, *Public Power, Politics and Technology in the Eisenhower and Kennedy Years: The Hanford Dual-Purpose Reactor Controversy, 1956-1962* (New York: Arno Press, 1979), 127-37
6. CH/FXG.
7. Arguments are in CH to Dear Colleague and attachment, 7 July 1961, Box 54 (H.R. 7476), HP.
8. CH/FXG, CH-HBA input to RWD.
9. 13 July, 17 July, 8 Aug., and 13 Sept. 1961, *Congressional Record*, 87th Cong. 1st sess., vol. 107, 12471, 12828, 14958, and 19217-19220.
10. Pendergrass, *Public Power, Politics and Technology in the Eisenhower and Kennedy Years*, 127-37.
11. Ibid.
12. Alex Radin/FXG, 6 Oct. 1985. See also Radin to CH, 23 July 1962, Box 54 [H.R. 11974], HP.
13. See 17 July 1962, *Congressional Record*, 87th Cong., 2nd sess., vol.108, 12860-61.
14. Ibid., 12826-12862; Open letter to Congress by the local chambers of commerce is in "Hanford file," APPA library, Wash., D.C. Lee editorials are in the (Feb.- Aug.) *Tri-City Herald*. See *New York Times*, 17 July 1962 for a favorable article. Hosmer's brochure is in Box 54 [H.R. 11974], HP.
15. See 13 July 1962, *Congressional Record*, 87th Cong., 2nd sess., vol. 108, 13505-12.
16. CH/FXG, CH-HBA input to RWD.
17. Jack Newman/FXG, 4 Nov. 1985.
18. See Dyke, *Mr. Atomic Energy*, 178-179. Van Zandt still refused to sign the conference report.
19. 17 July 1962, *Congressional Record*, 87th Cong., 2nd sess., vol. 108, 12845.
20. CH to Colleague, 12 Sept. 1962, Box 54 (H.R. 11974), HP; *Mr. Atomic Energy*, 180, 355 n. 37.
21. Morgan Dubrow/FXG, 20 Sept. 1984.
22. See U.S. Interior Dept. news release, [1964], "Fact Sheet: Pacific Northwest-Pacific Southwest Intertie," 11 pp., Box 4 (Intertie 2#); Federal Power Commission, "Report on the Review of the Pacific Northwest-Pacific Southwest Intertie, August 1966," typescript, Box 4 (Intertie Meeting), HP.
23. CH/FXG, CH-HBA input to RWD; PG&E pamphlet, *Pacific Intertie*, Box 4 (Pacific Intertie).
24. Ibid.
25. Even *Pacific Intertie* notes the triumph of peaceful co-existence with private power.
26. *Mr. Atomic Energy*, 274-75. *Pacific Intertie*, 3, sees LBJ as herald of "New Era of Cooperation."
27. CH/FXG, CH-HBA input to RWD; CH to LBJ, 29 July 1964, Box 4 (Intertie 2#), HP.
28. CH/FXG, CH-HBA input to RWD.
29. Ibid. In CH to LBJ, 29 July 1964, CH notes his meetings with all of the involved parties.
30. CH/FXG, CH-HBA input to RWD.
31. Ibid.
32. Ibid.; transcript, "Long Distance Call from Congressman Bernie Sisk and ... Holifield to Mr. Gerdes (P. G. & E.), Piedmont, California ... OLney 3-6423," n. d., Box 4 (Intertie Meeting), HP.
33. CH recalled his meeting with Gerdes in CH/FXG.
34. CH/FXG.

35. Ibid.

36. LBJ to CH, 11 Aug. 1964, Box 4 (Intertie); Udall to CH, 31 July 1967, Box 4 (Intertie #3), HP; *Pacific Intertie*, 18; 3 Sept. 1964, *Congressional Record*, 88th Cong., 2nd sess., vol. 110, 21627-28.

37. CH/FXG, CH-HBA input to RWD; *Pacific Intertie*, 1; U.S. Interior Dept., "Fact Sheet," 9-11.

38. CH/FXG, CH-HBA input to RWD. See Interior Dept. rpt. to H. Approp. Com. (GPO, 1964).

39. Committee on Government Operations, *Comptroller General Reports to Congress on Audits of Defense Contracts*, committee print, 89th Cong., 2nd sess. (Washington, D.C.: GPO, 23 Mar. 1966), 32.

40. Douglas Dahlin (subcommittee staff)/FXG, 9 Sept. 1984 noted Drew Pearson's criticisms.

41. CH/FXG, CH-HBA input to RWD.

42. Ibid.; Unna, "Government Operations Committee," 3.

43. James A. Lanigan/FXG, 20 Sept. 1985.

44. *Comptroller General ... on Audits of Defense Contracts*; Frederick C. Mosher, *The GAO: The Quest for Accountability in American Government* (Boulder, Colorado: Westview Press, 1979), 153-65.

45. *Comptroller General Reports to Congress on Audits of Defense Contracts*.

46. Ibid., 27-29.

47. Ibid., 32.

48. CH/FXG, CH-HBA input to RWD.

49. Ibid.; See also Mosher, *The GAO*, 153-65.

50. Elmer B. Staats/FXG, 20 Aug. 1985.

51. Ibid. See Staats, "The GAO: Gov't Watchdog, Analyst, Critic," *GAO Review* (Fall, 1972):1-10.

52. Staats/FXG, 20 Aug. 1985.

53. Ibid.; CH/FXG, CH-HBA input to RWD.

54. Dante Fascell/FXG, 23 Feb. 1984.

55. CH notes his acting chairmanship in Unna, "Government Operations Committee," 2.

56. CH/FXG, CH-HBA input to RWD. Box 13, HP, covers congressional reforms.

57. Nicholas Masters (telephone) interview with FXG, 18 Aug. 1985.

58. For background on the 1965 and 1970 reform efforts, see Roger H. Davidson and Walter J. Oleszek, *Congress Against Itself* (Bloomington, Indiana: Indiana University Press, 1977), 11, 52.

59. Ibid.; CH/FXG, CH-HBA input to RWD.

60. CH/FXG, CH-HBA input to RWD.

61. Ibid.

62. John Paul Ridgely (telephone) interview with FXG, 27 Sept. 1985.

63. CH/FXG, CH-HBA input to RWD. CH's and Ford's relationship was very productive.

64. Newman/FXG, 4 Apr. 1986.

Chapter 7: Who Shall Live?

1. CH/FXG, CH-HBA input to RWD; CH/RWD, 19 Feb. 1980.

2. CH/FXG, CH-HBA input to RWD; Hewlett and Duncan, *Nuclear Navy*, 382-83.

3. CH/FXG; CH/RWD.

4. See CH, "Atomic Bomb Tests: Bikini," pamphlet, [1947], Box 41 (Bikini Atom Tests), HP.

5. CH/FXG, CH-HBA input to RWD.

6. See, for example, H. Res. 591, 79th Cong., 2nd sess., 13 Apr. 1946, Box 51 [H. Res. 591], HP.

7. See Dawson, *Nuclear Power*, 68-70; similar NRECA speech, Dyke, *Mr. Atomic Energy*, 92.

8. Dyke, *Mr. Atomic Energy*, 101-102.

9. 15 July 1954, *Congressional Record*, 83rd Cong., 2nd sess., vol. 100, 10552.

10. Senate Committee on Foreign Relations, *Treaty on the Nonproliferation of Nuclear Weapons*, 90th Cong., 2nd sess., 26 Sept. 1968, S. Exec. Rept. 9.

11. See, for example, 24 Feb. 1949, *Congressional Record*, 81st Cong., 1st sess., vol. 95, 1536-38.

12. CH notes, in *East Los Angeles Gazette*, 2 Aug. 1945, A14-15, Box 1 (Biographical Material), HP.

13. *East Los Angeles Gazette*, 2 Aug. 1945, A14-A15.

14. Ibid.

15. Ibid.

16. CH visited Corregidor (Philippines)/Japan on Bikini trip. ("CH, "Atomic Bomb Tests: Bikini.")

17. Quoted from CH, "Atomic Bomb Tests: Bikini."

18. CH/FXG, CH-HBA input to RWD.

19. LASL/DOD, *The Effects of Atomic Weapons* (Wash., D.C., June 1950), revised Sept. 1950.

20. CH, "Atomic Warfare Leaves Mankind No Place to Hide," 24 Feb. 1949, *Congressional Record*.

21. Ibid.

22. On Ike's "massive retaliation" policy, see Alan Brinkley, Richard N. Current, Frank Freidel, and T. Harry Williams, *American History: A Survey*, 8th Edition (New York: McGraw-Hill, Inc., 1987), 874.

23. CH, "Power of 1952 Hydrogen Bomb," a combination press release and House floor speech, 12 Apr. 1954, 3, Box 79 [April 12, 1954, Speech--Floor, "Power of 1952 Model Hydrogen Bomb"], HP.

24. Robert A. Divine, *Blowing on the Wind: The Nuclear Test Ban Debate, 1954-1960* (New York: Oxford University Press, 1978), 4-8, 13.

25. Unna, "Full-Time Civil Defense Corps Urged," *Washington Post and Times Herald*, 30 Jan. 1955, Box 52 (Civil Defense Legislation), HP.

26. CH/FXG; CH/RWD, 8 Feb. 1982; "Tell the People the Facts ...," Box 79 (March 29, 1954, Speech--Floor, "Tell the People the Facts About Atomic-Hydrogen Weapons"), HP.

27. CH statement, 31 Jan. 1956, Box 79 (January 31, 1955 [sic], Statement--Re: Civil Defense), HP.

28. See Subcommittee on Military Operations, *Civil Defense for National Survival*, hearings, 84th Cong., 2nd sess. (Wash., D.C.: GPO, 1956), pts. 1-7; also 103-page H. Rept. No. 2946, 27 July 1956.

29. *Civil Defense for National Survival, Hearings*, pt. 2, 363, 372.

30. "Holifield Subcommittee Issues Civil Defense Report," press release, 26 July 1956, Box 79 (July 26, 1956, Press Release, "Holifield Subcommittee Issues Civil Defense Report"), HP.

31. 27 July 1956, *Congressional Record*, 84th Cong., 2nd sess., vol. 102, 15464.

32. H. Rept. No. 2946, 27 July 1956.

33. "Both Views of Civil Defense," *Los Angeles Times*, 4 Sept. 1956, I, 4; "Civil Defense Chief Hits Back at Critics of Program: Val Peterson Draws Reply by Rep. Holifield," 3 Sept. 1956, I, 2.

34. CH called in 1957 for cabinet-level Dept. of Civil Defense. (Dyke, *Mr. Atomic Energy*, 193-205.)

35. Quoted in "New Frontier's Backyard Shelters Another Case of 'Warmed Over Eisenhower,'" *I. F. Stone's Weekly*, 23 Oct. 1961, 2, Box 42 (Civil Defense 1961), HP.

36. CH to Theodore C. Sorenson (JFK spch. writer) 7 June 1961, Box 42 (Civil Defense 1961), HP.

37. CH's criticism of Kennedy's reference to "survival insurance" is in CH to Sorenson, 7 June 1961.

38. Sorenson, *Kennedy* (New York: Bantam Books, 1966), 693, 695; Dyke, *Mr. Atomic Energy*, 210.

39. Leon H. Weaver, *The Civil Defense Debate: Differing Perceptions of a Persistent Issue in National Security Policy* (East Lansing, Michigan: Michigan State University Press, 1967), 7.

40. CH/FXG, CH-HBA input to RWD.

41. Weaver, *Civil Defense Debate*, 7.

42. See *New York Times*, 30 Mar. 1982, II, 13; *New York Times*, 4 Mar. 1985, I, 9.

43. CH/FXG, CH-HBA input to RWD. See also Dyke, *Mr. Atomic Energy*, 210-13.

44. CH/FXG, CH-HBA input to RWD; Dyke, *Mr. Atomic Energy*, 194-95, 359 n. 23.

45. CH, "Congressional Hearings on Radioactive Fallout: Draft of Congressman Chet Holifield's Article for the *Bulletin of the Atomic Scientists*," typescript, 3 Sept. 1957, 1-2, Box 41 (1959 Fallout), HP.

46. Ibid., 3-4; JCAE Special Subcommittee on Radiation, *The Nature of Radioactive Fallout and Its Effect on Man*, hearings, 85th Cong., 1st sess. (Washington, D.C.: GPO, 1957).

47. CH/FXG, CH-HBA input to RWD; Dyke, *Mr. Atomic Energy*, 196.

48. 28 June 1957, *Congressional Record*, 85th Cong., 1st sess., vol. 103, pt. 8, 10569.

49. George T. Mazuzan and J. Samuel Walker, *Controlling the Atom: The Beginnings of Nuclear Regulation 1946-1962* (Los Angeles: The University of California Press, 1984), 48-53; Divine, *Blowing on the Wind*, 130-38; and "Congressional Hearings on Radioactive Fallout," 4-6.

50. 28 June 1957, *Congressional Record*, 85th Cong., 1st sess., vol. 103, pt. 8, 10571.

51. Ibid., 10570.

52. Ibid., 10570-71.

53. Dr. Ralph E. Lapp/FXG. Lapp is author of over 10 books and coauthored with Jack Schubert one of first layman texts, *Radiation: What It Is and How It Affects You* (New York: Viking Press, 1957).

54. Lapp interviews and communications with FXG.

55. Divine, *Blowing on the Wind*, 231, 238-39, 262.

56. The 1959 hearings are summarized in JCAE, *Fallout from Nuclear Weapons Tests: Summary-Analysis of Hearings, May 5-8, 1959*, 86th Cong., 1st sess., Committee print.

57. Ibid.; CH/RWD.

58. *Fallout From Nuclear Weapons Tests*.

59. Ibid.; Divine, *Blowing on the Wind*, 271-177; Mazuzan and Walker, *Controlling the Atom*, 255-56.

60. Divine, *Blowing on the Wind*, 272, 277.

61. Dyke, *Mr. Atomic Energy*, 200-201.

62. Divine, *Blowing on the Wind*, 277, notes that the severity of the criticism of CH's 1959 hearings "suggested that the hearings had succeeded in easing the fallout scare." (See also 275-76, 278.)

63. Dyke, *Mr. Atomic Energy*, 206, and 361 n. 48 re CH's "talk and test" position on nuclear testing.

64. CH/FXG, CH-HBA input to RWD; Dyke, *Mr. Atomic Energy*, 206 and 361, n. 48.

65. CH/FXG, CH-HBA input to RWD; CH's "talk and test" view in Dyke, *Mr. Atomic Energy*, 206.

66. CH/FXG, CH-HBA input to RWD. Dyke, *Mr. Atomic Energy*, 212.

67. Dyke, *Mr. Atomic Energy*, 204-205.

68. CH/FXG, CH-HBA input to RWD.

69. Ibid.; Divine, *Blowing on the Wind*, 27; William Sweet, *The Nuclear Age: Atomic Energy, Proliferation, and the Arms Race* (Washington, D.C.: Congressional Quarterly, Inc., 1988), 226, 229, 241.

Chapter 8: The Atom at Sea

1. For Rickover's wartime record see, for example, Clay Blair, Jr., *The Atomic Submarine and Admiral Rickover* (New York: Henry Holt & Co., 1954), 62-70.

2. Hewlett and Duncan, *Nuclear Navy*, 1-5, 12-14.

3. Ibid., 12, 41-43, 71-73. Joint Army-Navy Assessment Committee, *Japanese Naval and Merchant Shipping Losses During World War II By All Causes* [Washington, D.C.: GPO, Feb. 1947], iii-vii. This data is from the Naval Historical Center, Bldg. 57, Washington, D.C. 20374.

4. Hewlett and Duncan, *Nuclear Navy*, 10-12. Data on WW II submarines given to FXG and RWD by MS-HBA. More data: Naval Submarine League, P.O. Box 1146, Annadale, Virginia 22003.

5. CH was present at the 1946 BAKER test. ("Atomic Bomb Tests: Bikini.")

6. Hewlett and Anderson, *The New World*, 81-83; Hewlett and Duncan, *Nuclear Navy*, 15-51; Blair, *Atomic Submarine*, 15-18. See *Nuclear Navy*, 8-9, 13, 15, 19-21, for the Navy's early activities.

7. Hewlett and Duncan, *Nuclear Navy*, 32-35; Blair, *Atomic Submarine*, 21, 71-92.

8. Hewlett and Duncan, *Nuclear Navy*, 35-38, 49-51; Blair, *Atomic Submarine*, 15-38, 80-88.

9. See Rickover, Dunford, Rockwell, Barnes, and Shaw, "Some Problems in the Application of Nuclear Propulsion to Naval Vessels," a paper presented at the Annual Meeting of the Society of Naval Architects and Marine Engineers, New York City, 14-15 Nov. 1957.

10. CH/Douglass, vol. 3, 47; Unna, "Atomic Energy," 20.

11. Hewlett and Duncan, *Nuclear Navy*, 49-52, 74-76, 87, 88; Blair, *Atomic Submarine*, 117-121.

12. Hewlett and Duncan, *Nuclear Navy*, 88-92.

13. CH/FXG; CH/RWD. In *Journal of Reactor Science and Technology* (3 [June 1953]), Rickover noted that those without technical knowledge of reactors often made decisions. CH complained to J. Robert Oppenheimer that more engineers and fewer physicists were needed. (*Nuclear Navy*, 55.)

14. Hewlett and Duncan, *Atomic Shield*, 207, 212, 423. See also Hewlett and Duncan, *Nuclear Navy*, 76-87, 114-17, and Blair, *Atomic Submarine*, 142-145.

15. CH/FXG, CH-HBA input to RWD.

16. Ibid. Hewlett and Duncan, *Nuclear Navy*, 214.

17. CH/FXG, CH-HBA input to RWD.

18. CH/FXG, with additional CH-HBA input to RWD; *Nuclear Navy*, 231.

19. Hewlett and Duncan, *Nuclear Navy*, 174, 176, 273, 185-86; Hewlett and Duncan, *Atomic Shield*, 515; *Review of the U.S. Naval Nuclear Propulsion Program*, 32, 36.

20. The "Rickover approach" is described in Rickover, et. al., "Some Problems in the Application of Nuclear Propulsion to Naval Vessels," and in Hewlett and Duncan in *Nuclear Navy*, 384-91.

21. Hewlett and Duncan, *Nuclear Navy*, 222; Unna, "Atomic Energy," 19.

22. Hewlett and Jack M. Holl, *Atoms for Peace and War, 1953-1961: Eisenhower and the Atomic Energy Commission*, vol. III of *A History of the Atomic Energy Commission* (Los Angeles: University of California Press, 1989), 423; CH/FXG, CH-HBA input to RWD.

23. Hewlett and Duncan, *Nuclear Navy, 1946-1962*, 267-70, 280, 299, 310, 315, 370-73; Hewlett and Holl, *Atoms for Peace and War*, 521; *Review of the U.S. Naval Nuclear Propulsion Program*, 32-40, 48.

24. This is one of CH's contributions from his verbal and written comments on draft chapters.

25. CH, Jack Crawford, and John Conway/FXG, with additional CH-HBA input to RWD.

26. CH and Conway/FXG, CH-HBA input to RWD.

27. Hewlett and Duncan, *Nuclear Navy*, 363-365. See 364 for CH's statement aboard the *Skipjack*.

28. Ibid., 364-65.

29. CH/FXG. See also Subcommittee on Military Operations, *Organization and Management of Missile Programs*, hearings, 86th Cong., 1st sess. (Wash., D.C.: GPO, Sept. 1959), H. Rept. 1121.

30. Hewlett and Duncan, *Nuclear Navy*, 186-191, 390. See also Blair, *Atomic Submarine*, 193-258.

31. CH, "Atomic Bomb Tests: Bikini." CH lamented America's lack of preparedness for WW II.

32. CH/FXG, 10 Jan. 1986.

33. William Liscum Borden/FXG, 20 Sept. 1984; Borden, *There Will Be No Time: The Revolution in Strategy* (New York: The MacMillan Co., 1946), 144, and 43, 56, 84-87, 160-61, 198-99, 218-20, 225.

34. CH/FXG; CH/RWD, 19 Feb. 1980.

35. Hewlett and Duncan, *Nuclear Navy*, 223; Hewlett and Holl, *Atoms for Peace and War*, 520; CH/FXG, CH-HBA input to RWD;

36. CH/FXG, CH-HBA input to RWD; James Barr, *Polaris* (New York: Harcourt, Brace and Company, 1960); V. Adm. W. Raborn, Jr./Dr. J.T. Mason, Jr., 15 Sept. 1978, Navy's Oral History Proj.

37. CH/FXG, CH-HBA input to RWD; *Nuclear Navy*, 266-67, 308-309, 315, 371, 400.

38. Hewlett and Holl, *Atoms for Peace and War*, 244-45, 506.

39. Ibid., 244-45, 506-507.

40. CH/FXG, CH-HBA input to RWD; Hewlett and Holl, *Atoms for Peace and War*, 245, 506-508.

41. Dwight Ink/FXG, 15 Sept. 1985.

42. Ibid. See also Hewlett and Holl, *Atoms for Peace and War*, 507-508.

43. MS interviews/conversations with FXG and RWD.

44. Ink/FXG, 15 Sept. 1985.

45. Ibid.

46. *Savannah* was deactivated in 1971. See (JCAE Executive Director) Edward J. Bauser to All JCAE Members, 4 May 1971, Box 48 (Staff Memoranda 1971), HP; also Box 45 (Savanah (*sic*) JCAE).

47. CH/FXG, CH-HBA input to RWD. See hearing records of JCAE, 10 Mar. 1960 through 18 Mar. 1976, and of Armed Services Committee, 27 Apr. 1977 through 1 Mar. 1979.

48. CH, "Atomic Bomb Tests: Bikini."

49. "Nuclear Submarines Doom Large Surface Ships," *Western World* (May 1958).

50. There are numerous materials on CH's support for the nuclear navy dating from the mid 1960s in HP. See especially Box 45 (Nuclear Navy 1961-1968) and Box 49 (Nuclear Submarines 1971-1972).

51. Arguments against a surface fleet are in hearings on nuclear propulsion by JCAE (from 10 Mar. 1960 through 18 Mar. 1976) and Armed Services Committee (from 27 Apr. 1977 through 1 Mar. 1979).

52. Hewlett and Duncan, *Nuclear Navy*, 214, 266, 280-81, 401. See also *Review of the U.S. Naval Nuclear Propulsion Program*, June 1987, 26.

53. *Nuclear Navy*, 280-81, 401; *Review of the U.S. Naval Nuclear Propulsion Program*, June 1987, 25.

54. For commissioning and decommissioning dates of the *Long Beach* and *Enterprise*, see *Review of the U.S. Naval Nuclear Propulsion Program*, June 1991, 58-66.

55. For *Bainbridge* (DGN-25, redesignated CGN-25), see Hewlett and Duncan, *Nuclear Navy*, 274, 311-12, 355, 370. See also *Review of the U.S. Naval Nuclear Propulsion Program*, June 1987, 26, 40.

56. Hewlett and Duncan, *Nuclear Navy*, 370, 376. *Truxton* was essentially a duplicate of Bainbridge.

57. 22 Apr. 1964, *Congressional Record*, 88th Cong., 2nd sess., vol. 110, 8536.

58. JCAE, *Nuclear Propulsion for Naval Warships*, hearings, 5 May 1971-30 Sept. 1972, 92nd Cong., 1st and 2nd sess. (Washington, D.C.: GPO, 1972), Appendix 1, 143, covers McNamara's positions, etc.

59. See unclassified portion of *Tour of the USS Enterprise and Report on Joint AEC-Naval Reactor Program*, hearings, 31 Mar. 1962, 87th Cong., 2nd sess. (Washington, D.C.: GPO, 1962).

60. See JCAE, *Nuclear Propulsion for Naval Surface Vessels*, hearings, 30 and 31 Oct., 3 Nov. 1963, 88th Cong., 1st sess. (Washington, D.C.: GPO, 1964), and 37-page committee print (Dec. 1963). For Pastore's and CH's comments on *John F. Kennedy*, see Claude Witze, "Air Power in the News: Ten, Nine, Eight, HOLD," *Air Force and Space Digest* (Nov. 1964):17, Box 1 (Articles Mentioning), HP.

61. Conway and Bauser/FXG, CH-HBA input to RWD.

62. The 1963 JCAE hearings (*Nuclear Propulsion for Naval Surface Vessels*) contain McNamara's arguments. See also Hewlett and Duncan, *Nuclear Navy*, 371, 376, 451 n.55. A succinct criticism of McNamara based on ship performance in the 1962 Cuban Missile Crisis, is in *Nuclear Propulsion for Naval Warships*, 1971-1972 hearings, 92nd Cong., 2nd sess. (Washington: GPO, 1972), 134-135.

63. *Naval Nuclear Propulsion Program*, hearing, 7 Mar. 1966, 89th Cong., 2nd sess. (Washington, D.C.: GPO, 1966), III (Foreword), n. 6; "Information on Nuclear Warships and Their Performance in the Vietnam War," JCAE Press Release No. 510, 24 Apr. 1966, 1, Box 44 (1966 Misc. #1), HP.

64. "Information on Nuclear Warships ..."; Hewlett and Duncan, *Nuclear Navy*,371.

65. "Information on Nuclear Warships ...," 1. For recent status rpt., see DOE/DOD, *A Review of the U.S. Naval Nuclear Propulsion Program* (Wash., D.C.: GPO, June 1991), 58-66.

66. Ibid., 2.

67. "Statement by Congressman Chet Holifield, Vice Chairman ... on ... Aircraft Carrier JOHN F. KENNEDY," CH press release, 6 Sept. 1968, 1-4, Box 45 (1968 Atomic Energy Commission), HP.

68. CH/FXG, CH-HBA input to RWD; Hewlett and Duncan, *Nuclear Navy*, 362.

69. CH/FXG, CH-HBA input to RWD; Hewlett and Duncan, *Nuclear Navy*, 186-93.

70. Unna, "Atomic Energy," 24-25; Hewlett and Duncan, *Nuclear Navy*, 362.

71. CH/FXG, CH-HBA input to RWD.

72. Unna, "Atomic Energy," 25-26; CH/FXG, CH-HBA input to RWD.

73. Unna, "Atomic Energy," 26; CH/FXG; United Press International dispatch, 17 Dec. 1963.

74. CH/FXG, CH-HBA input to RWD.

75. Ibid.; Unna, "Atomic Energy," 19-20; Hewlett and Duncan, *Nuclear Navy*, 387-88.

76. CH/FXG; Jack Crawford/FXG; Hewlett and Duncan, *Nuclear Navy*, 385-86.

77. Ibid. See *Nuclear Navy*, 330-31, on quality assurance at Newport News Shipyard.

78. CH/FXG.

79. Ibid.

80. Ibid. On the MLF, CH wrote to John F. Kennedy, 26 Nov. 1960, Box 45 [Nuclear Weapons 1960-68], and to Lyndon B. Johnson, 3 Oct. 1964, Box 43 [Multi-lateral Nuclear Force], HP.

81. Unna, "Atomic Energy," 19.

Chapter 9: Swords into Plowshares

1. Sterling Cole/FXG, 3 Nov. 1985.

2. Hewlett and Holl, *Atoms for Peace and War*, 18, 162, 167.

3. Committee on Military Affairs, *Atomic Energy Act of 1946*, 5 Nov. 1945, H. Rept. 1186, 16-18.

4. Section 1(a), Atomic Energy Act of 1946, Public Law 79-585, 60 Stat. 755, 1 Aug. 1946.

5. CH/FXG, with additional CH-HBA input to RWD.

6. This passage, with minor editing, is taken from HBA member John Reich, "An Account of the Power Reactors Demonstration Program," unpublished typescript, 11, CH's files.

7. Green and Rosenthal, *Government of the Atom*, 236-38.

8. JCAE, *Atomic Power Development and Private Enterprise*, hearings, 24 June - 31 July 1953, 83rd Cong., 1st sess. (Washington, D.C.: GPO, 1953), 1-2 (**hereafter cited as** *1953 Hearings*); Dyke, *Mr. Atomic Energy*, 85; Dawson, *Nuclear Power*, 53-54; Green and Rosenthal, *Government of the Atom*, 123.

9. CH, 29 July 1953 speech (typescript), Box 79 (July 29, 1953, Speech--Floor, "Atomic Power Development"), HP; 29 July 1953, *Congressional Record*, 83rd Cong., 1st sess., vol. 99, 10426-10428. See also JCAE, *Atomic Energy and Private Enterprise*, committee print, 82nd Cong., 2nd sess. (Washington, D.C.: GPO, 1952), and Mazuzan and Walker, *Controlling the Atom*, 20.

10. *1953 Hearings*, 46.

11. Ibid.

12. Ibid., 94-95.

13. Quoted in Dawson, *Nuclear Power*, 59.

14. Box 79, HP, has many examples of speeches. See also Dyke, *Mr. Atomic Energy*, 87, 93, 95, 103.

15. 10 June 1953, *Congressional Record*, 83rd Cong., 1st sess., vol. 99, pt. 5, 6367.

16. 1 June 1953, *Congressional Record*, 83rd Cong., 1st sess., vol. 99, pt. 5, 5859.

17. 22 June 1953, *Congressional Record*, 83rd Cong., 1st sess., vol. 99, pt. 5, 7029-30.

18. Ibid., 7030.

19. Ibid., 7030-31.

20. See Box 79 (November 17, 1953, Speech before the Federation of American Scientists Re: Atomic Energy "Give-Away") and Box 79 (April 20, 1954, Press Release Re: Atomic Energy Bill), HP.

21. 27 Apr. 1954, *Congressional Record*, 83rd Cong., 2nd sess., vol. 100, pt. 4, 5599.

22. 1 Mar. 1954, *Congressional Record*, 83rd Cong., 2nd sess., vol. 100, pt. 2, 2439.

23. Eisenhower press release with 17 Feb. 1954 speech is in Box 41 (Correspondence, White House, 1954), HP. See also Green and Rosenthal, *Government of the Atom*, 125; Dawson, *Nuclear Power*, 67.

24. JCAE, *Amending the Atomic Energy Act of 1946, as Amended, and for Other Purposes: A Report to Accompany S. 3690*, 83rd Cong., 2nd sess. (Wash., D.C.: GPO, 1954), S. Rept. 1699, 10-31 and 32-94.

25. Dawson, *Nuclear Power*, 62-64, 66.

26. Minority report is in *Amending the Atomic Energy Act of 1946*, 105-138. See esp. 105-108.

27. JCAE, *Amending the Atomic Energy Act of 1946*, 109-112.

28. Ibid., 114-118.

29. Ibid., 126.

30. Ibid., 127

31. Ibid., 123-24.

32. Green and Rosenthal, *Government of the Atom*, 160-63; Dawson, *Nuclear Power*, 70.

33. Green and Rosenthal, *Government of the Atom*, 165-66; Dawson, *Nuclear Power*, 71.

34. 9 Aug. 1954, *Congressional Record*, 83rd Cong., 2nd sess., vol. 100, pt. 10, 13783-84.

35. Green and Rosenthal, *Government of the Atom*, 159-60; Dawson, *Nuclear Power*, 72.

36. Green and Rosenthal, *Government of the Atom*, 167.

37. CH/Douglass, vol. 2, 114-116.

38. Clay Cochran, "The Great Debate: The 1954 Atomic Energy Act Battle," *Rural Electrification Magazine* (Sept. 1954):17-18.

39. Murray, *Nuclear Policy for War and Peace*, 153-54; Aaron B. Wildavsky, *Dixon-Yates: A Study in Power Politics* (New Haven, Connecticut: Yale University Press, 1962), 13-14.

40. Wildavsky, *Dixon-Yates*, 15-21, 28, 31-49, 89-95.

41. Ibid., 22-28.

42. Ibid., 85-86, 99, 103, 106.

43. Ibid, 87-88. CH notes his role in a prepared statement (typescript) for a JCAE hearing, in Box 79 (June 4, 1954--Statement Re: Atomic Energy Bill), HP. See Wildavsky, *Dixon-Yates*, 135, 154-55.

44. 6 July 1954, *Congressional Record*, 83rd Cong., 2nd sess., vol. 100, 9866.

45. Ibid., 9867.

46. CH/RWD, 8 Feb. 1982; CH/Douglass, vol. 2, 128; Wildavsky, *Dixon-Yates*, 228-31.

47. Francis J. Cotter/FXG, 1 June 1983.

48. Ibid.

49. Wildavsky, *Dixon-Yates*, 134-35, 137-38. CH/Price filed minority report on the waiver decision.

50. Ibid., 264, 288, 317. See also press release, "Holifield Urges Appeal of Dixon-Yates Decision," and floor speech, "The Dixon-Yates Decision Should be Appealed," in Box 41 (Dixon-Yates #4), HP.

51. CH/Douglass, vol. 2, 125.

52. CH/FXG, CH-HBA input to RWD; CH/Douglass, vol. 3, 28, 32; Senate Committee on Interstate and Foreign Commerce, *Nomination of Lewis L. Strauss*, hearings, 17 Mar. - 14 May 1959, 86th Cong., 1st sess. (Wash., D.C.: GPO, 1959), 504-505, 536-37. For samples of Murray's views at the AEC, JCAE, *Accelerating Civilian Reactor Program*, hearings on S. 2725 and H.R. 10805, 23-29 May 1956, 84th Cong., 2nd sess. (Wash., D.C.: GPO, 1956), 109-12; JCAE, *Civilian Atomic Power Acceleration Program*, hearing, 28 June 1956, 84th Cong., 2nd sess. (Wash., D.C.: GPO, 1956), 45-46.

53. CH/RWD; Murray to Clinton Anderson, 29 June 1956, reprinted in JCAE, *Civilian Atomic Power Acceleration Program*, 45; Thomas E. Murray, *Nuclear Policy for War and Peace* (New York: The World Publishing Company, 1960), 162.

54. National Planning Association (NPA), Special Policy Committee on the Productive Uses of Nuclear Energy, *Summary of Findings--Policy Suggestions for the Future* (Wash., D.C.: NPA, 1957), 2-3.

Chapter 10: The Atom Goes into the Market

1. CH/FXG, CH-HBA input to RWD. CH's comments were partly influenced by his delight in reading "Rickover, Shippingport and Civilian Nuclear Power," *Nuclear Engineering International* (Dec. 1986):22-24, written by "two of his [Rickover's] former trainees."

2. Murray, *Nuclear Policy for War and Peace*, 157-60. For a technical history on Shippingport by NR, Westinghouse Bettis, and Duquesne Light Company personnel, see AEC, *The Shippingport Pressurized Water Reactor* (Reading, Massachusetts: Addison-Wesley Publishing Company, Inc., 1958).

3. Utilities' misunderstanding of the complexity of nuclear power is covered from an anti-nuclear perspective in James M. Jasper, *Nuclear Politics: Energy and the State in the United States, Sweden, and France* (Princeton, New Jersey: Princeton University Press, 1990), 62.

4. Dawson, *Nuclear Power*, 93-96. After gaining authorization powers, the JCAE reviewed all AEC programs in annual hearings. For example, see JCAE, *AEC Authorizing Legislation, FY 1963*, hearings, 9 July -15 Oct. 1963, 88th Cong., 2nd sess. (Wash., D.C.: GPO, 1963).

5. Dawson, *Nuclear Power*, 98-100. The annual *AEC Authorizing Legislation* hearing records often contained certain AEC reports/correspondence to the JCAE and other material as appendices.

6. MS/RWD, 1992. Dyke, *Mr. Atomic Energy*, 129-31, gives multiple reasons for Gore-Holifield.

7. See *Accelerating Civilian Reactor Program*, 4, 7; Dyke, *Mr. Atomic Energy*, 129, 339 n. 1. Minority report is in *Amending the Atomic Energy Act of 1946*, 105-138. Conf. minority rept. is in Box 79 (August 9, 1954, Statement, Melvin Price and Chet Holifield, Re: Atomic Energy Legislation), HP.

8. CH/FXG; Unna, "Atomic Energy," 27.

9. The original bill (S. 2725/H.R. 10805) is in JCAE, *Accelerating Civilian Reactor Program*, 1-3. The revised version is in JCAE, *Civilian Atomic Power Acceleration Program*, 2-3.

10. JCAE, *Civilian Atomic Power Acceleration Program*, 10.

11. CH/FXG; Green and Rosenthal, *Government of the Atom*, 135-36, 153-56.

12. CH/FXG; 4 July 1956, *Congressional Record*, 84th Cong., 2nd sess., vol. 102, 14276-286.

13. 17 July 1956, *Congressional Record*, 84th Cong., 2nd sess., vol. 102, 13195-99; CH, "The United States Must Lead in Atomic Power Development," typescript, 17 July 1956, 10-11, Box 79 (July 17, 1956, Press Release, "The United States Must Lead in Atomic Power Development"), HP.

14. 24 July 1956, *Congressional Record*, vol. 102, 14288; Green and Rosenthal, *Government of the Atom*, 155; 26 July 1956, *Congressional Record*, vol. 102, 14889-91; 27 July 1956, *Congressional Record*, vol. 102, 15454. A reprint of CH's 27 July 1956 speech, "Holifield Bill for Peacetime Atomic Power," is in Box 79 (July 27, 1956, Speech--Floor, "Holifield Bill for Peacetime Atomic Power"), HP.

15. See Green and Rosenthal, *Government of the Atom*, 152 n. 89.

16. CH's minority report is reprinted in 14 July 1956, *Congressional Record*, vol. 102, 14263. See also Mazuzan and Walker, *Controlling the Atom*, 209-11; Dawson, *Nuclear Power*, 128-30.

17. Dawson, *Nuclear Power*, 100-101; Green and Rosenthal, *Government of the Atom*, 258.

18. JCAE, *Congressional Review of Atomic Power Program*, hearings, 23 May and 10 June 1957, 85th Cong., 1st sess. (Wash., D.C.: GPO, 1957), 10; Green and Rosenthal, *Government of the Atom*, 176-77.

19. Green and Rosenthal, *Government of the Atom*, 175-80, 258; Dawson, *Nuclear Power*, 108.

20. Dyke, *Mr. Atomic Energy*, 265.

21. CH/FXG.

22. Conway/FXG, with additional HBA input to RWD.

23. Green and Rosenthal, *Government of the Atom*, 180-90; Dyke, *Mr. Atomic Energy*, 155-160; Dawson, *Nuclear Power*, 108-109, 114-15.

24. JCAE, *Proposed Expanded Civilian Nuclear Power Program*, 85th Cong., 1st sess. (Washington, D.C.: GPO, Aug. 1958), especially 4, 9.

25. CH used status data routinely included in hearings. 1970 data is in *Nuclear Reactors Built, or Planned in the United States* (as of 31 Dec. 1969), Appendix 4 of *AEC Authorizing Legislation, FY 1971--Part 3*, 11 Mar. 1970, 91st Cong., 2nd sess. (Washington, D.C.: GPO, 1970), 1572-1605.

26. The Ten-Year Plan, *Civilian Power Reactor Program--Plans for Development* (16 Feb. 1960), is in Appendix II of JCAE Subcommittee on Legislation, *AEC Authorizing Legislation, FY 1961*, hearings, 8 Mar. - 7 Apr. 1960, 86th Cong., 2nd sess. (Washington, D.C.: GPO, 1960), 474-89. See also Green and Rosenthal, *Government of the Atom*, 141-42, 151.

27. Mazuzan and Walker, *Controlling the Atom*, 407-426, devote their last chapter (XIV) to "Watershed: The 1962 Report to the President." See 408 for CH's reaction to the FY 1963 administration budget proposal. See also Green and Rosenthal, *Government of the Atom*, 264.

28. Mazuzan and Walker, *Controlling the Atom*, 407.

29. CH to Kennedy, 21 Feb. 1961 and 13 Feb. 1962, in Mazuzan and Walker, *Controlling the Atom*, 408, 410, who use letters from Kennedy Papers. HP copies could not be located.

30. Mazuzan and Walker, *Controlling the Atom*, 408-11; Green and Rosenthal, *Government of the Atom*, 264-65.

31. Dawson, *Nuclear Power*, 135; Mazuzan and Walker, *Controlling the Atom*, 414-15.

32. Mazuzan and Walker, *Controlling the Atom*, 412. Entire 1962 report is AEC, *Civilian Nuclear Power--A Report to the President--1962* (Washington, D.C.: GPO, 20 Nov. 1962).

33. Mazuzan and Walker, *Controlling the Atom*, 413, 416. They call the 1962 report "a milestone in the early history of nuclear development." (418) See also Dawson, *Nuclear Power*, 133, 135.

34. See Dawson, *Nuclear Power*, 133.

35. The JCAE hearings on the 1962 report are *AEC Authorizing Legislation, FY 1964*, hearings, 20-21 Feb. and 2-5 Apr. 1963, 88th Cong., 1st sess. (Washington, D.C.: GPO, 1962).

36. Mazuzan and Walker, *Controlling the Atom*, 416. Dyke, *Mr. Atomic Energy*, 265, posits that "Holifield could not have asked a more prominent authority to state in clearer terms what amounted to his own recommendations and program."

37. AEC, *Civilian Nuclear Power--The 1967 Supplement to the 1962 Report to the President* (Wash., D.C.: GPO, Feb. 1967). An "advance copy" is in JCAE, *AEC Authorizing Legislation, FY 1968--Part 2*, hearings, 14-15 Mar. 1967, 90th Cong., 1st sess. (Wash., D.C.: GPO, 1967), Appendix 8, 1149-1206.

38. Dante Fascell/FXG.

39. JCAE, *AEC Authorizing Legislation, FY 1967--Part 2*, hearings, 16 Feb. - 16 Mar. 1966, 89th Cong., 2nd sess. (Washington, D.C.: GPO, 1966), 633-54, especially 633-38.

40. Ibid., 638.

41. John W. Simpson/FXG.

42. Ibid.

43. Ibid.

44. Ibid.

45. CH/FXG.

46. JCAE, *AEC Authorizing Legislation, FY 1970--Part 2*, hearings, 24-25 Apr. 1969, 91st Cong., 1st sess. (Washington, D.C.: GPO, 1969), 983-992. Many reports provide data on plants planned, ordered, and built. For example, see Appendix 10 of JCAE, *Development, Growth and State of the Nuclear Industry*, special hearings, 5-6 Feb. 1974, 93rd Cong., 2nd sess. (Wash., D.C.: GPO, 1974), 489-602.

47. Los Angeles Chamber of Commerce, "Holifield Sees Nuclear Power Breakthrough," *Southern California Business* 27 Dec. 1965, 1, Box 43 (1965), HP; CH/FXG, CH-HBA input to RWD.

48. CH, "Remarks by Congressman Chet Holifield, Vice Chairman, JCAE at Groundbreaking of San Onofre Nuclear Power Plant, Camp Pendleton, San Diego, CA, Oct. 9, 1964." CH was the keynote speaker. This speech is in CH's personal bound copies of his speeches (*Chet Holifield Speeches, 1964-1965*, vol. IV, 22-28), and could not be found in Box 81, HP, covering 1962-1966 speeches.

49. Ibid.

50. John W. Simpson/FXG.

51. CH-MS discussions with FXG/RWD. See also JCAE, *AEC Authorizing Legislation, FY 1972--1972, Part 2*, hearing, 4 Mar. 1971, 92nd Cong., 1st sess. (Wash., D.C.: GPO, 1971), 595-612.

52. CH-MS discussions with FXG and RWD, with additional CH-HBA input to RWD.

53. Ibid.

54. Ibid. In CH/Douglass, vol. 3, 87, CH notes early intertwining of promotion and regulation.

55. CH-MS discussions with FXG and RWD, with additional CH-HBA input to RWD.

56. MS covered 12 factors in 1966-73 hearings; For samples, see JCAE, *AEC Authorizing Legislation, FY 1970--Part 2*, 975-1020 (esp. 1017); *FY 1968--Part 2*, 695-713, 756-764, 768-772, 788-789.

57. JCAE, *AEC Authorizing Legislation, FY 1970--Part 2*, 1018.

58. Ali B. Cambel, et. al., *Energy R&D and National Progress* (Washington, D.C.: GPO, 1965), was prepared for Steering Committee of the Interdepartmental Energy Study in response to a 15 Feb. 1963 directive from JFK. On govt./lab roles, *AEC Authorizing Legislation, FY 1967--Part 2*, 634-642, 644-655.

59. JCAE, *AEC Authorizing Legislation, FY 1967--Part 2*, 635.

60. Ibid.

61. CH-MS discussions with FXG.

62. CH-MS discussions with FXG and RWD, with additional CH-HBA input to RWD. For example, background information including AEC analytical and assessment documents on priorities of reactor concepts, see JCAE, *AEC Authorizing Legislation, FY 1970--Part 2*, 1029-1032, 1035-1073.

63. CH-MS discussions with FXG and RWD, with CH-HBA input to RWD, much of which was based on discussions in JCAE hearings 1965-1974. For example, see JCAE, *AEC Authorizing Legislation, FY 1972--Part 2*, 654-670, 759-777; JCAE, *AEC Authorizing Legislation, FY 1967--Part 2*, 634-654, 695-742, 798-820, 996-1002; JCAE, *AEC Authorizing Legislation, FY 1970--Part 2*, 277-280, 295-303.

64. MS discussions with FXG and RWD, with additional CH-HBA input to RWD.

65. Quoted in "'Toughness' Wins at the AEC," *Electrical World*, 174 (1 Dec. 1970):25.

66. Ibid., 25-26.

67. CH to R. B. Duffield, 24 June 1970, is in *AEC Authorizing Legislation, FY 1972--Part 2*, 656.

68. JCAE, *AEC Authorizing Legislation, FY 1973--Part 2*, 1149.

Chapter 11: Refining the Nuclear Enterprise

1. CH, "The Nation's Stake in Atomic Power," typescript speech, 25 Apr. 1961, 3, Box 80 (April 25, 1961, Speech--American Public Power Association, "The Nation's Stake in Atomic Power"), HP. CH's JCAE Special Subcommittee on Radiation held first hearings on nuclear waste disposal: *Industrial Radioactive Waste Disposal*, 28 Jan. - 3 Feb. 1959, 86th Cong., 1st sess. (Wash., D.C.: GPO, 1959).

2. MS discussions with FXG and RWD. Also relevant is Babcock and Wilcox (B&W), *Steam: Its Generation and Use*, provided by B&W, 161 East 42nd Street, New York, NY 10017.

3. On blackout, see CH, "Civilian Nuclear Power," typescript speech, Dec. 1965, 4, Box 81 (Dec. 1965 Speech--L. A. Chamber of Commerce, "Civilian Nuclear Power"), HP; CH, "Power and Policy," typescript speech, 15 Feb. 1971, 1-4, Box 84 (Nat. Rural Electric Cooperative Assn., Dallas, Feb. 15, 1971), HP; JCAE, *Licensing and Regulation of Nuclear Reactors*, hearings, 12-14 Sept. 1967, 90th Cong., 1st sess. (Washington, D.C.: GPO, 1968), 514; *AEC Authorizing Legislation, FY 1970--Part 2*, 981.

4. CH, "Radiation Hazards and the Public Interest," typescript speech, 27 Feb. 1957, 1, Box 80 (Speech--AFL-CIO Conference, "Radiation Hazards and the Public Interest"), HP.

5. CH, "The Nation's Stake in Atomic Power," 25 Apr. 1961, 3.

6. CH, "Radiation Hazards and the Public Interest," 27 Feb. 1957, 5.

7. MS/FXG; MS/RWD. Concerns on industry capabilities and potential to meet stringent safety standards were covered in almost all JCAE authorization hearings, 1965-1974. For example, see JCAE, *AEC Authorizing Legislation, FY 1970--Part 2*, 847-871, 975-762, and Appendixes 2, 3, and 4, 1490-1608.

8. CH/RWD, 8 Feb. 1982; Green and Rosenthal, *Government of the Atom*, 107; Harold L. Nieburg, *Nuclear Secrecy and Foreign Policy* (Washington, D.C.: Public Affairs Press, 1964), 55. CH refers to Ramey **(hereafter JTR)** as "a longtime personal friend" in Unna, "Atomic Energy," 18. In CH/Douglass, vol. 1, 66, he details JTR's experience and notes that he recommended him for AEC post.

9. JTR/FXG. In 1968, without advising JTR, CH worked out a deal with LBJ. JTR was finishing his first term, and LBJ's withdrawal from the 1968 race meant the Democrats might lose the election and JTR, up for reappointment to a partial term, might be forced out. To prevent this, CH arranged for Seaborg, whose term was also ending, to get the partial term. JTR was given the five-year term, to 1973, in exchange for a promise to LBJ to serve a full term. JTR remained until 1973, when Nixon chose not to reappoint him. (CH/FXG, CH-HBA input to RWD; Unna, "Atomic Energy," 18.)

10. CH/FXG; JTR/FXG.

11. MS/RWD, May 1991. Secretaries of the Navy were John Connolly, Fred Korth, and Paul Nitze.

12. MS, "AEC Views on Quality Assurance in the Civilian Reactor Program," Pittsburgh, PA, 2 Nov. 1966, reprinted in JCAE, *AEC Authorizing Legislation, FY 1968--Part 2*, Appendix 13, 1296-1303. JTR's companion speech, "Quality Assurance as a Matter of Public Policy in the Safety of Atomic Power Plants," is reprinted in Appendix 12, 1287-95. MS reiterates his views in JCAE, *Authorizing Legislation, FY 1974*, hearings, 93rd Cong., 1st sess. (Washington, D.C.: GPO, 1974), 1722.

13. JCAE, *AEC Authorizing Legislation, FY 1968--Part 2*, 762.

14. CH communications with FXG.

15. Ibid. CH participated in special JCAE hearings, *The Loss of the USS THRESHER*, 88th Cong., 1st and 2nd sess., 26-27 Jan. and 23 July 1963, and July 1964 (Washington, D.C.: GPO, 1963-1964).

16. Wallace B. Behnke/FXG, with additional Behnke input to RWD.

17. CH/FXG; JTR/FXG; MS/FXG. See JCAE, *AEC Authorizing Legislation, FY 1968--Part 2*, 763-64, 777, and *AEC Authorizing Legislation, FY 1970--Part 2*, 860-61 for similar CH and MS views.

18. CH/FXG; JTR/FXG; MS/FXG. See also *AEC Authorizing Legislation, FY 1968--Part 2*, 756-58.

19. CH/FXG, CH-HBA input to RWD; JTR/FXG; MS/FXG. CH notes "the 'defense in depth' approach adopted in nuclear engineering" in CH, "Civilian Nuclear Power," Dec. 1965, 4.

20. AEC, *Civilian Nuclear Power--The 1967 Supplement to the 1962 Report to the President*, 3.

21. Ibid., 3-4; CH/FXG.

22. Written commentary updated and clarified for RWD by HBA [October 1992].

23. Behnke/FXG, later Behnke input via HBA to RWD.

24. Quotes in 5 previous paragraphs are from Behnke/FXG, later Behnke input via HBA to RWD.

25. CH/FXG, CH-HBA input to RWD; JCAE, *AEC Authorizing Legislation, FY 1970--Part 2*, 847-871, 975-762; *AEC Authorizing Legislation, FY 1972--Part 2*, 561-670.

26. CH/FXG, with CH-HBA input to RWD; Rolph, *Nuclear Power and the Public Safety*, 70, 101-103; JCAE, *AEC Authorizing Legislation, FY 1970--Part 2*, 863-864. CH, Ramey, and MS were very frank in hearings. See CH in *AEC Authorizing Legislation, FY 1967--Part 2*, 636. See Ramey in *AEC Authorizing Legislation, FY 1974*, 1714. See MS in *AEC Authorizing Legislation, FY 1968--Part 2*, 762, 769, 778; *AEC Authorizing Legislation, FY 1969--Part 1*, hearings, 30 Jan. - 6 Feb. 1968, 90th Cong., 2nd sess. (Washington, D.C.: GPO, 1968), 81; and *AEC Authorizing Legislation, FY 1968--Part 2*, 776.

27. CH/FXG. CH compared nuclear, fossil, and coal power in JCAE, *Environmental Effects of Producing Electric Power--Part 1*, hearings, 28 Oct. - 7 Nov. 1969, 91st Cong., 1st sess. (Wash., D.C.: GPO, 1969), and *Part 2 (Vols. I and II)*, hearings, 27 Jan. - 26 Feb. 1970, 91st Cong., 2nd sess. (Wash., D.C.: GPO, 1970). CH also provided discussions in CH to Miss Laura Burts, 1 Nov. 1970, Box 22 (Pollution--1970); CH to Mr. T.V. Arredondo, 13 June 1972, Box 49 (JCAE Outgoing Correspondence [Blue Copies] 1972); and CH to Senator Lee Metcalf, 27 May 1969, Box 47 (Thermal Pollution), HP.

28. CH, "Important Factors in Power Planning for the Future," typescript speech, Los Angeles, CA, 4 May 1965, 7. Copy used is vol. IV (1964-1965), *Chet Holifield Speeches*, CH's personal library.

29. Passage could not be found; For example of EEI's very frequent testimony at JCAE hearings, see the special hearing in Dec. 1971, on *Nuclear Power and Related Energy Problems--1968 through 1970*.

30. Dyke, *Mr. Atomic Energy*, 81, notes that CH "leaned philosophically toward the public power persuasion." See also 92-93, 100-104, 109, 117, 119, 127-29, 134-35, 140-45, 148, 150-63, 165-67, 175-76.

31. CH, "The Nation's Stake in Atomic Power," 25 Apr. 1961, 7.

32. See JCAE, *Participation by Small Electrical Utilities in Nuclear Power--Parts 1 and 2*, hearings, 30 Apr. - 3 May 1968 and 11-13 June 1968, 90th Cong., 2nd sess. (Washington, D.C.: GPO, 1968).

33. CH covers Public Law 91-560 (1970 amendments) in "Power and Policy," 15 Feb. 1971, 5-6.

34. CH/FXG; MS/FXG; MS/RWD. The 20% is influenced heavily by plants of TVA and WPPSS.

35. CH/FXG; JCAE, *AEC Authorizing Legislation, FY 1970--Part 2*, 920-950, 1029-1033, 1047-1072.

36. CH-MS discussions with FXG and RWD, and subsequent CH-HBA input to RWD.

37. Ibid.

38. Ibid. By the 1950s, House members did 85-90% of JCAE work. (CH/Douglass, vol. 2, 106.)

39. CH-MS discussions with FXG and RWD, and subsequent CH-HBA input to RWD.

40. Ibid. In Unna, "Atomic Energy," 15-16, CH noted killing, as well as promoting, many projects.

41. CH/FXG; MS/FXG, 1985-1988.

42. Edward J. Bauser/FXG. In CH/Douglass, vol. 1, 66, CH called former Navy Captain Bauser "one of the most brilliant and most dedicated and loyal men that I have ever known."

43. Ibid.

44. CH/FXG; Unna, "Atomic Energy," 15. For other cancellations, see JCAE, *AEC Authorizing Legislation, FY 1965--Part 2*, hearings, 5 Feb.-4 Mar. 1964, 88th Cong., 2nd sess. (GPO, 1964), 411.

45. CH/FXG.

46. CH-JTR-MS discussions with FXG-RWD; *AEC Authorizing Legislation, FY 1971--Part 3*, 1154.

47. CH/FXG, MS/FXG, MS/RWD, with later CH-MS-HBA input to RWD. See status charts in JCAE, *AEC Authorizing Legislation, FY 1970--Part 2*, 847-871, 975-1020; *AEC Authorizing Legislation, FY 1972--Part 2*, 590-640, especially 595 for MS's "12 factors." See also Dawson, *Nuclear Power*, 146-47.

48. CH communications with FXG. Printed source for quote could not be found.

49. Ibid.

50. CH noted industry chose LWRs based on "commercial factors." (L.A. Chamber of Commerce, "Holifield Sees Nuclear Power Breakthrough," HP.) See also JCAE, *AEC Authorizing Legislation, FY 1973--Part 2*, hearings, 22-23 Feb. 1972, 92nd Cong., 2nd sess., (Wash., D.C.: GPO, 1972), 1137-1149.

51. See JCAE, *AEC Authorizing Legislation, FY 1969--Part 1*, hearings, 30 Jan.- 6 Feb. 1968, 90th Cong., 2nd sess. (Washington, D.C.: GPO, 1968), 123-130, 269-274, and hearing indexes to 1975.

52. CH-MS input to FXG-RWD, later CH-HBA input to RWD; JCAE, *AEC Authorizing Legislation, FY 1973--Part 2*, 1134-1142; "Holifield Calls for Caution in Reactor Licensing," *Nucleonics*, 24 (July 1966):17; "Holifield Outlines Views on Major Policy Questions," *Nuclear Industry*, 13 (June 1966):29-37; CH, "Recent Developments ... in Atomic Power," 8 June 1966, Box 81 (Speech--Edison Electric Institute, "Recent Developments and Future Challenges in Atomic Power"), HP.

53. CH/FXG, augmented by RWD, and MS-CH discussions in Nov. 1989 later provided to RWD.

54. The FPC estimate of 7% annual elect. growth is in JCAE, *AEC Authorizing Legislation, FY 1972--Part 2*, 556. On energy crisis, see JCAE, *AEC Authorizing Legislation, FY 1974*, 1718-19.

55. Elizabeth S. Rolph, *Nuclear Power and the Public Safety: A Study in Regulation* (Lexington, Massachusetts: Lexington Books, 1979), 62-63, 71, 91, 1002-103, 139. Among the major antinuclear works were Richard S. Lewis, *Nuclear-Power Rebellion* (New York: The Viking Press, 1972); H. P. Metzger, *The Atomic Power Establishment* (New York: Simon and Schuster, 1972); R. Curtis and E. Hogan, *Perils of the Peaceful Atom* (Garden City, New York: Doubleday & Co. Inc., 1969); and R. Nader and J. Abbotts, *The Menace of Atomic Energy* (New York: W. Norton and Co., 1977).

56. CH, MS, and FXG discussions, later CH-HBA to RWD. For samples of CH concerns, see JCAE, *AEC Authorizing Legislation, FY 1967--Part 2*, 654-718; *AEC Authorizing Legislation, FY 1968--Part 2*, 701-728, 767-791, 838-876; and JCAE, *AEC Authorizing Legislation, FY 1971--Part 3*, 1142-1190.

57. CH discussions with FXG. Source of this quote could not be located.

58. JTR/FXG.

59. Rolph, *Nuclear Power and the Public Safety*, 152, notes March 1973 for AEC 1,300 Mwe limit.

60. Communications/comments by HBA to RWD.

61. Rolph, *Nuclear Power and the Public Safety*, 152.

62. HBA input to RWD; Sweet, *The Nuclear Age*, 19; Jasper, *Nuclear Politics*, 117.

63. CH/FXG; MS/FXG.

64. CH/FXG.

Chapter 12: Toward Distant Horizons

1. Hewlett and Duncan, *Atomic Shield*, 29-30.

2. Ibid., 216-17, 497-98; Dawson, *Nuclear Power*, 42, 83-84, 88.

3. See Dawson, *Nuclear Power*, 88-89, EBR-II. See also CH's 1965 speech files, Box 81 (Speech--Dedication of EBR II) and Box 81 (Speech--Start-of-Construction Ceremonies for SEFOR Reactor), and 1969 speech file, Box 83 (Speech--Dedication of SEFOR Reactor), HP.

4. JCAE, *AEC Authorizing Legislation, FY 1971--Part 3*, 1317-18, 1418. For JCAE/AEC exchanges on alternate breeder studies, see JCAE, *AEC Authorizing Legislation, FY 1969--Part 1*, 132-141.

5. HBA input to FXG and RWD. For a summary on fast breeders, see James J. Pickard, *Nuclear Power Reactors* ("Geneva Series of the Peaceful Uses of Atomic Energy"; New York: D. Van Nostrand

Company, Inc., 1957), 310-374. See also John G. Yevick, *Fast Reactor Technology, Plant Design* (Cambridge, Massachusetts: MIT Press, Mar. 1966), and British Nuclear Energy Society, *Proceedings of the London Conference on Fast Breeder Reactors* (London: Pergamon Press, May 1966). On LMFBR, see Hewlett and Duncan, *Atomic Shield*, 29-30, 115, 206, 493-94.

6. Mazuzan and Walker, *Controlling the Atom*, 122-82. On Murray's leaks to JCAE, see 136-38.

7. Mazuzan and Walker, *Controlling the Atom*, 144, partially quote CH's 4 Aug. 1956 press release, Box 79 (Press Release, Re: Issuance of Construction Permit for Reactor at Monroe, Michigan), HP. See also Rolph, *Nuclear Power and the Public Safety*, 39-42; Dawson, *Nuclear Power*, 194.

8. CH/FXG; CH/RWD. USSR's BN-350 and France's Phoenix are discussed in JCAE, *AEC Authorizing Legislation, FY 1971--Part 3*, 1265-1266, 1268-1269 and noted in JCAE, *AEC Authorizing Legislation, FY 1972--Part 2*, 554 (Figure 5). For government role in energy R&D, see Ali B. Cambel, et. al., *Energy R&D and National Progress* (Washington, D.C.; GPO, 1965), 29-43. On govt./laboratory roles and capabilities, see *AEC Authorizing Legislation, FY 1967--Part 2*, 634-642, 644-655.

9. CH/FXG. For similar views, see 17 July 1956, *Congressional Record*, 84th Cong., 2nd sess., vol. 102, 13195-99; "Why LMFBR Now? Presentation by Congressman Chet Holifield of California," *The Time is Now*, publication by Westinghouse, [1971], 5, Box 48 (Fast Breeder Reactor 1971), HP.

10. For characteristics of the breeder, see Energy Research and Development Administration, *Final Environmental Statement of the Liquid Metal Fast Breeder Reactor Program*, (Washington, D.C.: GPO, Dec. 1975), ERDA-1535, 3 vols. See also Dawson, *Nuclear Power*, 151-67.

11. CH/FXG, CH-HBA input to RWD. On pros and cons of breeder development, see Annex, A-1 to 153 of AEC, *Environmental Statement, Liquid Metal Fast Breeder Reactor Demonstration Plant* (Wash., D.C.: GPO, Apr. 1972), WASH-1509, and *Final Environmental Statement of the Liquid Metal Fast Breeder Reactor Program*, (Wash., D.C.: GPO, Dec. 1975), ERDA-1535, IV, A-1 to C-36.

12. CH/FXG, with CH-HBA input to RWD. Jasper, *Nuclear Politics*, 51, notes that "In 1964 Milton Shaw became the AEC's director of reactor development, *with a mandate to develop a strong government program similar to Hyman Rickover's project on the submarine reactor*." (Emphasis added.)

13. Ibid. For MS on Navy/civilian differences: *AEC Authorizing Legislation, FY 1968--Part 2*, 557.

14. For MS on RDT centralization effort, see for example, JCAE, *AEC Authorizing Legislation, FY 1968--Part 2*, 758-69; *AEC Authorizing Legislation, FY 1967--Part 2*, 633-48; and *Authorizing Legislation, FY 1974--Part 3*, hearing, 14 Mar. 1973, 93rd Cong., 2nd sess. (Washington, D.C.: GPO, 1974), 1725.

15. CH/FXG; CH-HBA input to RW.

16. CH/FXG; CH/RWD; MS/FXG; MS/RWD.

17. CH, Price, Conway, and Bauser interviews and input to FXG and RWD.

18. MS/FXG; MS/RWD. See also JCAE, *AEC Authorizing Legislation, FY 1967--Part 2*, 653.

19. MS interview/conversations with RWD and written comments to RWD.

20. CH/FXG, with additional CH-HBA input to RWD.

21. MS and Crawford conversations with FXG and RWD, and HBA written comments to RWD.

22. For examples where breeder objectives are included/amplified, see Argonne National Laboratory Program Office, *Element 1 - Overall Plan of RDT's LMFBR Program Plan, Introduction* (Washington, D.C.: GPO), WASH-1101, 1; JCAE, *AEC Authorizing Legislation, FY 1967--Part 2*, Chart 37, 719; Enclosure 1 of *AEC Invitation for Proposals, Fourth Round, the LMFBR Demonstration Plant Program*; in AEC, *LMFBR Demonstration Plant Program, Proceedings of Senior Utility Steering Committee and Senior Utility Technical Advisory Panel for the LMFBR Demonstration Plant Program, April 1971 Through January 1972*, WASH-1201, 43-54; and on RDT Chart 21-RDT-228, briefing book.

23. MS/FXG; MS/RWD. For LMFBR Program Plan (1967-1968), see Appendix 17 of JCAE, *AEC Authorizing Legislation, FY 1969--Part 1*, 521-628. The plan became AEC Reports WASH-1101 through WASH-1110. An updated edition was completed in December 1973.

24. CH/FXG, CH-HBA input to RWD; JCAE, *AEC Authorizing Legislation, FY 1967--Part 2*, 642-46, for MS's discussion of ANL actions. CH declared "A central depository of power to manage and make decisions is imperative." He added: "The breeder reactor can not be constructed by a committee. This approach killed the Bolsa Chica power-desalting project in Southern California." (CH to Admiral Lewis L. Strauss, 11 June 1971, Box 48 [JCAE Outgoing Correspondence (Blue Copies) 1971], HP.)

25. CH/FXG, CH-HBA input to RWD; MS and Crawford discussions with FXG, subsequent input to RWD. See JCAE, *AEC Authorizing Legislation, FY 1967--Part 2*, 634, re cancellation of FARET.

26. CH, Bauser, and MS meetings with FXG, later input to RWD; MS conversations with RWD. See also JCAE, *AEC Authorizing Legislation, FY 1971--Part 3*, 1376-1396, 1399-1408.

27. CH/FXG, JTR/FXG, and MS/FXG, later HBA input to RWD.

28. CH/FXG and MS/FXG, with subsequent CH-HBA input to RWD.

29. Ibid. For examples, MS reported on FFTF in JCAE, *AEC Authorizing Legislation, FY 1968--Part 2*, 759, 766 (see chart especially), 769; *AEC Authorizing Legislation, FY 1969--Part 1*, 78-81; *AEC Authorizing Legislation, FY 1971--Part 3*, 1211-1243, 1273-1291, 1446-1451.

30. CH/FXG, CH-HBA input to RWD.

31. Concerns about FFTF were discussed often in hearings. For example, see JCAE, *AEC Authorizing Legislation, FY 1971--Part 3*, 1273-1275, 1275-1292, 1376-1380, 1391-1408.

32. CH/FXG, CH-HBA input to RWD.

33. Ibid.; MS input to RWD, 1991.

34. MS/FXG; MS-HBA input to RWD; *AEC Authorizing Legislation, FY 1972--Part 2*, 654-670.

35. MS/FXG, HBA comments to RWD. MS praised both Kintner and Evans for "an outstanding fuel effort" in JCAE, *AEC Authorizing Legislation, FY 1972--Part 2*, 775.

36. JCAE, *AEC Authorizing Legislation, FY 1970--Part 2*, 1159.

37. See JCAE, *AEC Authorizing Legislation, FY 1968--Part 2*, 768, for MS's comments.

38. HBA input to FXG and RWD. The role and other important information about the FFTF are provided in JCAE, *AEC Authorizing Legislation, FY 1968--Part 2*, 766-777.

39. "'Toughness' Wins at AEC," *Electrical World* 174 (1 Dec. 1970):25. MS's white paper was a long memorandum, MS to Commissioners Seaborg, Ramey, Johnson, Thompson, and Larson, "Problems in the Conduct of the FFTF Project at PNL," 24 Nov. 1969, provided to RWD from MS's personal files.

40. HBA input to FXG and RWD.

41. Ibid.; "'Toughness' Wins at AEC," *Electrical World*.

42. HBA input to FXG and RWD. See summary of RDT strengthening actions at AEC, Hanford and other key organizations in JCAE, *AEC Authorizing Legislation, FY 1973--Part 2*, 1146-49.

43. At every opportunity, CH emphasizes that the breeder **"demonstration plants are a necessary phase in [the] program"** (emphasis CH's) in CH, "Why LMFBR Now?"

44. CH/FXG, CH-HBA input to RWD. CH, "Electrical Energy and Pollution," 4 June 1971, *Congressional Record--House*, 92nd Cong., 1st sess., H4722-28, Box 26 (Presidential Energy Message, June 4, 1971), HP; JCAE, *AEC Authorizing Legislation, FY 1972--Part 4*, 3261-72.

45. CH/FXG, CH-HBA input to RWD. See also several JCAE *Authorizing Legislation* hearings, including *FY 1969--Part 1*, 79-89, 123-130, 137-146, 244-291, 521-628; *FY 1970--Part 2*, 1028-1245; and *FY 1971--Part 3*, 1202-1275, 1351-1358, 1375-1380, 1390-1419. See also AEC, *LMFBR Demonstration Plant Program, Proceedings of Senior Utility Steering Committee and Senior Utility Technical Advisory Panel for the Period April 1971 Through January 1972* (WASH-1201).

46. See JCAE, *AEC Authorizing Legislation, FY 1970--Part 2*, especially 1073-74, 1085-88.

47. CH/FXG, CH-HBA input to RWD; JCAE, *AEC Authorizing Legislation, FY 1970--Part 2*, 1088; JCAE, *AEC Authorizing Legislation, FY 1967--Part 2*, 971-1002. The 15-16 Mar. 1966 testimony was not a formal "Section 202" hearing, and in fact became part of the FY 1967 hearings (see 821-1002).

48. CH/FXG, CH-HBA input to RWD.

49. CH, "The 1970s--A Critical Era in Nuclear Power," speech typescript, 3 Dec. 1969, 3-4, Box 83 (Speech--Atomic Industrial Forum, "The 1970's--A Critical Era in Nuclear Power), HP. FXG inverted the last 2 paragraphs for dramatic effect. Several 1-sentence paragraphs are also combined.

50. CH, "The Need for a Comprehensive Energy Program," speech typescript, 18 Nov. 1970, 1, Box 83 (American Nuclear Society, Atomic Industrial Forum, November 18, 1970), HP.

51. JCAE, *Environmental Effects of Producing Electric Power--Part 2 (Vol. I)*, (see Ch. 11, n. 31), 1480; CH, "Electrical Energy and Pollution," H4722. CH sat in about 200 sets of hearings, many on the power industry. His and others' concerns led to the interagency study under S. David Freeman of the Office of Science and Technology, *Considerations Affecting Steam Power Plant Site Selection*, published Dec. 1968. See JCAE, *AEC Authorizing Legislation, FY 1970--Part 2*, 871-875; AEC, *Current Status and Future Technical and Economic Potential of Light Water Reactors*, WASH-1082, June 1967.

52. Unna, "Nixon," 3-4. CH has slightly revised this passage for clarity.

53. Ibid., 3; CH/RWD, 20 Feb. 1984.

54. CH/FXG, CH-HBA input to RWD.

55. CH input to FXG, with additional CH-HBA comments and input to RWD, 1991.

56. Paul McCracken to Glenn Seaborg, 8 Oct. 1970, provided to RWD from MS's personal files.

57. Seaborg to McCracken, 30 Oct. 1970, provided to RWD from MS's personal files.

58. CH/FXG, CH-HBA input to RWD.

59. CH recalled his plane trip in CH/FXG; CH/RWD, 20 Feb. 1984; Unna, "Nixon"; and CH/Douglass, vol. 2, 145-51. The quoted passage, edited for increased clarity and understanding by CH, is based on CH's original spoken comments in Unna, "Nixon," 4.

60. Unna, "Nixon," 4-5, slightly revised by CH and HBA for clarity.

61. Ibid., 5, substantially revised (and corrected) by CH and HBA for clarity.

62. Ibid., 5; CH/RWD, 20 Feb. 1984.

63. CH/FXG; CH/RWD; MS/FXG; MS/RWD.

64. Unna, "Nixon," 6; CH/FXG, with additional CH-HBA input to RWD.

65. Unna, "Nixon," 6-7; CH/FXG, JTR/FXG, and MS/FXG, with later CH-HBA input to RWD.

66. See 4 June 1971, *Congressional Record--House*, 92nd Cong., 1st sess., H4715-19, Box 26 (Presidential Energy Message, June 4, 1971), HP, for Nixon speech. See also JCAE, *AEC Authorizing Legislation, FY 1972--Part 4,* 3261-72. CH feels less that Nixon betrayed nuclear power than became side-tracked (Watergate) and made bad appointments, such as Ray. (CH/FXG; CH/RWD.) CH told Unna, however, that Nixon "fouled it up" by over-emphasizing industry's role. The breeder was killed in Ronald Reagan's term, although Reagan had long urged "that every effort be made to advance the technology of the breeder concept without delay." ([California] Governor Reagan to "Chet," 24 Mar. 1971, Box 48 [Fast Breeder Reactor 1971], HP.) CH praised LBJ, noting that he "will be honored in future histories for bringing to the attention of the people so dramatically the problems of environmental pollution." (JCAE, *Environmental Effects of Producing Electric Power--Part 1,* 485.)

67. CH/FXG, CH-HBA input to RWD.

68. MS/FXG; MS/RWD. **Members of the Senior Utility Steering Committee included** T. G. Ayers, President, Commonwealth Edison Co.; James Campell, President, Consumers Power Co.; E. K. Davis, Assistant General Manager, Sacramento Municipal Utility District; R. F. Gilkeson, CEO, Philadelphia Electric Co.; J. K. Horton, CEO, Southern California Edison Co.; W. G. Kuhns, President and CEO, General Public Utilities; C. F. Luce, Chairman and Chief Executive, Consolidated Edison Co.; J. M. Nelson, Superintendent, Seattle Department of Lighting; B. B. Parker, Executive Vice President, Duke Power Co.; Byron Price, General Manager, Eugene Water & Electric Co.; S. L. Sibley, President, Pacific Gas & Electric Co.; A. J. Wagner, Chairman, TVA; Frank Warren, President, Portland General Electric Co.; John Madgett, General Manager, Dairyland Power Cooperative; W. D. Crawford*, President, Edison Electric Institute; Alex Radin*, General Manager, American Public Power Association; and R. E. Hollingsworth, General Manager, AEC, Chairman, Steering Committee. **Members of the Senior Utility Technical Advisory Panel included** R. A. Baker, Vice President, Public Service Electric and Gas Co.; W. G. Behnke, Vice President, Commonwealth Edison Co.; W. J. Cahill, Jr., Vice President for Engineering, Consolidated Edison Co.; W. R. Gould, Vice President, Southern California Edison Co.; W. S. Lee III, Vice President, Engineering, Duke Power Co.; Larrey Minnick, Vice President, Yankee Atomic Electric Power Co.; R. C. Nyland, Assistant to Power Manager, Bonneville Power Administration; R. E. Reder, Nuclear Project Administrator, Nebraska Public Power District; A. C. Sugden, Vice President, Long Island Lighting Co.; J. Tillinghast, Executive Vice President, American Electric Power Service Corp.; H. Wagner, Consultant, Detroit Edison Co.; J. Watson, Manager of Power, TVA; Larry Hobart*, Assistant General Manager, American Public Power Association; J. Kearney*, Vice President, Edison Electric Institute; M. Shaw, Director, RDT, AEC, Chairman, Technical Panel; (Note: Names with an asterisk [*] following denote ex-officio members.)

69. Behnke/FXG, with additional Behnke-MS-HBA input to RWD.

70. MS/FXG; MS/RWD. See also AEC, *LMFBR Demonstration Plant Program, Proceedings of Senior Utility Steering Committee and Senior Utility Technical Advisory Panel for the Period April 1971 Through January 1972,* WASH-1201.

71. CH/FXG, CH-HBA input to RWD.

72. CH, "Fast Breeder Reactor Management Team Selected," House floor speech, 19 Jan. 1972, *Congressional Record--House,* H107-H108, Box 49 (Fast Breeder Reactor Speech, Congressional Record,

1-19-72), HP. See also "Commonwealth Edison - TVA Chosen For First Demo," *Nuclear News* (Feb. 1972):24. See also CH press release, 15 Jan. 1971 (*sic*), Box 49 (Fast Breeder Reactor 1972), HP,;

73. MS discussions with FXG and RWD. See also AEC press release, No. P-423, "AEC Highlights 1972," 8 Dec. 1972, Box 49 (Atomic Energy Commission 1972), HP.

74. MS/FXG; MS/RWD. 1972 was pivotal. BRC and PMC were formed, the Clinch River site was selected, Westinghouse was chosen as lead manufacturer, and there were progress hearings in Sept. 1972 and early 1973. See "AEC Highlights 1972"; "Activities and Accomplishments of the Joint Committee on Atomic Energy (1972)," [1973], 5-6, Box 49 (Joint Committee on Atomic Energy 1972); "Summary of Richard H. Sandler's May 1, 1973, Statement on the Contract for the LMFBR Demonstration Plant Project," [1973], Box 49 (Fast Breeder Reactor 1973 #2), HP.

75. CH/FXG, CH-HBA input to RWD. See also JCAE, *Proposed Changes in Basis for Cooperative Arrangement for the LMFBR*, hearings, 28 Feb. and 4 May 1973, 93rd Cong., 1st sess. (Washington, D.C.: GPO, 1973), 6-43.

76. See JCAE, *Proposed Changes in Basis for Cooperative Arrangement for the LMFBR*, 105-107.

77. CH and MS interviews/conversations with FXG and RWD.

78. CH/FXG, CH-HBA input to RWD.

79. The contract was executed in July 1973. (See "U.S. Breeder Program: Forging a Partnership of Strengths - Remarks by Thomas Nemzek, Director, Division of Reactor Research and Development, at the Atomic Industrial Forum Annual Conference, San Francisco, California, November 14, 1973," [title page on AEC press release letterhead], typescript, 3, Box 50 [Fast Breeder Reactor 1974], HP.)

Chapter 13: The Pitfalls of Politics

1. CH/FXG; CH/RWD. In Unna, "Atomic Energy," 31, CH posits that the new scheme was hatched by the oil industry: "the oil boys could have bought at a discount the $2 1/2 billion enrichment plants, upped the price on uranium fuel, and amortized their investment in a short time." For his and others' fears of "another Dixon-Yates," see "Ghost Rattles in Atom Plant Sale Proposal," *Long Beach Independent Press-Telegram*, 7 Dec. 1969, B-2, Box 47 (Uranium Enrichment Facilities 1970), HP, and Unna, "Nuclear Plant Controversy: Nixon's Plan to Sell Enriched Uranium Facilities Arouses Fear of Private Energy Combine," *Washington Post*, 16 Nov. 1969, A-3.

2. Oak Ridge was the first plant. (Hewlett and Anderson, *The New World*, 298-300). See Hewlett and Duncan, *Atomic Shield*, 532, 586 for origins of Portsmouth and Paducah plants. See also Dawson, *Nuclear Power*, 167-69, and AEC press release, No. M-255, "AEC Proceeds to Implement Presidential Decision on Uranium Enrichment," 10 Nov. 1969, 2, Box 47 [Uranium Enrichment Facilities], HP.

3. According to CH, "The [Nixon] administration man in charge was Peter Flanagan, a rich Wall Streeter who had been with the Atomic Institute." (Unna, "Atomic Energy," 29.)

4. Unna, "Atomic Energy," 29-30, edited for readability by CH and HBA. Meaning is unchanged.

5. CH/FXG, CH-HBA input to RWD. See also White House press release, 10 Nov. 1969, and AEC press release no. M-255, both in Box 47 (Uranium Enrichment Facilities), HP.

6. Unna, "Nuclear Plant Controversy: Nixon's Plan to Sell Enriched Uranium Facilities . . . ."

7. Ibid. In "Atoms: Dispute Over Plan to Sell U.S. Plants," *New York Times*, 16 Nov. 1969, Section IV, 6, Dr. Ralph E. Lapp noted that "No one expects the Government to get $2.3 billion for its plants, although this is their replacement cost." See also Robert B. Semple, Jr., "U.S. Plans to Sell Atom Fuel Plants: President Instructs AEC to Pave Way for Move--Value Put at $2 Billion," *New York Times*, 11 Nov. 1969, Section 1, 1 (front page) and Carroll Kilpatrick, "Uranium Plants to be Split From AEC; Nixon Hints Sale," *Washington Post*, 11 Nov. 1969, A-12. In a 8 Oct. 1971 letter to AEC Chairman Schlesinger (Box 49 [International Nuclear Power], HP), CH worried about a possible crisis in meeting foreign commitments for enriched uranium. See also JCAE, *AEC Authorizing Legislation, FY 1972--Part 2*, 589-594, for CH's views.

8. CH, Bauser, and MS conversations with FXG and RWD; "Holifield Condemns Nuclear Plant Plan," *New York Times*, 14 July 1970, Section 1, 27, and Dyke, *Mr. Atomic Energy*, 289-92.

9. MS/FXG; MS/RWD; Sweet, *The Nuclear Age*, 142-44, 185. See Dawson, *Nuclear Power*, 172, and Jasper, *Nuclear Politics*, 119, for the later Alabama gaseous diffusion venture.

10. CH/FXG, CH-HBA input to RWD. CH grilled Lilienthal at the 1963 JCAE "202" hearings. (Mazuzan and Walker, *Controlling the Atom*, 426.) CH notes: "I later summoned him as a witness to explain how his oil dealings in Iran might influence his views on a (*sic*) competitive nuclear power." (Unna, "Atomic Energy," 16.) On other points, see Dyke, *Mr. Atomic Energy*, 45-46, 84-89.

11. CH/FXG, Ink/FXG, and Crawford/FXG, with additional CH-HBA input to RWD.

12. Ibid.; CH/Douglass, vol. 3, 28; Murray, *Nuclear Policy for War and Peace*, 202-207. Murray, 76, 86 notes that he presented his nuclear testing views to the AEC and JCAE. It is unclear if this was when he called for hearings on effects of nuclear war. Murray was aware of AEC intransigence. (201)

13. CH/FXG and Ink/FXG, with additional CH-HBA input to RWD.

14. Ibid. Dawson, *Nuclear Power*, 132, also notes that "his [McCone's] relationship with the JCAE was one of cooperation." See Dyke, *Mr. Atomic Energy*, 260-71, on CH's influence with Kennedy.

15. CH/FXG, with additional CH-HBA input to RWD. Ramey worked well with both Seaborg and CH and JCAE members, and helped smooth relations between the two organizations.

16. Ibid. CH wrote to Treasury Secretary George P. Schultz about rumors that Schlesinger would become CIA head, noting "I sincerely believe that his contribution to our national need can be far more important in the direction of solving our basic electrical energy deficit." CH asked Schultz's help to retain Schlesinger. (CH to Schultz, 7 Dec. 1972, Box 49 [Fast Breeder Reactor 1973], HP.) Schlesinger's first speech before a large industry audience, "Expectations and Responsibilities of the Nuclear Industry," 30 Oct. 1971, conference banquet of the Joint Meeting of the Atomic Industrial Forum and the American Nuclear Society, Bal Harbour, Florida, published as AEC No. S-21-71 (from FXG's files), was blunt and upset many utility executives, but let them know his views on requirements needed for success. Many believed that he effectively followed through on the issues in this speech.

17. CH/FXG, with additional CH-HBA input to RWD.

18. Ibid. In CH/Douglass, vol. 3, 28-29, CH claimed that Ray "made life miserable for all of her commissioners--by withholding information from them, by making decisions and announcing them without consultation with them," and by withholding information necessary "to do a job."

19. Ibid. See also JCAE, *AEC Authorizing Legislation, FY 1974--Part 3*, 1720-23, 1730-46, 1750-54, and Fig. 24, 1745; and Dawson, *Nuclear Power*, 146.

20. CH/FXG, with additional CH-HBA input to RWD.

21. CH/FXG, Melvin Price/FXG, Bauser/FXG, and MS/FXG, with additional CH-HBA input to RWD. The quote is from meeting notes and was placed in preface of final WASH-1250 report, *The Safety of Nuclear Power Reactors (Light Water-Cooled) and Related Facilities*, July 1973.

22. CH, Bauser, and MS interviews/discussions with FXG, with CH-HBA comments to RWD.

23. Ibid.

24. For MS's comments on centralization and engineering excellence, see, for example, JCAE, *AEC Authorizing Legislation, FY 1967--Part 2*, 644, *FY 1972--Part 2*, 599, and *FY 1974--Part 3*, 1722-24.

25. CH/FXG, Bauser/FXG, and MS/FXG, with additional CH-HBA input to RWD. Jasper, *Nuclear Politics*, 53, concedes, as is argued here, that "the conflict [over safety R&D] arose partly from the national labs' organizational interests in continued funding." With his antinuclear bias, however, Jasper is sure the conflict was more about "contrasting assessments of the risk of accidents in LWRs." As examples of cancellations, see JCAE, *AEC Authorizing Legislation, FY 1967--Part 2*, 634.

26. CH/FXG, Bauser/FXG, Reich/FXG, Crawford/FXG, MS/FXG, with CH-HBA input to RWD.

27. JCAE, *AEC Authorizing Legislation, FY 1973--Part 2*, 1217. For liabilities of not satisfying AEC requirements, see JCAE, *AEC Authorizing Legislation, FY 1972--Part 2*, 594-619, and *AEC Authorizing Legislation, FY 1974--Part 3*, 1738-50.

28. CH/FXG, CH-HBA input to RWD.

29. Ibid. Rolph, *Nuclear Power and the Public Safety*, 94, 138, and 141, describes the role played by the Advisory Committee on Reactor Safeguards and environmental intervenors.

30. CH/FXG, with additional CH-HBA input to RWD. There is no printed record, but Gillette notes session in "Nuclear Safety (IV): Barriers to Communication," *Science* 177 (22 Sept. 1972):1082.

31. Schlesinger to Melvin Price, 25 Apr. 1972, provided from FXG's files.

32. See Robert Gillette, "Nuclear Safety (I): The Roots of Dissent," *Science* 177 (1 Sept. 1972):771-76; "Nuclear Safety (II): The Years of Delay," (8 Sept. 1972):867-71; "Nuclear Safety (III): Critics

Charge Conflicts of Interest," (15 Sept. 1972):970-75; and "Nuclear Safety (IV): Barriers to Communication," (22 Sept. 1972):1080-82.

33. CH/FXG and MS/FXG, with later CH-HBA input to RWD; Gillette, "Nuclear Safety (I)," 771, 774-75. Gillette termed the centralization effort as a "forceful new style of management from Washington," and defined MS's two major tasks as "to wean the industry from government support of water reactors, and to marshall his forces for a concerted thrust on the commission's prime objective--an economical breeder."

34. Orval Hansen to R.E. Hollingsworth, 3 October 1972, provided from FXG's files.

35. Hollingsworth to Orval Hanson, 17 Oct. 1972, 1-2, provided from FXG's files.

36. Ibid., 1, 2.

37. Ibid., 2.

38. CH/FXG, Bauser/FXG, Reich/FXG, Crawford/FXG, MS/FXG, with CH-HBA input to RWD.

39. Ibid.

40. JCAE, *Nuclear Reactor Safety--Part 1*, hearings, Phase I and Phase IIa, 23 Jan. 1973, 93rd Cong., 1st sess. (Wash., D.C.: GPO, 1973), 39; JCAE, *AEC Authorizing Legislation, FY 1974--Part 3*, 33. Rolph, *Nuclear Power and the Public Safety*, 94, notes that Schlesinger considered MS to be "the [safety] program's greatest champion."

41. JCAE, *Nuclear Reactor Safety--Part 1*, 39.

42. CH/FXG, with additional CH-HBA input to RWD.

43. JCAE, *Nuclear Reactor Safety--Part 1*, 7.

44. Ibid., 7-8.

45. Guzzo, *Is It True What They Say About Dixy?* 2, 4, 5, 32, 105.

46. CH/FXG; Bauser/FXG; Reich/FXG; Crawford/FXG; MS/FXG; CH-HBA and later MS input to RWD. CH and others were particularly incensed with the way Ray treated MS and other executives.

47. In Unna, "Atomic Energy," 18, CH says he "had real differences" with Ray." Strauss and Ray are compared in CH/Douglass, vol. 3, 28-29. Ray was a "misfit" who "could not work as one of a five-person commission." (46) On Ray's later defense of nuclear power, see Ray with Lou Guzzo, *Trashing the Planet: How Science Can Help Us Deal with Acid Rain, Depletion of the Ozone, and Nuclear Waste (Among Other Things)* (New York: Harper Perennial, 1990), esp. "Part III: Issues Nuclear," 93-156.

48. CH/FXG, Bauser/FXG, and Reich/FXG, with additional CH-HBA input to RWD.

49. Louis R. Guzzo, *Is It True What They Say About Dixy?* (Mercer Island, Washington: The Writing Works, Inc., 1980), 83-85.

50. Ibid., 12, 83-85. Gillette, "Nuclear Safety (I)," 771-72; CH/FXG, Bauser/FXG, MS/FXG, and Crawford/FXG, with CH-HBA input to RWD.

51. CH/FXG, CH-HBA input to RWD. Guzzo, *Is It True What They Say About Dixy?* 5, calls Ray a "marine biologist who had been known as an environmentalist most of her [career]."

52. CH/FXG; Bauser/FXG; MS/FXG; MS/RWD; CH-HBA input to RWD; Mary Russell, "AEC Reshuffle Would Shift Safety Effort Responsibility," *Washington Post*, 16 May 1973, A-3; Unna, "Atomic Energy," 18. Guzzo, *Is It True What They Say About Dixy?* 84-85, 99-100, 104, 112. Guzzo seems to suggest that a Ray-MS "clash" led to RDT's breakup. MS avers that no clash occurred; Ray simply avoided him.

53. MS/FXG, Crawford/FXG, with HBA input to RWD. MS's 4-page memo, provided by MS to RWD on 3 July 1991, is M. Shaw to R. E. Hollingsworth, "Implementation of Recent Reorganization Changes Affecting RDT," 8 June 1973, accompanied by a 9-page "Enclosure to Memorandum from M. Shaw to R. E. Hollingsworth dated 6/8/73."

54. CH-MS conversations with FXG-RWD. CH notes in 1974 that when Ramey, "a former [JCAE] staff director, a Democrat and personal friend, opposed Dr. Ray and told me of what had happened, she saw to it that Ramey was not reappointed when his term as Commissioner expired. I fought that one up to the White House but lost." (Unna, "Atomic Energy," 18.) Ray confirmed this. See Guzzo, *Is It True What They Say About Dixy?* 126-27.

55. CH/FXG, with additional CH-HBA input to RWD.

56. CH-MS conversations with FXG-RWD. Breeder changes are covered in GAO report to Congress, *The Liquid Metal Fast Breeder Reactor Program--Past, Present, and Future*, 28 Apr. 1975. Report was reviewed in Joint Economic Committee, *Fast Breeder Reactor Program*, hearings, 30 Apr. and

8 May 1975, 94th Congress, 1st sess. (Wash., D.C.: GPO, 1975), 3-72. A GAO letter report to Congress, *Comments on Energy Research and Development Adminstration's Proposed Arrangement for the Clinch River Breeder Reactor Demonstration Plant*, 4 Apr. 1975, was also in the hearings. See 306-23.

57. CH/FXG, Bauser/FXG, Crawford/FXG, and MS/FXG, with CH-HBA input to RWD.

58. Ibid.

59. CH/FXG, with additional CH-HBA input to RWD.

60. CH, "Problems of the Nuclear Age," speech typescript, 29 Sept. 1961, 6, Box 80 (Speech--State Bar of California, "Problems of the Nuclear Age"), HP. Dyke, *Mr. Atomic Energy*, 226-27, discusses CH's lead role in establishing the independent atomic safety and licensing boards.

61. CH, "Power and Policy," typescript speech, 15 Feb. 1971, 2-3, Box 84 (Nat. Rural Electric Cooperative Assn., Dallas, Feb. 15, 1971), HP.

62. Ibid.

63. CH/FXG, CH-HBA input to RWD; Dyke, *Mr. Atomic Energy*, 295-96; Unna, "Government Operations Committee," 16-17. Nixon's first 1971 proposal called for a Department of Natural Resources (DNR), but no action was taken. Nixon then asked for a Department of *Energy* and Natural Resources (DENR). See Richard M. Nixon, *Draft of Proposed Legislation to Promote More Effective Management of Certain Related Functions of the Executive Branch*, 29 June 1973, 93rd Cong. 1st sess. (Washington, D.C.: GPO, 1973), H. Doc. 93-119, and National Association of Conservation Districts, "Nixon Proposes Agency Shifts," newsletter, 10 July 1973, Box 60 (H.R. 9090), HP.

64. Dyke, *Mr. Atomic Energy*, 296-97. ERDA and NEC were part of the DENR proposal, but CH was working on a similar proposal in the Government Operations Committee. In Unna, "Government Operations Committee," 17, CH notes that he "proposed" ERDA. See materials in Boxes 60-61, HP.

65. Dyke, *Mr. Atomic Energy*, 297-302.

66. CH-HBA discussions with FXG and RWD. Of Ray, CH remembered that she "tried her best to neutralize the Joint Committee against me. But in the end, I also had something to say. . . . Miss Ray ended up at the State Department as an Assistant Secretary in charge of marine biology." (Unna, "Atomic Energy," 18-19.) CH would not consider Ray for ERDA. In a letter to Roy Ash, he stated the new ERDA head should be a person "who could work with people, not like the Chairman of the AEC, Dr. Ray, who put herself off from the others, but a team player who could come to Congress." CH tactfully put forward John Simpson, but Robert Seamans got the job. (Unna, "Government Operations Committee," 17-19.)

67. CH/FXG and MS/FXG, with additional CH-MS conversations with RWD.

68. Sweet, *The Nuclear Age*, 41-42, 142; Jasper, *Nuclear Politics*, 189-91.

69. MS/RWD; Sweet, *The Nuclear Age*, 42; Jasper, *Nuclear Politics*, 188, 193-94.   70. CH/FXG, with additional CH-HBA input to RWD.

Chapter 14: A Revolutionary Upheaval on Capitol Hill

1. See Box 13, HP, for many files on CH's role in Rules reform. He admired "the new programs for health, housing, education, and civil rights," but forecast "years of work to bring to fulfillment our policies and dreams." (CH, "Democratic Programs and Policies," typescript, 17 Sept. 1966, 5, 8, Box 81 [Speech for Warren Dawson Dinner in Norwalk, California, September 17, 1966], HP.) On monopoly, see, for example, CH and Pastore to U.S. Attorney General John Newton Mitchell, 24 Jan. 1969, Box 46 (JCAE Correspondence - 1969, Outgoing January - May), HP.

2. In the 1960s, CH declared that "I hope and pray that the Congress will pass a strong civil rights bill." (CH, "World Impact of Civil Rights Debate," speech typescript, n.d. [1965?], 1, Box 66 [Civil Rights (Riots) #2], HP.) In a 20 Oct. 1972 letter to Los Angeles resident Thomas B. Caldwell, CH noted that "I have always supported the rights of labor and fought for the civil rights of all citizens." (CH to Caldwell, Box 66 [Civil Rights - 1972], HP.) CH "led the floor debate on a bill to authorize appropriations to extend the Cabinet Committee on Opportunities for Spanish-Speaking People." ("Holifield Bill to Extend Committee on Opportunities for Spanish Speaking People Passed by House," CH press release, 7 July 1971, Box 84 [Holifield Bill to Extend Committee on Opportunities for Spanish Speaking People Passed by House], HP.) See Public Law 92-112, 16 Aug. 1971, in Box 58 (H.R. 7586 -Establish Cabinet

Committee on Opportunities for Spanish-Speaking People); "Spanish-Speaking Committee Bill Passed," CH press release, 18 Oct. 1973, Box 85 (Passage of Cabinet Committee Bill, October 18, 1973), HP.

3. CH/FXG, with additional CH-HBA input to RWD.

4. Unna, "Government Operations Committee," 12-14. For full discussion, see 12-16.

5. CH, "Riots, Crime, and Civil Responsibilities," speech typescript, 7 Sept. 1967, 8-9, 14, Box 82 (Emergency Operations Symposium Dinner Meeting Address - September 7, 1967), HP. See also "Rioting and Crime," typescript, n.d., Box 66 (Civil Rights [Riots] #2), HP, for speech excerpts.

6. See Box 45 (Uranium Mine Radiation), HP (a large file), and CH/Douglass, vol. 3, 73-74.

7. CH was "one of [Secretary of Labor W. Willard] Wirtz's harshest critics" on the uranium mine safety issue." (J.V. Reistrup, "Wirtz Says Many Uranium Mines Still Exceed Limit on Radiation," *Washington Post*, 9 Aug. 1967, newspaper clipping, in Box 45 [Uranium Mine Radiation], HP.)

8. CH/Douglass, vol. 3, 76. See AEC's WASH-1250 report, *The Safety of Nuclear Power Reactors (Light Water-Cooled) and Related Facilities* (Washington, D.C.: GPO, July 1973), I-20-32.

9. CH/Douglass, vol. 3, 65-67; CH to RWD, 22 Apr. 1980, private communication.

10. CH/Douglass, vol. 3, 78-79. A relevant discussion of "Can Nuclear Power Plants Explode Like Bombs?" is in Chapter 8 of AEC's WASH-1250 report, 8-1-3.

11. Even Sheldon Novick, who documents a military reactor accident at the beginning of *The Careless Atom* (Boston: Houghton Mifflin Company, 1969), 195, concedes that "there is no question but that the Joint Committee and the AEC are conscientious and acutely aware of the need for safety."

12. CH/FXG, MS/FXG, CH-MS input to RWD; Gillette, "Nuclear Safety (II)," 867. CH, other JCAE members like Hosmer, and MS discussed major safety test programs in nearly every JCAE annual hearing. See, *AEC Authorizing Legislation, FY 1968*, and for subsequent years through FY 1974.

13. A CH view of the opposition is in his speech at the annual ANS/AIF Conference in Washington, D.C., "The Need For A Comprehensive Energy Program," Appendix 16 of JCAE, *Nuclear Power and Related Energy Problems--1968 Through 1970*, 1094-1101. This speech is also in Box 83 (American Nuclear Society, Atomic Industrial Forum, Nov. 18, 1970), HP.

14. CH/FXG, with additional CH-HBA input to RWD.

15. JCAE, *Environmental Effects of Producing Electric Power-Part 2 (Vol. I)*, 1468-69.

16. Dr. Ralph E. Lapp/FXG, with additional CH-HBA input to RWD.

17. See 21 June 1943, *Congressional Record*, 78th Cong., 1st sess., vol. 89, pt. 5, 6223-6225.

18. CH/FXG, CH-HBA input to RWD. Representative B. F. Sisk (D-California) was a CH defender in CH's conflicts with Rosenthal and Nader. Also relevant is Box 57 (H.R. 18067 . . .), HP.

19. Ibid. Files in Boxes 57 and 58 and the files on Ralph Nader in Box 71 provide background.

20. Unna, "Government Operations Committee," 3.

21. Ibid., 8; Robert Walters, "Bill for Consumer Weakened Again," *Washington Star*, 7 Sept. 1971, Box 57 (H.R. 18067 - Establish Office of Consumer Affairs and a Consumer Protection Agency), HP.

22. Unna, "Government Operations Committee," 8-9. CH noted that he had been "personally lobbied by this man [Nader]--both through phone calls at home and office visits--more than I've been lobbied by anyone on anything for 10 years." (Quoted in "Holifield and Nader Trade Jabs," *Washington Post*, 3 Oct. 1971, and William B. Mead, "Nader is Seeking Consumer 'Tyrant' Holifield Charges," *Washington Evening Star*, 2 Oct. 1971, A-2, both in Box 57 (H.R. 18067 - Establish Office of Consumer Affairs and a Consumer Protection Agency), HP.

23. Unna, "Government Operations Committee," 9-10. CH reported a "clean" bill, H.R. 18067, out of his Subcommittee on Executive and Legislative Reorganization. See "Summary of H.R. 18067" and "Comparison of Major Features of Rosenthal [H.R. 6037], Dwyer [H.R. 13793] and Nixon Administration [H.R. 14758] Consumer Organization Bills," typescripts on subcommittee letterhead, in Box 57 (H.R. 18067 - Establish Office of Consumer Affairs and a Consumer Protection Agency), HP. Shirley Elder, "House Sends Consumer Bill to Senate," *Washington Star*, 15 Oct. 1971, in Box 57 (H.R. 18067 . . .), HP, analyzes votes.

24. Unna, "Government Operations Committee," 10-11; CH press release, "Holifield Says Nader Helped Kill Consumer Bill," 13 Oct. 1972, Box 71 (Ralph Nader--General), HP; Mead, "Nader is Seeking Consumer 'Tyrant' Holifield Charges."

25. "Holifield Erases Panels on Consumers, Privacy," *Washington Star*, 21 Mar. 1971, Box 71 (Ralph Nader--Consumer Study Group, Government Operations Committee), HP; Nader to CH, 19 Mar. 1971, Box 71 (Ralph Nader--Consumer Study Group, Government Operations Committee), HP.

26. CH/FXG, CH-HBA input to RWD.

27. CH rebutted Rosenthal's charges in a six-page press release, "Holifield Answers Challenge to His Committee Chairmanships in the Democratic Caucus of the House of Representatives," 23 Jan. 1973, Box 85 (Holifield Answers Rosenthal Challenge), HP.

28. Ibid., 2.

29. Ronald Sarro, "Holifield Decries 'Vendetta': Nader, Common Cause Named," and "House Panel Chairmen Get Lukewarm Backing," both in *Washington Evening Star and Daily News*, 24 Jan. 1973, A-16, Box 71 (Ralph Nader--General), HP.

30. Unna, "Government Operations Committee," 11; CH/FXG, CH-HBA input to RWD; CH press release, "Holifield's Consumer Protection Act Passes House," Box 85 (Holifield's Consumer Protection Bill Passes House, April 3, 1974), HP.

31. Unna, "Legislating," 13.

32. CH/FXG, CH-HBA input to RWD.

33. Ibid.; CH, et. al., to "Dear Colleague," 20 July 1970, Box 67 (Congressional Reform), HP. Minority staff had been proposed by House Repub. Conf. Chmn. Gerald R. Ford in the early 1960s.

34. CH/FXG, CH-HBA input to RWD; Unna, "Government Operations Committee," 16-17.

35. For a summary of Bolling's proposals, see House Select Committee on Committees, *Committee Reform Amendments of 1974--Part II*, report to accompany H. Res. 988, 93rd Cong., 2nd sess. (Washington, D.C.: GPO, 21 Mar. 1974), H. Rept. No. 93-916 Part II, 3-7. See also Committee on Post Office and Post Roads is reprinted in 8 Oct. 1974, *Congressional Record*, 93rd Cong., 2nd sess., vol. 120, 34413. For CH's concerns about reform and the dissolution of the JCAE, see especially 30 Sept. 1974, *Congressional Record*, 93rd Cong., 2nd sess., vol. 120, 32993-995 and Unna, "Legislating," 7-13.

36. Unna, "Legislating," 7; *Committee Reform Amendments of 1974--Part II*, 15, 72-74.

37. CH/FXG, CH-HBA input to RWD; similar quote in Unna, "Legislating," 11.

38. *Committee Organization in the House--Vol. 1 (Part 1) of 3 Vols.*, hearings, 2-18 May 1973, 93rd Cong., 1st sess. (Washington, D.C.: GPO, 1973), 178-79. In his formal presentation, Horton averred that "I find minority staffing on my own [Government Operations] committee fair and reasonable" and "I am very happy with the relationship the chairman and I have with regard to staffing." (176)

39. Ibid., 331. CH had Price and Jack Bridges with him, and Bridges gave the technical presentation. (322-34). CH's call for a Joint Committee on the Environment and Technology passed the House in May 1970. (Dyke, *Mr. Atomic Energy*, 239, 377 n.43; see also Box 59 [H.J. Res. 1117], HP.) Pastore drafted a bill for a similar committee but the Senate leadership did not support it.

40. 26 Sept. 1974, *Congressional Record*, 93rd Cong., 2nd sess., vol. 120, 32805. See 32804-806 for full speech, "Committee Reform or Committee Confusion." See also Box 85 (Remarks before ... Rules), HP. CH charged that the reforms would make Government Operations "the most hated committee in the House." (30 Sept. 1974, *Congressional Record*, 93rd Cong., 2nd sess., vol. 120, 32965.)

41. Unna, "Legislating," 11.

42. Ibid., 9; CH/FXG, with additional CH-HBA input to RWD.

43. In Unna, "Legislating," 8, CH relates that he told other House colleagues that Bolling's reforms "'will make the Rules Committee almost as tyrannical as in the days of Uncle Joe Cannon.'"

44. Bolling refers to his and CH's "Dear Colleague" letters in 8 Oct. 1974, *Congressional Record*, 93rd Cong., 2nd sess., vol. 120, 34413. CH letter is in Box 85 (Why H. Res. 988 Won't Work), HP. *Committee Reform Amendments of 1974: Explanation of H. Res. 988 as Adopted by the House of Representatives, October 8, 1974*, committee print, (Wash., D.C.: GPO, 1974), 1-5, 195-219, is helpful.

45. 30 Sept. 1974, *Congressional Record*, 93rd Cong., 2nd sess., vol. 120, 32992-994; *Committee Reform Amendments of 1974--Part 2*, open business meeting, 1-13 Mar. 1974, 444, 548-52.

46. Sweet, *Nuclear Age*, 30-31, 43.

47. Public Law 95-110, 91 STAT. 884, 20 Sept. 1977. In CH/Douglass, vol. 3, 55-56, CH acknowledged that his and Hosmer's retirements hurt the atomic energy program: "There has been no one yet who has come forward to take our place and fight as hard as we have fought."

48. 20 Dec. 1974, *Congressional Record*, 93rd Cong., 2nd sess., vol. 120, 41868-884.

Index